수능기출 전국연합 학력평가

하루 20분 30일 완성

미니 모의고사

고1 영어

KB212717

수능 모의고사 전문 출판
ip 입시플라이

하루 12문제·20분
영어 30일 완성

가볍게 하루 12문제씩 20분을 학습하면 수능 실전 감각을 키워줄 뿐 아니라 '영어 1등급을 위한 나만의 학습 루틴(routine)'이 됩니다. [30일 완성 미니모의고사]는 수능 영어 전 유형을 매일 골고루 풀 수 있도록 7개년 수능 및 모의평가와 [고1 학력평가] 중 우수한 문제만을 엄선 후 난이도별로 배치했습니다. 학습 부담 없는 30일 완성 미니모의고사로 수능·내신 '1등급의 감각을 유지'하세요.

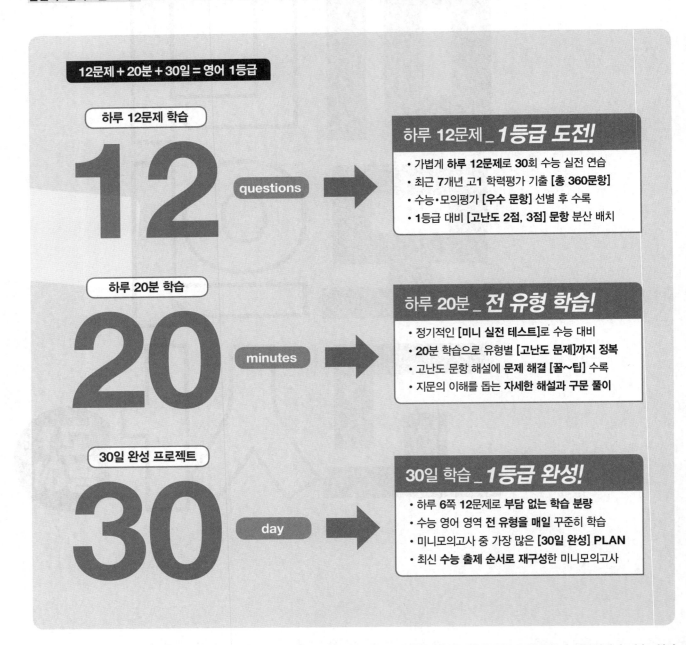

12문제 + 20분 + 30일 = 영어 1등급

하루 12문제 학습

12 questions →

하루 12문제_1등급 도전!
- 가볍게 **하루 12문제**로 30회 수능 실전 연습
- 최근 7개년 고1 학력평가 기출 [총 360문항]
- 수능·모의평가 [우수 문항] 선별 후 수록
- 1등급 대비 [고난도 2점, 3점] 문항 분산 배치

하루 20분 학습

20 minutes →

하루 20분_전 유형 학습!
- 정기적인 [미니 실전 테스트]로 수능 대비
- **20분 학습**으로 유형별 [고난도 문제]까지 정복
- 고난도 문항 해설에 문제 해결 [꿀~팁] 수록
- 지문의 이해를 돕는 **자세한 해설과 구문 풀이**

30일 완성 프로젝트

30 day →

30일 학습_1등급 완성!
- 하루 6쪽 12문제로 부담 없는 학습 분량
- 수능 영어 영역 전 유형을 매일 꾸준히 학습
- 미니모의고사 중 가장 많은 [30일 완성] PLAN
- 최신 수능 출제 순서로 재구성한 미니모의고사

※ 미니모의고사가 수능에서 반드시 필요한 이유는 대부분의 수험생들이 영어 과목을 주제(유형)별 위주로 학습하기 때문입니다. 수능 영어 전 유형을 골고루 풀어 볼 수 있는 미니 모의고사로 하루 12문제씩 학습하면 '실전 감각도 함께 쌓을 수' 있습니다.

Contents &
30 Day planner

고1 영어

- 날짜별로 정해진 **학습 분량에 맞춰 공부하고 학습 결과를 기록**합니다.
- **planner**를 이용해 학습 일정을 계획하고 **자신의 성적을 체크하면서 30일 완성으로 목표를** 세우세요.
- 가볍게 매일 20분씩 꾸준하게 학습을 하세요. 주어진 목표 시간 안에 문제를 푸는 연습은 수능 실전에서 자신감까지 **UP**해 줍니다.

차례	쪽수	학습 날짜		소요 시간	틀린 문제 & 복습할 문제	복습 날짜	
Day 01	004쪽	월	일			월	일
Day 02	010쪽	월	일			월	일
Day 03	016쪽	월	일			월	일
Day 04	022쪽	월	일			월	일
Day 05	028쪽	월	일			월	일
Day 06	034쪽	월	일			월	일
Day 07	040쪽	월	일			월	일
Day 08	046쪽	월	일			월	일
Day 09	052쪽	월	일			월	일
Day 10	058쪽	월	일			월	일
Day 11	064쪽	월	일			월	일
Day 12	070쪽	월	일			월	일
Day 13	076쪽	월	일			월	일
Day 14	082쪽	월	일			월	일
Day 15	088쪽	월	일			월	일
Day 16	094쪽	월	일			월	일
Day 17	100쪽	월	일			월	일
Day 18	106쪽	월	일			월	일
Day 19	112쪽	월	일			월	일
Day 20	118쪽	월	일			월	일
Day 21	124쪽	월	일			월	일
Day 22	130쪽	월	일			월	일
Day 23	136쪽	월	일			월	일
Day 24	142쪽	월	일			월	일
Day 25	148쪽	월	일			월	일
Day 26	154쪽	월	일			월	일
Day 27	160쪽	월	일			월	일
Day 28	166쪽	월	일			월	일
Day 29	172쪽	월	일			월	일
Day 30	178쪽	월	일			월	일

DAY 01

● 날짜 :　　월　　일　● 시작 시각 :　　시　　분　　초　● 목표 시간 : 20분

※ 점수 표기가 없는 문항은 모두 **2점**입니다.

01

고1 • 2023년 9월 18번

다음 글의 목적으로 가장 적절한 것은?

Dear Professor Sanchez,

My name is Ellis Wight, and I'm the director of the Alexandria Science Museum. We are holding a Chemistry Fair for local middle school students on Saturday, October 28. The goal of the fair is to encourage them to be interested in science through guided experiments. We are looking for college students who can help with the experiments during the event. I am contacting you to ask you to recommend some students from the chemistry department at your college who you think are qualified for this job. With their help, I'm sure the participants will have a great experience. I look forward to hearing from you soon.

Sincerely,
Ellis Wight

① 과학 박물관 내 시설 이용 제한을 안내하려고
② 화학 박람회 일정이 변경된 이유를 설명하려고
③ 중학생을 위한 화학 실험 특별 강연을 부탁하려고
④ 중학교 과학 수업용 실험 교재 집필을 의뢰하려고
⑤ 화학 박람회에서 실험을 도울 대학생 추천을 요청하려고

02

고1 • 2024년 3월 20번

다음 글에서 필자가 주장하는 바로 가장 적절한 것은?

Magic is what we all wish for to happen in our life. Do you love the movie *Cinderella* like me? Well, in real life, you can also create magic. Here's the trick. Write down all the real-time challenges that you face and deal with. Just change the challenge statement into positive statements. Let me give you an example here. If you struggle with getting up early in the morning, then write a positive statement such as "I get up early in the morning at 5:00 am every day." Once you write these statements, get ready to witness magic and confidence. You will be surprised that just by writing these statements, there is a shift in the way you think and act. Suddenly you feel more powerful and positive.

① 목표한 바를 꼭 이루려면 생각을 곧바로 행동으로 옮겨라.
② 자신감을 얻으려면 어려움을 긍정적인 진술로 바꿔 써라.
③ 어려운 일을 해결하려면 주변 사람에게 도움을 청하라.
④ 일상에서 자신감을 향상하려면 틈틈이 마술을 배워라.
⑤ 실생활에서 마주하는 도전을 피하지 말고 견뎌 내라.

03

다음 글의 주제로 가장 적절한 것은?

Managers of natural resources typically face market incentives that provide financial rewards for exploitation. For example, owners of forest lands have a market incentive to cut down trees rather than manage the forest for carbon capture, wildlife habitat, flood protection, and other ecosystem services. These services provide the owner with no financial benefits, and thus are unlikely to influence management decisions. But the economic benefits provided by these services, based on their non-market values, may exceed the economic value of the timber. For example, a United Nations initiative has estimated that the economic benefits of ecosystem services provided by tropical forests, including climate regulation, water purification, and erosion prevention, are over three times greater per hectare than the market benefits. Thus cutting down the trees is economically inefficient, and markets are not sending the correct "signal" to favor ecosystem services over extractive uses.

* exploitation: 이용 ** timber: 목재

① necessity of calculating the market values of ecosystem services

② significance of weighing forest resources' non-market values

③ impact of using forest resources to maximize financial benefits

④ merits of balancing forests' market and non-market values

⑤ ways of increasing the efficiency of managing natural resources

04

Wilbur Smith에 관한 다음 글의 내용과 일치하지 <u>않는</u> 것은?

Wilbur Smith was a South African novelist specialising in historical fiction. Smith wanted to become a journalist, writing about social conditions in South Africa, but his father was never supportive of his writing and forced him to get a real job. Smith studied further and became a tax accountant, but he finally turned back to his love of writing. He wrote his first novel, *The Gods First Make Mad*, and had received 20 rejections by 1962. In 1964, Smith published another novel, *When the Lion Feeds*, and it went on to be successful, selling around the world. A famous actor and film producer bought the film rights for *When the Lion Feeds*, although no movie resulted. By the time of his death in 2021 he had published 49 novels, selling more than 140 million copies worldwide.

① 역사 소설을 전문으로 하는 소설가였다.
② 아버지는 그가 글 쓰는 것을 지지하지 않았다.
③ 첫 번째 소설은 1962년까지 20번 거절당했다.
④ 소설 *When the Lion Feeds*는 영화화되었다.
⑤ 죽기 전까지 49편의 소설을 출간했다.

05

다음 글의 밑줄 친 부분 중, 어법상 틀린 것은? [3점]

The reduction of minerals in our food is the result of using pesticides and fertilizers ① that kill off beneficial bacteria, earthworms, and bugs in the soil that create many of the essential nutrients in the first place and prevent the uptake of nutrients into the plant. Fertilizing crops with nitrogen and potassium ② has led to declines in magnesium, zinc, iron and iodine. For example, there has been on average about a 30% decline in the magnesium content of wheat. This is partly due to potassium ③ being a blocker against magnesium absorption by plants. Lower magnesium levels in soil also ④ occurring with acidic soils and around 70% of the farmland on earth is now acidic. Thus, the overall characteristics of soil determine the accumulation of minerals in plants. Indeed, nowadays our soil is less healthy and so are the plants ⑤ grown on it.

* pesticide: 살충제

06 1등급 대비 고난도 2점 문제

다음 글의 밑줄 친 부분 중, 문맥상 낱말의 쓰임이 적절하지 않은 것은?

Honesty is a fundamental part of every strong relationship. Use it to your advantage by being open with what you feel and giving a ① truthful opinion when asked. This approach can help you escape uncomfortable social situations and make friends with honest people. Follow this simple policy in life — never lie. When you ② develop a reputation for always telling the truth, you will enjoy strong relationships based on trust. It will also be more difficult to manipulate you. People who lie get into trouble when someone threatens to ③ uncover their lie. By living true to yourself, you'll ④ avoid a lot of headaches. Your relationships will also be free from the poison of lies and secrets. Don't be afraid to be honest with your friends, no matter how painful the truth is. In the long term, lies with good intentions ⑤ comfort people much more than telling the truth.

* manipulate: (사람을) 조종하다

07

다음 빈칸에 들어갈 말로 가장 적절한 것을 고르시오.

There is nothing more fundamental to the human spirit than the need to be _____. It is the intuitive force that sparks our imaginations and opens pathways to life-changing opportunities. It is the catalyst for progress and personal freedom. Public transportation has been vital to that progress and freedom for more than two centuries. The transportation industry has always done more than carry travelers from one destination to another. It connects people, places, and possibilities. It provides access to what people need, what they love, and what they aspire to become. In so doing, it grows communities, creates jobs, strengthens the economy, expands social and commercial networks, saves time and energy, and helps millions of people achieve a better life.

* catalyst: 촉매, 기폭제

① secure
② mobile
③ exceptional
④ competitive
⑤ independent

08 1등급 대비 고난도 3점 문제

다음 빈칸에 들어갈 말로 가장 적절한 것을 고르시오. [3점]

In a study at Princeton University in 1992, research scientists looked at two different groups of mice. One group was made intellectually superior by modifying the gene for the glutamate receptor. Glutamate is a brain chemical that is necessary in learning. The other group was genetically manipulated to be intellectually inferior, also done by modifying the gene for the glutamate receptor. The smart mice were then raised in standard cages, while the inferior mice were raised in large cages with toys and exercise wheels and with lots of social interaction. At the end of the study, although the intellectually inferior mice were genetically handicapped, they were able to perform just as well as their genetic superiors. This was a real triumph for nurture over nature. Genes are turned on or off _____.

* glutamate: 글루타민산염　** manipulate: 조작하다

① by themselves for survival
② free from social interaction
③ based on what is around you
④ depending on genetic superiority
⑤ so as to keep ourselves entertained

09

다음 글에서 전체 흐름과 관계 <u>없는</u> 문장은?

Given the widespread use of emoticons in electronic communication, an important question is whether they help Internet users to understand emotions in online communication. ① Emoticons, particularly character-based ones, are much more ambiguous relative to face-to-face cues and may end up being interpreted very differently by different users. ② Nonetheless, research indicates that they are useful tools in online text-based communication. ③ One study of 137 instant messaging users revealed that emoticons allowed users to correctly understand the level and direction of emotion, attitude, and attention expression and that emoticons were a definite advantage in non-verbal communication. ④ In fact, there have been few studies on the relationships between verbal and nonverbal communication. ⑤ Similarly, another study showed that emoticons were useful in strengthening the intensity of a verbal message, as well as in the expression of sarcasm.

* ambiguous: 모호한　** verbal: 언어적인
*** sarcasm: 풍자

10 　1등급 대비 고난도 2점 문제

주어진 글 다음에 이어질 글의 순서로 가장 적절한 것을 고르시오.

In the Old Stone Age, small bands of 20 to 60 people wandered from place to place in search of food. Once people began farming, they could settle down near their farms.

(A) While some workers grew crops, others built new houses and made tools. Village dwellers also learned to work together to do a task faster.

(B) For example, toolmakers could share the work of making stone axes and knives. By working together, they could make more tools in the same amount of time.

(C) As a result, towns and villages grew larger. Living in communities allowed people to organize themselves more efficiently. They could divide up the work of producing food and other things they needed.

* dweller: 거주자

① (A) − (C) − (B)　　② (B) − (A) − (C)
③ (B) − (C) − (A)　　④ (C) − (A) − (B)
⑤ (C) − (B) − (A)

DAY 01

[11 ~ 12] 다음 글을 읽고, 물음에 답하시오.

Early hunter-gatherer societies had (a) <u>minimal</u> structure. A chief or group of elders usually led the camp or village. Most of these leaders had to hunt and gather along with the other members because the surpluses of food and other vital resources were seldom (b) <u>sufficient</u> to support a full-time chief or village council. The development of agriculture changed work patterns. Early farmers could reap 3-10 kg of grain from each 1 kg of seed planted. Part of this food/energy surplus was returned to the community and (c) <u>limited</u> support for nonfarmers such as chieftains, village councils, men who practice medicine, priests, and warriors. In return, the nonfarmers provided leadership and security for the farming population, enabling it to continue to increase food/energy yields and provide ever larger surpluses.

With improved technology and favorable conditions, agriculture produced consistent surpluses of the basic necessities, and population groups grew in size. These groups concentrated in towns and cities, and human tasks (d) <u>specialized</u> further. Specialists such as carpenters, blacksmiths, merchants, traders, and sailors developed their skills and became more efficient in their use of time and energy. The goods and services they provided brought about an (e) <u>improved</u> quality of life, a higher standard of living, and, for most societies, increased stability.

* reap: (농작물을) 베어들이다   ** chieftain: 수령, 두목

11

고1 · 2023년 6월 41번

윗글의 제목으로 가장 적절한 것은?

① How Agriculture Transformed Human Society
② The Dark Shadow of Agriculture: Repetition
③ How Can We Share Extra Food with the Poor?
④ Why Were Early Societies Destroyed by Agriculture?
⑤ The Advantages of Large Groups Over Small Groups in Farming

12

고1 · 2023년 6월 42번

밑줄 친 (a) ~ (e) 중에서 문맥상 낱말의 쓰임이 적절하지 <u>않은</u> 것은? [3점]

① (a)　　② (b)　　③ (c)　　④ (d)　　⑤ (e)

DAY 02

수능기출
전국연합학력평가 **20분 미니 모의고사**

● 날짜 :　　월　　일　● 시작 시각 :　　시　　분　　초　● 목표 시간 : 20분

※ 점수 표기가 없는 문항은 모두 2점입니다.

01

고1 · 2023년 9월 19번

다음 글에 나타난 'I'의 심경 변화로 가장 적절한 것은?

Gregg and I had been rock climbing since sunrise and had had no problems. So we took a risk. "Look, the first bolt is right there. I can definitely climb out to it. Piece of cake," I persuaded Gregg, minutes before I found myself pinned. It wasn't a piece of cake. The rock was deceptively barren of handholds. I clumsily moved back and forth across the cliff face and ended up with nowhere to go...but down. The bolt that would save my life, if I could get to it, was about two feet above my reach. My arms trembled from exhaustion. I looked at Gregg. My body froze with fright from my neck down to my toes. Our rope was tied between us. If I fell, he would fall with me.

＊ barren of: ～이 없는

① joyful　　　→ bored
② confident　→ fearful
③ nervous　　→ relieved
④ regretful　 → pleased
⑤ grateful　　→ annoyed

02

고1 · 2024년 6월 22번

다음 글의 요지로 가장 적절한 것은?

When it comes to helping out, you don't have to do much. All you have to do is come around and show that you care. If you notice someone who is lonely, you could go and sit with them. If you work with someone who eats lunch all by themselves, and you go and sit down with them, they will begin to be more social after a while, and they will owe it all to you. A person's happiness comes from attention. There are too many people out in the world who feel like everyone has forgotten them or ignored them. Even if you say hi to someone passing by, they will begin to feel better about themselves, like someone cares.

① 사소한 관심이 타인에게 도움이 될 수 있다.
② 사람마다 행복의 기준이 제각기 다르다.
③ 선행을 통해 자신을 되돌아볼 수 있다.
④ 원만한 대인 관계는 경청에서 비롯된다.
⑤ 현재에 대한 만족이 행복의 필수조건이다.

03

다음 글의 제목으로 가장 적절한 것은?

When people think about the development of cities, rarely do they consider the critical role of vertical transportation. In fact, each day, more than 7 billion elevator journeys are taken in tall buildings all over the world. Efficient vertical transportation can expand our ability to build taller and taller skyscrapers. Antony Wood, a Professor of Architecture at the Illinois Institute of Technology, explains that advances in elevators over the past 20 years are probably the greatest advances we have seen in tall buildings. For example, elevators in the Jeddah Tower in Jeddah, Saudi Arabia, under construction, will reach a height record of 660m.

① Elevators Bring Buildings Closer to the Sky
② The Higher You Climb, the Better the View
③ How to Construct an Elevator Cheap and Fast
④ The Function of the Ancient and the Modern City
⑤ The Evolution of Architecture: Solutions for Overpopulation

04

Green Tea Packaging Design Competition에 관한 다음 안내문의 내용과 일치하지 <u>않는</u> 것은?

Green Tea Packaging Design Competition

Take the opportunity to design the packaging box for brand-new green tea products of TIIS Tea in the competition!

Deadline: December 2, 2019, 6:00 p.m.
Participants: Lokota County residents only
Details
- Our company name "TIIS Tea" should appear on the design.
- The competition theme is "Go Green with Green Tea."
- Entries (JPG format only) should be submitted by email to designmanager@tiistea.com.

Evaluation Criteria
- Functionality
- Creativity
- Eco-friendliness

Awards
- 1st place: $1,000
- 2nd place: $500
- 3rd place: $250
  (The first-place winner's signature will be printed on the packaging box.)

Please visit www.tiistea.com to learn more about the competition.

① 신제품 녹차를 위한 포장 상자 디자인 대회이다.
② Lokota County 주민들만 참가할 수 있다.
③ 출품작은 직접 방문하여 제출해야 한다.
④ 평가 기준에 창의성이 포함된다.
⑤ 1등 수상자의 서명이 포장 상자에 인쇄될 것이다.

05

다음 글의 밑줄 친 부분 중, 어법상 틀린 것은? [3점]

An economic theory of Say's Law holds that everything that's made will get sold. The money from anything that's produced is used to ① buy something else. There can never be a situation ② which a firm finds that it can't sell its goods and so has to dismiss workers and close its factories. Therefore, recessions and unemployment are impossible. Picture the level of spending like the level of water in a bath. Say's Law applies ③ because people use all their earnings to buy things. But what happens if people don't spend all their money, saving some of ④ it instead? Savings are a 'leakage' of spending from the economy. You're probably imagining the water level now falling, so there's less spending in the economy. That would mean firms producing less and ⑤ dismissing some of their workers.

＊recession: 경기 후퇴

06

다음 글의 밑줄 친 부분 중, 문맥상 낱말의 쓰임이 적절하지 않은 것은? [3점]

Do you sometimes feel like you don't love your life? Like, deep inside, something is missing? That's because we are living someone else's life. We allow other people to ① influence our choices. We are trying to meet their expectations. Social pressure is deceiving — we are all impacted without noticing it. Before we realize we are losing ownership of our lives, we end up ② ignoring how other people live. Then, we can only see the greener grass — ours is never good enough. To regain that passion for the life you want, you must ③ recover control of your choices. No one but yourself can choose how you live. But, how? The first step to getting rid of expectations is to treat yourself ④ kindly. You can't truly love other people if you don't love yourself first. When we accept who we are, there's no room for other's ⑤ expectations.

07 1등급 대비 고난도 *3점* 문제

고1 · 2019년 11월 32번

다음 빈칸에 들어갈 말로 가장 적절한 것을 고르시오. [3점]

The title of Thomas Friedman's 2005 book, *The World Is Flat,* was based on the belief that globalization would inevitably bring us closer together. It has done that, but it has also inspired us _____ . When faced with perceived threats — the financial crisis, terrorism, violent conflict, refugees and immigration, the increasing gap between rich and poor — people cling more tightly to their groups. One founder of a famous social media company believed social media would unite us. In some respects it has, but it has simultaneously given voice and organizational ability to new cyber tribes, some of whom spend their time spreading blame and division across the World Wide Web. There seem now to be as many tribes, and as much conflict between them, as there have ever been. Is it possible for these tribes to coexist in a world where the concept of "us and them" remains?

① to build barriers
② to achieve equality
③ to abandon traditions
④ to value individualism
⑤ to develop technologies

08 1등급 대비 고난도 *2점* 문제

고1 · 2021년 3월 38번

글의 흐름으로 보아, 주어진 문장이 들어가기에 가장 적절한 곳을 고르시오.

> Meanwhile, improving by 1 percent isn't particularly notable, but it can be far more meaningful in the long run.

It is so easy to overestimate the importance of one defining moment and underestimate the value of making small improvements on a daily basis. Too often, we convince ourselves that massive success requires massive action. (①) Whether it is losing weight, winning a championship, or achieving any other goal, we put pressure on ourselves to make some earthshaking improvement that everyone will talk about. (②) The difference this tiny improvement can make over time is surprising. (③) Here's how the math works out: if you can get 1 percent better each day for one year, you'll end up thirty-seven times better by the time you're done. (④) Conversely, if you get 1 percent worse each day for one year, you'll decline nearly down to zero. (⑤) What starts as a small win or a minor failure adds up to something much more.

09 1등급 대비 고난도 2점 문제

다음 글의 내용을 한 문장으로 요약하고자 한다. 빈칸 (A), (B)에 들어갈 말로 가장 적절한 것은?

Nearly eight of ten U.S. adults believe there are "good foods" and "bad foods." Unless we're talking about spoiled stew, poison mushrooms, or something similar, however, no foods can be labeled as either good or bad. There are, however, combinations of foods that add up to a healthful or unhealthful diet. Consider the case of an adult who eats only foods thought of as "good" — for example, raw broccoli, apples, orange juice, boiled tofu, and carrots. Although all these foods are nutrient-dense, they do not add up to a healthy diet because they don't supply a wide enough variety of the nutrients we need. Or take the case of the teenager who occasionally eats fried chicken, but otherwise stays away from fried foods. The occasional fried chicken isn't going to knock his or her diet off track. But the person who eats fried foods every day, with few vegetables or fruits, and loads up on supersized soft drinks, candy, and chips for snacks has a bad diet.

↓

Unlike the common belief, defining foods as good or bad is not _____(A)_____ ; in fact, a healthy diet is determined largely by what the diet is _____(B)_____ .

	(A)		(B)
①	incorrect	……	limited to
②	appropriate	……	composed of
③	wrong	……	aimed at
④	appropriate	……	tested on
⑤	incorrect	……	adjusted to

[10 ~ 12] 다음 글을 읽고, 물음에 답하시오.

(A)

Once upon a time, there was a king who lived in a beautiful palace. While the king was away, a monster approached the gates of the palace. The monster was so ugly and smelly that the guards froze in shock. He passed the guards and sat on the king's throne. The guards soon came to their senses, went in, and shouted at the monster, demanding that (a) he get off the throne.

＊throne: 왕좌

(B)

Eventually the king returned. He was wise and kind and saw what was happening. He knew what to do. He smiled and said to the monster, "Welcome to my palace!" He asked the monster if (b) he wanted a cup of coffee. The monster began to grow smaller as he drank the coffee.

(C)

The king offered (c) him some take-out pizza and fries. The guards immediately called for pizza. The monster continued to get smaller with the king's kind gestures. (d) He then offered the monster a full body massage. As the guards helped with the relaxing massage, the monster became tiny. With another act of kindness to the monster, he just disappeared.

(D)

With each bad word the guards used, the monster grew more ugly and smelly. The guards got even angrier — they began to brandish their swords to scare the monster away from the palace. But (e) he just grew bigger and bigger, eventually taking up the whole room. He grew more ugly and smelly than ever.

＊brandish: 휘두르다

10

고1·2023년 3월 43번

주어진 글 (A)에 이어질 내용을 순서에 맞게 배열한 것으로 가장 적절한 것은?

① (B) − (D) − (C)   ② (C) − (B) − (D)

③ (C) − (D) − (B)   ④ (D) − (B) − (C)

⑤ (D) − (C) − (B)

12

고1·2023년 3월 45번

윗글에 관한 내용으로 적절하지 <u>않은</u> 것은?

① 왕이 없는 동안 괴물이 궁전 문으로 접근했다.

② 왕은 미소를 지으며 괴물에게 환영한다고 말했다.

③ 왕의 친절한 행동에 괴물의 몸이 계속 더 작아졌다.

④ 경비병들은 괴물을 마사지해 주기를 거부했다.

⑤ 경비병들은 겁을 주어 괴물을 쫓아내려 했다.

11

고1·2023년 3월 44번

밑줄 친 (a)~(e) 중에서 가리키는 대상이 나머지 넷과 <u>다른</u> 것은?

① (a)   ② (b)   ③ (c)   ④ (d)   ⑤ (e)

학습 Check! ▶ 몰라서 틀린 문항 × 표기 ▶ 헷갈렸거나 찍은 문항 △ 표기 ▶ ×, △ 문항은 다시 풀고 ✔ 표기를 하세요.

종료 시각	시 분 초	문항 번호	01	02	03	04	05	06	07	08	09	10	11	12
소요 시간	분 초	채점 결과												
초과 시간	분 초	틀린 문항 복습												

[Day 02] 미니 모의고사 015

01

고3 · 2023학년도 수능 18번

다음 글의 목적으로 가장 적절한 것은?

To whom it may concern,

My name is Michael Brown. I have been a bird-watcher since childhood. I have always enjoyed watching birds in my yard and identifying them by sight and sound. Yesterday, I happened to read an article about your club. I was surprised and excited to find out about a community of passionate bird-watchers who travel annually to go birding. I would love to join your club, but your website appears to be under construction. I could not find any information except for this contact email address. I would like to know how to sign up for the club. I look forward to your reply.

Sincerely,
Michael Brown

① 조류 관찰 클럽에 가입하는 방법을 문의하려고
② 조류 관찰 시 주의해야 할 사항을 전달하려고
③ 조류 관찰 협회의 새로운 규정을 확인하려고
④ 조류 관찰과 관련된 웹 사이트를 소개하려고
⑤ 조류 관찰 시 필요한 장비를 알아보려고

02 **1등급 대비 고난도 2점 문제**

고1 · 2020년 11월 21번

밑줄 친 **popped out of the box**가 다음 글에서 의미하는 바로 가장 적절한 것은?

With the Internet, everything changed. Product problems, overpromises, the lack of customer support, differential pricing — all of the issues that customers actually experienced from a marketing organization suddenly popped out of the box. No longer were there any controlled communications or even business systems. Consumers could generally learn through the Web whatever they wanted to know about a company, its products, its competitors, its distribution systems, and, most of all, its truthfulness when talking about its products and services. Just as important, the Internet opened up a forum for customers to compare products, experiences, and values with other customers easily and quickly. Now the customer had a way to talk back to the marketer and to do so through public forums instantly.

＊differential pricing: 가격 차등

① could not be kept secret anymore
② might disappear from public attention
③ were no longer available to marketers
④ became too complicated to understand
⑤ began to improve companies' reputations

03

다음 글의 주제로 가장 적절한 것은?

We tend to believe that we possess a host of socially desirable characteristics, and that we are free of most of those that are socially undesirable. For example, a large majority of the general public thinks that they are more intelligent, more fair-minded, less prejudiced, and more skilled behind the wheel of an automobile than the average person. This phenomenon is so reliable and ubiquitous that it has come to be known as the "Lake Wobegon effect," after Garrison Keillor's fictional community where "the women are strong, the men are good-looking, and all the children are above average." A survey of one million high school seniors found that 70% thought they were above average in leadership ability, and only 2% thought they were below average. In terms of ability to get along with others, *all* students thought they were above average, 60% thought they were in the top 10%, and 25% thought they were in the top 1%!

＊ubiquitous: 도처에 있는

① importance of having a positive self-image as a leader
② our common belief that we are better than average
③ our tendency to think others are superior to us
④ reasons why we always try to be above average
⑤ danger of prejudice in building healthy social networks

04

다음 도표의 내용과 일치하지 않는 것은?

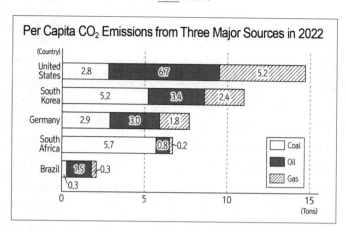

The above graph shows per capita CO_2 emissions from coal, oil, and gas by countries in 2022. ① The United States had the highest total per capita CO_2 emissions, even though its emissions from coal were the second lowest among the five countries shown. ② South Korea's total per capita CO_2 emissions were over 10 tons, ranking it the second highest among the countries shown. ③ Germany had lower CO_2 emissions per capita than South Korea in all three major sources respectively. ④ The per capita CO_2 emissions from coal in South Africa were over three times higher than those in Germany. ⑤ In Brazil, oil was the largest source of CO_2 emissions per capita among its three major sources, just as it was in the United States and Germany.

＊per capita: 1인당

05

다음 글의 밑줄 친 부분 중, 어법상 틀린 것은? [3점]

Positively or negatively, our parents and families are powerful influences on us. But even ① stronger, especially when we're young, are our friends. We often choose friends as a way of ② expanding our sense of identity beyond our families. As a result, the pressure to conform to the standards and expectations of friends and other social groups ③ is likely to be intense. Judith Rich Harris, who is a developmental psychologist, ④ arguing that three main forces shape our development: personal temperament, our parents, and our peers. The influence of peers, she argues, is much stronger than that of parents. "The world ⑤ that children share with their peers," she says, "is what shapes their behavior and modifies the characteristics they were born with, and hence determines the sort of people they will be when they grow up."

＊temperament: 기질

06

(A), (B), (C)의 각 네모 안에서 문맥에 맞는 낱말로 가장 적절한 것은?

From the beginning of human history, people have asked questions about the world and their place within it. For early societies, the answers to the most basic questions were found in (A) religion / science . Some people, however, found the traditional religious explanations inadequate, and they began to search for answers based on reason. This (B) consistency / shift marked the birth of philosophy, and the first of the great thinkers that we know of was Thales of Miletus. He used reason to inquire into the nature of the universe, and encouraged others to do likewise. He passed on to his followers not only his answers but also the process of thinking (C) rationally / irrationally , together with an idea of what kind of explanations could be considered satisfactory.

(A)	(B)	(C)
① religion	consistency	rationally
② religion	shift	irrationally
③ religion	shift	rationally
④ science	shift	irrationally
⑤ science	consistency	rationally

07 1등급 대비 고난도 2점 문제

다음 빈칸에 들어갈 말로 가장 적절한 것을 고르시오.

As the tenth anniversary of the terrorist attacks of September 11, 2001, approached, 9/11-related media stories peaked in the days immediately surrounding the anniversary date and then dropped off rapidly in the weeks thereafter. Surveys conducted during those times asked citizens to choose two "especially important" events from the past seventy years. Two weeks prior to the anniversary, before the media blitz began, about 30 percent of respondents named 9/11. But as the anniversary drew closer, and the media treatment intensified, survey respondents started identifying 9/11 in increasing numbers — to a high of 65 percent. Two weeks later, though, after reportage had decreased to earlier levels, once again only about 30 percent of the participants placed it among their two especially important events of the past seventy years. Clearly, the _____ of news coverage can make a big difference in the *perceived* significance of an issue among observers as they are exposed to the coverage.

* blitz: 대선전, 집중 공세

① accuracy
② tone
③ amount
④ source
⑤ type

08

다음 빈칸에 들어갈 말로 가장 적절한 것을 고르시오. [3점]

Most times a foreign language is spoken in film, subtitles are used to translate the dialogue for the viewer. However, there are occasions when foreign dialogue is left unsubtitled (and thus incomprehensible to most of the target audience). This is often done if the movie is seen mainly from the viewpoint of a particular character who does not speak the language. Such absence of subtitles allows the audience to feel a similar sense of incomprehension and alienation that the character feels. An example of this is seen in *Not Without My Daughter*. The Persian language dialogue spoken by the Iranian characters is not subtitled because the main character Betty Mahmoody does not speak Persian and the audience is _____.

* subtitle: 자막(을 넣다) ** incomprehensible: 이해할 수 없는

*** alienation: 소외

① seeing the film from her viewpoint
② impressed by her language skills
③ attracted to her beautiful voice
④ participating in a heated debate
⑤ learning the language used in the film

09

다음 글에서 전체 흐름과 관계 없는 문장은?

Developing a personal engagement with poetry brings a number of benefits to you as an individual, in both a personal and a professional capacity. ① Writing poetry has been shown to have physical and mental benefits, with expressive writing found to improve immune system and lung function, diminish psychological distress, and enhance relationships. ② Poetry has long been used to aid different mental health needs, develop empathy, and reconsider our relationship with both natural and built environments. ③ Poetry is also an incredibly effective way of actively targeting the cognitive development period, improving your productivity and scientific creativity in the process. ④ Poetry is considered to be an easy and useful means of expressing emotions, but you fall into frustration when you realize its complexity. ⑤ In short, poetry has a lot to offer, if you give it the opportunity to do so.

＊cognitive: 인지적인

10 [1등급 대비 고난도 2점 문제]

주어진 글 다음에 이어질 글의 순서로 가장 적절한 것을 고르시오.

To be successful, you need to understand the vital difference between believing you will succeed, and believing you will succeed easily.

(A) Unrealistic optimists, on the other hand, believe that success will happen to them — that the universe will reward them for all their positive thinking, or that somehow they will be transformed overnight into the kind of person for whom obstacles don't exist anymore.

(B) Put another way, it's the difference between being a realistic optimist, and an unrealistic optimist. Realistic optimists believe they will succeed, but also believe they have to make success happen — through things like careful planning and choosing the right strategies.

(C) They recognize the need for giving serious thought to how they will deal with obstacles. This preparation only increases their confidence in their own ability to get things done.

① (A) － (C) － (B)
② (B) － (A) － (C)
③ (B) － (C) － (A)
④ (C) － (A) － (B)
⑤ (C) － (B) － (A)

[11 ~ 12] 다음 글을 읽고, 물음에 답하시오.

Since the turn of the twentieth century we've believed in genetic causes of diagnoses — a theory called genetic determinism. Under this model, our genes (and subsequent health) are determined at birth. We are "destined" to inherit certain diseases based on the misfortune of our DNA. Genetic determinism doesn't (a) consider the role of family backgrounds, traumas, habits, or anything else within the environment. In this dynamic we are not (b) active participants in our own health and wellness. Why would we be? If something is predetermined, it's not (c) necessary to look at anything beyond our DNA. But the more science has learned about the body and its interaction with the environment around it (in its various forms, from our nutrition to our relationships to our racially oppressive systems), the more (d) simplistic the story becomes. We are not merely expressions of coding but products of a remarkable variety of interactions that are both within and outside of our control. Once we see beyond the narrative that genetics are (e) destiny, we can take ownership of our health. This allows us to see how "choiceless" we once were and empowers us with the ability to create real and lasting change.

* oppressive: 억압적인

11

윗글의 제목으로 가장 적절한 것은?

① Health Is in Our Hands, Not Only in Our Genes
② Genetics: A Solution to Enhance Human Wellness
③ How Did DNA Dominate Over Environment in Biology?
④ Never Be Confident in Your Health, but Keep Checking!
⑤ Why Scientific Innovation Affects Our Social Interactions

12

밑줄 친 (a) ~ (e) 중에서 문맥상 낱말의 쓰임이 적절하지 <u>않은</u> 것은? [3점]

① (a) ② (b) ③ (c) ④ (d) ⑤ (e)

DAY 03

학습 Check!   ▶ 몰라서 틀린 문항 × 표기   ▶ 헷갈렸거나 찍은 문항 △ 표기   ▶ ×, △ 문항은 다시 풀고 ✔ 표기를 하세요.

종료 시각	시 분 초	문항 번호	01	02	03	04	05	06	07	08	09	10	11	12
소요 시간	분 초	채점 결과												
초과 시간	분 초	틀린 문항 복습												

DAY 04

● 날짜 : 　월　 일 ● 시작 시각 : 　시　 분　 초 ● 목표 시간 : 20분

※ 점수 표기가 없는 문항은 모두 **2점**입니다.

01

고1 • 2022년 6월 20번

다음 글에서 필자가 주장하는 바로 가장 적절한 것은?

　Meetings encourage creative thinking and can give you ideas that you may never have thought of on your own. However, on average, meeting participants consider about one third of meeting time to be unproductive. But you can make your meetings more productive and more useful by preparing well in advance. You should create a list of items to be discussed and share your list with other participants before a meeting. It allows them to know what to expect in your meeting and prepare to participate.

① 회의 결과는 빠짐없이 작성해서 공개해야 한다.
② 중요한 정보는 공식 회의를 통해 전달해야 한다.
③ 생산성 향상을 위해 정기적인 평가회가 필요하다.
④ 모든 참석자의 동의를 받아서 회의를 열어야 한다.
⑤ 회의에서 다룰 사항은 미리 작성해서 공유해야 한다.

02

고1 • 2023년 3월 22번

다음 글의 요지로 가장 적절한 것은?

　When students are starting their college life, they may approach every course, test, or learning task the same way, using what we like to call "the rubber-stamp approach." Think about it this way: Would you wear a tuxedo to a baseball game? A colorful dress to a funeral? A bathing suit to religious services? Probably not. You know there's appropriate dress for different occasions and settings. Skillful learners know that "putting on the same clothes" won't work for every class. They are flexible learners. They have different strategies and know when to use them. They know that you study for multiple-choice tests differently than you study for essay tests. And they not only know what to do, but they also know how to do it.

① 숙련된 학습자는 상황에 맞는 학습 전략을 사용할 줄 안다.
② 선다형 시험과 논술 시험은 평가의 형태와 목적이 다르다.
③ 문화마다 특정 행사와 상황에 맞는 복장 규정이 있다.
④ 학습의 양보다는 학습의 질이 학업 성과를 좌우한다.
⑤ 학습 목표가 명확할수록 성취 수준이 높아진다.

03

Donato Bramante에 관한 다음 글의 내용과 일치하지 <u>않는</u> 것은?

Donato Bramante, born in Fermignano, Italy, began to paint early in his life. His father encouraged him to study painting. Later, he worked as an assistant of Piero della Francesca in Urbino. Around 1480, he built several churches in a new style in Milan. He had a close relationship with Leonardo da Vinci, and they worked together in that city. Architecture became his main interest, but he did not give up painting. Bramante moved to Rome in 1499 and participated in Pope Julius II's plan for the renewal of Rome. He planned the new Basilica of St. Peter in Rome — one of the most ambitious building projects in the history of humankind. Bramante died on April 11, 1514 and was buried in Rome. His buildings influenced other architects for centuries.

① Piero della Francesca의 조수로 일했다.
② Milan에서 새로운 양식의 교회들을 건축했다.
③ 건축에 주된 관심을 갖게 되면서 그림 그리기를 포기했다.
④ Pope Julius II의 Rome 재개발 계획에 참여했다.
⑤ 그의 건축물들은 다른 건축가들에게 영향을 끼쳤다.

04 [1등급 대비 고난도 3점 문제]

다음 글의 밑줄 친 부분 중, 어법상 틀린 것은? [3점]

"You are what you eat." That phrase is often used to ① <u>show</u> the relationship between the foods you eat and your physical health. But do you really know what you are eating when you buy processed foods, canned foods, and packaged goods? Many of the manufactured products made today contain so many chemicals and artificial ingredients ② <u>which</u> it is sometimes difficult to know exactly what is inside them. Fortunately, now there are food labels. Food labels are a good way ③ <u>to find</u> the information about the foods you eat. Labels on food are ④ <u>like</u> the table of contents found in books. The main purpose of food labels ⑤ <u>is</u> to inform you what is inside the food you are purchasing.

* manufactured: (공장에서) 제조된
** table of contents: (책 등의) 목차

05

다음 글의 밑줄 친 부분 중, 문맥상 낱말의 쓰임이 적절하지 <u>않은</u> 것은? [3점]

Plant growth is controlled by a group of hormones called auxins found at the tips of stems and roots of plants. Auxins produced at the tips of stems tend to accumulate on the side of the stem that is in the shade. Accordingly, the auxins ① <u>stimulate</u> growth on the shaded side of the plant. Therefore, the shaded side grows faster than the side facing the sunlight. This phenomenon causes the stem to bend and appear to be growing ② <u>towards</u> the light. Auxins have the ③ <u>opposite</u> effect on the roots of plants. Auxins in the tips of roots tend to limit growth. If a root is horizontal in the soil, the auxins will accumulate on the lower side and interfere with its development. Therefore, the lower side of the root will grow ④ <u>faster</u> than the upper side. This will, in turn, cause the root to bend ⑤ <u>downwards</u>, with the tip of the root growing in that direction.

06

다음 빈칸에 들어갈 말로 가장 적절한 것을 고르시오.

If we lived on a planet where nothing ever changed, there would be little to do. There would be nothing to figure out and there would be no reason for science. And if we lived in an unpredictable world, where things changed in random or very complex ways, we would not be able to figure things out. Again, there would be no such thing as science. But we live in an in-between universe, where things change, but according to _____. If I throw a stick up in the air, it always falls down. If the sun sets in the west, it always rises again the next morning in the east. And so it becomes possible to figure things out. We can do science, and with it we can improve our lives.

① age ② luck
③ belief ④ rules
⑤ interests

07 1등급 대비 고난도 3점 문제

다음 빈칸에 들어갈 말로 가장 적절한 것을 고르시오. [3점]

We're often told that newborns and infants are comforted by rocking because this motion is similar to what they experienced in the womb, and that they must take comfort in this familiar feeling. This may be true; however, to date there are no convincing data that demonstrate a significant relationship between the amount of time a mother moves during pregnancy and her newborn's response to rocking. Just as likely is the idea that newborns come to associate gentle rocking with being fed. Parents understand that rocking quiets a newborn, and they very often provide gentle, repetitive movement during feeding. Since the appearance of food is a primary reinforcer, newborns may _____ _____ because they have been conditioned through a process of associative learning.

* womb: 자궁 ** reinforcer: 강화물

① acquire a fondness for motion
② want consistent feeding
③ dislike severe rocking
④ remember the tastes of food
⑤ form a bond with their mothers

08 1등급 대비 고난도 3점 문제

글의 흐름으로 보아, 주어진 문장이 들어가기에 가장 적절한 곳을 고르시오. [3점]

> More recently, agriculture has in many places lost its local character, and has become incorporated into the global economy.

Earlier agricultural systems were integrated with and co-evolved with technologies, beliefs, myths and traditions as part of an integrated social system. (①) Generally, people planted a variety of crops in different areas, in the hope of obtaining a reasonably stable food supply. (②) These systems could only be maintained at low population levels, and were relatively non-destructive (but not always). (③) This has led to increased pressure on agricultural land for exchange commodities and export goods. (④) More land is being diverted from local food production to "cash crops" for export and exchange; fewer types of crops are raised, and each crop is raised in much greater quantities than before. (⑤) Thus, ever more land is converted from forest (and other natural systems) for agriculture for export, rather than using land for subsistence crops.

* subsistence crop: 자급자족용 작물

DAY 04

09

고1·2023년 9월 40번

다음 글의 내용을 한 문장으로 요약하고자 한다. 빈칸 (A), (B)에 들어갈 말로 가장 적절한 것은?

It's not news to anyone that we judge others based on their clothes. In general, studies that investigate these judgments find that people prefer clothing that matches expectations — surgeons in scrubs, little boys in blue — with one notable exception. A series of studies published in an article in June 2014 in the *Journal of Consumer Research* explored observers' reactions to people who broke established norms only slightly. In one scenario, a man at a black-tie affair was viewed as having higher status and competence when wearing a red bow tie. The researchers also found that valuing uniqueness increased audience members' ratings of the status and competence of a professor who wore red sneakers while giving a lecture. The results suggest that people judge these slight deviations from the norm as positive because they suggest that the individual is powerful enough to risk the social costs of such behaviors.

↓

A series of studies show that people view an individual _____(A)_____ when the individual only slightly _____(B)_____ the norm for what people should wear.

	(A)		(B)
①	positively	.....	challenges
②	negatively	.....	challenges
③	indifferently	.....	neglects
④	negatively	.....	meets
⑤	positively	.....	meets

[10 ~ 12] 다음 글을 읽고, 물음에 답하시오.

(A)

When I was 17, I discovered a wonderful thing. My father and I were sitting on the floor of his study. We were organizing his old papers. Across the carpet I saw a fat paper clip. Its rust dusted the cover sheet of a report of some kind. I picked it up. I started to read. Then I started to cry.

(B)

"Daddy," I said, handing him the pages, "this speech — how did you ever get permission to give it? And weren't you scared?" "Well, honey," he said, "I didn't ask for permission. I just asked myself, 'What is the most important challenge facing my generation?' I knew immediately. Then (a) I asked myself, 'And if I weren't afraid, what would I say about it in this speech?'"

(C)

It was a speech he had written in 1920, in Tennessee. Then only 17 himself and graduating from high school, he had called for equality for African Americans. (b) I marvelled, proud of him, and wondered how, in 1920, so young, so white, and in the deep South, where the law still separated black from white, (c) he had had the courage to deliver it. I asked him about it.

(D)

"I wrote it. And I delivered it. About half way through I looked out to see the entire audience of teachers, students, and parents stand up — and walk out. Left alone on the stage, (d) I thought to myself, 'Well, I guess I need to be sure to do only two things with my life: keep thinking for myself, and not get killed.'" He handed the speech back to me, and smiled. "(e) You seem to have done both," I said.

10

고1 • 2021년 6월 43번

주어진 글 (A)에 이어질 내용을 순서에 맞게 배열한 것으로 가장 적절한 것은?

① (B) − (D) − (C)   ② (C) − (B) − (D)
③ (C) − (D) − (B)   ④ (D) − (B) − (C)
⑤ (D) − (C) − (B)

12

고1 • 2021년 6월 45번

윗글에 관한 내용으로 적절하지 <u>않은</u> 것은?

① 아버지와 나는 서류를 정리하고 있었다.
② 나는 서재에서 발견한 것을 읽고 나서 울기 시작했다.
③ 아버지는 연설을 하기 위한 허락을 구하지 않았다.
④ 아버지가 연설문을 썼을 당시 17세였다.
⑤ 교사, 학생, 학부모 모두 아버지의 연설을 끝까지 들었다.

11

고1 • 2021년 6월 44번

밑줄 친 (a)~(e) 중에서 가리키는 대상이 나머지 넷과 <u>다른</u> 것은?

① (a)   ② (b)   ③ (c)   ④ (d)   ⑤ (e)

학습 Check!   ▶ 몰라서 틀린 문항 × 표기   ▶ 헷갈렸거나 찍은 문항 △ 표기   ▶ ×, △ 문항은 다시 풀고 ✔ 표기를 하세요.

종료 시각	시	분	초	문항 번호	01	02	03	04	05	06	07	08	09	10	11	12
소요 시간		분	초	채점 결과												
초과 시간		분	초	틀린 문항 복습												

● 날짜 : 월 일 ● 시작 시각 : 시 분 초 ● 목표 시간 : 20분　　　　　　　※ 점수 표기가 없는 문항은 모두 **2점**입니다.

01
고3 • 2018학년도 수능 18번

다음 글의 목적으로 가장 적절한 것은?

Dear Ms. Diane Edwards,

I am a teacher working at East End High School. I have read from your notice that the East End Seaport Museum is now offering a special program, the 2017 Bug Lighthouse Experience. The program would be a great opportunity for our students to have fun and experience something new. I estimate that 50 students and teachers from our school would like to participate in it. Would you please let me know if it is possible to make a group reservation for the program for Saturday, November 18? We don't want to miss this great opportunity. I look forward to hearing from you soon.

Best regards,
Joseph Loach

① 단체 관람 시 유의 사항을 안내하려고
② 교내 행사에 초청할 강사 추천을 부탁하려고
③ 프로그램 단체 예약이 가능한지를 문의하려고
④ 새로운 체험 학습 프로그램을 소개하려고
⑤ 견학 예정 인원수의 변경을 요청하려고

02
고1 • 2023년 6월 20번

다음 글에서 필자가 주장하는 바로 가장 적절한 것은?

Research shows that people who work have two calendars: one for work and one for their personal lives. Although it may seem sensible, having two separate calendars for work and personal life can lead to distractions. To check if something is missing, you will find yourself checking your to-do lists multiple times. Instead, organize all of your tasks in one place. It doesn't matter if you use digital or paper media. It's okay to keep your professional and personal tasks in one place. This will give you a good idea of how time is divided between work and home. This will allow you to make informed decisions about which tasks are most important.

① 결정한 것은 반드시 실행하도록 노력하라.
② 자신이 담당한 업무에 관한 전문성을 확보하라.
③ 업무 집중도를 높이기 위해 책상 위를 정돈하라.
④ 좋은 아이디어를 메모하는 습관을 길러라.
⑤ 업무와 개인 용무를 한 곳에 정리하라.

03

다음 글의 제목으로 가장 적절한 것은?

Many people make a mistake of only operating along the safe zones, and in the process they miss the opportunity to achieve greater things. They do so because of a fear of the unknown and a fear of treading the unknown paths of life. Those that are brave enough to take those roads less travelled are able to get great returns and derive major satisfaction out of their courageous moves. Being overcautious will mean that you will miss attaining the greatest levels of your potential. You must learn to take those chances that many people around you will not take, because your success will flow from those bold decisions that you will take along the way.

* tread: 밟다

① More Courage Brings More Opportunities
② Travel: The Best Way to Make Friends
③ How to Turn Mistakes into Success
④ Satisfying Life? Share with Others
⑤ Why Is Overcoming Fear So Hard?

04

다음 도표의 내용과 일치하지 <u>않는</u> 것은?

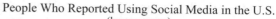
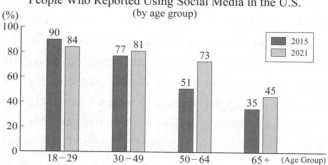

People Who Reported Using Social Media in the U.S.
(by age group)

The graph above shows the percentages of people in different age groups who reported using social media in the United States in 2015 and 2021. ① In each of the given years, the 18−29 group had the highest percentage of people who said they used social media. ② In 2015, the percentage of people who reported using social media in the 30−49 group was more than twice that in the 65 and older group. ③ The percentage of people who said they used social media in the 50−64 group in 2021 was 22 percentage points higher than that in 2015. ④ In 2021, except for the 65 and older group, more than four-fifths of people in each age group reported using social media. ⑤ Among all the age groups, only the 18−29 group showed a decrease in the percentage of people who reported using social media from 2015 to 2021.

05

다음 글의 밑줄 친 부분 중, 어법상 틀린 것은?

My dad worked very late hours as a musician — until about three in the morning — so he slept late on weekends. As a result, we didn't have much of a relationship when I was young other than him constantly nagging me to take care of chores like mowing the lawn and cutting the hedges, ① which I hated. He was a responsible man ② dealing with an irresponsible kid. Memories of how we interacted ③ seems funny to me today. For example, one time he told me to cut the grass and I decided ④ to do just the front yard and postpone doing the back, but then it rained for a couple days and the backyard grass became so high I had to cut it with a sickle. That took so long ⑤ that by the time I was finished, the front yard was too high to mow, and so on.

＊sickle: 낫

06 **1등급 대비 고난도 3점 문제**

다음 글의 밑줄 친 부분 중, 문맥상 낱말의 쓰임이 적절하지 않은 것은? [3점]

Detailed study over the past two or three decades is showing that the complex forms of natural systems are essential to their functioning. The attempt to ① straighten rivers and give them regular cross-sections is perhaps the most disastrous example of this form-and-function relationship. The natural river has a very ② irregular form: it curves a lot, spills across floodplains, and leaks into wetlands, giving it an ever-changing and incredibly complex shoreline. This allows the river to ③ prevent variations in water level and speed. Pushing the river into tidy geometry ④ destroys functional capacity and results in disasters like the Mississippi floods of 1927 and 1993 and, more recently, the unnatural disaster of Hurricane Katrina. A $50 billion plan to "let the river loose" in Louisiana recognizes that the ⑤ controlled Mississippi is washing away twenty-four square miles of that state annually.

＊geometry: 기하학 ＊＊capacity: 수용능력

07

다음 빈칸에 들어갈 말로 가장 적절한 것을 고르시오. [3점]

Good managers have learned to overcome the initial feelings of anxiety when assigning tasks. They are aware that no two people act in exactly the same way and so do not feel threatened if they see one employee going about a task differently than another. Instead, they focus on _____. If a job was successfully done, as long as people are working in a manner acceptable to the organization (for example, as long as salespeople are keeping to the company's ethical selling policy), then that's fine. If an acceptable final outcome wasn't achieved, then such managers respond by discussing it with the employee and analyzing the situation, to find out what training or additional skills that person will need to do the task successfully in the future.

* assign: (일·책임 등을) 맡기다

① the end result
② the welfare policy
③ the uniform procedure
④ the informal atmosphere
⑤ the employee's personality

08 1등급 대비 고난도 3점 문제

다음 빈칸에 들어갈 말로 가장 적절한 것을 고르시오. [3점]

Back in 1996, an American airline was faced with an interesting problem. At a time when most other airlines were losing money or going under, over 100 cities were begging the company to service their locations. However, that's not the interesting part. What's interesting is that the company turned down over 95 percent of those offers and began serving only four new locations. It turned down tremendous growth because _____. Sure, its executives wanted to grow each year, but they didn't want to grow too much. Unlike other famous companies, they wanted to set their own pace, one that could be sustained in the long term. By doing this, they established a safety margin for growth that helped them continue to thrive at a time when the other airlines were flailing.

* flail: 마구 흔들리다

① it was being faced with serious financial crises
② there was no specific long-term plan on marketing
③ company leadership had set an upper limit for growth
④ its executives worried about the competing airlines' future
⑤ the company had emphasized moral duties more than profits

09

다음 글에서 전체 흐름과 관계 <u>없는</u> 문장은?

In a single week, the sun delivers more energy to our planet than humanity has used through the burning of coal, oil, and natural gas through *all of human history*. And the sun will keep shining on our planet for billions of years. ① Our challenge isn't that we're running out of energy. ② It's that we have been focused on the wrong source — the small, finite one that we're using up. ③ Indeed, all the coal, natural gas, and oil we use today is just solar energy from millions of years ago, a very tiny part of which was preserved deep underground. ④ Our efforts to develop technologies that use fossil fuels have shown meaningful results. ⑤ Our challenge, and our opportunity, is to learn to efficiently and cheaply use the *much more abundant* source that is the new energy striking our planet each day from the sun.

10

주어진 글 다음에 이어질 글의 순서로 가장 적절한 것을 고르시오.
[3점]

The next time you're out under a clear, dark sky, look up. If you've picked a good spot for stargazing, you'll see a sky full of stars, shining and twinkling like thousands of brilliant jewels.

(A) It might be easier if you describe patterns of stars. You could say something like, "See that big triangle of bright stars there?" Or, "Do you see those five stars that look like a big letter W?"

(B) But this amazing sight of stars can also be confusing. Try and point out a single star to someone. Chances are, that person will have a hard time knowing exactly which star you're looking at.

(C) When you do that, you're doing exactly what we all do when we look at the stars. We look for patterns, not just so that we can point something out to someone else, but also because that's what we humans have always done.

① (A) − (C) − (B) ② (B) − (A) − (C)
③ (B) − (C) − (A) ④ (C) − (A) − (B)
⑤ (C) − (B) − (A)

[11 ～ 12] 다음 글을 읽고, 물음에 답하시오.

A quick look at history shows that humans have not always had the abundance of food that is enjoyed throughout most of the developed world today. In fact, there have been numerous times in history when food has been rather scarce. As a result, people used to eat more when food was available since the availability of the next meal was (a) questionable. Overeating in those times was essential to ensure survival, and humans received satisfaction from eating more than was needed for immediate purposes. On top of that, the highest pleasure was derived from eating the most calorie-dense foods, resulting in a (b) longer lasting energy reserve.

Even though there are parts of the world where, unfortunately, food is still scarce, most of the world's population today has plenty of food available to survive and thrive. However, this abundance is new, and your body has not caught up, still naturally (c) rewarding you for eating more than you need and for eating the most calorie-dense foods. These are innate habits and not simple addictions. They are self-preserving mechanisms initiated by your body, ensuring your future survival, but they are (d) irrelevant now. Therefore, it is your responsibility to communicate with your body regarding the new environment of food abundance and the need to (e) strengthen the inborn habit of overeating.

＊innate: 타고난

11

고1・2019년 9월 41번

윗글의 제목으로 가장 적절한 것은?

① Which Is Better, Tasty or Healthy Food?
② Simple Steps for a More Balanced Diet
③ Overeating: It's Rooted in Our Genes
④ How Calorie-dense Foods Ruin Our Bodies
⑤ Our Eating Habits Reflect Our Personalities

12 1등급 대비 고난도 3점 문제

고1・2019년 9월 42번

밑줄 친 (a) ～ (e) 중에서 문맥상 낱말의 쓰임이 적절하지 않은 것은? [3점]

① (a)　　② (b)　　③ (c)　　④ (d)　　⑤ (e)

학습 Check!

▶ 몰라서 틀린 문항 × 표기　▶ 헷갈렸거나 찍은 문항 △ 표기　▶ ×, △ 문항은 다시 풀고 ✔ 표기를 하세요.

종료 시각	시	분	초	문항 번호	01	02	03	04	05	06	07	08	09	10	11	12
소요 시간		분	초	채점 결과												
초과 시간		분	초	틀린 문항 복습												

DAY 06

● 날짜 : 　월　 　일　 ● 시작 시각 : 　시　 　분　 　초　 ● 목표 시간 : 20분

※ 점수 표기가 없는 문항은 모두 **2점**입니다.

01

고3 · 2022학년도 수능 19번

다음 글에 나타난 **Evelyn**의 심경 변화로 가장 적절한 것은?

It was Evelyn's first time to explore the Badlands of Alberta, famous across Canada for its numerous dinosaur fossils. As a young amateur bone-hunter, she was overflowing with anticipation. She had not travelled this far for the bones of common dinosaur species. Her life-long dream to find rare fossils of dinosaurs was about to come true. She began eagerly searching for them. After many hours of wandering throughout the deserted lands, however, she was unsuccessful. Now, the sun was beginning to set, and her goal was still far beyond her reach. Looking at the slowly darkening ground before her, she sighed to herself, "I can't believe I came all this way for nothing. What a waste of time!"

① confused　　→ scared

② discouraged → confident

③ relaxed　　 → annoyed

④ indifferent　→ depressed

⑤ hopeful　　→ disappointed

02

고1 · 2022년 6월 22번

다음 글의 요지로 가장 적절한 것은?

Your emotions deserve attention and give you important pieces of information. However, they can also sometimes be an unreliable, inaccurate source of information. You may feel a certain way, but that does not mean those feelings are reflections of the truth. You may feel sad and conclude that your friend is angry with you when her behavior simply reflects that she's having a bad day. You may feel depressed and decide that you did poorly in an interview when you did just fine. Your feelings can mislead you into thinking things that are not supported by facts.

① 자신의 감정으로 인해 상황을 오해할 수 있다.

② 자신의 생각을 타인에게 강요해서는 안 된다.

③ 인간관계가 우리의 감정에 영향을 미친다.

④ 타인의 감정에 공감하는 자세가 필요하다.

⑤ 공동체를 위한 선택에는 보상이 따른다.

03

고1 · 2021년 3월 24번

다음 글의 제목으로 가장 적절한 것은?

Think, for a moment, about something you bought that you never ended up using. An item of clothing you never ended up wearing? A book you never read? Some piece of electronic equipment that never even made it out of the box? It is estimated that Australians alone spend on average $10.8 billion AUD (approximately $9.99 billion USD) every year on goods they do not use — more than the total government spending on universities and roads. That is an average of $1,250 AUD (approximately $1,156 USD) for each household. All the things we buy that then just sit there gathering dust are waste — a waste of money, a waste of time, and waste in the sense of pure rubbish. As the author Clive Hamilton observes, 'The difference between the stuff we buy and what we use is waste.'

① Spending Enables the Economy
② Money Management: Dos and Don'ts
③ Too Much Shopping: A Sign of Loneliness
④ 3R's of Waste: Reduce, Reuse, and Recycle
⑤ What You Buy Is Waste Unless You Use It

04

고1 · 2023년 9월 26번

Bill Evans에 관한 다음 글의 내용과 일치하지 <u>않는</u> 것은?

American jazz pianist Bill Evans was born in New Jersey in 1929. His early training was in classical music. At the age of six, he began receiving piano lessons, later adding flute and violin. He earned bachelor's degrees in piano and music education from Southeastern Louisiana College in 1950. He went on to serve in the army from 1951 to 1954 and played flute in the Fifth Army Band. After serving in the military, he studied composition at the Mannes School of Music in New York. Composer George Russell admired his playing and hired Evans to record and perform his compositions. Evans became famous for recordings made from the late-1950s through the 1960s. He won his first Grammy Award in 1964 for his album *Conversations with Myself*. Evans' expressive piano works and his unique harmonic approach inspired a whole generation of musicians.

① 6세에 피아노 수업을 받기 시작했다.
② Southeastern Louisiana 대학에서 학위를 취득했다.
③ 군 복무 이후 뉴욕에서 작곡을 공부했다.
④ 작곡가 George Russell을 고용했다.
⑤ 1964년에 자신의 첫 번째 그래미상을 수상했다.

DAY 06

05

다음 글의 밑줄 친 부분 중, 어법상 틀린 것은? [3점]

　Are you honest with yourself about your strengths and weaknesses? Get to really know ① yourself and learn what your weaknesses are. Accepting your role in your problems ② mean that you understand the solution lies within you. If you have a weakness in a certain area, get educated and do ③ what you have to do to improve things for yourself. If your social image is terrible, look within yourself and take the necessary steps to improve ④ it, TODAY. You have the ability to choose how to respond to life. Decide today to end all the excuses, and stop ⑤ lying to yourself about what is going on. The beginning of growth comes when you begin to personally accept responsibility for your choices.

06

(A), (B), (C)의 각 네모 안에서 문맥에 맞는 낱말로 가장 적절한 것은?

　Intellectual humility is admitting you are human and there are limits to the knowledge you have. It involves (A) neglecting / recognizing that you possess cognitive and personal biases, and that your brain tends to see things in such a way that your opinions and viewpoints are favored above others. It is being willing to work to overcome those biases in order to be more objective and make informed decisions. People who display intellectual humility are more likely to be (B) receptive / resistant to learning from others who think differently than they do. They tend to be well-liked and respected by others because they make it clear that they (C) value / undervalue what other people bring to the table. Intellectually humble people want to learn more and are open to finding information from a variety of sources. They are not interested in trying to appear or feel superior to others.

	(A)	(B)	(C)
①	recognizing	receptive	value
②	recognizing	resistant	undervalue
③	recognizing	receptive	undervalue
④	neglecting	resistant	undervalue
⑤	neglecting	receptive	value

07 1등급 대비 고난도 2점 문제

다음 빈칸에 들어갈 말로 가장 적절한 것을 고르시오.

When reading another scientist's findings, think critically about the experiment. Ask yourself: Were observations recorded during or after the experiment? Do the conclusions make sense? Can the results be repeated? Are the sources of information reliable? You should also ask if the scientist or group conducting the experiment was unbiased. Being unbiased means that you have no special interest in the outcome of the experiment. For example, if a drug company pays for an experiment to test how well one of its new products works, there is a special interest involved: The drug company profits if the experiment shows that its product is effective. Therefore, the experimenters aren't _____. They might ensure the conclusion is positive and benefits the drug company. When assessing results, think about any biases that may be present!

① inventive
② objective
③ untrustworthy
④ unreliable
⑤ decisive

08 1등급 대비 고난도 3점 문제

글의 흐름으로 보아, 주어진 문장이 들어가기에 가장 적절한 곳을 고르시오. [3점]

> In the U.S. we have so many metaphors for time and its passing that we think of time as "a thing," that is "the weekend is almost gone," or "I haven't got the time."

There are some cultures that can be referred to as "people who live outside of time." The Amondawa tribe, living in Brazil, does not have a concept of time that can be measured or counted. (①) Rather they live in a world of serial events, rather than seeing events as being rooted in time. (②) Researchers also found that no one had an age. (③) Instead, they change their names to reflect their stage of life and position within their society, so a little child will give up their name to a newborn sibling and take on a new one. (④) We think such statements are objective, but they aren't. (⑤) We create these metaphors, but the Amondawa don't talk or think in metaphors for time.

＊metaphor: 은유　＊＊sibling: 형제자매

09 1등급 대비 고난도 3점 문제

다음 글의 내용을 한 문장으로 요약하고자 한다. 빈칸 (A), (B)에 들어갈 말로 가장 적절한 것은? [3점]

In a study, psychologist Laurence Steinberg of Temple University and his co-author, psychologist Margo Gardner divided 306 people into three age groups: young adolescents, with a mean age of 14; older adolescents, with a mean age of 19; and adults, aged 24 and older. Subjects played a computerized driving game in which the player must avoid crashing into a wall that appears, without warning, on the roadway. Steinberg and Gardner randomly assigned some participants to play alone or with two same-age peers looking on. Older adolescents scored about 50 percent higher on an index of risky driving when their peers were in the room — and the driving of early adolescents was fully twice as reckless when other young teens were around. In contrast, adults behaved in similar ways regardless of whether they were on their own or observed by others.

* reckless: 무모한

↓

The ____(A)____ of peers makes adolescents, but not adults, more likely to ____(B)____.

	(A)		(B)
①	presence	……	take risks
②	presence	……	behave cautiously
③	indifference	……	perform poorly
④	absence	……	enjoy adventures
⑤	absence	……	act independently

[10 ~ 12] 다음 글을 읽고, 물음에 답하시오.

(A)

A rich merchant lived alone in his house. Knowing that he was the only person living in the house, he was always prepared in case thieves came to his house. So, one day, when a thief entered his home, he remained calm and cool. Although he was awake, the merchant pretended to be in a deep sleep. He lay in bed and watched the thief in action. The thief had brought a new white sheet with (a) him to carry away the stolen goods.

(B)

(b) He then lay down and pretended to be asleep. When the thief had finished collecting as many valuables as he could, he hurriedly tied a knot in the white sheet which he thought was his. The merchant meanwhile ran out into the garden and yelled — "Thief! Thief!" with all the air in his lungs. The thief got nervous and quickly lifted the sheet. To (c) his surprise, the thin white sheet, filled with stolen goods, was torn apart.

(C)

All the stolen goods fell down on the floor creating a very loud and unpleasant noise. Seeing many people run towards him, the thief had to give up on all of the stolen goods. Leaving the goods behind in the house, he ran away in a hurry saying under his breath: "This man is such a skillful merchant; he is a businessman to the core. He has not only managed to save his valuables but has also taken away (d) my new sheet. He has stolen from a thief!" As he said that to himself, he ran away from the house.

(D)

He spread it out on the floor with the idea of putting all the stolen valuables into it, tying it, and carrying it away. While (e) he was busy gathering expensive-looking items from the merchant's luxurious house, the merchant quickly got out of the bed. Then he replaced the new white sheet with a similar looking white sheet, which was much weaker and much cheaper than the thief's one.

10

고1 · 2021년 9월 43번

주어진 글 (A)에 이어질 내용을 순서에 맞게 배열한 것으로 가장 적절한 것은?

① (B) − (D) − (C)   ② (C) − (B) − (D)
③ (C) − (D) − (B)   ④ (D) − (B) − (C)
⑤ (D) − (C) − (B)

11

고1 · 2021년 9월 44번

밑줄 친 (a)～(e) 중에서 가리키는 대상이 나머지 넷과 다른 것은?

① (a)   ② (b)   ③ (c)   ④ (d)   ⑤ (e)

12

고1 · 2021년 9월 45번

윗글에 관한 내용으로 적절하지 않은 것은?

① 상인은 도둑이 드는 상황에 항상 대비하고 있었다.
② 상인은 정원으로 뛰어나가 크게 소리쳤다.
③ 도둑이 훔친 물건들이 바닥에 떨어졌다.
④ 도둑은 상인의 물건들을 집밖으로 가지고 달아났다.
⑤ 상인의 보자기는 도둑의 보자기보다 값싼 것이었다.

학습 Check!   ▶ 몰라서 틀린 문항 × 표기   ▶ 헷갈렸거나 찍은 문항 △ 표기   ▶ ×, △ 문항은 다시 풀고 ✔ 표기를 하세요.

종료 시각	시 분 초	문항 번호	01	02	03	04	05	06	07	08	09	10	11	12
소요 시간	분 초	채점 결과												
초과 시간	분 초	틀린 문항 복습												

DAY 06

DAY 07

● 날짜 :　　월　　일　● 시작 시각 :　　시　　분　　초　● 목표 시간 : 20분

※ 점수 표기가 없는 문항은 모두 **2점**입니다.

01

고1 · 2022년 11월 18번

다음 글의 목적으로 가장 적절한 것은?

> Dear Mr. Krull,
>
> I have greatly enjoyed working at Trincom Enterprises as a sales manager. Since I joined in 2015, I have been a loyal and essential member of this company, and have developed innovative ways to contribute to the company. Moreover, in the last year alone, I have brought in two new major clients to the company, increasing the company's total sales by 5%. Also, I have voluntarily trained 5 new members of staff, totaling 35 hours. I would therefore request your consideration in raising my salary, which I believe reflects my performance as well as the industry average. I look forward to speaking with you soon.
>
> Kimberly Morss

① 부서 이동을 신청하려고
② 급여 인상을 요청하려고
③ 근무 시간 조정을 요구하려고
④ 기업 혁신 방안을 제안하려고
⑤ 신입 사원 연수에 대해 문의하려고

02

고3 · 2021학년도 수능 20번

다음 글에서 필자가 주장하는 바로 가장 적절한 것은?

Developing expertise carries costs of its own. We can become experts in some areas, like speaking a language or knowing our favorite foods, simply by living our lives, but in many other domains expertise requires considerable training and effort. What's more, expertise is domain specific. The expertise that we work hard to acquire in one domain will carry over only imperfectly to related ones, and not at all to unrelated ones. In the end, as much as we may want to become experts on everything in our lives, there simply isn't enough time to do so. Even in areas where we could, it won't necessarily be worth the effort. It's clear that we should concentrate our own expertise on those domains of choice that are most common and/or important to our lives, and those we actively enjoy learning about and choosing from.

① 자신에게 의미 있는 영역을 정해서 전문성을 키워야 한다.
② 전문성 함양에는 타고난 재능보다 노력과 훈련이 중요하다.
③ 전문가가 되기 위해서는 다양한 분야에 관심을 가져야 한다.
④ 전문성을 기르기 위해서는 구체적인 계획과 실천이 필수적이다.
⑤ 전문가는 일의 우선순위를 결정해서 업무를 수행해야 한다.

03

밑줄 친 put the glass down이 다음 글에서 의미하는 바로 가장 적절한 것은? [3점]

A psychology professor raised a glass of water while teaching stress management principles to her students, and asked them, "How heavy is this glass of water I'm holding?" Students shouted out various answers. The professor replied, "The absolute weight of this glass doesn't matter. It depends on how long I hold it. If I hold it for a minute, it's quite light. But, if I hold it for a day straight, it will cause severe pain in my arm, forcing me to drop the glass to the floor. In each case, the weight of the glass is the same, but the longer I hold it, the heavier it feels to me." As the class nodded their heads in agreement, she continued, "Your stresses in life are like this glass of water. If you still feel the weight of yesterday's stress, it's a strong sign that it's time to put the glass down."

① pour more water into the glass
② set a plan not to make mistakes
③ let go of the stress in your mind
④ think about the cause of your stress
⑤ learn to accept the opinions of others

04

다음 글의 주제로 가장 적절한 것은?

For creatures like us, evolution smiled upon those with a strong need to belong. Survival and reproduction are the criteria of success by natural selection, and forming relationships with other people can be useful for both survival and reproduction. Groups can share resources, care for sick members, scare off predators, fight together against enemies, divide tasks so as to improve efficiency, and contribute to survival in many other ways. In particular, if an individual and a group want the same resource, the group will generally prevail, so competition for resources would especially favor a need to belong. Belongingness will likewise promote reproduction, such as by bringing potential mates into contact with each other, and in particular by keeping parents together to care for their children, who are much more likely to survive if they have more than one caregiver.

① skills for the weak to survive modern life
② usefulness of belonging for human evolution
③ ways to avoid competition among social groups
④ roles of social relationships in children's education
⑤ differences between two major evolutionary theories

DAY 07

05 1등급 대비 고난도 2편 문제

다음 글의 밑줄 친 부분 중, 어법상 틀린 것은?

There is a reason the title "Monday Morning Quarterback" exists. Just read the comments on social media from fans discussing the weekend's games, and you quickly see how many people believe they could play, coach, and manage sport teams more ① successfully than those on the field. This goes for the boardroom as well. Students and professionals with years of training and specialized degrees in sport business may also find themselves ② being given advice on how to do their jobs from friends, family, or even total strangers without any expertise. Executives in sport management ③ have decades of knowledge and experience in their respective fields. However, many of them face criticism from fans and community members telling ④ themselves how to run their business. Very few people tell their doctor how to perform surgery or their accountant how to prepare their taxes, but many people provide feedback on ⑤ how sport organizations should be managed.

* boardroom: 이사회실

06

다음 글의 밑줄 친 부분 중, 문맥상 낱말의 쓰임이 적절하지 않은 것은? [3점]

We often ignore small changes because they don't seem to ① matter very much in the moment. If you save a little money now, you're still not a millionaire. If you study Spanish for an hour tonight, you still haven't learned the language. We make a few changes, but the results never seem to come ② quickly and so we slide back into our previous routines. The slow pace of transformation also makes it ③ easy to break a bad habit. If you eat an unhealthy meal today, the scale doesn't move much. A single decision is easy to ignore. But when we ④ repeat small errors, day after day, by following poor decisions again and again, our small choices add up to bad results. Many missteps eventually lead to a ⑤ problem.

07

다음 빈칸에 들어갈 말로 가장 적절한 것을 고르시오.

One outcome of motivation is behavior that takes considerable _____ . For example, if you are motivated to buy a good car, you will research vehicles online, look at ads, visit dealerships, and so on. Likewise, if you are motivated to lose weight, you will buy low-fat foods, eat smaller portions, and exercise. Motivation not only drives the final behaviors that bring a goal closer but also creates willingness to expend time and energy on preparatory behaviors. Thus, someone motivated to buy a new smartphone may earn extra money for it, drive through a storm to reach the store, and then wait in line to buy it.

＊preparatory: 준비의

① risk   ② effort
③ memory   ④ fortune
⑤ experience

08 1등급 대비 고난도 3점 문제

다음 빈칸에 들어갈 말로 가장 적절한 것을 고르시오. [3점]

There is a famous Spanish proverb that says, "The belly rules the mind." This is a clinically proven fact. Food is the original mind-controlling drug. Every time we eat, we bombard our brains with a feast of chemicals, triggering an explosive hormonal chain reaction that directly influences the way we think. Countless studies have shown that the positive emotional state induced by a good meal _____ .
It triggers an instinctive desire to repay the provider. This is why executives regularly combine business meetings with meals, why lobbyists invite politicians to attend receptions, lunches, and dinners, and why major state occasions almost always involve an impressive banquet. Churchill called this "dining diplomacy," and sociologists have confirmed that this principle is a strong motivator across all human cultures.

＊banquet: 연회

① leads us to make a fair judgement
② interferes with cooperation with others
③ does harm to serious diplomatic occasions
④ plays a critical role in improving our health
⑤ enhances our receptiveness to be persuaded

09

다음 글에서 전체 흐름과 관계 <u>없는</u> 문장은?

The Zeigarnik effect is commonly referred to as the tendency of the subconscious mind to remind you of a task that is incomplete until that task is complete. Bluma Zeigarnik was a Lithuanian psychologist who wrote in the 1920s about the effects of leaving tasks incomplete. ① She noticed the effect while watching waiters serve in a restaurant. ② The waiters would remember an order, however complicated, until the order was complete, but they would later find it difficult to remember the order. ③ Zeigarnik did further studies giving both adults and children puzzles to complete then interrupting them during some of the tasks. ④ They developed cooperation skills after finishing tasks by putting the puzzles together. ⑤ The results showed that both adults and children remembered the tasks that hadn't been completed because of the interruptions better than the ones that had been completed.

10 **1등급 대비 고난도 2점 문제**

주어진 글 다음에 이어질 글의 순서로 가장 적절한 것을 고르시오.

Roughly twenty years ago, brick-and-mortar stores began to give way to electronic commerce. For good or bad, the shift fundamentally changed consumers' perception of the shopping experience.

(A) Before long, the e-commerce book market naturally expanded to include additional categories, like CDs and DVDs. E-commerce soon snowballed into the enormous industry it is today, where you can buy everything from toilet paper to cars online.

(B) Nowhere was the shift more obvious than with book sales, which is how online bookstores got their start. Physical bookstores simply could not stock as many titles as a virtual bookstore could. There is only so much space available on a shelf.

(C) In addition to greater variety, online bookstores were also able to offer aggressive discounts thanks to their lower operating costs. The combination of lower prices and greater selection led to the slow, steady rise of online bookstores.

＊brick-and-mortar: 오프라인 거래의

① (A) − (C) − (B)　　② (B) − (A) − (C)
③ (B) − (C) − (A)　　④ (C) − (A) − (B)
⑤ (C) − (B) − (A)

[11 ~ 12] 다음 글을 읽고, 물음에 답하시오.

Marketers have known for decades that you buy what you see first. You are far more likely to purchase items placed at eye level in the grocery store, for example, than items on the bottom shelf. There is an entire body of research about the way "product placement" in stores influences your buying behavior. This gives you a chance to use product placement to your advantage. Healthy items like produce are often the (a) least visible foods at home. You won't think to eat what you don't see. This may be part of the reason why 85 percent of Americans do not eat enough fruits and vegetables.

If produce is (b) hidden in a drawer at the bottom of your refrigerator, these good foods are out of sight and mind. The same holds true for your pantry. I used to have a shelf lined with salty crackers and chips at eye level. When these were the first things I noticed, they were my (c) primary snack foods. That same shelf is now filled with healthy snacks, which makes good decisions (d) easy. Foods that sit out on tables are even more critical. When you see food every time you walk by, you are likely to (e) avoid it. So to improve your choices, leave good foods like apples and pistachios sitting out instead of crackers and candy.

＊produce: 농산물

11

윗글의 제목으로 가장 적절한 것은?

① Why We Need to Consider Food Placement
② Pleasure Does Not Come from What You Buy
③ Which Do You Believe, Visible or Invisible?
④ A Secret for Health: Eat Less, Move More
⑤ Three Effective Ways to Tidy Things Up

12

밑줄 친 (a) ~ (e) 중에서 문맥상 낱말의 쓰임이 적절하지 않은 것은? [3점]

① (a)　　② (b)　　③ (c)　　④ (d)　　⑤ (e)

학습 Check!　　▶ 몰라서 틀린 문항 ✕ 표기　▶ 헷갈렸거나 찍은 문항 △ 표기　▶ ✕, △ 문항은 다시 풀고 ✔ 표기를 하세요.

종료 시각	시	분	초	문항 번호	01	02	03	04	05	06	07	08	09	10	11	12
소요 시간		분	초	채점 결과												
초과 시간		분	초	틀린 문항 복습												

DAY 08

수능기출 전국연합학력평가 **20분 미니 모의고사**

● 날짜 :   월   일 ● 시작 시각 :   시   분   초 ● 목표 시간 : 20분   ※ 점수 표기가 없는 문항은 모두 2점입니다.

01

다음 글에 나타난 'I'의 심경 변화로 가장 적절한 것은?

It was two hours before the submission deadline and I still hadn't finished my news article. I sat at the desk, but suddenly, the typewriter didn't work. No matter how hard I tapped the keys, the levers wouldn't move to strike the paper. I started to realize that I would not be able to finish the article on time. Desperately, I rested the typewriter on my lap and started hitting each key with as much force as I could manage. Nothing happened. Thinking something might have happened inside of it, I opened the cover, lifted up the keys, and found the problem — a paper clip. The keys had no room to move. After picking it out, I pressed and pulled some parts. The keys moved smoothly again. I breathed deeply and smiled. Now I knew that I could finish my article on time.

① confident   → nervous
② frustrated   → relieved
③ bored   → amazed
④ indifferent → curious
⑤ excited   → disappointed

02

다음 글의 요지로 가장 적절한 것은?

We all negotiate every day, whether we realise it or not. Yet few people ever learn *how* to negotiate. Those who do usually learn the traditional, win-lose negotiating style rather than an approach that is likely to result in a win-win agreement. This old-school, adversarial approach may be useful in a one-off negotiation where you will probably not deal with that person again. However, such transactions are becoming increasingly rare, because most of us deal with the same people repeatedly — our spouses and children, our friends and colleagues, our customers and clients. In view of this, it's essential to achieve successful results for ourselves and maintain a healthy relationship with our negotiating partners at the same time. In today's interdependent world of business partnerships and long-term relationships, a win-win outcome is fast becoming the *only* acceptable result.

* adversarial: 적대적인

① 협상 상대의 단점뿐 아니라 장점을 철저히 분석해야 한다.
② 의사소통 과정에서 서로의 의도를 확인하는 것이 바람직하다.
③ 성공적인 협상을 위해 다양한 대안을 준비하는 것이 중요하다.
④ 양측에 유리한 협상을 통해 상대와 좋은 관계를 유지해야 한다.
⑤ 원만한 인간관계를 위해 상호독립성을 인정하는 것이 필요하다.

03

다음 글의 제목으로 가장 적절한 것은?

Mending and restoring objects often require even more creativity than original production. The preindustrial blacksmith made things to order for people in his immediate community; customizing the product, modifying or transforming it according to the user, was routine. Customers would bring things back if something went wrong; repair was thus an extension of fabrication. With industrialization and eventually with mass production, making things became the province of machine tenders with limited knowledge. But repair continued to require a larger grasp of design and materials, an understanding of the whole and a comprehension of the designer's intentions. "Manufacturers all work by machinery or by vast subdivision of labour and not, so to speak, by hand," an 1896 *Manual of Mending and Repairing* explained. "But all repairing *must* be done by hand. We can make every detail of a watch or of a gun by machinery, but the machine cannot mend it when broken, much less a clock or a pistol!"

① Still Left to the Modern Blacksmith: The Art of Repair
② A Historical Survey of How Repairing Skills Evolved
③ How to Be a Creative Repairperson: Tips and Ideas
④ A Process of Repair: Create, Modify, Transform!
⑤ Can Industrialization Mend Our Broken Past?

04

Undersea Walking Activity에 관한 다음 안내문의 내용과 일치하는 것은?

Undersea Walking Activity

Enjoy a fascinating underwater walk on the ocean floor. Witness wonderful marine life on foot!

Age Requirement
10 years or older

Operating Hours
from Tuesday to Sunday
9:00 a.m. – 4:00 p.m.

Price
$30 (insurance fee included)

What to Bring
swim suit and towel

Notes
• Experienced lifeguards accompany you throughout the activity.
• With a special underwater helmet, you can wear glasses during the activity.
• Reservations can be made on-site or online at www.seawalkwonder.com.

① 연중무휴로 운영된다.
② 가격에 보험료는 포함되어 있지 않다.
③ 숙련된 안전 요원이 활동 내내 동행한다.
④ 특수 수중 헬멧 착용 시 안경을 쓸 수 없다.
⑤ 현장 예약은 불가능하다.

05

다음 글의 밑줄 친 부분 중, 어법상 틀린 것은? [3점]

Each species of animals can detect a different range of odours. No species can detect all the molecules that are present in the environment ① in which it lives — there are some things that we cannot smell but which some other animals can, and vice versa. There are also differences between individuals, relating to the ability to smell an odour, or how ② pleasantly it seems. For example, some people like the taste of coriander — known as cilantro in the USA — while others find ③ it soapy and unpleasant. This effect has an underlying genetic component due to differences in the genes ④ controlling our sense of smell. Ultimately, the selection of scents detected by a given species, and how that odour is perceived, will depend upon the animal's ecology. The response profile of each species will enable it ⑤ to locate sources of smell that are relevant to it and to respond accordingly.

* coriander: 고수

06

(A), (B), (C)의 각 네모 안에서 문맥에 맞는 낱말로 가장 적절한 것은? [3점]

People have higher expectations as their lives get better. However, the higher the expectations, the more difficult it is to be satisfied. We can increase the satisfaction we feel in our lives by (A) controlling / raising our expectations. Adequate expectations leave room for many experiences to be pleasant surprises. The challenge is to find a way to have proper expectations. One way to do this is by keeping wonderful experiences (B) frequent / rare. No matter what you can afford, save great wine for special occasions. Make an elegantly styled silk blouse a special treat. This may seem like an act of denying your desires, but I don't think it is. On the contrary, it's a way to make sure that you can continue to experience (C) familiarity / pleasure. What's the point of great wines and great blouses if they don't make you feel great?

	(A)	(B)	(C)
①	controlling	frequent	pleasure
②	controlling	rare	familiarity
③	controlling	rare	pleasure
④	raising	frequent	familiarity
⑤	raising	rare	pleasure

07 1등급 대비 고난도 2점 문제

고1 · 2021년 6월 31번

다음 빈칸에 들어갈 말로 가장 적절한 것을 고르시오.

In a culture where there is a belief that you can have anything you truly want, there is no problem in choosing. Many cultures, however, do not maintain this belief. In fact, many people do not believe that life is about getting what you want. Life is about doing what you are *supposed* to do. The reason they have trouble making choices is they believe that what they may want is not related to what they are supposed to do. The weight of outside considerations is greater than their _____. When this is an issue in a group, we discuss what makes for good decisions. If a person can be unburdened from their cares and duties and, just for a moment, consider what appeals to them, they get the chance to sort out what is important to them. Then they can consider and negotiate with their external pressures.

① desires
② merits
③ abilities
④ limitations
⑤ worries

08 1등급 대비 고난도 3점 문제

고1 · 2021년 3월 39번

글의 흐름으로 보아, 주어진 문장이 들어가기에 가장 적절한 곳을 고르시오. [3점]

> Before a trip, research how the native inhabitants dress, work, and eat.

The continued survival of the human race can be explained by our ability to adapt to our environment. (①) While we may have lost some of our ancient ancestors' survival skills, we have learned new skills as they have become necessary. (②) Today, the gap between the skills we once had and the skills we now have grows ever wider as we rely more heavily on modern technology. (③) Therefore, when you head off into the wilderness, it is important to fully prepare for the environment. (④) How they have adapted to their way of life will help you to understand the environment and allow you to select the best gear and learn the correct skills. (⑤) This is crucial because most survival situations arise as a result of a series of events that could have been avoided.

* inhabitant: 주민

09 1등급 대비 고난도 2점 문제 · 고1 · 2018년 11월 40번

다음 글의 내용을 한 문장으로 요약하고자 한다. 빈칸 (A), (B)에 들어갈 말로 가장 적절한 것은?

We cannot predict the outcomes of sporting contests, which vary from week to week. This heterogeneity is a feature of sport. It is the uncertainty of the result and the quality of the contest that consumers find attractive. For the sport marketer, this is problematic, as the quality of the contest cannot be guaranteed, no promises can be made in relations to the result and no assurances can be given in respect of the performance of star players. Unlike consumer products, sport cannot and does not display consistency as a key feature of marketing strategies. The sport marketer therefore must avoid marketing strategies based solely on winning, and must instead focus on developing product extensions such as the facility, parking, merchandise, souvenirs, food and beverages rather than on the core product (that is, the game itself).

* heterogeneity: 이질성(異質性)

↓

Sport has the essential nature of being ___(A)___, which requires that its marketing strategies ___(B)___ products and services more than just the sports match.

	(A)		(B)
①	unreliable	……	feature
②	unreliable	……	exclude
③	risky	……	ignore
④	consistent	……	involve
⑤	consistent	……	promote

[10～12] 다음 글을 읽고, 물음에 답하시오.

(A)

A nurse took a tired, anxious soldier to the bedside. "Jack, your son is here," the nurse said to an old man lying on the bed. She had to repeat the words several times before the old man's eyes opened. Suffering from the severe pain because of heart disease, he barely saw the young uniformed soldier standing next to him. (a) He reached out his hand to the soldier.

(B)

Whenever the nurse came into the room, she heard the soldier say a few gentle words. The old man said nothing, only held tightly to (b) him all through the night. Just before dawn, the old man died. The soldier released the old man's hand and left the room to find the nurse. After she was told what happened, she went back to the room with him. The soldier hesitated for a while and asked, "Who was this man?"

(C)

She was surprised and asked, "Wasn't he your father?" "No, he wasn't. I've never met him before," the soldier replied. She asked, "Then why didn't you say something when I took you to (c) him?" He said, "I knew there had been a mistake, but when I realized that he was too sick to tell whether or not I was his son, I could see how much (d) he needed me. So, I stayed."

(D)

The soldier gently wrapped his fingers around the weak hand of the old man. The nurse brought a chair so that the soldier could sit beside the bed. All through the night the young soldier sat there, holding the old man's hand and offering (e) him words of support and comfort. Occasionally, she suggested that the soldier take a rest for a while. He politely said no.

10

주어진 글 (A)에 이어질 내용을 순서에 맞게 배열한 것으로 가장 적절한 것은?

① (B) – (D) – (C)　　　② (C) – (B) – (D)

③ (C) – (D) – (B)　　　④ (D) – (B) – (C)

⑤ (D) – (C) – (B)

11

밑줄 친 (a) ~ (e) 중에서 가리키는 대상이 나머지 넷과 다른 것은?

① (a)　　② (b)　　③ (c)　　④ (d)　　⑤ (e)

12

윗글에 관한 내용으로 적절하지 않은 것은?

① 노인은 심장병으로 극심한 고통을 겪고 있었다.

② 군인은 간호사를 찾기 위해 병실을 나갔다.

③ 군인은 노인과 이전에 만난 적이 있다고 말했다.

④ 간호사는 군인이 앉을 수 있도록 의자를 가져왔다.

⑤ 군인은 잠시 쉬라는 간호사의 제안을 정중히 거절하였다.

학습 Check!

▶ 몰라서 틀린 문항 × 표기　▶ 헷갈렸거나 찍은 문항 △ 표기　▶ ×, △ 문항은 다시 풀고 ✔ 표기를 하세요.

종료 시각	시　분　초	문항 번호	01	02	03	04	05	06	07	08	09	10	11	12
소요 시간	분　초	채점 결과												
초과 시간	분　초	틀린 문항 복습												

DAY 09

수능기출
전국연합학력평가 **20분 미니 모의고사**

● 날짜 : 　월　　일　● 시작 시각 :　시　　분　　초　● 목표 시간 : 20분

※ 점수 표기가 없는 문항은 모두 **2점**입니다.

01

고1 · 2021년 3월 18번

다음 글의 목적으로 가장 적절한 것은?

Dear members of Eastwood Library,

　Thanks to the Friends of Literature group, we've successfully raised enough money to remodel the library building. John Baker, our local builder, has volunteered to help us with the remodelling but he needs assistance. By grabbing a hammer or a paint brush and donating your time, you can help with the construction. Join Mr. Baker in his volunteering team and become a part of making Eastwood Library a better place! Please call 541-567-1234 for more information.

Sincerely,
Mark Anderson

---

① 도서관 임시 휴관의 이유를 설명하려고
② 도서관 자원봉사자 교육 일정을 안내하려고
③ 도서관 보수를 위한 모금 행사를 제안하려고
④ 도서관 공사에 참여할 자원봉사자를 모집하려고
⑤ 도서관에서 개최하는 글쓰기 대회를 홍보하려고

02

고1 · 2023년 9월 20번

다음 글에서 필자가 주장하는 바로 가장 적절한 것은?

　We are always teaching our children something by our words and our actions. They learn from seeing. They learn from hearing and from *overhearing*. Children share the values of their parents about the most important things in life. Our priorities and principles and our examples of good behavior can teach our children to take the high road when other roads look tempting. Remember that children do not learn the values that make up strong character simply by being *told* about them. They learn by seeing the people around them *act* on and *uphold* those values in their daily lives. Therefore show your child good examples of life by your action. In our daily lives, we can show our children that we respect others. We can show them our compassion and concern when others are suffering, and our own self-discipline, courage and honesty as we make difficult decisions.

① 자녀를 타인과 비교하는 말을 삼가야 한다.
② 자녀에게 행동으로 삶의 모범을 보여야 한다.
③ 칭찬을 통해 자녀의 바람직한 행동을 강화해야 한다.
④ 훈육을 하기 전에 자녀 스스로 생각할 시간을 주어야 한다.
⑤ 자녀가 새로운 것에 도전할 때 인내심을 가지고 지켜봐야 한다.

03

밑줄 친 refining ignorance가 다음 글에서 의미하는 바로 가장 적절한 것은?

Although not the explicit goal, the best science can really be seen as refining ignorance. Scientists, especially young ones, can get too obsessed with results. Society helps them along in this mad chase. Big discoveries are covered in the press, show up on the university's home page, help get grants, and make the case for promotions. But it's wrong. Great scientists, the pioneers that we admire, are not concerned with results but with the next questions. The highly respected physicist Enrico Fermi told his students that an experiment that successfully proves a hypothesis is a measurement; one that doesn't is a discovery. A discovery, an uncovering — of new ignorance. The Nobel Prize, the pinnacle of scientific accomplishment, is awarded, not for a lifetime of scientific achievement, but for a single discovery, a result. Even the Nobel committee realizes in some way that this is not really in the scientific spirit, and their award citations commonly honor the discovery for having "opened a field up," "transformed a field," or "taken a field in new and unexpected directions."

＊pinnacle: 정점

① looking beyond what is known towards what is left unknown

② offering an ultimate account of what has been discovered

③ analyzing existing knowledge with an objective mindset

④ inspiring scientists to publicize significant discoveries

⑤ informing students of a new field of science

04

다음 글의 주제로 가장 적절한 것은?

Every day, children explore and construct relationships among objects. Frequently, these relationships focus on how much or how many of something exists. Thus, children count — "One cookie, two shoes, three candles on the birthday cake, four children in the sandbox." Children compare — "Which has more? Which has fewer? Will there be enough?" Children calculate — "How many will fit? Now, I have five. I need one more." In all of these instances, children are developing a notion of quantity. Children reveal and investigate mathematical concepts through their own activities or experiences, such as figuring out how many crackers to take at snack time or sorting shells into piles.

① difficulties of children in learning how to count

② how children build mathematical understanding

③ why fingers are used in counting objects

④ importance of early childhood education

⑤ advantages of singing number songs

05

다음 글의 밑줄 친 부분 중, 어법상 틀린 것은? [3점]

There are many methods for finding answers to the mysteries of the universe, and science is only one of these. However, science is unique. Instead of making guesses, scientists follow a system ① designed to prove if their ideas are true or false. They constantly reexamine and test their theories and conclusions. Old ideas are replaced when scientists find new information ② that they cannot explain. Once somebody makes a discovery, others review it carefully before ③ using the information in their own research. This way of building new knowledge on older discoveries ④ ensure that scientists correct their mistakes. Armed with scientific knowledge, people build tools and machines that transform the way we live, making our lives ⑤ much easier and better.

06

다음 글의 밑줄 친 부분 중, 문맥상 낱말의 쓰임이 적절하지 않은 것은? [3점]

Hunting can explain how humans developed *reciprocal altruism* and *social exchange*. Humans seem to be unique among primates in showing extensive reciprocal relationships that can last years, decades, or a lifetime. Meat from a large game animal comes in quantities that ① exceed what a single hunter and his immediate family could possibly consume. Furthermore, hunting success is highly ② variable; a hunter who is successful one week might fail the next. These conditions ③ encourage food sharing from hunting. The costs to a hunter of giving away meat he cannot eat immediately are ④ high because he cannot consume all the meat himself and leftovers will soon spoil. The benefits can be large, however, when those who are given his food return the generous favor later on when he has failed to get food for himself. In essence, hunters can ⑤ store extra meat in the bodies of their friends and neighbors.

* reciprocal altruism: 상호 이타주의 ** primates: 영장류

07 [1등급 대비 고난도 2점 문제] 고1 · 2022년 3월 31번

다음 빈칸에 들어갈 말로 가장 적절한 것을 고르시오.

Generalization without specific examples that humanize writing is boring to the listener and to the reader. Who wants to read platitudes all day? Who wants to hear the words great, greater, best, smartest, finest, humanitarian, on and on and on without specific examples? Instead of using these 'nothing words,' leave them out completely and just describe the _____. There is nothing worse than reading a scene in a novel in which a main character is described up front as heroic or brave or tragic or funny, while thereafter, the writer quickly moves on to something else. That's no good, no good at all. You have to use less one word descriptions and more detailed, engaging descriptions if you want to make something real.

＊platitude: 상투적인 말

① similarities   ② particulars
③ fantasies   ④ boredom
⑤ wisdom

08 고1 · 2019년 6월 34번

다음 빈칸에 들어갈 말로 가장 적절한 것을 고르시오.

We are more likely to eat in a restaurant if we know that it is usually busy. Even when nobody tells us a restaurant is good, our herd behavior determines our decision-making. Let's suppose you walk toward two empty restaurants. You do not know which one to enter. However, you suddenly see a group of six people enter one of them. Which one are you more likely to enter, the empty one or the other one? Most people would go into the restaurant with people in it. Let's suppose you and a friend go into that restaurant. Now, it has eight people in it. Others see that one restaurant is empty and the other has eight people in it. So, _____ _____.

＊herd: 무리, 떼

① both restaurants are getting busier
② you and your friend start hesitating
③ your decision has no impact on others'
④ they reject what lots of other people do
⑤ they decide to do the same as the other eight

09

다음 글에서 전체 흐름과 관계 없는 문장은?

Although technology has the potential to increase productivity, it can also have a negative impact on productivity. For example, in many office environments workers sit at desks with computers and have access to the internet. ① They are able to check their personal e-mails and use social media whenever they want to. ② This can stop them from doing their work and make them less productive. ③ Introducing new technology can also have a negative impact on production when it causes a change to the production process or requires workers to learn a new system. ④ Using technology can enable businesses to produce more goods and to get more out of the other factors of production. ⑤ Learning to use new technology can be time consuming and stressful for workers and this can cause a decline in productivity.

10 1등급 대비 고난도 3점 문제

주어진 글 다음에 이어질 글의 순서로 가장 적절한 것을 고르시오.
[3점]

> Most people have a perfect time of day when they feel they are at their best, whether in the morning, evening, or afternoon.

(A) When your mind and body are less alert than at your "peak" hours, the muse of creativity awakens and is allowed to roam more freely. In other words, when your mental machinery is loose rather than standing at attention, the creativity flows.

(B) However, if the task you face demands creativity and novel ideas, it's best to tackle it at your "worst" time of day! So if you are an early bird, make sure to attack your creative task in the evening, and vice versa for night owls.

(C) Some of us are night owls, some early birds, and others in between may feel most active during the afternoon hours. If you are able to organize your day and divide your work, make it a point to deal with tasks that demand attention at your best time of the day.

* roam: (어슬렁어슬렁) 거닐다

① (A) − (C) − (B) ② (B) − (A) − (C)
③ (B) − (C) − (A) ④ (C) − (A) − (B)
⑤ (C) − (B) − (A)

[11 ~ 12] 다음 글을 읽고, 물음에 답하시오.

Like all humans, the first *Homo* species to begin the long difficult process of constructing a language from scratch almost certainly never said entirely what was on their minds. At the same time, these primitive hominins would not have simply made (a) random sounds or gestures. Instead, they would have used means to communicate that they believed others would understand. And they also thought their hearers could "fill in the gaps", and connect their knowledge of their culture and the world to interpret what was uttered.

These are some of the reasons why the (b) origins of human language cannot be effectively discussed unless conversation is placed at the top of the list of things to understand. Every aspect of human language has evolved, as have components of the human brain and body, to (c) engage in conversation and social life. Language did not fully begin when the first hominid uttered the first word or sentence. It began in earnest only with the first conversation, which is both the source and the (d) goal of language. Indeed, language changes lives. It builds society and expresses our highest aspirations, our basest thoughts, our emotions and our philosophies of life. But all language is ultimately at the service of human interaction. Other components of language — things like grammar and stories — are (e) crucial to conversation.

* hominin: 인간의 조상으로 분류되는 종족
** hominid: 사람과(科)의 동물

11

윗글의 제목으로 가장 적절한 것은?

① Various Communication Strategies of Our Ancestors
② Conversation: The Core of Language Development
③ Ending Conversation Without Offending Others
④ How Language Shapes the Way You Think
⑤ What Makes You a Good Communicator?

12 1등급 대비 고난도 3점 문제

밑줄 친 (a) ~ (e) 중에서 문맥상 낱말의 쓰임이 적절하지 않은 것은? [3점]

① (a)　　② (b)　　③ (c)　　④ (d)　　⑤ (e)

▶ 몰라서 틀린 문항 × 표기　▶ 헷갈렸거나 찍은 문항 △ 표기　▶ ×, △ 문항은 다시 풀고 ✔ 표기를 하세요.

종료 시각	시	분	초	문항 번호	01	02	03	04	05	06	07	08	09	10	11	12
소요 시간		분	초	채점 결과												
초과 시간		분	초	틀린 문항 복습												

● 날짜 : 　월　　일 ● 시작 시각 : 　시　　분　　초 ● 목표 시간 : 20분　　　　　　　　　　　　　　　※ 점수 표기가 없는 문항은 모두 2점입니다.

01

고3·2017학년도 수능 19번

다음 글에 드러난 **Breaden**의 심경 변화로 가장 적절한 것은?

All smiling, Breaden, a cute three-year-old boy, was walking along the aisle of snacks, bars, and sweets. It was the aisle of all kinds of temptation for him. "Wow!" he exclaimed. Right in front of his eyes were rows of delicious-looking chocolate bars waiting to be touched. His mom was holding his hand. Breaden, her only child, had always been the focus of her attention and she was cautious not to lose him in the market. Suddenly, she stopped to say hello to her friends. Breaden stopped, too. With his eyes wide open and his mouth watering, Breaden stretched out his arm and was about to grab a bar when he felt a tight grip on his hand. He looked up. "Breaden, not today!" He knew what that meant. "Okay, Mommy," he sighed. His shoulders fell.

① excited　　　 → disappointed
② embarrassed → satisfied
③ lonely　　　 → pleased
④ annoyed　　 → relieved
⑤ delighted　　→ jealous

02

고1·2022년 9월 22번

다음 글의 요지로 가장 적절한 것은?

A recent study from Carnegie Mellon University in Pittsburgh, called "When Too Much of a Good Thing May Be Bad," indicates that classrooms with too much decoration are a source of distraction for young children and directly affect their cognitive performance. Being visually overstimulated, the children have a great deal of difficulty concentrating and end up with worse academic results. On the other hand, if there is not much decoration on the classroom walls, the children are less distracted, spend more time on their activities, and learn more. So it's our job, in order to support their attention, to find the right balance between excessive decoration and the complete absence of it.

① 아이들의 집중을 돕기 위해 과도한 교실 장식을 지양할 필요가 있다.
② 아이들의 인성과 인지 능력을 균형 있게 발달시키는 것이 중요하다.
③ 아이들이 직접 교실을 장식하는 것은 창의력 발달에 도움이 된다.
④ 다양한 교실 활동은 아이들의 수업 참여도를 증진시킨다.
⑤ 풍부한 시각 자료는 아이들의 학습 동기를 높인다.

03

다음 글의 제목으로 가장 적절한 것은?

Success can lead you off your intended path and into a comfortable rut. If you are good at something and are well rewarded for doing it, you may want to keep doing it even if you stop enjoying it. The danger is that one day you look around and realize you're so deep in this comfortable rut that you can no longer see the sun or breathe fresh air; the sides of the rut have become so slippery that it would take a superhuman effort to climb out; and, effectively, you're stuck. And it's a situation that many working people worry they're in now. The poor employment market has left them feeling locked in what may be a secure, or even well-paying — but ultimately unsatisfying — job.

＊rut: 틀에 박힌 생활

① Don't Compete with Yourself
② A Trap of a Successful Career
③ Create More Jobs for Young People
④ What Difficult Jobs Have in Common
⑤ A Road Map for an Influential Employer

04

Margaret Knight에 관한 다음 글의 내용과 일치하지 <u>않는</u> 것은?

Margaret Knight was an exceptionally prolific inventor in the late 19th century; journalists occasionally compared her to Thomas Edison by nicknaming her "a woman Edison." From a young age, she built toys for her older brothers. After her father died, Knight's family moved to Manchester. Knight left school in 1850, at age 12, to earn money for her family at a nearby textile factory, where she witnessed a fellow worker injured by faulty equipment. That led her to create her first invention, a safety device for textile equipment, but she never earned money from the invention. She also invented a machine that cut, folded and glued flat-bottomed paper bags and was awarded her first patent in 1871 for it. It eliminated the need for workers to assemble them slowly by hand. Knight received 27 patents in her lifetime and entered the National Inventors Hall of Fame in 2006.

＊prolific: 다작(多作)의 ＊＊patent: 특허

① 기자들이 '여자 Edison'이라는 별명을 지어 주었다.
② 가족을 위해 돈을 벌려고 학교를 그만두었다.
③ 직물 장비에 쓰이는 안전장치를 발명하여 많은 돈을 벌었다.
④ 밑이 평평한 종이 가방을 자르고 접고 붙이는 기계를 발명했다.
⑤ 2006년에 국립 발명가 명예의 전당에 입성했다.

DAY 10

05 1등급 대비 고난도 3점 문제

고1 · 2018년 6월 28번

다음 글의 밑줄 친 부분 중, 어법상 틀린 것은? [3점]

Plastic is extremely slow to degrade and tends to float, ① which allows it to travel in ocean currents for thousands of miles. Most plastics break down into smaller and smaller pieces when exposed to ultraviolet (UV) light, ② forming microplastics. These microplastics are very difficult to measure once they are small enough to pass through the nets typically used to collect ③ themselves. Their impacts on the marine environment and food webs are still poorly understood. These tiny particles are known to be eaten by various animals and to get into the food chain. Because most of the plastic particles in the ocean ④ are so small, there is no practical way to clean up the ocean. One would have to filter enormous amounts of water to collect a ⑤ relatively small amount of plastic.

＊ degrade: 분해되다

06

고1 · 2020년 9월 30번

(A), (B), (C)의 각 네모 안에서 문맥에 맞는 낱말로 가장 적절한 것은? [3점]

Social connections are so essential for our survival and well-being that we not only cooperate with others to build relationships, we also compete with others for friends. And often we do both at the same time. Take gossip. Through gossip, we bond with our friends, sharing interesting details. But at the same time, we are (A) creating / forgiving potential enemies in the targets of our gossip. Or consider rival holiday parties where people compete to see who will attend *their* party. We can even see this (B) harmony / tension in social media as people compete for the most friends and followers. At the same time, competitive exclusion can also (C) generate / prevent cooperation. High school social clubs and country clubs use this formula to great effect: It is through selective inclusion *and exclusion* that they produce loyalty and lasting social bonds.

(A)	(B)	(C)
① creating	…… harmony	…… prevent
② creating	…… tension	…… generate
③ creating	…… tension	…… prevent
④ forgiving	…… tension	…… prevent
⑤ forgiving	…… harmony	…… generate

07 1등급 대비 고난도 2점 문제

다음 빈칸에 들어갈 말로 가장 적절한 것을 고르시오.

Face-to-face interaction is a uniquely powerful — and sometimes the only — way to share many kinds of knowledge, from the simplest to the most complex. It is one of the best ways to stimulate new thinking and ideas, too. Most of us would have had difficulty learning how to tie a shoelace only from pictures, or how to do arithmetic from a book. Psychologist Mihàly Csikszentmihàlyi found, while studying high achievers, that a large number of Nobel Prize winners were the students of previous winners: they had access to the same literature as everyone else, but _____ made a crucial difference to their creativity. Within organisations this makes conversation both a crucial factor for high-level professional skills and the most important way of sharing everyday information.

* arithmetic: 계산 ** literature: (연구) 문헌

① natural talent
② regular practice
③ personal contact
④ complex knowledge
⑤ powerful motivation

08 1등급 대비 고난도 3점 문제

글의 흐름으로 보아, 주어진 문장이 들어가기에 가장 적절한 곳을 고르시오. [3점]

> As children absorb more evidence from the world around them, certain possibilities become much more likely and more useful and harden into knowledge or beliefs.

According to educational psychologist Susan Engel, curiosity begins to decrease as young as four years old. By the time we are adults, we have fewer questions and more default settings. As Henry James put it, "Disinterested curiosity is past, the mental grooves and channels set." (①) The decline in curiosity can be traced in the development of the brain through childhood. (②) Though smaller than the adult brain, the infant brain contains millions more neural connections. (③) The wiring, however, is a mess; the lines of communication between infant neurons are far less efficient than between those in the adult brain. (④) The baby's perception of the world is consequently both intensely rich and wildly disordered. (⑤) The neural pathways that enable those beliefs become faster and more automatic, while the ones that the child doesn't use regularly are pruned away.

* default setting: 기본값 ** groove: 고랑
*** prune: 가지치기하다

DAY 10

09

다음 글의 내용을 한 문장으로 요약하고자 한다. 빈칸 (A), (B)에 들어갈 말로 가장 적절한 것은?

There is often a lot of uncertainty in the realm of science, which the general public finds uncomfortable. They don't want "informed guesses," they want certainties that make their lives easier, and science is often unequipped to meet these demands. In particular, the human body is fantastically complex, and some scientific answers can never be provided in black-or-white terms. All this is why the media tends to oversimplify scientific research when presenting it to the public. In their eyes, they're just "giving people what they want" as opposed to offering more accurate but complex information that very few people will read or understand. A perfect example of this is how people want definitive answers as to which foods are "good" and "bad." Scientifically speaking, there are no "good" and "bad" foods; rather, food quality exists on a continuum, meaning that some foods are *better* than others when it comes to general health and well-being.

* continuum: 연속(체)

↓

With regard to general health, science, by its nature, does not ___(A)___ the public's demands for certainty, which leads to the media giving less ___(B)___ answers to the public.

	(A)		(B)
①	satisfy	······	simple
②	satisfy	······	complicated
③	ignore	······	difficult
④	ignore	······	simple
⑤	reject	······	complicated

[10 ～ 12] 다음 글을 읽고, 물음에 답하시오.

(A)

Once, a farmer lost his precious watch while working in his barn. It may have appeared to be an ordinary watch to others, but it brought a lot of happy childhood memories to him. It was one of the most important things to (a) him. After searching for it for a long time, the old farmer became exhausted.

* barn: 헛간(곡물·건초 따위를 두는 곳)

(B)

The number of children looking for the watch slowly decreased and only a few tired children were left. The farmer gave up all hope of finding it and called off the search. Just when the farmer was closing the barn door, a little boy came up to him and asked the farmer to give him another chance. The farmer did not want to lose out on any chance of finding the watch so let (b) him in the barn.

(C)

After a little while the boy came out with the farmer's watch in his hand. (c) He was happily surprised and asked how he had succeeded to find the watch while everyone else had failed. He replied "I just sat there and tried listening for the sound of the watch. In silence, it was much easier to hear it and follow the direction of the sound." (d) He was delighted to get his watch back and rewarded the little boy as promised.

(D)

However, the tired farmer did not want to give up on the search for his watch and asked a group of children playing outside to help him. (e) He promised an attractive reward for the person who could find it. After hearing about the reward, the children hurried inside the barn and went through and round the entire pile of hay looking for the watch. After a long time searching for it, some of the children got tired and gave up.

10

고1 · 2022년 6월 43번

주어진 글 (A)에 이어질 내용을 순서에 맞게 배열한 것으로 가장 적절한 것은?

① (B) – (D) – (C)　　　② (C) – (B) – (D)

③ (C) – (D) – (B)　　　④ (D) – (B) – (C)

⑤ (D) – (C) – (B)

11

고1 · 2022년 6월 44번

밑줄 친 (a) ~ (e) 중에서 가리키는 대상이 나머지 넷과 다른 것은?

① (a)　　② (b)　　③ (c)　　④ (d)　　⑤ (e)

12

고1 · 2022년 6월 45번

윗글에 관한 내용으로 적절하지 <u>않은</u> 것은?

① 농부의 시계는 어린 시절의 행복한 기억을 불러일으켰다.

② 한 어린 소년이 농부에게 또 한 번의 기회를 달라고 요청했다.

③ 소년이 한 손에 농부의 시계를 들고 나왔다.

④ 아이들은 시계를 찾기 위해 헛간을 뛰쳐나왔다.

⑤ 아이들 중 일부는 지쳐서 시계 찾기를 포기했다.

DAY 10

DAY 11

수능기출 전국연합학력평가 **20분 미니 모의고사**

● 날짜 :   월   일 ● 시작 시각 :   시   분   초 ● 목표 시간 : 20분

※ 점수 표기가 없는 문항은 모두 **2점**입니다.

01

고1 · 2022년 3월 20번

다음 글에서 필자가 주장하는 바로 가장 적절한 것은?

When I was in the army, my instructors would show up in my barracks room, and the first thing they would inspect was our bed. It was a simple task, but every morning we were required to make our bed to perfection. It seemed a little ridiculous at the time, but the wisdom of this simple act has been proven to me many times over. If you make your bed every morning, you will have accomplished the first task of the day. It will give you a small sense of pride and it will encourage you to do another task and another. By the end of the day, that one task completed will have turned into many tasks completed. If you can't do little things right, you will never do the big things right.

*barracks room: (병영의) 생활관 **accomplish: 성취하다

① 숙면을 위해서는 침대를 깔끔하게 관리해야 한다.
② 일의 효율성을 높이려면 협동심을 발휘해야 한다.
③ 올바른 습관을 기르려면 정해진 규칙을 따라야 한다.
④ 건강을 유지하기 위해서는 기상 시간이 일정해야 한다.
⑤ 큰일을 잘 이루려면 작은 일부터 제대로 수행해야 한다.

02

고1 · 2023년 6월 22번

다음 글의 요지로 가장 적절한 것은?

The promise of a computerized society, we were told, was that it would pass to machines all of the repetitive drudgery of work, allowing us humans to pursue higher purposes and to have more leisure time. It didn't work out this way. Instead of more time, most of us have less. Companies large and small have off-loaded work onto the backs of consumers. Things that used to be done for us, as part of the value-added service of working with a company, we are now expected to do ourselves. With air travel, we're now expected to complete our own reservations and check-in, jobs that used to be done by airline employees or travel agents. At the grocery store, we're expected to bag our own groceries and, in some supermarkets, to scan our own purchases.

*drudgery: 고된 일

① 컴퓨터 기반 사회에서는 여가 시간이 더 늘어난다.
② 회사 업무의 전산화는 업무 능률을 향상시킨다.
③ 컴퓨터화된 사회에서 소비자는 더 많은 일을 하게 된다.
④ 온라인 거래가 모든 소비자들을 만족시키기에는 한계가 있다.
⑤ 산업의 발전으로 인해 기계가 인간의 일자리를 대신하고 있다.

03

고3 · 2018학년도 수능 22번

다음 글의 주제로 가장 적절한 것은?

Sensory-specific satiety is defined as a decrease in appetite, or the subjective liking for the food that is consumed, with little change in the hedonics of uneaten food. As a result of sensory-specific satiety, when people consume a variety of foods, they tend to overeat. A greater variety of food leads people to eat more than they would otherwise. So, being full and feeling sated are separate matters. The recovery of appetite or the motivation to eat is apparent to anyone who has consumed a large meal and is quite full, and does not require additional energy or nutrients to meet their daily needs, but decides to consume additional calories after seeing the dessert cart. Small changes in the sensory properties of foods are sufficient to increase food intake. For example, subjects who were presented with different shapes of pasta showed increased hedonic ratings and increased energy consumption relative to subjects eating only a single shape of pasta.

＊satiety: 포만(감) ＊＊hedonics: 쾌락
＊＊＊sated: 충분히 만족한

① necessity of consuming a varied diet in daily life
② reasons for people's rejection of unfamiliar foods
③ changes in people's preference for basic food items
④ impact of food variety on the amount of food people consume
⑤ importance of maintaining food diversity to prevent overeating

04

고1 · 2022년 6월 29번

다음 글의 밑줄 친 부분 중, 어법상 틀린 것은?

Despite all the high-tech devices that seem to deny the need for paper, paper use in the United States ① has nearly doubled recently. We now consume more paper than ever: 400 million tons globally and growing. Paper is not the only resource ② that we are using more of. Technological advances often come with the promise of ③ using fewer materials. However, the reality is that they have historically caused more materials use, making us ④ dependently on more natural resources. The world now consumes far more "stuff" than it ever has. We use twenty-seven times more industrial minerals, such as gold, copper, and rare metals, than we ⑤ did just over a century ago. We also each individually use more resources. Much of that is due to our high-tech lifestyle.

＊copper: 구리

05

다음 글의 밑줄 친 부분 중, 문맥상 낱말의 쓰임이 적절하지 않은 것은? [3점]

It is widely believed that certain herbs somehow magically improve the work of certain organs, and "cure" specific diseases as a result. Such statements are unscientific and groundless. Sometimes herbs appear to work, since they tend to ① increase your blood circulation in an aggressive attempt by your body to eliminate them from your system. That can create a ② temporary feeling of a high, which makes it seem as if your health condition has improved. Also, herbs can have a placebo effect, just like any other method, thus helping you feel better. Whatever the case, it is your body that has the intelligence to ③ regain health, and not the herbs. How can herbs have the intelligence needed to direct your body into getting healthier? That is impossible. Try to imagine how herbs might come into your body and intelligently ④ fix your problems. If you try to do that, you will see how impossible it seems. Otherwise, it would mean that herbs are ⑤ less intelligent than the human body, which is truly hard to believe.

＊placebo effect: 위약 효과

06 1등급 대비 고난도 3점 문제

다음 빈칸에 들어갈 말로 가장 적절한 것을 고르시오. [3점]

Creativity is a skill we usually consider uniquely human. For all of human history, we have been the most creative beings on Earth. Birds can make their nests, ants can make their hills, but no other species on Earth comes close to the level of creativity we humans display. However, just in the last decade we have acquired the ability to do amazing things with computers, like developing robots. With the artificial intelligence boom of the 2010s, computers can now recognize faces, translate languages, take calls for you, write poems, and beat players at the world's most complicated board game, to name a few things. All of a sudden, we must face the possibility that our ability to be creative is not _____.

① unrivaled
② learned
③ universal
④ ignored
⑤ challenged

07

다음 빈칸에 들어갈 말로 가장 적절한 것을 고르시오. [3점]

Scientists believe that the frogs' ancestors were water-dwelling, fishlike animals. The first frogs and their relatives gained the ability to come out on land and enjoy the opportunities for food and shelter there. But they _____. A frog's lungs do not work very well, and it gets part of its oxygen by breathing through its skin. But for this kind of "breathing" to work properly, the frog's skin must stay moist. And so the frog must remain near the water where it can take a dip every now and then to keep from drying out. Frogs must also lay their eggs in water, as their fishlike ancestors did. And eggs laid in the water must develop into water creatures, if they are to survive. For frogs, metamorphosis thus provides the bridge between the water-dwelling young forms and the land-dwelling adults.

* metamorphosis: 탈바꿈

① still kept many ties to the water
② had almost all the necessary organs
③ had to develop an appetite for new foods
④ often competed with land-dwelling species
⑤ suffered from rapid changes in temperature

08

다음 글에서 전체 흐름과 관계 <u>없는</u> 문장은?

Whose story it is affects *what* the story is. Change the main character, and the focus of the story must also change. If we look at the events through another character's eyes, we will interpret them differently. ① We'll place our sympathies with someone new. ② When the conflict arises that is the heart of the story, we will be praying for a different outcome. ③ Consider, for example, how the tale of Cinderella would shift if told from the viewpoint of an evil stepsister. ④ We know Cinderella's kingdom does not exist, but we willingly go there anyway. ⑤ *Gone with the Wind* is Scarlett O'Hara's story, but what if we were shown the same events from the viewpoint of Rhett Butler or Melanie Wilkes?

* sympathy: 공감

09 1등급 대비 고난도 3점 문제
고1 · 2021년 11월 37번

주어진 글 다음에 이어질 글의 순서로 가장 적절한 것을 고르시오. [3점]

> Literary works, by their nature, suggest rather than explain; they imply rather than state their claims boldly and directly.

(A) What a text implies is often of great interest to us. And our work of figuring out a text's implications tests our analytical powers. In considering what a text suggests, we gain practice in making sense of texts.

(B) But whatever the proportion of a work's showing to telling, there is always something for readers to interpret. Thus we ask the question "What does the text suggest?" as a way to approach literary interpretation, as a way to begin thinking about a text's implications.

(C) This broad generalization, however, does not mean that works of literature do not include direct statements. Depending on when they were written and by whom, literary works may contain large amounts of direct telling and lesser amounts of suggestion and implication.

① (A) − (C) − (B)
② (B) − (A) − (C)
③ (B) − (C) − (A)
④ (C) − (A) − (B)
⑤ (C) − (B) − (A)

10
고1 · 2021년 6월 40번

다음 글의 내용을 한 문장으로 요약하고자 한다. 빈칸 (A), (B)에 들어갈 말로 가장 적절한 것은?

> A woman named Rhonda who attended the University of California at Berkeley had a problem. She was living near campus with several other people — none of whom knew one another. When the cleaning people came each weekend, they left several rolls of toilet paper in each of the two bathrooms. However, by Monday all the toilet paper would be gone. It was a classic tragedy-of-the-commons situation: because some people took more toilet paper than their fair share, the public resource was destroyed for everyone else. After reading a research paper about behavior change, Rhonda put a note in one of the bathrooms asking people not to remove the toilet paper, as it was a shared item. To her great satisfaction, one roll reappeared in a few hours, and another the next day. In the other note-free bathroom, however, there was no toilet paper until the following weekend, when the cleaning people returned.

↓

> A small _____(A)_____ brought about a change in the behavior of the people who had taken more of the _____(B)_____ goods than they needed.

	(A)		(B)
①	reminder	······	shared
②	reminder	······	recycled
③	mistake	······	stored
④	mistake	······	borrowed
⑤	fortune	······	limited

[11 ~ 12] 다음 글을 읽고, 물음에 답하시오.

Many high school students study and learn inefficiently because they insist on doing their homework while watching TV or listening to loud music. These same students also typically (a) interrupt their studying with repeated phone calls, trips to the kitchen, video games, and Internet surfing. Ironically, students with the greatest need to concentrate when studying are often the ones who surround themselves with the most distractions. These teenagers argue that they can study *better* with the TV or radio (b) playing. Some professionals actually (c) oppose their position. They argue that many teenagers can actually study productively under less-than-ideal conditions because they've been exposed repeatedly to "background noise" since early childhood. These educators argue that children have become (d) used to the sounds of the TV, video games, and loud music. They also argue that insisting students turn off the TV or radio when doing homework will not necessarily improve their academic performance. This position is certainly not generally shared, however. Many teachers and learning experts are (e) convinced by their own experiences that students who study in a noisy environment often learn inefficiently.

11

윗글의 제목으로 가장 적절한 것은?

① Successful Students Plan Ahead
② Studying with Distractions: Is It Okay?
③ Smart Devices as Good Learning Tools
④ Parents & Teachers: Partners in Education
⑤ Good Habits: Hard to Form, Easy to Break

12 1등급 대비 고난도 3점 문제

밑줄 친 (a) ~ (e) 중에서 문맥상 낱말의 쓰임이 적절하지 않은 것은? [3점]

① (a)　　② (b)　　③ (c)　　④ (d)　　⑤ (e)

학습 Check! ▶ 몰라서 틀린 문항 × 표기　▶ 헷갈렸거나 찍은 문항 △ 표기　▶ ×, △ 문항은 다시 풀고 ✔ 표기를 하세요.

종료 시각	시 분 초	문항 번호	01	02	03	04	05	06	07	08	09	10	11	12
소요 시간	분 초	채점 결과												
초과 시간	분 초	틀린 문항 복습												

● 날짜 :　　월　　일 ● 시작 시각 :　　시　　분　　초 ● 목표 시간 : 20분　　　　　※ 점수 표기가 없는 문항은 모두 2점입니다.

01

고1 · 2023년 3월 18번

다음 글의 목적으로 가장 적절한 것은?

To whom it may concern,

I am a resident of the Blue Sky Apartment. Recently I observed that the kid zone is in need of repairs. I want you to pay attention to the poor condition of the playground equipment in the zone. The swings are damaged, the paint is falling off, and some of the bolts on the slide are missing. The facilities have been in this terrible condition since we moved here. They are dangerous to the children playing there. Would you please have them repaired? I would appreciate your immediate attention to solve this matter.

Yours sincerely,
Nina Davis

① 아파트의 첨단 보안 설비를 홍보하려고
② 아파트 놀이터의 임시 폐쇄를 공지하려고
③ 아파트 놀이터 시설의 수리를 요청하려고
④ 아파트 놀이터 사고의 피해 보상을 촉구하려고
⑤ 아파트 공용 시설 사용 시 유의 사항을 안내하려고

02

고1 · 2023년 9월 21번

밑줄 친 **fall silently in the woods**가 다음 글에서 의미하는 바로 가장 적절한 것은? [3점]

Most people have no doubt heard this question: If a tree falls in the forest and there is no one there to hear it fall, does it make a sound? The correct answer is no. Sound is more than pressure waves, and indeed there can be no sound without a hearer. And similarly, scientific communication is a two-way process. Just as a signal of any kind is useless unless it is perceived, a published scientific paper (signal) is useless unless it is both received *and* understood by its intended audience. Thus we can restate the axiom of science as follows: A scientific experiment is not complete until the results have been published *and understood*. Publication is no more than pressure waves unless the published paper is understood. Too many scientific papers fall silently in the woods.

＊ axiom: 자명한 이치

① fail to include the previous study
② end up being considered completely false
③ become useless because they are not published
④ focus on communication to meet public demands
⑤ are published yet readers don't understand them

03

다음 글의 제목으로 가장 적절한 것을 고르시오.

As a system for transmitting specific factual information without any distortion or ambiguity, the sign system of honey-bees would probably win easily over human language every time. However, language offers something more valuable than mere information exchange. Because the meanings of words are not invariable and because understanding always involves interpretation, the act of communicating is always a joint, creative effort. Words can carry meanings beyond those consciously intended by speakers or writers because listeners or readers bring their own perspectives to the language they encounter. Ideas expressed imprecisely may be more intellectually stimulating for listeners or readers than simple facts. The fact that language is not always reliable for causing precise meanings to be generated in someone else's mind is a reflection of its powerful strength as a medium for creating new understanding. It is the inherent ambiguity and adaptability of language as a meaning-making system that makes the relationship between language and thinking so special.

* distortion: 왜곡, 곡해

① Erase Ambiguity in Language Production!
② Not Creative but Simple: The Way Language Works
③ Communication as a Universal Goal in Language Use
④ What in Language Creates Varied Understanding?
⑤ Language: A Crystal-Clear Looking Glass

04

Willow Valley Hot Air Balloon Ride에 관한 다음 안내문의 내용과 일치하는 것은?

Willow Valley Hot Air Balloon Ride

Enjoy the best views of Willow Valley from the sky with our hot air balloon ride!

• **Capacity**: up to 8 people including a pilot

• **Time Schedule**

Spring & Summer (from April to September)	5:00 a.m. − 7:00 a.m.
Autumn & Winter (from October to March)	6:00 a.m. − 8:00 a.m.

※ Duration of Flight: about 1 hour

• **Fee**: $150 per person (insurance not included)

• **Note**
− Reservations are required and must be made online.
− You can get a full refund up to 24 hours in advance.
− Visit www.willowvalleyballoon.com for more information.

---

① 조종사를 제외하고 8인까지 탈 수 있다.
② 여름에는 오전 6시에 시작한다.
③ 요금에 보험이 포함되어 있다.
④ 예약은 온라인으로 해야 한다.
⑤ 환불은 예외 없이 불가능하다.

DAY 12

05

다음 글의 밑줄 친 부분 중, 어법상 틀린 것은? [3점]

Although there is usually a correct way of holding and playing musical instruments, the most important instruction to begin with is ① that they are not toys and that they must be looked after. ② Allow children time to explore ways of handling and playing the instruments for themselves before showing them. Finding different ways to produce sounds ③ are an important stage of musical exploration. Correct playing comes from the desire ④ to find the most appropriate sound quality and find the most comfortable playing position so that one can play with control over time. As instruments and music become more complex, learning appropriate playing techniques becomes ⑤ increasingly relevant.

06

(A), (B), (C)의 각 네모 안에서 문맥에 맞는 낱말로 가장 적절한 것은?

The brain makes up just two percent of our body weight but uses 20 percent of our energy. In newborns, it's no less than 65 percent. That's partly why babies sleep all the time — their growing brains (A) warn / exhaust them — and have a lot of body fat, to use as an energy reserve when needed. Our muscles use even more of our energy, about a quarter of the total, but we have a lot of muscle. Actually, per unit of matter, the brain uses by far (B) more / less energy than our other organs. That means that the brain is the most expensive of our organs. But it is also marvelously (C) creative / efficient. Our brains require only about four hundred calories of energy a day — about the same as we get from a blueberry muffin. Try running your laptop for twenty-four hours on a muffin and see how far you get.

	(A)	(B)	(C)
①	warn	······ less	······ efficient
②	warn	······ more	······ efficient
③	exhaust	······ more	······ efficient
④	exhaust	······ more	······ creative
⑤	exhaust	······ less	······ creative

07 1등급 대비 고난도 2점 문제　고1 · 2022년 6월 31번

다음 빈칸에 들어갈 말로 가장 적절한 것을 고르시오.

One of the big questions faced this past year was how to keep innovation rolling when people were working entirely virtually. But experts say that digital work didn't have a negative effect on innovation and creativity. Working within limits pushes us to solve problems. Overall, virtual meeting platforms put more constraints on communication and collaboration than face-to-face settings. For instance, with the press of a button, virtual meeting hosts can control the size of breakout groups and enforce time constraints; only one person can speak at a time; nonverbal signals, particularly those below the shoulders, are diminished; "seating arrangements" are assigned by the platform, not by individuals; and visual access to others may be limited by the size of each participant's screen. Such _____ are likely to stretch participants beyond their usual ways of thinking, boosting creativity.

① restrictions
② responsibilities
③ memories
④ coincidences
⑤ traditions

08 1등급 대비 고난도 2점 문제　고1 · 2023년 6월 38번

글의 흐름으로 보아, 주어진 문장이 들어가기에 가장 적절한 곳을 고르시오.

> Yet we know that the face that stares back at us from the glass is not the same, cannot be the same, as it was 10 minutes ago.

Sometimes the pace of change is far slower. (①) The face you saw reflected in your mirror this morning probably appeared no different from the face you saw the day before — or a week or a month ago. (②) The proof is in your photo album: Look at a photograph taken of yourself 5 or 10 years ago and you see clear differences between the face in the snapshot and the face in your mirror. (③) If you lived in a world without mirrors for a year and then saw your reflection, you might be surprised by the change. (④) After an interval of 10 years without seeing yourself, you might not at first recognize the person peering from the mirror. (⑤) Even something as basic as our own face changes from moment to moment.

＊peer: 응시하다

09 1등급 대비 고난도 2편 문제

고1 · 2022년 9월 40번

다음 글의 내용을 한 문장으로 요약하고자 한다. 빈칸 (A), (B)에 들어갈 말로 가장 적절한 것은?

My colleagues and I ran an experiment testing two different messages meant to convince thousands of resistant alumni to make a donation. One message emphasized the opportunity to do good: donating would benefit students, faculty, and staff. The other emphasized the opportunity to feel good: donors would enjoy the warm glow of giving. The two messages were equally effective: in both cases, 6.5 percent of the unwilling alumni ended up donating. Then we combined them, because two reasons are better than one. Except they weren't. When we put the two reasons together, the giving rate dropped below 3 percent. Each reason alone was more than twice as effective as the two combined. The audience was already skeptical. When we gave them different kinds of reasons to donate, we triggered their awareness that someone was trying to persuade them — and they shielded themselves against it.

* alumni: 졸업생 ** skeptical: 회의적인

In the experiment mentioned above, when the two different reasons to donate were given   (A)   , the audience was less likely to be   (B)   because they could recognize the intention to persuade them.

	(A)		(B)
①	simultaneously	……	convinced
②	separately	……	confused
③	frequently	……	annoyed
④	separately	……	satisfied
⑤	simultaneously	……	offended

[10 ～ 12] 다음 글을 읽고, 물음에 답하시오.

(A)

One day a young man was walking along a road on his journey from one village to another. As he walked he noticed a monk working in the fields. The young man turned to the monk and said, "Excuse me. Do you mind if I ask (a) you a question?" "Not at all," replied the monk.

* monk: 수도승

(B)

A while later a middle-aged man journeyed down the same road and came upon the monk. "I am going to the village in the valley," said the man. "Do you know what it is like?" "I do," replied the monk, "but first tell (b) me about the village where you came from." "I've come from the village in the mountains," said the man. "It was a wonderful experience. I felt as though I was a member of the family in the village."

(C)

"I am traveling from the village in the mountains to the village in the valley and I was wondering if (c) you knew what it is like in the village in the valley." "Tell me," said the monk, "what was your experience of the village in the mountains?" "Terrible," replied the young man. "I am glad to be away from there. I found the people most unwelcoming. So tell (d) me, what can I expect in the village in the valley?" "I am sorry to tell you," said the monk, "but I think your experience will be much the same there." The young man lowered his head helplessly and walked on.

(D)

"Why did you feel like that?" asked the monk. "The elders gave me much advice, and people were kind and generous. I am sad to have left there. And what is the village in the valley like?" he asked again. "(e) I think you will find it much the same," replied the monk. "I'm glad to hear that," the middle-aged man said smiling and journeyed on.

10

주어진 글 (A)에 이어질 내용을 순서에 맞게 배열한 것으로 가장 적절한 것은?

① (B) − (D) − (C)   ② (C) − (B) − (D)

③ (C) − (D) − (B)   ④ (D) − (B) − (C)

⑤ (D) − (C) − (B)

12

윗글에 관한 내용으로 적절하지 <u>않은</u> 것은?

① 한 수도승이 들판에서 일하고 있었다.

② 중년 남자는 골짜기에 있는 마을로 가는 중이었다.

③ 수도승은 골짜기에 있는 마을에 대해 질문받았다.

④ 수도승의 말을 듣고 젊은이는 고개를 숙였다.

⑤ 중년 남자는 산속에 있는 마을을 떠나서 기쁘다고 말했다.

DAY 12

11

밑줄 친 (a) ~ (e) 중에서 가리키는 대상이 나머지 넷과 <u>다른</u> 것은?

① (a)   ② (b)   ③ (c)   ④ (d)   ⑤ (e)

학습 Check!

▶ 몰라서 틀린 문항 ✕ 표기 ▶ 헷갈렸거나 찍은 문항 △ 표기 ▶ ✕, △ 문항은 다시 풀고 ✔ 표기를 하세요.

종료 시각	시 분 초	문항 번호	01	02	03	04	05	06	07	08	09	10	11	12
소요 시간	분 초	채점 결과												
초과 시간	분 초	틀린 문항 복습												

DAY 13

수능기출 전국연합학력평가 **20분 미니 모의고사**

● 날짜 :   월   일   ● 시작 시각 :   시   분   초   ● 목표 시간 : 20분

※ 점수 표기가 없는 문항은 모두 **2점**입니다.

01

고1 · 2023년 6월 19번

다음 글에 드러난 'I'의 심경 변화로 가장 적절한 것은?

　When I woke up in our hotel room, it was almost midnight. I didn't see my husband nor daughter. I called them, but I heard their phones ringing in the room. Feeling worried, I went outside and walked down the street, but they were nowhere to be found. When I decided I should ask someone for help, a crowd nearby caught my attention. I approached, hoping to find my husband and daughter, and suddenly I saw two familiar faces. I smiled, feeling calm. Just then, my daughter saw me and called, "Mom!" They were watching the magic show. Finally, I felt all my worries disappear.

① anxious　　　→ relieved
② delighted　　→ unhappy
③ indifferent　　→ excited
④ relaxed　　　→ upset
⑤ embarrassed　→ proud

02

고1 · 2022년 9월 20번

다음 글에서 필자가 주장하는 바로 가장 적절한 것은?

　Experts on writing say, "Get rid of as many words as possible." Each word must do something important. If it doesn't, get rid of it. Well, this doesn't work for speaking. It takes more words to introduce, express, and adequately elaborate an idea in speech than it takes in writing. Why is this so? While the reader can reread, the listener cannot rehear. Speakers do not come equipped with a replay button. Because listeners are easily distracted, they will miss many pieces of what a speaker says. If they miss the crucial sentence, they may never catch up. This makes it necessary for speakers to talk *longer* about their points, using more words on them than would be used to express the same idea in writing.

① 연설 시 중요한 정보는 천천히 말해야 한다.
② 좋은 글을 쓰려면 간결한 문장을 사용해야 한다.
③ 말하기 전에 신중히 생각하는 습관을 길러야 한다.
④ 글을 쓸 때보다 말할 때 더 많은 단어를 사용해야 한다.
⑤ 청중의 이해를 돕기 위해 미리 연설문을 제공해야 한다.

03

다음 글의 요지로 가장 적절한 것은?

The old saying is that "knowledge is power," but when it comes to scary, threatening news, research suggests the exact opposite. Frightening news can actually rob people of their inner sense of control, making them less likely to take care of themselves and other people. Public health research shows that when the news presents health-related information in a pessimistic way, people are actually less likely to take steps to protect themselves from illness as a result. A news article that's intended to warn people about increasing cancer rates, for example, can result in fewer people choosing to get screened for the disease because they're so terrified of what they might find. This is also true for issues such as climate change. When a news story is all doom and gloom, people feel depressed and become less interested in taking small, personal steps to fight ecological collapse.

① 두려움을 주는 뉴스는 사람들이 문제에 덜 대처하게 할 수 있다.
② 정보를 전달하는 시기에 따라 뉴스의 영향력이 달라질 수 있다.
③ 지속적인 환경 문제 보도가 사람들의 인식 변화를 가져온다.
④ 정보 제공의 지연은 정확한 문제 인식에 방해가 될 수 있다.
⑤ 출처가 불분명한 건강 정보는 사람들에게 유익하지 않다.

04

다음 도표의 내용과 일치하지 <u>않는</u> 것은?

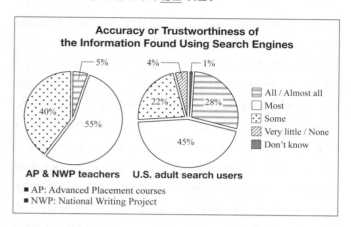

The two pie charts above show how much of the information found using search engines is considered to be accurate or trustworthy by two groups of respondents (AP & NWP teachers and U.S. adult search users) in 2012. ① As for AP & NWP teachers, five percent say that "All / Almost all" of the information found using search engines is accurate or trustworthy, while 28 percent of U.S. adult search users say the same. ② The largest percentage of both AP & NWP teachers and U.S. adult search users answer that "Most" of the information is accurate or trustworthy. ③ In addition, 40 percent of AP & NWP teachers say that "Some" of the information is accurate or trustworthy, and more than 30 percent of U.S. adult search users respond the same. ④ U.S. adult search users saying that "Very little / None" of the information found using search engines is accurate or trustworthy account for less than five percent. ⑤ The percentage of U.S. adult search users who answer "Don't know" is only one percent.

05

다음 글의 밑줄 친 부분 중, 어법상 틀린 것은? [3점]

The belief that humans have morality and animals don't is such a longstanding assumption that it could well be called a habit of mind, and bad habits, as we all know, are extremely hard ① to break. A lot of people have caved in to this assumption because it is easier to deny morality to animals than to deal with the complex effects of the possibility ② that animals have moral behavior. The historical tendency, framed in the outdated dualism of us versus them, ③ is strong enough to make a lot of people cling to the status quo. Denial of who animals are ④ convenient allows for maintaining false stereotypes about the cognitive and emotional capacities of animals. Clearly a major paradigm shift is needed, because the lazy acceptance of habits of mind has a strong influence on ⑤ how animals are understood and treated.

＊dualism: 이원론(二元論)　＊＊status quo: 현재 상태

06

다음 글의 밑줄 친 부분 중, 문맥상 낱말의 쓰임이 적절하지 않은 것은? [3점]

While moving is difficult for everyone, it is particularly stressful for children. They lose their sense of security and may feel disoriented when their routine is disrupted and all that is ① familiar is taken away. Young children, ages 3-6, are particularly affected by a move. Their understanding at this stage is quite literal, and it is ② easy for them to imagine beforehand a new home and their new room. Young children may have worries such as "Will I still be me in the new place?" and "Will my toys and bed come with us?" It is important to establish a balance between validating children's past experiences and focusing on helping them ③ adjust to the new place. Children need to have opportunities to share their backgrounds in a way that ④ respects their past as an important part of who they are. This contributes to building a sense of community, which is essential for all children, especially those in ⑤ transition.

07 1등급 대비 고난도 2점 문제

다음 빈칸에 들어갈 말로 가장 적절한 것을 고르시오.

One of the most important aspects of providing good care is making sure that an animal's needs are being met consistently and predictably. Like humans, animals need a sense of control. So an animal who may get enough food but doesn't know when the food will appear and can see no consistent schedule may experience distress. We can provide a sense of control by ensuring that our animal's environment is _____ : there is always water available and always in the same place. There is always food when we get up in the morning and after our evening walk. There will always be a time and place to eliminate, without having to hold things in to the point of discomfort. Human companions can display consistent emotional support, rather than providing love one moment and withholding love the next. When animals know what to expect, they can feel more confident and calm.

*eliminate: 배설하다

① silent   ② natural
③ isolated   ④ dynamic
⑤ predictable

08

다음 빈칸에 들어갈 말로 가장 적절한 것을 고르시오. [3점]

There is a major problem with _____
_____. To determine the number of objects by counting, such as determining how many apples there are on a table, many children would touch or point to the first apple and say "one," then move on to the second apple and say "two," and continue in this manner until all the apples are counted. If we start at 0, we would have to touch nothing and say "zero," but then we would have to start touching apples and calling out "one, two, three" and so on. This can be very confusing because there would be a need to stress when to touch and when not to touch. If a child accidentally touches an apple while saying "zero," then the total number of apples will be off by 1.

① counting from 0
② numbering in reverse order
③ adding up the numbers given
④ learning words through games
⑤ saying numbers in a loud voice

09

고1 · 2022년 6월 35번

다음 글에서 전체 흐름과 관계 없는 문장은?

According to Marguerite La Caze, fashion contributes to our lives and provides a medium for us to develop and exhibit important social virtues. ① Fashion may be beautiful, innovative, and useful; we can display creativity and good taste in our fashion choices. ② And in dressing with taste and care, we represent both self-respect and a concern for the pleasure of others. ③ There is no doubt that fashion can be a source of interest and pleasure which links us to each other. ④ Although the fashion industry developed first in Europe and America, today it is an international and highly globalized industry. ⑤ That is, fashion provides a sociable aspect along with opportunities to imagine oneself differently — to try on different identities.

＊virtue: 가치

10 1등급 대비 고난도 2점 문제

고1 · 2020년 9월 37번

주어진 글 다음에 이어질 글의 순서로 가장 적절한 것을 고르시오.

Mirrors and other smooth, shiny surfaces reflect light. We see reflections from such surfaces because the rays of light form an image on the retina of our eyes.

(A) Keep your eyes on the reflected image while you are writing and not on your paper. After a little practice, it will be easier to write "backwards." When your friend receives such a message he will be able to read it by holding the paper up to a mirror.

(B) Stand a mirror upright on the table, so that a piece of paper on the table can be clearly seen in the mirror. Now write a message that looks right when you look in the mirror.

(C) Such images are always reversed. Look at yourself in a mirror, wink your right eye and your left eye seems to wink back at you. You can use a mirror to send a coded message to a friend.

＊retina: (눈의) 망막

① (A) − (C) − (B) ② (B) − (A) − (C)
③ (B) − (C) − (A) ④ (C) − (A) − (B)
⑤ (C) − (B) − (A)

[11 ~ 12] 다음 글을 읽고, 물음에 답하시오.

Researchers brought two groups of 11-year-old boys to a summer camp at Robbers Cave State Park in Oklahoma. The boys were strangers to one another and upon arrival at the camp, were randomly separated into two groups. The groups were kept apart for about a week. They swam, camped, and hiked. Each group chose a name for itself, and the boys printed their group's name on their caps and T-shirts. Then the two groups met. A series of athletic competitions were set up between them. Soon, each group considered the other an (a) enemy. Each group came to look down on the other. The boys started food fights and stole various items from members of the other group. Thus, under competitive conditions, the boys quickly (b) drew sharp group boundaries.

The researchers next stopped the athletic competitions and created several apparent emergencies whose solution (c) required cooperation between the two groups. One such emergency involved a leak in the pipe supplying water to the camp. The researchers assigned the boys to teams made up of members of both groups. Their job was to look into the pipe and fix the leak. After engaging in several such (d) cooperative activities, the boys started playing together without fighting. Once cooperation replaced competition and the groups (e) started to look down on each other, group boundaries melted away as quickly as they had formed.

* apparent: ~인 것으로 보이는

11

고1·2019년 3월 41번

윗글의 제목으로 가장 적절한 것은?

① How Are Athletic Competitions Helpful for Teens?
② Preparation: The Key to Preventing Emergencies
③ What Makes Group Boundaries Disappear?
④ Respect Individual Differences in Teams
⑤ Free Riders: Headaches in Teams

12 1등급 대비 고난도 2점 문제

고1·2019년 3월 42번

밑줄 친 (a) ~ (e) 중에서 문맥상 낱말의 쓰임이 적절하지 <u>않은</u> 것은?

① (a)　　② (b)　　③ (c)　　④ (d)　　⑤ (e)

DAY 14

● 날짜 :   월   일   ● 시작 시각 :   시   분   초   ● 목표 시간 : 20분

※ 점수 표기가 없는 문항은 모두 **2점**입니다.

01

고1 · 2022년 6월 18번

다음 글의 목적으로 가장 적절한 것은?

Dear Boat Tour Manager,

On March 15, my family was on one of your Glass Bottom Boat Tours. When we returned to our hotel, I discovered that I left behind my cell phone case. The case must have fallen off my lap and onto the floor when I took it off my phone to clean it. I would like to ask you to check if it is on your boat. Its color is black and it has my name on the inside. If you find the case, I would appreciate it if you would let me know.

Sincerely,
Sam Roberts

① 제품의 고장 원인을 문의하려고
② 분실물 발견 시 연락을 부탁하려고
③ 시설물의 철저한 관리를 당부하려고
④ 여행자 보험 가입 절차를 확인하려고
⑤ 분실물 센터 확장의 필요성을 건의하려고

02

고3 · 2021학년도 수능 21번

밑줄 친 **the role of the 'lion's historians'**가 다음 글에서 의미하는 바로 가장 적절한 것은?

There is an African proverb that says, 'Till the lions have their historians, tales of hunting will always glorify the hunter'. The proverb is about power, control and law making. Environmental journalists have to play the role of the 'lion's historians'. They have to put across the point of view of the environment to people who make the laws. They have to be the voice of wild India. The present rate of human consumption is completely unsustainable. Forest, wetlands, wastelands, coastal zones, eco-sensitive zones, they are all seen as disposable for the accelerating demands of human population. But to ask for any change in human behaviour — whether it be to cut down on consumption, alter lifestyles or decrease population growth — is seen as a violation of human rights. But at some point human rights become 'wrongs'. It's time we changed our thinking so that there is no difference between the rights of humans and the rights of the rest of the environment.

① uncovering the history of a species' biological evolution
② urging a shift to sustainable human behaviour for nature
③ fighting against widespread violations of human rights
④ rewriting history for more underrepresented people
⑤ restricting the power of environmental lawmakers

03

다음 글의 제목으로 가장 적절한 것은?

Diversity, challenge, and conflict help us maintain our imagination. Most people assume that conflict is bad and that being in one's "comfort zone" is good. That is not exactly true. Of course, we don't want to find ourselves without a job or medical insurance or in a fight with our partner, family, boss, or coworkers. One bad experience can be sufficient to last us a lifetime. But small disagreements with family and friends, trouble with technology or finances, or challenges at work and at home can help us think through our own capabilities. Problems that need solutions force us to use our brains in order to develop creative answers. Navigating landscapes that are varied, that offer trials and occasional conflicts, is more helpful to creativity than hanging out in landscapes that pose no challenge to our senses and our minds. Our two million-year history is packed with challenges and conflicts.

① Technology: A Lens to the Future
② Diversity: A Key to Social Unification
③ Simple Ways to Avoid Conflicts with Others
④ Creativity Doesn't Come from Playing It Safe
⑤ There Are No Challenges That Can't Be Overcome

04

Gary Becker에 관한 다음 글의 내용과 일치하지 <u>않는</u> 것은?

Gary Becker was born in Pottsville, Pennsylvania in 1930 and grew up in Brooklyn, New York City. His father, who was not well educated, had a deep interest in financial and political issues. After graduating from high school, Becker went to Princeton University, where he majored in economics. He was dissatisfied with his economic education at Princeton University because "it didn't seem to be handling real problems." He earned a doctor's degree in economics from the University of Chicago in 1955. His doctoral paper on the economics of discrimination was mentioned by the Nobel Prize Committee as an important contribution to economics. Since 1985, Becker had written a regular economics column in *Business Week*, explaining economic analysis and ideas to the general public. In 1992, he was awarded the Nobel Prize in economic science.

＊discrimination: 차별

① New York City의 Brooklyn에서 자랐다.
② 아버지는 금융과 정치 문제에 깊은 관심이 있었다.
③ Princeton University에서의 경제학 교육에 만족했다.
④ 1955년에 경제학 박사 학위를 취득했다.
⑤ *Business Week*에 경제학 칼럼을 기고했다.

05 1등급 대비 고난도 3점 문제

다음 글의 밑줄 친 부분 중, 어법상 틀린 것은? [3점]

Improved consumer water consciousness may be the cheapest way ① to save the most water, but it is not the only way consumers can contribute to water conservation. With technology progressing faster than ever before, there ② are plenty of devices that consumers can install in their homes to save more. More than 35 models of high-efficiency toilets are on the U.S. market today, some of ③ them use less than 1.3 gallons per flush. Starting at $200, these toilets are affordable and can help the average consumer save hundreds of gallons of water per year. Appliances ④ officially approved as most efficient are tagged with the Energy Star logo to alert the shopper. Washing machines with that rating use 18 to 25 gallons of water per load, compared with older machines that use 40 gallons. High-efficiency dishwashers save ⑤ even more water. These machines use up to 50 percent less water than older models.

06

(A), (B), (C)의 각 네모 안에서 문맥에 맞는 낱말로 가장 적절한 것은? [3점]

Many successful people tend to keep a good bedtime routine. They take the time just before bed to reflect on or write down three things that they are (A) regretful / thankful for that happened during the day. Keeping a diary of things that they appreciate reminds them of the progress they made that day in any aspect of their lives. It serves as a key way to stay motivated, especially when they experience a (B) hardship / success. In such case, many people fall easily into the trap of replaying negative situations from a hard day. But regardless of how badly their day went, successful people typically (C) avoid / employ that trap of negative self-talk. That is because they know it will only create more stress.

(A)	(B)	(C)
① regretful	hardship	avoid
② regretful	success	employ
③ thankful	hardship	avoid
④ thankful	success	avoid
⑤ thankful	hardship	employ

07 1등급 대비 고난도 3점 문제

다음 빈칸에 들어갈 말로 가장 적절한 것을 고르시오. [3점]

Our homes aren't just ecosystems, they're unique ones, hosting species that are adapted to indoor environments and pushing evolution in new directions. Indoor microbes, insects, and rats have all evolved the ability to survive our chemical attacks, developing resistance to antibacterials, insecticides, and poisons. German cockroaches are known to have developed a distaste for glucose, which is commonly used as bait in roach traps. Some indoor insects, which have fewer opportunities to feed than their outdoor counterparts, seem to have developed the ability to survive when food is limited. Dunn and other ecologists have suggested that as the planet becomes more developed and more urban, more species will _____. Over a long enough time period, indoor living could drive our evolution, too. Perhaps my indoorsy self represents the future of humanity.

＊glucose: 포도당　＊＊bait: 미끼

① produce chemicals to protect themselves
② become extinct with the destroyed habitats
③ evolve the traits they need to thrive indoors
④ compete with outside organisms to find their prey
⑤ break the boundaries between wildlife and humans

08 1등급 대비 고난도 3점 문제

글의 흐름으로 보아, 주어진 문장이 들어가기에 가장 적절한 곳을 고르시오. [3점]

> Other individuals prefer integrating work and family roles all day long.

Boundaries between work and home are blurring as portable digital technology makes it increasingly possible to work anywhere, anytime. Individuals differ in how they like to manage their time to meet work and outside responsibilities. (①) Some people prefer to separate or segment roles so that boundary crossings are minimized. (②) For example, these people might keep separate email accounts for work and family and try to conduct work at the workplace and take care of family matters only during breaks and non-work time. (③) We've even noticed more of these "segmenters" carrying two phones — one for work and one for personal use. (④) Flexible schedules work well for these individuals because they enable greater distinction between time at work and time in other roles. (⑤) This might entail constantly trading text messsages with children from the office, or monitoring emails at home and on vacation, rather than returning to work to find hundreds of messages in their inbox.

＊entail: 수반하다

09

고1 · 2020년 11월 40번

다음 글의 내용을 한 문장으로 요약하고자 한다. 빈칸 (A), (B)에 들어갈 말로 가장 적절한 것은?

In their study in 2007 Katherine Kinzler and her colleagues at Harvard showed that our tendency to identify with an in-group to a large degree begins in infancy and may be innate. Kinzler and her team took a bunch of five-month-olds whose families only spoke English and showed the babies two videos. In one video, a woman was speaking English. In the other, a woman was speaking Spanish. Then they were shown a screen with both women side by side, not speaking. In infant psychology research, the standard measure for affinity or interest is attention — babies will apparently stare longer at the things they like more. In Kinzler's study, the babies stared at the English speakers longer. In other studies, researchers have found that infants are more likely to take a toy offered by someone who speaks the same language as them. Psychologists routinely cite these and other experiments as evidence of our built-in evolutionary preference for "our own kind."

* affinity: 애착

↓

Infants' more favorable responses to those who use a ___(A)___ language show that there can be a(n) ___(B)___ tendency to prefer in-group members.

	(A)		(B)
①	familiar	……	inborn
②	familiar	……	acquired
③	foreign	……	cultural
④	foreign	……	learned
⑤	formal	……	innate

[10 ~ 12] 다음 글을 읽고, 물음에 답하시오.

(A)

Once upon a time, there lived a young king who had a great passion for hunting. His kingdom was located at the foot of the Himalayas. Once every year, he would go hunting in the nearby forests. (a) He would make all the necessary preparations, and then set out for his hunting trip.

(B)

Seasons changed. A year passed by. And it was time to go hunting once again. The king went to the same forest as the previous year. (b) He used his beautiful deerskin drum to round up animals. But none came. All the animals ran for safety, except one doe. She came closer and closer to the drummer. Suddenly, she started fearlessly licking the deerskin drum.

* round up: ~을 몰다 ** doe: 암사슴

(C)

Like all other years, the hunting season had arrived. Preparations began in the palace and the king got ready for (c) his hunting trip. Deep in the forest, he spotted a beautiful wild deer. It was a large stag. His aim was perfect. When he killed the deer with just one shot of his arrow, the king was filled with pride. (d) The proud hunter ordered a hunting drum to be made out of the skin of the deer.

* stag: 수사슴

(D)

The king was surprised by this sight. An old servant had an answer to this strange behavior. "The deerskin used to make this drum belonged to her mate, the deer who we hunted last year. This doe is mourning the death of her mate," (e) the man said. Upon hearing this, the king had a change of heart. He had never realized that an animal, too, felt the pain of loss. He made a promise, from that day on, to never again hunt wild animals.

* mourn: 애도하다

10

고1 • 2021년 3월 43번

주어진 글 (A)에 이어질 내용을 순서에 맞게 배열한 것으로 가장 적절한 것은?

① (B) − (D) − (C) 　② (C) − (B) − (D)
③ (C) − (D) − (B) 　④ (D) − (B) − (C)
⑤ (D) − (C) − (B)

12

고1 • 2021년 3월 45번

윗글에 관한 내용으로 적절하지 <u>않은</u> 것은?

① 왕은 매년 근처의 숲으로 사냥 여행을 갔다.
② 암사슴은 북 치는 사람으로부터 도망갔다.
③ 왕은 화살로 단번에 수사슴을 맞혔다.
④ 한 나이 든 신하가 암사슴의 행동의 이유를 알고 있었다.
⑤ 왕은 다시는 야생 동물을 사냥하지 않겠다고 약속했다.

11

고1 • 2021년 3월 44번

밑줄 친 (a) ∼ (e) 중에서 가리키는 대상이 나머지 넷과 <u>다른</u> 것은?

① (a)　　② (b)　　③ (c)　　④ (d)　　⑤ (e)

학습 Check!				▶ 몰라서 틀린 문항 × 표기		▶ 헷갈렸거나 찍은 문항 △ 표기		▶ ×, △ 문항은 다시 풀고 ✔ 표기를 하세요.							
종료 시각	시	분	초	문항 번호	01	02	03	04	05	06	07	08	09	10	11	12
소요 시간		분	초	채점 결과												
초과 시간		분	초	틀린 문항 복습												

[해설편 p.058]

DAY **15**

수능기출
전국연합학력평가 **20분 미니 모의고사**

● 날짜 : 　월　　일 ● 시작 시각 : 　시　　분　　초 ● 목표 시간 : 20분

※ 점수 표기가 없는 문항은 모두 2점입니다.

01

다음 글에 드러난 Matthew의 심경 변화로 가장 적절한 것은?

One Saturday morning, Matthew's mother told Matthew that she was going to take him to the park. A big smile came across his face. As he loved to play outside, he ate his breakfast and got dressed quickly so they could go. When they got to the park, Matthew ran all the way over to the swing set. That was his favorite thing to do at the park. But the swings were all being used. His mother explained that he could use the slide until a swing became available, but it was broken. Suddenly, his mother got a phone call and she told Matthew they had to leave. His heart sank.

① embarrassed → indifferent
② excited → disappointed
③ cheerful → ashamed
④ nervous → touched
⑤ scared → relaxed

02

다음 글에서 필자가 주장하는 바로 가장 적절한 것은?

You already have a business and you're about to launch your blog so that you can sell your product. Unfortunately, here is where a 'business mind' can be a bad thing. Most people believe that to have a successful business blog promoting a product, they have to stay strictly 'on the topic.' If all you're doing is shamelessly promoting your product, then who is going to want to read the latest thing you're writing about? Instead, you need to give some useful or entertaining information away for free so that people have a reason to keep coming back. Only by doing this can you create an interested audience that you will then be able to sell to. So, the best way to be successful with a business blog is to write about things that your audience will be interested in.

① 인터넷 게시물에 대한 윤리적 기준을 세워야 한다.
② 블로그를 전문적으로 관리할 인력을 마련해야 한다.
③ 신제품 개발을 위해 상업용 블로그를 적극 활용해야 한다.
④ 상품에 대한 고객들의 반응을 정기적으로 분석할 필요가 있다.
⑤ 상업용 블로그는 사람들이 흥미 있어 할 정보를 제공해야 한다.

03

다음 글의 요지로 가장 적절한 것은?

It's important that you think independently and fight for what you believe in, but there comes a time when it's wiser to stop fighting for your view and move on to accepting what a trustworthy group of people think is best. This can be extremely difficult. But it's smarter, and ultimately better for you to be open-minded and have faith that the conclusions of a trustworthy group of people are better than whatever you think. If you can't understand their view, you're probably just blind to their way of thinking. If you continue doing what you think is best when all the evidence and trustworthy people are against you, you're being dangerously confident. The truth is that while most people can become incredibly open-minded, some can't, even after they have repeatedly encountered lots of pain from betting that they were right when they were not.

① 대부분의 사람들은 진리에 도달하지 못하고 고통을 받는다.
② 맹목적으로 다른 사람의 의견을 받아들이는 것은 위험하다.
③ 남을 설득하기 위해서는 타당한 증거로 주장을 뒷받침해야 한다.
④ 믿을만한 사람이 누구인지 판단하려면 열린 마음을 가져야 한다.
⑤ 자신의 의견이 최선이 아닐 수 있다는 것을 인정하는 것이 필요하다.

04

Turtle Island Boat Tour에 관한 다음 안내문의 내용과 일치하지 <u>않는</u> 것은?

Turtle Island Boat Tour

The fantastic Turtle Island Boat Tour invites you to the beautiful sea world.

Dates: From June 1 to August 31, 2024

Tour Times

Weekdays	1 p.m. – 5 p.m.
Weekends	9 a.m. – 1 p.m.
	1 p.m. – 5 p.m.

※ Each tour lasts four hours.

Tickets & Booking
- $50 per person for each tour
  (Only those aged 17 and over can participate.)
- Bookings must be completed no later than 2 days before the day of the tour.
- No refunds after the departure time
- Each tour group size is limited to 10 participants.

Activities
- Snorkeling with a professional diver
- Feeding tropical fish

※ Feel free to explore our website, www.snorkelingti.com.

---

① 주말에는 하루에 두 번 운영된다.
② 17세 이상만 참가할 수 있다.
③ 당일 예약이 가능하다.
④ 출발 시간 이후에는 환불이 불가능하다.
⑤ 전문 다이버와 함께 하는 스노클링 활동이 있다.

05 1등급 대비 고난도 3점 문제

다음 글의 밑줄 친 부분 중, 어법상 틀린 것은? [3점]

In perceiving changes, we tend to regard the most recent ① ones as the most revolutionary. This is often inconsistent with the facts. Recent progress in telecommunications technologies is not more revolutionary than ② what happened in the late nineteenth century in relative terms. Moreover, in terms of the consequent economic and social changes, the Internet revolution has not been as ③ important as the washing machine and other household appliances. These things, by vastly reducing the amount of work needed for household chores, ④ allowing women to enter the labor market and virtually got rid of professions like domestic service. We should not "put the telescope backward" when we look into the past and underestimate the old and overestimate the new. This leads us ⑤ to make all sorts of wrong decisions about national economic policy, corporate policies, and our own careers.

06

다음 글의 밑줄 친 부분 중, 문맥상 낱말의 쓰임이 적절하지 않은 것은?

Advertisers often displayed considerable facility in ① adapting their claims to the market status of the goods they promoted. Fleischmann's yeast, for instance, was used as an ingredient for cooking homemade bread. Yet more and more people in the early 20th century were buying their bread from stores or bakeries, so consumer demand for yeast ② increased. The producer of Fleischmann's yeast hired the J. Walter Thompson advertising agency to come up with a different marketing strategy to ③ boost sales. No longer the "Soul of Bread," the Thompson agency first turned yeast into an important source of vitamins with significant health ④ benefits. Shortly thereafter, the advertising agency transformed yeast into a natural laxative. ⑤ Repositioning yeast helped increase sales.

＊laxative: 완하제(배변을 쉽게 하는 약·음식·음료)

07

다음 빈칸에 들어갈 말로 가장 적절한 것을 고르시오.

_____ provides a change to the environment for journalists. Newspaper stories, television reports, and even early online reporting (prior to communication technology such as tablets and smartphones) required one central place to which a reporter would submit his or her news story for printing, broadcast, or posting. Now, though, a reporter can shoot video, record audio, and type directly on their smartphones or tablets and post a news story instantly. Journalists do not need to report to a central location where they all contact sources, type, or edit video. A story can be instantaneously written, shot, and made available to the entire world. The news cycle, and thus the job of the journalist, never takes a break. Thus the "24-hour" news cycle that emerged from the rise of cable TV is now a thing of the past. The news "cycle" is really a constant.

① Mobility
② Sensitivity
③ Creativity
④ Accuracy
⑤ Responsibility

08 1등급 대비 고난도 3점 문제

다음 빈칸에 들어갈 말로 가장 적절한 것을 고르시오. [3점]

Due to technological innovations, music can now be experienced by more people, for more of the time than ever before. Mass availability has given individuals unheard-of control over their own sound-environment. However, it has also confronted them with the simultaneous availability of countless genres of music, in which they have to orient themselves. People start filtering out and organizing their digital libraries like they used to do with their physical music collections. However, there is the difference that the choice lies in their own hands. Without being restricted to the limited collection of music-distributors, nor being guided by the local radio program as a 'preselector' of the latest hits, the individual actively has to _____ _____. The search for the right song is thus associated with considerable effort.

＊simultaneous: 동시의

① choose and determine his or her musical preferences
② understand the technical aspects of recording sessions
③ share unique and inspiring playlists on social media
④ interpret lyrics with background knowledge of the songs
⑤ seek the advice of a voice specialist for better performances

09

다음 글에서 전체 흐름과 관계 <u>없는</u> 문장은?

Who hasn't used a cup of coffee to help themselves stay awake while studying? Mild stimulants commonly found in tea, coffee, or sodas possibly make you more attentive and, thus, better able to remember. ① However, you should know that stimulants are as likely to have negative effects on memory as they are to be beneficial. ② Even if they could improve performance at some level, the ideal doses are currently unknown. ③ If you are wide awake and well-rested, mild stimulation from caffeine can do little to further improve your memory performance. ④ In contrast, many studies have shown that drinking tea is healthier than drinking coffee. ⑤ Indeed, if you have too much of a stimulant, you will become nervous, find it difficult to sleep, and your memory performance will suffer.

＊stimulant: 자극제　＊＊dose: 복용량

10 [1등급 대비 고난도 3점 문제]

주어진 글 다음에 이어질 글의 순서로 가장 적절한 것을 고르시오.
[3점]

Natural processes form minerals in many ways. For example, hot melted rock material, called magma, cools when it reaches the Earth's surface, or even if it's trapped below the surface. As magma cools, its atoms lose heat energy, move closer together, and begin to combine into compounds.

(A) Also, the size of the crystals that form depends partly on how rapidly the magma cools. When magma cools slowly, the crystals that form are generally large enough to see with the unaided eye.

(B) During this process, atoms of the different compounds arrange themselves into orderly, repeating patterns. The type and amount of elements present in a magma partly determine which minerals will form.

(C) This is because the atoms have enough time to move together and form into larger crystals. When magma cools rapidly, the crystals that form will be small. In such cases, you can't easily see individual mineral crystals.

＊compound: 화합물

① (A) － (C) － (B)　　② (B) － (A) － (C)
③ (B) － (C) － (A)　　④ (C) － (A) － (B)
⑤ (C) － (B) － (A)

[11 ~ 12] 다음 글을 읽고, 물음에 답하시오.

As kids, we worked hard at learning to ride a bike; when we fell off, we got back on again, until it became second nature to us. But when we try something new in our adult lives we'll usually make just one attempt before judging whether it's (a) worked. If we don't succeed the first time, or if it feels a little awkward, we'll tell ourselves it wasn't a success rather than giving it (b) another shot.

That's a shame, because repetition is central to the process of rewiring our brains. Consider the idea that your brain has a network of neurons. They will (c) connect with each other whenever you remember to use a brain-friendly feedback technique. Those connections aren't very (d) reliable at first, which may make your first efforts a little hit-and-miss. You might remember one of the steps involved, and not the others. But scientists have a saying: "neurons that fire together, wire together." In other words, repetition of an action (e) blocks the connections between the neurons involved in that action. That means the more times you try using that new feedback technique, the more easily it will come to you when you need it.

11

윗글의 제목으로 가장 적절한 것은?

① Repeat and You Will Succeed
② Be More Curious, Be Smarter
③ Play Is What Makes Us Human
④ Stop and Think Before You Act
⑤ Growth Is All About Keeping Balance

DAY 15

12

밑줄 친 (a) ~ (e) 중에서 문맥상 낱말의 쓰임이 적절하지 <u>않은</u> 것은?

① (a)　　② (b)　　③ (c)　　④ (d)　　⑤ (e)

학습 Check!　▶ 몰라서 틀린 문항 × 표기　▶ 헷갈렸거나 찍은 문항 △ 표기　▶ ×, △ 문항은 다시 풀고 ✔ 표기를 하세요.

종료 시각	시 분 초	문항 번호	01	02	03	04	05	06	07	08	09	10	11	12
소요 시간	분 초	채점 결과												
초과 시간	분 초	틀린 문항 복습												

[Day 15] 미니 모의고사　093

DAY 16

수능기출
전국연합학력평가 **20분 미니 모의고사**

● 날짜 :　　월　　일　● 시작 시각 :　　시　　분　　초　● 목표 시간 : 20분

※ 점수 표기가 없는 문항은 모두 2점입니다.

01

고1 · 2023년 6월 18번

다음 글의 목적으로 가장 적절한 것은?

ACC Travel Agency Customers:

Have you ever wanted to enjoy a holiday in nature? This summer is the best time to turn your dream into reality. We have a perfect travel package for you. This travel package includes special trips to Lake Madison as well as massage and meditation to help you relax. Also, we provide yoga lessons taught by experienced instructors. If you book this package, you will enjoy all this at a reasonable price. We are sure that it will be an unforgettable experience for you. If you call us, we will be happy to give you more details.

① 여행 일정 변경을 안내하려고
② 패키지 여행 상품을 홍보하려고
③ 여행 상품 불만족에 대해 사과하려고
④ 여행 만족도 조사 참여를 부탁하려고
⑤ 패키지 여행 업무 담당자를 모집하려고

02 1등급 대비 고난도 2점 문제

고1 · 2021년 9월 21번

밑줄 친 "matter out of place"가 다음 글에서 의미하는 바로 가장 적절한 것은?

Nothing is trash by nature. Anthropologist Mary Douglas brings back and analyzes the common saying that dirt is "matter out of place." Dirt is relative, she emphasizes. "Shoes are not dirty in themselves, but it is dirty to place them on the dining-table; food is not dirty in itself, but it is dirty to leave pots and pans in the bedroom, or food all over clothing; similarly, bathroom items in the living room; clothing lying on chairs; outdoor things placed indoors; upstairs things downstairs, and so on." Sorting the dirty from the clean — removing the shoes from the table, putting the dirty clothing in the washing machine — involves systematic ordering and classifying. Eliminating dirt is thus a positive process.

① something that is completely broken
② a tiny dust that nobody notices
③ a dirty but renewable material
④ what can be easily replaced
⑤ a thing that is not in order

03

고1 · 2022년 3월 24번

다음 글의 제목으로 가장 적절한 것은?

Our ability to accurately recognize and label emotions is often referred to as *emotional granularity*. In the words of Harvard psychologist Susan David, "Learning to label emotions with a more nuanced vocabulary can be absolutely transformative." David explains that if we don't have a rich emotional vocabulary, it is difficult to communicate our needs and to get the support that we need from others. But those who are able to distinguish between a range of various emotions "do much, much better at managing the ups and downs of ordinary existence than those who see everything in black and white." In fact, research shows that the process of labeling emotional experience is related to greater emotion regulation and psychosocial well-being.

* nuanced: 미묘한 차이가 있는

① True Friendship Endures Emotional Arguments
② Detailed Labeling of Emotions Is Beneficial
③ Labeling Emotions: Easier Said Than Done
④ Categorize and Label Tasks for Efficiency
⑤ Be Brave and Communicate Your Needs

04

고3 · 2019학년도 수능 26번

Marjorie Kinnan Rawlings에 관한 다음 글의 내용과 일치하지 않는 것은?

Marjorie Kinnan Rawlings, an American author born in Washington, D.C. in 1896, wrote novels with rural themes and settings. While she was young, one of her stories appeared in *The Washington Post*. After graduating from university, Rawlings worked as a journalist while simultaneously trying to establish herself as a fiction writer. In 1928, she purchased an orange grove in Cross Creek, Florida. This became the source of inspiration for some of her writings which included *The Yearling* and her autobiographical book, *Cross Creek*. In 1939, *The Yearling*, which was about a boy and an orphaned baby deer, won the Pulitzer Prize for Fiction. Later, in 1946, *The Yearling* was made into a film of the same name. Rawlings passed away in 1953, and the land she owned at Cross Creek has become a Florida State Park honoring her achievements.

* grove: 과수원

① Washington, D.C.에서 태어난 미국 작가이다.
② 그녀의 이야기 중 하나가 *The Washington Post*에 실렸다.
③ 대학교를 졸업한 후 저널리스트로 일했다.
④ *The Yearling*이라는 소설은 다른 제목으로 영화화되었다.
⑤ Cross Creek에 소유했던 땅은 Florida 주립 공원이 되었다.

DAY 16

05

다음 글의 밑줄 친 부분 중, 어법상 틀린 것은? [3점]

There have been occasions ① in which you have observed a smile and you could sense it was not genuine. The most obvious way of identifying a genuine smile from an insincere ② one is that a fake smile primarily only affects the lower half of the face, mainly with the mouth alone. The eyes don't really get involved. Take the opportunity to look in the mirror and manufacture a smile ③ using the lower half your face only. When you do this, judge ④ how happy your face really looks — is it genuine? A genuine smile will impact on the muscles and wrinkles around the eyes and less noticeably, the skin between the eyebrow and upper eyelid ⑤ are lowered slightly with true enjoyment. The genuine smile can impact on the entire face.

06

(A), (B), (C)의 각 네모 안에서 문맥에 맞는 낱말로 가장 적절한 것은?

How does a leader make people feel important? First, by listening to them. Let them know you respect their thinking, and let them (A) silence / voice their opinions. As an added bonus, you might learn something! A friend of mine once told me about the CEO of a large company who told one of his managers, "There's nothing you could possibly tell me that I haven't already thought about before. Don't ever tell me what you think unless I ask you. Is that understood?" Imagine the (B) improvement / loss of self-esteem that manager must have felt. It must have discouraged him and negatively affected his performance. On the other hand, when you make a person feel a great sense of importance, he or she will feel on top of the world — and the level of energy will (C) decrease / increase rapidly.

	(A)	(B)	(C)
①	silence	improvement	decrease
②	silence	loss	increase
③	voice	improvement	decrease
④	voice	loss	decrease
⑤	voice	loss	increase

07 1등급 대비 고난도 3점 문제

다음 빈칸에 들어갈 말로 가장 적절한 것을 고르시오. [3점]

Since a great deal of day-to-day academic work is boring and repetitive, you need to be well motivated to keep doing it. A mathematician sharpens her pencils, works on a proof, tries a few approaches, gets nowhere, and finishes for the day. A writer sits down at his desk, produces a few hundred words, decides they are no good, throws them in the bin, and hopes for better inspiration tomorrow. To produce something worthwhile — if it ever happens — may require years of such _____ labor. The Nobel Prize-winning biologist Peter Medawar said that about four-fifths of his time in science was wasted, adding sadly that "nearly all scientific research leads nowhere." What kept all of these people going when things were going badly was their passion for their subject. Without such passion, they would have achieved nothing.

＊proof: (수학) 증명

① cooperative
② productive
③ fruitless
④ dangerous
⑤ irregular

08 1등급 대비 고난도 3점 문제

글의 흐름으로 보아, 주어진 문장이 들어가기에 가장 적절한 곳을 고르시오. [3점]

> Nevertheless, language is enormously important in human life and contributes largely to our ability to cooperate with each other in dealing with the world.

Should we use language to understand mind or mind to understand language? (①) Analytic philosophy historically assumes that language is basic and that mind would make sense if proper use of language was appreciated. (②) Modern cognitive science, however, rightly judges that language is just one aspect of mind of great importance in human beings but not fundamental to all kinds of thinking. (③) Countless species of animals manage to navigate the world, solve problems, and learn without using language, through brain mechanisms that are largely preserved in the minds of humans. (④) There is no reason to assume that language is fundamental to mental operations. (⑤) Our species *homo sapiens* has been astonishingly successful, which depended in part on language, first as an effective contributor to collaborative problem solving and much later, as collective memory through written records.

＊appreciate: (제대로) 인식하다

09

고1·2023년 3월 40번

다음 글의 내용을 한 문장으로 요약하고자 한다. 빈칸 (A), (B)에 들어갈 말로 가장 적절한 것은?

To help decide what's risky and what's safe, who's trustworthy and who's not, we look for *social evidence*. From an evolutionary view, following the group is almost always positive for our prospects of survival. "If everyone's doing it, it must be a sensible thing to do," explains famous psychologist and best selling writer of *Influence*, Robert Cialdini. While we can frequently see this today in product reviews, even subtler cues within the environment can signal trustworthiness. Consider this: when you visit a local restaurant, are they busy? Is there a line outside or is it easy to find a seat? It is a hassle to wait, but a line can be a powerful cue that the food's tasty, and these seats are in demand. More often than not, it's good to adopt the practices of those around you.

* subtle: 미묘한 ** hassle: 성가신 일

↓

We tend to feel safe and secure in ___(A)___ when we decide how to act, particularly when faced with ___(B)___ conditions.

	(A)		(B)
①	numbers	·····	uncertain
②	numbers	·····	unrealistic
③	experiences	·····	unrealistic
④	rules	·····	uncertain
⑤	rules	·····	unpleasant

[10 ~ 12] 다음 글을 읽고, 물음에 답하시오.

(A)

A merchant in a small town had identical twin sons. The boys worked for their father in the store he owned and when he died, they took over the store. Everything went well until the day a twenty-dollar bill disappeared. One of the brothers had left the bill on the counter and walked outside with a friend. When he returned, the money was gone. (a) He asked his older brother, "Did you see that twenty-dollar bill on the counter?"

(B)

Then one day a man from another state stopped by the store. He walked in and asked the younger brother, "How long have you been here?" (b) He replied that he'd been there all his life. The customer said, "Twenty years ago I came into this town in a boxcar. I hadn't eaten for three days. I came into this store and saw a twenty-dollar bill on the counter. I put it in my pocket and walked out. All these years I haven't been able to forgive myself. So I had to come back to return it."

(C)

His older brother replied that he had not. But (c) the young man kept questioning him. "Twenty-dollar bills just don't get up and walk away! Surely you must have seen it!" There was subtle accusation in (d) his voice. Anger began to rise. Hatred set in. Before long, bitterness divided the twins. They refused to speak. They finally decided they could no longer work together and a dividing wall was built down the center of the store. For twenty years the hostility grew, spreading to their families and the community.

(D)

The customer was amazed to see tears well up in the eyes of the man. "Would you please go next door and tell that same story to (e) the man in the store?" the younger brother said. Then the customer was even more amazed to see the two middle-aged men hugging each other and weeping together in the front of the store. After twenty years, the brokenness was repaired. The wall of anger that divided them came down.

10

고1・2020년 9월 43번

주어진 글 (A)에 이어질 내용을 순서에 맞게 배열한 것으로 가장 적절한 것은?

① (B) − (D) − (C) ② (C) − (B) − (D)
③ (C) − (D) − (B) ④ (D) − (B) − (C)
⑤ (D) − (C) − (B)

11

고1・2020년 9월 44번

밑줄 친 (a)～(e) 중에서 가리키는 대상이 나머지 넷과 다른 것은?

① (a)   ② (b)   ③ (c)   ④ (d)   ⑤ (e)

12

고1・2020년 9월 45번

윗글에 관한 내용으로 적절하지 않은 것은?

① 쌍둥이 형제는 아버지의 가게를 물려받았다.
② 카운터 위에 놓여진 20달러 지폐가 없어졌다.
③ 손님은 20년 만에 가게에 다시 방문했다.
④ 쌍둥이 형제의 가게 중앙에 벽이 세워졌다.
⑤ 쌍둥이 형제는 끝까지 화해하지 못했다.

DAY 16

학습 Check! ▶ 몰라서 틀린 문항 × 표기 ▶ 헷갈렸거나 찍은 문항 △ 표기 ▶ ×, △ 문항은 다시 풀고 ✔ 표기를 하세요.

종료 시각	시 분 초	문항 번호	01	02	03	04	05	06	07	08	09	10	11	12
소요 시간	분 초	채점 결과												
초과 시간	분 초	틀린 문항 복습												

[Day 16] 미니 모의고사 099

DAY 17

수능기출 전국연합학력평가 **20분 미니 모의고사**

● 날짜 : 월 일 ● 시작 시각 : 시 분 초 ● 목표 시간 : 20분

※ 점수 표기가 없는 문항은 모두 **2점**입니다.

01

고3 · 2020학년도 수능 20번

다음 글에서 필자가 주장하는 바로 가장 적절한 것은?

Probably the biggest roadblock to play for adults is the worry that they will look silly, improper, or dumb if they allow themselves to truly play. Or they think that it is irresponsible, immature, and childish to give themselves regularly over to play. Nonsense and silliness come naturally to kids, but they get pounded out by norms that look down on "frivolity." This is particularly true for people who have been valued for performance standards set by parents or the educational system, or measured by other cultural norms that are internalized and no longer questioned. If someone has spent his adult life worried about always appearing respectable, competent, and knowledgeable, it can be hard to let go sometimes and become physically and emotionally free. The thing is this: You have to give yourself permission to improvise, to mimic, to take on a long-hidden identity.

* frivolity: 경박함 ** improvise: 즉흥적으로 하다

① 어른도 규범에 얽매이지 말고 자유롭게 놀이를 즐겨야 한다.
② 아동에게 사회 규범을 내면화할 수 있는 놀이를 제공해야 한다.
③ 개인의 창의성을 극대화할 수 있는 놀이 문화를 조성해야 한다.
④ 타인의 시선을 의식하지 않고 자신의 목표 달성에 매진해야 한다.
⑤ 어른을 위한 잠재력 계발 프로그램에서 놀이의 비중을 늘려야 한다.

02

고1 · 2020년 11월 22번

다음 글의 요지로 가장 적절한 것은?

FOBO, or Fear of a Better Option, is the anxiety that something better will come along, which makes it undesirable to commit to existing choices when making a decision. It's an affliction of abundance that drives you to keep all of your options open and to avoid risks. Rather than assessing your options, choosing one, and moving on with your day, you delay the inevitable. It's not unlike hitting the snooze button on your alarm clock only to pull the covers over your head and fall back asleep. As you probably found out the hard way, if you hit snooze enough times, you'll end up being late and racing for the office, your day and mood ruined. While pressing snooze feels so good at the moment, it ultimately demands a price.

* affliction: 고통

① 적당한 수준의 불안감은 업무 수행에 도움이 된다.
② 성급한 의사 결정은 의도하지 않은 결과를 초래한다.
③ 반복되는 실수를 줄이기 위해서는 신중함이 요구된다.
④ 더 나은 선택을 위해 결정을 미루는 것은 결국 해가 된다.
⑤ 규칙적인 생활 습관은 직장에서의 성공 가능성을 높인다.

03 1등급 대비 고난도 2점 문제

다음 글의 주제로 가장 적절한 것은?

As the social and economic situation of countries got better, wage levels and working conditions improved. Gradually people were given more time off. At the same time, forms of transport improved and it became faster and cheaper to get to places. England's industrial revolution led to many of these changes. Railways, in the nineteenth century, opened up now famous seaside resorts such as Blackpool and Brighton. With the railways came many large hotels. In Canada, for example, the new coast-to-coast railway system made possible the building of such famous hotels as Banff Springs and Chateau Lake Louise in the Rockies. Later, the arrival of air transport opened up more of the world and led to tourism growth.

① factors that caused tourism expansion
② discomfort at a popular tourist destination
③ importance of tourism in society and economy
④ negative impacts of tourism on the environment
⑤ various types of tourism and their characteristics

04

다음 도표의 내용과 일치하지 <u>않는</u> 것은?

Health Spending as a Share of GDP for Selected OECD Countries [2018]

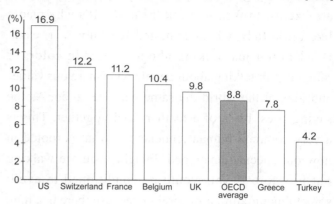

The above graph shows health spending as a share of GDP for selected OECD countries in 2018. ① On average, OECD countries were estimated to have spent 8.8 percent of their GDP on health care. ② Among the given countries above, the US had the highest share, with 16.9 percent, followed by Switzerland at 12.2 percent. ③ France spent more than 11 percent of its GDP, while Turkey spent less than 5 percent of its GDP on health care. ④ Belgium's health spending as a share of GDP sat between that of France and the UK. ⑤ There was a 3 percentage point difference in the share of GDP spent on health care between the UK and Greece.

DAY 17

05

다음 글의 밑줄 친 부분 중, 어법상 틀린 것은?

We usually get along best with people who we think are like us. In fact, we seek them out. It's why places like Little Italy, Chinatown, and Koreatown ① exist. But I'm not just talking about race, skin color, or religion. I'm talking about people who share our values and look at the world the same way we ② do. As the saying goes, birds of a feather flock together. This is a very common human tendency ③ what is rooted in how our species developed. Imagine you are walking out in a forest. You would be conditioned to avoid something unfamiliar or foreign because there is a high likelihood that ④ it would be interested in killing you. Similarities make us ⑤ relate better to other people because we think they'll understand us on a deeper level than other people.

* species: 종(생물 분류의 기초 단위)

06 1등급 대비 고난도 2점 문제

다음 글의 밑줄 친 부분 중, 문맥상 낱말의 쓰임이 적절하지 않은 것은?

People are innately inclined to look for causes of events, to form explanations and stories. That is one reason storytelling is such a ① persuasive medium. Stories resonate with our experiences and provide examples of new instances. From our experiences and the stories of others we tend to form ② generalizations about the way people behave and things work. We attribute causes to events, and as long as these cause-and-effect ③ pairings make sense, we use them for understanding future events. Yet these causal attributions are often mistaken. Sometimes they implicate the ④ wrong causes, and for some things that happen, there is no single cause. Rather, there is a complex chain of events that all contribute to the result; if any one of the events would not have occurred, the result would be ⑤ similar. But even when there is no single causal act, that doesn't stop people from assigning one.

* resonate: 떠올리게 하다
** implicate: 연관시키다

07

다음 빈칸에 들어갈 말로 가장 적절한 것을 고르시오.

We don't send telegraphs to communicate anymore, but it's a great metaphor for giving advance notice. Sometimes, you must inform those close to you of upcoming change by conveying important information well in advance. There's a huge difference between saying, "From now on, we will do things differently," which doesn't give people enough time to understand and accept the change, and saying something like, "Starting next month, we're going to approach things differently." Telegraphing empowers people to _____. Telegraphing involves the art of seeing an upcoming event or circumstance and giving others enough time to process and accept the change. Telegraph anything that will take people out of what is familiar and comfortable to them. This will allow processing time for them to accept the circumstances and make the most of what's happening.

① unite
② adapt
③ object
④ compete
⑤ recover

08　1등급 대비 고난도 3점 문제

다음 빈칸에 들어갈 말로 가장 적절한 것을 고르시오. [3점]

Recently I was with a client who had spent almost five hours with me. As we were parting for the evening, we reflected on what we had covered that day. Even though our conversation was very collegial, I noticed that my client was holding one leg at a right angle to his body, seemingly wanting to take off on its own. At that point I said, "You really do have to leave now, don't you?" "Yes," he admitted. "I am so sorry. I didn't want to be rude but I have to call London and I only have five minutes!" Here was a case where my client's language and most of his body revealed nothing but positive feelings. His feet, however, were _____ _____, and they clearly told me that as much as he wanted to stay, duty was calling.

＊collegial: 평등하게 책임을 지는

① a signal of his politeness
② the subject of the conversation
③ expressing interest in my words
④ the most honest communicators
⑤ stepping excitedly onto the ground

DAY 17

09

다음 글에서 전체 흐름과 관계 <u>없는</u> 문장은?

The fast-paced evolution of Information and Communication Technologies (ICTs) has radically transformed the dynamics and business models of the tourism and hospitality industry. ① This leads to new levels/forms of competitiveness among service providers and transforms the customer experience through new services. ② Creating unique experiences and providing convenient services to customers leads to satisfaction and, eventually, customer loyalty to the service provider or brand (i.e., hotels). ③ In particular, the most recent *technological* boost received by the tourism sector is represented by mobile applications. ④ Increasing competitiveness among service providers does not necessarily mean promoting quality of customer services. ⑤ Indeed, empowering tourists with mobile access to services such as hotel reservations, airline ticketing, and recommendations for local attractions generates strong interest and considerable profits.

* hospitality industry: 서비스업(호텔·식당업 등)

10

주어진 글 다음에 이어질 글의 순서로 가장 적절한 것을 고르시오. [3점]

Maybe you've heard this joke: "How do you eat an elephant?" The answer is "one bite at a time."

(A) Common crystal habits include squares, triangles, and six-sided hexagons. Usually crystals form when liquids cool, such as when you create ice cubes. Many times, crystals form in ways that do not allow for perfect shapes. If conditions are too cold, too hot, or there isn't enough source material, they can form strange, twisted shapes.

(B) So, how do you "build" the Earth? That's simple, too: one atom at a time. Atoms are the basic building blocks of crystals, and since all rocks are made up of crystals, the more you know about atoms, the better. Crystals come in a variety of shapes that scientists call *habits*.

(C) But when conditions are right, we see beautiful displays. Usually, this involves a slow, steady environment where the individual atoms have plenty of time to join and fit perfectly into what's known as the *crystal lattice*. This is the basic structure of atoms that is seen time after time.

① (A) − (C) − (B)　　② (B) − (A) − (C)
③ (B) − (C) − (A)　　④ (C) − (A) − (B)
⑤ (C) − (B) − (A)

[11 ~ 12] 다음 글을 읽고, 물음에 답하시오.

A bedroom temperature of around 65 degrees Fahrenheit (18.3°C) is ideal for the sleep of most people, assuming standard bedding and clothing. This (a) surprises many, as it sounds just a little too cold for comfort. Of course, that specific temperature will vary depending on the individual in question and their gender and age. But like calorie recommendations, it's a good target for the average human being. Most of us set bedroom temperatures higher than are ideal for good sleep and this likely contributes to (b) lower quantity and quality of sleep than you are otherwise capable of getting. Lower than 55 degrees Fahrenheit can be harmful rather than helpful to sleep, unless warm bedding or nightclothes are used. However, most of us fall into the (c) opposite category of setting a controlled bedroom temperature that is too high: 70 or 72 degrees. Sleep clinicians treating patients who can't sleep at night will often ask about room temperature, and will advise patients to (d) raise their current thermostat set-point by 3 to 5 degrees from that which they currently use.

Anyone disbelieving of the influence of temperature on sleep can explore some related experiments on this topic. Scientists have, for example, gently warmed the feet or the body of rats to encourage blood to rise to the surface of the skin and release heat, thereby decreasing core body temperature. The rats fell asleep far (e) faster than was otherwise normal.

＊thermostat: 온도 조절 장치

11

윗글의 제목으로 가장 적절한 것은?

① Signs of Sleep Problems
② Stay Cool for Better Sleep
③ Turn Up the Heat in Your Room
④ How to Correct Bad Sleeping Posture
⑤ A Key to Quality Sleep: Clean Bedding

12

밑줄 친 (a) ~ (e) 중에서 문맥상 낱말의 쓰임이 적절하지 않은 것은? [3점]

① (a)　　② (b)　　③ (c)　　④ (d)　　⑤ (e)

학습 Check!　▶ 몰라서 틀린 문항 × 표기　▶ 헷갈렸거나 찍은 문항 △ 표기　▶ ×, △ 문항은 다시 풀고 ✔ 표기를 하세요.

종료 시각	시 분 초	문항 번호	01	02	03	04	05	06	07	08	09	10	11	12
소요 시간	분 초	채점 결과												
초과 시간	분 초	틀린 문항 복습												

DAY 18

● 날짜 :   월   일 ● 시작 시각 :   시   분   초 ● 목표 시간 : 20분

※ 점수 표기가 없는 문항은 모두 2점입니다.

01

고1 · 2021년 6월 18번

다음 글의 목적으로 가장 적절한 것은?

Dear Mr. Jones,

I am James Arkady, PR Director of KHJ Corporation. We are planning to redesign our brand identity and launch a new logo to celebrate our 10th anniversary. We request you to create a logo that best suits our company's core vision, 'To inspire humanity.' I hope the new logo will convey our brand message and capture the values of KHJ. Please send us your logo design proposal once you are done with it. Thank you.

Best regards,
James Arkady

① 회사 로고 제작을 의뢰하려고
② 변경된 회사 로고를 홍보하려고
③ 회사 비전에 대한 컨설팅을 요청하려고
④ 회사 창립 10주년 기념품을 주문하려고
⑤ 회사 로고 제작 일정 변경을 공지하려고

02

고3 · 2022학년도 수능 23번

다음 글의 주제로 가장 적절한 것은? [3점]

Scientists *use* paradigms rather than believing them. The use of a paradigm in research typically addresses related problems by employing shared concepts, symbolic expressions, experimental and mathematical tools and procedures, and even some of the same theoretical statements. Scientists need only understand *how* to use these various elements in ways that others would accept. These elements of shared practice thus need not presuppose any comparable unity in scientists' beliefs about what they are doing when they use them. Indeed, one role of a paradigm is to enable scientists to work successfully without having to provide a detailed account of what they are doing or what they believe about it. Thomas Kuhn noted that scientists "can agree in their *identification* of a paradigm without agreeing on, or even attempting to produce, a full *interpretation* or *rationalization* of it. Lack of a standard interpretation or of an agreed reduction to rules will not prevent a paradigm from guiding research."

① difficulty in drawing novel theories from existing paradigms
② significant influence of personal beliefs in scientific fields
③ key factors that promote the rise of innovative paradigms
④ roles of a paradigm in grouping like-minded researchers
⑤ functional aspects of a paradigm in scientific research

03

고1 · 2022년 11월 24번

다음 글의 제목으로 가장 적절한 것은?

Have you ever brought up an idea or suggestion to someone and heard them immediately say "No, that won't work."? You may have thought, "He/she didn't even give it a chance. How do they know it won't work?" When you are right about something, you close off the possibility of another viewpoint or opportunity. Being right about something means that "it is the way it is, period." You may be correct. Your particular way of seeing it may be true with the facts. However, considering the other option or the other person's point of view can be beneficial. If you see their side, you will see something new or, at worse, learn something about how the other person looks at life. Why would you think everyone sees and experiences life the way you do? Besides how boring that would be, it would eliminate all new opportunities, ideas, invention, and creativity.

① The Value of Being Honest
② Filter Out Negative Points of View
③ Keeping Your Word: A Road to Success
④ Being Right Can Block New Possibilities
⑤ Look Back When Everyone Looks Forward

04

고1 · 2022년 6월 26번

Claude Bolling에 관한 다음 글의 내용과 일치하지 <u>않는</u> 것은?

Pianist, composer, and big band leader, Claude Bolling, was born on April 10, 1930, in Cannes, France, but spent most of his life in Paris. He began studying classical music as a youth. He was introduced to the world of jazz by a schoolmate. Later, Bolling became interested in the music of Fats Waller, one of the most excellent jazz musicians. Bolling became famous as a teenager by winning the Best Piano Player prize at an amateur contest in France. He was also a successful film music composer, writing the music for more than one hundred films. In 1975, he collaborated with flutist Rampal and published *Suite for Flute and Jazz Piano Trio*, which he became most well-known for. He died in 2020, leaving two sons, David and Alexandre.

① 1930년에 프랑스에서 태어났다.
② 학교 친구를 통해 재즈를 소개받았다.
③ 20대에 Best Piano Player 상을 받았다.
④ 성공적인 영화 음악 작곡가였다.
⑤ 1975년에 플루트 연주자와 협업했다.

[Day 18] 미니 모의고사   107

05

다음 글의 밑줄 친 부분 중, 어법상 틀린 것은? [3점]

Although praise is one of the most powerful tools available for improving young children's behavior, it is equally powerful for improving your child's self-esteem. Preschoolers believe what their parents tell ① them in a very profound way. They do not yet have the cognitive sophistication to reason ② analytically and reject false information. If a preschool boy consistently hears from his mother ③ that he is smart and a good helper, he is likely to incorporate that information into his self-image. Thinking of himself as a boy who is smart and knows how to do things ④ being likely to make him endure longer in problem-solving efforts and increase his confidence in trying new and difficult tasks. Similarly, thinking of himself as the kind of boy who is a good helper will make him more likely to volunteer ⑤ to help with tasks at home and at preschool.

* profound: 뜻 깊은   ** sophistication: 정교화(함)

06 1등급 대비 고난도 3점 문제

(A), (B), (C)의 각 네모 안에서 문맥에 맞는 낱말로 가장 적절한 것은? [3점]

School assignments have typically required that students work alone. This emphasis on (A) collective / individual productivity reflected an opinion that independence is a necessary factor for success. Having the ability to take care of oneself without depending on others was considered a requirement for everyone. Consequently, teachers in the past (B) more / less often arranged group work or encouraged students to acquire teamwork skills. However, since the new millennium, businesses have experienced more global competition that requires improved productivity. This situation has led employers to insist that newcomers to the labor market provide evidence of traditional independence but also interdependence shown through teamwork skills. The challenge for educators is to ensure individual competence in basic skills while (C) adding / decreasing learning opportunities that can enable students to also perform well in teams.

* competence: 능력

	(A)		(B)		(C)
①	individual	⋯⋯	less	⋯⋯	adding
②	collective	⋯⋯	less	⋯⋯	decreasing
③	individual	⋯⋯	less	⋯⋯	decreasing
④	collective	⋯⋯	more	⋯⋯	decreasing
⑤	individual	⋯⋯	more	⋯⋯	adding

07 [1등급 대비 고난도 2점 문제]

다음 빈칸에 들어갈 말로 가장 적절한 것을 고르시오.

One big difference between science and stage magic is that while magicians hide their mistakes from the audience, in science you make your mistakes in public. You show them off so that everybody can learn from them. This way, you get the advantage of everybody else's experience, and not just your own idiosyncratic path through the space of mistakes. This, by the way, is another reason why we humans are so much smarter than every other species. It is not that our brains are bigger or more powerful, or even that we have the ability to reflect on our own past errors, but that we _____ that our individual brains have earned from their individual histories of trial and error.

＊idiosyncratic: (개인에게) 특유한

① share the benefits
② overlook the insights
③ develop creative skills
④ exaggerate the achievements
⑤ underestimate the knowledge

08 [1등급 대비 고난도 3점 문제]

글의 흐름으로 보아, 주어진 문장이 들어가기에 가장 적절한 곳을 고르시오. [3점]

> What we need is a reliable and reproducible method for measuring the relative hotness or coldness of objects rather than the rate of energy transfer.

We often associate the concept of temperature with how hot or cold an object feels when we touch it. In this way, our senses provide us with a qualitative indication of temperature. (①) Our senses, however, are unreliable and often mislead us. (②) For example, if you stand in bare feet with one foot on carpet and the other on a tile floor, the tile feels colder than the carpet *even though both are at the same temperature*. (③) The two objects feel different because tile transfers energy by heat at a higher rate than carpet does. (④) Your skin "measures" the rate of energy transfer by heat rather than the actual temperature. (⑤) Scientists have developed a variety of thermometers for making such quantitative measurements.

＊thermometer: 온도계

09

고1 · 2022년 3월 40번

다음 글의 내용을 한 문장으로 요약하고자 한다. 빈칸 (A), (B)에 들어갈 말로 가장 적절한 것은?

The common blackberry (*Rubus allegheniensis*) has an amazing ability to move manganese from one layer of soil to another using its roots. This may seem like a funny talent for a plant to have, but it all becomes clear when you realize the effect it has on nearby plants. Manganese can be very harmful to plants, especially at high concentrations. Common blackberry is unaffected by damaging effects of this metal and has evolved two different ways of using manganese to its advantage. First, it redistributes manganese from deeper soil layers to shallow soil layers using its roots as a small pipe. Second, it absorbs manganese as it grows, concentrating the metal in its leaves. When the leaves drop and decay, their concentrated manganese deposits further poison the soil around the plant. For plants that are not immune to the toxic effects of manganese, this is very bad news. Essentially, the common blackberry eliminates competition by poisoning its neighbors with heavy metals.

* manganese: 망가니즈(금속 원소) ** deposit: 축적물

↓

The common blackberry has an ability to ___(A)___ the amount of manganese in the surrounding upper soil, which makes the nearby soil quite ___(B)___ for other plants.

	(A)		(B)
①	increase	……	deadly
②	increase	……	advantageous
③	indicate	……	nutritious
④	reduce	……	dry
⑤	reduce	……	warm

[10 ~ 12] 다음 글을 읽고, 물음에 답하시오.

(A)

Long ago, an old man built a grand temple at the center of his village. People traveled to worship at the temple. So the old man made arrangements for food and accommodation inside the temple itself. He needed someone who could look after the temple, so (a) he put up a notice: Manager needed.

(B)

When that young man left the temple, the old man called him and asked, "Will you take care of this temple?" The young man was surprised by the offer and replied, "I have no experience caring for a temple. I'm not even educated." The old man smiled and said, "I don't want any educated man. I want a qualified person." Confused, the young man asked, "But why do (b) you consider me a qualified person?"

(C)

The old man replied, "I buried a brick on the path to the temple. I watched for many days as people tripped over that brick. No one thought to remove it. But you dug up that brick." The young man said, "I haven't done anything great. It's the duty of every human being to think about others. (c) I only did my duty." The old man smiled and said, "Only people who know their duty and perform it are qualified people."

(D)

Seeing the notice, many people went to the old man. But he returned all the applicants after interviews, telling them, "I need a qualified person for this work." The old man would sit on the roof of (d) his house every morning, watching people go through the temple doors. One day, (e) he saw a young man come to the temple.

10

고1 · 2023년 9월 43번

주어진 글 (A)에 이어질 내용을 순서에 맞게 배열한 것으로 가장 적절한 것은?

① (B) − (D) − (C) ② (C) − (B) − (D)
③ (C) − (D) − (B) ④ (D) − (B) − (C)
⑤ (D) − (C) − (B)

11

고1 · 2023년 9월 44번

밑줄 친 (a) ~ (e) 중에서 가리키는 대상이 나머지 넷과 다른 것은?

① (a) ② (b) ③ (c) ④ (d) ⑤ (e)

12

고1 · 2023년 9월 45번

윗글에 관한 내용으로 적절하지 않은 것은?

① 노인은 마을 중심부에 사원을 지었다.
② 젊은이가 사원을 나설 때 노인이 그를 불렀다.
③ 젊은이는 노인의 제안에 놀랐다.
④ 노인은 사원으로 통하는 길에 묻혀있던 벽돌을 파냈다.
⑤ 공고를 보고 많은 사람들이 노인을 찾아갔다.

DAY 18

DAY 19

● 날짜 :   월   일 ● 시작 시각 :   시   분   초 ● 목표 시간 : 20분

※ 점수 표기가 없는 문항은 모두 **2점**입니다.

01

고1 · 2021년 9월 20번

다음 글에서 필자가 주장하는 바로 가장 적절한 것은?

As you set about to write, it is worth reminding yourself that while you ought to have a point of view, you should avoid telling your readers what to think. Try to hang a question mark over it all. This way you allow your readers to think for themselves about the points and arguments you're making. As a result, they will feel more involved, finding themselves just as committed to the arguments you've made and the insights you've exposed as you are. You will have written an essay that not only avoids passivity in the reader, but is interesting and gets people to think.

① 저자의 독창적인 견해를 드러내야 한다.
② 다양한 표현으로 독자에게 감동을 주어야 한다.
③ 독자가 능동적으로 사고할 수 있도록 글을 써야 한다.
④ 독자에게 가치판단의 기준점을 명확히 제시해야 한다.
⑤ 주관적 관점을 배제하고 사실을 바탕으로 글을 써야 한다.

02

고3 · 2021학년도 수능 22번

다음 글의 요지로 가장 적절한 것은?

Prior to file-sharing services, music albums landed exclusively in the hands of music critics before their release. These critics would listen to them well before the general public could and preview them for the rest of the world in their reviews. Once the internet made music easily accessible and allowed even advanced releases to spread through online social networks, availability of new music became democratized, which meant critics no longer had unique access. That is, critics and laypeople alike could obtain new music simultaneously. Social media services also enabled people to publicize their views on new songs, list their new favorite bands in their social media bios, and argue over new music endlessly on message boards. The result was that critics now could access the opinions of the masses on a particular album before writing their reviews. Thus, instead of music reviews guiding popular opinion toward art (as they did in preinternet times), music reviews began to reflect — consciously or subconsciously — public opinion.

* laypeople: 비전문가

① 미디어 환경의 변화로 음악 비평이 대중의 영향을 받게 되었다.
② 인터넷의 발달로 다양한 장르의 음악을 접하는 것이 가능해졌다.
③ 비평가의 음악 비평은 자신의 주관적인 경험을 기반으로 한다.
④ 오늘날 새로운 음악은 대중의 기호를 확인한 후에 공개된다.
⑤ 온라인 환경의 대두로 음악 비평의 질이 전반적으로 상승하였다.

03

다음 글의 주제로 가장 적절한 것은?

The interaction of workers from different cultural backgrounds with the host population might increase productivity due to positive externalities like knowledge spillovers. This is only an advantage up to a certain degree. When the variety of backgrounds is too large, fractionalization may cause excessive transaction costs for communication, which may lower productivity. Diversity not only impacts the labour market, but may also affect the quality of life in a location. A tolerant native population may value a multicultural city or region because of an increase in the range of available goods and services. On the other hand, diversity could be perceived as an unattractive feature if natives perceive it as a distortion of what they consider to be their national identity. They might even discriminate against other ethnic groups and they might fear that social conflicts between different foreign nationalities are imported into their own neighbourhood.

＊externality: 외부 효과 ＊＊fractionalization: 분열

① roles of culture in ethnic groups
② contrastive aspects of cultural diversity
③ negative perspectives of national identity
④ factors of productivity differences across countries
⑤ policies to protect minorities and prevent discrimination

04

다음 도표의 내용과 일치하지 <u>않는</u> 것은?

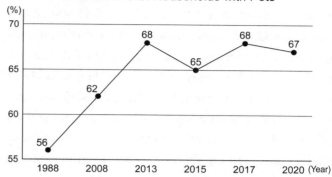

Percent of U.S. Households with Pets

The graph above shows the percent of households with pets in the United States (U.S.) from 1988 to 2020. ① In 1988, more than half of U.S. households owned pets, and more than 6 out of 10 U.S. households owned pets from 2008 to 2020. ② In the period between 1988 and 2008, pet ownership increased among U.S. households by 6 percentage points. ③ From 2008 to 2013, pet ownership rose an additional 6 percentage points. ④ The percent of U.S. households with pets in 2013 was the same as that in 2017, which was 68 percent. ⑤ In 2015, the rate of U.S. households with pets was 3 percentage points lower than in 2020.

05

다음 글의 밑줄 친 부분 중, 어법상 틀린 것은? [3점]

The human brain, it turns out, has shrunk in mass by about 10 percent since it ① peaked in size 15,000-30,000 years ago. One possible reason is that many thousands of years ago humans lived in a world of dangerous predators ② where they had to have their wits about them at all times to avoid being killed. Today, we have effectively domesticated ourselves and many of the tasks of survival — from avoiding immediate death to building shelters to obtaining food — ③ has been outsourced to the wider society. We are smaller than our ancestors too, and it is a characteristic of domestic animals ④ that they are generally smaller than their wild cousins. None of this may mean we are dumber — brain size is not necessarily an indicator of human intelligence — but it may mean that our brains today are wired up differently, and perhaps more efficiently, than ⑤ those of our ancestors.

06 [1등급 대비 고난도 3점 문제]

다음 글의 밑줄 친 부분 중, 문맥상 낱말의 쓰임이 적절하지 않은 것은? [3점]

Rejection is an everyday part of our lives, yet most people can't handle it well. For many, it's so painful that they'd rather not ask for something at all than ask and ① risk rejection. Yet, as the old saying goes, if you don't ask, the answer is always no. Avoiding rejection ② negatively affects many aspects of your life. All of that happens only because you're not ③ tough enough to handle it. For this reason, consider rejection therapy. Come up with a ④ request or an activity that usually results in a rejection. Working in sales is one such example. Asking for discounts at the stores will also work. By deliberately getting yourself ⑤ welcomed you'll grow a thicker skin that will allow you to take on much more in life, thus making you more successful at dealing with unfavorable circumstances.

* deliberately: 의도적으로

07

다음 빈칸에 들어갈 말로 가장 적절한 것을 고르시오.

People differ in how quickly they can reset their biological clocks to overcome jet lag, and the speed of recovery depends on the _____ of travel. Generally, it's easier to fly westward and lengthen your day than it is to fly eastward and shorten it. This east-west difference in jet lag is sizable enough to have an impact on the performance of sports teams. Studies have found that teams flying westward perform significantly better than teams flying eastward in professional baseball and college football. A more recent study of more than 46,000 Major League Baseball games found additional evidence that eastward travel is tougher than westward travel.

* jet lag: 시차로 인한 피로감

① direction
② purpose
③ season
④ length
⑤ cost

08 1등급 대비 고난도 3점 문제

다음 빈칸에 들어갈 말로 가장 적절한 것을 고르시오. [3점]

Over time, babies construct expectations about what sounds they will hear when. They hold in memory the sound patterns that occur on a regular basis. They make hypotheses like, "If I hear *this* sound first, it probably will be followed by *that* sound." Scientists conclude that much of babies' skill in learning language is due to their _____. For babies, this means that they appear to pay close attention to the patterns that repeat in language. They remember, in a systematic way, how often sounds occur, in what order, with what intervals, and with what changes of pitch. This memory store allows them to track, within the neural circuits of their brains, the frequency of sound patterns and to use this knowledge to make predictions about the meaning in patterns of sounds.

① lack of social pressures
② ability to calculate statistics
③ desire to interact with others
④ preference for simpler sounds
⑤ tendency to imitate caregivers

09

다음 글에서 전체 흐름과 관계 <u>없는</u> 문장은?

The Barnum Effect is the phenomenon where someone reads or hears something very general but believes that it applies to them. ① These statements appear to be very personal on the surface but in fact, they are true for many. ② Human psychology allows us to want to believe things that we can identify with on a personal level and even seek information where it doesn't necessarily exist, filling in the blanks with our imagination for the rest. ③ This is the principle that horoscopes rely on, offering data that appears to be personal but probably makes sense to countless people. ④ Reading daily horoscopes in the morning is beneficial as they provide predictions about the rest of the day. ⑤ Since the people reading them want to believe the information so badly, they will search for meaning in their lives that make it true.

* horoscope: 별자리 운세

10

주어진 글 다음에 이어질 글의 순서로 가장 적절한 것을 고르시오.

Students work to get good grades even when they have no interest in their studies. People seek job advancement even when they are happy with the jobs they already have.

(A) It's like being in a crowded football stadium, watching the crucial play. A spectator several rows in front stands up to get a better view, and a chain reaction follows.

(B) And if someone refuses to stand, he might just as well not be at the game at all. When people pursue goods that are positional, they can't help being in the rat race. To choose not to run is to lose.

(C) Soon everyone is standing, just to be able to see as well as before. Everyone is on their feet rather than sitting, but no one's position has improved.

* rat race: 치열하고 무의미한 경쟁

① (A) − (C) − (B) ② (B) − (A) − (C)
③ (B) − (C) − (A) ④ (C) − (A) − (B)
⑤ (C) − (B) − (A)

[11 ~ 12] 다음 글을 읽고, 물음에 답하시오.

Many advertisements cite statistical surveys. But we should be (a) cautious because we usually do not know how these surveys are conducted. For example, a toothpaste manufacturer once had a poster that said, "More than 80% of dentists recommend *Smiley Toothpaste*." This seems to say that most dentists (b) prefer *Smiley Toothpaste* to other brands. But it turns out that the survey questions allowed the dentists to recommend more than one brand, and in fact another competitor's brand was recommended just as often as *Smiley Toothpaste*! No wonder the UK Advertising Standards Authority ruled in 2007 that the poster was (c) misleading and it could no longer be displayed.

A similar case concerns a well-known cosmetics firm marketing a cream that is supposed to rapidly reduce wrinkles. But the only evidence provided is that "76% of 50 women agreed." But what this means is that the evidence is based on just the personal opinions from a small sample with no objective measurement of their skin's condition. Furthermore, we are not told how these women were selected. Without such information, the "evidence" provided is pretty much (d) useful. Unfortunately, such advertisements are quite typical, and as consumers we just have to use our own judgment and (e) avoid taking advertising claims too seriously.

11

고1 · 2019년 6월 41번

윗글의 제목으로 가장 적절한 것은?

① The Link between Advertisements and the Economy
② Are Statistical Data in Advertisements Reliable?
③ Statistics in Advertisements Are Objective!
④ The Bright Side of Public Advertisements
⑤ Quality or Price, Which Matters More?

12 1등급 대비 고난도 3점 문제

고1 · 2019년 6월 42번

밑줄 친 (a) ~ (e) 중에서 문맥상 낱말의 쓰임이 적절하지 않은 것은? [3점]

① (a)　　② (b)　　③ (c)　　④ (d)　　⑤ (e)

DAY 19

학습 Check! ▶ 몰라서 틀린 문항 × 표기 ▶ 헷갈렸거나 찍은 문항 △ 표기 ▶ ×, △ 문항은 다시 풀고 ✔ 표기를 하세요.

종료 시각	시 분 초	문항 번호	01	02	03	04	05	06	07	08	09	10	11	12
소요 시간	분 초	채점 결과												
초과 시간	분 초	틀린 문항 복습												

[Day 19] 미니 모의고사 **117**

DAY 20

수능기출
전국연합학력평가 **20분 미니 모의고사**

● 날짜 : 　월　　일　● 시작 시각 : 　시　　분　　초　● 목표 시간 : 20분

※ 점수 표기가 없는 문항은 모두 2점입니다.

01

고1 · 2021년 11월 18번

다음 글의 목적으로 가장 적절한 것은?

To the school librarian,

I am Kyle Thomas, the president of the school's English writing club. I have planned activities that will increase the writing skills of our club members. One of the aims of these activities is to make us aware of various types of news media and the language used in printed newspaper articles. However, some old newspapers are not easy to access online. It is, therefore, my humble request to you to allow us to use old newspapers that have been stored in the school library. I would really appreciate it if you grant us permission.

Yours truly,
Kyle Thomas

① 도서관 이용 시간 연장을 건의하려고
② 신청한 도서의 대출 가능 여부를 문의하려고
③ 도서관에 보관 중인 자료 현황을 조사하려고
④ 글쓰기 동아리 신문의 도서관 비치를 부탁하려고
⑤ 도서관에 있는 오래된 신문의 사용 허락을 요청하려고

02 1등급 대비 고난도 3점 문제

고1 · 2022년 11월 21번

밑줄 친 challenge this sacred cow가 다음 글에서 의미하는 바로 가장 적절한 것은? [3점]

Our language helps to reveal our deeper assumptions. Think of these revealing phrases: When we accomplish something important, we say it took "blood, sweat, and tears." We say important achievements are "hard-earned." We recommend a "hard day's work" when "day's work" would be enough. When we talk of "easy money," we are implying it was obtained through illegal or questionable means. We use the phrase "That's easy for you to say" as a criticism, usually when we are seeking to invalidate someone's opinion. It's like we all automatically accept that the "right" way is, inevitably, the harder one. In my experience this is hardly ever questioned. What would happen if you do challenge this sacred cow? We don't even pause to consider that something important and valuable could be made easy. What if the biggest thing keeping us from doing what matters is the false assumption that it has to take huge effort?

* invalidate: 틀렸음을 입증하다

① resist the tendency to avoid any hardship
② escape from the pressure of using formal language
③ doubt the solid belief that only hard work is worthy
④ abandon the old notion that money always comes first
⑤ break the superstition that holy animals bring good luck

03

고1·2023년 9월 24번

다음 글의 제목으로 가장 적절한 것은?

We think we are shaping our buildings. But really, our buildings and development are also shaping us. One of the best examples of this is the oldest-known construction: the ornately carved rings of standing stones at Göbekli Tepe in Turkey. Before these ancestors got the idea to erect standing stones some 12,000 years ago, they were hunter-gatherers. It appears that the erection of the multiple rings of megalithic stones took so long, and so many successive generations, that these innovators were forced to settle down to complete the construction works. In the process, they became the first farming society on Earth. This is an early example of a society constructing something that ends up radically remaking the society itself. Things are not so different in our own time.

* ornately: 화려하게   ** megalithic: 거석의

① Buildings Transform How We Live!
② Why Do We Build More Than We Need?
③ Copying Ancient Buildings for Creativity
④ Was Life Better in Hunter-gatherer Times?
⑤ Innovate Your Farm with New Constructions

04

고3·2023학년도 수능 27번

다음 Renovation Notice의 내용과 일치하지 <u>않는</u> 것은?

Renovation Notice

At the Natural Jade Resort, we are continually improving our facilities to better serve our guests. Therefore, we will be renovating some areas of the resort, according to the schedule below.

Renovation Period: November 21 to December 18, 2022
  • Renovations will take place every day from 9:00 a.m. to 5:00 p.m.

Areas to be Closed: Gym and indoor swimming pool

Further Information
  • All outdoor leisure activities will be available as usual.
  • Guests will receive a 15% discount for all meals in the restaurant.
  • Guests may use the tennis courts for free.

We will take all possible measures to minimize noise and any other inconvenience. We sincerely appreciate your understanding.

① 보수 공사는 2022년 11월 21일에 시작된다.
② 보수 공사는 주말에만 진행될 것이다.
③ 체육관과 실내 수영장은 폐쇄될 것이다.
④ 모든 야외 레저 활동은 평소와 같이 가능할 것이다.
⑤ 손님은 무료로 테니스장을 이용할 수 있다.

DAY 20

05

다음 글의 밑줄 친 부분 중, 어법상 틀린 것은? [3점]

Non-verbal communication is not a substitute for verbal communication. Rather, it should function as a supplement, ① serving to enhance the richness of the content of the message that is being passed across. Non-verbal communication can be useful in situations ② where speaking may be impossible or inappropriate. Imagine you are in an uncomfortable position while talking to an individual. Non-verbal communication will help you ③ get the message across to him or her to give you some time off the conversation to be comfortable again. Another advantage of non-verbal communication is ④ what it offers you the opportunity to express emotions and attitudes properly. Without the aid of non-verbal communication, there are several aspects of your nature and personality that will not be adequately expressed. So, again, it does not substitute verbal communication but rather ⑤ complements it.

* supplement: 보충

06

(A), (B), (C)의 각 네모 안에서 문맥에 맞는 낱말로 가장 적절한 것은? [3점]

Recent research suggests that evolving humans' relationship with dogs changed the structure of both species' brains. One of the various (A) physical / psychological changes caused by domestication is a reduction in the size of the brain: 16 percent for horses, 34 percent for pigs, and 10 to 30 percent for dogs. This is because once humans started to take care of these animals, they no longer needed various brain functions in order to survive. Animals who were fed and protected by humans did not need many of the skills required by their wild ancestors and (B) developed / lost the parts of the brain related to those capacities. A similar process occurred for humans, who seem to have been domesticated by wolves. About 10,000 years ago, when the role of dogs was firmly established in most human societies, the human brain also (C) expanded / shrank by about 10 percent.

	(A)		(B)		(C)
①	physical	······	developed	······	expanded
②	physical	······	lost	······	expanded
③	physical	······	lost	······	shrank
④	psychological	······	developed	······	shrank
⑤	psychological	······	lost	······	shrank

07 [1등급 대비 고난도 3점 문제]

고1 · 2022년 6월 32번

다음 빈칸에 들어갈 말로 가장 적절한 것을 고르시오. [3점]

The law of demand is that the demand for goods and services increases as prices fall, and the demand falls as prices increase. *Giffen goods* are special types of products for which the traditional law of demand does not apply. Instead of switching to cheaper replacements, consumers demand more of giffen goods when the price increases and less of them when the price decreases. Taking an example, rice in China is a giffen good because people tend to purchase less of it when the price falls. The reason for this is, when the price of rice falls, people have more money to spend on other types of products such as meat and dairy and, therefore, change their spending pattern. On the other hand, as rice prices increase, people _____.

① order more meat
② consume more rice
③ try to get new jobs
④ increase their savings
⑤ start to invest overseas

08 [1등급 대비 고난도 2점 문제]

고1 · 2022년 3월 39번

글의 흐름으로 보아, 주어진 문장이 들어가기에 가장 적절한 곳을 고르시오.

> Since the dawn of civilization, our ancestors created myths and told legendary stories about the night sky.

We are connected to the night sky in many ways. (①) It has always inspired people to wonder and to imagine. (②) Elements of those narratives became embedded in the social and cultural identities of many generations. (③) On a practical level, the night sky helped past generations to keep track of time and create calendars — essential to developing societies as aids to farming and seasonal gathering. (④) For many centuries, it also provided a useful navigation tool, vital for commerce and for exploring new worlds. (⑤) Even in modern times, many people in remote areas of the planet observe the night sky for such practical purposes.

＊embed: 깊이 새겨 두다 ＊＊commerce: 무역

DAY 20

09

다음 글의 내용을 한 문장으로 요약하고자 한다. 빈칸 (A), (B)에 들어갈 말로 가장 적절한 것은?

One way that music could express emotion is simply through a learned association. Perhaps there is nothing naturally sad about a piece of music in a minor key, or played slowly with low notes. Maybe we have just come to hear certain kinds of music as sad because we have learned to associate them in our culture with sad events like funerals. If this view is correct, we should have difficulty interpreting the emotions expressed in culturally unfamiliar music. Totally opposed to this view is the position that the link between music and emotion is one of resemblance. For example, when we feel sad we move slowly and speak slowly and in a low-pitched voice. Thus when we hear slow, low music, we hear it as sad. If this view is correct, we should have little difficulty understanding the emotion expressed in culturally unfamiliar music.

↓

It is believed that emotion expressed in music can be understood through a(n) ____(A)____ learned association or it can be understood due to the ____(B)____ between music and emotion.

	(A)		(B)
①	culturally	······	similarity
②	culturally	······	balance
③	socially	······	difference
④	incorrectly	······	connection
⑤	incorrectly	······	contrast

[10 ~ 12] 다음 글을 읽고, 물음에 답하시오.

(A)

A boy had a place at the best school in town. In the morning, his granddad took him to the school. When (a) he went onto the playground with his grandson, the children surrounded them. "What a funny old man," one boy smirked. A girl with brown hair pointed at the pair and jumped up and down. Suddenly, the bell rang and the children ran off to their first lesson.

＊smirk: 히죽히죽 웃다

(B)

In some schools the children completely ignored the old man and in others, they made fun of (b) him. When this happened, he would turn sadly and go home. Finally, he went onto the tiny playground of a very small school, and leant against the fence, exhausted. The bell rang, and the crowd of children ran out onto the playground. "Sir, are you all right? Shall I bring you a glass of water?" a voice said. "We've got a bench in the playground — come and sit down," another voice said. Soon a young teacher came out onto the playground.

(C)

The old man greeted (c) him and said: "Finally, I've found my grandson the best school in town." "You're mistaken, sir. Our school is not the best — it's small and cramped." The old man didn't argue with the teacher. Instead, he made arrangements for his grandson to join the school, and then the old man left. That evening, the boy's mom said to (d) him: "Dad, you can't even read. How do you know you've found the best teacher of all?" "Judge a teacher by his pupils," the old man replied.

＊cramped: 비좁은

(D)

The old man took his grandson firmly by the hand, and led him out of the school gate. "Brilliant, I don't have to go to school!" the boy exclaimed. "You do, but not this one," his granddad replied. "I'll find you a school myself." Granddad took his grandson back to his own house, asked grandma to look after him, and went off to look for a teacher (e) <u>himself</u>. Every time he spotted a school, the old man went onto the playground, and waited for the children to come out at break time.

10

고1·2022년 9월 43번

주어진 글 (A)에 이어질 내용을 순서에 맞게 배열한 것으로 가장 적절한 것은?

① (B) − (D) − (C)　　② (C) − (B) − (D)

③ (C) − (D) − (B)　　④ (D) − (B) − (C)

⑤ (D) − (C) − (B)

11

고1·2022년 9월 44번

밑줄 친 (a) ~ (e) 중에서 가리키는 대상이 나머지 넷과 <u>다른</u> 것은?

① (a)　　② (b)　　③ (c)　　④ (d)　　⑤ (e)

12

고1·2022년 9월 45번

윗글에 관한 내용으로 적절하지 <u>않은</u> 것은?

① 갈색 머리 소녀가 노인과 소년을 향해 손가락질했다.

② 노인은 지쳐서 울타리에 기댔다.

③ 노인은 선생님과 논쟁을 벌였다.

④ 노인은 글을 읽을 줄 몰랐다.

⑤ 소년은 학교에 가지 않아도 된다고 소리쳤다.

DAY 20

학습 Check!

▶ 몰라서 틀린 문항 × 표기　▶ 헷갈렸거나 찍은 문항 △ 표기　▶ ×, △ 문항은 다시 풀고 ✔ 표기를 하세요.

종료 시각	시 분 초	문항 번호	01	02	03	04	05	06	07	08	09	10	11	12
소요 시간	분 초	채점 결과												
초과 시간	분 초	틀린 문항 복습												

DAY 21

수능기출
전국연합학력평가 **20분 미니 모의고사**

● 날짜 :　　월　　일　● 시작 시각 :　　시　　분　　초　● 목표 시간 : 20분

※ 점수 표기가 없는 문항은 모두 2점입니다.

01

고3 · 2023학년도 수능 20번

다음 글에서 필자가 주장하는 바로 가장 적절한 것은?

At every step in our journey through life we encounter junctions with many different pathways leading into the distance. Each choice involves uncertainty about which path will get you to your destination. Trusting our intuition to make the choice often ends up with us making a suboptimal choice. Turning the uncertainty into numbers has proved a potent way of analyzing the paths and finding the shortcut to your destination. The mathematical theory of probability hasn't eliminated risk, but it allows us to manage that risk more effectively. The strategy is to analyze all the possible scenarios that the future holds and then to see what proportion of them lead to success or failure. This gives you a much better map of the future on which to base your decisions about which path to choose.

* junction: 분기점　** suboptimal: 차선의

① 성공적인 삶을 위해 미래에 대한 구체적인 계획을 세워야 한다.
② 중요한 결정을 내릴 때에는 자신의 직관에 따라 판단해야 한다.
③ 더 나은 선택을 위해 성공 가능성을 확률적으로 분석해야 한다.
④ 빠른 목표 달성을 위해 지름길로 가고자 할 때 신중해야 한다.
⑤ 인생의 여정에서 선택에 따른 결과를 스스로 책임져야 한다.

02

고1 · 2022년 3월 22번

다음 글의 요지로 가장 적절한 것은?

Many people view sleep as merely a "down time" when their brain shuts off and their body rests. In a rush to meet work, school, family, or household responsibilities, people cut back on their sleep, thinking it won't be a problem, because all of these other activities seem much more important. But research reveals that a number of vital tasks carried out during sleep help to maintain good health and enable people to function at their best. While you sleep, your brain is hard at work forming the pathways necessary for learning and creating memories and new insights. Without enough sleep, you can't focus and pay attention or respond quickly. A lack of sleep may even cause mood problems. In addition, growing evidence shows that a continuous lack of sleep increases the risk for developing serious diseases.

* vital: 매우 중요한

① 수면은 건강 유지와 최상의 기능 발휘에 도움이 된다.
② 업무량이 증가하면 필요한 수면 시간도 증가한다.
③ 균형 잡힌 식단을 유지하면 뇌 기능이 향상된다.
④ 불면증은 주위 사람들에게 부정적인 영향을 미친다.
⑤ 꿈의 내용은 깨어 있는 시간 동안의 경험을 반영한다.

03

다음 글의 주제로 가장 적절한 것은?

  The most remarkable and unbelievable consequence of melting ice and rising seas is that together they are a kind of time machine, so real that they are altering the duration of our day. It works like this: As the glaciers melt and the seas rise, gravity forces more water toward the equator. This changes the shape of the Earth ever so slightly, making it fatter around the middle, which in turns slows the rotation of the planet similarly to the way a ballet dancer slows her spin by spreading out her arms. The slowdown isn't much, just a few thousandths of a second each year, but like the barely noticeable jump of rising seas every year, it adds up. When dinosaurs lived on the Earth, a day lasted only about twenty-three hours.

① cause of rising temperatures on the Earth
② principles of planets maintaining their shapes
③ implications of melting ice on marine biodiversity
④ way to keep track of time without using any device
⑤ impact of melting ice and rising seas on the length of a day

04

Kenner High School's Water Challenge에 관한 다음 안내문의 내용과 일치하는 것은?

Kenner High School's Water Challenge

  Kenner High School's Water Challenge is a new contest to propose measures against water pollution. Please share your ideas for dealing with water pollution!

Submission
− **How**: Submit your proposal by email to admin@khswater.edu.
− **When**: September 5, 2022 to September 23, 2022

Details
− Participants must enter in teams of four and can only join one team.
− Submission is limited to one proposal per team.
− Participants must use the proposal form provided on the website.

Prizes
− 1 s t: $50 gift certificate
− 2nd: $30 gift certificate
− 3rd: $10 gift certificate

Please visit www.khswater.edu to learn more about the challenge.

---

① 제안서는 직접 방문하여 제출해야 한다.
② 9월 23일부터 제안서를 제출할 수 있다.
③ 제안서는 한 팀당 4개까지 제출할 수 있다.
④ 제공된 제안서 양식을 사용해야 한다.
⑤ 2등은 10달러의 상품권을 받는다.

05 1등급 대비 고난도 3점 문제

고1 · 2017년 3월 28번

다음 글의 밑줄 친 부분 중, 어법상 틀린 것은? [3점]

Take time to read the comics. This is worthwhile not just because they will make you laugh but ① because they contain wisdom about the nature of life. *Charlie Brown* and *Blondie* are part of my morning routine and help me ② to start the day with a smile. When you read the comics section of the newspaper, ③ cutting out a cartoon that makes you laugh. Post it wherever you need it most, such as on your refrigerator or at work — so that every time you see it, you will smile and feel your spirit ④ lifted. Share your favorites with your friends and family so that everyone can get a good laugh, too. Take your comics with you when you go to visit sick friends ⑤ who can really use a good laugh.

06

고1 · 2021년 3월 30번

다음 글의 밑줄 친 부분 중, 문맥상 낱말의 쓰임이 적절하지 않은 것은? [3점]

When the price of something fundamental drops greatly, the whole world can change. Consider light. Chances are you are reading this sentence under some kind of artificial light. Moreover, you probably never thought about whether using artificial light for reading was worth it. Light is so ① cheap that you use it without thinking. But in the early 1800s, it would have cost you four hundred times what you are paying now for the same amount of light. At that price, you would ② notice the cost and would think twice before using artificial light to read a book. The ③ increase in the price of light lit up the world. Not only did it turn night into day, but it allowed us to live and work in big buildings that ④ natural light could not enter. Nearly nothing we have today would be ⑤ possible if the cost of artificial light had not dropped to almost nothing.

* artificial: 인공의

07

다음 빈칸에 들어갈 말로 가장 적절한 것을 고르시오.

If you follow science news, you will have noticed that _____ among animals has become a hot topic in the mass media. For example, in late 2007 the science media widely reported a study by Claudia Rutte and Michael Taborsky suggesting that rats display what they call "generalized reciprocity." They each provided help to an unfamiliar and unrelated individual, based on their own previous experience of having been helped by an unfamiliar rat. Rutte and Taborsky trained rats in a cooperative task of pulling a stick to obtain food for a partner. Rats who had been helped previously by an unknown partner were more likely to help others. Before this research was conducted, generalized reciprocity was thought to be unique to humans.

① friction
② diversity
③ hierarchy
④ cooperation
⑤ independence

08 1등급 대비 고난도 3점 문제

다음 빈칸에 들어갈 말로 가장 적절한 것을 고르시오. [3점]

If you ask a physicist how long it would take a marble to fall from the top of a ten-story building, he will likely answer the question by assuming that the marble falls in a vacuum. In reality, the building is surrounded by air, which applies friction to the falling marble and slows it down. Yet the physicist will point out that the friction on the marble is so small that its effect is negligible. Assuming the marble falls in a vacuum simplifies the problem without substantially affecting the answer. Economists make assumptions for the same reason: Assumptions can simplify the complex world and make it easier to understand. To study the effects of international trade, for example, we might assume that the world consists of only two countries and that each country produces only two goods. By doing so, we can _____. Thus, we are in a better position to understand international trade in the complex world.

＊negligible: 무시할 수 있는

① prevent violations of consumer rights
② understand the value of cultural diversity
③ guarantee the safety of experimenters in labs
④ focus our thinking on the essence of the problem
⑤ realize the differences between physics and economics

09

다음 글에서 전체 흐름과 관계 <u>없는</u> 문장은?

Internet activist Eli Pariser noticed how online search algorithms encourage our human tendency to grab hold of everything that confirms the beliefs we already hold, while quietly ignoring information that doesn't match those beliefs. ① We set up a so-called "filter-bubble" around ourselves, where we are constantly exposed only to that material that we agree with. ② We are never challenged, never giving ourselves the opportunity to acknowledge the existence of diversity and difference. ③ Creating a difference that others don't have is a way to succeed in your field, leading to the creation of innovations. ④ In the best case, we become naive and sheltered, and in the worst, we become radicalized with extreme views, unable to imagine life outside our particular bubble. ⑤ The results are disastrous: intellectual isolation and the real distortion that comes with believing that the little world we create for ourselves is *the* world.

* naive: 세상을 모르는 ** radicalize: 과격하게 만들다
*** distortion: 왜곡

10 1등급 대비 고난도 3점 문제

주어진 글 다음에 이어질 글의 순서로 가장 적절한 것을 고르시오. [3점]

The basic difference between an AI robot and a normal robot is the ability of the robot and its software to make decisions, and learn and adapt to its environment based on data from its sensors.

(A) For instance, if faced with the same situation, such as running into an obstacle, then the robot will always do the same thing, such as go around the obstacle to the left. An AI robot, however, can do two things the normal robot cannot: make decisions and learn from experience.

(B) It will adapt to circumstances, and may do something different each time a situation is faced. The AI robot may try to push the obstacle out of the way, or make up a new route, or change goals.

(C) To be a bit more specific, the normal robot shows deterministic behaviors. That is, for a set of inputs, the robot will always produce the same output.

* deterministic: 결정론적인

① (A) − (C) − (B)　　　② (B) − (A) − (C)
③ (B) − (C) − (A)　　　④ (C) − (A) − (B)
⑤ (C) − (B) − (A)

[11 ~ 12] 다음 글을 읽고, 물음에 답하시오.

U.K. researchers say a bedtime of between 10 p.m. and 11 p.m. is best. They say people who go to sleep between these times have a (a) lower risk of heart disease. Six years ago, the researchers collected data on the sleep patterns of 80,000 volunteers. The volunteers had to wear a special watch for seven days so the researchers could collect data on their sleeping and waking times. The scientists then monitored the health of the volunteers. Around 3,000 volunteers later showed heart problems. They went to bed earlier or later than the (b) ideal 10 p.m. to 11 p.m. timeframe.

One of the authors of the study, Dr. David Plans, commented on his research and the (c) effects of bedtimes on the health of our heart. He said the study could not give a certain cause for their results, but it suggests that early or late bedtimes may be more likely to disrupt the body clock, with (d) positive consequences for cardiovascular health. He said that it was important for our body to wake up to the morning light, and that the worst time to go to bed was after midnight because it may (e) reduce the likelihood of seeing morning light which resets the body clock. He added that we risk cardiovascular disease if our body clock is not reset properly.

＊disrupt: 혼란케 하다　＊＊cardiovascular: 심장 혈관의

11

윗글의 제목으로 가장 적절한 것은?

① The Best Bedtime for Your Heart
② Late Bedtimes Are a Matter of Age
③ For Sound Sleep: Turn Off the Light
④ Sleeping Patterns Reflect Personalities
⑤ Regular Exercise: A Miracle for Good Sleep

12

밑줄 친 (a) ~ (e) 중에서 문맥상 낱말의 쓰임이 적절하지 않은 것은?

① (a)　　② (b)　　③ (c)　　④ (d)　　⑤ (e)

DAY 22

수능기출 전국연합학력평가 **20분 미니 모의고사**

● 날짜 :　　월　　일　 ● 시작 시각 :　　시　　분　　초　 ● 목표 시간 : 20분　　　　　　　　　　　　　　　　　　　　※ 점수 표기가 없는 문항은 모두 **2점**입니다.

01

고1 · 2022년 9월 18번

다음 글의 목적으로 가장 적절한 것은?

Dear Parents/Guardians,

Class parties will be held on the afternoon of Friday, December 16th, 2022. Children may bring in sweets, crisps, biscuits, cakes, and drinks. We are requesting that children do not bring in home-cooked or prepared food. All food should arrive in a sealed packet with the ingredients clearly listed. Fruit and vegetables are welcomed if they are pre-packed in a sealed packet from the shop. Please DO NOT send any food into school containing nuts as we have many children with severe nut allergies. Please check the ingredients of all food your children bring carefully. Thank you for your continued support and cooperation.

Yours sincerely,

Lisa Brown, Headteacher

① 학급 파티 일정 변경을 공지하려고
② 학교 식당의 새로운 메뉴를 소개하려고
③ 학생의 특정 음식 알레르기 여부를 조사하려고
④ 학부모의 적극적인 학급 파티 참여를 독려하려고
⑤ 학급 파티에 가져올 음식에 대한 유의 사항을 안내하려고

02

고1 · 2021년 9월 23번

다음 글의 주제로 가장 적절한 것은?

Vegetarian eating is moving into the mainstream as more and more young adults say no to meat, poultry, and fish. According to the American Dietetic Association, "approximately planned vegetarian diets are healthful, are nutritionally adequate, and provide health benefits in the prevention and treatment of certain diseases." But health concerns are not the only reason that young adults give for changing their diets. Some make the choice out of concern for animal rights. When faced with the statistics that show the majority of animals raised as food live in confinement, many teens give up meat to protest those conditions. Others turn to vegetarianism to support the environment. Meat production uses vast amounts of water, land, grain, and energy and creates problems with animal waste and resulting pollution.

＊ poultry: 가금류(닭·오리·거위 등)

① reasons why young people go for vegetarian diets
② ways to build healthy eating habits for teenagers
③ vegetables that help lower your risk of cancer
④ importance of maintaining a balanced diet
⑤ disadvantages of plant-based diets

03

고1 · 2021년 11월 24번

다음 글의 제목으로 가장 적절한 것은?

In modern times, society became more dynamic. Social mobility increased, and people began to exercise a higher degree of choice regarding, for instance, their profession, their marriage, or their religion. This posed a challenge to traditional roles in society. It was less evident that one needed to commit to the roles one was born into when alternatives could be realized. Increasing control over one's life choices became not only possible but desired. Identity then became a problem. It was no longer almost ready-made at birth but something to be discovered. Traditional role identities prescribed by society began to appear as masks imposed on people whose real self was to be found somewhere underneath.

＊impose: 부여하다

① What Makes Our Modern Society So Competitive?
② How Modern Society Drives Us to Discover Our Identities
③ Social Masks: A Means to Build Trustworthy Relationships
④ The More Social Roles We Have, the Less Choice We Have
⑤ Increasing Social Mobility Leads Us to a More Equal Society

04

고3 · 2020학년도 수능 29번

다음 글의 밑줄 친 부분 중, 어법상 틀린 것은?

Speculations about the meaning and purpose of prehistoric art ① <u>rely</u> heavily on analogies drawn with modern-day hunter-gatherer societies. Such primitive societies, ② <u>as</u> Steven Mithen emphasizes in *The Prehistory of the Modern Mind*, tend to view man and beast, animal and plant, organic and inorganic spheres, as participants in an integrated, animated totality. The dual expressions of this tendency are *anthropomorphism* (the practice of regarding animals as humans) and *totemism* (the practice of regarding humans as animals), both of ③ <u>which</u> spread through the visual art and the mythology of primitive cultures. Thus the natural world is conceptualized in terms of human social relations. When considered in this light, the visual preoccupation of early humans with the nonhuman creatures ④ <u>inhabited</u> their world becomes profoundly meaningful. Among hunter-gatherers, animals are not only good to eat, they are also *good to think about*, as Claude Lévi-Strauss has observed. In the practice of totemism, he has suggested, an unlettered humanity "broods upon ⑤ <u>itself</u> and its place in nature."

＊speculation: 고찰 ＊＊analogy: 유사점
＊＊＊brood: 곰곰이 생각하다

05

(A), (B), (C)의 각 네모 안에서 문맥에 맞는 낱말로 가장 적절한 것은? [3점]

We notice repetition among confusion, and the opposite: we notice a break in a repetitive pattern. But how do these arrangements make us feel? And what about "perfect" regularity and "perfect" chaos? Some repetition gives us a sense of security, in that we know what is coming next. We like some (A) predictability / unpredictability. We arrange our lives in largely repetitive schedules. Randomness, in organization or in events, is more challenging and more frightening for most of us. With "perfect" chaos we are (B) excited / frustrated by having to adapt and react again and again. But "perfect" regularity is perhaps even more horrifying in its monotony than randomness is. It (C) denies / implies a cold, unfeeling, mechanical quality. Such perfect order does not exist in nature; there are too many forces working against each other. Either extreme, therefore, feels threatening.

	(A)	(B)	(C)
①	predictability	…… excited	…… denies
②	predictability	…… frustrated	…… implies
③	predictability	…… frustrated	…… denies
④	unpredictability	…… excited	…… implies
⑤	unpredictability	…… frustrated	…… implies

06 1등급 대비 고난도 2점 문제

다음 빈칸에 들어갈 말로 가장 적절한 것을 고르시오.

Research has confirmed that athletes are less likely to participate in unacceptable behavior than are non-athletes. However, moral reasoning and good sporting behavior seem to decline as athletes progress to higher competitive levels, in part because of the increased emphasis on winning. Thus winning can be _____ _____ in teaching character development. Some athletes may want to win so much that they lie, cheat, and break team rules. They may develop undesirable character traits that can enhance their ability to win in the short term. However, when athletes resist the temptation to win in a dishonest way, they can develop positive character traits that last a lifetime. Character is a learned behavior, and a sense of fair play develops only if coaches plan to teach those lessons systematically.

* trait: 특성

① a piece of cake
② a one-way street
③ a bird in the hand
④ a fish out of water
⑤ a double-edged sword

07 1등급 대비 고난도 3점 문제 고1 · 2023년 6월 32번

다음 빈칸에 들어갈 말로 가장 적절한 것을 고르시오. [3점]

Think of the brain as a city. If you were to look out over a city and ask "where is the economy located?" you'd see there's no good answer to the question. Instead, the economy emerges from the interaction of all the elements — from the stores and the banks to the merchants and the customers. And so it is with the brain's operation: it doesn't happen in one spot. Just as in a city, no neighborhood of the brain _____ _____. In brains and in cities, everything emerges from the interaction between residents, at all scales, locally and distantly. Just as trains bring materials and textiles into a city, which become processed into the economy, so the raw electrochemical signals from sensory organs are transported along superhighways of neurons. There the signals undergo processing and transformation into our conscious reality.

* electrochemical: 전기화학의

① operates in isolation
② suffers from rapid changes
③ resembles economic elements
④ works in a systematic way
⑤ interacts with another

08 1등급 대비 고난도 2점 문제 고1 · 2019년 6월 38번

글의 흐름으로 보아, 주어진 문장이 들어가기에 가장 적절한 곳을 고르시오.

> When the boy learned that he had misspelled the word, he went to the judges and told them.

Some years ago at the national spelling bee in Washington, D.C., a thirteen-year-old boy was asked to spell *echolalia*, a word that means a tendency to repeat whatever one hears. (①) Although he misspelled the word, the judges misheard him, told him he had spelled the word right, and allowed him to advance. (②) So he was eliminated from the competition after all. (③) Newspaper headlines the next day called the honest young man a "spelling bee hero," and his photo appeared in *The New York Times*. (④) "The judges said I had a lot of honesty," the boy told reporters. (⑤) He added that part of his motive was, "I didn't want to feel like a liar."

* spelling bee: 단어 철자 맞히기 대회

09

다음 글의 내용을 한 문장으로 요약하고자 한다. 빈칸 (A), (B)에 들어갈 말로 가장 적절한 것은? [3점]

Have you noticed that some coaches get the most out of their athletes while others don't? A poor coach will tell you what you did wrong and then tell you not to do it again: "Don't drop the ball!" What happens next? The images you see in your head are images of you dropping the ball! Naturally, your mind recreates what it just "saw" based on what it's been told. Not surprisingly, you walk on the court and drop the ball. What does the good coach do? He or she points out what could be improved, but will then tell you how you could or should perform: "I know you'll catch the ball perfectly this time." Sure enough, the next image in your mind is you *catching* the ball and *scoring* a goal. Once again, your mind makes your last thoughts part of reality — but this time, that "reality" is positive, not negative.

↓

Unlike ineffective coaches, who focus on players' ___(A)___, effective coaches help players improve by encouraging them to ___(B)___ successful plays.

	(A)		(B)
①	scores	······	complete
②	scores	······	remember
③	mistakes	······	picture
④	mistakes	······	ignore
⑤	strengths	······	achieve

[10~12] 다음 글을 읽고, 물음에 답하시오.

(A)

On my daughter Marie's 8th birthday, she received a bunch of presents from her friends at school. That evening, with her favorite present, a teddy bear, in her arms, we went to a restaurant to celebrate her birthday. Our server, a friendly woman, noticed my daughter holding the teddy bear and said, "My daughter loves teddy bears, too." Then, we started chatting about (a) her family.

(B)

When Marie came back out, I asked her what she had been doing. She said that she gave her teddy bear to our server so that she could give it to (b) her daughter. I was surprised at her sudden action because I could see how much she loved that bear already. (c) She must have seen the look on my face, because she said, "I can't imagine being stuck in a hospital bed. I just want her to get better soon."

(C)

I felt moved by Marie's words as we walked toward the car. Then, our server ran out to our car and thanked Marie for her generosity. The server said that (d) she had never had anyone doing anything like that for her family before. Later, Marie said it was her best birthday ever. I was so proud of her empathy and warmth, and this was an unforgettable experience for our family.

(D)

The server mentioned during the conversation that her daughter was in the hospital with a broken leg. (e) She also said that Marie looked about the same age as her daughter. She was so kind and attentive all evening, and even gave Marie cookies for free. After we finished our meal, we paid the bill and began to walk to our car when unexpectedly Marie asked me to wait and ran back into the restaurant.

10

고1 · 2022년 11월 43번

주어진 글 (A)에 이어질 내용을 순서에 맞게 배열한 것으로 가장 적절한 것은?

① (B) – (D) – (C)
② (C) – (B) – (D)
③ (C) – (D) – (B)
④ (D) – (B) – (C)
⑤ (D) – (C) – (B)

11

고1 · 2022년 11월 44번

밑줄 친 (a) ~ (e) 중에서 가리키는 대상이 나머지 넷과 다른 것은?

① (a) ② (b) ③ (c) ④ (d) ⑤ (e)

12

고1 · 2022년 11월 45번

윗글에 관한 내용으로 적절하지 않은 것은?

① Marie는 테디 베어를 팔에 안고 식당에 갔다.
② 'I'는 Marie의 갑작스러운 행동에 놀랐다.
③ 종업원은 Marie의 관대함에 고마워했다.
④ 종업원은 자신의 딸이 팔이 부러져서 병원에 있다고 말했다.
⑤ 종업원은 Marie에게 쿠키를 무료로 주었다.

▶ 몰라서 틀린 문항 ✕ 표기 ▶ 헷갈렸거나 찍은 문항 △ 표기 ▶ ✕, △ 문항은 다시 풀고 ✔ 표기를 하세요.

종료 시각	시 분 초	문항 번호	01	02	03	04	05	06	07	08	09	10	11	12
소요 시간	분 초	채점 결과												
초과 시간	분 초	틀린 문항 복습												

DAY 23

수능기출
전국연합학력평가 **20분 미니 모의고사**

● 날짜 : 　월　　일　● 시작 시각 : 　시　　분　　초　● 목표 시간 : **20분**

※ 점수 표기가 없는 문항은 모두 **2점**입니다.

01

고1 · 2023년 3월 19번

다음 글에 드러난 'I'의 심경 변화로 가장 적절한 것은?

On a two-week trip in the Rocky Mountains, I saw a grizzly bear in its native habitat. At first, I felt joy as I watched the bear walk across the land. He stopped every once in a while to turn his head about, sniffing deeply. He was following the scent of something, and slowly I began to realize that this giant animal was smelling me! I froze. This was no longer a wonderful experience; it was now an issue of survival. The bear's motivation was to find meat to eat, and I was clearly on his menu.

* scent: 냄새

① sad　　　　→ angry
② delighted → scared
③ satisfied　→ jealous
④ worried　 → relieved
⑤ frustrated → excited

02

고1 · 2021년 11월 20번

다음 글에서 필자가 주장하는 바로 가장 적절한 것은?

Some experts estimate that as much as half of what we communicate is done through the way we move our bodies. Paying attention to the nonverbal messages you send can make a significant difference in your relationship with students. In general, most students are often closely tuned in to their teacher's body language. For example, when your students first enter the classroom, their initial action is to look for their teacher. Think about how encouraging and empowering it is for a student when that teacher has a friendly greeting and a welcoming smile. Smiling at students — to let them know that you are glad to see them — does not require a great deal of time or effort, but it can make a significant difference in the classroom climate right from the start of class.

① 교사는 학생 간의 상호 작용을 주의 깊게 관찰해야 한다.
② 수업 시 교사는 학생의 수준에 맞는 언어를 사용해야 한다.
③ 학생과의 관계에서 교사는 비언어적 표현에 유의해야 한다.
④ 학교는 학생에게 다양한 역할 경험의 기회를 제공해야 한다.
⑤ 교사는 학생 안전을 위해 교실의 물리적 환경을 개선해야 한다.

03

고1 · 2020년 9월 22번

다음 글의 요지로 가장 적절한 것은?

Learners function within complex developmental, cognitive, physical, social, and cultural systems. Research and theory from diverse fields have contributed to an evolving understanding that all learners grow and learn in culturally defined ways in culturally defined contexts. While humans share basic brain structures and processes, as well as fundamental experiences such as relationships with family, age-related stages, and many more, each of these phenomena is shaped by an individual's precise experiences. Learning does not happen in the same way for all people because cultural influences are influential from the beginning of life. These ideas about the intertwining of learning and culture have been supported by research on many aspects of learning and development.

＊ intertwine: 뒤얽히다

① 문화 다양성에 대한 체계적 연구가 필요하다.
② 개인의 문화적 경험이 학습에 영향을 끼친다.
③ 인간의 뇌 구조는 학습을 통해 복잡하게 진화했다.
④ 원만한 대인관계 형성은 건강한 성장의 토대가 된다.
⑤ 학습 발달 단계에 적합한 자극을 제공하는 것이 좋다.

04

고1 · 2022년 11월 25번

다음 도표의 내용과 일치하지 <u>않는</u> 것은?

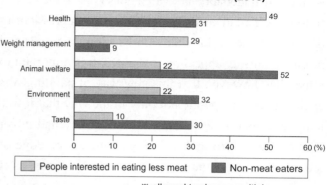

Reasons for People Interested in Eating Less Meat and Non-meat Eaters in the UK (2018)

※ allowed to choose multiple reasons

The graph above shows the survey results on reasons for people interested in eating less meat and those eating no meat in the UK in 2018. ① For the group of people who are interested in eating less meat, health is the strongest motivator for doing so. ② For the group of non-meat eaters, animal welfare accounts for the largest percentage among all reasons, followed by environment, health, and taste. ③ The largest percentage point difference between the two groups is in animal welfare, whereas the smallest difference is in environment. ④ The percentage of non-meat eaters citing taste is four times higher than that of people interested in reducing their meat consumption citing taste. ⑤ Weight management ranks the lowest for people who don't eat meat, with less than 10 percent.

05 1등급 대비 고난도 3점 문제

다음 글의 밑줄 친 부분 중, 어법상 틀린 것은? [3점]

Impressionist paintings are probably most popular; it is an easily understood art which does not ask the viewer ① to work hard to understand the imagery. Impressionism is 'comfortable' to look at, with its summer scenes and bright colours ② appealing to the eye. It is important to remember, however, that this new way of painting was challenging to its public not only in the way that it was made but also in ③ that was shown. They had never seen ④ such 'informal' paintings before. The edge of the canvas cut off the scene in an arbitrary way, as if snapped with a camera. The subject matter included modernization of the landscape; railways and factories. Never before had these subjects been considered ⑤ appropriate for artists.

06

다음 글의 밑줄 친 부분 중, 문맥상 낱말의 쓰임이 적절하지 않은 것은? [3점]

Bazaar economies feature an apparently flexible price-setting mechanism that sits atop more enduring ties of shared culture. Both the buyer and seller are aware of each other's ① restrictions. In Delhi's bazaars, buyers and sellers can ② assess to a large extent the financial constraints that other actors have in their everyday life. Each actor belonging to a specific economic class understands what the other sees as a necessity and a luxury. In the case of electronic products like video games, they are not a ③ necessity at the same level as other household purchases such as food items. So, the seller in Delhi's bazaars is careful not to directly ask for very ④ low prices for video games because at no point will the buyer see possession of them as an absolute necessity. Access to this type of knowledge establishes a price consensus by relating to each other's preferences and limitations of belonging to a ⑤ similar cultural and economic universe.

* constraint: 압박 ** consensus: 일치

07

다음 빈칸에 들어갈 말로 가장 적절한 것을 고르시오. [3점]

In small towns the same workman makes chairs and doors and tables, and often the same person builds houses. And it is, of course, impossible for a man of many trades to be skilled in all of them. In large cities, on the other hand, because many people make demands on each trade, one trade alone — very often even less than a whole trade — is enough to support a man. For instance, one man makes shoes for men, and another for women. And there are places even where one man earns a living by only stitching shoes, another by cutting them out, and another by sewing the uppers together. Such skilled workers may have used simple tools, but their _____ did result in more efficient and productive work.

* trade: 직종

① specialization
② criticism
③ competition
④ diligence
⑤ imagination

08 1등급 대비 고난도 3점 문제

다음 빈칸에 들어갈 말로 가장 적절한 것을 고르시오. [3점]

Focusing on the differences among societies conceals a deeper reality: their similarities are greater and more profound than their dissimilarities. Imagine studying two hills while standing on a ten-thousand-foot-high plateau. Seen from your perspective, one hill appears to be three hundred feet high, and the other appears to be nine hundred feet. This difference may seem large, and you might focus your attention on what local forces, such as erosion, account for the difference in size. But this narrow perspective misses the opportunity to study the other, more significant geological forces that created what are actually two very similar mountains, one 10,300 feet high and the other 10,900 feet. And when it comes to human societies, people have been standing on a ten-thousand-foot plateau, letting the differences among societies _____.

* erosion: 침식

① prove the uniqueness of each society
② prevent cross-cultural understanding
③ mask the more overwhelming similarities
④ change their perspective on what diversity is
⑤ encourage them to step out of their mental frame

09

다음 글에서 전체 흐름과 관계 <u>없는</u> 문장은?

Today's music business has allowed musicians to take matters into their own hands. ① Gone are the days of musicians waiting for a gatekeeper (someone who holds power and prevents you from being let in) at a label or TV show to say they are worthy of the spotlight. ② In today's music business, you don't need to ask for permission to build a fanbase and you no longer need to pay thousands of dollars to a company to do it. ③ There are rising concerns over the marketing of child musicians using TV auditions. ④ Every day, musicians are getting their music out to thousands of listeners without any outside help. ⑤ They simply deliver it to the fans directly, without asking for permission or outside help to receive exposure or connect with thousands of listeners.

10

주어진 글 다음에 이어질 글의 순서로 가장 적절한 것을 고르시오.

With nearly a billion hungry people in the world, there is obviously no single cause.

(A) The reason people are hungry in those countries is that the products produced there can be sold on the world market for more than the local citizens can afford to pay for them. In the modern age you do not starve because you have no food, you starve because you have no money.

(B) However, far and away the biggest cause is poverty. Seventy-nine percent of the world's hungry live in nations that are net exporters of food. How can this be?

(C) So the problem really is that food is, in the grand scheme of things, too expensive and many people are too poor to buy it. The answer will be in continuing the trend of lowering the cost of food.

＊net exporter: 순 수출국　＊＊scheme: 체계, 조직

① (A) − (C) − (B)　　② (B) − (A) − (C)
③ (B) − (C) − (A)　　④ (C) − (A) − (B)
⑤ (C) − (B) − (A)

[11 ~ 12] 다음 글을 읽고, 물음에 답하시오.

If you were afraid of standing on balconies, you would start on some lower floors and slowly work your way up to higher ones. It would be easy to face a fear of standing on high balconies in a way that's totally controlled. Socializing is (a) trickier. People aren't like inanimate features of a building that you just have to be around to get used to. You have to interact with them, and their responses can be unpredictable. Your feelings toward them are more complex too. Most people's self-esteem isn't going to be affected that much if they don't like balconies, but your confidence can (b) suffer if you can't socialize effectively.

It's also harder to design a tidy way to gradually face many social fears. The social situations you need to expose yourself to may not be (c) available when you want them, or they may not go well enough for you to sense that things are under control. The progression from one step to the next may not be clear, creating unavoidable large (d) decreases in difficulty from one to the next. People around you aren't robots that you can endlessly experiment with for your own purposes. This is not to say that facing your fears is pointless when socializing. The principles of gradual exposure are still very (e) useful. The process of applying them is just messier, and knowing that before you start is helpful.

11 1등급 대비 고난도 2점 문제

고1 · 2021년 6월 41번

윗글의 제목으로 가장 적절한 것은?

① How to Improve Your Self-Esteem
② Socializing with Someone You Fear: Good or Bad?
③ Relaxation May Lead to Getting Over Social Fears
④ Are Social Exposures Related with Fear of Heights?
⑤ Overcoming Social Anxiety Is Difficult; Try Gradually!

12

고1 · 2021년 6월 42번

밑줄 친 (a) ~ (e) 중에서 문맥상 낱말의 쓰임이 적절하지 <u>않은</u> 것은?

① (a)　　② (b)　　③ (c)　　④ (d)　　⑤ (e)

DAY 23

학습 Check!　　▶ 몰라서 틀린 문항 × 표기　▶ 헷갈렸거나 찍은 문항 △ 표기　▶ ×, △ 문항은 다시 풀고 ✔ 표기를 하세요.

종료 시각	시	분	초	문항 번호	01	02	03	04	05	06	07	08	09	10	11	12
소요 시간		분	초	채점 결과												
초과 시간		분	초	틀린 문항 복습												

DAY 24

● 날짜 :   월   일   ● 시작 시각 :   시   분   초   ● 목표 시간 : 20분

※ 점수 표기가 없는 문항은 모두 2점입니다.

01

고1·2021년 3월 20번

다음 글에서 필자가 주장하는 바로 가장 적절한 것은?

At a publishing house and at a newspaper you learn the following: *It's not a mistake if it doesn't end up in print.* It's the same for email. Nothing bad can happen if you haven't hit the Send key. What you've written can have misspellings, errors of fact, rude comments, obvious lies, but it doesn't matter. If you haven't sent it, you still have time to fix it. You can correct any mistake and nobody will ever know the difference. This is easier said than done, of course. Send is your computer's most attractive command. But before you hit the Send key, make sure that you read your document carefully one last time.

① 중요한 이메일은 출력하여 보관해야 한다.
② 글을 쓸 때에는 개요 작성부터 시작해야 한다.
③ 이메일을 전송하기 전에 반드시 검토해야 한다.
④ 업무와 관련된 컴퓨터 기능을 우선 익혀야 한다.
⑤ 업무상 중요한 내용은 이메일보다는 직접 전달해야 한다.

02

고1·2021년 6월 23번

다음 글의 주제로 가장 적절한 것은?

Curiosity makes us much more likely to view a tough problem as an interesting challenge to take on. A stressful meeting with our boss becomes an opportunity to learn. A nervous first date becomes an exciting night out with a new person. A colander becomes a hat. In general, curiosity motivates us to view stressful situations as challenges rather than threats, to talk about difficulties more openly, and to try new approaches to solving problems. In fact, curiosity is associated with a less defensive reaction to stress and, as a result, less aggression when we respond to irritation.

＊colander: (음식 재료의 물을 빼는 데 쓰는) 체

① importance of defensive reactions in a tough situation
② curiosity as the hidden force of positive reframes
③ difficulties of coping with stress at work
④ potential threats caused by curiosity
⑤ factors that reduce human curiosity

03

다음 도표의 내용과 일치하지 <u>않는</u> 것은?

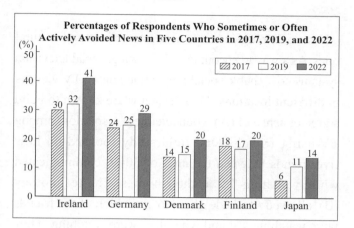

Percentages of Respondents Who Sometimes or Often Actively Avoided News in Five Countries in 2017, 2019, and 2022

The above graph shows the percentages of the respondents in five countries who sometimes or often actively avoided news in 2017, 2019, and 2022. ① For each of the three years, Ireland showed the highest percentage of the respondents who sometimes or often actively avoided news, among the countries in the graph. ② In Germany, the percentage of the respondents who sometimes or often actively avoided news was less than 30% in each of the three years. ③ In Denmark, the percentage of the respondents who sometimes or often actively avoided news in 2019 was higher than that in 2017 but lower than that in 2022. ④ In Finland, the percentage of the respondents who sometimes or often actively avoided news in 2019 was lower than that in 2017, which was also true for Japan. ⑤ In Japan, the percentage of the respondents who sometimes or often actively avoided news did not exceed 15% in each of the three years.

04

2023 Drone Racing Championship에 관한 다음 안내문의 내용과 일치하지 <u>않는</u> 것은?

2023 Drone Racing Championship

Are you the best drone racer? Then take the opportunity to prove you are the one!

When & Where
• 6 p.m. – 8 p.m., Sunday, July 9
• Lakeside Community Center

Requirements
• Participants: High school students only
• Bring your own drone for the race.

Prize
• $500 and a medal will be awarded to the winner.

Note
• The first 10 participants will get souvenirs.

For more details, please visit www.droneracing.com or call 313-6745-1189.

① 7월 9일 일요일에 개최된다.
② 고등학생만 참가할 수 있다.
③ 자신의 드론을 가져와야 한다.
④ 상금과 메달이 우승자에게 수여될 것이다.
⑤ 20명의 참가자가 기념품을 받을 것이다.

05

다음 글의 밑줄 친 부분 중, 어법상 틀린 것은? [3점]

The most noticeable human characteristic projected onto animals is ① that they can talk in human language. Physically, animal cartoon characters and toys ② made after animals are also most often deformed in such a way as to resemble humans. This is achieved by ③ showing them with humanlike facial features and deformed front legs to resemble human hands. In more recent animated movies the trend has been to show the animals in a more "natural" way. However, they still use their front legs ④ like human hands (for example, lions can pick up and lift small objects with one paw), and they still talk with an appropriate facial expression. A general strategy that is used to make the animal characters more emotionally appealing, both to children and adults, ⑤ are to give them enlarged and deformed childlike features.

＊deform: 변형하다　＊＊paw: (동물의) 발

06

(A), (B), (C)의 각 네모 안에서 문맥에 맞는 낱말로 가장 적절한 것은?

New technologies create new interactions and cultural rules. As a way to encourage TV viewing, social television systems now enable social interaction among TV viewers in different locations. These systems are known to build a greater sense of (A) connectedness / isolation among TV-using friends. One field study focused on how five friends between the ages of 30-36 communicated while watching TV at their homes. The technology (B) allowed / forbade them to see which of the friends were watching TV and what they were watching. They chose how to communicate via social television — whether through voice chat or text chat. The study showed a strong preference for text over voice. Users offered two key reasons for (C) disliking / favoring text chat. First, text chat required less effort and attention, and was more enjoyable than voice chat. Second, study participants viewed text chat as more polite.

	(A)	(B)	(C)
①	connectedness	allowed	disliking
②	connectedness	forbade	disliking
③	connectedness	allowed	favoring
④	isolation	forbade	favoring
⑤	isolation	allowed	disliking

07 1등급 대비 고난도 2점 문제

다음 빈칸에 들어갈 말로 가장 적절한 것을 고르시오.

Humans are champion long-distance runners. As soon as a person and a chimp start running they both get hot. Chimps quickly overheat; humans do not, because they are much better at shedding body heat. According to one leading theory, ancestral humans lost their hair over successive generations because less hair meant cooler, more effective long-distance running. That ability let our ancestors outmaneuver and outrun prey. Try wearing a couple of extra jackets — or better yet, fur coats — on a hot humid day and run a mile. Now, take those jackets off and try it again. You'll see what a difference _____ makes.

* shed: 떨어뜨리다   ** outmaneuver: ~에게 이기다

① hot weather
② a lack of fur
③ muscle strength
④ excessive exercise
⑤ a diversity of species

08 1등급 대비 고난도 3점 문제

글의 흐름으로 보아, 주어진 문장이 들어가기에 가장 적절한 곳을 고르시오. [3점]

> But after this brief moment of rest, the pendulum swings back again and therefore part of the total energy is then given in the form of kinetic energy.

In general, kinetic energy is the energy associated with motion, while potential energy represents the energy which is "stored" in a physical system. Moreover, the total energy is always conserved. (①) But while the total energy remains unchanged, the kinetic and potential parts of the total energy can change all the time. (②) Imagine, for example, a pendulum which swings back and forth. (③) When it swings, it sweeps out an arc and then slows down as it comes closer to its highest point, where the pendulum does not move at all. (④) So at this point, the energy is completely given in terms of potential energy. (⑤) So as the pendulum swings, kinetic and potential energy constantly change into each other.

* pendulum: 추(錘)   ** arc: 호(弧)

DAY 24

09 1등급 대비 고난도 3점 문제

다음 글의 내용을 한 문장으로 요약하고자 한다. 빈칸 (A), (B)에 들어갈 말로 가장 적절한 것은? [3점]

Nancy Lowry and David Johnson conducted an experiment to study a teaching environment where fifth and sixth graders were assigned to interact on a topic. With one group, the discussion was led in a way that built an agreement. With the second group, the discussion was designed to produce disagreements about the right answer. Students who easily reached an agreement were less interested in the topic, studied less, and were less likely to visit the library to get additional information. The most noticeable difference, though, was revealed when teachers showed a special film about the discussion topic — during lunch time! Only 18 percent of the agreement group missed lunch time to see the film, but 45 percent of the students from the disagreement group stayed for the film. The thirst to fill a knowledge gap — to find out who was right within the group — can be more powerful than the thirst for slides and jungle gyms.

⬇

According to the experiment above, students' interest in a topic _____(A)_____ when they are encouraged to _____(B)_____ .

	(A)		(B)
①	increases	······	differ
②	increases	······	approve
③	increases	······	cooperate
④	decreases	······	participate
⑤	decreases	······	argue

[10 ~ 12] 다음 글을 읽고, 물음에 답하시오.

(A)

James Walker was a renowned wrestler and he made his living through wrestling. In his town, there was a tradition in which the leader of the town chose a day when James demonstrated his skills. The leader announced one day that James would exhibit his skills as a wrestler and asked the people if there was anyone to challenge (a) him for the prize money.

(B)

When James saw the old man, he was speechless. Like everyone else, he thought that the old man had a death wish. The old man asked James to come closer since (b) he wanted to say something to him. James moved closer and the old man whispered, "I know it is impossible for me to win but my children are starving at home. Can you lose this competition to me so I can feed them with the prize money?"

(C)

Everyone was looking around in the crowd when an old man stood up and said with a shaking voice, "I will enter the contest against (c) him." Everyone burst out laughing thinking that it was a joke. James would crush him in a minute. According to the law, the leader could not stop someone who of his own free will entered the competition, so he allowed the old man to challenge the wrestler.

(D)

James thought he had an excellent opportunity to help a man in distress. (d) He did a couple of moves so that no one would suspect that the competition was fixed. However, he did not use his full strength and allowed the old man to win. The old man was overjoyed when he received the prize money. That night James felt the most victorious (e) he had ever felt.

10

고1 · 2020년 11월 43번

주어진 글 (A)에 이어질 내용을 순서에 맞게 배열한 것으로 가장 적절한 것은?

① (B) − (D) − (C)   ② (C) − (B) − (D)
③ (C) − (D) − (B)   ④ (D) − (B) − (C)
⑤ (D) − (C) − (B)

12

고1 · 2020년 11월 45번

윗글에 관한 내용으로 적절하지 <u>않은</u> 것은?

① James는 레슬링으로 생계를 유지했다.
② James는 노인을 보고 말문이 막혔다.
③ 노인의 아이들은 집에서 굶주리고 있었다.
④ 지도자는 노인이 James와 겨루는 것을 말렸다.
⑤ James는 노인과의 시합에서 전력을 다하지 않았다.

DAY 24

11

고1 · 2020년 11월 44번

밑줄 친 (a)～(e) 중에서 가리키는 대상이 나머지 넷과 <u>다른</u> 것은?

① (a)   ② (b)   ③ (c)   ④ (d)   ⑤ (e)

학습 Check!   ▶ 몰라서 틀린 문항 ✕ 표기   ▶ 헷갈렸거나 찍은 문항 △ 표기   ▶ ✕, △ 문항은 다시 풀고 ✔ 표기를 하세요.

종료 시각	시	분	초	문항 번호	01	02	03	04	05	06	07	08	09	10	11	12
소요 시간		분	초	채점 결과												
초과 시간		분	초	틀린 문항 복습												

DAY 25

● 날짜 :   월   일 ● 시작 시각 :   시   분   초 ● 목표 시간 : 20분

※ 점수 표기가 없는 문항은 모두 2점입니다.

01

고1 · 2020년 11월 18번

다음 글의 목적으로 가장 적절한 것은?

To whom it may concern:

I was born and raised in the city of Boulder and have enjoyed our scenic natural spaces for my whole life. The land through which the proposed Pine Hill walking trail would cut is home to a variety of species. Wildlife faces pressure from development, and these animals need space where they can hide from human activity. Although trails serve as a wonderful source for us to access the natural world and appreciate the wildlife within it, if we continue to destroy habitats with excess trails, the wildlife will stop using these areas. Please reconsider whether the proposed trail is absolutely necessary.

Sincerely,
Tyler Stuart

① 환경 보호 캠페인 참여를 부탁하려고
② 지역 관광 프로그램에 대해 문의하려고
③ 산책로 조성 계획의 재고를 요청하려고
④ 보행자 안전을 위해 인도 설치를 건의하려고
⑤ 야생 동물 보호구역 관리의 문제점을 지적하려고

02

고1 · 2020년 6월 22번

다음 글의 요지로 가장 적절한 것은?

A goal-oriented mind-set can create a "yo-yo" effect. Many runners work hard for months, but as soon as they cross the finish line, they stop training. The race is no longer there to motivate them. When all of your hard work is focused on a particular goal, what is left to push you forward after you achieve it? This is why many people find themselves returning to their old habits after accomplishing a goal. The purpose of setting goals is to win the game. The purpose of building systems is to continue playing the game. True long-term thinking is goal-less thinking. It's not about any single accomplishment. It is about the cycle of endless refinement and continuous improvement. Ultimately, it is your commitment to the process that will determine your progress.

① 발전은 한 번의 목표 성취가 아닌 지속적인 개선 과정에 의해 결정된다.
② 결승선을 통과하기 위해 장시간 노력해야 원하는 바를 얻을 수 있다.
③ 성공을 위해서는 구체적인 목표를 설정하는 것이 중요하다.
④ 지난 과정을 끊임없이 반복하는 것이 성공의 지름길이다.
⑤ 목표 지향적 성향이 강할수록 발전이 빠르게 이루어진다.

03

고1·2021년 11월 26번

Bessie Coleman에 관한 다음 글의 내용과 일치하지 <u>않는</u> 것은?

Bessie Coleman was born in Texas in 1892. When she was eleven, she was told that the Wright brothers had flown their first plane. Since that moment, she dreamed about the day she would soar through the sky. At the age of 23, Coleman moved to Chicago, where she worked at a restaurant to save money for flying lessons. However, she had to travel to Paris to take flying lessons because American flight schools at the time admitted neither women nor Black people. In 1921, she finally became the first Black woman to earn an international pilot's license. She also studied flying acrobatics in Europe and made her first appearance in an airshow in New York in 1922. As a female pioneer of flight, she inspired the next generation to pursue their dreams of flying.

* flying acrobatics: 곡예 비행

① 11살 때 Wright 형제의 첫 비행 소식을 들었다.
② 비행 수업을 듣기 위해 파리로 가야 했다.
③ 국제 조종사 면허를 딴 최초의 흑인 여성이 되었다.
④ 유럽에서 에어쇼에 첫 출현을 했다.
⑤ 다음 세대가 비행의 꿈을 추구하도록 영감을 주었다.

04

고1·2021년 6월 28번

Virtual Idea Exchange에 관한 다음 안내문의 내용과 일치하는 것은?

Virtual Idea Exchange

Connect in real time and have discussions about the upcoming school festival.

☐ **Goal**
• Plan the school festival and share ideas for it.

☐ **Participants**: Club leaders only

☐ **What to Discuss**
• Themes   • Ticket sales   • Budget

☐ **Date & Time**: 5 to 7 p.m. on Friday, June 25th, 2021

☐ **Notes**
• Get the access link by text message 10 minutes before the meeting and click it.
• Type your real name when you enter the chatroom.

---

① 동아리 회원이라면 누구나 참여 가능하다.
② 티켓 판매는 논의 대상에서 제외된다.
③ 회의는 3시간 동안 열린다.
④ 접속 링크를 문자로 받는다.
⑤ 채팅방 입장 시 동아리명으로 참여해야 한다.

05 1등급 대비 고난도 3점 문제

다음 글의 밑줄 친 부분 중, 어법상 틀린 것은? [3점]

You may have seen headlines in the news about some of the things machines powered by artificial intelligence can do. However, if you were to consider all the tasks ① that AI-powered machines could actually perform, it would be quite mind-blowing! One of the key features of artificial intelligence ② is that it enables machines to learn new things, rather than requiring programming specific to new tasks. Therefore, the core difference between computers of the future and ③ those of the past is that future computers will be able to learn and self-improve. In the near future, smart virtual assistants will know more about you than your closest friends and family members ④ are. Can you imagine how that might change our lives? These kinds of changes are exactly why it is so important ⑤ to recognize the implications that new technologies will have for our world.

06

다음 글의 밑줄 친 부분 중, 문맥상 낱말의 쓰임이 적절하지 않은 것은?

Europe's first *Homo sapiens* lived primarily on large game, particularly reindeer. Even under ideal circumstances, hunting these fast animals with spear or bow and arrow is an ① uncertain task. The reindeer, however, had a ② weakness that mankind would mercilessly exploit: it swam poorly. While afloat, it is uniquely ③ vulnerable, moving slowly with its antlers held high as it struggles to keep its nose above water. At some point, a Stone Age genius realized the enormous hunting ④ advantage he would gain by being able to glide over the water's surface, and built the first boat. Once the ⑤ laboriously overtaken and killed prey had been hauled aboard, getting its body back to the tribal camp would have been far easier by boat than on land. It would not have taken long for mankind to apply this advantage to other goods.

＊exploit: 이용하다   ＊＊haul: 끌어당기다

07 1등급 대비 고난도 2점 문제

다음 빈칸에 들어갈 말로 가장 적절한 것을 고르시오.

Individuals who perform at a high level in their profession often have instant credibility with others. People admire them, they want to be like them, and they feel connected to them. When they speak, others listen — even if the area of their skill has nothing to do with the advice they give. Think about a world-famous basketball player. He has made more money from endorsements than he ever did playing basketball. Is it because of his knowledge of the products he endorses? No. It's because of what he can do with a basketball. The same can be said of an Olympic medalist swimmer. People listen to him because of what he can do in the pool. And when an actor tells us we should drive a certain car, we don't listen because of his expertise on engines. We listen because we admire his talent. _____ connects. If you possess a high level of ability in an area, others may desire to connect with you because of it.

*endorsement: (유명인의 텔레비전 등에서의 상품) 보증 선전

① Patience   ② Sacrifice
③ Honesty   ④ Excellence
⑤ Creativity

08

다음 빈칸에 들어갈 말로 가장 적절한 것을 고르시오. [3점]

Everything in the world around us was finished in the mind of its creator before it was started. The houses we live in, the cars we drive, and our clothing — all of these began with an idea. Each idea was then studied, refined and perfected before the first nail was driven or the first piece of cloth was cut. Long before the idea was turned into a physical reality, the mind had clearly pictured the finished product. The human being designs his or her own future through much the same process. We begin with an idea about how the future will be. Over a period of time we refine and perfect the vision. Before long, our every thought, decision and activity are all working in harmony to bring into existence what we _____.

*refine: 다듬다

① didn't even have the potential to accomplish
② have mentally concluded about the future
③ haven't been able to picture in our mind
④ considered careless and irresponsible
⑤ have observed in some professionals

09

주어진 글 다음에 이어질 글의 순서로 가장 적절한 것을 고르시오.
[3점]

According to legend, once a vampire bites a person, that person turns into a vampire who seeks the blood of others. A researcher came up with some simple math, which proves that these highly popular creatures can't exist.

(A) In just two-and-a-half years, the original human population would all have become vampires with no humans left. But look around you. Have vampires taken over the world? No, because there's no such thing.

(B) If the first vampire came into existence that day and bit one person a month, there would have been two vampires by February 1st, 1600. A month later there would have been four, the next month eight, then sixteen, and so on.

(C) University of Central Florida physics professor Costas Efthimiou's work breaks down the myth. Suppose that on January 1st, 1600, the human population was just over five hundred million.

① (A) − (C) − (B)　　② (B) − (A) − (C)
③ (B) − (C) − (A)　　④ (C) − (A) − (B)
⑤ (C) − (B) − (A)

10

글의 흐름으로 보아, 주어진 문장이 들어가기에 가장 적절한 곳을 고르시오.

However, do not assume that a product is perfectly complementary, as customers may not be completely locked in to the product.

A "complementary good" is a product that is often consumed alongside another product. (①) For example, popcorn is a complementary good to a movie, while a travel pillow is a complementary good for a long plane journey. (②) When the popularity of one product increases, the sales of its complementary good also increase. (③) By producing goods that complement other products that are already (or about to be) popular, you can ensure a steady stream of demand for your product. (④) Some products enjoy perfect complementary status — they *have* to be consumed together, such as a lamp and a lightbulb. (⑤) For example, although motorists may seem required to purchase gasoline to run their cars, they can switch to electric cars.

[11 ~ 12] 다음 글을 읽고, 물음에 답하시오.

The market's way of telling a firm about its failures is harsh and brief. Not only are complaints less expensive to handle but they also can cause the seller to (a) improve. The seller may learn something as well. I remember a cosmetics company that received complaints about sticky sunblock lotion. At the time, all such lotions were more or less sticky, so the risk of having customers buy products from a rival company was not (b) great. But this was also an opportunity. The company managed to develop a product that was not sticky and captured 20 percent of the market in its first year. Another company had the (c) opposite problem. Its products were not sticky enough. The company was a Royal Post Office in Europe and the product was a stamp. The problem was that the stamp didn't stick to the envelope. Management contacted the stamp producer who made it clear that if people just moistened the stamps properly, they would stick to any piece of paper. What to do? Management didn't take long to come to the conclusion that it would be (d) less costly to try to educate its customers to wet each stamp rather than to add more glue. The stamp producer was told to add more glue and the problem didn't occur again.

Since it is better for the firm to have buyers complain rather than go elsewhere, it is important to make it (e) easier for dissatisfied customers to complain.

＊stamp: 우표

11

윗글의 제목으로 가장 적절한 것은?

① Designs That Matter the Most to Customers
② Complaints: Why Firms Should Welcome Them
③ Cheap Prices Don't Necessarily Mean Low Quality
④ More Sticky or Less Sticky: An Unsolved Problem
⑤ Treat Your Competitors Like Friends, Not Enemies

12 1등급 대비 고난도 3점 문제

밑줄 친 (a) ~ (e) 중에서 문맥상 낱말의 쓰임이 적절하지 않은 것은? [3점]

① (a) ② (b) ③ (c) ④ (d) ⑤ (e)

DAY 25

DAY 26

수능기출
전국연합학력평가 **20분 미니 모의고사**

● 날짜 :   월   일   ● 시작 시각 :   시   분   초   ● 목표 시간 : 20분

※ 점수 표기가 없는 문항은 모두 **2점**입니다.

01

고3 · 2021학년도 수능 19번

다음 글에 드러난 'I'의 심경 변화로 가장 적절한 것은?

Once again, I had lost the piano contest to my friend. When I learned that Linda had won, I was deeply troubled and unhappy. My body was shaking with uneasiness. My heart beat quickly and my face became reddish. I had to run out of the concert hall to settle down. Sitting on the stairs alone, I recalled what my teacher had said. "Life is about winning, not necessarily about winning against others but winning at being you. And the way to win is to figure out who you are and do your best." He was absolutely right. I had no reason to oppose my friend. Instead, I should focus on myself and my own improvement. I breathed out slowly. My hands were steady now. At last, my mind was at peace.

① grateful   → sorrowful
② upset   → calm
③ envious   → doubtful
④ surprised   → disappointed
⑤ bored   → relieved

02 1등급 대비 고난도 3점 문제

고1 · 2020년 6월 21번

밑줄 친 **by reading a body language dictionary**가 의미하는 바로 가장 적절한 것은? [3점]

Authentic, effective body language is more than the sum of individual signals. When people work from this rote-memory, dictionary approach, they stop seeing the bigger picture, all the diverse aspects of social perception. Instead, they see a person with crossed arms and think, "Reserved, angry." They see a smile and think, "Happy." They use a firm handshake to show other people "who is boss." Trying to use body language by reading a body language dictionary is like trying to speak French by reading a French dictionary. Things tend to fall apart in an inauthentic mess. Your actions seem robotic; your body language signals are disconnected from one another. You end up confusing the very people you're trying to attract because your body language just rings false.

① by learning body language within social context
② by comparing body language and French
③ with a body language expert's help
④ without understanding the social aspects
⑤ in a way people learn their native language

03

다음 글의 제목으로 가장 적절한 것은?

　Few people will be surprised to hear that poverty tends to create stress: a 2006 study published in the American journal *Psychosomatic Medicine*, for example, noted that a lower socioeconomic status was associated with higher levels of stress hormones in the body. However, richer economies have their own distinct stresses. The key issue is time pressure. A 1999 study of 31 countries by American psychologist Robert Levine and Canadian psychologist Ara Norenzayan found that wealthier, more industrialized nations had a faster pace of life — which led to a higher standard of living, but at the same time left the population feeling a constant sense of urgency, as well as being more prone to heart disease. In effect, fast-paced productivity creates wealth, but it also leads people to feel time-poor when they lack the time to relax and enjoy themselves.

*prone: 걸리기 쉬운

① Why Are Even Wealthy Countries Not Free from Stress?
② In Search of the Path to Escaping the Poverty Trap
③ Time Management: Everything You Need to Know
④ How Does Stress Affect Human Bodies?
⑤ Sound Mind Wins the Game of Life!

04 **1등급 대비 고난도 3점 문제**

다음 글의 밑줄 친 부분 중, 어법상 틀린 것은? [3점]

　Although it is obvious that part of our assessment of food is its visual appearance, it is perhaps surprising ① how visual input can override taste and smell. People find it very ② difficult to correctly identify fruit-flavoured drinks if the colour is wrong, for instance an orange drink that is coloured green. Perhaps even more striking ③ is the experience of wine tasters. One study of Bordeaux University students of wine and wine making revealed that they chose tasting notes appropriate for red wines, such as 'prune and chocolate', when they ④ gave white wine coloured with a red dye. Experienced New Zealand wine experts were similarly tricked into thinking ⑤ that the white wine Chardonnay was in fact a red wine, when it had been coloured with a red dye.

*override: ~에 우선하다　**prune: 자두

DAY 26

05 1등급 대비 고난도 2점 문제 고1 · 2021년 11월 30번

다음 글의 밑줄 친 부분 중, 문맥상 낱말의 쓰임이 적절하지 <u>않은</u> 것은?

For species approaching extinction, zoos can act as a last chance for survival. ① <u>Recovery</u> programs are established to coordinate the efforts of field conservationists and wildlife authorities. As populations of those species ② <u>diminish</u> it is not unusual for zoos to start captive breeding programs. Captive breeding acts to protect against extinction. In some cases captive-bred individuals may be released back into the wild, supplementing wild populations. This is most successful in situations where individuals are at greatest threat during a ③ <u>particular</u> life stage. For example, turtle eggs may be removed from high-risk locations until after they hatch. This may ④ <u>increase</u> the number of turtles that survive to adulthood. Crocodile programs have also been successful in protecting eggs and hatchlings, ⑤ <u>capturing</u> hatchlings once they are better equipped to protect themselves.

* captive breeding: 포획 사육　** hatch: 부화하다

06 고1 · 2023년 9월 31번

다음 빈칸에 들어갈 말로 가장 적절한 것을 고르시오.

Many people are terrified to fly in airplanes. Often, this fear stems from a lack of control. The pilot is in control, not the passengers, and this lack of control instills fear. Many potential passengers are so afraid they choose to drive great distances to get to a destination instead of flying. But their decision to drive is based solely on emotion, not logic. Logic says that statistically, the odds of dying in a car crash are around 1 in 5,000, while the odds of dying in a plane crash are closer to 1 in 11 million. If you're going to take a risk, especially one that could possibly involve your well-being, wouldn't you want the odds in your favor? However, most people choose the option that will cause them the least amount of _____. Pay attention to the thoughts you have about taking the risk and make sure you're basing your decision on facts, not just feelings.

* instill: 스며들게 하다

① anxiety　　　　　② boredom
③ confidence　　　 ④ satisfaction
⑤ responsibility

07

고1 · 2022년 9월 34번

다음 빈칸에 들어갈 말로 가장 적절한 것을 고르시오. [3점]

In the studies of Colin Cherry at the Massachusetts Institute for Technology back in the 1950s, his participants listened to voices in one ear at a time and then through both ears in an effort to determine whether we can listen to two people talk at the same time. One ear always contained a message that the listener had to repeat back (called "shadowing") while the other ear included people speaking. The trick was to see if you could totally focus on the main message and also hear someone talking in your other ear. Cleverly, Cherry found it was impossible for his participants to know whether the message in the other ear was spoken by a man or woman, in English or another language, or was even comprised of real words at all! In other words, people could not _____.

① decide what they should do in the moment
② remember a message with too many words
③ analyze which information was more accurate
④ speak their own ideas while listening to others
⑤ process two pieces of information at the same time

08

고1 · 2019년 3월 35번

다음 글에서 전체 흐름과 관계 <u>없는</u> 문장은?

Public speaking is audience centered because speakers "listen" to their audiences during speeches. They monitor audience feedback, the verbal and nonverbal signals an audience gives a speaker. ① Audience feedback often indicates whether listeners understand, have interest in, and are ready to accept the speaker's ideas. ② This feedback assists the speaker in many ways. ③ It helps the speaker know when to slow down, explain something more carefully, or even tell the audience that she or he will return to an issue in a question-and-answer session at the close of the speech. ④ It is important for the speaker to memorize his or her script to reduce on-stage anxiety. ⑤ Audience feedback assists the speaker in creating a respectful connection with the audience.

* verbal: 언어적인

09

다음 글의 내용을 한 문장으로 요약하고자 한다. 빈칸 (A), (B)에 들어갈 말로 가장 적절한 것은? [3점]

According to a study of Swedish adolescents, an important factor of adolescents' academic success is how they respond to challenges. The study reports that when facing difficulties, adolescents exposed to an authoritative parenting style are less likely to be passive, helpless, and afraid to fail. Another study of nine high schools in Wisconsin and northern California indicates that children of authoritative parents do well in school, because these parents put a lot of effort into getting involved in their children's school activities. That is, authoritative parents are significantly more likely to help their children with homework, to attend school programs, to watch their children in sports, and to help students select courses. Moreover, these parents are more aware of what their children do and how they perform in school. Finally, authoritative parents praise academic excellence and the importance of working hard more than other parents do.

↓

The studies above show that the children of authoritative parents often succeed academically, since they are more _____(A)_____ to deal with their difficulties and are affected by their parents' _____(B)_____ involvement.

	(A)		(B)
①	likely	......	random
②	willing	......	minimal
③	willing	......	active
④	hesitant	......	unwanted
⑤	hesitant	......	constant

[10 ~ 12] 다음 글을 읽고, 물음에 답하시오.

(A)

A long time ago, a farmer in a small town had a neighbor who was a hunter. The hunter owned a few fierce and poorly-trained hunting dogs. They jumped the fence frequently and chased the farmer's lambs. The farmer asked his neighbor to keep (a) his dogs in check, but his words fell on deaf ears. One day when the dogs jumped the fence, they attacked and severely injured several of the lambs.

(B)

To protect his sons' newly acquired playmates, the hunter built a strong doghouse for his dogs. The dogs never bothered the farmer's lambs again. Out of gratitude for the farmer's generosity toward (b) his children, the hunter often invited the farmer for feasts. In turn, the farmer offered him lamb meat and cheese he had made. The farmer quickly developed a strong friendship with (c) him.

(C)

"All right, I will offer you a solution that keeps your lambs safe and will also turn your neighbor into a good friend." Having heard the judge's solution, the farmer agreed. As soon as the farmer reached home, he immediately put the judge's suggestions to the test. (d) He selected three of the cutest lambs from his farm. He then presented them to his neighbor's three small sons. The children accepted with joy and began to play with them.

(D)

The farmer had had enough by this point. He went to the nearest city to consult a judge. After listening carefully to his story, the judge said, "I could punish the hunter and instruct (e) him to keep his dogs chained or lock them up. But you would lose a friend and gain an enemy. Which would you rather have for a neighbor, a friend or an enemy?" The farmer replied that he preferred a friend.

10

고1 · 2019년 11월 43번

주어진 글 (A)에 이어질 내용을 순서에 맞게 배열한 것으로 가장 적절한 것은?

① (B) – (D) – (C)   ② (C) – (B) – (D)

③ (C) – (D) – (B)   ④ (D) – (B) – (C)

⑤ (D) – (C) – (B)

12

고1 · 2019년 11월 45번

윗글의 농부에 관한 내용으로 적절하지 <u>않은</u> 것은?

① 그의 양이 사냥개의 공격을 받았다.

② 사냥꾼에게 양고기와 치즈를 받았다.

③ 재판관의 해결책에 동의했다.

④ 세 명의 아들을 둔 이웃이 있었다.

⑤ 도시로 조언을 구하러 갔다.

11

고1 · 2019년 11월 44번

밑줄 친 (a)~(e) 중에서 가리키는 대상이 나머지 넷과 <u>다른</u> 것은?

① (a)   ② (b)   ③ (c)   ④ (d)   ⑤ (e)

DAY 26

학습 Check!

▶ 몰라서 틀린 문항 × 표기   ▶ 헷갈렸거나 찍은 문항 △ 표기   ▶ ×, △ 문항은 다시 풀고 ✔ 표기를 하세요.

종료 시각	시 분 초	문항 번호	01	02	03	04	05	06	07	08	09	10	11	12
소요 시간	분 초	채점 결과												
초과 시간	분 초	틀린 문항 복습												

DAY 27

● 날짜 :　　월　　일　● 시작 시각 :　　시　　분　　초　● 목표 시간 : 20분　　　　　　　　※ 점수 표기가 없는 문항은 모두 **2점**입니다.

01
고3 · 2019학년도 수능 20번

다음 글에서 필자가 주장하는 바로 가장 적절한 것은?

　War is inconceivable without *some* image, or concept, of the enemy. It is the presence of the enemy that gives meaning and justification to war. 'War follows from feelings of hatred', wrote Carl Schmitt. 'War has its own strategic, tactical, and other rules and points of view, but they all presuppose that the political decision has already been made as to who the enemy is'. The concept of the enemy is fundamental to the moral assessment of war: 'The basic aim of a nation at war in establishing an image of the enemy is to distinguish as sharply as possible the act of killing from the act of murder'. However, we need to be cautious about thinking of war and the image of the enemy that informs it in an abstract and uniform way. Rather, both must be seen for the cultural and contingent phenomena that they are.

*contingent: 불확정적인

① 전쟁과 적을 추상적이고 획일적으로 개념화하는 것을 경계해야 한다.
② 적에 따라 다양한 전략과 전술을 수립하고 적용해야 한다.
③ 보편적 윤리관에 기초하여 적의 개념을 정의해야 한다.
④ 전쟁 예방에 도움이 되는 정치적 결정을 해야 한다.
⑤ 어떠한 경우에도 전쟁을 정당화하지 말아야 한다.

02
고1 · 2021년 11월 23번

다음 글의 주제로 가장 적절한 것은?

　We used to think that the brain never changed, but according to the neuroscientist Richard Davidson, we now know that this is not true — specific brain circuits grow stronger through regular practice. He explains, "Well-being is fundamentally no different than learning to play the cello. If one practices the skills of well-being, one will get better at it." What this means is that you can actually train your brain to become more grateful, relaxed, or confident, by repeating experiences that evoke gratitude, relaxation, or confidence. Your brain is shaped by the thoughts you repeat. The more neurons fire as they are activated by repeated thoughts and activities, the faster they develop into neural pathways, which cause lasting changes in the brain. Or in the words of Donald Hebb, "Neurons that fire together wire together." This is such an encouraging premise: bottom line — we can intentionally create the habits for the brain to be happier.

*evoke: (감정을) 불러일으키다　**premise: 전제

① possibility of forming brain habits for well-being
② role of brain circuits in improving body movements
③ importance of practice in playing musical instruments
④ effect of taking a break on enhancing memory capacity
⑤ difficulty of discovering how neurons in the brain work

03

다음 도표의 내용과 일치하지 <u>않는</u> 것은?

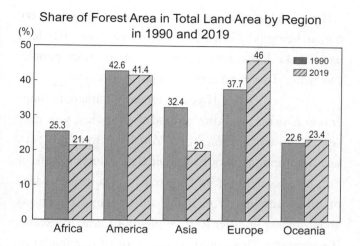

Share of Forest Area in Total Land Area by Region in 1990 and 2019

The above graph shows the share of forest area in total land area by region in 1990 and 2019. ① Africa's share of forest area in total land area was over 20% in both 1990 and 2019. ② The share of forest area in America was 42.6% in 1990, which was larger than that in 2019. ③ The share of forest area in Asia declined from 1990 to 2019 by more than 10 percentage points. ④ In 2019, the share of forest area in Europe was the largest among the five regions, more than three times that in Asia in the same year. ⑤ Oceania showed the smallest gap between 1990 and 2019 in terms of the share of forest area in total land area.

04 1등급 대비 고난도 2점 문제

다음 글의 밑줄 친 부분 중, 어법상 <u>틀린</u> 것은?

Bad lighting can increase stress on your eyes, as can light that is too bright, or light that shines ① <u>directly</u> into your eyes. Fluorescent lighting can also be ② <u>tiring</u>. What you may not appreciate is that the quality of light may also be important. Most people are happiest in bright sunshine — this may cause a release of chemicals in the body ③ <u>that</u> bring a feeling of emotional well-being. Artificial light, which typically contains only a few wavelengths of light, ④ <u>do</u> not seem to have the same effect on mood that sunlight has. Try experimenting with working by a window or ⑤ <u>using</u> full spectrum bulbs in your desk lamp. You will probably find that this improves the quality of your working environment.

* fluorescent lighting: 형광등

DAY 27

05 1등급 대비 고난도 3점 문제

다음 글의 밑줄 친 부분 중, 문맥상 낱말의 쓰임이 적절하지 않은 것은? [3점]

The major philosophical shift in the idea of selling came when industrial societies became more affluent, more competitive, and more geographically spread out during the 1940s and 1950s. This forced business to develop ① closer relations with buyers and clients, which in turn made business realize that it was not enough to produce a quality product at a reasonable price. In fact, it was equally ② essential to deliver products that customers actually wanted. Henry Ford produced his best-selling T-model Ford in one color only (black) in 1908, but in modern societies this was no longer ③ possible. The modernization of society led to a marketing revolution that ④ strengthened the view that production would create its own demand. Customers, and the desire to ⑤ meet their diverse and often complex needs, became the focus of business.

* affluent: 부유한

06

다음 빈칸에 들어갈 말로 가장 적절한 것을 고르시오.

Here's the unpleasant truth: we are all biased. Every human being is affected by unconscious biases that lead us to make incorrect assumptions about other people. Everyone. To a certain extent, bias is a(n) _____ _____. If you're an early human, perhaps *Homo Erectus*, walking around the jungles, you may see an animal approaching. You have to make very fast assumptions about whether that animal is safe or not, based solely on its appearance. The same is true of other humans. You make split-second decisions about threats in order to have plenty of time to escape, if necessary. This could be one root of our tendency to categorize and label others based on their looks and their clothes.

① necessary survival skill
② origin of imagination
③ undesirable mental capacity
④ barrier to relationships
⑤ challenge to moral judgment

07

다음 빈칸에 들어갈 말로 가장 적절한 것을 고르시오.

If you've ever made a poor choice, you might be interested in learning how to break that habit. One great way to trick your brain into doing so is to sign a "Ulysses Contract." The name of this life tip comes from the Greek myth about Ulysses, a captain whose ship sailed past the island of the Sirens, a tribe of dangerous women who lured victims to their death with their irresistible songs. Knowing that he would otherwise be unable to resist, Ulysses instructed his crew to stuff their ears with cotton and tie him to the ship's mast to prevent him from turning their ship towards the Sirens. It worked for him and you can do the same thing by _____. For example, if you want to stay off your cellphone and concentrate on your work, delete the apps that distract you or ask a friend to change your password!

* lure: 유혹하다 ** mast: 돛대

① letting go of all-or-nothing mindset
② finding reasons why you want to change
③ locking yourself out of your temptations
④ building a plan and tracking your progress
⑤ focusing on breaking one bad habit at a time

08

다음 글에서 전체 흐름과 관계 <u>없는</u> 문장은? [3점]

Health and the spread of disease are very closely linked to how we live and how our cities operate. The good news is that cities are incredibly resilient. Many cities have experienced epidemics in the past and have not only survived, but advanced. ① The nineteenth and early-twentieth centuries saw destructive outbreaks of cholera, typhoid, and influenza in European cities. ② Doctors such as Jon Snow, from England, and Rudolf Virchow, of Germany, saw the connection between poor living conditions, overcrowding, sanitation, and disease. ③ A recognition of this connection led to the replanning and rebuilding of cities to stop the spread of epidemics. ④ In spite of reconstruction efforts, cities declined in many areas and many people started to leave. ⑤ In the mid-nineteenth century, London's pioneering sewer system, which still serves it today, was built as a result of understanding the importance of clean water in stopping the spread of cholera.

* resilient: 회복력이 있는 ** sewer system: 하수 처리 시스템

09

주어진 글 다음에 이어질 글의 순서로 가장 적절한 것을 고르시오. [3점]

> Understanding how to develop respect for and a knowledge of other cultures begins with reexamining the golden rule: "I treat others in the way I want to be treated."

(A) It can also create a frustrating situation where we believe we are doing what is right, but what we are doing is not being interpreted in the way in which it was meant. This miscommunication can lead to problems.

(B) In a multicultural setting, however, where words, gestures, beliefs, and views may have different meanings, this rule has an unintended result; it can send a message that my culture is better than yours.

(C) This rule makes sense on some level; if we treat others as well as we want to be treated, we will be treated well in return. This rule works well in a monocultural setting, where everyone is working within the same cultural framework.

① (A) − (C) − (B)   ② (B) − (A) − (C)
③ (B) − (C) − (A)   ④ (C) − (A) − (B)
⑤ (C) − (B) − (A)

10

글의 흐름으로 보아, 주어진 문장이 들어가기에 가장 적절한 곳을 고르시오. [3점]

> Grown-ups rarely explain the meaning of new words to children, let alone how grammatical rules work.

Our brains are constantly solving problems. (①) Every time we learn, or remember, or make sense of something, we solve a problem. (②) Some psychologists have characterized all infant language-learning as problem-solving, extending to children such scientific procedures as "learning by experiment," or "hypothesis-testing." (③) Instead they use the words or the rules in conversation and leave it to children to figure out what is going on. (④) In order to learn language, an infant must make sense of the contexts in which language occurs; problems must be solved. (⑤) We have all been solving problems of this kind since childhood, usually without awareness of what we are doing.

[11 ～ 12] 다음 글을 읽고, 물음에 답하시오.

Claims that local food production cut greenhouse gas emissions by reducing the burning of transportation fuel are usually not well founded. Transport is the source of only 11 percent of greenhouse gas emissions within the food sector, so reducing the distance that food travels after it leaves the farm is far (a) less important than reducing wasteful energy use on the farm. Food coming from a distance can actually be better for the (b) climate, depending on how it was grown. For example, field-grown tomatoes shipped from Mexico in the winter months will have a smaller carbon footprint than (c) local winter tomatoes grown in a greenhouse. In the United Kingdom, lamb meat that travels 11,000 miles from New Zealand generates only one-quarter the carbon emissions per pound compared to British lamb because farmers in the United Kingdom raise their animals on feed (which must be produced using fossil fuels) rather than on clover pastureland.

When food does travel, what matters most is not the (d) distance traveled but the travel mode (surface versus air), and most of all the load size. Bulk loads of food can travel halfway around the world by ocean freight with a smaller carbon footprint, per pound delivered, than foods traveling just a short distance but in much (e) larger loads. For example, 18-wheelers carry much larger loads than pickup trucks so they can move food 100 times as far while burning only one-third as much gas per pound of food delivered.

* freight: 화물 운송

11

윗글의 제목으로 가장 적절한 것은?

① Shorten the Route, Cut the Cost
② Is Local Food Always Better for the Earth?
③ Why Mass Production Ruins the Environment
④ New Technologies: What Matters in Agriculture
⑤ Reduce Food Waste for a Smaller Carbon Footprint

12 1등급 대비 고난도 2점 문제

밑줄 친 (a) ～ (e) 중에서 문맥상 낱말의 쓰임이 적절하지 않은 것은?

① (a)   ② (b)   ③ (c)   ④ (d)   ⑤ (e)

DAY 27

▶ 몰라서 틀린 문항 × 표기   ▶ 헷갈렸거나 찍은 문항 △ 표기   ▶ ×, △ 문항은 다시 풀고 ✔ 표기를 하세요.

종료 시각	시	분	초	문항 번호	01	02	03	04	05	06	07	08	09	10	11	12
소요 시간		분	초	채점 결과												
초과 시간		분	초	틀린 문항 복습												

DAY 28

수능기출 전국연합학력평가 20분 미니 모의고사

※ 점수 표기가 없는 문항은 모두 **2점**입니다.

● 날짜 :　월　　일 ● 시작 시각 :　시　　분　　초 ● 목표 시간 : 20분

01

고1・2022년 11월 19번

다음 글에 드러난 'I'의 심경 변화로 가장 적절한 것은?

On one beautiful spring day, I was fully enjoying my day off. I arrived at the nail salon, and muted my cellphone so that I would be disconnected for the hour and feel calm and peaceful. I was so comfortable while I got a manicure. As I left the place, I checked my cellphone and saw four missed calls from a strange number. I knew immediately that something bad was coming, and I called back. A young woman answered and said that my father had fallen over a stone and was injured, now seated on a bench. I was really concerned since he had just recovered from his knee surgery. I rushed getting into my car to go see him.

① nervous → confident
② relaxed → worried
③ excited → indifferent
④ pleased → jealous
⑤ annoyed → grateful

02

고1・2020년 3월 22번

다음 글의 요지로 가장 적절한 것은?

Practically anything of value requires that we take a risk of failure or being rejected. This is the price we all must pay for achieving the greater rewards lying ahead of us. To take risks means you will succeed sometime but never to take a risk means that you will never succeed. Life is filled with a lot of risks and challenges and if you want to get away from all these, you will be left behind in the race of life. A person who can never take a risk can't learn anything. For example, if you never take the risk to drive a car, you can never learn to drive. If you never take the risk of being rejected, you can never have a friend or partner. Similarly, by not taking the risk of attending an interview, you will never get a job.

① 위험을 무릅쓰지 않으면 아무 것도 얻지 못한다.
② 자신이 잘하는 일에 집중하는 것이 효율적이다.
③ 잦은 실패 경험은 도전할 의지를 잃게 한다.
④ 위험 요소가 있으면 미리 피하는 것이 좋다.
⑤ 부탁을 자주 거절하면 신뢰를 잃는다.

03

다음 글의 제목으로 가장 적절한 것은?

Different parts of the brain's visual system get information on a need-to-know basis. Cells that help your hand muscles reach out to an object need to know the size and location of the object, but they don't need to know about color. They need to know a little about shape, but not in great detail. Cells that help you recognize people's faces need to be extremely sensitive to details of shape, but they can pay less attention to location. It is natural to assume that anyone who sees an object sees everything about it — the shape, color, location, and movement. However, one part of your brain sees its shape, another sees color, another detects location, and another perceives movement. Consequently, after localized brain damage, it is possible to see certain aspects of an object and not others. Centuries ago, people found it difficult to imagine how someone could see an object without seeing what color it is. Even today, you might find it surprising to learn about people who see an object without seeing where it is, or see it without seeing whether it is moving.

① Visual Systems Never Betray Our Trust!
② Secret Missions of Color-Sensitive Brain Cells
③ Blind Spots: What Is Still Unknown About the Brain
④ Why Brain Cells Exemplify Nature's Recovery Process
⑤ Separate and Independent: Brain Cells' Visual Perceptions

04

Silversmithing Class에 관한 다음 안내문의 내용과 일치하지 않는 것은?

Silversmithing Class

Kingston Club is offering a fine jewelry making class. Don't miss this great chance to make your own jewelry!

When & Where
- Saturday, October 21, 2023 (2 p.m. to 4 p.m.)
- Kingston Club studio

Registration
- Available only online
- Dates: October 1 – 14, 2023
- Fee: $40 (This includes all tools and materials.)
- Registration is limited to 6 people.

Note
- Participants must be at least 16 years old.
- No refund for cancellation on the day of the class

---

① 두 시간 동안 진행된다.
② 10월 1일부터 등록할 수 있다.
③ 등록 인원은 6명으로 제한된다.
④ 참가 연령에 제한이 없다.
⑤ 수업 당일 취소 시 환불이 불가하다.

05 1등급 대비 고난도 3점 문제
고1・2017년 11월 29번

(A), (B), (C)의 각 네모 안에서 문맥에 맞는 낱말로 가장 적절한 것은? [3점]

Everyone knows a young person who is impressively "street smart" but does poorly in school. We think it is a waste that one who is so (A) | intelligent / unintelligent | about so many things in life seems unable to apply that intelligence to academic work. What we don't realize is that schools and colleges might be at fault for missing the opportunity to draw such street smarts and guide them toward good academic work. Nor do we consider one of the major reasons why schools and colleges (B) | accept / overlook | the intellectual potential of street smarts: the fact that we associate those street smarts with anti-intellectual concerns. We associate the educated life, the life of the mind, too (C) | narrowly / widely | with subjects and texts that we consider inherently weighty and academic.

	(A)	(B)	(C)
①	intelligent	accept	widely
②	intelligent	overlook	narrowly
③	unintelligent	overlook	widely
④	unintelligent	overlook	narrowly
⑤	unintelligent	accept	widely

06 1등급 대비 고난도 2점 문제
고1・2019년 9월 30번

다음 글의 밑줄 친 부분 중, 문맥상 낱말의 쓰임이 적절하지 <u>않은</u> 것은?

Technological development often forces change, and change is uncomfortable. This is one of the main reasons why technology is often resisted and why some perceive it as a ① threat. It is important to understand our natural ② hate of being uncomfortable when we consider the impact of technology on our lives. As a matter of fact, most of us prefer the path of ③ least resistance. This tendency means that the true potential of new technologies may remain ④ unrealized because, for many, starting something new is just too much of a struggle. Even our ideas about how new technology can enhance our lives may be ⑤ encouraged by this natural desire for comfort.

07

다음 빈칸에 들어갈 말로 가장 적절한 것을 고르시오. [3점]

One CEO in one of Silicon Valley's most innovative companies has what would seem like a boring, creativity-killing routine. He holds a three-hour meeting that starts at 9:00 A.M. one day a week. It is never missed or rescheduled at a different time. It is mandatory — so much so that even in this global firm all the executives know never to schedule any travel that will conflict with the meeting. At first glance there is nothing particularly unique about this. But what *is* unique is the quality of ideas that come out of _____. Because the CEO has eliminated the mental cost involved in planning the meeting or thinking about who will or won't be there, people can focus on creative problem solving.

① consumer complaints
② the regular meetings
③ traveling experiences
④ flexible working hours
⑤ the financial incentives

08

다음 글에서 전체 흐름과 관계 없는 문장은?

Training and conditioning for baseball focuses on developing strength, power, speed, quickness and flexibility. ① Before the 1980s, strength training was not an important part of conditioning for a baseball player. ② People viewed baseball as a game of skill and technique rather than strength, and most managers and coaches saw strength training as something for bodybuilders, not baseball players. ③ Unlike more isolated bodybuilding exercises, athletic exercises train as many muscle groups and functions as possible at the same time. ④ They feared that weight lifting and building large muscles would cause players to lose flexibility and interfere with quickness and proper technique. ⑤ Today, though, experts understand the importance of strength training and have made it part of the game.

09 1등급 대비 고난도 2점 문제

고1 · 2021년 3월 40번

다음 글의 내용을 한 문장으로 요약하고자 한다. 빈칸 (A), (B)에 들어갈 말로 가장 적절한 것은?

In one study, researchers asked pairs of strangers to sit down in a room and chat. In half of the rooms, a cell phone was placed on a nearby table; in the other half, no phone was present. After the conversations had ended, the researchers asked the participants what they thought of each other. Here's what they learned: when a cell phone was present in the room, the participants reported the quality of their relationship was worse than those who'd talked in a cell phone-free room. The pairs who talked in the rooms with cell phones thought their partners showed less empathy. Think of all the times you've sat down to have lunch with a friend and set your phone on the table. You might have felt good about yourself because you didn't pick it up to check your messages, but your unchecked messages were still hurting your connection with the person sitting across from you.

* empathy: 공감

↓

The presence of a cell phone _____(A)_____ the connection between people involved in conversations, even when the phone is being _____(B)_____.

	(A)		(B)
①	weakens	......	answered
②	weakens	......	ignored
③	renews	......	answered
④	maintains	......	ignored
⑤	maintains	......	updated

[10～12] 다음 글을 읽고, 물음에 답하시오.

(A)

One day a poor man brought a bunch of grapes to a prince as a gift. He was very excited to be able to bring a gift for (a) him because he was too poor to afford more. He placed the grapes beside the prince and said, "Oh, Prince, please accept this small gift from me." His face beamed with happiness as he offered his small gift.

(B)

If the prince had offered the grapes to them, they might have made funny faces and shown their distaste for the grapes. That would have hurt the feelings of that poor man. He thought to himself that it would be better to eat all of them cheerfully and please (b) him. He did not want to hurt the feelings of that poor man. Everyone around him was moved by his thoughtfulness.

(C)

The prince thanked him politely. As the man looked at him expectantly, the prince ate one grape. Then (c) he ate another one. Slowly the prince finished the whole bunch of grapes by himself. He did not offer grapes to anyone near him. The man who brought those grapes to (d) him was very pleased and left. The close friends of the prince who were around him were very surprised.

(D)

Usually the prince shared whatever he had with others. He would offer them whatever he was given and they would eat it together. This time was different. Without offering it to anyone, (e) he finished the bunch of grapes by himself. One of the friends asked, "Prince! How come you ate all the grapes by yourself and did not offer them to any one of us?" He smiled and said that he ate all the grapes by himself because the grapes were too sour.

10

고1 · 2021년 11월 43번

주어진 글 (A)에 이어질 내용을 순서에 맞게 배열한 것으로 가장 적절한 것은?

① (B) − (D) − (C) ② (C) − (B) − (D)
③ (C) − (D) − (B) ④ (D) − (B) − (C)
⑤ (D) − (C) − (B)

11

고1 · 2021년 11월 44번

밑줄 친 (a)～(e) 중에서 가리키는 대상이 나머지 넷과 다른 것은?

① (a)   ② (b)   ③ (c)   ④ (d)   ⑤ (e)

12

고1 · 2021년 11월 45번

윗글의 왕자에 관한 내용으로 적절하지 않은 것은?

① 가난한 남자에게 포도 한 송이를 선물로 받았다.
② 가난한 남자의 감정을 상하게 하고 싶지 않았다.
③ 곁에 있던 어떤 이에게도 포도를 권하지 않았다.
④ 가지고 있는 어떤 것이든 평소에 다른 사람들과 나눴다.
⑤ 포도가 너무 시어서 혼자 다 먹지 못했다.

DAY 28

학습 Check!

▶ 몰라서 틀린 문항 × 표기 ▶ 헷갈렸거나 찍은 문항 △ 표기 ▶ ×, △ 문항은 다시 풀고 ✔ 표기를 하세요.

종료 시각	시 분 초	문항 번호	01	02	03	04	05	06	07	08	09	10	11	12
소요 시간	분 초	채점 결과												
초과 시간	분 초	틀린 문항 복습												

DAY 29

● 날짜 :   월   일   ● 시작 시각 :   시   분   초   ● 목표 시간 : 20분

※ 점수 표기가 없는 문항은 모두 2점입니다.

01

고1 · 2021년 9월 18번

다음 글의 목적으로 가장 적절한 것은?

Dear Mr. Dennis Brown,

We at G&D Restaurant are honored and delighted to invite you to our annual Fall Dinner. The annual event will be held on October 1st, 2021 at our restaurant. At the event, we will be introducing new wonderful dishes that our restaurant will be offering soon. These delicious dishes will showcase the amazing talents of our gifted chefs. Also, our chefs will be providing cooking tips, ideas on what to buy for your kitchen, and special recipes. We at G&D Restaurant would be more than grateful if you can make it to this special occasion and be part of our celebration. We look forward to seeing you. Thank you so much.

Regards,
Marcus Lee, Owner - G&D Restaurant

① 식당 개업을 홍보하려고
② 식당의 연례행사에 초대하려고
③ 신입 요리사 채용을 공고하려고
④ 매장 직원의 실수를 사과하려고
⑤ 식당 만족도 조사 참여를 부탁하려고

02

고1 · 2020년 11월 20번

다음 글에서 필자가 주장하는 바로 가장 적절한 것은?

When I was in high school, we had students who could study in the coffee shop and not get distracted by the noise or everything happening around them. We also had students who could not study if the library was not super quiet. The latter students suffered because even in the library, it was impossible to get the type of complete silence they sought. These students were victims of distractions who found it very difficult to study anywhere except in their private bedrooms. In today's world, it is impossible to run away from distractions. Distractions are everywhere, but if you want to achieve your goals, you must learn how to tackle distractions. You cannot eliminate distractions, but you can learn to live with them in a way that ensures they do not limit you.

① 자신에게 적합한 시간 관리법을 찾아야 한다.
② 집중을 방해하는 요인에 대처할 줄 알아야 한다.
③ 학습 공간과 휴식 공간을 명확하게 분리해야 한다.
④ 집중력 향상을 위해 정돈된 학습환경을 유지해야 한다.
⑤ 공공장소에서 타인에게 피해를 주는 행동을 삼가야 한다.

03

밑줄 친 a slap in our own face가 다음 글에서 의미하는 바로 가장 적절한 것은? [3점]

When it comes to climate change, many blame the fossil fuel industry for pumping greenhouse gases, the agricultural sector for burning rainforests, or the fashion industry for producing excessive clothes. But wait, what drives these industrial activities? Our consumption. Climate change is a summed product of each person's behavior. For example, the fossil fuel industry is a popular scapegoat in the climate crisis. But why do they drill and burn fossil fuels? We provide them strong financial incentives: some people regularly travel on airplanes and cars that burn fossil fuels. Some people waste electricity generated by burning fuel in power plants. Some people use and throw away plastic products derived from crude oil every day. Blaming the fossil fuel industry while engaging in these behaviors is a slap in our own face.

＊scapegoat: 희생양

① giving the future generation room for change
② warning ourselves about the lack of natural resources
③ refusing to admit the benefits of fossil fuel production
④ failing to recognize our responsibility for climate change
⑤ starting to deal with environmental problems individually

04

다음 글의 요지로 가장 적절한 것은?

Rather than attempting to punish students with a low grade or mark in the hope it will encourage them to give greater effort in the future, teachers can better motivate students by considering their work as incomplete and then requiring additional effort. Teachers at Beachwood Middle School in Beachwood, Ohio, record students' grades as A, B, C, or I (Incomplete). Students who receive an I grade are required to do additional work in order to bring their performance up to an acceptable level. This policy is based on the belief that students perform at a failure level or submit failing work in large part because teachers accept it. The Beachwood teachers reason that if they no longer accept substandard work, students will not submit it. And with appropriate support, they believe students will continue to work until their performance is satisfactory.

① 학생에게 평가 결과를 공개하는 것은 학습 동기를 떨어뜨린다.
② 학생에게 추가 과제를 부여하는 것은 학업 부담을 가중시킨다.
③ 지속적인 보상은 학업 성취도에 장기적으로 부정적인 영향을 준다.
④ 학생의 자기주도적 학습 능력은 정서적으로 안정된 학습 환경에서 향상된다.
⑤ 학생의 과제가 일정 수준에 도달하도록 개선 기회를 주면 동기 부여에 도움이 된다.

DAY 29

05

다음 도표의 내용과 일치하지 <u>않는</u> 것은?

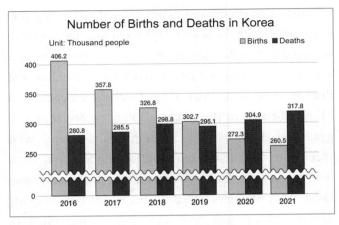

Number of Births and Deaths in Korea

Unit: Thousand people   ▫ Births ■ Deaths

The above graph shows the number of births and deaths in Korea from 2016 to 2021. ① The number of births continued to decrease throughout the whole period. ② The gap between the number of births and deaths was the largest in 2016. ③ In 2019, the gap between the number of births and deaths was the smallest, with the number of births slightly larger than that of deaths. ④ The number of deaths increased steadily during the whole period, except the period from 2018 to 2019. ⑤ In 2021, the number of deaths was larger than that of births for the first time.

06

다음 글의 밑줄 친 부분 중, 어법상 틀린 것은? [3점]

Like whole individuals, cells have a life span. During their life cycle (cell cycle), cell size, shape, and metabolic activities can change dramatically. A cell is "born" as a twin when its mother cell divides, ① producing two daughter cells. Each daughter cell is smaller than the mother cell, and except for unusual cases, each grows until it becomes as large as the mother cell ② was. During this time, the cell absorbs water, sugars, amino acids, and other nutrients and assembles them into new, living protoplasm. After the cell has grown to the proper size, its metabolism shifts as it either prepares to divide or matures and ③ differentiates into a specialized cell. Both growth and development require a complex and dynamic set of interactions involving all cell parts. ④ What cell metabolism and structure should be complex would not be surprising, but actually, they are rather simple and logical. Even the most complex cell has only a small number of parts, each ⑤ responsible for a distinct, well-defined aspect of cell life.

＊metabolic: 물질대사의 ＊＊protoplasm: 원형질

07

다음 빈칸에 들어갈 말로 가장 적절한 것을 고르시오.

Remember that _____ is always of the essence. If an apology is not accepted, thank the individual for hearing you out and leave the door open for if and when he wishes to reconcile. Be conscious of the fact that just because someone accepts your apology does not mean she has fully forgiven you. It can take time, maybe a long time, before the injured party can completely let go and fully trust you again. There is little you can do to speed this process up. If the person is truly important to you, it is worthwhile to give him or her the time and space needed to heal. Do not expect the person to go right back to acting normally immediately.

* reconcile: 화해하다

① curiosity
② independence
③ patience
④ creativity
⑤ honesty

08 **1등급 대비 고난도 3점 문제**

다음 빈칸에 들어갈 말로 가장 적절한 것을 고르시오. [3점]

For many people, *ability* refers to intellectual competence, so they want everything they do to reflect how smart they are — writing a brilliant legal brief, getting the highest grade on a test, writing elegant computer code, saying something exceptionally wise or witty in a conversation. You could also define ability in terms of a particular skill or talent, such as how well one plays the piano, learns a language, or serves a tennis ball. Some people focus on their ability to be attractive, entertaining, up on the latest trends, or to have the newest gadgets. However ability may be defined, a problem occurs when _____ _____. The performance becomes the *only* measure of the person; nothing else is taken into account. An outstanding performance means an outstanding person; an average performance means an average person. Period.

① it is the sole determinant of one's self-worth
② you are distracted by others' achievements
③ there is too much competition in one field
④ you ignore feedback about a performance
⑤ it is not accompanied by effort

09 1등급 대비 고난도 3점 문제

고1 · 2019년 11월 37번

주어진 글 다음에 이어질 글의 순서로 가장 적절한 것을 고르시오. [3점]

> Many studies have shown that people's health and subjective well-being are affected by ethnic relations. Members of minority groups in general have poorer health outcomes than the majority group.

(A) One possible answer is stress. From multiple physiological studies, we know that encounters with members of other ethnic-racial categories, even in the relatively safe environment of laboratories, trigger stress responses.

(B) But that difference remains even when obvious factors, such as social class and access to medical services are controlled for. This suggests that dominance relations have their own effect on people's health. How could that be the case?

(C) Minority individuals have many encounters with majority individuals, each of which may trigger such responses. However minimal these effects may be, their frequency may increase total stress, which would account for part of the health disadvantage of minority individuals.

① (A) − (C) − (B)   ② (B) − (A) − (C)
③ (B) − (C) − (A)   ④ (C) − (A) − (B)
⑤ (C) − (B) − (A)

10 1등급 대비 고난도 3점 문제

고1 · 2020년 9월 38번

글의 흐름으로 보아, 주어진 문장이 들어가기에 가장 적절한 곳을 고르시오. [3점]

> The few times that they do occur, it is the possessor who tries to make someone leave the circle.

Reciprocity can be explored in captivity by handing one chimpanzee a large amount of food, such as a watermelon or leafy branch, and then observing what follows. (①) The owner will be center stage, with a group of others around him or her, soon to be followed by newly formed groups around those who obtained a sizable share, until all food has been distributed. (②) Beggars may complain and cry, but aggressive conflicts are rare. (③) She will hit them over their head with her branch or bark at them in a high-pitched voice until they leave her alone. (④) Whatever their rank, possessors control the food flow. (⑤) Once chimpanzees enter reciprocity mode, their social rank no longer matters.

* reciprocity: 호혜주의, 상호의 이익

[11 ~ 12] 다음 글을 읽고, 물음에 답하시오.

In a society that rejects the consumption of insects there are some individuals who overcome this rejection, but most will continue with this attitude. It may be very (a) difficult to convince an entire society that insects are totally suitable for consumption. However, there are examples in which this (b) reversal of attitudes about certain foods has happened to an entire society. Several examples in the past 120 years from European-American society are: considering lobster a luxury food instead of a food for servants and prisoners; considering sushi a safe and delicious food; and considering pizza not just a food for the rural poor of Sicily. In Latin American countries, where insects are already consumed, a portion of the population hates their consumption and (c) associates it with poverty. There are also examples of people who have had the habit of consuming them and (d) encouraged that habit due to shame, and because they do not want to be categorized as poor or uncivilized. According to Esther Katz, an anthropologist, if the consumption of insects as a food luxury is to be promoted, there would be more chances that some individuals who do not present this habit overcome ideas under which they were educated. And this could also help to (e) revalue the consumption of insects by those people who already eat them.

11

고1 · 2022년 9월 41번

윗글의 제목으로 가장 적절한 것은?

① The More Variety on the Table, The Healthier You Become
② Edible or Not? Change Your Perspectives on Insects
③ Insects: A Key to Solve the World Food Shortage
④ Don't Let Uniqueness in Food Culture Disappear
⑤ Experiencing Various Cultures by Food

12

고1 · 2022년 9월 42번

밑줄 친 (a) ~ (e) 중에서 문맥상 낱말의 쓰임이 적절하지 <u>않은</u> 것은?

① (a)　　② (b)　　③ (c)　　④ (d)　　⑤ (e)

DAY 29

DAY 30

수능기출
전국연합학력평가 **20분 미니 모의고사**

● 날짜 :　월　일　● 시작 시각 :　시　분　초　● 목표 시간 : 20분

※ 점수 표기가 없는 문항은 모두 2점입니다.

01

고1 · 2023년 3월 20번

다음 글에서 필자가 주장하는 바로 가장 적절한 것은?

　It is difficult for any of us to maintain a constant level of attention throughout our working day. We all have body rhythms characterised by peaks and valleys of energy and alertness. You will achieve more, and feel confident as a benefit, if you schedule your most demanding tasks at times when you are best able to cope with them. If you haven't thought about energy peaks before, take a few days to observe yourself. Try to note the times when you are at your best. We are all different. For some, the peak will come first thing in the morning, but for others it may take a while to warm up.

＊alertness: 기민함

① 부정적인 감정에 에너지를 낭비하지 말라.
② 자신의 신체 능력에 맞게 운동량을 조절하라.
③ 자기 성찰을 위한 아침 명상 시간을 확보하라.
④ 생산적인 하루를 보내려면 일을 균등하게 배분하라.
⑤ 자신의 에너지가 가장 높은 시간을 파악하여 활용하라.

02

고1 · 2020년 11월 23번

다음 글의 주제로 가장 적절한 것은?

　The use of renewable sources of energy to produce electricity has increasingly been encouraged as a way to harmonize the need to secure electricity supply with environmental protection objectives. But the use of renewable sources also comes with its own consequences, which require consideration. Renewable sources of energy include a variety of sources such as hydropower and ocean-based technologies. Additionally, solar, wind, geothermal and biomass renewable sources also have their own impact on the environment. Hydropower dams, for example, have an impact on aquatic ecosystems and, more recently, have been identified as significant sources of greenhouse emissions. Wind, solar, and biomass also cause negative environmental impacts, such as visual pollution, intensive land occupation and negative effects on bird populations.

＊geothermal: 지열의　＊＊biomass: 에너지로 사용 가능한 생물체

① environmental side effects of using renewable energy sources
② practical methods to meet increasing demand for electricity
③ negative impacts of the use of traditional energy sources
④ numerous ways to obtain renewable sources of energy
⑤ effective procedures to reduce greenhouse emissions

03

고1 · 2021년 9월 26번

Paul Laurence Dunbar에 관한 다음 글의 내용과 일치하지 않는 것은?

Paul Laurence Dunbar, an African-American poet, was born on June 27, 1872. By the age of fourteen, Dunbar had poems published in the *Dayton Herald*. While in high school he edited his high school newspaper. Despite being a fine student, Dunbar was financially unable to attend college and took a job as an elevator operator. In 1893, Dunbar published his first book, *Oak and Ivy*, at his own expense. In 1895, he published the second book, *Majors and Minors*, which brought him national and international recognition. The poems written in standard English were called "majors," and those in dialect were termed "minors." Although the "major" poems in standard English outnumber those written in dialect, it was the dialect poems that brought Dunbar the most attention.

① 14세쯤에 *Dayton Herald*에 시를 발표했다.
② 고등학교 재학 시 학교 신문을 편집했다.
③ 재정상의 이유로 대학에 진학하지 못했다.
④ 두 번째 출판한 책으로 국내외에서 인정받게 되었다.
⑤ 표준 영어로 쓴 시들로 가장 큰 주목을 받았다.

04 [1등급 대비 고난도 3점 문제]

고1 · 2016년 11월 29번

(A), (B), (C)의 각 네모 안에서 문맥에 맞는 낱말로 가장 적절한 것은? [3점]

Feeling and emotion are crucial for everyday decision making. The neuroscientist Antonio Damasio studied people who were perfectly normal in every way except for brain injuries that damaged their emotional systems. As a result, they were (A) able / unable to make decisions or function effectively in the world. While they could describe exactly how they should have been functioning, they couldn't determine where to live, what to eat, and what products to buy and use. This finding (B) contradicts / supports the common belief that decision making is the heart of rational, logical thought. But modern research shows that the affective system provides critical (C) assistance / interference to your decision making by helping you make rapid selections between good and bad, reducing the number of things to be considered.

	(A)		(B)		(C)
①	able	……	contradicts	……	assistance
②	unable	……	contradicts	……	assistance
③	unable	……	contradicts	……	interference
④	unable	……	supports	……	interference
⑤	able	……	supports	……	interference

DAY **30**

05

다음 글의 밑줄 친 부분 중, 문맥상 낱말의 쓰임이 적절하지 않은 것은? [3점]

Suppose we know that Paula suffers from a severe phobia. If we reason that Paula is afraid either of snakes or spiders, and then ① establish that she is not afraid of snakes, we will conclude that Paula is afraid of spiders. However, our conclusion is reasonable only if Paula's fear really does concern either snakes or spiders. If we know only that Paula has a phobia, then the fact that she's not afraid of snakes is entirely ② consistent with her being afraid of heights, water, dogs or the number thirteen. More generally, when we are presented with a list of alternative explanations for some phenomenon, and are then persuaded that all but one of those explanations are ③ unsatisfactory, we should pause to reflect. Before ④ denying that the remaining explanation is the correct one, consider whether other plausible options are being ignored or overlooked. The fallacy of false choice misleads when we're insufficiently attentive to an important hidden assumption, that the choices which have been made explicit exhaust the ⑤ sensible alternatives.

* plausible: 그럴듯한   ** fallacy: 오류

06 **1등급 대비 고난도 2점 문제**

다음 빈칸에 들어갈 말로 가장 적절한 것을 고르시오.

People engage in typical patterns of interaction based on the relationship between their roles and the roles of others. Employers are expected to interact with employees in a certain way, as are doctors with patients. In each case, actions are restricted by the role responsibilities and obligations associated with individuals' positions within society. For instance, parents and children are linked by certain rights, privileges, and obligations. Parents are responsible for providing their children with the basic necessities of life — food, clothing, shelter, and so forth. These expectations are so powerful that not meeting them may make the parents vulnerable to charges of negligence or abuse. Children, in turn, are expected to do as their parents say. Thus, interactions within a relationship are functions not only of the individual personalities of the people involved but also of the role requirements associated with the _____ they have.

* vulnerable: 비난받기 쉬운   ** negligence: 태만

① careers
② statuses
③ abilities
④ motivations
⑤ perspectives

07 [1등급 대비 고난도 3점 문제]

다음 글에서 전체 흐름과 관계 <u>없는</u> 문장은? [3점]

Sensory nerves have specialized endings in the tissues that pick up a particular sensation. If, for example, you step on a sharp object such as a pin, nerve endings in the skin will transmit the pain sensation up your leg, up and along the spinal cord to the brain. ① While the pain itself is unpleasant, it is in fact acting as a protective mechanism for the foot. ② That is, you get used to the pain so the capacity with which you can avoid pain decreases. ③ Within the brain, nerves will connect to the area that controls speech, so that you may well shout 'ouch' or something rather less polite. ④ They will also connect to motor nerves that travel back down the spinal cord, and to the muscles in your leg that now contract quickly to lift your foot away from the painful object. ⑤ Sensory and motor nerves control almost all functions in the body — from the beating of the heart to the movement of the gut, sweating and just about everything else.

* spinal cord: 척수   ** gut: 장

08

글의 흐름으로 보아, 주어진 문장이 들어가기에 가장 적절한 곳을 고르시오. [3점]

> It has been observed that at each level of transfer, a large proportion, 80 − 90 percent, of the potential energy is lost as heat.

Food chain means the transfer of food energy from the source in plants through a series of organisms with the repeated process of eating and being eaten. (①) In a grassland, grass is eaten by rabbits while rabbits in turn are eaten by foxes. (②) This is an example of a simple food chain. (③) This food chain implies the sequence in which food energy is transferred from producer to consumer or higher trophic level. (④) Hence the number of steps or links in a sequence is restricted, usually to four or five. (⑤) The shorter the food chain or the nearer the organism is to the beginning of the chain, the greater the available energy intake is.

* trophic: 영양의

09

다음 글의 내용을 한 문장으로 요약하고자 한다. 빈칸 (A), (B)에 들어갈 말로 가장 적절한 것은?

One of the most powerful tools to find meaning in our lives is reflective journaling — thinking back on and writing about what has happened to us. In the 1990s, Stanford University researchers asked undergraduate students on spring break to journal about their most important personal values and their daily activities; others were asked to write about only the good things that happened to them in the day. Three weeks later, the students who had written about their values were happier, healthier, and more confident about their ability to handle stress than the ones who had only focused on the good stuff. By reflecting on how their daily activities supported their values, students had gained a new perspective on those activities and choices. Little stresses and hassles were now demonstrations of their values in action. Suddenly, their lives were full of meaningful activities. And all they had to do was reflect and write about it — positively reframing their experiences with their personal values.

＊hassle: 귀찮은 일

↓

Journaling about daily activities based on what we believe to be _____(A)_____ can make us feel that our life is meaningful by _____(B)_____ our experiences in a new way.

	(A)		(B)
①	factual	······	rethinking
②	worthwhile	······	rethinking
③	outdated	······	generalizing
④	objective	······	generalizing
⑤	demanding	······	describing

[10~12] 다음 글을 읽고, 물음에 답하시오.

(A)

"Grandma," asked Amy, "are angels real?" "Some people say so," said Grandmother. Amy told Grandmother that she had seen them in pictures. But (a) she also wanted to know if her grandmother had ever actually seen an angel. Her grandmother said she had, but they looked different than in pictures. "Then, I am going to find one!" said Amy. "That's good! But I will go with you, because you're too little," said Grandmother. Amy complained, "But you walk so slowly." "I can walk faster than you think!" Grandmother replied, with a smile.

(B)

"That was not an angel!" said Amy. "No, indeed!" said Grandmother. So Amy walked ahead again. Then, (b) she met a beautiful woman who wore a dress as white as snow. "You must be an angel!" cried Amy. "You dear little girl, do I really look like an angel?" (c) she asked. "You are an angel!" replied Amy. But suddenly the woman's face changed when Amy stepped on her dress by mistake. "Go away, and go back to your home!" she shouted.

(C)

So they started, Amy leaping and running. Then, she saw a horse coming towards them. On the horse sat a wonderful lady. When Amy saw her, the woman sparkled with jewels and gold, and her eyes were brighter than diamonds. "Are you an angel?" asked Amy. The lady gave no reply, but stared coldly at (d) her, leaving without saying a word.

(D)

As Amy stepped back from the woman, she stumbled and fell. (e) <u>She</u> lay in the dusty road and sobbed. "I am tired! Will you take me home, Grandma?" she asked. "Sure! That is what I came for," Grandmother said in a warm voice. They started to walk along the road. Suddenly Amy looked up and said, "Grandma, you are not an angel, are you?" "Oh, honey," said Grandmother, "I'm not an angel." "Well, Grandma, you are an angel to me because you always stay by my side," said Amy.

＊stumble: 비틀거리다   ＊＊sob: 흐느끼다

10

고1·2020년 6월 43번

주어진 글 (A)에 이어질 내용을 순서에 맞게 배열한 것으로 가장 적절한 것은?

① (B) − (D) − (C)
② (C) − (B) − (D)
③ (C) − (D) − (B)
④ (D) − (B) − (C)
⑤ (D) − (C) − (B)

11

고1·2020년 6월 44번

밑줄 친 (a) ~ (e) 중에서 가리키는 대상이 나머지 넷과 다른 것은?

① (a)　　② (b)　　③ (c)　　④ (d)　　⑤ (e)

12

고1·2020년 6월 45번

윗글의 Amy에 관한 내용으로 적절하지 않은 것은?

① 천사를 찾고 싶어했다.
② 한 여자의 드레스를 밟았다.
③ 말을 탄 여자로부터 친절한 대답을 들었다.
④ 할머니에게 집에 데려다 달라고 부탁했다.
⑤ 할머니를 천사라고 생각했다.

DAY 30

▶ 몰라서 틀린 문항 × 표기   ▶ 헷갈렸거나 찍은 문항 △ 표기   ▶ ×, △ 문항은 다시 풀고 ✔ 표기를 하세요.

종료 시각	시	분	초	문항 번호	01	02	03	04	05	06	07	08	09	10	11	12
소요 시간		분	초	채점 결과												
초과 시간		분	초	틀린 문항 복습												

MEMO

DAY 01
01⑤ 02② 03② 04④ 05④ 06⑤
07② 08③ 09④ 10④ 11① 12③

DAY 02
01② 02① 03① 04③ 05② 06②
07① 08② 09② 10④ 11④ 12④

DAY 03
01① 02① 03② 04④ 05④ 06③
07③ 08① 09④ 10③ 11① 12④

DAY 04
01⑤ 02① 03③ 04② 05④ 06④
07① 08③ 09① 10② 11② 12⑤

DAY 05
01③ 02⑤ 03① 04④ 05③ 06③
07① 08③ 09④ 10② 11③ 12⑤

DAY 06
01⑤ 02① 03⑤ 04④ 05② 06①
07② 08④ 09① 10④ 11② 12④

DAY 07
01② 02① 03③ 04② 05④ 06③
07② 08⑤ 09④ 10③ 11① 12⑤

DAY 08
01② 02④ 03① 04③ 05② 06③
07① 08④ 09① 10④ 11② 12③

DAY 09
01④ 02② 03① 04② 05④ 06④
07② 08⑤ 09④ 10⑤ 11② 12⑤

DAY 10
01① 02① 03② 04③ 05③ 06②
07③ 08⑤ 09② 10④ 11② 12④

DAY 11
01⑤ 02③ 03④ 04④ 05⑤ 06①
07① 08④ 09⑤ 10① 11② 12③

DAY 12
01③ 02⑤ 03④ 04④ 05③ 06③
07① 08② 09① 10② 11④ 12⑤

DAY 13
01① 02④ 03① 04③ 05④ 06②
07⑤ 08① 09④ 10⑤ 11③ 12⑤

DAY 14
01② 02② 03④ 04③ 05③ 06③
07③ 08⑤ 09① 10② 11⑤ 12②

DAY 15
01② 02⑤ 03⑤ 04③ 05④ 06②
07① 08① 09④ 10② 11① 12⑤

DAY 16
01② 02⑤ 03② 04④ 05⑤ 06⑤
07③ 08⑤ 09① 10④ 11⑤ 12⑤

DAY 17
01① 02④ 03① 04⑤ 05③ 06⑤
07② 08④ 09④ 10② 11② 12④

DAY 18
01① 02⑤ 03④ 04③ 05④ 06①
07① 08⑤ 09① 10④ 11③ 12④

DAY 19
01③ 02① 03② 04⑤ 05③ 06⑤
07① 08② 09④ 10① 11② 12④

DAY 20
01⑤ 02③ 03① 04② 05④ 06③
07② 08② 09① 10④ 11③ 12③

DAY 21
01③ 02① 03⑤ 04④ 05③ 06③
07④ 08④ 09③ 10④ 11① 12④

DAY 22
01⑤ 02① 03② 04④ 05② 06⑤
07① 08② 09③ 10④ 11③ 12④

DAY 23
01② 02③ 03② 04④ 05③ 06④
07① 08③ 09③ 10② 11⑤ 12④

DAY 24
01③ 02② 03④ 04⑤ 05⑤ 06③
07② 08⑤ 09① 10② 11② 12④

DAY 25
01③ 02① 03④ 04④ 05④ 06⑤
07④ 08② 09⑤ 10⑤ 11② 12④

DAY 26
01② 02④ 03① 04④ 05⑤ 06①
07⑤ 08④ 09③ 10⑤ 11④ 12②

DAY 27
01① 02① 03④ 04④ 05④ 06①
07③ 08④ 09⑤ 10③ 11② 12⑤

DAY 28
01② 02① 03⑤ 04④ 05② 06⑤
07② 08③ 09② 10③ 11② 12⑤

DAY 29
01② 02② 03④ 04⑤ 05⑤ 06④
07③ 08① 09② 10③ 11② 12④

DAY 30
01⑤ 02① 03⑤ 04② 05④ 06②
07② 08④ 09② 10② 11③ 12③

수능기출 베스트셀러
리얼 오리지널

수능기출 전국연합 학력평가
하루 20분 30일 완성

미니 모의고사

30 Days completed

2030
하루 20분   30일 완성

The Real series ipsifly provide questions in previous real test and
you can practice as real college scholastic ability test.

고1 영어
해설편

- 최신 **7개년 수능·모의평가 및 고1 학력평가** 문제 중 **우수 문항 총 360제 수록**
- 가볍게 하루 **12문제**를 20분씩 학습하는 [30일 완성] mini 모의고사
- 매일 영어 영역 [전 유형을 골고루] 풀 수 있는 체계적인 문항 배치
- 지문의 이해를 돕는 [구문 풀이와 자세한 해설] 및 고난도 문제 해결 꿀팁

수능 모의고사 전문 출판
입시플라이

DAY 01
01⑤ 02② 03② 04④ 05④ 06⑤
07② 08③ 09④ 10④ 11① 12③

DAY 02
01② 02① 03① 04③ 05② 06②
07① 08② 09② 10④ 11④ 12④

DAY 03
01① 02① 03② 04④ 05④ 06③
07③ 08① 09④ 10③ 11① 12④

DAY 04
01⑤ 02① 03③ 04② 05④ 06④
07① 08③ 09① 10② 11② 12⑤

DAY 05
01③ 02⑤ 03① 04④ 05③ 06③
07① 08③ 09④ 10② 11③ 12⑤

DAY 06
01⑤ 02① 03⑤ 04④ 05② 06①
07② 08④ 09① 10④ 11② 12④

DAY 07
01② 02① 03③ 04② 05④ 06③
07② 08⑤ 09④ 10③ 11① 12⑤

DAY 08
01② 02④ 03① 04③ 05② 06③
07① 08④ 09① 10④ 11② 12③

DAY 09
01④ 02② 03① 04② 05④ 06④
07② 08⑤ 09④ 10⑤ 11② 12⑤

DAY 10
01① 02① 03② 04③ 05③ 06②
07③ 08⑤ 09② 10④ 11② 12④

DAY 11
01⑤ 02③ 03④ 04④ 05⑤ 06①
07① 08④ 09⑤ 10① 11② 12③

DAY 12
01③ 02⑤ 03④ 04④ 05③ 06③
07① 08② 09① 10② 11④ 12⑤

DAY 13
01① 02④ 03① 04③ 05④ 06②
07⑤ 08① 09④ 10⑤ 11③ 12⑤

DAY 14
01② 02② 03④ 04③ 05③ 06③
07③ 08⑤ 09① 10② 11⑤ 12②

DAY 15
01② 02⑤ 03⑤ 04③ 05④ 06②
07① 08① 09④ 10② 11① 12⑤

DAY 16
01② 02⑤ 03② 04④ 05⑤ 06⑤
07③ 08⑤ 09① 10② 11⑤ 12⑤

DAY 17
01① 02④ 03① 04⑤ 05③ 06⑤
07② 08④ 09④ 10② 11② 12④

DAY 18
01① 02⑤ 03④ 04③ 05④ 06①
07① 08⑤ 09① 10④ 11③ 12④

DAY 19
01③ 02① 03② 04⑤ 05③ 06⑤
07① 08② 09④ 10① 11② 12④

DAY 20
01⑤ 02③ 03① 04② 05④ 06③
07② 08② 09① 10④ 11③ 12③

DAY 21
01③ 02① 03⑤ 04④ 05③ 06③
07④ 08④ 09③ 10④ 11① 12④

DAY 22
01⑤ 02① 03② 04④ 05② 06⑤
07① 08② 09③ 10④ 11③ 12④

DAY 23
01② 02③ 03② 04④ 05③ 06④
07① 08③ 09③ 10② 11⑤ 12④

DAY 24
01③ 02② 03④ 04⑤ 05⑤ 06③
07② 08⑤ 09① 10② 11② 12④

DAY 25
01③ 02① 03④ 04④ 05④ 06⑤
07④ 08② 09⑤ 10⑤ 11② 12④

DAY 26
01② 02④ 03① 04④ 05⑤ 06①
07⑤ 08④ 09③ 10⑤ 11④ 12②

DAY 27
01① 02① 03④ 04④ 05④ 06①
07③ 08④ 09⑤ 10③ 11② 12⑤

DAY 28
01② 02① 03⑤ 04④ 05② 06⑤
07② 08③ 09② 10③ 11② 12⑤

DAY 29
01② 02② 03④ 04⑤ 05⑤ 06④
07③ 08① 09② 10③ 11② 12④

DAY 30
01⑤ 02① 03⑤ 04② 05④ 06②
07② 08④ 09② 10② 11③ 12③

하루 20분 30일 완성
미니모의고사 고1 영어
해설편

Contents

● **Day 01** │ 20분 미니 모의고사	002쪽
● **Day 02** │ 20분 미니 모의고사	006쪽
● **Day 03** │ 20분 미니 모의고사	010쪽
● **Day 04** │ 20분 미니 모의고사	014쪽
● **Day 05** │ 20분 미니 모의고사	018쪽
● **Day 06** │ 20분 미니 모의고사	022쪽
● **Day 07** │ 20분 미니 모의고사	026쪽
● **Day 08** │ 20분 미니 모의고사	030쪽
● **Day 09** │ 20분 미니 모의고사	034쪽
● **Day 10** │ 20분 미니 모의고사	038쪽
● **Day 11** │ 20분 미니 모의고사	042쪽
● **Day 12** │ 20분 미니 모의고사	046쪽
● **Day 13** │ 20분 미니 모의고사	050쪽
● **Day 14** │ 20분 미니 모의고사	054쪽
● **Day 15** │ 20분 미니 모의고사	058쪽
● **Day 16** │ 20분 미니 모의고사	062쪽
● **Day 17** │ 20분 미니 모의고사	066쪽
● **Day 18** │ 20분 미니 모의고사	070쪽
● **Day 19** │ 20분 미니 모의고사	075쪽
● **Day 20** │ 20분 미니 모의고사	079쪽
● **Day 21** │ 20분 미니 모의고사	083쪽
● **Day 22** │ 20분 미니 모의고사	087쪽
● **Day 23** │ 20분 미니 모의고사	091쪽
● **Day 24** │ 20분 미니 모의고사	095쪽
● **Day 25** │ 20분 미니 모의고사	099쪽
● **Day 26** │ 20분 미니 모의고사	103쪽
● **Day 27** │ 20분 미니 모의고사	107쪽
● **Day 28** │ 20분 미니 모의고사	111쪽
● **Day 29** │ 20분 미니 모의고사	115쪽
● **Day 30** │ 20분 미니 모의고사	119쪽

수록된 정답률은 실제와 차이가 있을
수 있습니다. 문제 난도를 파악하는데
참고용으로 활용하시기 바랍니다.

DAY 01 › 20분 미니 모의고사

01 ⑤	02 ②	03 ②	04 ④	05 ④
06 ⑤	07 ②	08 ③	09 ④	10 ④
11 ①	12 ③			

---

01 학생 인력 추천 요청
정답률 86% | 정답 ⑤

다음 글의 목적으로 가장 적절한 것은?

① 과학 박물관 내 시설 이용 제한을 안내하려고
② 화학 박람회 일정이 변경된 이유를 설명하려고
③ 중학생을 위한 화학 실험 특별 강연을 부탁하려고
④ 중학교 과학 수업용 실험 교재 집필을 의뢰하려고
☑ 화학 박람회에서 실험을 도울 대학생 추천을 요청하려고

[본문 해석]

Sanchez 교수님께

제 이름은 Ellis Wight이고 Alexandria 과학 박물관의 관장입니다. 저희는 10월 28일 토요일에 지역 중학교 학생을 위한 화학 박람회를 개최합니다. 이 박람회의 목적은 안내자가 있는 실험을 통해 학생들이 과학에 관한 관심을 갖도록 장려하는 것입니다. 저희는 행사 기간 동안 실험을 도와줄 수 있는 대학생을 모집하고자 합니다. 저는 이 일에 적합하다고 생각되는 귀교의 화학과 학생 몇 명을 추천해 달라는 요청을 드리고자 연락드렸습니다. 그 학생들의 도움으로 참가자들이 훌륭한 경험을 하게 될 것이라 확신합니다. 빠른 시일 내에 귀하로부터 연락 받기를 기대하겠습니다.

Ellis Wight 드림

Why? 왜 정답일까?

박람회에서 진행할 실험을 도와줄 화학과 학생을 추천해달라는(I am contacting you to ask you to recommend some students from the chemistry department at your college who you think are qualified for this job.) 내용이므로, 글의 목적으로 가장 적절한 것은 ⑤ '화학 박람회에서 실험을 도울 대학생 추천을 요청하려고'이다.

- **hold** ⓥ 개최하다
- **fair** ⓝ 박람회
- **experiment** ⓝ 실험
- **department** ⓝ 학과, 부서
- **chemistry** ⓝ 화학
- **local** ⓐ 지역의, 지역의
- **recommend** ⓥ 추천하다
- **qualified for** ~에 적합한, 자격을 갖춘

구문 풀이

9행 I am contacting you to ask you to recommend some students
「ask + 목적어 + to부정사 : ~이 …하기를 요청하다」 선행사
from the chemistry department at your college [who (you think) are
주격 관·대↲ 삽입절 동사
qualified for this job].

---

02 긍정적인 진술의 마법
정답률 73% | 정답 ②

다음 글에서 필자가 주장하는 바로 가장 적절한 것은?

① 목표한 바를 꼭 이루려면 생각을 곧바로 행동으로 옮겨라.
☑ 자신감을 얻으려면 어려움을 긍정적인 진술로 바꿔 써라.
③ 어려운 일을 해결하려면 주변 사람에게 도움을 청하라.
④ 일상에서 자신감을 향상하려면 틈틈이 마술을 배워라.
⑤ 실생활에서 마주하는 도전을 피하지 말고 견뎌 내라.

[본문 해석]

마법은 우리 모두 자신의 삶에서 일어나기를 바라는 바이다. 여러분도 나처럼 *신데렐라* 영화를 사랑하는가? 그러면, 실제 삶에서, 여러분도 마법을 만들 수 있다. 여기 그 요령이 있다. 여러분이 직면하고 처리하는 모든 실시간의 어려움을 적어라. 그 어려움에 관한 진술을 긍정적인 진술로 바꾸어라. 여기서 여러분에게 한 예시를 제시하겠다. 만약 여러분이 아침 일찍 일어나는 것에 어려움을 겪는다면, 그러면 '나는 매일 일찍 아침 5시에 일어난다.'와 같은 긍정적인 진술을 써라. 일단 여러분이 이러한 진술을 적는다면, 마법과 자신감을 목격할 준비를 하라. 여러분은 단지 이러한 진술을 적음으로써 여러분이 생각하고 행동

하는 방식에 변화가 있다는 것에 놀랄 것이다. 어느 순간 여러분은 더 강력하고 긍정적이라고 느끼게 된다.

Why? 왜 정답일까?

일상생활에서 마법을 이루는 방법으로 긍정적인 진술 작성을 제시하고 있기 때문에(Just change the challenge statement into positive statements.), 필자가 주장하는 바로 가장 적절한 것은 ② '자신감을 얻으려면 어려움을 긍정적인 진술로 바꿔 써라.'이다.

- **magic** ⓝ 마법, 마술
- **statement** ⓝ 진술
- **struggle** ⓥ 어려움을 겪다
- **confidence** ⓝ 자신감
- **shift** ⓝ 변화
- **challenge** ⓝ 어려움, 도전
- **positive** ⓐ 긍정적인
- **witness** ⓥ 목격하다
- **surprise** ⓥ 놀라게 하다
- **powerful** ⓐ 강력한

구문 풀이

11행 You will be surprised that just by writing these statements,
조동사 + 동사원형 수동태 →종속접속사
there is a shift in the way you think and act.
관계부사 the way(= how)

---

03 산림 자원의 비시장적 가치를 고려할 필요성
정답률 49% | 정답 ②

다음 글의 주제로 가장 적절한 것은?

① necessity of calculating the market values of ecosystem services
생태계 도움의 시장 가치 산정의 필요성
☑ significance of weighing forest resources' non-market values
산림 자원의 비시장적 가치를 따져 보는 것의 의의
③ impact of using forest resources to maximize financial benefits
재정적 이익을 극대화하기 위한 산림 자원 이용의 영향
④ merits of balancing forests' market and non-market values
숲의 시장 가치와 비시장 가치의 균형을 맞추는 장점
⑤ ways of increasing the efficiency of managing natural resources
천연자원 관리의 효율성을 높이는 방법

[본문 해석]

천연자원의 관리자는 일반적으로 이용에 재정적 보상을 제공하는 시장 인센티브에 직면한다. 예를 들어, 삼림 지대의 소유자는 탄소 포집, 야생 동물 서식지, 홍수 방어 및 다른 생태계 도움을 위해 숲을 관리하기보다 나무를 베어 내는 시장 인센티브를 가지고 있다. 이러한 (생태계) 도움은 소유자에게 어떠한 재정적 이익도 제공하지 않으므로, 관리 결정에 영향을 미칠 것 같지 않다. 그러나 이러한 도움이 제공하는 경제적 이익은, 그것의 비시장적 가치에 근거하여, 목재의 경제적 가치를 초과할 수도 있다. 예를 들어, 유엔의 한 계획은 기후 조절, 수질 정화 및 침식 방지를 포함하여 열대 우림이 제공하는 생태계 도움의 경제적 이익이 시장 이익보다 헥타르당 3배보다 더 크다고 추정했다. 따라서 나무를 베는 것은 경제적으로 비효율적인데, 시장은 채취하는 사용보다 생태계 도움을 선호하게 하는 올바른 '신호'를 보내지 않고 있다.

Why? 왜 정답일까?

글 중간의 But 뒤로, 목재의 비시장적 가치가 시장적 가치를 넘어설 수도 있기 때문에(But the economic benefits provided by these services, based on their non-market values, may exceed the economic value of the timber.) 목재 채취가 경제적으로 비효율적일 수 있지만 이에 대한 올바른 시장 신호가 부족하다고 한다. 이러한 지적에 비추어볼 때, 글의 요지로 가장 적절한 것은 ② '산림 자원의 비시장적 가치를 따져 보는 것의 의의'이다.

- **natural resource** 천연 자원
- **reward** ⓝ 보상
- **carbon capture** 탄소 포집
- **habitat** ⓝ 서식지
- **ecosystem** ⓝ 생태계
- **timber** ⓝ 목재
- **estimate** ⓥ 추정하다
- **regulation** ⓝ 조절, 규제
- **prevention** ⓝ 방지, 예방
- **inefficient** ⓐ 비효율적인
- **extractive** ⓐ 채취의, 채광의
- **weigh** ⓥ (결정을 내리기 전에) 따져보다
- **financial** ⓐ 금전적인
- **exploitation** ⓝ 이용
- **wildlife** ⓝ 야생 동물
- **protection** ⓝ 보호
- **exceed** ⓥ 초과하다
- **initiative** ⓝ 계획
- **tropical** ⓐ 열대의
- **purification** ⓝ 정화
- **erosion** ⓝ 침식
- **favor A over B** B보다 A를 선호하다
- **significance** ⓝ 중요성, 의의
- **merit** ⓝ 이득

구문 풀이

11행 For example, a United Nations initiative has estimated that
접속새(~것)
the economic benefits of ecosystem services provided by tropical
주어 과거분사구

forests, including climate regulation, water purification, and erosion prevention, are over three times greater per hectare than the market benefits.

동사(복수)← / 배수사+비교급+ / than : 몇 배 더 ~한,

Why? 왜 정답일까?

and 앞뒤로 2개의 절이 연결되는 구조로, 첫 번째 주어인 **Lower magnesium levels** 뒤로 동사가 필요하기 때문에 **occurring**을 **occur**로 고쳐야 한다. 따라서 어법상 틀린 것은 ④이다.

Why? 왜 오답일까?

① pesticides and fertilizers를 꾸미는 주격 관계대명사로 **that**을 썼다.
② 주어가 동명사구인 'Fertilizing crops ~'이므로 단수 취급하여 **has**를 썼다.
③ 전치사처럼 쓰이는 **due to**(~ 때문에) 뒤로 동명사 또는 명사를 써야 하므로 **being**을 썼다. potassium은 being의 의미상 주어이다.
⑤ the plants가 '키워지는' 대상이므로 수동의 의미를 나타내는 과거분사 **grown**을 썼다.

---

04 Wilbur Smith의 생애
정답률 82% | 정답 ④

Wilbur Smith에 관한 다음 글의 내용과 일치하지 않는 것은?

① 역사 소설을 전문으로 하는 소설가였다.
② 아버지는 그가 글 쓰는 것을 지지하지 않았다.
③ 첫 번째 소설은 1962년까지 20번 거절당했다.
✓ 소설 *When the Lion Feeds*는 영화화되었다.
⑤ 죽기 전까지 49편의 소설을 출간했다.

[본문 해석]

『Wilbur Smith는 역사 소설을 전문으로 하는 남아프리카 소설가였다.』 Smith는 남아프리카의 사회 환경에 관해 글을 쓰는 언론인이 되고 싶었으나, 『그의 아버지는 그가 글을 쓰는 것을 절대로 지지하지 않았고 그가 현실적인 직업을 갖도록 강요했다.』 Smith는 더 공부하여 세금 회계사가 되었으나 결국에는 그가 사랑하는 글 쓰는 일로 돌아왔다. 『그는 첫 번째 소설, *The Gods First Make Mad*를 썼고 1962년까지 20번의 거절을 당했다.』 1964년에 Smith는 또 다른 소설, *When the Lion Feeds*를 출간했고, 그것이 전 세계에 팔리면서 성공을 거두었다. 『비록 영화화되지는 않았지만, 한 유명한 배우이자 영화 제작자가 *When the Lion Feeds*에 대한 영화 판권을 샀다.』 『2021년 죽기 전까지 그는 49편의 소설을 출간했으며 전 세계적으로 1억 4천만 부 이상을 판매했다.』

「」: ②의 근거 일치 / 「」: ③의 근거 일치 / 「」: ④의 근거 불일치 / 「」: ⑤의 근거 일치

Why? 왜 정답일까?

'A famous actor and film producer bought the film rights for *When the Lion Feeds*, although no movie resulted.'에서 소설 *When the Lion Feeds*의 영화 판권은 팔렸지만, 실제로 이것이 영화화되지는 않았다고 하므로, 내용과 일치하지 않는 것은 ④ '소설 *When the Lion Feeds*는 영화화되었다.'이다.

Why? 왜 오답일까?

① 'Wilbur Smith was a South African novelist specialising in historical fiction.'의 내용과 일치한다.
② '~ his father was never supportive of his writing ~'의 내용과 일치한다.
③ 'He wrote his first novel, *The Gods First Make Mad*, and had received 20 rejections by 1962.'의 내용과 일치한다.
⑤ 'By the time of his death in 2021 he had published 49 novels, ~'의 내용과 일치한다.

- novelist ⓝ 소설가
- be supportive of ~을 지지하다
- turn back to ~로 돌아오다
- historical ⓐ 역사적인
- tax accountant 세무사
- rejection ⓝ 거절

구문 풀이

13행 By the time of his death in 2021 he had published 49 novels,
~할 무렵 / 과거완료
selling more than 140 million copies worldwide.
분사구문(그리고 ~하다)

---

05 살충제와 비료의 사용으로 초래된 결과
정답률 45% | 정답 ④

다음 글의 밑줄 친 부분 중, 어법상 틀린 것은? [3점]

[본문 해석]

우리의 식품 속 미네랄의 감소는 우선적으로 많은 필수 영양소를 만들어 내는 토양에 있는 이로운 박테리아, 지렁이 그리고 벌레를 죽이고 식물이 영양소를 흡수하는 것을 막는 살충제와 비료를 사용한 결과이다. 농작물에 질소와 포타슘으로 비료를 주는 것은 마그네슘, 아연, 철 그리고 아이오딘의 감소로 이어져 왔다. 예를 들어 밀의 마그네슘 함량에서 평균적으로 약 30%의 감소가 있었다. 이는 부분적으로 식물이 마그네슘을 흡수하는 데 포타슘이 방해물이 되기 때문이다. 토양의 마그네슘 수치 감소는 산성 토양에서도 나타나는데, 지구상에 있는 농지의 약 70%가 현재 산성이다. 따라서 토양의 전반적인 특성은 식물 속 미네랄의 축적을 결정한다. 실제로 오늘날 우리의 토양은 덜 건강하고 그 위에서 길러진 식물도 그러하다.

- reduction ⓝ 감소
- in the first place 애초에, 우선
- fertilize ⓥ 비옥하게 하다, 비료를 주다
- absorption ⓝ 흡수
- characteristic ⓝ 특징, 특성
- essential ⓐ 필수적인, 본질적인
- uptake ⓝ 흡수, 활용
- decline ⓝ 감소 ⓥ 감소하다
- acidic ⓐ 산성의
- accumulation ⓝ 축적

구문 풀이

15행 Indeed, nowadays our soil is less healthy and so are the plants grown on it.
「so+동사+주어 : 동의 구문(~도 그렇다)

★★★ 1등급 대비 고난도 2점 문제

06 정직의 중요성
정답률 42% | 정답 ⑤

다음 글의 밑줄 친 부분 중, 문맥상 낱말의 쓰임이 적절하지 않은 것은?

[본문 해석]

정직은 모든 굳건한 관계의 근본적인 부분이다. 자신이 느끼는 바에 대해 솔직하게 말하고, 질문을 받았을 때 ① 정직한 의견을 줌으로써 그것을 여러분에게 유리하게 사용하라. 이 접근법은 여러분이 불편한 사회적 상황에서 벗어나고 정직한 사람들과 친구가 될 수 있도록 도와줄 수 있다. 삶에서 다음과 같은 분명한 방침을 따르라 — 절대로 거짓말을 하지 말라. 항상 진실만을 말한다는 평판이 ② 쌓이면, 여러분은 신뢰를 바탕으로 굳건한 관계를 누릴 것이다. (누군가가) 여러분을 조종하는 것도 더 어려워질 것이다. 거짓말을 하는 사람은 누군가가 거짓말을 ③ 폭로하겠다고 위협하면 곤경에 처하게 된다. 자신에게 진실하게 삶으로써, 여러분은 많은 골칫거리를 ④ 피할 것이다. 또한 여러분의 관계에는 거짓과 비밀이라는 해악이 없을 것이다. 진실이 아무리 고통스러울지라도 친구들에게 정직하게 대하는 것을 두려워하지 말라. 장기적으로 보면, 선의의 거짓말은 진실을 말하는 것보다 사람들에게 훨씬 더 많이 ⑤ 위안을 준다 (→ 상처를 준다).

Why? 왜 정답일까?

이 글의 주제는 정직함의 중요성(Honesty is a fundamental part of every strong relationship.)이고 ⑤가 포함된 바로 앞 문장에서 진실이 아무리 고통스러워도 정직하게 대하는 것을 두려워하지 말라는 내용으로 볼 때, 거짓말은 결국에는 더 큰 상처가 된다는 뜻을 나타낼 수 있도록 comfort를 hurt로 고치는 것이 적절하다.

- fundamental ⓐ 근본적인
- truthful ⓐ 정직한
- uncomfortable ⓐ 불편한
- reputation ⓝ 평판
- get into trouble 곤경에 처하다
- uncover ⓥ 폭로하다
- in the long term 장기적으로 보면
- to one's advantage ~에게 유리하게
- approach ⓝ 접근법
- policy ⓝ 방침, 정책
- manipulate ⓥ 조종하다
- threaten to ~하겠다고 위협하다
- no matter how 아무리 ~할지라도
- good intentions 선의

구문 풀이

4행 This approach can help you escape uncomfortable social situations and make friends with honest people.
준사역동사 / 원형부정사1 / 원형부정사2

★★ 문제 해결 꿀~팁 ★★

▶ 많이 틀린 이유는?
최다 오답인 ③의 uncover는 '폭로하다'라는 뜻으로 얼핏 주제와 반대되는 내용의 단어처럼 보이지만, 문맥 속에서는 거짓말을 '폭로하겠다'는 위협을 받으면 곤경에

처할 수 있다는 의미를 나타낸다. 이는 '관계에서 정직할 필요가 있다'는 주제를 뒷받침하기 위한 근거 중 하나이다.

▶ 문제 해결 방법은?
어휘 문제에서는 각 선택지의 단어 뜻을 정확히 알고 있는 것도 중요하지만 그 단어의 문맥적 쓰임을 파악하는 능력 또한 중요하다는 데 유의한다.

---

07 이동을 통한 인간의 진보와 자유 실현 정답률 45% | 정답 ②

다음 빈칸에 들어갈 말로 가장 적절한 것을 고르시오.

① secure – 안정되려는
✓ mobile – 이동하려는
③ exceptional – 특출나려는
④ competitive – 경쟁하려는
⑤ independent – 독립하려는

[본문 해석]

인간의 정신에는 이동하려는 욕구보다 더 근본적인 것은 없다. 그것은 우리의 상상력을 자극하고 삶을 변화시킬 기회로 가는 길을 열어주는 직관적인 힘이다. 그것은 진보와 개인의 자유의 촉매이다. 대중교통은 2세기 넘게 그 진보와 자유에 없어서는 안 될 것이었다. 운송 산업은 항상 한 목적지에서 다른 목적지로 이동하는 사람들을 실어 나르는 것 이상의 일을 해 왔다. 그것은 사람, 장소 그리고 가능성을 연결해 준다. 그것은 사람들이 필요로 하는 것과 좋아하는 것과 되고자 열망하는 것에 대한 접근성을 제공해 준다. 그렇게 하면서 그것은 공동체를 성장시키고, 일자리를 창출하고, 경제를 강화하고, 사회와 상업 네트워크를 확장하고, 시간과 에너지를 절약해 주며 수백만 명의 사람들이 더 나은 삶을 누릴 수 있도록 돕는다.

Why? 왜 정답일까?

'Public transportation has been vital ~' 이하로 인간의 이동을 가능케 하는 수단인 대중교통이 인간의 진보와 자유에 없어서는 안 될 것이었다는 설명이 제시되고 있다. 이를 근거로 볼 때, 빈칸이 포함된 문장 또한 인간의 '이동'이 매우 근본적이고 중요하다는 의미를 나타내야 한다. 따라서 빈칸에 들어갈 말로 가장 적절한 것은 ② '이동하려는'이다.

- fundamental ⓐ 근본적인
- spark ⓥ 자극하다, 유발하다
- public transportation 대중교통
- aspire ⓥ 열망하다
- secure ⓐ 안정된
- intuitive ⓐ 직관적인
- progress ⓝ 진보, 진전
- vital ⓐ 없어서는 안 되는, 필수적인
- strengthen ⓥ 강화하다
- exceptional ⓐ 특출난, 이례적인

구문 풀이

2행 It is the intuitive force [that sparks our imaginations and opens pathways to life-changing opportunities].
대명사 / 선행사 / 주격 관·대 동사1 / 동사2

★★★ **1등급 대비 고난도 3점 문제**

08 지적 능력 발달에 있어 천성보다 중요한 양육 정답률 44% | 정답 ③

다음 빈칸에 들어갈 말로 가장 적절한 것을 고르시오. [3점]

① by themselves for survival – 생존을 위해 스스로
② free from social interaction – 사회적 상호작용 없이
✓ based on what is around you – 여러분 주변에 있는 것에 따라
④ depending on genetic superiority – 유전적 우월성에 따라
⑤ so as to keep ourselves entertained – 우리 자신을 계속 즐겁게 하기 위해

[본문 해석]

1992년 프린스턴 대학의 한 연구에서, 연구 과학자들은 두 개의 다른 쥐 집단을 관찰했다. 한 집단은 글루타민산염 수용체에 대한 유전자를 변형함으로써 지적으로 우월하게 만들어졌다. 글루타민산염은 학습에 필수적인 뇌 화학 물질이다. 다른 집단도 역시 글루타민산염 수용체에 대한 유전자를 변형함으로써, 지적으로 열등하도록 유전적으로 조작되었다. 그 후 똑똑한 쥐들은 표준 우리에서 길러진 반면에 열등한 쥐들은 장난감과 운동용 쳇바퀴가 있고 사회적 상호작용이 많은 큰 우리에서 길러졌다. 연구가 끝날 무렵, 비록 지적 능력이 떨어지는 쥐들이 유전적으로 장애가 있었지만, 그들은 딱 유전적인 우월군들만큼 잘 수행할 수 있었다. 이것은 천성(선천적 성질)에 대한 양육(후천적 환경)의 진정한 승리였다. 유전자는 여러분 주변에 있는 것에 따라 작동하거나 멈춘다.

Why? 왜 정답일까?

빈칸이 있는 문장 바로 앞에서 양육, 즉 후천적 환경이 타고난 천성을 이겼다(a real triumph for nurture over nature)는 말로 연구 결과를 정리하고 있다. 따라서 빈칸에 들어갈 말로 가장 적절한 것은 '환경, 양육'과 같은 의미의 ③ '여러분 주변에 있는 것에 따라'이다.

- intellectually ⓐⓓ 지적으로
- receptor ⓝ 수용체
- inferior ⓐ 열등한
- triumph ⓝ 승리
- modify ⓥ 수정하다, 바꾸다
- genetically ⓐⓓ 유전적으로
- handicapped ⓐ 장애가 있는
- free from ~ 없이, ~을 면하여

구문 풀이

5행 The other group was genetically manipulated to be intellectually inferior, (which was) also done by modifying the gene for the glutamate receptor.
선행사 / 생략(계속적 용법) / 과거분사

★★ **문제 해결 꿀~팁** ★★

▶ 많이 틀린 이유는?
지적으로 우월하게(superior) 만들어진 쥐와 열등하게(inferior) 만들어진 쥐를 비교하는 실험 내용상 '유전적 우월함'을 언급하는 ④가 정답처럼 보인다. 하지만 실험의 결과를 보면, 결국 유전적으로 지능이 우월하게 만들어진 쥐와 열등하게 만들어진 쥐 사이에 차이가 없었다는 것이 핵심이다. 따라서 '유전적 우월함에 따라' 유전자가 작동하거나 작동하지 않을 수 있다는 의미를 완성하는 ④는 빈칸에 적절하지 않다.

▶ 문제 해결 방법은?
유전적으로 유도된 지능 차이보다도, 다른 어떤 요인이 쥐의 수행에 영향을 미칠 수 있었는지 살펴봐야 한다. 글 중반부를 보면, 열등한 쥐들이 자란 환경은 우월한 쥐들이 자란 환경에 비해 사회적 상호작용이 활발한 공간이었다고 한다. 나아가 빈칸 앞에서는 이 실험 결과가 유전보다도 양육, 즉 후천적 환경(nurture)의 중요성을 말해 준다고 한다. 따라서 빈칸에도 '환경'과 관련된 내용이 들어가야 한다.

---

09 이모티콘의 유용성 정답률 58% | 정답 ④

다음 글에서 전체 흐름과 관계 없는 문장은?

[본문 해석]

전자 통신에서 이모티콘이 널리 사용되고 있다는 점을 고려할 때, 중요한 문제는 인터넷 사용자들이 온라인상의 의사소통에서 감정을 이해하는 데 그것들이 도움을 주는가의 여부이다. ① 이모티콘, 특히 문자를 기반으로 한 것들은, 면대면을 통한 단서에 비해 훨씬 더 모호하며 결국 다른 사용자들에 의해 매우 다르게 해석될 수 있다. ② 그럼에도 불구하고, 연구는 그것들이 온라인상의 텍스트 기반 의사소통에서 유용한 도구라는 것을 보여준다. ③ 137명의 즉석 메시지 사용자들을 대상으로 한 연구는 이모티콘이 사용자들로 하여금 감정, 태도, 관심 표현의 정도와 방향을 정확하게 이해할 수 있게 해주고 이모티콘이 비언어적 의사소통에서 확실한 장점이라는 것을 밝혀냈다. ④ 사실, 언어적 의사소통과 비언어적 의사소통 간의 관계에 관한 연구는 거의 없었다. ⑤ 마찬가지로, 또 다른 연구는 이모티콘이 풍자의 표현에서 뿐만 아니라, 언어적 메시지의 강도를 강화하는 데 유용하다는 것을 보여주었다.

Why? 왜 정답일까?

이모티콘이 텍스트를 기반으로 하는 인터넷상의 의사소통에서 유용하다는 내용을 다룬 글로, ④는 언어적 의사소통과 비언어적 의사소통의 관계만을 언급하여 흐름에서 벗어난다. 따라서 무관한 문장은 ④이다.

- widespread ⓐ 널리 퍼진
- relative to ~에 비하여
- interpret ⓥ 해석하다
- strengthen ⓥ 강화하다
- electronic ⓐ 전자상의
- face-to-face ⓐ 면대면의
- definite ⓐ 확실한
- intensity ⓝ 강도

구문 풀이

1행 Given the widespread use of emoticons in electronic communication, an important question is whether they help Internet users to understand emotions in online communication.
~을 고려할 때(= Considering) / 주어 / 동사접속사(~인지 아닌지) / 준사역동사 / 목적어 / 목적격 보어

★★★ 1등급 대비 고난도 2점 문제

10 농경 생활로 인한 인간 사회의 변화
정답률 36% | 정답 ④

주어진 글 다음에 이어질 글의 순서로 가장 적절한 것을 고르시오.

① (A) – (C) – (B)
② (B) – (A) – (C)
③ (B) – (C) – (A)
✔④ (C) – (A) – (B)
⑤ (C) – (B) – (A)

[본문 해석]

구석기 시대에는 20 ~ 60명의 작은 무리가 먹을 것을 찾아 여기저기 돌아다녔다. 일단 농사를 짓기 시작하면서, 사람들은 자신의 농경지 근처에 정착할 수 있었다.

(C) 그 결과, 도시와 마을이 더 커졌다. 공동체 생활을 통해 사람들은 더 효율적으로 조직될 수 있었다. 그들은 식량과 자신들에게 필요한 다른 것들을 생산하는 일을 나눌 수 있었다.

(A) 어떤 노동자들은 농작물을 재배하는 한편, 다른 노동자들은 새로운 집을 짓고 도구를 만들었다. 마을 거주자들은 또한 일을 더 빨리 하려고 함께 일하는 법도 익혔다.

(B) 예를 들어, 도구 제작자들은 돌도끼와 돌칼을 만드는 작업을 함께 할 수 있었다. 그들은 함께 일하여 같은 시간 안에 더 많은 도구를 만들 수 있었다.

Why? 왜 정답일까?

농경이 시작되면서 사람들이 정착할 수 있었다는 내용의 주어진 글 뒤로, '그 결과' 도시와 마을이 생기고 사람들이 일을 분배할 수 있게 되었다고 설명하는 (C)가 먼저 연결된다. 이어서 (A)는 (C)에서 언급된 '분업'이 어떻게 이루어졌는지 언급하며, 사람들이 함께 일하는 법 또한 배우게 되었다고 이야기한다. (B)에서는 '함께 작업'하는 상황의 예를 제시하며 (A)를 보충 설명한다. 따라서 글의 순서로 가장 적절한 것은 ④ '(C) – (A) – (B)'이다.

- **Old Stone Age** 구석기 시대
- **wander** ⓥ 돌아다니다, 배회하다
- **in search of** ~을 찾아서
- **crop** ⓝ 작물
- **work together** 함께 일하다, 협력하다
- **axe** ⓝ 도끼
- **community** ⓝ 공동체, 지역사회
- **efficiently** [ad] 효율적으로
- **band** ⓝ (소규모) 무리
- **from place to place** 여기저기
- **settle down** 정착하다
- **dweller** ⓝ 거주자
- **share** ⓥ 나누다, 공유하다
- **as a result** 그 결과
- **organize** ⓥ 조직하다, 정리하다
- **divide up** ~을 나누다

구문 풀이

[3행] Once people began farming, they could settle down near their farms.
접속사(일단 ~한다면)

★★ 문제 해결 꿀~팁 ★★

▶ 많이 틀린 이유는?

글을 자세히 읽지 않고 연결어 중심으로만 보면, (B)가 주어진 글의 예시(For example)이고 (C)가 전체 글의 결론(As a result)일 것이라고 잘못 추론할 수 있다. 하지만, 내용적 단서가 중요하다. 주어진 글은 사람들이 농경을 시작하며 정착했다는 내용인데, (B)는 갑자기 '도구 제작자'를 언급하며, 이들이 업무를 분업해 담당했다는 설명을 제시하고 있다. 서로 전혀 다른 키워드로 보아 (B)가 주어진 글에 대한 예시라고 보기 어렵기 때문에 ②를 답으로 고르는 것은 적절하지 않다.

▶ 문제 해결 방법은?

사람들이 농경지 근처에 정착하여 살게 되면서, 마을이 성장하고 분업화가 일어나 (C), 누구는 농사를 짓고 누구는 도구를 만드는 한편 공동 작업도 활성화되었으며 (A), 공동 작업으로 더 쉽고 빠른 작업이 가능해졌다(B)는 흐름이다.

11-12 농업 발전과 생활 변화

[본문 해석]

초기 수렵 채집인 사회는 (a) 최소한의 구조만 가지고 있었다. 추장이나 장로 그룹이 주로 캠프나 마을을 이끌었다. 식량과 기타 필수 자원의 잉여분이 전임 추장이나 마을 의회를 지원할 만큼 (b) 충분한 경우가 드물었기 때문에 대부분의 이러한 지도자들은 다른 구성원들과 함께 사냥과 채집을 해야 했다. 『농업의 발전은 작업 패턴을 변화시켰다.』 초기 농부들은 심은 씨앗 1kg마다 3–10kg

---

의 곡물을 수확할 수 있었다. 이 식량/에너지 잉여분의 일부는 지역 사회에 환원되었고 족장, 마을 의회, 의술가, 사제, 전사와 같은 비농민에 대한 지원을 (c) 제한했다(→ 제공했다). 『그 대가로, 비농민들은 농업 인구에게 리더십과 안보를 제공하여, 그들이 식량/에너지 생산량을 지속적으로 늘리고 항상 더 많은 잉여를 제공할 수 있게 하였다.』——「」: 12번의 근거

개선된 기술과 유리한 조건으로, 농업은 기본 생필품의 지속적인 흑자를 창출했고, 인구 집단은 규모가 커졌다. 이러한 집단은 마을과 도시에 집중되었고, 인간의 업무는 더욱 (d) 전문화되었다. 목수, 대장장이, 상인, 무역업자, 선원과 같은 전문가들은 기술을 계발하고 자신의 시간과 에너지 사용을 더 효율적으로 하게 되었다. 『그들이 제공한 재화와 서비스로 인해 삶의 질 (e) 향상, 생활 수준 개선, 그리고 대부분의 사회에서 안정성의 향상을 가져왔다.』——「」: 11번의 근거

- **hunter-gatherer** ⓝ 수렵 채집인
- **vital** ⓐ 필수적인, 매우 중요한
- **reap** ⓥ (농작물을) 베어들이다
- **practice medicine** 의술을 행하다
- **security** ⓝ 안보
- **basic necessity** 기본 필수품
- **carpenter** ⓝ 목수
- **sailor** ⓝ 선원
- **stability** ⓝ 안정성
- **surplus** ⓝ 잉여, 흑자
- **sufficient** ⓐ 충분한
- **chieftain** ⓝ 수령, 두목
- **warrior** ⓝ 전사
- **yield** ⓝ 수확량
- **concentrate** ⓥ 집중되다
- **blacksmith** ⓝ 대장장이
- **bring about** ~을 야기하다, 초래하다

구문 풀이

[25행] The goods and services [they provided] brought about
주어 / 동사
an improved quality of life, a higher standard of living, and, for most
목적어1 / 목적어2
societies, increased stability.
목적어3

11 제목 파악
정답률 61% | 정답 ①

윗글의 제목으로 가장 적절한 것은?

✔① How Agriculture Transformed Human Society
농업은 어떻게 인간 사회를 바꿨나
② The Dark Shadow of Agriculture: Repetition
농업의 어두운 그늘: 반복
③ How Can We Share Extra Food with the Poor?
우리는 가난한 사람들과 남은 음식을 어떻게 나눌 수 있을까?
④ Why Were Early Societies Destroyed by Agriculture?
왜 초기 사회는 농업으로 파괴되었나?
⑤ The Advantages of Large Groups Over Small Groups in Farming
농업에 있어 대규모 집단이 소규모 집단보다 유리한 점

Why? 왜 정답일까?

농업 이전 사회에서는 비교적 단순했던 사회 구조가 농업 이후로 어떻게 변화했는지 설명하는 내용이다. 우선 작업의 패턴이 변하고(The development of agriculture changed work patterns.), 잉여 생산물이 늘어남에 따라 사회 규모도 바뀌면서 삶의 질도 향상되었다(~ an improved quality of life, a higher standard of living, and, for most societies, increased stability.)는 설명이 주를 이룬다. 따라서 글의 제목으로 가장 적절한 것은 ① '농업은 어떻게 인간 사회를 바꿨나'이다.

12 어휘 추론
정답률 58% | 정답 ③

밑줄 친 (a) ~ (e) 중에서 문맥상 낱말의 쓰임이 적절하지 않은 것은? [3점]

① (a) ② (b) ✔③ (c) ④ (d) ⑤ (e)

Why? 왜 정답일까?

In return 앞뒤는 농민이 비농민에게 무언가를 해준 '보답으로' 비농민 또한 농민에게 안보를 제공하여 생산에 집중하게 했다는 내용이다. 즉 (c)는 농민의 잉여 생산물이 비농민에 대한 지원을 '제공하는 데' 쓰였다는 의미일 것이므로, limited 대신 provided를 써야 자연스럽다. 따라서 문맥상 낱말의 쓰임이 적절하지 않은 것은 ③ '(c)'이다.

DAY 02 〉 20분 미니 모의고사

01 ②	02 ①	03 ①	04 ③	05 ②
06 ②	07 ①	08 ②	09 ②	10 ④
11 ④	12 ④			

---

01 암벽 등반 중 위기를 맞이한 필자 일행
정답률 69% | 정답 ②

다음 글에 나타난 'I'의 심경 변화로 가장 적절한 것은?

① joyful → bored
　즐거운　　지루한
② confident → fearful ✓
　자신 있는　　겁에 질린
③ nervous → relieved
　긴장한　　안도한
④ regretful → pleased
　후회하는　　즐거운
⑤ grateful → annoyed
　고마운　　짜증 난

[본문 해석]

Gregg와 나는 일출 이후에 암벽 등반을 하고 있었고, 아무런 문제가 없었다. 그래서 우리는 위험을 감수했다. "봐, 첫 번째 볼트가 바로 저기야. 난 분명히 거기까지 올라갈 수 있어. 식은 죽 먹기야."라고 나는 Gregg를 설득했고, 얼마 지나지 않아 나는 내가 꼼짝 못하게 되었다는 것을 알게 되었다. 그것은 식은 죽 먹기가 아니었다. 그 바위는 믿을 수 없게도 손으로 잡을 곳이 없었다. 나는 서툴게 절벽 면을 이리저리 가로질러 보았지만 갈 곳이… 결국 아래쪽밖에는 없었다. 만약 내가 거기까지 갈 수 있다면, 내 목숨을 구해줄 볼트는 내 손이 닿을 수 있는 곳에서 약 2피트 위에 있었다. 내 팔은 극도의 피로로 떨렸다. 나는 Gregg를 쳐다보았다. 내 몸은 목에서부터 발끝까지 공포로 얼어붙었다. 우리 사이에 밧줄이 묶여 있었다. 내가 떨어지면, 그도 나와 함께 떨어질 것이었다.

Why? 왜 정답일까?

첫 번째 볼트까지 쉽게 오를 수 있다며 자신했던(I can definitely climb out to it. Piece of cake. ~) 필자가 생각과 다른 현실에 공포감에 휩싸였다(My body froze with fright ~)는 내용이다. 따라서 'I'의 심경 변화로 가장 적절한 것은 ② '자신 있는 → 겁에 질린'이다.

- sunrise ⓝ 일출
- bolt ⓝ 볼트, 나사못
- piece of cake 식은 죽 먹기, 몹시 쉬운 일
- deceptively ⓐⓓ 현혹될 정도로
- clumsily ⓐⓓ 서툴게
- cliff ⓝ 절벽
- exhaustion ⓝ 피로
- fright ⓝ 공포
- fearful ⓐ 겁에 질린
- take a risk 위험을 감수하다
- definitely ⓐⓓ 확실히, 분명히
- pinned ⓐ 고정된
- handhold ⓝ 손으로 잡을 수 있는 곳
- back and forth 이리저리
- end up with 결국 ~에 처하다
- freeze ⓥ 얼어붙다
- confident ⓐ 자신 있는
- regretful ⓐ 유감스러운, 후회하는

구문 풀이

8행 The bolt [that would save my life], (if I could get to it), was
　　　주어　주격 관·대　　　　　　　　삽입절　　동사(단수)
about two feet above my reach.
대략, 약

---

02 사소한 관심의 영향
정답률 89% | 정답 ①

다음 글의 요지로 가장 적절한 것은?

① 사소한 관심이 타인에게 도움이 될 수 있다. ✓
② 사람마다 행복의 기준이 제각기 다르다.
③ 선행을 통해 자신을 되돌아볼 수 있다.
④ 원만한 대인 관계는 경청에서 비롯된다.
⑤ 현재에 대한 만족이 행복의 필수조건이다.

[본문 해석]

도움을 주는 것에 관해서 당신은 많은 것을 할 필요는 없다. 그저 다가가서 관심을 갖고 있다는 것을 보여주기만 하면 된다. 외로운 사람을 발견하면 가서 함께 앉아 있으면 된다. 혼자서 점심을 먹는 사람과 함께 일한다면, 그리고 그 사람에게 다가가서 함께 앉는다면 얼마 지나지 않아 그 사람은 더 사교적으로 변하기 시작할 것이고, 이 모든 것을 당신 덕분이라고 할 것이다. 한 사람의 행복은 관심에서 비롯된다. 세상에는 모든 이가 자신을 잊었거나 무시한다고 느끼는 사람들이 너무 많다. 지나가는 사람들에게 인사만 건네도, 누군가 (그들에게) 관심을 가져주는 것처럼, 그들은 자기 자신에 대해 기분이 좋아지기 시작할 것이다.

Why? 왜 정답일까?

도움은 많은 것을 해줄 필요가 없고, 관심을 갖고 있다는 것을 보여주기만 하면 된다(When it comes to helping out, you don't have to do much.)고 말하고 있기 때문에, 글의 요지로 가장 적절한 것은 ① '사소한 관심이 타인에게 도움이 될 수 있다.'이다.

- notice ⓥ 알아차리다
- social ⓐ 사회적인
- attention ⓝ 관심
- lonely ⓐ 외로운
- owe ⓥ 빚지다
- pass by 지나가다

구문 풀이

4행 If you work with someone who eats lunch all by themselves,
　　　　가정법　　　　　　　주격관계대명사
and you go and sit down with them, they will begin to be more social
　동사1　동사2
after a while, and they will owe it all to you.
곧(= soon)

---

03 고층 건물 건축에 이바지하는 엘리베이터
정답률 73% | 정답 ①

다음 글의 제목으로 가장 적절한 것은?

① Elevators Bring Buildings Closer to the Sky ✓
　엘리베이터는 빌딩이 하늘에 더 가까워지게 만든다
② The Higher You Climb, the Better the View
　더 높이 오를수록 경치가 더 좋다
③ How to Construct an Elevator Cheap and Fast
　엘리베이터를 싸고 빠르게 짓는 방법
④ The Function of the Ancient and the Modern City
　고대 및 현대 도시의 기능
⑤ The Evolution of Architecture: Solutions for Overpopulation
　건축의 진화 : 인구 과잉의 해결책

[본문 해석]

사람들은 도시 발전에 대해 생각할 때, 수직 운송 수단의 중요한 역할을 거의 고려하지 않는다. 실제로 매일 70억 회 이상의 엘리베이터 이동이 전 세계 높은 빌딩에서 이루어진다. 효율적인 수직 운송 수단은 점점 더 높은 고층 건물을 만들 수 있는 우리의 능력을 확장시킬 수 있다. Illinois 공과대학의 건축학과 교수인 Antony Wood는 지난 20년 간 엘리베이터의 발전은 아마도 우리가 높은 건물에서 봐 왔던 가장 큰 발전이라고 설명한다. 예를 들어, 건설 중인 사우디아라비아 Jeddah의 Jeddah Tower에 있는 엘리베이터는 660미터라는 기록적인 높이에 이를 것이다.

Why? 왜 정답일까?

'Efficient vertical transportation can expand our ability to build taller and taller skyscrapers.'에서 수직 운송 수단, 즉 엘리베이터가 더 높은 고층 건물을 짓도록 도와준다고 언급하는 것으로 보아, 글의 제목으로 가장 적절한 것은 ① '엘리베이터는 빌딩이 하늘에 더 가까워지게 만든다'이다.

- critical ⓐ 중요한
- transportation ⓝ 운송, 수송
- skyscraper ⓝ 고층 건물
- overpopulation ⓝ 인구 과잉
- vertical ⓐ 수직의
- expand ⓥ 확장하다
- under construction 건설 중인

구문 풀이

1행 When people think about the development of cities,
rarely do they consider the critical role of vertical transportation.
「부정어구 + 조동사 + 주어 + 동사원형 : 도치 구문」

---

04 녹차 포장 디자인 대회
정답률 96% | 정답 ③

Green Tea Packaging Design Competition에 관한 다음 안내문의 내용과 일치하지 않는 것은?

① 신제품 녹차를 위한 포장 상자 디자인 대회이다.
② Lokota County 주민들만 참가할 수 있다.
③ 출품작은 직접 방문하여 제출해야 한다. ✓
④ 평가 기준에 창의성이 포함된다.
⑤ 1등 수상자의 서명이 포장 상자에 인쇄될 것이다.

[본문 해석]

Green Tea Packaging Design Competition
(녹차 포장 디자인 대회)

「대회에서 TIIS Tea의 신제품 녹차 포장 상자를 디자인할 기회를 잡으세요!」 ←「」: ①의 근거 일치

마감일시: 2019년 12월 2일 오후 6시

「**참가자:** Lokota County 주민들만」 ←「」: ②의 근거 일치

세부사항
· 저희 회사명 'TIIS Tea'가 디자인에 보여야 합니다.
· 대회 주제는 '녹차로 친환경하기'입니다.
· 「출품작(JPG 포맷으로만)은 designmanager @tiistea.com으로 이메일을 통해 제출해야 합니다.」 ←「」: ③의 근거 불일치

평가 기준
· 기능성   · 「창의성」   · 친환경성 ←「」: ④의 근거 일치

상
· 1등: 1,000달러   · 2등: 500달러   · 3등: 250달러
「(1등 수상자의 서명이 포장 상자에 인쇄될 것입니다.)」 ←「」: ⑤의 근거 일치

대회에 관해 더 많이 알고 싶으시면 www.tiistea.com을 방문하세요.

Why? 왜 정답일까?

'Entries (JPG format only) should be submitted by email to designmanager @tiistea.com.'에서 출품작은 JPG 포맷으로 이메일을 통해 제출되어야 한다고 안내하므로, 안내문의 내용과 일치하지 않는 것은 ③ '출품작은 직접 방문하여 제출해야 한다.'이다.

Why? 왜 오답일까?

① 'Take the opportunity to design the packaging box for brand-new green tea products of TIIS Tea in the competition!'의 내용과 일치한다.
② 'Participants: Lokota County residents only'의 내용과 일치한다.
④ 'Evaluation Criteria / Creativity'의 내용과 일치한다.
⑤ '(The first-place winner's signature will be printed on the packaging box.)'의 내용과 일치한다.

· **packaging** ⓝ 포장
· **deadline** ⓝ 마감일
· **appear** ⓥ 나타나다
· **entry** ⓝ 출품작
· **criteria** ⓝ 기준
· **signature** ⓝ 서명
· **product** ⓝ 상품
· **participant** ⓝ 참가자
· **theme** ⓝ 주제
· **submit** ⓥ 제출하다
· **functionality** ⓝ 기능성

---

05 Say의 법칙   정답률 48% | 정답 ②

다음 글의 밑줄 친 부분 중, 어법상 틀린 것은? [3점]

[본문 해석]

경제이론인 Say의 법칙은 만들어진 모든 물품이 팔리기 마련이라고 주장한다. 모든 생산된 물품으로부터 나오는 돈은 다른 물품을 사는 데 사용된다. 한 회사가 물품을 팔 수 없게 되어서 직원들을 해고하고 공장의 문을 닫아야 하는 상황은 절대 있을 수 없다. 따라서, 경기 후퇴와 실업은 불가능하다. 지출의 정도를 욕조 안의 물 높이로 상상해 보아라. 사람들이 그들의 모든 수입을 물품을 사는 데 사용하기 때문에 Say의 법칙이 적용된다. 하지만 만약 사람들이 그들의 돈을 전부 사용하는 대신, 돈의 일부를 모은다면 무슨 일이 일어날까? 저축은 경제로부터 지출이 '누수'되는 것이다. 당신은 아마 물의 높이가 지금 낮아져서 경제에서 지출이 적어지는 것을 상상하고 있을 것이다. 그것은 회사들이 더 적게 생산하고 일부 직원들을 해고한다는 의미일 것이다.

Why? 왜 정답일까?

뒤에 'a firm finds that ~'과 같이 주어, 동사, 목적어를 모두 갖춘 완전한 문장이 연결되고 있다. 이 경우 관계대명사가 아닌 관계부사를 써야 하므로, **which**를 **where**로 바꾸어야 한다. 따라서 어법상 틀린 것은 ②이다.

Why? 왜 오답일까?

① 「be used to + 동사원형(~하기 위해 사용되다)」의 **buy**가 적절히 쓰였다.
③ 뒤에 'people use ~'라는 절이 나오므로, 접속사 **because**가 적절히 쓰였다.
④ 앞에 나온 **money**는 불가산명사로, 대명사로 받을 경우 단수 취급하므로 **it**이 적절히 쓰였다.
⑤ and 앞에 **producing**이라는 동명사가 있으므로 and 뒤에 **dismissing**이 적절히 쓰였다. 「mean + 동명사(~하는 것을 뜻하다)」를 기억해 둔다.

· **hold** ⓥ (주로 뒤에 that절과 함께) 주장하다
· **unemployment** ⓝ 실업
· **savings** ⓝ 저축(액)
· **spending** ⓝ 지출
· **dismiss** ⓥ 해고하다, 내보내다
· **earnings** ⓝ 수입, 소득
· **leakage** ⓝ 누수, 누출

구문 풀이

3행 There can never be a situation [where a firm finds {that it sell
　　　　　　　　　　　　　　　선행사　　관계부사　주어　동사
its goods and so has to dismiss workers and close its factories}].
　　　　　　　　　　　　　　　{ }: 목적어

---

06 삶을 사랑하는 법   정답률 61% | 정답 ②

다음 글의 밑줄 친 부분 중, 문맥상 낱말의 쓰임이 적절하지 않은 것은? [3점]

[본문 해석]

당신은 가끔 삶을 사랑하지 않는다고 느끼는가? 마치 마음 깊은 곳에서 뭔가가 빠진 것처럼? 왜냐하면 우리가 타인의 삶을 살고 있기 때문이다. 우리는 타인이 우리의 선택에 ① 영향을 주도록 허용한다. 우리는 그들의 기대감을 만족시키기 위해 노력하고 있다. 사회적 압력은 (우리를) 현혹시켜서, 우리 모두는 그것을 눈치채지도 못한 채 영향을 받는다. 우리의 삶에 대한 소유권을 잃어가고 있다는 것을 깨닫기도 전에, 우리는 결국 다른 사람들이 어떻게 사는지를 ② 무시하게(→ 부러워하게) 된다. 그러면, 우리는 더 푸른 잔디(타인의 삶이 더 좋아보이는 것)만 볼 수 있게 되어, 우리의 삶은 (만족할 만큼) 충분히 좋아질 수 없다. 당신이 원하는 삶에 대한 열정을 되찾기 위해서는 당신의 선택에 대한 통제력을 ③ 회복해야 한다. 당신 자신을 제외한 그 누구도 당신이 어떻게 살지를 선택할 수 없다. 하지만 어떻게 해야 할까? 기대감을 버리는 첫 단계는 자기 자신에게 ④ 친절하게 대하는 것이다. 자신을 먼저 사랑하지 않으면 다른 사람을 진정으로 사랑할 수 없다. 우리가 우리 있는 그대로를 받아들일 때, 타인의 ⑤ 기대를 위한 여지는 남지 않는다.

Why? 왜 정답일까?

타인의 기대를 만족시키는 삶을 살아갈 때에는 삶을 사랑할 수 없기에 자신을 친절하게 대하며 삶에 대한 주도권을 회복해 나가야 한다는 내용의 글이다. 흐름상 ② 앞뒤는 타인의 삶을 살다 보면 자신의 삶에 대한 통제력을 잃었음을 알기도 전에 이미 타인의 삶을 더 좋게 보고 '부러워하게' 된다는 문맥이므로, **ignoring**을 **envying**으로 고쳐야 한다. 따라서 문맥상 낱말의 쓰임이 적절하지 않은 것은 ②이다.

· **missing** ⓐ 빠진, 실종된
· **meet the expectation** 기대를 충족하다
· **impact** ⓥ 영향을 미치다
· **recover** ⓥ 회복하다
· **influence** ⓥ 영향을 미치다 ⓝ 영향
· **deceiving** ⓐ 현혹시키는, 속이는
· **ownership** ⓝ 소유권
· **get rid of** ~을 없애다

구문 풀이

11행 No one but yourself can choose {how you live}.
　　　~을 제외하고(= except)　　{ }: 간접의문문(어떻게 ~할지)

★★★ 1등급 대비 고난도 3점 문제

07 세계화로 강화된 집단 간 장벽   정답률 34% | 정답 ①

다음 빈칸에 들어갈 말로 가장 적절한 것을 고르시오. [3점]

✓ ① to build barriers – 장벽을 쌓도록
② to achieve equality – 평등을 성취하도록
③ to abandon traditions – 전통을 버리도록
④ to value individualism – 개인주의를 중시하도록
⑤ to develop technologies – 기술을 발전시키도록

[본문 해석]

Thomas Friedman의 2005년 저서의 제목인 *The World Is Flat*은 세계화가 필연적으로 우리를 더 가깝게 만들 것이라는 믿음에 근거하였다. 그것(세계화)은 그렇게 해왔지만 또한 우리가 장벽을 쌓도록 해왔다. 금융 위기, 테러 행위, 폭력적 분쟁, 난민과 이민자, 증가하는 빈부 격차 같은 인지된 위협들에 직면할 때, 사람들은 자신의 집단에 더 단단히 달라붙는다. 한 유명 소셜 미디어 회사 설립자는 소셜 미디어가 우리를 결합시킬 것이라고 믿었다. 어떤 면에서는 그래 왔지만 그것은 동시에 새로운 사이버 부족들에게 목소리와 조직력을 부여해 왔고, 이들 중 일부는 월드 와이드 웹(World Wide Web)에서 비난과 분열을 퍼뜨리는 데 그들의 시간을 보낸다. 지금까지 그래 온 만큼이나 현재 많은 부족들,

그리고 그들 사이의 많은 분쟁이 존재하는 것처럼 보인다. '우리와 그들'이라는 개념이 남아 있는 세계에서 이러한 부족들이 공존하는 것이 가능할까?

Why? 왜 정답일까?

세계화로 인해 각 집단은 가까워질 것으로 기대되었지만 한편으로 서로 간 단절이 심화되었다는 점을 지적한 글이다. 특히 마지막 두 문장에서 사이버 상의 각 부족들 별로 아직도 많은 분쟁이 존재하고 있으며 '우리'와 '그들'이라는 구별이 여전히 남아 있음(There seem now to be as many tribes, and as much conflict between them, ~.)을 언급하므로, 빈칸에 들어갈 말로 가장 적절한 것은 ① '장벽을 쌓도록'이다.

- inevitably **ad** 필연적으로, 불가피하게
- threat **n** 위협
- conflict **n** 분쟁, 갈등
- gap between rich and poor 빈부격차
- founder **n** 설립자
- organizational **a** 조직(상)의
- equality **n** 평등
- inspire **v** 고무하다, 자극하다
- crisis **n** 위기
- refugee **n** 난민
- cling to **v** ~에 달라붙다
- simultaneously **ad** 동시에
- coexist **v** 공존하다
- individualism **n** 개인주의

구문 풀이

10행 In some respects it has (united us), but it has simultaneously
생략(앞 문장에 나옴)
given voice and organizational ability to new cyber tribes, some of
목적격 관·대   선행사
whom spend their time spreading blame and division across the
「spend + 시간 + 동명사 : ~하는 데 …을 들이다」
World Wide Web.

★★ 문제 해결 꿀~팁 ★★

▶ 많이 틀린 이유는?
글 중간의 'it has simultaneously given voice and organizational ability to new cyber tribes'를 긍정적으로 해석하면 세계화가 새로운 사이버 부족에게 각자의 목소리를 낼 수 있게 도왔다는 의미로 보아 ④를 답으로 고를 수 있다. 하지만 이 문장의 'some of whom ~'에서 결국 자기만의 목소리를 내기 시작한 사이버 부족들이 서로 헐뜯고 분열되어 간다는 부정적인 결과에 주목하고 있으므로, '개인주의를 중시한다'는 부분적인 진술을 빈칸에 넣기는 부적합하다.

▶ 문제 해결 방법은?
결론에 따르면 이 글은 세계화와 소셜 미디어 발달로 생겨난 집단 간의 '갈등(conflict)'에 주목하고 있다. 따라서 세계화가 서로간의 '장벽을 세우는 데' 일조했다는 의미의 ①이 빈칸에 가장 적절하다.

★★★ 1등급 대비 고난도 2점 문제

08 작은 발전으로 이루는 큰 변화   정답률 36% | 정답 ②

글의 흐름으로 보아, 주어진 문장이 들어가기에 가장 적절한 곳을 고르시오.

[본문 해석]

결정적인 한순간의 중요성을 과대평가하고 매일 작은 발전을 이루는 것의 가치를 과소평가하기는 매우 쉽다. 너무 자주 우리는 거대한 성공에는 거대한 행동이 필요하다고 스스로를 납득시킨다. ① 체중을 줄이는 것이든, 결승전에서 이기는 것이든, 혹은 어떤 다른 목표를 달성하는 것이든 간에, 우리는 모두가 이야기하게 될 지축을 흔들 만한 발전을 이루도록 우리 스스로에게 압력을 가한다. ② 한편, 1퍼센트 발전하는 것은 특별히 눈에 띄지는 않지만, 장기적으로는 훨씬 더 의미가 있을 수 있다. 시간이 지남에 따라 이 작은 발전이 이룰 수 있는 변화는 놀랍다. ③ 다음과 같이 계산이 이루어지는데, 만일 여러분이 1년 동안 매일 1퍼센트씩 더 나아질 수 있다면, 끝마칠 때 즈음 여러분은 결국 37배 더 나아질 것이다. ④ 역으로, 1년 동안 매일 1퍼센트씩 나빠지면 여러분은 거의 0까지 떨어질 것이다. ⑤ 작은 승리나 사소한 패배로 시작한 것은 쌓여서 훨씬 더 큰 무언가가 된다.

Why? 왜 정답일까?

② 앞에서는 우리가 작은 변화의 가치를 과소평가하고 거대한 발전에 맞는 거대한 행동을 해나가도록 스스로를 압박한다는 내용이 주를 이룬다. 이에 이어 주어진 문장은 Meanwhile로 흐름을 전환하며 '1퍼센트만큼' 작게 발전하는 것이 당장은 눈에 띄지 않아도 장기적으로는 큰 의미를 가질 수 있다고 설명한다. ② 뒤의 문장은 주어진 문장에서 언급한 '1퍼센트의 발전'을 this tiny improvement라는 말로 바꾸며 '작은 발전'으로 인한 변화가 시간이 지난 후에는 놀라울 수 있음을 환기시킨다. 따라서 주어진 문장이 들어가기에 가장 적절한 곳은 ②이다.

- meanwhile **ad** 한편
- in the long run 장기적으로
- underestimate **v** 과소평가하다
- convince **v** 납득시키다, 설득하다
- put pressure on ~에 압박을 가하다
- tiny **a** 극히 작은
- decline **v** 떨어지다, 감소하다
- notable **a** 눈에 띄는, 두드러지는
- overestimate **v** 과대평가하다
- on a daily basis 매일
- massive **a** 거대한
- earthshaking **a** 극히 중대한
- conversely **ad** 역으로

구문 풀이

8행 (Whether it is losing weight, winning a championship, or
주어└동사 동명사 보어1   동명사 보어2
achieving any other goal), we put pressure on ourselves to make
동명사 보어3   ( ) : 부사절(~이든 …이든)
some earthshaking improvement [that everyone will talk about].
선행사   목적격 관계대명사

★★ 문제 해결 꿀~팁 ★★

▶ 많이 틀린 이유는?
최다 오답인 ④ 앞뒤는 Conversely를 기점으로 매일 조금씩 1년 동안 발전하는 경우와 나빠지는 경우가 적절히 대비를 이루는 맥락이다. 따라서 ④에 주어진 문장을 넣기에는 부적절하다.

▶ 문제 해결 방법은?
② 앞에서는 거창한 결과를 이룩하려면 거창한 행동이 필요하다고 생각한다는 내용이 주를 이루는데, ② 뒤에서는 '이 작은 발전(this tiny improvement)'에 관해 언급한다.
즉 ② 앞뒤 내용이 서로 상충하므로 Meanwhile(한편)으로 시작하며 흐름을 반전하는 주어진 문장이 ②에 들어가야 한다.

★★★ 1등급 대비 고난도 2점 문제

09 식단의 좋고 나쁨   정답률 53% | 정답 ②

다음 글의 내용을 한 문장으로 요약하고자 한다. 빈칸 (A), (B)에 들어갈 말로 가장 적절한 것은?

	(A)		(B)
①	incorrect 부정확한	······	limited to ~에 한정된
✓②	appropriate 적절한	······	composed of ~로 구성되는
③	wrong 틀린	······	aimed at ~을 목표로 하는
④	appropriate 적절한	······	tested on ~에 시험된
⑤	incorrect 부정확한	······	adjusted to ~에 맞춰진

[본문 해석]

미국 성인 10명 중 거의 8명이 '좋은 음식'과 '나쁜 음식'이 있다고 믿는다. 하지만, 우리가 상한 스튜, 독버섯, 또는 이와 유사한 것에 관해 이야기하고 있지 않는 한, 어떤 음식도 좋고 나쁨으로 분류될 수 없다. 하지만, 결국 건강에 좋은 식단이나 건강에 좋지 않은 식단이 되는 음식들의 조합이 있다. 가령 생브로콜리, 사과, 오렌지 주스, 삶은 두부와 당근과 같이 '좋은' 음식이라고 생각되는 음식만 먹는 성인의 경우를 생각해보라. 비록 이 모든 음식들이 영양이 풍부하지만, 그것들은 우리가 필요로 하는 충분히 다양한 영양소를 공급하진 않기에 결국 건강한 식단이 되지 않는다. 또는 튀긴 치킨을 가끔 먹지만, 다른 경우에는 튀긴 음식을 멀리하는 십 대의 경우를 예로 들어보자. 가끔 먹는 튀긴 치킨은 이 십 대의 식단을 궤도에서 벗어나게 하지 않을 것이다. 하지만 채소나 과일을 거의 먹지 않으면서 매일 튀긴 음식을 먹고, 간식으로 초대형 탄산음료, 사탕, 그리고 감자 칩으로 배를 가득 채우는 사람은 식단이 나쁜 것이다.

➡ 일반적인 믿음과 달리, 음식을 좋고 나쁨으로 정의하는 것은 (A) 적절하지 않고, 사실 건강에 좋은 식단이란 대체로 그 식단이 무엇으로 (B) 구성되는지에 의해 결정된다.

Why? 왜 정답일까?

첫 세 문장에서 음식을 절대적으로 좋고 나쁘다고 분류할 수는 없고(~ no foods can be labeled as either good or bad.), 그 조합이 중요하다(There are, however, combinations of foods that add up to a healthful or unhealthful diet.)고 말한다. 따라서 요약문의 빈칸 (A), (B)에 들어갈 말로 가장 적절한 것은 ② '(A) appropriate(적절한), (B) composed of(~로 구성되는)'이다.

- nearly **ad** 거의
- unless **conj** ~하지 않는 한

- spoiled ⓐ 상한
- label A as B A를 B라고 분류하다
- add up to 결국 ~이 되다
- broccoli ⓝ 브로콜리
- nutrient-dense ⓐ 영양이 풍부한
- nutrient ⓝ 영양분
- otherwise ⓐⓓ 그렇지 않으면
- load up on ~로 배를 가득 채우다

- poison mushroom 독버섯
- combination ⓝ 조합
- healthful ⓐ 건강에 좋은
- tofu ⓝ 두부
- a wide variety of 매우 다양한
- occasionally ⓐⓓ 가끔
- stay away from ~을 멀리하다
- composed of ~로 구성된

구문 풀이

2행 Unless we're talking about spoiled stew, poison mushrooms,
접속사(~하지 않는 한)
or something similar, however, no foods can be labeled as either
「A + be labeled as + B : A가 B라고 분류되다」
good or bad.

★★ 문제 해결 꿀~팁 ★★

▶ 많이 틀린 이유는?
두 번째 문장에서 음식을 절대적으로 좋고 나쁘다고 분류할 수 없다고 언급하는 것으로 보아, 음식의 분류가 '부정확하지' 않다, 즉 '정확하다'는 의미를 완성하는 ①과 ⑤의 incorrect를 (A)에 넣기는 부적절하다.

▶ 문제 해결 방법은?
글 초반에 however가 두 번 연속해 등장하여 주제를 강조한다. Consider 이하는 이 주제에 대한 사례이므로 결론만 가볍게 확인하며 읽어도 충분하다.

10-12 친절로 없어진 괴물

[본문 해석]

(A)
옛날 옛적에, 아름다운 궁전에 사는 한 왕이 있었다. 『왕이 없는 동안, 한 괴물이 궁전 문으로 접근했다.』 그 괴물이 너무 추하고 냄새가 나서 경비병들은 충격으로 얼어붙었다. 괴물은 경비병들을 지나 왕의 왕좌에 앉았다. 경비병들은 곧 정신을 차리고 안으로 들어가 괴물을 향해 소리치며 (a) 그에게 왕좌에서 내려올 것을 요구했다.
「: 12번 ①의 근거 일치」

(D)
경비병들이 나쁜 말을 사용할 때마다, 그 괴물은 더 추해졌고, 더 냄새가 났다. 『경비병들은 한층 더 화가 났다. 그들은 그 괴물을 겁주어 궁전에서 쫓아내려고 칼을 휘두르기 시작했다.』 하지만 (e) 그는 그저 점점 더 커져서 결국 방 전체를 차지했다. 그는 그 어느 때보다 더 추해졌고, 더 냄새가 났다.
「: 12번 ⑤의 근거 일치」

(B)
마침내 왕이 돌아왔다. 그는 현명하고 친절했으며, 무슨 일이 일어나고 있는지 알았다. 그는 어떻게 해야 할지 알고 있었다. 『그는 미소를 지으며 그 괴물에게 "나의 궁전에 온 것을 환영하오!"라고 말했다.』 왕은 그 괴물에게 (b) 그가 커피 한 잔을 원하는지 물었다. 괴물은 그 커피를 마시면서 더 작아지기 시작했다.
「: 12번 ②의 근거 일치」

(C)
왕은 (c) 그에게 약간의 테이크아웃 피자와 감자튀김을 제안했다. 경비병들은 즉시 피자를 시켰다. 『그 괴물은 왕의 친절한 행동에 몸이 계속 더 작아졌다.』 그리고 나서 (d) 그는 괴물에게 전신 마사지를 제공해 주었다. 『경비병들이 편안한 마사지를 도와주자 그 괴물은 매우 작아졌다.』 그 괴물에게 또 한 번의 친절한 행동을 베풀자, 그는 바로 사라졌다.
「: 12번 ③의 근거 일치」
「: 12번 ④의 근거 불일치」

- approach ⓥ 다가오다, 접근하다
- ugly ⓐ 추한
- in shock 충격을 받아
- come to one's senses 정신을 차리다
- get off ~을 떠나다
- take-out ⓐ 사서 가지고 가는
- gesture ⓝ 몸짓, (감정의) 표시, 표현
- brandish ⓥ 휘두르다
- take up ~을 차지하다

- gate ⓝ 문
- smelly ⓐ 냄새 나는, 악취가 나는
- throne ⓝ 왕좌
- shout at ~을 향해 소리치다
- wise ⓐ 현명한
- call for ~을 시키다, ~을 요구하다
- tiny ⓐ 아주 작은
- scare away ~을 겁주어 쫓아버리다
- than ever 그 어느 때보다

구문 풀이

(A) 6행 The guards soon came to their senses, went in, and shouted
at the monster, demanding that he (should) get off the throne.
요구 동사   생략   동사원형

(D) 4행 But he just grew bigger and bigger, eventually taking up the
「비교급 + and + 비교급 : 점점 더 ~한」   분사구문(그리고 ~하다)
whole room.

10 글의 순서 파악
정답률 77% | 정답 ④

주어진 글 (A)에 이어질 내용을 순서에 맞게 배열한 것으로 가장 적절한 것은?

① (B) – (D) – (C)
② (C) – (B) – (D)
③ (C) – (D) – (B)
④ (D) – (B) – (C) ✓
⑤ (D) – (C) – (B)

Why? 왜 정답일까?

왕이 없을 때 어느 괴물이 왕좌에 대신 앉아버렸다는 내용의 (A) 뒤에는, 경비병들이 괴물을 위협하며 쫓아내려 했으나 오히려 괴물의 몸집이 점점 커질 뿐이었다는 내용의 (D), 왕이 돌아와서는 사태를 파악하고 괴물에게 친절을 베풀기 시작했다는 내용의 (B), 왕이 음식과 마사지 등 친절한 행동을 보탤 때마다 괴물이 점점 작아져서 마침내는 없어졌다는 내용의 (C)가 차례로 연결되어야 한다. 따라서 글의 순서로 가장 적절한 것은 ④ '(D) – (B) – (C)'이다.

11 지칭 추론
정답률 75% | 정답 ④

밑줄 친 (a) ~ (e) 중에서 가리키는 대상이 나머지 넷과 다른 것은?

① (a)   ② (b)   ③ (c)   ④ (d) ✓   ⑤ (e)

Why? 왜 정답일까?

(a), (b), (c), (e)는 the monster, (d)는 the king을 가리키므로, (a) ~ (e) 중에서 가리키는 대상이 다른 하나는 ④ '(d)'이다.

12 세부 내용 파악
정답률 83% | 정답 ④

윗글에 관한 내용으로 적절하지 않은 것은?

① 왕이 없는 동안 괴물이 궁전 문으로 접근했다.
② 왕은 미소를 지으며 괴물에게 환영한다고 말했다.
③ 왕의 친절한 행동에 괴물의 몸이 계속 더 작아졌다.
④ 경비병들은 괴물을 마사지해 주기를 거부했다. ✓
⑤ 경비병들은 겁을 주어 괴물을 쫓아내려 했다.

Why? 왜 정답일까?

(C) 'As the guards helped with the relaxing massage, ~'에서 경비병들은 괴물을 마사지해주기를 거부하지 않고, 오히려 마사지를 도와줬음을 알 수 있다. 따라서 내용과 일치하지 않는 것은 ④ '경비병들은 괴물을 마사지해 주기를 거부했다.'이다.

Why? 왜 오답일까?

① (A) 'While the king was away, a monster approached the gates of the palace.'의 내용과 일치한다.
② (B) 'He smiled and said to the monster, "Welcome to my palace!"'의 내용과 일치한다.
③ (C) 'The monster continued to get smaller with the king's kind gestures.'의 내용과 일치한다.
⑤ (D) 'The guards ~ began to brandish their swords to scare the monster away from the palace.'의 내용과 일치한다.

DAY 02

DAY 03 〉 20분 미니 모의고사

01 ①	02 ①	03 ②	04 ④	05 ④
06 ③	07 ③	08 ①	09 ④	10 ③
11 ①	12 ④			

---

01 | 조류 관찰 클럽 가입 방법 문의 　　정답률 98% | 정답 ①

다음 글의 목적으로 가장 적절한 것은?

☑ 조류 관찰 클럽에 가입하는 방법을 문의하려고
② 조류 관찰 시 주의해야 할 사항을 전달하려고
③ 조류 관찰 협회의 새로운 규정을 확인하려고
④ 조류 관찰과 관련된 웹 사이트를 소개하려고
⑤ 조류 관찰 시 필요한 장비를 알아보려고

[본문 해석]
관계자분께

제 이름은 Michael Brown입니다. 저는 어렸을 때부터 조류 관찰자였습니다. 저는 항상 저의 뜰에서 새들을 관찰하여 모습과 소리로 새들을 식별하기를 즐겼습니다. 어제 저는 우연히 귀하의 클럽에 대한 기사를 읽었습니다. 저는 매년 조류 관찰을 하러 다니는 열정적인 조류 관찰자들의 공동체에 대해 알게 되어 놀라고 신났습니다. 저는 귀하의 클럽에 가입하기를 몹시 원하지만, 귀하의 웹 사이트가 공사 중인 것 같습니다. 이 이메일 주소 외에 다른 정보를 찾을 수가 없었습니다. 클럽에 가입하는 방법을 알고 싶습니다. 귀하의 답장을 기다리겠습니다.

Michael Brown 드림

Why? 왜 정답일까?

'I would like to know how to sign up for the club.'에서 클럽에 가입할 방법을 알고 싶다고 하므로, 글의 목적으로 가장 적절한 것은 ① '조류 관찰 클럽에 가입하는 방법을 문의하려고'이다.

- **childhood** ⓝ 어린 시절
- **identify** ⓥ 식별하다, 알아보다
- **surprised** ⓐ 놀란
- **community** ⓝ 공동체
- **annually** 〔ad〕 해마다
- **appear to** ~인 것 같다
- **except for** ~을 제외하고
- **look forward to** ~을 고대하다
- **yard** ⓝ 뜰, 마당
- **sight** ⓝ 모습, 광경, 시야, 시력
- **find out** ~을 알아내다
- **passionate** ⓐ 열정적인
- **birding** ⓝ 조류 관찰
- **under construction** 공사 중인
- **sign up for** ~에 가입하다
- **reply** ⓝ 응답

구문 풀이

6행 I was surprised and excited to find out about a community
　　　 감정 형용사　　　　　　부사적 용법(~해서)
of passionate bird-watchers who travel annually to go birding.
　　　　　　　　　　　　　　주격 관계대명사

★★★ 1등급 대비 고난도 2점 문제

02 | 인터넷의 등장으로 변화한 소비자의 구매 방법 　정답률 41% | 정답 ①

밑줄 친 popped out of the box가 다음 글에서 의미하는 바로 가장 적절한 것은?

☑ could not be kept secret anymore – 더 이상 비밀로 지켜질 수 없었다
② might disappear from public attention – 대중의 관심에서 사라질 수도 있었다
③ were no longer available to marketers – 마케터들에게 더 이상 이용 가능하지 않았다
④ became too complicated to understand – 너무 복잡해서 이해할 수 없었다
⑤ began to improve companies' reputations – 회사의 명성을 높이기 시작했다

[본문 해석]
인터넷의 등장으로 모든 것이 변했다. 제품 문제, 과잉 약속, 고객 지원 부족, 가격 차등과 같은, 소비자들이 마케팅 조직으로부터 실제로 경험했던 모든 문제가 갑자기 상자 밖으로 튀어나왔다. 통제된 의사소통이나 사업 체계조차 더는 존재하지 않았다. 소비자들은 한 회사와 그곳의 제품, 경쟁사, 유통 체계,

---

그리고 무엇보다도 그 회사의 제품과 서비스에 관해 이야기할 때의 진정성에 대해 그들이 알고 싶어 하는 것은 무엇이든 대개 인터넷을 통해 알 수 있었다. 그만큼이나 중요하게도, 인터넷은 소비자들이 제품, 경험 그리고 가치를 다른 소비자들과 쉽고 빠르게 비교할 수 있는 장(場)을 열었다. 이제 소비자는 마케터에게 대응하고, 즉시 공론의 장을 통해 그렇게 할 수단을 가졌다.

Why? 왜 정답일까?

'Just as important, ~' 이하로 인터넷이 등장하면서 소비자들은 제품 정보나 사용 경험을 자유롭게 공유하고 비교할 뿐 아니라 마케터들에게도 대응할 수 있는 공론의 장을 갖게 되었다고 언급한다. 따라서 밑줄 친 부분의 의미로 가장 적절한 것은 소비자들이 마케팅 조직과의 관계에서 경험했던 문제가 '이전처럼 묻혀 있지 못하고' 겉으로 나타나기 시작했다는 뜻의 ① '더 이상 비밀로 지켜질 수 없었다'이다.

- **pop out of** ~ 밖으로 튀어나오다
- **distribution** ⓝ 유통, 분배
- **talk back to** ~에 대응하다, 말대답하다
- **disappear** ⓥ 사라지다
- **reputation** ⓝ 명성
- **competitor** ⓝ 경쟁자
- **truthfulness** ⓝ 진정성
- **instantly** 〔ad〕 즉시
- **complicated** ⓐ 복잡한

구문 풀이

7행 Consumers could generally learn through the Web {whatever
　　　　동사구　　　　　　　　　　　　　　복합관계대명사(~하는: 무엇이든지)
they wanted to know about a company, its products, its competitors,
　　　　　　　전치사　　 목적어1　　　　 목적어2　　　 목적어3
its distribution systems, and, most of all, its truthfulness when talking
　　목적어4　　　　　　　　　　　　　 목적어5　　　　　　 분사구문(~할 때)
about its products and services}. 〔 〕: 문장의 목적어

★★ 문제 해결 꿀~팁 ★★

▶ **많이 틀린 이유는?**
인터넷 시대가 도래하면서 소비자들은 이전까지 서로 공유하지 못했던 제품 사용 경험이나 서비스에 대한 정보를 자유롭게 나눌 수 있게 되었다는 내용이다. ③은 인터넷 시대 이후 소비자들이 마케팅 회사와 겪는 문제를 마케터들이 접할 수 없게 되었다는 의미로, 글의 내용과 무관하다.

▶ **문제 해결 방법은?**
소비자들이 그간 겪었던 문제가 '상자 밖으로 튀어나와' 인터넷에서 논의되기 시작했다는 것이 글의 핵심적인 내용이므로, 밑줄 부분은 문제가 '더 이상 비밀이 아니게 되었다'는 의미로 이해할 수 있다.

---

03 | 자신을 평균 이상으로 보는 경향 　　정답률 66% | 정답 ②

다음 글의 주제로 가장 적절한 것은?

① importance of having a positive self-image as a leader
　리더로서 긍정적인 자아상을 갖는 것의 중요성
☑ our common belief that we are better than average
　우리가 평균보다 낫다는 일반적인 믿음
③ our tendency to think others are superior to us
　남들이 우리보다 낫다고 생각하는 우리의 경향성
④ reasons why we always try to be above average
　우리가 늘 평균보다 나아지려고 노력하는 이유
⑤ danger of prejudice in building healthy social networks
　건전한 사회적 네트워크를 구축할 때 편견의 위험성

[본문 해석]
우리는 우리가 사회적으로 바람직한 특성들을 많이 지니고 있고, 사회적으로 바람직하지 않은 특성들 대부분은 지니고 있지 않다고 믿는 경향이 있다. 예를 들어, 대다수의 일반 대중들은 자신이 보통 사람보다 더 지적이고, 더 공정하고, 편견을 덜 가지고, 자동차를 운전할 때 더 능숙하다고 생각한다. 이 현상은 너무 신뢰할 수 있고 어디서나 볼 수 있기 때문에 '여성들은 강하고, 남성들은 잘생겼으며, 모든 아이들은 평균 이상'인 Garrison Keillor의 허구적인 공동체의 이름을 따서 'Lake Wobegon effect'라고 알려지게 되었다. 고등학교 졸업반 학생 100만 명을 대상으로 한 설문조사에서, (학생들의) 70%는 자신이 리더십 능력에 있어 평균 이상이라고 생각했고, 2%만이 자신이 평균 이하라고 생각했다는 것을 발견했다. 다른 사람들과 잘 지내는 능력에 있어서, 모든 학생들은 자신이 평균 이상이라고 생각했고, 60%는 자신이 상위 10%에 속한다고 생각했고, 25%는 자신이 상위 1%에 속한다고 생각했다!

Why? 왜 정답일까?

사람들은 스스로 바람직한 특성은 더 많이 가지고 있고, 바람직하지 않은 특성은 덜 가지고 있다고 믿는 경향이 있음(We tend to believe that we possess a host of socially desirable characteristics, and that we are free of most of those that are socially undesirable.)을 설명하는 글이다. 뒤에 이어지는 여러 예시에도 사람들이 스스로를 특정 항목에서 '평균 이상'이라고 생각한다는 내용이 주를 이룬다. 따라서 글의 주제로 가장 적절한 것은 ② '우리가 평균보다 낮다는 일반적인 믿음'이다.

- **possess** ⓥ 지니다, 소유하다
- **desirable** ⓐ 바람직한
- **fair-minded** ⓐ 공정한
- **skilled** ⓐ 능숙한
- **automobile** ⓝ 자동차
- **reliable** ⓐ 믿을 만한
- **fictional** ⓐ 허구의
- **self-image** ⓝ 자아상
- **a host of** 여러, 다수의
- **characteristic** ⓝ 특성
- **prejudiced** ⓐ 고정 관념이 있는
- **behind the wheel** 운전할 때, 핸들을 잡은
- **phenomenon** ⓝ 현상
- **ubiquitous** ⓐ 도처에 있는
- **good-looking** ⓐ 잘생긴
- **superior to** ~보다 우월한

구문 풀이

1행 We tend to believe {that we possess a host of socially
{ } : to believe의 목적절
desirable characteristics}, and {that we are free of most of those that
대명사(= characteristics)
are socially undesirable}.

---

04 2022년 국가별 1인당 이산화 탄소 배출량 정답률 79% | 정답 ④

다음 도표의 내용과 일치하지 않는 것은?

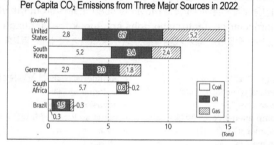

Per Capita CO$_2$ Emissions from Three Major Sources in 2022

(Country)	Coal	Oil	Gas
United States	2.8	6.7	5.2
South Korea	5.2	3.4	2.4
Germany	2.9	3.0	1.8
South Africa	5.7	0.8	0.2
Brazil	1.5	0.3	0.3

[본문 해석]
위 그래프는 2022년의 국가별 석탄, 석유, 천연가스에서 나온 1인당 이산화 탄소 배출량을 보여 준다. ① 석탄에서 나온 배출량은 보여진 다섯 개의 국가 중 두 번째로 낮았음에도 불구하고, 미국은 가장 높은 1인당 이산화 탄소 총배출량을 가졌다. ② 한국의 1인당 이산화 탄소 총배출량은 10톤이 넘고, 보여진 국가 중 두 번째로 높은 순위를 차지했다. ③ 독일은 한국보다 각각의 모든 세 가지 주요한 원천에서 더 낮은 1인당 이산화 탄소 배출량을 가졌다. ④ 남아프리카 공화국의 석탄으로부터의 1인당 이산화 탄소 배출량은 독일의 그것보다 세 배보다 더 높았다. ⑤ 브라질에서 석유는 브라질의 세 가지 주요한 원천 중에서 1인당 이산화 탄소 배출량의 가장 큰 원천이었고, 그것은 미국과 독일에서도 마찬가지였다.

Why? 왜 정답일까?

남아프리카 공화국의 석탄으로부터의 1인당 이산화 탄소 배출량은 5.7톤이고, 독일의 석탄으로부터의 1인당 이산화 탄소 배출량은 2.9톤이기 때문에 도표의 내용과 일치하지 않는 것은 ④이다.

- **emission** ⓝ 배출량
- **rank** ⓥ 순위에 들다
- **source** ⓝ 원천
- **per capita** 1인당
- **major** ⓐ 주요한

구문 풀이

2행 The United States had the highest total per capita CO$_2$
최상급
emissions, even though its emissions from coal were the second
비록   주어
lowest among the five countries shown.

---

05 또래 친구들이 우리에게 끼치는 영향 정답률 49% | 정답 ④

다음 글의 밑줄 친 부분 중, 어법상 틀린 것은? [3점]

[본문 해석]
긍정적이든 부정적이든, 우리의 부모님과 가족은 우리에게 강력한 영향을 미친다. 하지만 특히 우리가 어렸을 때, 훨씬 더 강한 영향을 주는 것은 우리의

친구들이다. 가족의 범위를 넘어서 우리의 (자아) 정체감을 확장하는 방법으로 우리는 흔히 친구들을 선택한다. 그 결과, 친구와 다른 사회 집단의 기준과 기대에 부합해야 한다는 압박감이 거세질 가능성이 있다. 발달 심리학자 Judith Rich Harris는 세 가지 주요한 힘이 우리의 발달을 형성한다고 주장하는데, 바로 개인적인 기질, 우리의 부모님, 우리의 또래들이다. 또래들의 영향은 부모의 영향보다 훨씬 더 강하다고 그녀는 주장한다. "아이들이 그들의 또래들과 공유하는 세상은 그들의 행동을 형성하는 것이고, 그들이 가지고 태어난 특성을 수정하는 것이며, 따라서 그들이 자라서 어떤 사람이 될지를 결정하는 것이다."라고 그녀는 말한다.

Why? 왜 정답일까?

주어인 Judith Rich Harris 뒤로 주어를 부연하는 관계절이 잇따른 후, 주어에 이어지는 동사가 나와야 하므로 arguing을 argues로 고쳐야 한다. 따라서 어법상 틀린 것은 ④이다.

Why? 왜 오답일까?

① 형용사 보어가 앞에 나와 주어와 동사가 도치된 구조이다. 즉 주어 our friends, 동사 are와 연결되어 보어 역할을 하는 비교급 형용사 stronger가 바르게 쓰였다.
② a way of(~할 방법으로)에 연결되는 동명사 expanding이 바르게 쓰였다.
③ 주어가 the pressure라는 단수 명사이므로 단수 동사 is가 알맞게 쓰였다. 'to conform ~'은 주어를 보충 설명한다.
⑤ 뒤에 나오는 관계절 'children share ~'가 목적어가 없는 불완전한 구조인 것으로 보아 that은 목적격 관계대명사로 알맞게 쓰였다.

- **positively** ⓐⓓ 긍정적으로
- **expand** ⓥ 확장하다
- **conform to** ⓥ ~에 부합하다, 순응하다
- **developmental** ⓐ 발달과 관련된
- **hence** ⓐⓓ 따라서, 이런 이유로
- **negatively** ⓐⓓ 부정적으로
- **sense of identity** ⓝ 정체감
- **intense** ⓐ 거센, 강력한
- **modify** ⓥ 수정하다

구문 풀이

2행 But even stronger, (especially when we're young), are
보어(도치) ( ) : 삽입절   동사
our friends.
주어(복수)

---

06 철학과 이성적 사고 과정의 태동 정답률 54% | 정답 ③

(A), (B), (C)의 각 네모 안에서 문맥에 맞는 낱말로 가장 적절한 것은?

	(A)	(B)	(C)
①	religion 종교	consistency 일관성	rationally 이성적으로
②	religion 종교	shift 변화	irrationally 비이성적으로
③ ✓	religion 종교	shift 변화	rationally 이성적으로
④	science 과학	shift 변화	irrationally 비이성적으로
⑤	science 과학	consistency 일관성	rationally 이성적으로

[본문 해석]
인류 역사의 시작부터 사람들은 세상과 세상 속 자신들의 위치에 관하여 질문해 왔다. 초기 사회에서는, 가장 기본적인 의문에 대한 대답이 (A) 종교에서 발견되었다. 그러나 몇몇 사람들은 전통적인 종교적 설명이 불충분하다는 것을 알게 되었고, 이성에 근거하여 답을 찾기 시작하였다. 이러한 (B) 변화는 철학의 탄생을 보여주었고, 우리가 아는 위대한 사상가들 중 최초의 사람은 밀레토스의 탈레스였다. 그는 우주의 본질을 탐구하기 위해 이성을 사용하였고, 다른 사람들도 이와 같이 하도록 권장하였다. 그는 자신의 추종자들에게 자신의 대답뿐만 아니라, 어떤 설명이 만족스럽다고 여겨질 수 있는가에 대한 생각과 함께 (C) 이성적으로 사고하는 과정도 전수해 주었다.

Why? 왜 정답일까?

(A) 'Some people, however, found the traditional religious explanations inadequate ~'에서 만물에 대한 전통적 설명이 '종교적'이었음을 드러내므로, (A)에는 'religion'이 적절하다.

(B) '~ they began to search for answers based on reason.'에서 종교적 설명에 불충분함을 느낀 사람들은 이성 쪽으로 '옮겨가기' 시작했다고 하므로, (B)에는 이를 요약할 말로 'shift'를 쓰는 것이 적절하다.

(C) 'He used reason to inquire into the nature of the universe, and encouraged others to do likewise.'에서 탈레스 이후 이성에 기반을 둔 사고

과정이 발달하기 시작하였음을 이야기하므로, (C)에는 'rationally'가 적절하다. 정답은 ③ '(A) religion(종교) – (B) shift(변화) – (C) rationally(이성적으로)'이다.

- **basic** ⓐ 기초적인, 기본적인
- **religious** ⓐ 종교적인
- **reason** ⓝ 이성
- **encourage** ⓥ 권장하다, 장려하다
- **satisfactory** ⓐ 만족스러운
- **traditional** ⓐ 전통적인
- **inadequate** ⓐ 불충분한
- **nature** ⓝ 본질, 본성
- **pass on** ~을 전수하다

구문 풀이

11행 He passed on to his followers not only his answers but also
주어 동사(~을 전수하다)   「not only+A(목적어1)+but also+
the process of thinking rationally, together with an idea of what kind
B(목적어2) : A뿐 아니라 B도」   전치사(동격) ← 의문사(어떤)
of explanations could be considered satisfactory.

★★★ 1등급 대비 고난도 2점 문제

07 사건의 중요성 인식에 영향을 주는 뉴스 보도의 양   정답률 44% | 정답 ③

다음 빈칸에 들어갈 말로 가장 적절한 것을 고르시오.
① accuracy – 정확성
② tone – 어조
☑ amount – 양
④ source – 근원
⑤ type – 유형

[본문 해석]

2001년 9월 11일 테러리스트 공격의 10주년 추모일이 다가오면서, 9/11 관련 언론 기사(의 양)가 추모일 바로 전후로 정점에 이르렀고, 그 후 몇 주 동안 급격히 줄어들었다. 그 시기 동안 실시된 조사는 시민들에게 지난 70년 동안 있었던 '특히 중요한' 두 가지 사건을 선택하도록 요청했다. 미디어 대선전이 시작되기 전인 추모일 2주 전, 응답자의 약 30퍼센트가 9/11을 언급했다. 그러나 추모일이 더 가까워지고, 미디어 보도가 증가함에 따라, 더 많은 응답자들이 9/11을 선택하기 시작했고, 그 수가 65퍼센트까지 올랐다. 그러나 보도가 2주 후에 이전 수준으로 줄어들자, 다시 한 번 참가자의 약 30퍼센트만이 그것을 지난 70년 동안의 특히 중요한 두 가지 사건으로 선택했다. 명백하게, 뉴스 보도의 양은 관찰자들이 그 보도에 노출될 때 그들 사이에서 *인지된* 문제의 중요성에 있어 큰 차이를 만들 수 있다.

Why? 왜 정답일까?

빈칸 앞의 두 문장에서 9/11 추모일이 가까워지면서 미디어 보도가 증가하자 사람들은 9/11을 '특히 중요한' 사건으로 더 많이 언급했지만, 미디어 보도가 다시 이전 수준으로 감소하자 9/11 보도를 중요한 사건으로 꼽는 사람들이 줄어들었다고 설명한다. 즉 어떤 사건에 대해 뉴스 보도가 '얼마나 많이' 이루어지는가에 따라 사건에 대한 사람들의 인식이 달라질 수 있다는 내용의 글이므로, 빈칸에 들어갈 말로 가장 적절한 것은 ③ '양'이다.

- **immediately** ⓐⓓ 바로 옆에
- **drop off** ⓥ 줄다
- **intensify** ⓥ (정도, 빈도, 강도가) 심해지다
- **perceive** ⓥ 인지하다
- **accuracy** ⓝ 정확성
- **anniversary** ⓝ 기념일
- **prior to** ~에 앞서
- **reportage** ⓝ 보도
- **significance** ⓝ 중요성

구문 풀이

12행 Two weeks later, though, after reportage had decreased to
부사(하지만) 시간 접속사(~한 후에)   과거완료
earlier levels, once again only about 30 percent of the participants
주어
placed it among their two especially important events of the past
동사
seventy years.

★★ 문제 해결 꿀~팁 ★★

▶ 많이 틀린 이유는?
예시 내용을 일반화하여 빈칸에 들어갈 말을 찾아야 하는데, 글에서 9/11 테러 사건이 '얼마나 많이' 보도되었는지를 언급하고 있을 뿐, 보도의 구체적인 유형을 나누고 있지는 않으므로 ⑤는 답으로 부적합하다.
▶ 문제 해결 방법은?
'the media treatment intensified ~', 'after reportage had decreased to earlier levels ~' 등을 참고하면 보도의 '양'이 곧 사건에 대한 사람들의 인식에 영향을 주는 요인임을 알 수 있다.

08 영화 속 외국어 대화에 자막이 없을 때의 효과   정답률 59% | 정답 ①

다음 빈칸에 들어갈 말로 가장 적절한 것을 고르시오. [3점]
☑ seeing the film from her viewpoint – 그녀의 시각에서 영화를 보고 있게
② impressed by her language skills – 그녀의 언어 능력에 감명받게
③ attracted to her beautiful voice – 그녀의 아름다운 목소리에 이끌리게
④ participating in a heated debate – 열띤 토론에 참여하게
⑤ learning the language used in the film – 영화에서 사용된 언어를 배우고 있게

[본문 해석]

영화에서 외국어가 사용되는 대부분의 경우 관객을 위해 대화를 통역하려고 자막이 사용된다. 하지만 외국어 대화가 자막 없이 (그리하여 대부분의 주요 대상 관객이 이해하지 못하게) 처리되는 경우가 있다. 영화가 그 언어를 할 줄 모르는 특정한 등장인물의 관점에서 주로 보여지는 경우에 흔히 이렇게 처리된다. 그러한 자막의 부재는 관객이 그 등장인물이 느끼는 것과 비슷한 몰이해와 소외의 감정을 느끼게 한다. 이것의 한 예를 *Not Without My Daughter*에서 볼 수 있다. 주인공 Betty Mahmoody가 페르시아어를 하지 못하기 때문에 이란인 등장인물들이 하는 페르시아어 대화에는 자막이 없으며, 관객은 그녀의 시각에서 영화를 보고 있게 된다.

Why? 왜 정답일까?

외국어 대화가 자막 없이 사용되는 경우는 그 언어를 할 줄 모르는 특정 등장인물의 시점에서 사건을 보게 만든다(~ if the movie is seen mainly from the viewpoint of a particular character who does not speak the language.)는 설명으로 보아, 빈칸에 들어갈 말로 가장 적절한 것은 ① '그녀의 시각에서 영화를 보고 있게'이다.

- **foreign** ⓐ 외국의, 낯선
- **translate** ⓥ 번역하다, 통역하다
- **viewer** ⓝ 관객
- **incomprehensible** ⓐ 이해할 수 없는
- **viewpoint** ⓝ 관점, 시점
- **alienation** ⓝ 소외
- **subtitle** ⓝ (영화·텔레비전 화면의) 자막
- **dialogue** ⓝ 대화
- **occasion** ⓝ 경우, 때
- **target audience** 주요 대상 관객
- **absence** ⓝ 부재
- **attract** ⓥ 끌어당기다

구문 풀이

3행 However, there are occasions [when foreign dialogue is left
선행사(경우) 관계부사   5형식 수동태
unsubtitled (and thus incomprehensible to most of the target
보어1(과거분사)   보어2(형용사)
audience)].

09 시 쓰기의 이점   정답률 62% | 정답 ④

다음 글에서 전체 흐름과 관계 없는 문장은?

[본문 해석]

시와의 개인적 관계를 발전시키는 것은 개인적인 능력과 전문적인 능력 모두에 한 개인으로서의 여러분에게 많은 이점을 가져다준다. ① 표현적 글쓰기가 면역 체계와 폐 기능을 향상시키고, 심리적 고통을 줄이고, 관계를 증진시킨다고 밝혀지면서, 시 쓰기는 신체적, 정신적 이점을 지닌 것으로 알려져 왔다. ② 시는 여러 정신 건강에 필요한 것들을 지원하고, 공감 능력을 개발하고, 자연 환경과 만들어진 환경 둘 다와의 관계를 재고하기 위해 오랫동안 사용되었다. ③ 시는 또한 인지 발달 시기를 적극적으로 겨냥하는 놀랍도록 효과적인 방법이며, 그 과정에서 여러분의 생산성과 과학적 창의력을 향상시킨다. ④ 시는 감정을 표현하는 쉽고 유용한 수단으로 여겨지지만, 여러분은 그것의 복잡성을 알면 좌절에 빠진다. ⑤ 간단히 말해서, 여러분이 그럴 기회를 준다면 시는 많은 것을 제공해줄 수 있다.

Why? 왜 정답일까?

시 쓰기의 이점을 두루 열거하는 글인데, ④는 시의 복잡함을 알면 우리가 좌절에 빠질 수 있다는 내용이므로 흐름상 어색하다. 따라서 전체 흐름과 관계 없는 문장은 ④이다.

- **engagement** ⓝ 관계, 참여
- **capacity** ⓝ 능력, 역량
- **lung** ⓝ 폐
- **distress** ⓝ 고통
- **empathy** ⓝ 공감, 감정 이입
- **cognitive** ⓐ 인지적인
- **frustration** ⓝ 좌절
- **poetry** ⓝ 시
- **immune system** 면역 체계
- **diminish** ⓥ 줄이다, 감소시키다
- **enhance** ⓥ 향상시키다
- **incredibly** ⓐⓓ 믿을 수 없을 정도로, 놀랍도록
- **productivity** ⓝ 생산성
- **complexity** ⓝ 복잡성

구문 풀이

1행 Developing a personal engagement with poetry brings
　　　　동명사구 주어　　　　　　　　　　　　　　동사(단수)
a number of benefits to you as an individual, in both a personal and
「a number of + 복수 명사 : 많은 ~」
a professional capacity.

★★★ 1등급 대비 고난도 2쩜 문제

10 현실적인 낙관론자와 비현실적인 낙관론자　　정답률 35% | 정답 ③

주어진 글 다음에 이어질 글의 순서로 가장 적절한 것을 고르시오.

① (A) – (C) – (B)　　　　② (B) – (A) – (C)
✔ (B) – (C) – (A)　　　　④ (C) – (A) – (B)
⑤ (C) – (B) – (A)

[본문 해석]

성공하려면 당신은 당신이 성공할 것이라고 믿는 것과 당신이 쉽게 성공할 것이라고 믿는 것 사이의 중요한 차이를 이해할 필요가 있다.

(B) 다시 말해서, 그것은 현실적인 낙관주의자가 되는 것과 비현실적인 낙관주의자가 되는 것 사이의 차이이다. 현실적인 낙관주의자들은 그들이 성공할 것이라고 믿을 뿐만 아니라, 그들이 신중한 계획과 적절한 전략을 선택하는 일 등을 통해 성공이 일어나도록 만들어야 한다고 믿는다.

(C) 그들은 그들이 장애물을 다룰 방법에 대해 심각하게 고려할 필요가 있다는 것을 인식한다. 이런 준비만이 일을 수행하는 그들 자신의 능력에 대한 자신감을 높여 준다.

(A) 반면에, 비현실적인 낙관론자들은 성공이 그들에게 일어날 것이라고, 즉 우주가 그들에게 자신의 모든 긍정적인 사고에 대해 보상할 것이라고 믿거나, 혹은 어떤 식으로든 그들이 하룻밤 사이에 장애물이 더 이상 없는 그런 종류의 사람으로 변모할 것이라고 믿는다.

Why? 왜 정답일까?

스스로 성공하리라 믿는 것과 쉽게 성공하리라고 믿는 것 사이의 차이를 구별할 필요가 있다고 언급한 주어진 글 뒤에는, 이를 현실적인 낙관론과 비현실적인 낙관론의 차이로 다시 언급하며 현실적인 낙관론자들에 관해 구체적으로 설명하기 시작하는 (B), 설명을 이어가는 (C), on the other hand로 흐름을 반전시키며 비현실적인 낙관론자에 관해 언급하는 (A)가 차례로 이어져야 자연스럽다. 따라서 글의 순서로 가장 적절한 것은 ③ '(B) – (C) – (A)'이다.

- **vital** ⓐ 중요한
- **optimist** ⓝ 낙관론자
- **transform** ⓥ 변모하다
- **obstacle** ⓝ 장애물
- **strategy** ⓝ 전략
- **unrealistic** ⓐ 비현실적인
- **somehow** [ad] 어떤 식으로든
- **overnight** [ad] 하룻밤 사이에
- **put another way** 다시 말해서
- **preparation** ⓝ 준비

구문 풀이

4행 Unrealistic optimists, on the other hand, believe that success
　　　　주어　　　　　　　　　　　　　　　동사　접속사1
will happen to them — that the universe will reward them for all their
　　　　　　　　접속사2
positive thinking, or that somehow they will be transformed overnight
　　　　　　　接속사3　　　　　　　　　　조동사 수동태
into the kind of person [for whom obstacles don't exist anymore].
선행사　　　　　「전치사 + 목적격 관계대명사」　자동사

★★ 문제 해결 꿀~팁 ★★

▶ 많이 틀린 이유는?
(B) 이후 단락의 순서를 정확하게 잡는 것이 풀이의 관건이다. (C)의 They 뒤에서 'giving serious thought to how they will deal with obstacles'는 (B)의 'they have to make success happen'에 이어진다. 즉 현실적 낙관주의자는 성공하기 위해서 자신이 장애물을 처리해야 함을 이해하고 있으며, 구체적 처리 방법을 고민하는 사람들이라는 설명이 (B) – (C)에 연달아 제시된다.

▶ 문제 해결 방법은?
순서 문제에서 대명사와 연결어는 중요한 단서이다. (A)의 on the other hand를 통해 이 글이 크게 보아 '현실적 낙관주의자 vs. 비현실적 낙관주의자'를 대조하는 글임을 파악한 뒤, (C)의 They가 둘 중 어느 대상을 가리키는지를 파악하는 데 주력하면 쉽게 답을 고를 수 있다.

11-12 단순히 유전자의 산물이 아닌 인간

[본문 해석]

20세기로 전환된 이래로 우리는 진단의 유전적인 원인, 즉 유전자 결정론이라 불리는 이론을 믿어 왔다. 이 모델 하에서 우리의 유전자(와 차후의 건강)은 태어날 때 결정된다. 우리는 자신의 DNA의 불행을 바탕으로 특정 질병을 물려받을 '운명'이다. 유전자 결정론은 가정 환경, 정신적 충격, 습관 또는 환경 내의 다른 어떤 것의 역할을 (a) 고려하지 않는다. 이 역학 관계에서 우리는 우리 자신의 건강과 안녕에 있어 (b) 능동적인 참여자가 아니다. 우리가 왜 그러겠는가? 만약 무언가가 미리 결정되어 있다면 우리의 DNA를 넘어서 어떤 것을 보는 것이 (c) 필요하지 않다. 하지만 과학이 신체와 (우리의 영양에서부터 관계, 그리고 인종적으로 억압적인 시스템에 이르기까지 다양한 형태인) 신체 주변 환경과의 상호 작용에 대해 더 많이 알게 될수록, 이야기는 더욱 (d) 단순해진다(→ 복잡해진다). 「우리는 단지 (유전적) 코딩의 표현이 아니라 우리의 통제 내부와 외부 모두에 있는 놀랍도록 다양한 상호 작용의 산물이다.」「일단 우리가 유전자가 (e) 운명이라는 이야기를 넘어서 보게 된다면 우리는 자신의 건강에 대한 소유권을 가질 수 있다. 이것은 우리가 한때 얼마나 '선택권이 없는' 상태였는지 알 수 있게 해 주며 우리에게 실제적이고 지속적인 변화를 만들어 낼 수 있는 능력을 부여한다.」——「」: 11번의 근거

- **genetic** ⓐ 유전적인
- **subsequent** ⓐ 차후의, 그다음의
- **predetermined** ⓐ 미리 결정된
- **simplistic** ⓐ 단순한
- **take ownership of** ~을 갖다, 소유하다
- **diagnosis** ⓝ 진단, 진찰
- **inherit** ⓥ 물려받다
- **racially** [ad] 인종적으로
- **remarkable** ⓐ 놀랄 만한

구문 풀이

23행 　　　　　　　　→「allow + A + to부정사 : A가 ~하도록 하다」
This allows us to see how "choiceless" we once were and
　　　　　　　　　　　「의문사 + 주어 + 동사 : 간접의문문」
empowers us with the ability to create real and lasting change.
「empowers A with B : A가 B할 능력을 부여하다」

11 제목 파악　　정답률 50% | 정답 ①

윗글의 제목으로 가장 적절한 것은?

✔ Health Is in Our Hands, Not Only in Our Genes
건강은 유전자에만 있는 것이 아니라 우리 손 안에 있다
② Genetics: A Solution to Enhance Human Wellness
유전학: 인간 건강을 증진하는 데 있어 해결책
③ How Did DNA Dominate Over Environment in Biology?
어떻게 DNA가 생물학에서 환경을 지배하였을까?
④ Never Be Confident in Your Health, but Keep Checking!
건강을 과신하지 말고, 계속 점검하세요
⑤ Why Scientific Innovation Affects Our Social Interactions
왜 과학적 혁신은 사회적 상호작용에 영향을 미치는가

Why? 왜 정답일까?

마지막 세 문장에서 인간은 단순히 유전자의 산물이 아니며, 자신의 건강을 직접 통제하고 관리할 수 있는 존재임을 설명하고 있다(Once we see beyond the narrative that genetics are destiny, we can take ownership of our health). 따라서 글의 제목으로 가장 적절한 것은 ① '건강은 유전자에만 있는 것이 아니라 우리 손 안에 있다'이다.

12 어휘 추론　　정답률 57% | 정답 ④

밑줄 친 (a) ~ (e) 중에서 문맥상 낱말의 쓰임이 적절하지 않은 것은? [3점]

① (a)　② (b)　③ (c)　✔ (d)　⑤ (e)

Why? 왜 정답일까?

(d)가 포함된 'But the more science ~' 문장을 기점으로 글의 흐름이 반전되고 있다. 앞에서는 인간의 신체와 건강이 유전자에 의해 '운명적으로' 결정된다고 보는 유전자 결정론의 시각을 설명하는 반면, 뒤에서는 인간이 단순한 유전자의 발현이 아니라 건강을 위한 행동을 선택할 수 있는 존재라는 내용이 이어지고 있다. 이러한 흐름으로 볼 때, 유전자 외의 다른 요소를 고려하기 시작하면 건강에 대한 이해가 더 '복잡해진다'는 의미로 (d)의 simplistic을 complex로 고쳐야 한다. 따라서 문맥상 낱말의 쓰임이 적절하지 않은 것은 ④ '(d)'이다.

DAY 04 · 20분 미니 모의고사

01 ⑤	02 ①	03 ③	04 ②	05 ④
06 ④	07 ①	08 ③	09 ①	10 ②
11 ②	12 ⑤			

---

01 회의 안건을 사전에 작성해 공유하기 정답률 88% | 정답 ⑤

다음 글에서 필자가 주장하는 바로 가장 적절한 것은?
① 회의 결과는 빠짐없이 작성해서 공개해야 한다.
② 중요한 정보는 공식 회의를 통해 전달해야 한다.
③ 생산성 향상을 위해 정기적인 평가회가 필요하다.
④ 모든 참석자의 동의를 받아서 회의를 열어야 한다.
☑ 회의에서 다룰 사항은 미리 작성해서 공유해야 한다.

[본문 해석]
회의는 창의적 사고를 촉진하며, 당신이 혼자서는 절대 떠올리지 못했을 만한 아이디어들을 당신에게 제공할 수 있다. 그러나, 평균적으로, 회의 참석자들은 회의 시간의 대략 3분의 1 정도를 비생산적으로 여긴다. 하지만 당신은 사전에 잘 준비함으로써 회의를 더 생산적이고 유용하게 만들 수 있다. 당신은 논의하게 될 사항들의 목록을 만들어 그 목록을 회의 전에 다른 회의 참석자들에게 공유해야 한다. 그것은 참석자들이 회의에서 무엇을 기대할지를 알고 회의 참석을 준비할 수 있도록 만들어 준다.

Why? 왜 정답일까?
'You should create a list of items to be discussed and share your list with other participants before a meeting.'에서 회의 전 논의 사항을 미리 작성해 공유하는 것이 좋다고 하므로, 필자가 주장하는 바로 가장 적절한 것은 ⑤ '회의에서 다룰 사항은 미리 작성해서 공유해야 한다.'이다.

- encourage ⓥ 촉진하다, 격려하다
- on average 평균적으로
- consider ⓥ 여기다
- unproductive ⓐ 비생산적인
- discuss ⓥ 논의하다
- allow ⓥ 허락하다, 허가하다
- creative ⓐ 창의적인
- participant ⓝ 참가자
- meeting time 회의 시간
- productive ⓐ 생산적인
- expect ⓥ 기대하다

구문 풀이

8행 It allows them to know {what to expect in your meeting} and
  동사   목적어 목적격 보어1   { } : 명사구(무엇을 ~할지)
(to) prepare to participate.
목적격 보어2

---

02 숙련된 학습자의 융통성 정답률 83% | 정답 ①

다음 글의 요지로 가장 적절한 것은?
☑ 숙련된 학습자는 상황에 맞는 학습 전략을 사용할 줄 안다.
② 선다형 시험과 논술 시험은 평가의 형태와 목적이 다르다.
③ 문화마다 특정 행사와 상황에 맞는 복장 규정이 있다.
④ 학습의 양보다는 학습의 질이 학업 성과를 좌우한다.
⑤ 학습 목표가 명확할수록 성취 수준이 높아진다.

[본문 해석]
대학 생활을 시작할 때 학생들은 우리가 '고무도장 방식(잘 살펴보지도 않고 무조건 승인 또는 처리하는 방식)'이라고 부르고자 하는 방법을 이용하여 모든 과목, 시험, 또는 학습 과제를 똑같은 방식으로 접근할지도 모른다. 그것을 이렇게 생각해 보라. 여러분은 야구 경기에 턱시도를 입고 가겠는가? 장례식에 화려한 드레스를 입고 가겠는가? 종교 예식에 수영복을 입고 가겠는가? 아마 아닐 것이다. 다양한 행사와 상황마다 적합한 옷이 있음을 여러분은 알고 있다. 숙련된 학습자는 '같은 옷을 입는 것'이 모든 수업에 효과가 있지 않을 것이라는 걸 알고 있다. 그들은 유연한 학습자이다. 그들은 다양한 전략을 갖고 있으며 그것을 언제 사용해야 하는지 안다. 그들은 선다형 시험은 논술 시험을 위해 학습하는 것과는 다르게 학습한다는 것을 안다. 그리고 그들은 무엇을 해야 하는지 알고 있을 뿐만 아니라, 그것을 어떻게 해야 하는지도 알고 있다.

Why? 왜 정답일까?
숙련된 학습자는 상황마다 적절한 학습 전략이 있음을 알고 이를 융통성 있게 사용한다 (Skillful learners know that "putting on the same clothes" won't work for every class. They are flexible learners. They have different strategies and know when to use them.)는 내용이다. 따라서 글의 요지로 가장 적절한 것은 ① '숙련된 학습자는 상황에 맞는 학습 전략을 사용할 줄 안다.'이다.

- course ⓝ 수업, 강좌
- colorful ⓐ 화려한, 색색의
- bathing suit 수영복
- appropriate ⓐ 적절한
- skillful ⓐ 숙련된
- strategy ⓝ 전략
- rubber-stamp ⓝ 고무도장
- funeral ⓝ 장례식
- religious service 종교 의식
- occasion ⓝ 상황, 경우
- flexible ⓐ 융통성 있는
- multiple-choice test 선다형 시험

구문 풀이

1행 When students are starting their college life, they may
approach every course, test, or learning task the same way, using
                                                              분사구문
what we like to call "the rubber-stamp approach."
관계 └불완전한 문장   to call의 보어
대명사   (to call의 목적어가 없음)

---

03 Donato Bramante의 생애 정답률 96% | 정답 ③

Donato Bramante에 관한 다음 글의 내용과 일치하지 않는 것은?
① Piero della Francesca의 조수로 일했다.
② Milan에서 새로운 양식의 교회들을 건축했다.
☑ 건축에 주된 관심을 갖게 되면서 그림 그리기를 포기했다.
④ Pope Julius II의 Rome 재개발 계획에 참여했다.
⑤ 그의 건축물들은 다른 건축가들에게 영향을 끼쳤다.

[본문 해석]
이탈리아의 Fermignano에서 태어난 Donato Bramante는 그의 인생에서 일찍이 그림을 그리기 시작했다. 그의 아버지는 그가 그림을 공부하도록 격려해 주었다. 「나중에, 그는 Urbino에서 Piero della Francesca의 조수로 일했다.」「1480년경, 그는 Milan에서 몇몇 교회들을 새로운 양식으로 건축했다.」 그는 Leonardo da Vinci와 친밀한 관계를 맺었으며, 그들은 그 도시에서 함께 작업했다. 「건축이 그의 주요한 관심사가 되었지만, 그는 그림을 포기하지 않았다.」「Bramante는 1499년에 Rome으로 이주해서 교황 Julius 2세의 Rome 재개발 계획에 참여했다.」 그는 Rome의 성 베드로 대성당의 새로운 바실리카를 구상했는데, 그것은 인류 역사상 가장 야심찬 건축 프로젝트 중 하나였다. Bramante는 1514년 4월 11일에 사망했으며 Rome에 묻혔다. 「그의 건축물들은 여러 세기 동안 다른 건축가들에게 영향을 끼쳤다.」

Why? 왜 정답일까?
'Architecture became his main interest, but he did not give up painting.'에서 Bramante는 건축이 주된 관심사가 된 후에도 그림을 놓지 않았다고 하므로, 내용과 일치하지 않는 것은 ③ '건축에 주된 관심을 갖게 되면서 그림 그리기를 포기했다.'이다.

Why? 왜 오답일까?
① 'Later, he worked as an assistant of Piero della Francesca in Urbino.'의 내용과 일치한다.
② 'Around 1480, he built several churches in a new style in Milan.'의 내용과 일치한다.
④ 'Bramante ~ participated in Pope Julius II's plan for the renewal of Rome.'의 내용과 일치한다.
⑤ 'His buildings influenced other architects for centuries.'의 내용과 일치한다.

- close ⓐ 친밀한
- renewal ⓝ 재개발, 회복
- bury ⓥ 묻다, 매장하다
- architecture ⓝ 건축
- ambitious ⓐ 야심찬

구문 풀이

10행 He planned the new Basilica of St. Peter in Rome — {one of
the most ambitious building projects in the history of humankind}.
  { } : 동격(the new Basilica)

★★★ 1등급 대비 고난도 3점 문제

04 식품 라벨을 통한 식품 정보 습득
정답률 51% | 정답 ②

다음 글의 밑줄 친 부분 중, 어법상 틀린 것은? [3점]

[본문 해석]

'당신이 먹는 것이 바로 당신이다(사람은 먹는 대로 이루어진다).' 그 구절은 흔히 여러분이 먹는 음식과 여러분의 신체적 건강 사이의 관계를 보여주기 위해 사용된다. 하지만 여러분은 가공식품, 통조림 식품, 포장 판매 식품을 살 때 자신이 무엇을 먹고 있는지 정말 아는가? 오늘날 만들어진 제조 식품 중 다수가 너무 많은 화학물질과 인공적인 재료를 함유하고 있어서 때로는 정확히 그 안에 무엇이 들어 있는지 알기가 어렵다. 다행히도, 이제는 식품 라벨이 있다. 식품 라벨은 여러분이 먹는 식품에 관한 정보를 알아내는 좋은 방법이다. 식품 라벨은 책에서 볼 수 있는 목차와 같다. 식품 라벨의 주된 목적은 여러분이 구입하고 있는 식품 안에 무엇이 들어 있는지 여러분에게 알려주는 것이다.

Why? 왜 정답일까?

'~ it is sometimes difficult ~'가 완전한 문장이므로 뒤에 불완전한 절이 나올 때 쓰는 관계대명사 which는 ② 자리에 나올 수 없다. 앞에 so many가 나오는 것으로 볼 때, 전체 문장은 'so ~ that …(너무 ~해서 …하다)' 구문임을 알 수 있다. 따라서 which를 결과의 부사절을 이끄는 접속사 that으로 고쳐야 한다. 어법상 틀린 것은 ②이다.

Why? 왜 오답일까?

① 'be used + to부정사(~하기 위해 사용되다)' 구문이 바르게 쓰였다.
③ a good way를 꾸미는 형용사적 용법으로 to부정사구인 to find가 바르게 쓰였다.
④ be동사 뒤에서 보어 역할을 하는 전명구를 이루기 위해 전치사 like(~처럼)가 바르게 쓰였다.
⑤ 주어가 The main purpose라는 단수 명사이므로 단수 동사 is가 바르게 쓰였다.

- **phrase** ⓝ 구절
- **processed** ⓐ 가공된
- **packaged** ⓐ 포장된
- **artificial** ⓐ 인공의
- **purpose** ⓝ 목적
- **physical** ⓐ 신체적인, 물리적인
- **canned** ⓐ 통조림으로 된
- **contain** ⓥ 함유하다
- **ingredient** ⓝ 재료

구문 풀이

5행 Many of the manufactured products made today contain
　　　 주어　　　　　　　　　　　과거분사　　　동사(복수)
so many chemicals and artificial ingredients that it is sometimes
so ~　　　　　　　　　　　　　　　　that … : 너무 ~해서 …하다
difficult to know exactly what is inside them.

★★ 문제 해결 꿀~팁 ★★

▶ **많이 틀린 이유는?**
④의 like는 동사뿐 아니라 '~처럼'이라는 의미의 전치사로 쓰여 뒤에 명사구를 수반할 수 있다는 점을 기억해 둔다. 또한 ⑤는 주어와 동사의 수 일치를 묻는 경우로 핵심 주어와 수식어구를 구별하는 것이 풀이의 관건이다.

▶ **문제 해결 방법은?**
② 'which vs. that'은 빈출되는 어법 사항이다. 둘 다 관계대명사로서 뒤에 불완전한 절을 수반할 수 있지만, that의 경우 접속사로도 쓰일 수 있기 때문에 뒤에 완전한 문장이 나오면 which가 아닌 that을 쓴다는 데 주의한다.

05 옥신의 작용과 식물 생장
정답률 47% | 정답 ④

다음 글의 밑줄 친 부분 중, 문맥상 낱말의 쓰임이 적절하지 않은 것은? [3점]

[본문 해석]

식물의 성장은 식물의 줄기와 뿌리의 끝에서 발견되는 옥신이라고 불리는 호르몬 그룹에 의해 조절된다. 줄기의 끝에서 생산된 옥신은 그늘진 곳에 있는 줄기 옆면에 축적되는 경향이 있다. 따라서, 옥신은 식물의 그늘진 면에서의 성장을 ① 촉진한다. 그러므로 그늘진 면은 햇빛을 마주하는 면보다 더 빨리 자란다. 이 현상은 줄기가 휘어지고 빛을 ② 향해 성장하는 것처럼 보이게 한다. 옥신은 식물의 뿌리에서는 ③ 반대 효과를 나타낸다. 뿌리 끝에 있는 옥신은 성장을 억제하는 경향이 있다. 만약 뿌리가 토양 속에서 수평이라면, 옥신은 아래쪽에 축적되어 그것의 발달을 방해할 것이다. 그러므로 뿌리 아래쪽은 위쪽보다 ④ 더 빠르게(→ 더 느리게) 자라게 된다. 이것은 결과적으로 뿌리가 ⑤ 아래로 휘어지게 하고, 뿌리 끝부분은 그쪽으로 자라난다.

Why? 왜 정답일까?

식물 생장에 있어 옥신의 작용 방식을 설명한 글이다. 줄기에 작용하는 옥신은 어두운 쪽의 성장을 자극하므로 식물은 마치 빛을 '향해' 작용하는 것처럼 보이게 되지만, 뿌리에서는 상황이 '반대'라고 한다. 즉, 뿌리 아래쪽에 축적된 옥신은 아래쪽의 성장을 오히려 '방해해서' 위쪽보다 '더 천천히' 자라게 만들 것이라는 내용을 추론할 수 있다. 따라서 문맥상 낱말의 쓰임이 적절하지 않은 것은 ④이며, faster를 slower로 바꿔야 한다.

- **tip** ⓝ 끝부분
- **accumulate** ⓥ 축적되다, 쌓이다
- **stimulate** ⓥ 자극하다, 촉진하다
- **bend** ⓥ 구부러지다
- **horizontal** ⓐ 수평적인
- **interfere with** ~을 방해하다
- **downward(s)** ⓐⓓ 아래로
- **stem** ⓝ 줄기
- **accordingly** ⓐⓓ 따라서
- **phenomenon** ⓝ 현상
- **limit** ⓥ 제한하다
- **soil** ⓝ 토양, 흙
- **in turn** 한편, 결국, 차례로

구문 풀이

14행 This will, in turn, cause the root to bend downwards,
with the tip of the root growing in that direction.
「with + 명사 + 분사 : ~이 …한 채로」

06 우리 세계에서 과학이 가능한 이유
정답률 67% | 정답 ④

다음 빈칸에 들어갈 말로 가장 적절한 것을 고르시오.

① age – 나이
② luck – 행운
③ belief – 믿음
✔ rules – 법칙
⑤ interests – 흥미

[본문 해석]

우리가 만일 그 어떤 것도 변한 적이 없는 행성 위에 살았더라면, 할 일이 거의 없었을 것이다. 알아내야 할 것도 없고 과학이 있을 이유도 없었을 것이다. 그리고 만일 우리가 만물이 무작위로 혹은 아주 복잡하게 변하는 예측 불가한 세계에 살았더라면, 우리는 상황을 알 수 없었을 것이다. 다시 한 번, 과학 같은 것은 없었을 것이다. 하지만 우리는 만물이 변하기는 하되 법칙에 따라 변하는 중간 세계에 살고 있다. 내가 만일 막대를 공중에 던지면 이는 항상 떨어진다. 태양은 서쪽으로 지면 항상 다음날 아침 동쪽에서 뜬다. 그래서 상황을 예측하는 것이 가능해진다. 우리는 과학을 할 수 있고, 과학을 가지고 삶을 개선해 나갈 수 있다.

Why? 왜 정답일까?

빈칸 앞의 문장에서 현재의 반대를 상상하는 가정법 과거 구문을 통해 만일 우리가 무작위로 혹은 매우 복잡한 방식으로 만물이 변하는 세계에 살았더라면 과학 같은 것은 없었을 것(And if we lived in an unpredictable world, where things changed in random or very complex ways, we would not be able to figure things out.)이라고 말하는데, 빈칸 문장은 현실은 다행히도 그렇지 않고 만물이 변하기는 하되 일정한 '법칙'에 따라 변한다는 내용을 피력하고 있다. 따라서 빈칸에 들어갈 말로 가장 적절한 것은 ④ '법칙'이다. 빈칸 뒤에 나오는 막대 및 태양의 예에서 변화에는 반드시 정해진 패턴이나 결과가 있어 예측이 가능하다는 점을 부연하고 있다.

- **planet** ⓝ 행성
- **unpredictable** ⓐ 예측할 수 없는
- **complex** ⓐ 복잡한
- **universe** ⓝ 우주
- **set** ⓥ (해 또는 달이) 지다
- **figure out** 알아내다
- **random** ⓐ 무작위의
- **in-between** 중간의
- **according to** ~에 따라
- **improve** ⓥ 개선하다, 향상시키다

구문 풀이

4행 And if we lived in an unpredictable world, [where things
　　　 「if + 주어 + 과거 동사　　　　　　　　　　관계부사
changed / in random or very complex ways], we would not be able
　　　　　　　　　　　　　　　　　　　주어 + would + 동사원형 : 가정법 과거」
to figure things out.

★★★ 1등급 대비 고난도 3점 문제

07 신생아가 부드러운 흔들림을 좋아하는 이유
정답률 27% | 정답 ①

다음 빈칸에 들어갈 말로 가장 적절한 것을 고르시오. [3점]

✔ acquire a fondness for motion – 움직임을 좋아하게 되고
② want consistent feeding – 계속 젖을 먹고 싶어 하고
③ dislike severe rocking – 너무 심한 흔들림을 싫어하고

④ remember the tastes of food – 음식의 맛을 기억하고
⑤ form a bond with their mothers – 엄마와 유대감을 형성하고

[본문 해석]

신생아와 유아는 흔들림에 의해 편안해지는데, 이것은 이런 움직임이 자궁 안에서 그들이 경험했던 것과 유사하기 때문이고, 그들이 이런 친숙한 느낌에서 편안해지는 것이 틀림없다는 말을 자주 듣는다. 이것은 사실일 수 있지만, 현재까지 임신 기간에 엄마가 움직이는 시간의 양과 흔들림에 대한 신생아의 반응 사이에 상당한 관계가 있음을 입증하는 설득력 있는 데이터는 없다. 신생아가 부드러운 흔들림을 젖을 먹는 것과 연관시키게 된다는 생각도 그만큼 가능할 법하다. 부모는 흔들어 주는 것이 신생아를 달래 준다는 것을 알고 있어서, 그들은 젖을 주는 동안 부드럽고 반복적인 움직임을 매우 자주 제공한다. 음식의 등장은 일차 강화물이기 때문에, 신생아는 움직임을 좋아하게 되고, 그 이유는 그들이 연관 학습의 과정을 통해 조건화되어 왔기 때문이다.

Why? 왜 정답일까?

신생아가 부드러운 흔들림을 좋아하는 이유에 관해 다룬 글로, 'Just as likely is the idea ~'에서 아이들은 흔들림을 젖 먹는 것과 연관 짓게 되면서 흔들림을 좋아하게 될 수도 있다는 견해를 제시한다. 이어서 엄마가 아이에게 젖을 먹이는 동안 보통 아이를 편안하게 해주기 위해서 아이를 흔들어 주는 과정에서 젖, 즉 음식이 흔들림을 '좋아하게' 되는 강화물로 기능하게 된다는 설명이 나온다. 따라서 빈칸에 들어갈 말로 가장 적절한 것은 ① '움직임을 좋아하게 되고'이다.

- newborn ⓝ 신생아
- comfort ⓝ 안락, 편안
- motion ⓝ 움직임
- womb ⓝ 자궁
- convincing ⓐ 설득력 있는
- significant ⓐ 상당한, 유의미한
- associate A with B A와 B를 연관시키다
- quiet ⓥ 진정시키다, 조용하게 하다
- appearance ⓝ 등장
- reinforcer ⓝ 강화물
- process ⓝ 과정, 절차
- consistent ⓐ 계속되는
- dislike ⓥ 싫어하다
- infant ⓝ 유아
- rock ⓥ 흔들다
- similar ⓐ 비슷한, 유사한
- to date 지금까지
- demonstrate ⓥ 입증하다
- pregnancy ⓝ 임신 (기간)
- gentle ⓐ 부드러운
- repetitive ⓐ 반복적인
- primary ⓐ 일차적인, 주요한
- condition ⓥ 조건화하다
- fondness ⓝ 좋아함
- feed ⓝ (아기의) 우유
- severe ⓐ 심한, 가혹한

구문 풀이

1행 We're often told {that newborns and infants are comforted
동사구(~을 듣다) 접속사1 주어 동사(수동태)
by rocking because this motion is similar to what they experienced
접속사(~ 때문에) ~와 비슷한 관계대명사(~것)
in the womb}, and {that they must take comfort in this familiar feeling}.
접속사2 주어 동사 { } : 문장의 목적어

★★ 문제 해결 꿀~팁 ★★

▶ 많이 틀린 이유는?
첫 문장에서 'newborns and infants are comforted by rocking'을 통해 신생아나 유아는 흔들림을 좋아한다는 전제를 제시했다. 이후 'because this motion is similar to ~'와 '~ associate gentle rocking with being fed.'에서 신생아가 흔들림을 좋아하는 이유를 밝히고 있다. 따라서 결론에 해당하는 빈칸에는 전제이자 요지인 ①이 들어가야 한다. ②와 ④는 둘 다 '움직임을 좋아하는' 특성에 관한 언급 없이 '먹는 것'과 관련된 내용만을 제시하므로 오답이다.

▶ 문제 해결 방법은?
더 자세히 살펴보면, 이 글은 신생아들이 흔들림을 좋아하는 이유에 관한 통념을 반박하고 새로운 견해를 제시하는 글로, however가 흐름의 전환을 이끈다. 글을 꼼꼼히 읽기 전에 이런 연결사 중심으로 구조를 파악해 두면 핵심 내용을 쉽게 이해하는 데 도움이 된다.

★★★ 1등급 대비 고난도 3점 문제

| **08** 농업 체제의 변화 | 정답률 43% | 정답 ③ |

글의 흐름으로 보아, 주어진 문장이 들어가기에 가장 적절한 곳을 고르시오. [3점]

[본문 해석]

초기의 농업 시스템은 통합된 사회 시스템의 일부로서 기술, 신념, 신화 그리고 전통과 통합되고 함께 발전했다. ① 일반적으로 사람들은 상당히 안정적인 식량 공급을 얻기를 기대하며 여러 지역에 다양한 작물을 심었다. ② 이 시스템은 낮은 인구 수준에서만 유지될 수 있었고, 비교적 파괴적이지 않았다(항상 그런 것은 아니지만). ③ 더 최근에는 농업이 많은 곳에서 그 지역적 특성을 잃고 세계 경제에 통합되어 왔다. 이로 인해 교환 상품과 수출 상품을 위한 농경지에 대한 압력이 증가하게 되었다. ④ 더 많은 땅이 지역 식량 생산에서 수출과 교환을 위한 '환금 작물'로 전환되고 있는데, 더 적은 종류의 작물이 재배되고, 각 작물은 이전보다 훨씬 더 많은 양으로 재배된다. ⑤ 따라서 자급자족용 작물을 위해 땅을 사용하기보다는, 수출을 위한 농업을 위해 어느 때보다 더 많은 토지가 산림(그리고 다른 자연 시스템)으로부터 전환된다.

Why? 왜 정답일까?

③ 앞에서 초기의 농업 시스템은 사회 시스템의 일부로 여러 다른 체계와 통합되어 발전하면서 식량 공급을 주 목적으로 했고 파괴성이 덜했다고 설명한다. 이어서 **More recently**로 시작하는 주어진 문장은 '더 최근'의 시점으로 넘어와 농업은 지역적 특성을 잃고 세계 경제에 통합되어 왔다는 사실을 제시한다. ③ 뒤에서는 주어진 문장과 같은 상황이 되었기 때문에 교환 상품이나 수출 상품을 재배할 농경지가 더 많이 필요해졌고, 재배되는 작물의 종류는 줄어들었으며, 환금 작물 중심의 농업이 이루어지고 있다는 내용이 이어진다. 따라서 주어진 문장이 들어가기에 가장 적절한 곳은 ③이다.

- agriculture ⓝ 농업
- integrate ⓥ 통합하다
- stable ⓐ 안정적인
- commodity ⓝ 상품
- convert ⓥ 전환하다, 개조하다
- incorporate A into B A를 B에 통합시키다
- in the hope of ~라는 희망으로
- non-destructive ⓐ 파괴적이지 않은
- divert ⓥ 전환시키다, 다른 데로 돌리다

구문 풀이

13행 More land is being diverted from local food production to
주어 동사(현재진행 수동태) 「from + A + to + B : A에서 B로」
"cash crops" for export and exchange; fewer types of crops are raised,
비교급 수식 부사 주어1 동사1
and each crop is raised in much greater quantities than before.
주어2 동사2 비교급 형용사

★★ 문제 해결 꿀~팁 ★★

▶ 많이 틀린 이유는?
농경 변천에 관한 글로, 흐름을 잘 파악해야 한다. 최다 오답인 ④ 앞에서 교환 및 수출 작물용 농경지에 대한 압박이 커졌다고 하는데, ④ 뒤에서는 이를 '환금 작물'이라는 용어로 바꾸며 식량보다는 무역 수익을 위한 농경이 많이 이루어지는 상황임을 설명하고 있다. 즉 ④ 앞뒤로 흐름 전환이나 논리적 공백이 발생하지 않으므로 ④에 주어진 문장을 넣을 필요가 없다.

▶ 문제 해결 방법은?
③ 앞에서 초기 농업은 안정적 식량 확보를 주된 목적으로 했다고 설명하는데, ③ 뒤에서는 '이로 인해' 교환 작물 또는 수출 작물을 키워야 한다는 압력이 커진다고 언급한다. 두 내용은 서로 상충하므로, ③에 '최근의 농업' 이야기로 흐름을 전환하는 문장이 들어가야 함을 알 수 있다.

| **09** 규범에서 약간 벗어난 옷차림을 좋게 보는 우리들 | 정답률 50% | 정답 ① |

다음 글의 내용을 한 문장으로 요약하고자 한다. 빈칸 (A), (B)에 들어갈 말로 가장 적절한 것은?

(A)	(B)	(A)	(B)
✓① positively 긍정적으로	challenges 도전할	② negatively 부정적으로	challenges 도전할
③ indifferently 무관심하게	neglects 등한시할	④ negatively 부정적으로	meets 일치할
⑤ positively 긍정적으로	meets 일치할		

[본문 해석]

우리가 남들을 옷으로 판단한다는 것은 누구에게도 새로운 일이 아니다. 일반적으로, 이러한 판단을 조사하는 연구는 사람들이 수술복을 입은 외과 의사, 파란 옷을 입은 남자아이와 같이 예상에 맞는 의복이되 눈에 띄는 예외가 하나 있는 것을 선호한다는 것을 발견한다. *Journal of Consumer Research*의 2014년 6월 논문에 실린 일련의 연구는 확립된 규범을 아주 약간 어긴 사람들에 대한 관찰자들의 반응을 탐구했다. 한 시나리오에서는, 정장 차림의 행사에서 한 남자가 빨간 나비 넥타이를 맸을 때 더 높은 지위와 능력을 지녔다고 여겨졌다. 연구자들은 또한, 독특함을 중시하는 것이 강의 중에 빨간 운동화를 신은 교수의 지위와 역량에 대한 청중들의 평가를 높였다는 것을 발견했다. 그 결과들은 사람들이 이런 식으로 규범을 약간 어긴 것을 긍정적으로 판단한다는 것을 시사하는데, 왜냐하면 그것들은 그 사람이 그러한 행동으로 인한 사회적 비용을

감수할 만큼 충분히 강하다는 것을 암시하기 때문이다.

➡ 일련의 연구는 사람들이 무엇을 입을지에 대한 규범에 개인이 아주 약간 (B) 도전할 때 사람들이 그 사람을 (A) 긍정적으로 본다는 것을 나타낸다.

Why? 왜 정답일까?

의복에 대한 규범을 살짝 어기는 사람이 더 긍정적으로 여겨진다(people judge these slight deviations from the norm as positive)는 연구를 소개하는 글이다. 따라서 요약문의 빈칸 (A), (B)에 들어갈 말로 가장 적절한 것은 ① '(A) positively(긍정적으로), (B) challenges(도전할)'이다.

- in general 일반적으로
- match ⓥ 일치하다, 맞다, 부합하다
- scrubs ⓝ 수술복
- exception ⓝ 예외
- reaction ⓝ 반응
- black-tie affair 격식을 차리는 모임
- uniqueness ⓝ 독특함, 고유함
- powerful ⓐ 영향력 있는, 강력한
- challenge ⓥ 반박하다, 도전하다
- neglect ⓥ 등한시하다, 소홀히 하다
- investigate ⓥ 연구하다, 조사하다
- surgeon ⓝ 외과 의사
- notable ⓐ 눈에 띄는
- explore ⓥ 탐구하다
- established ⓐ 확립된, 정해진
- bow tie 나비 넥타이
- deviation ⓝ 일탈
- risk ⓥ 위태롭게 하다
- negatively ⓐⓓ 부정적으로

구문 풀이

11행 The researchers also found that valuing uniqueness
　　　　　　　　　　　　　접속사　　　동명사구 주어
increased audience members' ratings of the status and competence
동사
of a professor [who wore red sneakers while giving a lecture].
　　　　　　　　└→ 주격 관·대　　　분사구문(= while he or she gave ~)

10-12 아버지의 연설문을 보고 감동한 필자

[본문 해석]

(A)
17살 때 나는 놀라운 물건을 발견했다. 아버지와 나는 서재 바닥에 앉아 있었다. 『우리는 아버지의 오래된 서류들을 정리하고 있었다.』 나는 카펫 너머에 있는 두꺼운 종이 클립을 보았다. 그것의 녹이 어떤 보고서의 표지를 더럽혔다. 나는 그것을 집어 들었다. 『나는 읽기 시작했다. 그러고 나서 나는 울기 시작했다.』
　　　　　　　　　　　　　　　　　　　　『 』: 12번 ②의 근거 일치

(C)
『그것은 1920년 Tennessee 주에서 아버지가 썼던 연설문이었다. 아버지는 당시 단지 17살에 고등학교를 졸업했을 뿐인데 아프리카계 미국인들을 위한 평등을 요구했다.』 아버지를 자랑스럽게 여기면서 (b) 나는 놀라워했고, 1920년에 법으로 백인과 흑인을 여전히 분리시키고 있었던 최남부 지역에서 그렇게 어리고 백인이었던 (c) 그가 어떻게 그 연설을 할 용기를 가지고 있었는지 궁금했다. 나는 그에게 그것에 관해 물었다.
　　　　　　　　　　『 』: 12번 ④의 근거 일치

(B)
아빠에게 서류를 건네 드리며 "아빠, 이 연설, 어떻게 이렇게 하도록 허락을 받으셨나요? 두렵지 않으셨나요?"라고 말했다. "아들아," 그가 말했다. "『난 허락을 구하지 않았단다.』 단지 '우리 세대가 직면하고 있는 가장 중요한 도전 과제는 무엇인가?'라고 나 자신에게 물었어. 난 즉시 알았어. 그 뒤 '내가 두려워하지 않는다면, 이 연설에서 이것에 대해 무엇을 말할까?'라고 (a) 나는 스스로에게 물었어."
　　　『 』: 12번 ③의 근거 일치

(D)
"난 글을 썼어. 그리고 연설을 했어. 『대략 반쯤 연설을 했을 때 교사, 학생, 학부모로 이루어진 전체 청중이 일어나더니 나가 버리는 것을 바라보았어.』 무대에 홀로 남겨진 채 '그래, 내 인생에서 두 가지만 확실히 해내면 되겠구나. 계속 스스로 생각하는 것과 죽임을 당하지 않는 것.'이라고 (d) 나는 마음속으로 생각했어." 아버지는 연설문을 나에게 돌려주며 미소 지으셨다. "(e) 아빠는 그 두 가지 모두를 해내신 것 같네요."라고 나는 말했다.
　　　　　『 』: 12번 ⑤의 근거 불일치

- study ⓝ 서재
- permission ⓝ 허락
- call for ~을 요구하다, 필요로 하다
- marvel ⓥ 놀라다
- courage ⓝ 용기
- entire ⓐ 전체의
- rust ⓝ 녹
- generation ⓝ 세대
- equality ⓝ 평등
- separate ⓥ 분리시키다
- deliver ⓥ (연설이나 강연을) 하다

구문 풀이

(B) 7행 And if I weren't afraid, what would I say about it in this
　　　　　「if + 주어 + 과거 동사 ~, 조동사 과거형 + 주어 + 동사원형 ~ : 가정법 과거 의문문」
speech?

(C) 4행 I marvelled, (being) proud of him, and wondered {how, in
　　　　　동사1　생략(분사구문)　　　　　　　동사2　의문사
1920, (being) so young, so white, and in the deep South, where the
　　　생략(분사구문 : he 보충 설명)　　　　　　선행사　　　관계부사
law still separated black from white, he had had the courage to
　　　　　　　　　　　　　　　　　　　주어　　동사
deliver it}.[　] : 목적어(간접의문문)

(D) 4행 Left alone on the stage, I thought to myself, 'Well, I guess
　　　　　분사구문
(that) I need to be sure to do only two things with my life: keep thinking
생략(접속사)　　　　　　　　　　　　　　　　　　　　　동격(= two things)
for myself, and not get killed.'

---

10 글의 순서 파악
정답률 68% | 정답 ②

주어진 글 (A)에 이어질 내용을 순서에 맞게 배열한 것으로 가장 적절한 것은?

① (B) – (D) – (C) 　✓② (C) – (B) – (D)
③ (C) – (D) – (B) 　④ (D) – (B) – (C)
⑤ (D) – (C) – (B)

Why? 왜 정답일까?

필자가 아버지와 서재를 정리하다가 아버지가 17살 때 썼던 연설문을 발견했다는 내용의 (A) 뒤에는, 연설문을 읽은 필자가 아버지에게 어떻게 그런 연설을 할 용기를 냈는지 물었다는 내용의 (C)가 연결된다. 이어서 (B)에서 아버지는 아들인 필자의 물음에 답하기 시작하고, (D)에서는 답을 마무리한다. 따라서 글의 순서로 가장 적절한 것은 ② '(C) – (B) – (D)'이다.

---

11 지칭 추론
정답률 44% | 정답 ②

밑줄 친 (a) ~ (e) 중에서 가리키는 대상이 나머지 넷과 다른 것은?

① (a) 　✓② (b) 　③ (c) 　④ (d) 　⑤ (e)

Why? 왜 정답일까?

(a), (c), (d), (e)는 My father, (b)는 필자인 'I'를 가리키므로, (a) ~ (e) 중에서 가리키는 대상이 다른 하나는 ② '(b)'이다.

---

12 세부 내용 파악
정답률 68% | 정답 ⑤

윗글에 관한 내용으로 적절하지 않은 것은?

① 아버지와 나는 서류를 정리하고 있었다.
② 나는 서재에서 발견한 것을 읽고 나서 울기 시작했다.
③ 아버지는 연설을 하기 위한 허락을 구하지 않았다.
④ 아버지가 연설문을 썼을 당시 17세였다.
✓⑤ 교사, 학생, 학부모 모두 아버지의 연설을 끝까지 들었다.

Why? 왜 정답일까?

(D) 'About half way through I looked out to see the entire audience of teachers, students, and parents stand up—and walk out.'에 따르면 필자의 아버지가 절반쯤 연설을 진행했을 때 교사, 학생, 학부모 등 전체 관중이 모두 일어나 나갔다고 하므로, 내용과 일치하지 않는 것은 ⑤ '교사, 학생, 학부모 모두 아버지의 연설을 끝까지 들었다.'이다.

Why? 왜 오답일까?

① (A) 'We were organizing his old papers.'의 내용과 일치한다.
② (A) 'I started to read. Then I started to cry.'의 내용과 일치한다.
③ (B) 'I didn't ask for permission.'의 내용과 일치한다.
④ (C) 'It was a speech he had written in 1920, in Tennessee. Then only 17 himself and graduating from high school, ~'의 내용과 일치한다.

DAY 05 — 20분 미니 모의고사

01 ③	02 ⑤	03 ①	04 ④	05 ③
06 ③	07 ①	08 ③	09 ④	10 ②
11 ③	12 ⑤			

01 프로그램 단체 예약 문의
정답률 92% | 정답 ③

다음 글의 목적으로 가장 적절한 것은?

① 단체 관람 시 유의 사항을 안내하려고
② 교내 행사에 초청할 강사 추천을 부탁하려고
✔ 프로그램 단체 예약이 가능한지를 문의하려고
④ 새로운 체험 학습 프로그램을 소개하려고
⑤ 견학 예정 인원수의 변경을 요청하려고

[본문 해석]

Diane Edwards 귀하,

저는 East End 고등학교에서 근무하는 교사입니다. 귀하의 공고문에서 East End 항구 박물관이 현재 '2017 Bug 등대 체험'이라는 특별한 프로그램을 제공하고 있다는 내용을 읽었습니다. 그 프로그램은 우리 학생들이 즐거운 시간을 보내며 새로운 것을 경험할 수 있는 훌륭한 기회가 될 것입니다. 제가 추산하기로는 우리 학교 학생 및 교사 50명이 그 프로그램에 참여하고 싶어 합니다. 11월 18일 토요일 해당 프로그램에 단체 예약을 하는 것이 가능한지 알려 주시겠습니까? 이 좋은 기회를 놓치고 싶지 않습니다. 귀하로부터 곧 소식을 듣기를 고대합니다.

Joseph Loach 드림

Why? 왜 정답일까?

'Would you please let me know if it is possible to make a group reservation for the program for Saturday, November 18?'에서 11월 18일 토요일에 프로그램 단체 예약이 가능한지 알려달라고 하므로, 글의 목적으로 가장 적절한 것은 ③ '프로그램 단체 예약이 가능한지를 문의하려고'이다.

- **notice** ⓝ (보통 공공장소에 붙이는) 공고문
- **estimate** ⓥ 추산하다, 추정하다
- **look forward to** ~을 고대하다
- **opportunity** ⓝ 기회
- **group reservation** 단체 예약

구문 풀이

3행 I have read (from your notice) [that the East End Seaport
접속새(~것)
Museum is now offering a special program, the 2017 Bug Lighthouse
[ ] : have read의 목적어   a special program과 동격
Experience].

02 업무와 개인 용무를 한 곳에 정리하기
정답률 78% | 정답 ⑤

다음 글에서 필자가 주장하는 바로 가장 적절한 것은?

① 결정한 것은 반드시 실행하도록 노력하라.
② 자신이 담당한 업무에 관한 전문성을 확보하라.
③ 업무 집중도를 높이기 위해 책상 위를 정돈하라.
④ 좋은 아이디어를 메모하는 습관을 길러라.
✔ 업무와 개인 용무를 한 곳에 정리하라.

[본문 해석]

연구는 일하는 사람들이 두 개의 달력을 가지고 있다는 것을 보여준다. 하나는 업무를 위한 달력이고 하나는 개인적인 삶을 위한 달력이다. 비록 이것이 현명해 보일지도 모르지만, 업무와 개인적인 삶을 위한 두 개의 별도의 달력을 갖는 것은 주의를 산만하게 할 수 있다. 누락된 것이 있는지를 확인하고자 당신은 자신이 할 일 목록을 여러 번 확인하고 있다는 것을 깨닫게 될 것이다. 그렇게 하는 대신에, 당신의 모든 일들을 한 곳에 정리하라. 당신이 디지털 매체를 사용하든 종이 매체를 사용하든 중요하지 않다. 당신의 업무와 개인 용무를 한 곳에 둬도 괜찮다. 이것은 당신에게 일과 가정 사이에 시간이 어떻게 나눠지는 지에 대해 잘 알게 해줄 것이다. 이것은 어떤 일이 가장 중요한지에 대해 잘 알고 결정하게 할 것이다.

Why? 왜 정답일까?

개인 용무와 일을 한 곳에 정리하라고(~ keep your professional and personal tasks in one place.) 조언하는 글이므로, 필자가 주장하는 바로 가장 적절한 것은 ⑤ '업무와 개인 용무를 한 곳에 정리하라.'이다.

- **sensible** ⓐ 분별 있는, 현명한
- **distraction** ⓝ 주의 분산
- **organize** ⓥ 정리하다
- **make an informed decision** 잘 알고 결정하다
- **separate** ⓐ 별개의
- **multiple** ⓐ 여럿의, 다수의
- **divide** ⓥ 나누다, 분배하다

구문 풀이

5행 To check if something is missing, you will find yourself
목적(~하려면) 접속새(~인지 아닌지)   동사   목적어
checking your to-do lists multiple times.
목적격 보어

03 용기가 불러오는 기회
정답률 65% | 정답 ①

다음 글의 제목으로 가장 적절한 것은?

✔ More Courage Brings More Opportunities – 더 큰 용기가 더 많은 기회를 부른다
② Travel: The Best Way to Make Friends – 여행: 친구를 사귀는 가장 좋은 방법
③ How to Turn Mistakes into Success – 실수를 성공으로 바꾸는 방법
④ Satisfying Life? Share with Others – 만족스러운 삶? 남들과 나누라
⑤ Why Is Overcoming Fear So Hard? – 공포를 극복하는 것은 왜 이리 어려울까?

[본문 해석]

많은 사람들이 안전 구역에서만 움직이는 실수를 저지르고, 그 과정에서 더 위대한 일들을 달성할 기회를 놓친다. 그들은 미지의 세계에 대한 두려움과 알려지지 않은 삶의 경로를 밟는 것에 대한 두려움 때문에 그렇게 한다. 사람들이 잘 다니지 않는 길을 택할 만큼 충분히 용감한 사람들은 엄청난 보상을 받을 수 있고 용감한 행동으로부터 큰 만족감을 끌어낼 수 있다. 지나치게 조심하는 것은 잠재력의 최고 수준을 달성하는 것을 놓친다는 의미일 것이다. 여러분은 주변에 있는 많은 사람들이 선택하지 않을 기회를 택하는 법을 배워야 하는데, 왜냐하면 여러분의 성공은 삶의 과정에서 여러분이 내릴 용감한 결정으로부터 나올 것이기 때문이다.

Why? 왜 정답일까?

결론을 제시하는 마지막 문장에서 많은 기회와 성공은 용기에서 파생되므로 더 과감해질 필요가 있다(You must learn to take those chances that many people around you will not take, because your success will flow from those bold decisions that you will take along the way.)고 조언하므로, 글의 제목으로 가장 적절한 것은 ① '더 큰 용기가 더 많은 기회를 부른다'이다.

- **safe zone** 안전 구역
- **brave** ⓐ 용감한
- **derive** ⓥ 끌어내다, 도출하다
- **overcautious** ⓐ 지나치게 조심하는
- **potential** ⓝ 잠재력
- **unknown** ⓐ 미지의, 알지 못하는
- **return** ⓝ 보상
- **courageous** ⓐ 용감한
- **attain** ⓥ 달성하다, 얻다
- **satisfying** ⓐ 만족스러운

구문 풀이

5행 Those that are brave enough to take those roads less travelled
「형/부 + enough + to부정사 : ~할 만큼 충분히 …한」   과거분사
are able to get great returns and derive major satisfaction out of
their courageous moves.

04 미국 내의 연령대별 소셜 미디어 사용자 비율
정답률 77% | 정답 ④

다음 도표의 내용과 일치하지 않는 것은?

People Who Reported Using Social Media in the U.S.
(by age group)

Age Group	2015	2021
18-29	90	84
30-49	77	81
50-64	51	73
65+	35	45

[본문 해석]

위 그래프는 2015년과 2021년에 미국에서 소셜 미디어를 사용한다고 보고한 다양한 연령 집단 내 사람들의 비율을 보여 준다. ① 주어진 각각의 해에, 18 ~ 29세 집단에서 소셜 미디어를 사용한다고 말한 사람들의 비율이 제일 높았다. ② 2015년에 30 ~ 49세 집단에서 소셜 미디어를 사용한다고 보고한 사람들의 비율은 65세 이상 집단의 두 배 이상이었다. ③ 2021년에 50 ~ 64세 집단에서 소셜 미디어를 사용한다고 말한 사람들의 비율은 2015년보다 22퍼센트포인트 더 높았다. ④ 2021년에 65세 이상 집단을 제외한 각 연령 집단에서 5분의 4가 넘는 사람들이 소셜 미디어를 사용한다고 보고했다. ⑤ 모든 연령 집단 중에서 18~29세 집단만이 2015년에서 2021년까지 소셜 미디어를 사용한다고 보고한 사람들의 비율에서 감소를 보였다.

Why? 왜 정답일까?

도표에 따르면 2021년에 미국에서 소셜 미디어를 사용하고 있다고 보고한 50~64세 인구는 73%인데, 이는 5분의 4인 80%에 미치지 못하는 수치이다. 따라서 도표와 일치하지 않는 것은 ④이다.

- **social media** 소셜 미디어
- **more than** ~ 이상
- **decrease** ⓝ 감소
- **given** ⓐ 주어진 [prep] ~을 고려하면
- **except for** ~을 제외하고

---

05 | 아버지에 대한 기억 | 정답률 62% | 정답 ③

다음 글의 밑줄 친 부분 중, 어법상 틀린 것은?

[본문 해석]

나의 아버지는 음악가로 매우 늦게, 새벽 3시 정도까지 일했고, 그래서 아버지는 주말마다 늦잠을 잤다. 그 결과, 아버지가 잔디 깎기와 울타리 덤불 자르기처럼 내가 싫어했던 허드렛일을 하라고 계속 나에게 잔소리한 것을 제외하고는 내가 어렸을 때 우리는 많은 관계를 가지지 못했다. 그는 무책임한 아이를 다루는 책임감 있는 사람이었다. 우리가 소통했던 방식에 대한 기억들이 현재 나에게는 우스워 보인다. 예를 들어, 한번은 아버지가 나에게 잔디를 깎으라고 말했고, 나는 앞뜰만 하기로 하고 뒤뜰을 하는 것은 미루기로 결심했으나, 그러고 나서 며칠 동안 비가 내렸고 뒤뜰의 잔디가 너무 길게 자라서 나는 그것을 낫으로 베어내야만 했다. 그 일은 너무 오래 걸려서 내가 끝냈을 때쯤에는 앞뜰의 잔디가 깎기에 너무 길었고, 그런 일이 계속되었다.

Why? 왜 정답일까?

복수 주어 Memories에 맞춰 단수형 seems를 복수형인 seem으로 고쳐야 하므로, 어법상 틀린 것은 ③이다.

Why? 왜 오답일까?

① 선행사 chores를 보충 설명하는 관계대명사로서 which를 쓴 것은 어법상 맞다.
② 명사 a responsible man을 꾸미면서 뒤에 목적어인 an irresponsible kid를 수반하므로 능동을 나타내는 현재분사 dealing을 쓴 것은 어법상 맞다.
④ 동사 decided의 목적어 역할을 하는 to부정사구로서 to do를 쓴 것은 어법상 맞다.
⑤ 'so ~ that …(너무 ~해서 …하다)' 구문이므로 접속사 that을 쓴 것은 어법상 맞다.

- **constantly** [ad] 계속, 끊임없이
- **mow** ⓥ (잔디나 풀을) 깎다, 베다
- **deal with** ~을 다루다, 처리하다
- **postpone** ⓥ 미루다, 연기하다
- **nag** ⓥ 잔소리하다, 바가지를 긁다
- **hedge** ⓝ 울타리
- **irresponsible** ⓐ 무책임한

구문 풀이

3행 As a result, we didn't have much of a relationship when I was
young / other than him constantly nagging me to take care of chores
like mowing the lawn and cutting the hedges, which I hated.

★★★ 1등급 대비 고난도 3점 문제

06 | 자연계의 복잡한 형태 | 정답률 34% | 정답 ③

다음 글의 밑줄 친 부분 중, 문맥상 낱말의 쓰임이 적절하지 않은 것은? [3점]

[본문 해석]

지난 20년 혹은 30년 동안의 상세한 연구는 자연계의 복잡한 형태가 그 기능에 필수적이라는 것을 보여주고 있다. 강을 ① 직선화하고 규칙적인 횡단면으로 만들고자 하는 시도는 아마도 이러한 형태 — 기능 관계의 가장 피해 막심한 사례가 될 수 있다. 자연 발생적인 강은 매우 ② 불규칙한 형태를 가지고 있다. 그것은 많이 굽이치고, 범람원을 가로질러 넘쳐 흐르고, 습지로 스며 들어가서 끊임없이 바뀌고 엄청나게 복잡한 강가를 만든다. 이것은 강의 수위와 속도 변화를 ③ 막을(→ 조절할) 수 있게 한다. 강을 질서정연한 기하학적 형태에 맞춰 넣는 것은 기능적 수용 능력을 ④ 파괴하고 1927년과 1993년의 미시시피 강의 홍수와 더 최근인 허리케인 Katrina와 같은 비정상적인 재난을 초래한다. 루이지애나에서 "강이 자유롭게 흐르도록 두라(let the river loose)"라는 500억 달러 계획은 ⑤ 통제된 미시시피 강이 매년 그 주의 24제곱마일을 유실시키고 있다는 것을 인정한 것이다.

Why? 왜 정답일까?

첫 문장에서 자연계의 복잡한 형태는 자연계가 기능하는 데 필수적이라는 주제를 제시하고 있다. 'The natural river ~'에서 자연 발생적인 강이 예시로 나오는데, 이러한 강이 매우 복잡한 형태를 띠고 있지만 바로 그 형태로 인해 물의 수위 변화와 속도를 조절할 수 있다는 내용이 이어져야 하므로 ③의 prevent를 accommodate로 고쳐야 한다. 따라서 문맥상 낱말의 쓰임이 적절하지 않은 것은 ③이다.

- **essential** ⓐ 필수적인
- **straighten** ⓥ 바로 펴다, 똑바르게 하다
- **irregular** ⓐ 불규칙한
- **spill** ⓥ 흐르다, 쏟아지다
- **incredibly** [ad] 엄청나게, 믿을 수 없게
- **attempt** ⓝ 노력, 시도
- **disastrous** ⓐ 처참한, 피해 막심한
- **curve** ⓥ 굽이치다
- **leak into** ~에 새어 들어가다
- **annually** [ad] 매년, 연마다

구문 풀이

3행 The attempt to straighten rivers and give them regular
주어 / 형용사적 용법1 / 형용사적 용법2
cross-sections is perhaps the most disastrous example of this
동사(단수) / 주격 보어
form-and-function relationship.

★★ 문제 해결 꿀~팁 ★★

▶ 많이 틀린 이유는?
자연의 복잡한 형태가 자연의 기능 수행에 도움이 된다는 다소 생소한 내용의 지문이다. 특히 글의 마지막 부분에서 강의 모양을 인위적으로 변형시키려 하다가는 이례적인 재난이 야기될 수 있어서 루이지애나 주 등에서 강의 모양을 '통제하려는' 시도를 그만두고 있다는 내용이 제시된다. 이러한 맥락으로 보아 최다 오답인 ⑤ 'controlled'는 적절하게 쓰였다.

▶ 문제 해결 방법은?
③이 포함된 문장에서 주어인 This는 앞 문장 내용, 즉 자연 발생적인 강이 복잡한 형태를 띤다는 내용을 받는다. 이러한 복잡한 형태가 자연의 기능 수행에 도움이 되는 요소임을 고려하면, 복잡한 형태가 강의 수위나 속도 변화를 '막아버린다'는 설명은 흐름상 어색하다.

---

07 | 업무의 결과를 보고 상황을 파악하는 관리자들 | 정답률 42% | 정답 ①

다음 빈칸에 들어갈 말로 가장 적절한 것을 고르시오. [3점]

✓① the end result - 최종 결과
② the welfare policy - 복지 정책
③ the uniform procedure - 획일적인 절차
④ the informal atmosphere - 격식에 얽매이지 않는 분위기
⑤ the employee's personality - 직원의 성격

[본문 해석]

좋은 관리자들은 업무를 맡길 때의 초기 불안감을 극복하는 것을 배워왔다. 그들은 어떤 두 사람도 정확히 똑같은 방식으로 행동하지 않는다는 것을 알고 있고, 그래서 한 직원이 다른 사람과 다르게 업무를 시작하는 것을 보더라도 두려움을 느끼지 않는다. 대신에, 그들은 최종 결과에 초점을 맞춘다. 만약 어떤 업무가 성공적으로 처리되었다면, 사람들이 조직에 수용될 만한 방식으로 일을 하는 한(예컨대, 판매원들이 회사의 윤리적 판매 정책을 준수하는 한) 그것은 괜찮다. 만약 수용할 만한 최종 결과가 성취되지 않았다면, 그러한 관리자들은 그 직원과 논의하고 상황을 분석하는 것으로 대응하여, 그 사람이 미래에 그 업무를 성공적으로 수행하기 위해 어떤 훈련이나 추가적인 기술을 필요로 하는지를 알아낸다.

Why? 왜 정답일까?

빈칸 뒤의 예문에서 관리자들은 업무의 결과, 즉 일이 결국 잘 처리되었는지 혹은 그렇지

않았는지를 보고 직원과 상황에 대한 판단을 내린다고 이야기하므로, 빈칸에 들어갈 말로 가장 적절한 것은 ① '최종 결과'이다.

- **initial** ⓐ 초기의, 처음의
- **threatened** ⓐ 위협감을 느끼는
- **successfully** ⓐⅾ 성공적으로
- **acceptable** ⓐ 수용될만한, 용인되는
- **respond** ⓥ 대응하다, 응답하다
- **additional** ⓐ 추가적인, 추가의
- **uniform** ⓐ 획일적인, 균일한, 한결같은
- **personality** ⓝ 성격
- **anxiety** ⓝ 불안, 걱정, 염려
- **focus on** ~에 집중하다
- **manner** ⓝ 방식
- **ethical** ⓐ 윤리적인, 도덕적인
- **analyze** ⓥ 분석하다
- **welfare** ⓝ 복지
- **informal** ⓐ 격식에 얽매이지 않은

구문 풀이

2행 They are aware {that no two people act in exactly the same
동사 　접속사　　　　　　　　　　　　　　　　　{ } : 명사절
way} and so do not feel threatened if they see one employee
　　　　　　동사2　　　　　　　　　　　　　　지각동사
going about a task differently than another.
현재분사(시작하다)　　　　　　　　　~와는 달리, 다르게

★★★ 1등급 대비 고난도 3점 문제

08 한 항공사의 어려운 시기 성장 비결　　정답률 34% | 정답 ③

다음 빈칸에 들어갈 말로 가장 적절한 것을 고르시오. [3점]

① it was being faced with serious financial crises
　그것이 심각한 재정 위기에 직면해 있었기
② there was no specific long-term plan on marketing
　마케팅에 관한 구체적인 장기 계획이 없었기
☑ company leadership had set an upper limit for growth
　회사 지도부가 성장의 상한치를 설정했기
④ its executives worried about the competing airlines' future
　회사 경영진이 경쟁 항공사의 미래를 걱정했기
⑤ the company had emphasized moral duties more than profits
　회사가 이익보다도 도덕적 의무를 강조했기

[본문 해석]

1996년에 한 미국 항공사가 흥미로운 문제에 직면했다. 대부분의 다른 항공사들이 손해를 보거나 파산하던 시기에, 100개가 넘는 도시가 그 회사에 그들의 지역에 취항할 것을 부탁하고 있었다. 하지만, 그것이 흥미로운 부분은 아니다. 흥미로운 것은 회사는 그 제안 중 95퍼센트 넘게 거절했고 네 개의 새로운 지역만 취항을 시작했다는 점이다. 회사는 엄청난 성장을 거절했는데 회사 지도부가 성장의 상한치를 설정했기 때문이다. 물론, 그 경영진들은 매년 성장하기를 원했지만, 너무 많이 성장하는 것을 원하지는 않았다. 다른 유명한 회사들과는 달리, 그들은 장기간 지속될 수 있는 것, 즉 자신만의 속도를 정하기를 원했다. 이렇게 함으로써 그들은 다른 항공사들이 마구 흔들리던 시기에 그들이 계속 번창하는 데 도움이 됐던, 성장의 안전이 보장되는 여유를 설정했다.

Why? 왜 정답일까?

'Sure, its executives wanted to grow each year, but they didn't want to grow too much. Unlike other famous companies, they wanted to set their own pace, ~'에 따르면 경쟁사가 고전하는 가운데 홀로 취항요청을 받았던 항공사의 경영진들은 과한 성장보다는 회사 나름의 속도대로 오래 지속되는 성장을 바랐다고 한다. 이를 근거로 할 때, 회사의 성장이 과해지지 않도록 조절하는 '상한치'가 있었을 것임을 추론할 수 있다. 따라서 빈칸에 들어갈 말로 가장 적절한 것은 ③ '회사 지도부가 성장의 상한치를 설정했기'이다.

- **go under** 파산하다
- **tremendous** 엄청난
- **establish** ⓥ 설정하다, 확립하다
- **thrive** ⓥ 번창하다
- **emphasize** ⓥ 강조하다
- **turn down** ~을 거절하다
- **executive** ⓝ 경영진, 운영진, 간부
- **margin** ⓝ 여유, 여지
- **crisis** ⓝ 위기

구문 풀이

11행 Unlike other famous companies, they wanted to set
전치사(~와는 달리)　→부정대명사(=pace)　　　　주어　　　동사구
their own pace, one [that could be sustained in the long term].
목적어　　　　　　　　주격 관·대　조동사 수동태

★★ 문제 해결 꿀~팁 ★★

▶ 많이 틀린 이유는?
글에 따르면 미국의 한 항공사는 100개가 넘는 지역으로부터 취항 제의를 받았음에도 '회사 나름의 속도에 맞게' 성장하려는 원칙을 고수하고자 네 군데에서만 새로

취항을 시작했다. 경쟁 항공사를 신경 썼다는 내용은 언급되지 않으므로 ④는 답으로 적절하지 않다.

▶ 문제 해결 방법은?
'didn't want to grow too much', 'set their own pace' 등 핵심 표현을 재진술한 말이 빈칸에 들어가야 한다.

09 태양에너지의 효율적 활용 방법 연구의 필요성　　정답률 61% | 정답 ④

다음 글에서 전체 흐름과 관계 없는 문장은?

[본문 해석]

단 한 주 만에, 태양은 *모든 인간의 역사*에 걸쳐 인간이 석탄, 석유, 그리고 천연가스의 연소를 통해 사용해 온 것보다 더 많은 에너지를 지구에 전달한다. 그리고 태양은 수십억 년 동안 계속하여 지구를 비출 것이다. ① 우리의 당면 과제는 에너지가 고갈되고 있다는 것이 아니다. ② 그것은 우리가 잘못된 원천 — 우리가 고갈시키고 있는 (양이) 적고 한정적인 것 — 에 집중하고 있다는 것이다. ③ 사실, 우리가 오늘날 사용하고 있는 모든 석탄, 천연가스, 그리고 석유는 수백만 년 전에 온 태양에너지일 뿐이며, 그것의 극히 일부분만이 지하 깊은 곳에 보존되어 있었다. ④ 화석 연료를 사용하는 기술을 개발하기 위한 우리의 노력은 의미 있는 결과를 거둬왔다. ⑤ 우리의 당면 과제이자 기회는 태양으로부터 매일 지구에 도달하는 새로운 에너지인 *훨씬 더 풍부한* 원천을 효율적이고도 저비용으로 사용하는 것을 배우는 것이다.

Why? 왜 정답일까?

에너지 분야에서의 과제는 화석 연료가 고갈되어 가고 있다는 사실이 아니라, 모든 인류 역사상 가장 방대한 에너지원으로 기능해 왔던 태양에너지를 어떻게 효율적으로 사용할지 알아내는 것이라는 내용의 글이다. ①, ②, ③, ⑤는 모두 주제를 적절히 보충 설명하지만, ④는 화석 연료 사용 기술에 관해 논하고 있어 흐름에서 벗어난다. 따라서 전체 흐름과 관계 없는 문장은 ④이다.

- **planet** ⓝ 지구, 행성
- **burn** ⓥ (연료가) 타다, 쓰이다
- **shine on** ~을 비추다
- **run out of** ~이 고갈되다
- **use up** 고갈시키다, 다 써 버리다
- **tiny** ⓐ 아주 작은, 아주 적은
- **fossil fuel** 화석 연료
- **efficiently** ⓐⅾ 효율적으로
- **abundant** ⓐ 풍부한
- **humanity** ⓝ 인류, 인간
- **coal** ⓝ 석탄
- **billion** ⓝ 10억
- **finite** ⓐ 한정적인, 유한한
- **solar** ⓐ 태양의
- **preserve** ⓥ 보존하다
- **meaningful** ⓐ 의미 있는
- **cheaply** ⓐⅾ 싸게, 저렴하게
- **strike** ⓥ (어떤 표면에) 부딪치다

구문 풀이

13행 Our challenge, and our opportunity, is to learn
　　　　　　주어　　　　　　　　　　동사 주격 보어
to efficiently and cheaply use the *much more abundant* source
명사적 용법(to+부사+동사원형 : 분리부정사)　　　　　　선행사
[that is the new energy striking our planet each day from the sun].
　　　　　　　　　　　　　　　현재분사

10 패턴을 찾는 인간의 특성　　정답률 50% | 정답 ②

주어진 글 다음에 이어질 글의 순서로 가장 적절한 것을 고르시오. [3점]

① (A) − (C) − (B)　　　　☑ (B) − (A) − (C)
③ (B) − (C) − (A)　　　　④ (C) − (A) − (B)
⑤ (C) − (B) − (A)

[본문 해석]

다음에 여러분이 맑고 어두운 하늘 아래에 있을 때 위를 올려다보아라. 만약 여러분이 별을 보기에 좋은 장소를 골랐다면, 수천 개의 광채가 나는 보석처럼 빛나고 반짝거리는 별로 가득한 하늘을 보게 될 것이다.

(B) 하지만 이 놀라운 별들의 광경은 또한 혼란스러울 수도 있다. 어떤 사람에게 별 하나를 가리켜 보라. 아마 그 사람은 여러분이 어떤 별을 보고 있는지를 정확하게 알기 어려울 것이다.

(A) 만약 여러분이 별의 패턴을 묘사한다면 그것은 더 쉬워질 수도 있다. "저기 큰 삼각형을 이루는 밝은 별들이 보이세요?"와 같은 말을 할 수 있을 것이다. 혹은, "대문자 W처럼 보이는 저 다섯 개의 별이 보이세요?"라고 말할 수도 있을 것이다.

(C) 여러분이 그렇게 하면, 여러분은 우리가 별을 바라볼 때 우리 모두가 하는 것을 정확하게 하고 있는 것이다. 우리는 다른 사람에게 어떤 것을 가리켜 보여주기 위해서뿐만 아니라, 그렇게 하는 것이 우리 인간이 항상 해왔던 것이기도 하기 때문에 패턴을 찾는다.

Why? 왜 정답일까?

밤하늘 가득한 별을 바라보라는 내용으로 시작하는 주어진 글 뒤에는, 어떤 사람에게 별 하나를 가리킨다면 정확히 어떤 별인지 파악하기 어려워할 것이라는 내용의 (B), 이때 별의 일정한 패턴을 묘사해주면 이해를 도울 수 있다는 내용의 (A), 이렇듯 패턴을 찾는 것이 인간 행동의 특징이라는 결론을 내리는 (C)가 차례로 이어지는 것이 자연스럽다. 따라서 글의 순서로 가장 적절한 것은 ② '(B) – (A) – (C)'이다.

- **spot** ⓝ 특정한 곳
- **twinkle** ⓥ 반짝거리다
- **describe** ⓥ 묘사하다
- **sight** ⓝ 보기, 봄
- **point out** 가리키다
- **exactly** ⓐⓓ 정확히
- **stargazing** ⓝ 별 보기
- **brilliant** ⓐ 눈부신, 훌륭한
- **amazing** ⓐ 놀라운
- **confuse** ⓥ 혼란시키다, 혼란스럽게 만들다
- **chances are that** ~할 가능성이 있다

구문 풀이

10행 Chances are, that person will have a hard time knowing
~할 가능성이 있다 「have a hard time + 동명사 : ~하는 데 어려움이 있다」
exactly which star you're looking at.
의문형용사(어떤)

11-12 음식이 부족하던 시절 인간의 자기 보호 기제로 시작된 과식

[본문 해석]

역사를 빠르게 살펴보면 인간은 오늘날 대부분의 발전된 세상에서 즐기는 음식의 풍부함을 항상 누렸던 것은 아님을 알 수 있다. 사실, 역사적으로 음식이 꽤 부족했던 수많은 시기가 있었다. 그 결과, 사람들은 다음번 식사의 가능성이 (a) 확실치 않았기 때문에 음식이 있을 때 더 많이 먹곤 했다. 그 시기의 과식은 생존을 보장하는 데 필수적이었고, 인간은 당장의 목적에 필요한 것보다 더 많이 먹는 것에서 만족을 얻었다. 더욱이, 가장 큰 기쁨은 가장 칼로리가 높은 음식을 먹는 것으로부터 얻어졌고, 이는 (b) 더 오래 지속되는 에너지 비축을 초래했다.

비록 불행하게도 음식이 여전히 부족한 세계의 일부 지역들이 있지만, 오늘날 세계 인구 대부분은 생존과 번영을 위해 이용 가능한 많은 음식을 가지고 있다. 『그러나 이러한 풍요로움은 새로운 것이고, 당신의 몸은 따라잡지 못하여, 당신이 필요한 것보다 더 많이 먹고 가장 칼로리가 높은 음식을 먹는 것에 대해 여전히 자연스럽게 (c) 보상한다. 이것들은 타고난 습관이지 단순한 중독이 아니다.』 ┗━━┛: 11번의 근거 『그것들은 당신의 몸에서 시작된 자기 보호 기제이고, 당신의 미래 생존을 보장해 주지만, 그것들은 이제 (d) 부적절하다.』 그러므로 음식이 풍부한 새로운 환 ┗━━┛: 12번의 근거 경과 타고난 과식 습관을 (e) 강화시킬(→ 변화시킬) 필요와 관련하여 당신의 몸과 대화하는 것은 당신의 책임이다.

- **abundance** ⓝ 풍부함
- **scarce** ⓐ 부족한
- **questionable** ⓐ 확실치 않은, 의심스러운
- **derive A from B** B에서 A를 얻다
- **reserve** ⓝ 비축(물)
- **catch up** ~을 따라잡다
- **self-preserving** 자기 보존의
- **irrelevant** ⓐ 부적절한, 관계없는
- **inborn** ⓐ 타고난
- **ruin** ⓥ 망치다
- **numerous** ⓐ 수많은
- **availability** ⓝ 이용 가능성
- **overeating** ⓝ 과식
- **calorie-dense** 칼로리가 높은
- **thrive** ⓥ 번영하다
- **addiction** ⓝ 중독
- **initiate** ⓥ 시작하다
- **regarding** prep ~에 관련하여
- **rooted in** ~에 뿌리박힌

구문 풀이

1행 A quick look at history shows that humans have not always
주어 동사 접속사 부분부정(늘 ~해 왔던 것은 아니다)
had the abundance of food [that is enjoyed throughout most of the
선행사 주격 관계대명사
developed world today].

---

11 제목 파악 정답률 50% | 정답 ③

윗글의 제목으로 가장 적절한 것은?

① Which Is Better, Tasty or Healthy Food?
맛있는 음식 또는 건강한 음식, 무엇이 더 좋은가
② Simple Steps for a More Balanced Diet
보다 균형잡힌 식단을 향한 간단한 단계들
✓③ Overeating: It's Rooted in Our Genes
과식: 그것은 우리 유전자에 뿌리박혀 있다
④ How Calorie-dense Foods Ruin Our Bodies
칼로리가 높은 음식이 어떻게 우리 몸을 망치는가
⑤ Our Eating Habits Reflect Our Personalities
우리의 식습관은 우리 성격을 반영한다

Why? 왜 정답일까?

'However, this abundance is new, and your body has not caught up, still naturally rewarding you for eating more than you need ~. These are innate habits and not simple addictions.'에서 음식의 풍요는 그 역사가 짧기에 우리 몸은 여전히 음식이 부족한 시대에 그랬던 것처럼 필요한 양 이상의 음식을 먹고, 이는 중독이 아니라 그저 타고난 습관의 일부라는 내용을 언급하고 있다. 따라서 글의 제목으로 가장 적절한 것은 ③ '과식: 그것은 우리 유전자에 뿌리박혀 있다'이다.

★★★ 1등급 대비 고난도 3점 문제

12 어휘 추론 정답률 39% | 정답 ⑤

밑줄 친 (a) ~ (e) 중에서 문맥상 낱말의 쓰임이 적절하지 <u>않은</u> 것은? [3점]
① (a) ② (b) ③ (c) ④ (d) ✓⑤ (e)

Why? 왜 정답일까?

'They are self-preserving mechanisms initiated by your body, ensuring your future survival, but they are irrelevant now.'에서 과식은 우리 몸을 보호하려는 기제에서 출발했지만 음식이 풍요로워진 현대에 이르러서는 무의미한 습관임을 설명하고 있다. 이 맥락에 비추어볼 때, 타고난 과식 습관을 '강화하기'보다는 '변화시킬' 필요가 크다는 내용이 이어져야 하므로, (e)의 strengthen을 change로 바꾸는 것이 적절하다. 따라서 문맥상 낱말의 쓰임이 적절하지 않은 것은 ⑤ '(e)'이다.

★★ 문제 해결 꿀~팁 ★★

▶ 많이 틀린 이유는?
과식 습관의 유래를 설명한 글로, 수험생들에게 다소 친숙하지 않은 내용을 다루고 있다. (c)가 포함된 문장의 '~ this abundance is new, and your body has not caught up ~'에서 현대인은 음식의 풍요를 누리고 있지만 몸이 아직 이에 맞게 발달하지 못하여 영양이 부족했던 과거와 마찬가지로 필요한 양 이상을 먹는다는 핵심 내용을 언급하고 있다. 이 문장을 근거로 할 때, 과식의 습관은 본래 미래 생존을 보장하기 위한 보호기제로 시작되었지만 현대에는 '부적절하다'는 의미를 나타내는 (d)는 맥락에 적합하다.
▶ 문제 해결 방법은?
장문 어휘 문제에서는 각 선택지가 서로 다른 선택지에 대한 근거를 제시한다. (d)가 포함된 문장에서 과식의 습관을 '부적절하다'고 언급하므로, 이에 비추어볼 때 이 습관을 '강화해야' 한다고 언급하는 (e)는 맥락상 부자연스럽다.

DAY 06 · 20분 미니 모의고사

01 ⑤	02 ①	03 ⑤	04 ④	05 ②
06 ①	07 ②	08 ④	09 ①	10 ④
11 ②	12 ④			

---

01 진기한 공룡 화석을 찾지 못해 실망한 Evelyn
정답률 91% | 정답 ⑤

다음 글에 나타난 Evelyn의 심경 변화로 가장 적절한 것은?

① confused → scared
혼란스러운 / 무서워하는
② discouraged → confident
낙담한 / 자신에 찬
③ relaxed → annoyed
느긋한 / 성가신
④ indifferent → depressed
무관심한 / 낙심한
✔ hopeful → disappointed
기대하는 / 실망스러운

[본문 해석]

캐나다 전역에서 수많은 공룡 화석으로 유명한 앨버타주의 Badlands를 탐험하는 것이 Evelyn에게는 처음이었다. 젊은 아마추어 (공룡) 뼈 발굴자로서, 그녀는 기대감으로 가득 차 있었다. 그녀는 흔한 공룡 종의 뼈를 위해서 이렇게 멀리까지 이동하지 않았다. 진기한 공룡 화석을 발견하고자 하는 그녀의 평생에 걸친 꿈이 막 실현되려 하고 있었다. 그녀는 열심히 그것들을 찾기 시작했다. 하지만 황량한 땅을 여러 시간 헤매고 다닌 후에도 그녀는 성과를 얻지 못했다. 이제 해가 지기 시작하고 있었고, 그녀의 목표는 여전히 멀리 손이 닿지 않는 곳에 있었다. 천천히 어두워지는 앞의 지면을 바라보면서 그녀는 혼자 한숨을 쉬며 말했다. "이렇게 먼 길을 와서 아무것도 얻지 못하다니 믿을 수가 없어. 무슨 시간 낭비란 말인가!"

Why? 왜 정답일까?

however 앞에서 Evelyn은 진기한 공룡 뼈를 찾을 수 있을 것이라는 기대에 부풀어 있었지만(~ she was overflowing with anticipation.), however 뒤에 따르면 아무런 성과도 얻지 못해 한숨을 쉬며(sighed) 시간을 낭비했음을 한탄했다(What a waste of time!). 따라서 Evelyn의 심경 변화로 가장 적절한 것은 ⑤ '기대하는 → 실망스러운'이다.

- explore ⓥ 탐사하다
- fossil ⓝ 화석
- anticipation ⓝ 기대
- rare ⓐ 보기 드문, 희귀한
- wander ⓥ 돌아다니다
- reach ⓝ (닿을 수 있는) 거리
- numerous ⓐ 수많은
- overflow with ~이 넘쳐나다
- life-long ⓐ 평생의, 긴 세월의
- eagerly ⓐⓓ 열심히, 열렬히
- deserted ⓐ 황량한, 사람이 없는
- discouraged ⓐ 낙담한

구문 풀이

5행 Her life-long dream to find rare fossils of dinosaurs
주어 / 형용사적 용법
was about to come true.
「be about to + 동사원형 : ~할 참이다」

---

02 상황을 오해하게 하는 감정
정답률 82% | 정답 ①

다음 글의 요지로 가장 적절한 것은?

✔ 자신의 감정으로 인해 상황을 오해할 수 있다.
② 자신의 생각을 타인에게 강요해서는 안 된다.
③ 인간관계가 우리의 감정에 영향을 미친다.
④ 타인의 감정에 공감하는 자세가 필요하다.
⑤ 공동체를 위한 선택에는 보상이 따른다.

[본문 해석]

당신의 감정은 주목할 만하고 당신에게 중요한 정보를 준다. 그러나, 감정은 또한 가끔 신뢰할 수 없고, 부정확한 정보의 원천이 될 수도 있다. 당신이 특정하게 느낄지 모르지만, 그것은 그러한 감정들이 사실의 반영이라는 뜻은 아니다. 친구의 행동이 단지 그 친구가 안 좋은 날을 보내고 있음을 나타낼 때에도, 당신이 슬프기 때문에 그녀가 당신에게 화가 났다고 결론을 내릴지도 모른다. 당신은 기분이 우울해서 면접에서 잘했을 때도 못했다고 판단할지도 모른다. 당신의 감정은 당신을 속여 사실에 의해 뒷받침되지 않는 것들을 생각하게 할 수 있다.

Why? 왜 정답일까?

'However, they can also sometimes be an unreliable, inaccurate source of information.'와 'Your feelings can mislead you into thinking things that are not supported by facts.'을 통해, 감정이 상황을 오해하게 하는 경우가 생길 수 있다는 중심 내용을 파악할 수 있으므로, 글의 요지로 가장 적절한 것은 ① '자신의 감정으로 인해 상황을 오해할 수 있다.'이다.

- deserve ⓥ ~을 받을 만하다
- inaccurate ⓐ 부정확한
- reflection ⓝ 반영
- behavior ⓝ 행동, 태도
- decide ⓥ 결정하다
- interview ⓝ 면접
- support ⓥ 뒷받침하다, 지지하다
- unreliable ⓐ 믿을 만하지 않은
- source of information 정보 출처
- conclude ⓥ 결론 짓다
- depressed ⓐ 우울한
- poorly ⓐⓓ 좋지 못하게
- mislead A into B A를 속여 B하게 하다

구문 풀이

10행 Your feelings can mislead you into thinking things [that are
「mislead + A + into + B : A를 잘못 인도해 B하게 하다」 / 선행사 / 주격 관·대
not supported by facts].

---

03 구입 이후 사용하지 않아 낭비가 된 물건들
정답률 77% | 정답 ⑤

다음 글의 제목으로 가장 적절한 것은?

① Spending Enables the Economy
소비가 경제를 가능케 한다
② Money Management: Dos and Don'ts
돈 관리: 해야 할 일과 하지 말아야 할 일
③ Too Much Shopping: A Sign of Loneliness
너무 많은 쇼핑: 외로움의 신호
④ 3R's of Waste: Reduce, Reuse, and Recycle
쓰레기의 3R: 줄이고, 다시 쓰고, 재활용하자
✔ What You Buy Is Waste Unless You Use It
당신이 사는 것은 당신이 그것을 이용하지 않는 한 낭비이다

[본문 해석]

여러분이 사 놓고 결국 한 번도 사용하지 않았던 물건에 대해 잠시 생각해 봐라. 결국 한 번도 입지 않은 옷 한 벌? 한 번도 읽지 않은 책 한 권? 심지어 상자에서 꺼내 보지도 않은 어떤 전자 기기? 호주인들만 봐도 사용하지 않는 물건에 매년 평균 108억 호주 달러(약 99억 9천 미국 달러)를 쓰는 것으로 추산되는데, 이는 대학과 도로에 사용하는 정부 지출 총액을 넘는 금액이다. 그 금액은 각 가구당 평균 1,250 호주 달러(약 1,156 미국 달러)이다. 우리가 사고 나서 제자리에서 먼지를 뒤집어쓰고 있는 모든 물건은 낭비인데, 돈 낭비, 시간 낭비, 그리고 순전히 쓸모없는 물건이라는 의미에서 낭비이다. 작가인 Clive Hamilton이 말하는 것처럼 "우리가 사는 물건에서 우리가 사용하는 것을 뺀 것은 낭비이다".

Why? 왜 정답일까?

사고 나서 한 번도 사용하지 않아 먼지만 쌓이고 있는 물건은 모두 낭비라는 내용의 글로, 마지막 두 문장이 주제를 잘 제시한다(All the things we buy that then just sit there gathering dust are waste ~. ~ 'The difference between the stuff we buy and what we use is waste.') 따라서 글의 제목으로 가장 적절한 것은 ⑤ '당신이 사는 것은 당신이 그것을 이용하지 않는 한 낭비이다'이다.

- end up 결국 ~하다
- equipment ⓝ 기기, 장비
- gather ⓥ 모으다
- rubbish ⓝ 쓰레기
- difference ⓝ 뺀 것, (양의) 차이
- electronic ⓐ 전자의
- approximately ⓐⓓ 대략
- waste ⓝ 낭비, 쓰레기
- observe ⓥ 말하다, 관찰하다

구문 풀이

11행 All the things [(that) we buy] [that then just sit there
주어(선행사) / 목적격 관계대명사 / 주격 관계대명사
gathering dust] are waste — a waste of money, a waste of time, and
분사구문(~하면서) / 동사(복수) 보어 / 동격(보어 보충 설명)
waste in the sense of pure rubbish.

---

04 Bill Evans의 생애
정답률 80% | 정답 ④

Bill Evans에 관한 다음 글의 내용과 일치하지 않는 것은?

① 6세에 피아노 수업을 받기 시작했다.
② Southeastern Louisiana 대학에서 학위를 취득했다.
③ 군 복무 이후 뉴욕에서 작곡을 공부했다.

☑ 작곡가 George Russell을 고용했다.
⑤ 1964년에 자신의 첫 번째 그래미상을 수상했다.

[본문 해석]

미국인 재즈 피아니스트 Bill Evans는 뉴저지에서 1929년에 태어났다. 그의 초기 교육은 클래식 음악이었다. 『그는 6세에 피아노 수업을 받기 시작해서, 나중에 플루트와 바이올린도 추가했다.』 『그는 1950년에 Southeastern Louisiana 대학에서 피아노와 음악 교육에서 학사 학위를 취득했다.』 그는 1951에서 1954년까지 군 복무를 하며 제5군악대에서 플루트를 연주했다. 『군 복무 이후 그는 뉴욕에 있는 Mannes School of Music에서 작곡을 공부했다.』 『작곡가 George Russell은 그의 연주에 감탄하여 Evans를 고용해 자신의 곡을 녹음하고 연주하게 했다.』 Evans는 1950년대 후반부터 1960년대 동안 만들어진 음반으로 유명해졌다. 『그는 자신의 앨범 *Conversations with Myself*로 1964년에 자신의 첫 번째 그래미상을 수상했다.』 Evans의 표현이 풍부한 피아노 작품과 그의 독특한 화성적 접근은 전 세대의 음악가들에게 영감을 주었다.

Why? 왜 정답일까?

'Composer George Russell admired his playing and hired Evans to record and perform his compositions.'에서 Evans는 작곡가 George Russell을 고용한 것이 아니고, 그에게 고용되어 그의 음악을 녹음하고 연주했다고 한다. 따라서 내용과 일치하지 않는 것은 ④ '작곡가 George Russell을 고용했다.'이다.

Why? 왜 오답일까?

① 'At the age of six, he began receiving piano lessons, ~'의 내용과 일치한다.
② 'He earned bachelor's degrees in piano and music education from Southeastern Louisiana College in 1950.'의 내용과 일치한다.
③ 'After serving in the military, he studied composition at the Mannes School of Music in New York.'의 내용과 일치한다.
⑤ 'He won his first Grammy Award in 1964 ~'의 내용과 일치한다.

- **add** ⓥ 추가하다
- **bachelor's degree** 학사 학위
- **military** ⓝ 군대 ⓐ 군사적인
- **admire** ⓥ 감탄하다, 존경하다
- **expressive** ⓐ 표현이 풍부한
- **earn** ⓥ 얻다, 취득하다, 벌다
- **serve in the army** 군 복무하다
- **composition** ⓝ 작곡
- **recording** ⓝ 음반, 녹음
- **harmonic** ⓐ (음악) 화성의

구문 풀이

9행 Composer George Russell admired his playing and hired <동사1> <동사2>
Evans to record and perform his compositions.
<목적(~하기 위해)>

---

05 약점 파악의 중요성   정답률 59% | 정답 ②

다음 글의 밑줄 친 부분 중, 어법상 틀린 것은? [3점]

[본문 해석]

자신의 강점 및 약점에 관해 스스로에게 솔직한가? 진정 자신을 알고 단점이 무엇인지 파악하라. 문제에 있어 자신의 역할을 받아들이는 것은 자신 안에 해결책이 있다는 것을 안다는 뜻이다. 특정 분야에 약점이 있다면, 교육을 받고 스스로 상황을 나아지게 하기 위해 해야 할 일을 해라. 만일 당신의 사회적 이미지가 심히 나쁘다면, 자신을 들여다보고 '당장 오늘' 그 이미지를 나아지게 하기 위해 필요한 조치를 취하라. 당신은 삶에 어떻게 반응할 것인지를 선택할 능력이 있다. 오늘 모든 변명을 끝내기로 결심하고 상황이 어떻게 돌아가는가에 대해 스스로에게 거짓말하는 일을 관둬라. 성장의 시작은 당신이 선택에 대한 책임을 직접 지기 시작할 때 온다.

Why? 왜 정답일까?

주어가 동명사구인 'Accepting ~'이므로 동사는 단수로 써야 하고, 이에 따라 복수동사인 mean을 means로 바꿔야 한다. 어법상 틀린 것은 ②이다.

Why? 왜 오답일까?

① 명령문에서 동사원형 앞에 생략된 주어는 You이다. 따라서 명령문의 목적어에 you가 나오면 반드시 재귀대명사인 yourself로 쓴다.
③ 앞에 선행사가 없고 뒤에 'have to do'의 목적어가 없는 불완전한 절이 나오므로 관계대명사 what을 쓴 것은 적절하다.

---

④ 맥락상 대명사가 'social image'라는 단수 명사를 받으므로 it을 쓴 것은 적절하다.
⑤ 타동사 stop은 동명사 목적어와 함께 쓰일 때 '~하기를 관두다, 멈추다'라는 뜻이다. 'stop+to부정사(~하기 위해 멈추다)'와 구별해 둔다.

- **strength** ⓝ 강점
- **accept** ⓥ 받아들이다, 수용하다
- **certain** ⓐ 특정한
- **social** ⓐ 사회의, 사회적인
- **respond to** ~에 응답하다
- **growth** ⓝ 성장
- **responsibility** ⓝ 책임
- **weakness** ⓝ 약점
- **role** ⓝ 역할
- **improve** ⓥ 나아지게 하다, 향상시키다
- **necessary** ⓐ 필요한
- **excuse** ⓝ 변명
- **personally** ⓐⓓ 직접, 개인적으로

구문 풀이

3행 Accepting your role in your problems means that you
<주어(동명사)> <동사(단수)> <접속사>
understand the solution lies within you.
<(접속사 that 생략)> <자동사(~에 있다)>

---

06 지적 겸손의 개념   정답률 62% | 정답 ①

(A), (B), (C)의 각 네모 안에서 문맥에 맞는 낱말로 가장 적절한 것은?

	(A)		(B)		(C)
☑	recognizing 인식하는 것	……	receptive 수용적인	……	value 존중한다
②	recognizing 인식하는 것	……	resistant 저항하는	……	undervalue 경시한다
③	recognizing 인식하는 것	……	receptive 수용적인	……	undervalue 경시한다
④	neglecting 무시하는 것	……	resistant 저항하는	……	undervalue 경시한다
⑤	neglecting 무시하는 것	……	receptive 수용적인	……	value 존중한다

[본문 해석]

지적 겸손이란 여러분이 인간이고 여러분이 가진 지식에 한계가 있다는 것을 인정하는 것이다. 이것은 여러분이 인지적이고 개인적인 편견을 가지고 있고, 여러분의 두뇌가 자신의 의견과 견해를 다른 것보다 선호하는 방식으로 사물을 바라보는 경향이 있다고 (A) 인식하는 것을 포함한다. 이것은 더 객관적이되고 정보에 근거한 결정들을 내리기 위해 그러한 편견들을 극복하고자 기꺼이 노력하는 것이다. 지적 겸손을 보이는 사람들은 자신들이 생각하는 것과 다르게 생각하는 다른 사람들에게 배우는 것에 더 (B) 수용적일 것이다. 그들은 다른 사람들이 제시하는 것을 (C) 존중한다는 것을 분명히 하기 때문에 다른 사람들에게 호감을 사고 존경받는 경향이 있다. 지적으로 겸손한 사람들은 더 많은 것을 배우고 싶어 하고 다양한 출처로부터 정보를 찾는 것에 개방적이다. 그들은 다른 사람들보다 우월하게 보이거나 느끼려고 애쓰는 데 관심이 없다.

Why? 왜 정답일까?

(A) 앞에서 자기 지식에 한계가 있음을 인정하는 것이 지적 겸손이라고 설명하는 것으로 보아, (A)에는 지적 겸손 안에 자신의 편견을 '인식한다'는 행동이 포함된다는 뜻의 recognizing이 들어가야 적절하다.
(B) 앞에서 지적 겸손을 보이는 이들은 자신의 편견을 극복하고자 기꺼이 노력한다는 내용이 나오는 것으로 보아, (B)에는 이들이 타인에게 배움을 얻는 데 '수용적'이라는 뜻의 receptive가 들어가야 적절하다.
(C) 마지막 두 문장에서 지적으로 겸손한 사람들은 더 많이 배우고 싶어 하며, 다양한 출처로부터 정보를 취하고자 하고, 타인보다 우월해 보이는 데 관심을 두지 않는다고 언급하는 것으로 보아, (C)에는 이들이 타인의 견해를 '존중한다'는 뜻의 value가 들어가야 적절하다. 따라서 각 네모 안에서 문맥에 맞는 낱말로 가장 적절한 것은 ① '(A) recognizing (인식하는 것) – (B) receptive(수용적인) – (C) value(존중한다)'이다.

- **humility** ⓝ 겸손
- **recognize** ⓥ 인식하다, 깨닫다
- **cognitive** ⓐ 인지적인
- **favor** ⓥ 선호하다
- **objective** ⓐ 객관적인
- **receptive** ⓐ 수용적인
- **bring to the table** ⓥ ~을 제시하다
- **neglect** ⓥ 무시하다, 소홀히 하다
- **possess** ⓥ 지니다, 가지다
- **bias** ⓝ 편견
- **overcome** ⓥ 극복하다
- **informed decision** ⓝ 정보에 근거한 결정
- **resistant** ⓐ ~에 저항하는
- **superior** ⓐ 우월한

구문 풀이

8행 People [who display intellectual humility] are more likely to be
<주어> ['be likely+to부정사 : ~하는 경향이 있다]
receptive to learning from others [who think differently than they do].
<~에 수용적인> <선행사> <=think>

DAY 06

★★★ 1등급 대비 고난도 2점 문제

07 실험을 비판적으로 바라보기   정답률 39% | 정답 ②

다음 빈칸에 들어갈 말로 가장 적절한 것을 고르시오.

① inventive – 독창적이지
② objective – 객관적이지 ✔
③ untrustworthy – 믿을 수 없는지
④ unreliable – 신뢰성이 없는지
⑤ decisive – 결정적이지

[본문 해석]

다른 과학자의 실험 결과물을 읽을 때, 그 실험에 대해 비판적으로 생각하라. 당신 자신에게 물어라. 관찰들이 실험 도중에 혹은 후에 기록되었나? 결론이 합리적인가? 그 결과들은 반복될 수 있는가? 정보의 출처는 신뢰할만한가? 당신은 실험을 수행한 그 과학자나 그룹이 한쪽으로 치우치지 않았는지도 물어야 한다. 한쪽으로 치우치지 않음은 당신이 실험의 결과로 특별한 이익을 얻지 않는다는 것을 의미한다. 예를 들면, 만약 한 제약 회사가 그 회사의 새로운 제품 중 하나가 얼마나 잘 작용하는지 시험해보기 위한 실험 비용을 지불한다면, 특별한 이익이 관련된 것이다. 즉 만약 실험이 그 제품이 효과 있음을 보여준다면, 그 제약 회사는 이익을 본다. 따라서, 그 실험자들은 <u>객관적이지</u> 않다. 그들은 결론이 긍정적이며 제약 회사에 이익을 주도록 보장할지도 모른다. 결과들을 평가할 때, 있을 수 있는 어떤 치우침에 대해 생각하라!

Why? 왜 정답일까?

첫 문장에서 실험을 비판적으로 바라보라고 조언한 후 'You should also ask if the scientist or group conducting the experiment was unbiased.', 'When assessing results, think about any biases that may be present!'에서 특히 실험이 어느 한쪽으로 편향되지는 않았는지 확인해야 한다는 조언을 보태고 있다. 따라서 빈칸에 들어갈 말로 가장 적절한 것은 실험이 '객관적이지' 않을 수 있으므로 주의가 필요함을 상기시키는 ② '객관적이지'이다.

- critically [ad] 비판적으로
- make sense [v] 합리적이다
- conduct [v] 수행하다
- interest [n] 이익
- profit [v] 이득을 보다 [n] 이득
- ensure [v] 보장하다
- inventive [a] 독창적인
- untrustworthy [a] 믿을 만하지 않은
- observation [n] 관찰
- reliable [a] 신뢰성 있는, 믿을 만한
- unbiased [a] 편파적이지 않은
- outcome [n] 결과
- experimenter [n] 실험자
- assess [v] 평가하다
- objective [a] 객관적인
- decisive [a] 결정적인

구문 풀이

5행 You should also ask if the scientist or group conducting the experiment was unbiased.
(접속사(~인지 아닌지)) (주어) (현재분사구) (동사)

★★ 문제 해결 꿀~팁 ★★

▶ 많이 틀린 이유는?
빈칸 앞에 aren't라는 부정 표현이 나오므로 빈칸에 주제와 반대되는 말이 들어가야 하는데, ③의 untrustworthy와 ④의 unreliable은 모두 '신뢰성이 없다'는 의미로 그 자체로 주제를 나타낸다.

▶ 문제 해결 방법은?
앞 문장의 내용을 충실히 이해하면 쉽게 답을 고를 수 있다. 앞에서 제약 회사가 연구에 돈을 대는 경우 '특별한 이익이 관련된다'고 언급하는데, 이는 바꾸어 말하면 연구의 '객관성'이 떨어진다는 뜻이다.

★★★ 1등급 대비 고난도 3점 문제

08 Amondawa 부족의 독특한 시간 관념   정답률 38% | 정답 ④

글의 흐름으로 보아, 주어진 문장이 들어가기에 가장 적절한 곳을 고르시오. [3점]

[본문 해석]

'시간 밖에서 사는 사람들'이라고 부를 수 있는 어떤 문화가 있다. 브라질에 사는 Amondawa 부족에게는 측정되거나 셀 수 있는 시간이라는 개념이 없다. ① 오히려 그들은 사건이 시간에 뿌리를 두고 있다고 간주하기보다는 연속되는 사건의 세상에서 산다. ② 연구자들은 또한 나이가 있는 사람이 아무도 없다는 것을 알아냈다. ③ 대신에 그들은 자신들의 생애 단계와 사회 내 위치를 반영하기 위해 이름을 바꾸어서 어린아이는 자신의 이름을 갓 태어난 형제자매에게 넘겨주고 새로운 이름을 갖는다. ④ 미국에는 시간과 시간의 흐름에 관한 매우 많은 은유가 있어서 우리는 시간을 '물건'으로 간주하는데, 즉 "주말이 거의 다 지나갔다."라거나 "나는 시간이 없다."라는 식이다. 우리는 그러한 말들이 객관적이라고 생각하지만, 그렇지 않다. ⑤ 우리는 이런 은유를 만들어 내지만, Amondawa 사람들은 시간을 은유적으로 말하거나 생각하지 않는다.

Why? 왜 정답일까?

Amondawa 부족의 독특한 시간 관념을 소개한 글이다. ④ 앞에서는 이들이 사건을 시간별로 파악하기보다는 그저 연속된 사건 속에 살며 나이도 세지 않는다는 내용을 제시한다. 반면 주어진 문장은 미국의 예를 들어 시간과 시간의 흐름을 물건처럼 느끼게 하는 많은 은유가 있다고 언급하는데, ④ 뒤에서는 '이러한 은유적인 말들'이 객관적으로 보이더라도 Amondawa 부족의 관점에는 적용될 수 없다는 이야기임을 덧붙이고 있다. 따라서 주어진 문장이 들어가기에 가장 적절한 곳은 ④이다.

- passing [n] (시간의) 흐름, 경과
- refer to A as B [v] A를 B라고 부르다
- measure [v] 측정하다
- reflect [v] 반영하다
- objective [a] 객관적인
- think of A as B [v] A를 B라고 간주하다
- tribe [n] 부족
- rooted in ~에 뿌리를 둔
- statement [n] 말, 진술

구문 풀이

1행 In the U.S. we have so many metaphors for time and its
「so ~ that … : 너무 ~해서 …하다」
passing that we think of time as "a thing," that is "the weekend is
「think of + A + as + B : A를 B라고 간주하다」 → 즉, 다시 말해
almost gone," or "I haven't got the time."

★★ 문제 해결 꿀~팁 ★★

▶ 많이 틀린 이유는?
⑤의 these metaphors가 주어진 문장의 따옴표 구절과 이어진다고 보면 ⑤를 답으로 고르기 쉽지만, 앞에 나오는 such statements 또한 가리키는 바가 불분명함을 염두에 두어야 한다.

▶ 문제 해결 방법은?
④ 뒤의 such statements가 가리키는 바에 주목해야 한다. 앞에서 '진술'로 받을 만한 말이 따로 나오지 않았는데 바로 '이러한 진술'이라는 언급을 이어가는 부적절하며, 마침 주어진 문장이 따옴표로 다양한 구절을 제시하고 있는 것으로 볼 때, such statement 앞에 주어진 문장이 나와야 함을 알 수 있다.

★★★ 1등급 대비 고난도 3점 문제

09 또래의 존재가 청소년의 행동에 미치는 영향   정답률 41% | 정답 ①

다음 글의 내용을 한 문장으로 요약하고자 한다. 빈칸 (A), (B)에 들어갈 말로 가장 적절한 것은? [3점]

	(A)		(B)
✔ ①	presence 존재	……	take risks 위험을 감수하다
②	presence 존재	……	behave cautiously 조심스럽게 행동하다
③	indifference 무관심	……	perform poorly 잘하지 못하다
④	absence 부재	……	enjoy adventures 모험을 즐기다
⑤	absence 부재	……	act independently 독립적으로 행동하다

[본문 해석]

한 연구에서, Temple 대학교의 심리학자 Laurence Steinberg와 공동 저자인 심리학자 Margo Gardner는 306명의 사람들을 세 연령 집단(평균 나이 14세인 어린 청소년, 평균 나이 19세인 나이가 더 많은 청소년, 그리고 24세 이상인 성인)으로 나누었다. 피실험자들은 게임 참가자가 도로에 경고 없이 나타나는 벽에 충돌하는 것을 피해야 하는 컴퓨터 운전 게임을 했다. Steinberg와 Gardner는 무작위로 몇몇 참가자들을 혼자 혹은 두 명의 같은 나이 또래들이 지켜보는 가운데 게임을 하게 했다. 나이가 더 많은 청소년들은 그들의 또래들이 같은 방에 있을 때 위험 운전 지수에서 약 50퍼센트 더 높은 점수를 기록했고, 어린 청소년들의 운전은 다른 어린 십대들이 주변에 있을 때 무려 두 배 더 무모했다. 대조적으로, 성인들은 그들이 혼자 있든지 혹은 다른 사람이 보고 있든지 상관없이 유사한 방식으로 행동했다.

➡ 성인들은 그렇지 않지만, 또래들의 (A) <u>존재</u>는 청소년들이 더 (B) <u>위험</u>을 감수하게 만든다.

Why? 왜 정답일까?

연구를 소개한 글이므로 결론을 제시하는 마지막 두 문장을 주의 깊게 독해하면, 청소년 집단은 또래들이 있을 때 훨씬 더 무모한 게임을 했으며, 어른들은 별 영향이 없었다는 내용이 나온다. 따라서 요약문의 빈칸 (A), (B)에 들어갈 말로 가장 적절한 것은 ① '(A) presence(존재), (B) take risks(위험을 감수하다)'이다.

- co-author 공동 저자
- adolescent ⓝ 청소년
- crash into ~에 충돌하다
- observe ⓥ 관찰하다
- indifference ⓝ 무관심
- independently ⓐⓓ 독립적으로
- divide ⓥ 나누다
- mean ⓐ 평균의
- regardless of ~에 상관없이
- cautiously ⓐⓓ 조심스럽게
- poorly ⓐⓓ 저조하게, 형편없이

구문 풀이

11행 Older adolescents scored about 50 percent higher on an
　　　　　　주어1　　　　　　　　　　동사1
index of risky driving when their peers were in the room — and
the driving of early adolescents was fully twice as reckless when
　　　　　　주어2　　　　　　　　　동사2　　「배수사 + as + 원급 + (as ~) :
other young teens were around.　　　　　　　　　(~보다) … 배 더 ~한」

★★ 문제 해결 꿀~팁 ★★

▶ 많이 틀린 이유는?
크게 보아 '연구 – 결과'의 구조를 이루는 글로, 성인과 청소년 집단을 대조하는 In contrast 앞뒤에서 어른과 달리 청소년들은 또래가 있을 때 더 무모한(reckless) 운전을 했다는 결론을 제시하고 있다. 최다 오답인 ②의 (B) 'behave cautiously'는 결론의 핵심어 reckless와 정반대의 의미를 나타내므로 답으로 적절치 않다.

▶ 문제 해결 방법은?
두 집단을 비교하여 설명하는 글에서는 각 집단의 특성과 관련된 핵심어를 먼저 찾은 뒤 요약문 및 선택지와 맞춰보도록 한다.

10-12 도둑을 솜씨 좋게 골탕먹인 상인

[본문 해석]

(A)
부유한 상인이 자신의 집에 혼자 살았다. 그 집에 사는 사람이 자기밖에 없다는 것을 알았기 때문에, 「그는 자신의 집에 도둑이 드는 상황에 항상 대비하고 있었다.」 「 」: 12번 ①의 근거 일치 그래서 어느 날, 도둑이 집에 들어왔을 때, 그는 차분하고 침착했다. 비록 상인은 깨어 있었지만, 깊이 잠든 척했다. 그는 침대에 누워서 도둑이 움직이는 것을 지켜보았다. 도둑은 훔친 물건들을 운반하기 위해 흰 새 보자기를 (a) 그와 함께 가지고 왔다.

(D)
그는 훔친 귀중품들을 모두 넣어 묶은 뒤 운반할 생각으로 그것을 바닥에 펼쳐 놓았다. (e) 그가 상인의 호화로운 집에서 비싸게 보이는 물건을 모으느라 분주한 사이, 상인은 재빨리 침대에서 일어났다. 「그리고 나서 그는 도둑의 흰 새 보자기를 비슷하게 생긴 흰 보자기로 바꾸었는데, 이것은 도둑의 것보다 훨씬 약하고 값싼 것이었다.」 「 」: 12번 ⑤의 근거 일치

(B)
그리고 나서 (b) 그(상인)는 누워서 자는 척했다. 도둑이 가능한 한 많은 귀중품들을 훔치는 것을 마쳤을 때, 그는 자신의 것이라고 생각했던 흰 보자기의 매듭을 서둘러 묶었다. 「그 동안에 상인은 정원으로 뛰어나가 있는 힘껏 소리 쳤다. — "도둑이야! 도둑!"」 「 」: 12번 ②의 근거 일치 도둑은 초조해져서 서둘러서 보자기를 들어올렸다. (c) 그가 놀랍게도 훔친 물건들로 가득 찬 얇은 흰 보자기가 찢어졌다.

(C)
「훔친 모든 물건들이 바닥에 떨어져 아주 크고 불쾌한 소리를 냈다.」 「 」: 12번 ③의 근거 일치 많은 사람들이 자신에게 달려드는 것을 보고 도둑은 훔친 모든 물건들을 포기해야만 했다. 「그 물건들을 집에 남겨두고 떠나면서, 그는 서둘러 도망치며 작은 목소리로 말했다.」 「 」: 12번 ④의 근거 불일치 "이 사람은 교묘한 상인이야. 그는 뼛속까지 장사꾼이야. 그는 그의 귀중품들을 지켜냈을 뿐만 아니라, (d) 내 새 보자기도 빼앗았다고. 그는 도둑한테서 훔쳤어!" 이렇게 혼잣말을 하면서 그는 집밖으로 뛰쳐나갔다.

- merchant ⓝ 상인
- in action 활동을 하는
- pretend ⓥ ~인 체하다
- valuable ⓝ 귀중품 ⓐ 귀한, 가치 있는

- tie a knot 매듭을 묶다
- to one's surprise ~로서는 놀랍게도
- unpleasant ⓐ 불쾌한
- under one's breath 낮은 목소리로
- spread out 펼치다
- yell ⓥ 소리치다
- tear apart 찢다
- give up on ~을 포기하다, 단념하다
- to the core 속속들이, 완전히

구문 풀이

(B) 2행 When the thief had finished collecting as many valuables as
　　　　　접속사(~할 때)　　　　동사(과거완료)
he could, he hurriedly tied a knot in the white sheet [which (he thought)
　　　　　　　　동사(과거)　　　　　　　　선행사　↖　( ): 삽입절
was his].
(D) 3행 While he was busy gathering expensive-looking items from
　　　　　　　　　「be busy + 동명사 : ~하느라 바쁘다」
the merchant's luxurious house, the merchant quickly got out of the bed.

---

10 글의 순서 파악　　　　정답률 66% | 정답 ④

주어진 글 (A)에 이어질 내용을 순서에 맞게 배열한 것으로 가장 적절한 것은?

① (B) – (D) – (C)　　　　② (C) – (B) – (D)
③ (C) – (D) – (B)　　　　✔ (D) – (B) – (C)
⑤ (D) – (C) – (B)

Why? 왜 정답일까?

혼자 살아서 도둑이 드는 상황에 늘 대비하고 있던 상인이 어느 날 정말 집에 도둑이 든 것을 알았다는 내용의 (A) 뒤로, 도둑이 귀한 물건을 찾느라 분주한 사이 상인이 도둑의 흰 보자기를 다른 것으로 바꾸어 놓았다는 (D)가 연결된다. 이어서 (B)에서는 도둑이 갈 채비를 하자 상인이 밖으로 나가 도둑이 들었다며 소리를 질렀고 이에 도둑이 바삐 움직이다가 보자기가 찢어졌다는 내용이 전개된다. 마지막으로 (C)는 보자기가 찢어지는 바람에 물건이 모두 떨어졌고, 도둑은 모든 것을 포기한 채 상인이 한 수 위임을 인정하고 떠났다는 결말을 제시한다. 따라서 글의 순서로 가장 적절한 것은 ④ '(D) – (B) – (C)' 이다.

11 지칭 추론　　　　정답률 47% | 정답 ②

밑줄 친 (a) ~ (e) 중에서 가리키는 대상이 나머지 넷과 다른 것은?

① (a)　　✔ (b)　　③ (c)　　④ (d)　　⑤ (e)

Why? 왜 정답일까?

(a), (c), (d), (e)는 the thief, (b)는 the merchant를 가리키므로, (a) ~ (e) 중에서 가리키는 대상이 다른 하나는 ② '(b)'이다.

12 세부 내용 파악　　　　정답률 68% | 정답 ④

윗글에 관한 내용으로 적절하지 않은 것은?

① 상인은 도둑이 드는 상황에 항상 대비하고 있었다.
② 상인은 정원으로 뛰어나가 크게 소리쳤다.
③ 도둑이 훔친 물건들이 바닥에 떨어졌다.
✔ 도둑은 상인의 물건들을 집밖으로 가지고 달아났다.
⑤ 상인의 보자기는 도둑의 보자기보다 값싼 것이었다.

Why? 왜 정답일까?

(C) 'Leaving the goods behind in the house, he ran away in a hurry ~' 에서 도둑은 훔치려던 물건을 모두 집에 두고 황급히 달아났다고 하므로, 내용과 일치하지 않는 것은 ④ '도둑은 상인의 물건들을 집밖으로 가지고 달아났다.'이다.

Why? 왜 오답일까?

① (A) '~ he was always prepared in case thieves came to his house.'의 내용과 일치한다.
② (B) 'The merchant meanwhile ran out into the garden and yelled ~'의 내용과 일치한다.
③ (C) 'All the stolen goods fell down on the floor ~'의 내용과 일치한다.
⑤ (D) '~ a similar looking white sheet, which was much weaker and much cheaper than the thief's one.'의 내용과 일치한다.

DAY 06

DAY 07 — 20분 미니 모의고사

01 ②	02 ①	03 ③	04 ②	05 ④
06 ③	07 ②	08 ⑤	09 ④	10 ③
11 ①	12 ⑤			

---

01 급여 인상 요청
정답률 79% | 정답 ②

다음 글의 목적으로 가장 적절한 것은?

① 부서 이동을 신청하려고
② 급여 인상을 요청하려고 ✓
③ 근무 시간 조정을 요구하려고
④ 기업 혁신 방안을 제안하려고
⑤ 신입 사원 연수에 대해 문의하려고

[본문 해석]

친애하는 Krull씨께

저는 Trincom Enterprises에서 영업 매니저로 일하는 것을 매우 즐겨 왔습니다. 2015년에 입사한 이후, 저는 이 회사의 충성스럽고 필수적인 구성원이었고, 회사에 기여할 혁신적인 방법들을 개발해 왔습니다. 게다가, 저는 작년 한 해만 두 개의 주요 고객사를 회사에 새로 유치하여 회사의 총매출을 5% 증가시켰습니다. 또한 저는 신규 직원 5명을 자발적으로 교육해 왔고 그 합계가 35시간이 되었습니다. 따라서 저는 제 급여를 인상하는 것을 고려해 주시기를 요청드리며, 이것이 업계 평균뿐만 아니라 제 성과도 반영한다고 믿습니다. 귀하와 곧 이야기하기를 기대합니다.

Kimberly Morss 드림

Why? 왜 정답일까?

'I would therefore request your consideration in raising my salary, ~'에서 급여 인상을 고려해달라는 요청이 나오므로, 글의 목적으로 가장 적절한 것은 ② '급여 인상을 요청하려고'이다.

- **enterprise** ⓝ 기업
- **loyal** ⓐ 충성스러운
- **innovative** ⓐ 혁신적인
- **voluntarily** ⓐⓓ 자원해서
- **sales manager** 영업 매니저
- **essential** ⓐ 핵심적인, 필수적인
- **increase** ⓥ 증가시키다
- **raise** ⓥ 올리다, 높이다

구문 풀이

10행 I would therefore request your consideration in raising my salary, which (I believe) reflects my performance as well as the industry average.
선행사 / 주격 관·대 / 동사 / ( ): 삽입절

---

02 전문성 개발에 있어 선택과 집중의 중요성
정답률 75% | 정답 ①

다음 글에서 필자가 주장하는 바로 가장 적절한 것은?

① 자신에게 의미 있는 영역을 정해서 전문성을 키워야 한다. ✓
② 전문성 함양에는 타고난 재능보다 노력과 훈련이 중요하다.
③ 전문가가 되기 위해서는 다양한 분야에 관심을 가져야 한다.
④ 전문성을 기르기 위해서는 구체적인 계획과 실천이 필수적이다.
⑤ 전문가는 일의 우선순위를 결정해서 업무를 수행해야 한다.

[본문 해석]

전문성을 개발하는 데는 그 자체의 비용이 수반된다. 우리는 언어를 말하거나 우리가 가장 좋아하는 음식을 아는 것과 같은 어떤 분야에서는 그냥 삶을 살아감으로써 전문가가 될 수 있지만, 다른 많은 분야에서는 전문성이 상당한 훈련과 노력을 요구한다. 게다가 전문성이란 특정한 영역에만 국한된다. 우리가 한 영역에서 열심히 노력해서 얻는 전문성은 관련 영역으로 오직 불완전하게 이어질 뿐이며, 관련이 없는 영역으로는 전혀 이어지지 않을 것이다. 결국, 우리가 우리 삶의 모든 것에서 전문가가 되기를 원한다고 해도, 그렇게 할 충분한 시간이 없다. 우리가 그렇게 할 수 있는 분야에서조차, 그만한 노력을 기울일 가치가 반드시 있는 것은 아닐 것이다. 우리가 우리의 삶에 가장 흔하며 중요한 선택 영역과 우리가 배우고 선택하는 것을 적극적으로 즐기는 영역에 우리의 전문성을 집중해야만 하는 것은 분명하다.

Why? 왜 정답일까?

마지막 문장인 'It's clear that we should concentrate our own expertise on those domains of choice that are most common and/or important to our lives, and those we actively enjoy learning about and choosing from.'에서 우리는 삶에 있어 중요하거나 우리가 배우면서 즐거워할 수 있는 영역을 선택하여 전문성을 집중적으로 키워야 한다고 언급하고 있다. 따라서 필자가 주장하는 바로 가장 적절한 것은 ① '자신에게 의미 있는 영역을 정해서 전문성을 키워야 한다.'이다.

- **expertise** ⓝ 전문성
- **considerable** ⓐ 상당한
- **carry over** (다른 상황에서 계속) 이어지다
- **domain** ⓝ 영역
- **specific** ⓐ 특정한
- **concentrate** ⓥ 집중하다

구문 풀이

8행 In the end, as much as we may want to become experts on everything in our lives, there simply isn't enough time to do so.
문두의 「as + 원급 + as」; 양보 구문(~에도 불구하고)
동사 / 주어 「enough + 명 + to부정사 : ~하기에 충분한 …」

---

03 스트레스 관리의 원칙
정답률 80% | 정답 ③

밑줄 친 put the glass down이 다음 글에서 의미하는 바로 가장 적절한 것은? [3점]

① pour more water into the glass – 잔에 물을 더 부어야
② set a plan not to make mistakes – 실수하지 않기 위해 계획을 세워야
③ let go of the stress in your mind – 마음속에서 스트레스를 떨쳐내야 ✓
④ think about the cause of your stress – 스트레스의 원인을 생각해 보아야
⑤ learn to accept the opinions of others – 다른 사람들의 의견을 받아들이는 법을 배워야

[본문 해석]

한 심리학 교수가 학생들에게 스트레스 관리 원칙을 가르치던 중 물이 든 유리잔을 들어 올리고 "제가 들고 있는 이 물 잔의 무게는 얼마나 될까요?"라고 물었다. 학생들은 다양한 대답을 외쳤다. 그 교수가 답했다. "이 잔의 절대 무게는 중요하지 않습니다. 이는 제가 이 잔을 얼마나 오래 들고 있느냐에 달려 있죠. 만약 제가 이것을 1분 동안 들고 있다면, 꽤 가볍죠. 하지만, 만약 제가 이것을 하루종일 들고 있다면 이것은 제 팔에 심각한 고통을 야기하고 잔을 바닥에 떨어뜨릴 수 밖에 없게 할 것입니다. 각 사례에서 잔의 무게는 같지만, 제가 오래 들고 있을수록 그것은 저에게 더 무겁게 느껴지죠." 학생들은 동의하며 고개를 끄덕였고, 교수는 이어 말했다. "여러분이 인생에서 느끼는 스트레스들도 이 물 잔과 같습니다. 만약 아직도 어제 받은 스트레스의 무게를 느낀다면, 그것은 잔을 내려놓아야 할 때라는 강한 신호입니다."

Why? 왜 정답일까?

물 잔의 무게를 느낄 때 중요한 것은 잔의 절대적 무게가 아니라 얼마나 오래 들고 있는지(It depends on how long I hold it.)이며, 같은 잔이라고 할지라도 더 오래 들고 있을수록 더 무겁게 느껴진다(the longer I hold it, the heavier it feels to me.)고 한다. 이를 스트레스 상황에 적용하면, 스트레스의 무게가 더 무겁게 느껴질수록 그 스트레스를 오래 안고 있었다는 뜻이므로 '스트레스를 떨쳐내기' 위해 노력해야 한다는 것을 알 수 있다. 따라서 밑줄 친 부분이 의미하는 바로 가장 적절한 것은 ③ '마음속에서 스트레스를 떨쳐내야'이다.

- **principle** ⓝ 원칙, 원리
- **nod** ⓥ 끄덕이다
- **put down** ~을 내려놓다
- **let go of** ~을 내려놓다, 버리다, 포기하다
- **severe** ⓐ 심각한
- **in agreement** 동의하며
- **pour** ⓥ 쏟다, 붓다

구문 풀이

7행 But, if I hold it for a day straight, it will cause severe pain in my arm, forcing me to drop the glass to the floor.
접속사(조건) / 동사(현재) / 동사(미래) / 분사구문(= and will force ~)

---

04 인간 진화와 소속 욕구
정답률 59% | 정답 ②

다음 글의 주제로 가장 적절한 것은?

① skills for the weak to survive modern life
약자가 현대 생활에서 생존하는 기술

✓ usefulness of belonging for human evolution
인간 진화에 있어 소속의 유용성
③ ways to avoid competition among social groups
사회적 집단 간의 경쟁을 피하는 방법
④ roles of social relationships in children's education
아이들의 교육에 있어 사회적 관계의 역할
⑤ differences between two major evolutionary theories
두 가지 주요 진화론의 차이

[본문 해석]

우리(인간)와 같은 창조물에게 있어, 진화는 강한 소속 욕구를 가진 이들에게 미소지어 주었다. 생존과 번식은 자연 선택에 의한 성공의 기준이고, 다른 사람들과 관계를 형성하는 것은 생존과 번식 모두에 유용할 수 있다. 집단은 자원을 공유하고, 아픈 구성원을 돌보고, 포식자를 쫓아버리고, 적에 맞서서 함께 싸우고, 효율성을 향상시키기 위해 일을 나누고, 많은 다른 방식으로 생존에 기여한다. 특히, 한 개인과 한 집단이 같은 자원을 원하면, 집단이 일반적으로 우세하고, 그래서 자원에 대한 경쟁은 소속하려는 욕구를 특별히 좋아할 것이다. 마찬가지로 소속되어 있다는 것은 이를테면 잠재적인 짝을 서로 만나게 해주거나, 특히 부모가 자녀를 돌보기 위해 함께 있도록 하면서 번식을 촉진시키는데, 자녀들은 한 명 이상의 돌보는 이가 있으면 훨씬 더 생존하기 쉬울 것이다.

Why? 왜 정답일까?

첫 문장인 'For creatures like us, evolution smiled upon those with a strong need to belong.'에서 진화의 과정은 강한 소속 욕구를 지닌 이들을 선호했다는 주제를 제시한 후, 소속 욕구가 진화에 어떤 식으로 도움이 되었는지 구체적으로 부연하고 있다. 따라서 글의 주제로 가장 적절한 것은 ② '인간 진화에 있어 소속의 유용성'이다.

- reproduction ⓝ 번식, 재생
- natural selection 자연 선택
- fight against ~에 맞서 싸우다
- belongingness ⓝ 소속, 귀속, 친밀감
- criterion ⓝ 기준
- scare off ~을 겁주어 쫓아버리다
- prevail ⓥ 우세하다
- caregiver ⓝ 양육자

구문 풀이

5행 Groups can share resources, care for sick members,
                      동사1   동사2
scare off predators, fight together against enemies, divide tasks
동사3   동사4   동사5
so as to improve efficiency, and contribute to survival in many other
목적(~하기 위해)   동사6
ways.

★★★ 1등급 대비 고난도 2점 문제

05 사후 비판을 유독 많이 듣는 스포츠 업계 사람들   정답률 33% | 정답 ④

다음 글의 밑줄 친 부분 중, 어법상 틀린 것은?

[본문 해석]

'Monday Morning Quarterback(월요일 아침 쿼터백: 일이 이미 있고 난 뒤 이러쿵저러쿵하는 사람)'이라는 명칭이 존재하는 이유가 있다. 주말 경기에 대해 토론하는 팬들의 소셜 미디어의 댓글만 읽어봐도, 여러분은 얼마나 많은 사람들이 경기장에 있는 이들보다 자기가 더 성공적으로 경기를 뛰고, 감독하고, 스포츠팀을 관리할 수 있다고 믿는지 금방 알 수 있다. 이것은 이사회실에서도 마찬가지이다. 스포츠 사업에서 수년간의 훈련을 받고 전문 학위를 가진 학생들과 전문가들 또한, 전문 지식이 전혀 없는 친구나 가족이나 혹은 심지어 생판 남으로부터 어떻게 일해야 할지에 관해 충고를 듣고 있는 자신을 발견할지도 모른다. 스포츠 경영 임원진들은 각자 자기 분야에서 수십 년의 지식과 경험을 가지고 있다. 하지만, 그들 중 많은 사람들이 자신에게 사업 운영 방식을 알려주는 팬들과 지역 사회 구성원들의 비난에 직면한다. 의사에게 수술하는 방법을 알려주거나, 회계사에게 세금을 준비하는 방법을 알려주는 사람은 거의 없지만, 스포츠 조직이 어떻게 관리되어야 하는지에 대한 피드백은 많은 이들이 제공한다.

Why? 왜 정답일까?

telling의 의미상 주어가 fans and community members인데, 목적어는 many of them(= executives)이므로, 둘은 서로 다른 대상을 지칭한다. 재귀대명사는 주어와 목적어가 일치할 때만 쓰므로, themselves 대신 them을 써야 어법상 맞다. 따라서 어법상 틀린 것은 ④이다.

Why? 왜 오답일까?

① 동사구인 could play, coach, and manage를 꾸미기 위해 부사 more successfully를 쓴 것이다.

---

② may also find의 목적어인 themselves가 '충고를 듣는' 입장이므로, 수동을 나타내는 「being + 과거분사」 형태를 적절하게 썼다.
③ 복수 명사 주어인 Executives에 맞춰 복수 동사 have를 쓴 것은 어법상 맞다.
⑤ 완전한 문장인 sport organizations should be managed를 이끌기 위해 의문부사 how(어떻게)를 쓴 것은 어법상 맞다.

- boardroom ⓝ 이사회실
- specialized ⓐ 전문화된
- expertise ⓝ 전문 지식
- respective ⓐ 각자의
- criticism ⓝ 비평
- accountant ⓝ 회계사
- organization ⓝ 조직, 단체
- professional ⓝ 전문가
- total stranger 생판 남
- executive ⓝ 임원, 중역
- face ⓥ 마주하다, 직면하다
- run ⓥ (가게나 사업을) 운영하다
- tax ⓝ 세금

구문 풀이

15행 Very few people tell their doctor how to perform surgery or
       ~하는 사람은 거의 없다   간접목적어1   직접목적어1 →4형식 동사
their accountant how to prepare their taxes, but many people
간접목적어2   직접목적어2
provide feedback on how sport organizations should be managed.

★★ 문제 해결 꿀~팁 ★★

▶ 많이 틀린 이유는?
themselves가 사람이므로 '충고를 주는' 주체처럼 보여서 ②를 고르기 쉽다. 하지만 문맥을 보면, 이들은 일을 어떻게 할지에 대한 충고를 남에게 '받는' 입장이 맞다.
▶ 문제 해결 방법은?
재귀대명사를 쓰려면, 행위를 나타내는 동사 또는 준동사를 기준으로 (의미상) 주어와 목적어가 같아야 한다. 여기서는 현재분사 telling을 중심으로 판단해야 하는데, 현재분사의 의미상 주어는 분사가 꾸미는 명사이고, 목적어는 분사 뒤에 나오는 명사이므로, 두 대상이 같은지 다른지 비교하면 된다.

06 작은 변화를 무시하기 쉬운 이유   정답률 61% | 정답 ③

다음 글의 밑줄 친 부분 중, 문맥상 낱말의 쓰임이 적절하지 <u>않은</u> 것은? [3점]

[본문 해석]

우리는 흔히 작은 변화들이 당장은 크게 ① 중요한 것 같지 않아서 그것들을 무시한다. 지금 돈을 약간 모아도, 여러분은 여전히 백만장자가 아니다. 오늘 밤에 스페인어를 한 시간 동안 공부해도, 여러분은 여전히 그 언어를 익힌 것은 아니다. 우리는 약간의 변화를 만들어 보지만, 그 결과는 결코 ② 빨리 오지 않는 것 같고 그래서 우리는 이전의 일상으로 다시 빠져든다. 변화의 느린 속도는 또한 나쁜 습관을 버리기 ③ 쉽게(→ 어렵게) 만든다. 오늘 몸에 좋지 않은 음식을 먹어도 체중계는 크게 움직이지 않는다. 하나의 결정은 무시하기 쉽다. 하지만 우리가 잘못된 결정을 반복적으로 따라 작은 오류를 날마다 ④ 반복한다면, 우리의 작은 선택들이 모여 좋지 않은 결과를 만들어낸다. 많은 실수는 결국 ⑤ 문제로 이어진다.

Why? 왜 정답일까?

'We make a few changes, but the results never seem to come quickly and so we slide back into our previous routines.'에서 우리가 변화를 시도하더라도 바로 변화가 나타나는 것이 아니기에 우리는 다시 변화 이전의 일상으로 돌아가게 된다고 설명한다. 이에 비추어 볼 때, 변화가 느리게 찾아온다는 점은 나쁜 습관을 버리기 '어렵게' 만든다는 의미가 되도록 ③의 easy를 difficult로 바꾸어야 한다. 문맥상 낱말의 쓰임이 적절하지 않은 것은 ③이다.

- ignore ⓥ 무시하다
- in the moment 당장, 지금
- slide back into ~로 돌아가다, 복귀하다
- routine ⓝ 일상
- break a bad habit 나쁜 습관을 버리다
- scale ⓝ 체중계, 저울
- add up to (합이) 결국 ~이 되다
- eventually ⓐⓓ 결국
- matter ⓥ 중요하다
- millionaire ⓝ 백만장자
- previous ⓐ 이전의
- transformation ⓝ 변화
- unhealthy ⓐ 몸에 좋지 않은, 건강하지 않은
- decision ⓝ 결정
- misstep ⓝ 실수, 잘못된 조치

구문 풀이

7행 The slow pace of transformation also makes it easy
                                        5형식 동사 목적격 보어 →가목적어
to break a bad habit.
진목적어

07 동기 부여의 효과
정답률 62% | 정답 ②

다음 빈칸에 들어갈 말로 가장 적절한 것을 고르시오.
① risk - 위험
✔ effort - 노력
③ memory - 기억
④ fortune - 행운
⑤ experience - 경험

[본문 해석]

동기 부여의 한 가지 결과는 상당한 노력을 필요로 하는 행동이다. 예를 들어, 만약 좋은 차를 사고자 하는 동기가 있다면, 당신은 온라인으로 차들을 검색하고, 광고를 자세히 보며, 자동차 대리점들을 방문하는 일 등을 할 것이다. 마찬가지로, 살을 빼려는 동기가 있다면, 당신은 저지방 식품을 사고, 더 적게 먹으며, 운동을 할 것이다. 동기 부여는 목표를 더 가까이 가져 오는 최종적인 행동을 이끌 뿐만 아니라, 준비 행동에 시간과 에너지를 쓸 의지를 만들기도 한다. 따라서 새 스마트폰을 사고자 하는 동기가 있는 사람은 그것을 위해 추가적인 돈을 벌고, 가게에 가기 위해 폭풍 속에 운전하며, 그것을 사려고 줄을 서서 기다릴지도 모른다.

Why? 왜 정답일까?

'Motivation not only drives the final behaviors that bring a goal closer but also creates willingness to expend time and energy on preparatory behaviors.'에서 동기 부여는 목표가 가까워지게 만들 행동을 이끌어낼 뿐 아니라 준비 행동에 시간과 에너지를 들일 의지를 만들어내기도 한다고 이야기하는데, 이는 결국 목표를 위해 '노력'을 기울이도록 유도한다는 말이므로, 빈칸에 들어갈 말로 가장 적절한 것은 ② '노력'이다.

- outcome ⓝ 결과
- considerable ⓐ 상당한
- lose weight 살을 빼다
- drive ⓥ 이끌다, 유도하다
- willingness ⓝ 기꺼이 ~하려는 마음, 의지
- motivation ⓝ 동기 부여, 동기
- dealership ⓝ 대리점
- portion ⓝ (음식의) 1인분
- behavior ⓝ 행동
- expend ⓥ (시간·노력·비용을) 들이다, 쓰다

구문 풀이

7행 Motivation not only drives the final behaviors [that bring a
　　　　　　　　　└ not only + A +
goal closer] but also creates willingness [to expend time and energy
　　　but also + B : A뿐 아니라 B도」
on preparatory behaviors].

★★★ 1등급 대비 고난도 3점 문제

08 음식이 마음에 미치는 영향
정답률 37% | 정답 ⑤

다음 빈칸에 들어갈 말로 가장 적절한 것을 고르시오. [3점]
① leads us to make a fair judgement
　우리가 공정한 판단을 내리게 유도한다
② interferes with cooperation with others
　타인과의 협력을 방해한다
③ does harm to serious diplomatic occasions
　심각한 외교 상황에 해를 끼친다
④ plays a critical role in improving our health
　우리의 건강을 증진하는 데 중요한 역할을 한다
✔ enhances our receptiveness to be persuaded
　설득되는 데 대한 우리의 수용성을 높인다

[본문 해석]

'배가 마음을 다스린다'라고 하는 유명한 스페인 속담이 있다. 이것은 임상적으로 증명된 사실이다. 음식은 원래 마음을 지배하는 약이다. 우리가 먹을 때마다 우리는 자신의 두뇌에 화학 물질의 향연을 퍼부어 우리가 생각하는 방식에 직접적으로 영향을 미치는 폭발적인 호르몬 연쇄 반응을 유발한다. 수많은 연구는 근사한 식사로 유도된 긍정적인 감정 상태가 설득되는 데 대한 우리의 수용성을 높인다는 것을 보여주었다. 그것은 그 제공자에게 보답하려는 본능적인 욕구를 유발한다. 이것이 경영진이 정기적으로 업무 회의와 식사를 결합하는 이유이고, 로비스트들이 정치인들을 환영회, 점심 식사, 저녁 식사에 참석하도록 초대하는 이유이고, 주요 국가 행사가 거의 항상 인상적인 연회를 포함하는 이유이다. Churchill은 이것을 '식사 외교'라고 불렀고, 사회학자들은 이 원리가 모든 인류 문화에 걸쳐 강력한 동기 부여물이라는 것을 확인해 왔다.

Why? 왜 정답일까?

첫 세 문장에서 스페인 속담을 예로 들며 음식이 마음을 지배한다(Food is the original mind-controlling drug.)는 것이 사실이라는 점을 언급하고, 빈칸 뒤에서는 이러한 이유로 각종 업무 상황에 연회와 식사가 포함된다고 설명한다. 따라서 빈칸에 들어갈 말

로 가장 적절한 것은 근사한 식사로 긍정적인 감정 상태에 이르렀을 때의 결과를 적절히 유추한 ⑤ '설득되는 데 대한 우리의 수용성을 높인다'이다.

- proverb ⓝ 속담
- drug ⓝ 약, 마약
- feast ⓝ 향연
- explosive ⓐ 폭발적인
- induce ⓥ 유도하다
- desire ⓝ 욕구, 갈망
- executive ⓝ 경영진
- reception ⓝ 환영회
- banquet ⓝ 연회, 만찬
- confirm ⓥ 사실임을 보여주다, 확인해 주다
- interfere with ⓥ ~을 방해하다
- enhance ⓥ 높이다, 향상시키다
- clinically ⓐⓓ 임상적으로
- bombard A with B ⓥ A에 B를 퍼붓다
- trigger ⓥ 유발하다
- countless ⓐ 수많은
- instinctive ⓐ 본능적인
- repay ⓥ 갚다, 보답하다
- politician ⓝ 정치인, 정치가
- impressive ⓐ 인상적인
- diplomacy ⓝ 외교
- principle ⓝ 원리
- do harm to ⓥ ~에 해를 끼치다
- receptiveness ⓝ 수용성, 감수성

구문 풀이

3행 Every time we eat, we bombard our brains with a feast of
　　　　～할 때마다　　　　　　　　「bombard + A + with + B : A에 B를 퍼붓다」
chemicals, triggering an explosive hormonal chain reaction [that
　분사구문(그리고 ~하다)　　　　　　　　선행사　　　　주격 관계대명사 ←┘
directly influences the way we think].

★★ 문제 해결 꿀~팁 ★★

▶ 많이 틀린 이유는?
'배가 마음을 지배한다'는 말이 있듯이 사람은 특히 근사한 식사를 하면 감정과 사고 과정에 영향을 받아 '설득되기 쉬운' 상태가 되고, 이 때문에 '식사 외교'라는 말이 등장할 만큼 다양한 사회적 상황에 식사가 수반된다는 내용을 다룬 글이다. ②는 근사한 식사가 도리어 '사람들 간 협력을 방해한다'는 의미를 나타내므로 주제와 상반된다.

▶ 문제 해결 방법은?
빈칸 바로 뒤의 문장에서 a good meal을 It으로 받아 근사한 식사는 식사를 제공해준 사람에게 보답하려는 본능을 일깨운다고 언급하고 있다. 이를 근거로 볼 때, 좋은 식사를 대접받으면 '(상대방의) 부탁에 설득될 가능성이 높아진다'는 내용이 빈칸에 들어가야 한다.

09 Zeigarnik 효과
정답률 65% | 정답 ④

다음 글에서 전체 흐름과 관계 없는 문장은?

[본문 해석]

Zeigarnik 효과는 보통 당신에게 끝나지 않은 과업이 끝날 때까지 그 과업을 상기시켜주는 잠재의식의 경향을 일컫는다. Bluma Zeigarnik는 1920년대에 과업을 완성하지 못한 채로 남겨두는 것이 주는 효과에 대해 쓴 리투아니아 심리학자이다. ① 그녀는 한 식당에서 웨이터들이 서빙하는 것을 보던 중 그 효과를 알아차렸다. ② 웨이터들은 아무리 복잡하더라도 주문이 끝날 때까지 주문을 기억했는데, 나중에는 그 주문을 기억하는 것이 어렵다는 것을 알았다. ③ Zeigarnik는 어른들과 아이들 둘 다에게 완성할 퍼즐을 주고 나서 그 과업들 중 몇몇을 하는 도중 그들을 방해하는 후속 연구를 했다. ④ 그들은 퍼즐을 같이 맞춤으로써 과업들을 마친 후에 협동 기술을 발달시켰다. ⑤ 결과에 따르면 어른들과 아이들 둘 다 방해로 인해 완성되지 못한 과업들을 완성된 것보다 더 잘 기억했다.

Why? 왜 정답일까?

과업이 미완성 상태로 남겨져 있다면 오래 기억된다는 심리적 효과에 관한 글이다. ①과 ②는 식당 웨이터를 대상으로 한 관찰 내용을 언급하고, ③과 ⑤는 어른들과 아이들에게 퍼즐 과업을 주었던 후속 연구를 언급하고 있다. 하지만 ④는 퍼즐 과업과 협동 기술을 연관지어 설명하므로 흐름에서 벗어난다. 따라서 전체 흐름과 관계 없는 문장은 ④이다.

- refer to 나타내다
- subconscious ⓐ 잠재의식의
- incomplete ⓐ 미완성된
- interrupt ⓥ 방해하다, 끼어들다
- tendency ⓝ 경향
- remind A of B A에게 B를 상기시키다
- complicated ⓐ 복잡한
- put together 조립하다, 만들다

구문 풀이

6행 The waiters would remember an order, (however complicated),
　　　　　　　　　　　　　　　　　　　　　　( ) : 삽입절
until the order was complete, but they would later find it difficult
　　　　　　　　　　　　　　　　　　　　　　5형식 동사　목적격 보어
to remember the order.
└ 진목적어 　→ 가목적어

★★★ 1등급 대비 고난도 2점 문제

10 전자 상거래의 성장   정답률 42% | 정답 ③

주어진 글 다음에 이어질 글의 순서로 가장 적절한 것을 고르시오.

① (A) – (C) – (B)   ② (B) – (A) – (C)
✔ (B) – (C) – (A)   ④ (C) – (A) – (B)
⑤ (C) – (B) – (A)

[본문 해석]

대략 20년 전 오프라인 거래 상점이 전자 상거래(온라인)로 바뀌기 시작했다. 좋든 나쁘든 간에 그 변화는 쇼핑 경험에 대한 소비자의 인식을 근본적으로 바꾸었다.

(B) 그 변화가 책 판매보다 더 분명한 곳은 없었는데, 그렇게 해서 온라인 서점이 시작되었다. 물리적인 서점은 가상 서점이 할 수 있는 만큼 많은 서적을 그야말로 구비할 수 없었다. 딱 책꽂이 위의 공간만큼이 이용 가능했다.

(C) 더 많은 다양성뿐만 아니라 온라인 서점은 또한 더 낮은 운영비 덕분에 대단히 적극적으로 할인을 제공할 수 있었다. 더 싼 가격과 더 많은 선택의 결합은 온라인 서점의 느리지만 꾸준한 상승으로 이어졌다.

(A) 머지않아 전자 상거래 책 시장은 CD와 DVD 같은 추가적인 항목을 포함하도록 자연스럽게 확장되었다. 전자 상거래는 곧 오늘날의 거대 산업으로 눈덩이처럼 불어났고, 여기서 여러분은 화장실 휴지에서 자동차까지 모든 것을 온라인으로 살 수 있다.

Why? 왜 정답일까?

주어진 글은 약 20년 전 전자 상거래가 시작되어 쇼핑에 대한 인식을 변화시켰다는 일반적인 내용을 제시한다. 이어서 (B)는 특히 온라인 서점의 사례를 언급하며, 물리적 점점에 비해 온라인 서점이 공간적 이점을 지녔다고 설명한다. (C)는 온라인 서점이 또한 가격 우위를 지녔음을 언급하고, (A)는 온라인 서점 분야가 CD, DVD 등으로 확장되었음을 설명한다. 따라서 글의 순서로 가장 적절한 것은 ③ '(B) – (C) – (A)'이다.

- **roughly** [ad] 약, 대략
- **give way to** ~로 바뀌다
- **perception** [n] 인식
- **e-commerce** [n] 전자 상거래
- **expand** [v] 확장되다
- **snowball** [v] 눈덩이처럼 커지다
- **title** [n] 서적, 출판물
- **offer** [v] 제공하다
- **operating cost** 운영비
- **brick-and-mortar** [a] 오프라인 거래의
- **electronic commerce** 전자 상거래
- **before long** 머지않아, 오래지 않아
- **naturally** [ad] 자연스럽게
- **additional** [a] 추가의
- **enormous** [a] 거대한
- **obvious** [a] 분명한
- **shelf** [n] 책꽂이
- **aggressive** [a] 공격적인, 적극적인
- **combination** [n] 결합

구문 풀이

10행 Nowhere was the shift more obvious than with book sales,
「장소 부사구+동사+주어: 도치 구문」
which is how online bookstores got their start.
계속적 용법(선행사: 앞 문장)

★★ 문제 해결 꿀~팁 ★★

▶ 많이 틀린 이유는?
(B) 이후 (A)와 (C)의 순서를 잘 잡는 것이 관건이다. (B)에서 온라인 서점이 오프라인 서점보다 책을 다양하게 구비했다는 장점을 소개한 후, (A)는 온라인 서점 시장이 다른 부문으로 확장되었다는 내용을, (C)는 온라인 서점의 추가적 장점을 언급한다. 흐름상 (C)에서 온라인 서점의 장점에 관한 설명을 마무리하고, (A)에서 이 장점을 바탕으로 다른 상품 분야로의 확장이 가능했다는 결론을 내리는 것이 자연스럽다. 따라서 ② '(B) – (A) – (C)'는 답으로 부적절하다.

▶ 문제 해결 방법은?
(B)의 as many titles as a virtual bookstore가 (C)의 greater variety로 연결된다. 이어서 (C)의 결론인 the slow, steady rise of online bookstores가 (A)의 the e-commerce book market naturally expanded to include additional categories로 연결되며, 온라인 서점 사업이 책을 넘어 CD, DVD 등 다양한 부문으로 확장되었다는 최종적 결론에 이르고 있다.

11-12 식단 개선을 위한 조언

[본문 해석]

마케팅 담당자들은 당신이 먼저 보는 것을 산다는 것을 수십 년 동안 알고 있었

다. 예를 들어, 아래쪽 선반에 있는 상품보다 식료품점의 눈높이에 놓여져 있는 상품을 구매할 가능성이 훨씬 더 높다. 매장에서의 '제품 배치'가 구매 행동에 영향을 미치는 방식에 대한 매우 많은 연구가 있다. 이것은 당신에게 유리하게 제품 배치를 사용할 기회를 준다. 농산물과 같은 건강한 식품은 종종 집에서 (a) 가장 덜 눈에 띄는 음식이다. 「당신은 보이지 않는 것을 먹으려고 생각하지 않을 것이다.」 ┌ :12번의 근거 이것이 85%의 미국인들이 과일과 채소를 충분히 먹지 않는 이유 중 일부일지도 모른다.

만약 농산물이 냉장고 아래쪽에 있는 서랍에 (b) 숨겨져 있으면, 이 좋은 음식들은 시야와 마음에서 벗어나 있다. 식료품 저장실에도 마찬가지다. 나는 눈높이에 짠 크래커와 칩이 줄지어 놓여 있는 선반을 가지고 있었다. 이것들이 내게 먼저 눈에 띄는 것이었을 때, 그것들이 나의 (c) 주된 간식이었다. 그 동일한 선반은 이제 건강에 좋은 간식으로 가득 차 있어, 좋은 결정을 내리기 (d) 쉽게 해준다. 식탁에 나와 있는 음식들은 훨씬 더 중요하다. 당신이 지나갈 때마다 음식을 보면, 당신은 그것을 (e) 피하기(→ 먹기) 쉽다. 「따라서 당신의 선택을 개선하기 위해, 크래커와 사탕 대신 사과와 피스타치오 같은 좋은 음식이 나와 있게 해라.」 ┌ :11번의 근거

- **grocery store** 식료품점
- **placement** [n] 배치
- **to one's advantage** ~에게 유리하게
- **primary** [a] 주된
- **critical** [a] 중요한
- **a body of** 많은
- **influence** [v] 영향을 미치다 [n] 영향
- **pantry** [n] 식료품 저장실
- **filled with** ~로 가득 찬
- **tidy up** [v] ~을 정리하다

구문 풀이

23행 So to improve your choices, leave good foods like apples
목적(~하기 위해)   5형식 동사   목적어
and pistachios sitting out instead of crackers and candy.
목적격 보어(현재분사)   → 전치사(~ 대신에)

11 제목 파악   정답률 72% | 정답 ①

윗글의 제목으로 가장 적절한 것은?

✔ Why We Need to Consider Food Placement
왜 우리는 식품 배치를 고려할 필요가 있는가
② Pleasure Does Not Come from What You Buy
기쁨은 당신이 사는 것에서 오지 않는다
③ Which Do You Believe, Visible or Invisible?
보이는 것과 보이지 않는 것 중 무엇을 믿는가?
④ A Secret for Health: Eat Less, Move More
건강을 위한 비결: 더 적게 먹고, 더 많이 움직여라
⑤ Three Effective Ways to Tidy Things Up
물건을 깔끔하게 정리하는 세 가지 효과적인 방법

Why? 왜 정답일까?

첫 단락에서 제품 배치가 소비자의 구매 행위에 미치는 영향을 언급한 후, 이를 음식 선택에 적용시킬 수 있다는 조언을 담은 글이다. 마지막 문장 'So to improve your choices, leave good foods like apples and pistachios sitting out instead of crackers and candy.'에서 더 건강한 음식을 먹는 식단으로 나아가기 위해서는 크래커나 사탕 대신 사과와 피스타치오 등 건강에 좋은 음식을 눈 앞에 보이도록 꺼내 두어야 한다고 언급하고 있으므로, 글의 제목으로 가장 적절한 것은 ① '왜 우리는 식품 배치를 고려할 필요가 있는가'이다.

12 어휘 추론   정답률 50% | 정답 ⑤

밑줄 친 (a) ~ (e) 중에서 문맥상 낱말의 쓰임이 적절하지 않은 것은? [3점]

① (a)   ② (b)   ③ (c)   ④ (d)   ✔ (e)

Why? 왜 정답일까?

'You won't think to eat what you don't see.'에서 눈에 보이지 않는 음식은 먹지 않는다고 언급하는 것으로 보아, 역으로 식탁에 나와 있는 음식은 우리가 '먹기' 좋다는 내용이 이어져야 한다. 따라서 (e)의 avoid를 eat으로 고쳐야 한다. 문맥상 낱말의 쓰임이 적절하지 않은 것은 ⑤ '(e)'이다.

DAY 07

DAY 08 · 20분 미니 모의고사

01 ②	02 ④	03 ①	04 ③	05 ②
06 ③	07 ①	08 ④	09 ①	10 ④
11 ②	12 ③			

---

01 뉴스 마감 전 고장 난 타자기를 고치고 안도한 필자
정답률 90% | 정답 ②

다음 글에 나타난 'I'의 심경 변화로 가장 적절한 것은?

① confident → nervous
　자신 있는　　긴장한
② frustrated → relieved
　절망한　　안도한
③ bored → amazed
　지루한　　놀란
④ indifferent → curious
　무관심한　　호기심 많은
⑤ excited → disappointed
　신난　　실망한

[본문 해석]

제출 마감 시간 두 시간 전이었고 나는 여전히 나의 뉴스 기사를 끝내지 못했다. 나는 책상에 앉았는데, 갑자기 타자기가 작동하지 않았다. 내가 아무리 세게 키를 두드려도, 레버는 종이를 두드리러 움직이지 않았다. 나는 내가 제시간에 그 기사를 끝낼 수 없으리라는 것을 깨닫기 시작했다. 필사적으로, 나는 타자기를 내 무릎 위에 올려놓고 각각의 키를 최대한 센 힘으로 누르기 시작했다. 아무 일도 일어나지 않았다. 타자기 내부에 무슨 일이 일어났을지도 모르겠다고 생각하면서, 나는 그 덮개를 열고, 키들을 들어 올리고, 문제를 발견했다 — 종이 집혔었다. 키들이 움직일 공간이 없었다. 그것을 집어서 꺼낸 후에, 나는 몇 개의 부품들을 누르고 당겼다. 키들이 매끄럽게 다시 움직였다. 나는 깊게 숨을 내쉬고 미소 지었다. 이제는 내가 제시간에 기사를 끝낼 수 있음을 알았다.

Why? 왜 정답일까?

뉴스 마감을 앞두고 타자기가 작동하지 않아 기사를 끝내지 못할까봐 절망했던(~ I would not be able to finish the article on time.) 필자가 무사히 타자기를 고치고 안도의 미소를 지었다(I breathed deeply and smiled.)는 내용의 글이다. 따라서 'I'의 심경 변화로 가장 적절한 것은 ② '절망한 → 안도한'이다.

- **strike** ⓥ 치다, 때리다, 두드리다
- **lift up** 들어올리다
- **frustrated** ⓐ 좌절한
- **desperately** [ad] 필사적으로
- **smoothly** [ad] 부드럽게

구문 풀이

6행 Desperately, I rested the typewriter on my lap and started
　　　부사(문장 수식)
hitting each key with as much force as I could manage.
　　　「as + 원급 + as + 주어 + can[could] : ~할 수 있는 한 최대로」

---

02 서로에게 좋은 결과를 얻기 위한 협상의 기술
정답률 83% | 정답 ④

다음 글의 요지로 가장 적절한 것은?

① 협상 상대의 단점뿐 아니라 장점을 철저히 분석해야 한다.
② 의사소통 과정에서 서로의 의도를 확인하는 것이 바람직하다.
③ 성공적인 협상을 위해 다양한 대안을 준비하는 것이 중요하다.
④ 양측에 유리한 협상을 통해 상대와 좋은 관계를 유지해야 한다.
⑤ 원만한 인간관계를 위해 상호독립성을 인정하는 것이 필요하다.

[본문 해석]

우리 모두는 우리가 알든 모르든 매일 협상한다. 하지만 이제까지 *어떻게* 협상하는지를 배운 사람은 거의 없다. (협상 방식을) 배우는 사람들은 대개 양쪽 모두에 유리한 합의를 도출할 가능성이 있는 접근법보다는, 이기고 지는 쪽이 생기는 전통적인 협상 방식을 배운다. 이런 구식의 적대적인 접근법은 아마도 여러분이 그 사람을 다시 상대하지 않을 일회성 협상에서는 유용할지도 모른다. 하지만 우리 대부분은 배우자와 자녀, 친구와 동료, 고객과 의뢰인같이 동일한 사람들을 반복적으로 상대하기 때문에, 이런 식의 거래는 점점 더 드물어지고 있다. 이러한 관점에서, 우리 자신을 위해 성공적인 결과를 얻어내는 동시에 협상 파트너들과 건전한 관계를 유지하는 것이 중요하다. 오늘날 비즈니스 파트너십과 장기적 관계의 상호 의존적인 세계에서, 양측에 유리한 성과는 수용 가능한 *유일한* 결과로 빠른 속도로 자리잡고 있다.

Why? 왜 정답일까?

협상 시 서로에게 모두 유리한 성과를 도출하면서 상대와 건전한 관계를 유지해야 한다(~ it's essential to achieve successful results for ourselves and maintain a healthy relationship with our negotiating partners at the same time.)고 조언하는 글이다. 따라서 글의 요지로 가장 적절한 것은 ④ '양측에 유리한 협상을 통해 상대와 좋은 관계를 유지해야 한다.'이다.

- **whether ~ or not** ~이든 아니든
- **old-school** ⓐ 구식의
- **one-off** ⓐ 단 한 번의
- **increasingly** [ad] 점점 더
- **spouse** ⓝ 배우자
- **maintain** ⓥ 유지하다
- **long-term** ⓐ 장기의
- **agreement** ⓝ 합의, 동의
- **adversarial** ⓐ 적대적인
- **transaction** ⓝ 거래
- **repeatedly** [ad] 반복해서
- **essential** ⓐ 필수적인, 아주 중요한
- **interdependent** ⓐ 상호 의존적인
- **acceptable** ⓐ 수용 가능한

구문 풀이

5행 This old-school, adversarial approach may be useful in
a one-off negotiation [where you will probably not deal with that
　　　　　　　선행사(상황)　　　관계부사
person again].

---

03 산업화 이후에도 인간의 작업으로 남은 수리
정답률 46% | 정답 ①

다음 글의 제목으로 가장 적절한 것은?

① Still Left to the Modern Blacksmith: The Art of Repair
　현대 대장장이에게 여전히 남아있는 것: 수리의 기술
② A Historical Survey of How Repairing Skills Evolved
　수리의 기술이 어떻게 발전했는가에 관한 역사적 조사
③ How to Be a Creative Repairperson: Tips and Ideas
　창의적인 수리공이 되는 방법: 조언과 아이디어
④ A Process of Repair: Create, Modify, Transform!
　수리의 과정: 만들고 수정하고 변형하라!
⑤ Can Industrialization Mend Our Broken Past?
　산업화는 우리의 망가진 과거를 고칠 수 있을까?

[본문 해석]

물건을 고치고 복원하는 것에는 흔히 최초 제작보다 훨씬 더 많은 창의력이 필요하다. 산업화 이전의 대장장이는 가까이에 사는 마을 사람들을 위해 주문에 따라 물건을 만들었고, 제품을 주문 제작하는 것, 즉 사용자에게 맞게 그것을 수정하거나 변형하는 일이 일상적이었다. 고객들은 뭔가 잘못되면 물건을 다시 가져다주곤 했고, 따라서 수리는 제작의 연장이었다. 산업화와 결국 대량 생산이 이루어지면서, 물건을 만드는 것은 제한된 지식을 지닌 기계 관리자의 영역이 되었다. 그러나 수리에는 설계와 재료에 대한 더 큰 이해, 즉 전체에 대한 이해와 설계자의 의도에 대한 이해가 계속 요구되었다. 1896년의 *Manual of Mending and Repairing*의 설명에 따르면, "제조업자들은 모두 기계나 방대한 분업으로 일하고, 말하자면 수작업으로 일하지는 않는다." "그러나 모든 수리는 손으로 *해야 한다.* 우리는 기계로 손목시계나 총의 모든 세부적인 것을 만들 수 있지만, 고장 났을 때 기계는 그것을 고칠 수 없으며, 시계나 권총은 말할 것도 없다!"

Why? 왜 정답일까?

산업화 이전과 이후의 물건 제작과 수리를 대조해 설명한 글이다. 산업화 이전에는 제작과 수리가 모두 인간 대장장이의 작업 영역에 있었던 반면, 산업화 이후에는 제작이 기계에 맡겨지고 수리가 인간의 일로 남았다. 특히 'But repair continued to require a larger grasp of design and materials, an understanding ~'에서 수리는 계속해서 폭넓은 이해를 요구했다고 설명하고, 'But all repairing *must* be done by hand.'에서는 수리가 인간의 손으로 이루어져야 한다는 인용구를 제시한다. 따라서 글의 제목으로 가장 적절한 것은 ① '현대 대장장이에게 여전히 남아있는 것: 수리의 기술'이다.

- **mend** ⓥ 고치다
- **modify** ⓥ 수정하다
- **fabrication** ⓝ 제작
- **industrialization** ⓝ 산업화
- **province** ⓝ 영역
- **comprehension** ⓝ 이해
- **preindustrial** ⓐ 산업화 이전의
- **extension** ⓝ 연장
- **tender** ⓝ 감시인, 관리자
- **mass production** 대량 생산
- **grasp** ⓝ 이해
- **subdivision** ⓝ 세분

구문 풀이

2행 The preindustrial blacksmith made things to order for people
in his immediate community; customizing the product, {modifying or
　　　　　　　　　　　　　　　주어(동명사구)
transforming it according to the user}, was routine.
{ }: 주어 동격　　　동사(단수)

---

04 | 해저 걷기 활동 안내　　　정답률 83% | 정답 ③

Undersea Walking Activity에 관한 다음 안내문의 내용과 일치하는 것은?

① 연중무휴로 운영된다.
② 가격에 보험료는 포함되어 있지 않다.
✓③ 숙련된 안전 요원이 활동 내내 동행한다.
④ 특수 수중 헬멧 착용 시 안경을 쓸 수 없다.
⑤ 현장 예약은 불가능하다.

[본문 해석]

해저 걷기 활동

해저에서 매력적인 수중 걷기를 즐기세요. 걸어 다니며 멋진 바다 생물을 직접 보세요!

연령 요건
10세 이상

영업시간
『화요일부터 일요일까지』—「」: ①의 근거 불일치
오전 9시부터 오후 4시까지

가격
『$30 (보험료 포함)』—「」: ②의 근거 불일치

준비물
수영복과 수건

주의 사항
• 『숙련된 안전 요원이 활동 내내 여러분과 동행합니다.』—「」: ③의 근거 일치
• 『특수 수중 헬멧 착용 시 여러분은 활동 중에 안경을 쓸 수 있습니다.』—「」: ④의 근거 불일치
• 『예약은 현장 또는 www.seawalkwonder.com에서 온라인으로 가능합니다.』
　　　　　　　　　　　　—「」: ⑤의 근거 불일치

Why? 왜 정답일까?

'Experienced lifeguards accompany you throughout the activity.'에서 숙련된 안전 요원이 활동 내내 동행한다고 하므로, 안내문의 내용과 일치하는 것은 ③ '숙련된 안전 요원이 활동 내내 동행한다.'이다.

Why? 왜 오답일까?

① 'from Tuesday to Sunday'에서 월요일이 휴무일임을 알 수 있다.
② '$30 (insurance fee included)'에서 입장 가격에 보험료가 포함돼 있다고 하였다.
④ 'With a special underwater helmet, you can wear glasses during the activity.'에서 특수 헬멧을 쓰면 안경 착용이 가능하다고 하였다.
⑤ 'Reservations can be made on-site ~'에서 현장 예약도 가능하다고 하였다.

● **fascinating** ⓐ 매혹적인
● **operating hour** 운영 시간
● **experienced** ⓐ 숙련된
● **accompany** ⓥ 동행하다
● **on-site** [ad] 현장에서 ⓐ 현장의
● **ocean floor** 해저
● **insurance fee** 보험료
● **lifeguard** ⓝ 안전 요원
● **throughout** [prep] ~ 내내

---

05 | 동물의 냄새 감지　　　정답률 54% | 정답 ②

다음 글의 밑줄 친 부분 중, 어법상 틀린 것은? [3점]

[본문 해석]

각 종의 동물들은 서로 다른 범주의 냄새를 감지할 수 있다. 어떤 종도 그것이 살고 있는 환경에 존재하는 모든 분자를 감지할 수는 없는데, 우리는 냄새를 맡을 수 없지만 몇몇 다른 동물들은 냄새를 맡을 수 있는 몇 가지 것들이 있고, 그 반대의 경우도 있다. 어떤 냄새를 맡을 수 있는 능력이나 그것이 얼마나 좋은 느낌을 주는지와 관련된 개체들 사이의 차이 역시 존재한다. 예를 들어, 어떤 사람들은 미국에서 고수(cilantro)라고 알려진 고수(coriander)의 맛을 좋아하는 반면, 다른 사람들은 그것이 비누 맛이 나고 불쾌하다고 여긴다. 이러한 결과에는 우리의 후각을 조절하는 유전자 차이로 인한 내재된 유전적 요소가 있다. 궁극적으로, 특정 종에 의해 감지된 냄새들의 집합 그리고 그 냄새가 어떻게 인식되는가는 그 동물의 생태에 달려 있을 것이다. 각 종의 반응 도표는 그 종이 자신과 관련된 냄새의 원천을 찾고 그에 따라 반응할 수 있게 해 줄 것이다.

Why? 왜 정답일까?

how가 이끄는 간접의문문의 어순은 'how＋형/부＋주어＋동사'인데, 이때 형용사나

부사 중 무엇을 쓸지는 동사에 따라 결정된다. 여기서는 뒤에 형용사 보어를 취하는 2형식 동사 seems가 나온 것으로 보아 부사 pleasantly 대신 형용사 pleasant를 써야 한다. 따라서 어법상 틀린 것은 ②이다.

Why? 왜 오답일까?

① 뒤에 나오는 'it lives'가 완전한 1형식 문장이므로 '전치사＋관계대명사' 형태의 in which를 써서 관계절을 연결한 것은 적절하다. 앞에 나온 the environment가 장소의 선행사이므로 이때 in which는 where로 바꿀 수 있다.
③ 앞에 나온 단수명사 the taste of coriander를 받기 위해 단수대명사 it이 바르게 쓰였다.
④ 뒤에 our sense of smell이라는 목적어가 나오는 것으로 보아 능동을 나타내는 현재분사 controlling이 바르게 쓰였다. 이 'controlling ~'은 the genes를 꾸민다.
⑤ 'enable＋목적어＋to부정사(~이 …할 수 있게 하다)'의 5형식 구조를 완성하기 위해 to locate가 바르게 쓰였다.

● **detect** ⓥ 감지하다, 알아차리다
● **molecule** ⓝ 분자
● **relate to** ~와 관련되다
● **unpleasant** ⓐ 불쾌한
● **genetic** ⓐ 유전적인
● **ecology** ⓝ 생태
● **accordingly** [ad] 그에 따라
● **odour** ⓝ 냄새, 악취
● **vice versa** 그 반대도 마찬가지다
● **soapy** ⓐ 비누 같은
● **underlying** ⓐ 내재된, 근본적인
● **component** ⓝ 구성 요소
● **response profile** 반응 도표

구문 풀이

12행 Ultimately, the selection of scents detected by a given
　　　　　　　　　　　　　주어1　　　　　　　과거분사
species, and how that odour is perceived, will depend upon the
　　　　주어2(간접의문문)　　　　　　　동사
animal's ecology.

---

06 | 기대감을 통제하여 행복감을 높이기　　　정답률 55% | 정답 ③

(A), (B), (C)의 각 네모 안에서 문맥에 맞는 낱말로 가장 적절한 것은? [3점]

	(A)	(B)	(C)
①	controlling 통제함	frequent 흔한	pleasure 즐거움
②	controlling 통제함	rare 드문	familiarity 익숙함
✓③	controlling 통제함	rare 드문	pleasure 즐거움
④	raising 높임	frequent 흔한	familiarity 익숙함
⑤	raising 높임	rare 드문	pleasure 즐거움

[본문 해석]

사람들은 삶이 나아질수록 더 높은 기대감을 지닌다. 하지만 기대감이 더 높아질수록 만족감을 느끼기는 더욱 어려워진다. 우리들은 기대감을 (A) 통제함으로써 삶에서 느끼는 만족감을 향상시킬 수 있다. 적절한 기대감은 많은 경험들이 즐거운 놀라움이 될 여지를 남긴다. 문제는 적절한 기대감을 가지는 방법을 찾는 것이다. 이것을 위한 한 가지 방법은 멋진 경험들을 (B) 드문 상태로 유지하는 것이다. 당신이 무엇이든 살 여유가 있더라도, 특별한 경우를 위해 훌륭한 와인을 아껴두어라. 품위 있는 스타일의 실크 블라우스를 특별한 즐거움으로 만들라. 이것은 당신의 욕구를 자제하는 행동처럼 보일 수도 있지만, 내 생각은 그렇지 않다. 반대로, 그것은 당신이 (C) 즐거움을 계속해서 경험할 수 있도록 보장해 주는 방법이다. 멋진 와인과 멋진 블라우스가 당신을 기분 좋게 만들지 못한다면 무슨 의미가 있겠는가?

Why? 왜 정답일까?

(A) '~ the higher the expectations, the more difficult it is to be satisfied.'에서 삶에 대한 기대감이 높아지면 만족이나 행복을 느끼기는 더 어려워진다고 이야기하므로, 만족감을 높이려면 역으로 기대감을 '통제하면' 된다는 내용을 유추할 수 있다. 따라서 (A)에는 controlling이 적절하다.
(B) 와인과 블라우스의 예를 통해 멋진 경험을 적절히 '아껴' 두면 적절한 기대감 수준을 유지할 수 있다는 것을 알 수 있으므로, (B)에는 rare가 적절하다.
(C) (B)가 있는 문장에서 멋진 경험이 드물어지면 기대감의 수준이 적절히 유지되면서 삶의 '만족감'이 높아진다는 것을 알 수 있으므로, (C)에는 pleasure가 적절하다. 따라서 각 네모 안에서 문맥에 맞는 낱말로 가장 적절한 것은 ③ '(A) controlling(통제함) – (B) rare(드문) – (C) pleasure(즐거움)'이다.

● **expectation** ⓝ 기대감, 기대
● **raise** ⓥ 올리다
● **satisfaction** ⓝ 만족
● **adequate** ⓐ 적절한, 충분한

[문제편 p.049]

- **proper** ⓐ 적절한, 적당한, 제대로 된
- **occasion** ⓝ (특별한) 일, 행사, 의식
- **treat** ⓝ 큰 기쁨, 만족을 주는 것
- **make sure** 보장하다, 확실히 하다
- **frequent** ⓐ 빈번한
- **elegantly** ⓐⓓ 품위 있게, 우아하게
- **deny** ⓥ 자제하다, 부인하다, 부정하다

구문 풀이

2행 However, {the higher} the expectations (are), {the more difficult}
「{the + 비교급} ~, {the + 비교급} … : ~할수록 더 …하다」 생략
it is to be satisfied.
가주어   진주어

8행 No matter what you can afford, save great wine for special
= Whatever(무엇을 ~하든지 간에)   명령문
occasions.

★★★ 1등급 대비 고난도 2점 문제

07   원하는 것과 해야 할 것   정답률 41% | 정답 ①

다음 빈칸에 들어갈 말로 가장 적절한 것을 고르시오.

✓① desires – 욕망
② merits – 장점
③ abilities – 능력
④ limitations – 한계
⑤ worries – 걱정

[본문 해석]

당신이 진정으로 원하는 것은 무엇이든지 가질 수 있다고 믿는 문화에서는 선택이 문제가 안 된다. 그러나 많은 문화들은 이러한 믿음을 유지하지 못한다. 사실, 많은 사람들은 삶이란 당신이 원하는 것을 얻는 것이라고 믿지 않는다. 인생은 당신이 **해야** 할 것을 하는 것이다. 그들이 선택을 하는 데 있어 어려움을 겪는 이유는 그들이 원하는 것이 그들이 해야 할 일과 관련이 없다고 믿기 때문이다. 외적으로 고려할 문제의 비중이 그들의 욕망보다 더 크다. 이것이 어떤 집단에서 논의 대상이 될 때, 우리는 어떤 것이 좋은 결정인지 의논을 한다. 만약 어떤 사람이 걱정과 의무로부터 벗어나 자신에게 호소하는 것이 무엇인지를 잠시 동안 생각해 볼 수 있다면, 그들은 자신에게 무엇이 중요한지를 가려낼 기회를 얻게 된다. 그러고 나서 그들은 외적인 부담에 대해 고려하고 협상할 수 있다.

Why? 왜 정답일까?

첫 두 문장에 따르면 많은 문화권에서 원하는 것을 다 가질 수 있다는 믿음이 유지되지 못한다고 한다. 이를 근거로 할 때, 빈칸이 포함된 문장은 '원하는 것' 이외에 고려할 문제가 더 많다는 의미여야 한다. 따라서 빈칸에 들어갈 말로 가장 적절한 것은 ① '욕망'이다.

- **maintain** ⓥ 유지하다
- **weight** ⓝ 비중, 무게
- **negotiate** ⓥ 협상하다
- **desire** ⓝ 욕망
- **limitation** ⓝ 한계
- **have trouble ~ing** ~하는 데 어려움을 겪다
- **consideration** ⓝ 고려 사항
- **external** ⓐ 외부적인
- **merit** ⓝ 장점

구문 풀이

1행 In a culture [where there is a belief {that you can have anything
선행사   관계부사   { } : 동격(= a belief)
you truly want}], there is no problem in choosing.
동사   주어

★★ 문제 해결 꿀~팁 ★★

▶ 많이 틀린 이유는?
이 글은 우리가 원하는 바를 모두 성취하지 못하고 해야 하는 일 등 외부적 요소를 고려하여 선택을 하는 경우가 대부분이라는 내용을 다루고 있다. '능력'에 관해서는 중요하게 언급되지 않으므로 ③은 빈칸에 부적절하다.

▶ 문제 해결 방법은?
'what you want'와 'what you are *supposed* to do'가 두 가지 핵심 소재인데, 빈칸 문장의 outside consideration은 이중 'what you are *supposed* to do'와 같은 말이다. 따라서 빈칸에는 'what you want'를 달리 표현하는 말이 들어가야 한다.

★★★ 1등급 대비 고난도 3점 문제

08   현지 환경을 미리 조사하고 대비하기   정답률 54% | 정답 ④

글의 흐름으로 보아, 주어진 문장이 들어가기에 가장 적절한 곳을 고르시오. [3점]

[본문 해석]

인류의 지속적인 생존은 환경에 적응하는 우리의 능력으로 설명될 수 있을 것이다. ① 우리가 고대 조상들의 생존 기술 중 일부를 잃어버렸을지도 모르지만, 새로운 기술이 필요해지면서 우리는 새로운 기술을 배웠다. ② 오늘날 우리가 현대 기술에 더 크게 의존함에 따라 한때 우리가 가졌던 기술과 현재 우리가 가진 기술 사이의 간극이 어느 때보다 더 커졌다. ③ 그러므로, 미지의 땅으로 향할 때에는 그 환경에 대해 충분히 준비하는 것이 중요하다. ④ 떠나기 전에, 토착 주민들이 어떻게 옷을 입고 일하고 먹는지를 조사하라. 그들이 어떻게 자신들의 생활 방식에 적응했는가는 여러분이 그 환경을 이해하도록 도울 것이고, 여러분이 최선의 장비를 선별하고 적절한 기술을 배우도록 해 줄 것이다. ⑤ 생존이 걸린 대부분의 상황이 피할 수도 있었던 일련의 사건의 결과로 발생하기 때문에 이것은 중요하다.

Why? 왜 정답일까?

④ 앞의 두 문장에서 현대 기술에 대한 우리의 의존도가 높아짐에 따라 과거의 기술과 오늘날의 기술 간에 격차가 더 벌어졌으므로 잘 모르는 곳에 갈 때에는 그 환경에 대한 충분한 준비가 필요하다고 언급한다. 이에 대한 구체적인 조언으로서 주어진 문장은 떠나기 전 '토착 주민'의 옷, 음식, 일하는 문화 등을 조사하라고 언급한다. ④ 뒤의 문장은 주어진 문장의 '토착 주민'을 they로 언급하며 이들이 나름의 삶의 방식에 어떻게 적응해 있는지를 파악하면 그 환경을 이해하는 데 도움이 될 것이라고 설명한다. 따라서 주어진 문장이 들어가기에 가장 적절한 곳은 ④이다.

- **adapt to** ~에 적응하다
- **rely on** ~에 의존하다
- **wilderness** ⓝ 황무지
- **arise** ⓥ 발생하다, 일어나다
- **ancestor** ⓝ 조상
- **heavily** ⓐⓓ 심하게, 많이
- **crucial** ⓐ 매우 중요한
- **as a result of** ~의 결과로

구문 풀이

12행 How they have adapted to their way of life will help you
주어(간접의문문 : 어떻게 ~하는지)   「help + 목적어 +
to understand the environment and allow you to select the best gear
to부정사 : ~이 …하는 데 도움이 되다」
and (to) learn the correct skills.
「allow + 목적어 + to부정사 : ~이 …하게 하다」

★★ 문제 해결 꿀~팁 ★★

▶ 많이 틀린 이유는?
인간은 환경에 맞추어 계속 적응하고 변하는데, 오늘날 인간은 기술에 대한 의존도가 커서 과거와의 간극이 더욱 벌어졌기에 미지의 땅으로 나아갈 때에는 항상 환경에 대한 대비와 조사가 필요하다는 내용의 글이다. 특히 최다 오답인 ③ 앞뒤로 '과거 기술과 현대 기술의 간극이 커져서 → 새로운 곳으로 갈 때 환경을 잘 알아봐야 한다'라는 내용이 적절한 인과 관계로 연결되어 있다. 따라서 주어진 문장을 ③에 넣는 것은 부적절하다.

▶ 문제 해결 방법은?
④ 뒤의 문장에 they가 나오므로 앞에서 they로 받을 만한 복수 명사가 언급되어야 한다. ④ 앞의 문장에는 적절한 복수 명사가 없는 반면, 주어진 문장에는 the native inhabitants가 있다. 따라서 이 they에 '토착 주민'을 넣어서 읽어 보고 맥락이 자연스러운지 확인해 보면 답을 찾을 수 있다.

★★★ 1등급 대비 고난도 2점 문제

09   스포츠의 불확실성과 스포츠 마케팅 전략   정답률 35% | 정답 ①

다음 글의 내용을 한 문장으로 요약하고자 한다. 빈칸 (A), (B)에 들어갈 말로 가장 적절한 것은?

(A)	(B)	(A)	(B)
✓① unreliable 불확실한	feature 특징으로 삼다	② unreliable 불확실한	exclude 제외시키다
③ risky 위험한	ignore 무시하다	④ consistent 일관된	involve 포함시키다
⑤ consistent 일관된	promote 홍보하다		

[본문 해석]

우리는 스포츠 경기의 결과를 예측할 수 없고, 이것은 매주 달라진다. 이러한 이질성이 스포츠의 특징이다. 바로 그 결과의 불확실성과 경기의 수준을 소비자들은 매력적으로 여긴다. 스포츠 마케팅 담당자에게 있어 이것은 문제가 되는데, 왜냐하면 경기의 수준이 보장될 수 없고, (경기의) 결과와 관련하여 어떠한 약속도 할 수 없으며 스타 선수의 경기력에 대해 어떠한 확신도 주어질 수 없기 때문이다. 소비재와 다르게, 스포츠는 마케팅 전략의 중요한 특징인 일관

성을 보여 줄 수도 없고 보여 주지도 않는다. 따라서 스포츠 마케팅 담당자는 순전히 승리에만 기반한 마케팅 전략을 피해야 하고, 대신에 핵심 제품(즉, 시합 그 자체)보다는 시설, 주차, 상품, 기념품, 식음료와 같은 제품 확장 개발에 집중해야만 한다.

➡ 스포츠는 (A) 불확실하다는 본질적 속성을 갖고 있으며, 이는 스포츠의 마케팅 전략이 단지 경기보다는 상품과 서비스를 (B) 특징으로 삼도록 요구한다.

Why? 왜 정답일까?

첫 문장과 마지막 문장에서 스포츠는 그 경기 결과를 장담할 수 없는 불확실성(We cannot predict the outcomes of sporting contests ~)을 지니고 있기 때문에 스포츠 마케팅 담당자는 경기 자체보다는 확장 상품에 집중하는 전략을 취할 필요가 있음(The sport marketer therefore ~ must instead focus on developing product extensions ~)이 언급되고 있다. 따라서 요약문의 빈칸 (A), (B)에 들어갈 말로 가장 적절한 것은 ① '(A) unreliable(불확실한), (B) feature(특징으로 삼다)'이다.

- predict ⓥ 예측하다
- feature ⓝ 특징 ⓥ 특징으로 삼다
- problematic ⓐ 문제가 있는
- assurance ⓝ 확신, 장담
- solely ⓐⓓ 순전히, 오로지, 단지
- merchandise ⓝ 상품, 물품
- vary ⓥ (상황에 따라) 달라지다
- uncertainty ⓝ 불확실성
- in relation to ~에 관하여
- consistency ⓝ 일관성, 한결같음
- facility ⓝ (특정 목적이나 활동을 위한) 시설
- souvenir ⓝ 기념품

구문 풀이

3행 It is the uncertainty of the result and the quality of the contest that consumers find attractive.
「It is + 강조하는 말 + that ~ : 강조 구문」
5형식 동사 목적격 보어

5행 For the sport marketer, this is problematic, / as the quality
주어 동사 이유 접속사← 주어1
of the contest cannot be guaranteed, no promises can be made in
동사1 주어2 동사2
relation to the result and no assurances can be given in respect of
주어3 동사3(조동사 수동태)
the performance of star players.

★★ 문제 해결 꿀~팁 ★★

▶ 많이 틀린 이유는?
스포츠 마케팅이라는 낯선 소재를 다루고 있는 데다 구문이 까다로워 읽기 어려운 지문이다. Unlike로 시작하는 문장에서 스포츠는 일관성을 보여 주지 않는다고 하므로, (A)에 consistent를 제시한 ④는 오답이다.

▶ 문제 해결 방법은?
요약문은 글의 핵심 결론을 한 문장으로 나타낸 것이므로, 이 문제 또한 마지막 두 문장을 주의 깊게 읽고 답을 고르도록 한다.

10-12 모르는 노인의 임종을 지킨 군인

[본문 해석]

(A)
한 간호사가 피곤하고 불안해하는 군인을 침대 곁으로 데려갔다. "Jack, 당신 아들이 왔어요."라고 간호사가 침대에 누워있는 노인에게 말했다. 그 노인이 눈을 뜨기 전에 그녀는 그 말을 여러 번 반복해야 했다. 『심장병 때문에 극심한 고통을 겪고 있던 그는 제복을 입은 젊은 군인이 자기 옆에 선 것을 간신히 알았다.』(a) 그는 손을 그 군인에게 뻗었다.

(D)
그 군인은 노인의 병약한 손을 부드럽게 감쌌다. 『간호사는 군인이 침대 옆에 앉을 수 있도록 의자를 가져왔다.』 밤새 젊은 군인은 거기에 앉아, 노인의 손을 잡고 (e) 그에게 지지와 위로의 말을 건넸다. 『가끔, 그녀는 군인에게 잠시 쉬라고 제안했다. 그는 정중하게 거절했다.』

(B)
간호사가 병실에 들어올 때마다, 그녀는 그 군인이 상냥한 말을 하는 것을 들었다. 밤새도록 (b) 그에게 손만 꼭 잡힌 채로 노인은 아무 말도 하지 않았다. 동트기 직전에, 그 노인은 죽었다. 『그 군인은 노인의 손을 놓고 간호사를 찾기 위해 병실을 나갔다.』 그녀가 무슨 일이 있었는지 들은 후, 그녀는 그와 함께 병실로 돌아갔다. 군인은 잠시 머뭇거리고는 "그분은 누구였나요?"라고 물었다.

(C)
그녀는 깜짝 놀라서 물었다. "그가 당신의 아버지가 아니었나요?" "아니요.

저는 그분을 이전에 만난 적이 없어요."라고 군인이 대답했다.』 그녀는 물었다. "그러면 내가 당신을 (c) 그에게 안내했을 때 왜 아무 말도 하지 않았나요?" 그가 말했다. "저는 실수가 있었다는 것을 알았지만, 그분이 너무도 위독해서 제가 아들인지 아닌지 구별할 수 없다는 걸 알게 되었을 때, 저는 (d) 그가 얼마나 저를 필요로 하는지 알 수 있었습니다. 그래서 저는 머물렀습니다."

- severe ⓐ 극심한
- reach out one's hand 손을 뻗다
- hesitate ⓥ 주저하다
- barely ⓐⓓ 간신히 ~하다, 거의 못 ~하다
- dawn ⓝ 새벽

구문 풀이

(A) 5행 Suffering from the severe pain because of heart disease, he
분사구문 전치사(~ 때문에)
barely saw the young uniformed soldier standing next to him.
지각동사 목적어 현재분사
(D) 2행 The nurse brought a chair so that the soldier could sit beside
접속사(~하도록)
the bed.

10 글의 순서 파악 정답률 77% | 정답 ④

주어진 글 (A)에 이어질 내용을 순서에 맞게 배열한 것으로 가장 적절한 것은?
① (B) − (D) − (C) ② (C) − (B) − (D)
③ (C) − (D) − (B) ④ (D) − (B) − (C)
⑤ (D) − (C) − (B)

Why? 왜 정답일까?

간호사가 한 군인을 임종이 임박한 노인에게 데려갔다는 내용의 (A) 뒤로, 군인이 노인 곁에 밤새 있었다는 내용의 (D), 마침내 노인이 임종한 뒤 군인이 그 노인이 누구였는지 물었다는 내용의 (B), 간호사가 놀라서 왜 노인 곁에 있었는지 묻고 군인이 답했다는 내용의 (C)가 순서대로 이어져야 자연스럽다. 따라서 글의 순서로 가장 적절한 것은 ④ '(D) − (B) − (C)'이다.

11 지칭 추론 정답률 64% | 정답 ②

밑줄 친 (a) ~ (e) 중에서 가리키는 대상이 나머지 넷과 다른 것은?
① (a) ② (b) ③ (c) ④ (d) ⑤ (e)

Why? 왜 정답일까?

(a), (c), (d), (e)는 the old man, (b)는 the soldier를 가리키므로, (a) ~ (e) 중에서 가리키는 대상이 다른 하나는 ② '(b)'이다.

12 세부 내용 파악 정답률 75% | 정답 ③

윗글에 관한 내용으로 적절하지 않은 것은?
① 노인은 심장병으로 극심한 고통을 겪고 있었다.
② 군인은 간호사를 찾기 위해 병실을 나갔다.
③ 군인은 노인과 이전에 만난 적이 있다고 말했다.
④ 간호사는 군인이 앉을 수 있도록 의자를 가져왔다.
⑤ 군인은 잠시 쉬라는 간호사의 제안을 정중히 거절하였다.

Why? 왜 정답일까?

(C) "No, he wasn't. I've never met him before."에서 군인은 노인을 만난 적이 없다고 말하므로, 내용과 일치하지 않는 것은 ③ '군인은 노인과 이전에 만난 적이 있다고 말했다.'이다.

Why? 왜 오답일까?

① (A) 'Suffering from the severe pain because of heart disease, ~'의 내용과 일치한다.
② (B) 'The soldier ~ left the room to find the nurse.'의 내용과 일치한다.
④ (D) 'The nurse brought a chair so that the soldier could sit beside the bed.'의 내용과 일치한다.
⑤ (D) 'Occasionally, she suggested that the soldier take a rest for a while. He politely said no.'의 내용과 일치한다.

DAY 08

DAY 09 · 20분 미니 모의고사

01 ④	02 ②	03 ①	04 ②	05 ④
06 ④	07 ②	08 ⑤	09 ④	10 ⑤
11 ②	12 ⑤

---

01 · 도서관 공사 자원봉사 모집
정답률 90% | 정답 ④

다음 글의 목적으로 가장 적절한 것은?

① 도서관 임시 휴관의 이유를 설명하려고
② 도서관 자원봉사자 교육 일정을 안내하려고
③ 도서관 보수를 위한 모금 행사를 제안하려고
✓ ④ 도서관 공사에 참여할 자원봉사자를 모집하려고
⑤ 도서관에서 개최하는 글쓰기 대회를 홍보하려고

[본문 해석]

Eastwood 도서관 회원들께,

Friends of Literature 모임 덕분에, 우리는 도서관 건물을 리모델링하기 위한 충분한 돈을 성공적으로 모았습니다. 우리 지역의 건축업자인 John Baker 씨가 우리의 리모델링을 돕기로 자원했지만, 그는 도움이 필요합니다. 망치나 페인트 붓을 쥐고 시간을 기부함으로써, 여러분은 공사를 도울 수 있습니다. Baker 씨의 자원봉사 팀에 동참하여 Eastwood 도서관을 더 좋은 곳으로 만드는 데 참여하십시오! 더 많은 정보를 원하시면 541-567-1234로 전화해 주십시오.

Mark Anderson 드림

Why? 왜 정답일까?

'By grabbing a hammer or a paint brush and donating your time, you can help with the construction. Join Mr. Baker in his volunteering team ~'에서 자원봉사 팀에 참여하여 도서관 공사에 도움이 되어 달라고 언급하는 것으로 볼 때, 글의 목적으로 가장 적절한 것은 ④ '도서관 공사에 참여할 자원봉사자를 모집하려고'이다.

- **raise** ⓥ (돈을) 모으다
- **assistance** ⓝ 도움
- **construction** ⓝ 공사, 건설
- **volunteer** ⓥ 자원하다
- **grab** ⓥ 쥐다

구문 풀이

6행 By grabbing a hammer or a paint brush and donating your
「by+동명사1 +   동명사2: ~하고 …함으로써」
time, you can help with the construction.

---

02 · 자녀에게 행동으로 모범을 보이기
정답률 93% | 정답 ②

다음 글에서 필자가 주장하는 바로 가장 적절한 것은?

① 자녀를 타인과 비교하는 말을 삼가야 한다.
✓ ② 자녀에게 행동으로 삶의 모범을 보여야 한다.
③ 칭찬을 통해 자녀의 바람직한 행동을 강화해야 한다.
④ 훈육을 하기 전에 자녀 스스로 생각할 시간을 주어야 한다.
⑤ 자녀가 새로운 것에 도전할 때 인내심을 가지고 지켜봐야 한다.

[본문 해석]

우리는 항상 우리 자녀에게 말과 행동으로 무언가를 가르치고 있다. 그들은 보는 것으로부터 배운다. 그들은 듣거나 우연히 들은 것으로부터 배운다. 아이들은 인생에서 가장 중요한 것에 관한 부모의 가치관을 공유한다. 우리의 우선순위와 원칙, 그리고 훌륭한 행동에 대한 본보기는 우리 자녀가 다른 길이 유혹적으로 보일 때 올바른 길로 가도록 가르칠 수 있다. 아이들은 확고한 인격을 구성하는 가치를 단순히 그것에 관해 들어서 배우지 않는다는 것을 기억하라. 그들은 주변 사람들이 일상생활에서 그러한 가치를 좇아 행동하고 유지하는 것을 보면서 배운다. 그러므로 여러분의 자녀에게 행동으로 삶의 모범을 보이라. 우리 일상생활에서, 우리는 자녀에게 우리가 타인을 존중하는 것을 보여줄 수 있다. 우리는 타인이 괴로워할 때 우리의 연민과 걱정을, 어려운 결정을 할 때 우리 자신의 자제력과 용기와 정직을 그들에게 보여줄 수 있다.

Why? 왜 정답일까?

글 중반부에서 행동을 통해 자녀에게 삶의 본보기를 보여주라고(Therefore show your child good examples of life by your action.) 조언하는 것으로 볼 때, 필자가 주장하는 바로 가장 적절한 것은 ② '자녀에게 행동으로 삶의 모범을 보여야 한다.'이다.

- **overhear** ⓥ 엿듣다, 우연히 듣다
- **priority** ⓝ 우선순위
- **take the high road** 확실한 길로 가다
- **act on** ~에 따라 행동하다
- **compassion** ⓝ 연민
- **suffer** ⓥ 고통받다, 괴로워하다
- **value** ⓝ 가치 ⓥ 중시하다
- **principle** ⓝ 원칙
- **tempting** ⓐ 유혹적인, 솔깃한
- **uphold** ⓥ 유지하다, 떠받치다
- **concern** ⓝ 걱정, 우려
- **self-discipline** ⓝ 자제

구문 풀이

8행 Remember that children do not learn the values [that make
      접속사   선행사   주격 관·대
up strong character] simply by being *told* about them.
                                    동명사의 수동태(~되는 것)

---

03 · 과학적 발견의 의미
정답률 52% | 정답 ①

밑줄 친 refining ignorance가 다음 글에서 의미하는 바로 가장 적절한 것은?

✓ ① looking beyond what is known towards what is left unknown
알려진 대상 너머로 모르는 채로 남겨져 있는 쪽을 보는
② offering an ultimate account of what has been discovered
발견된 대상에 대해 완전한 설명을 제공하는
③ analyzing existing knowledge with an objective mindset
객관적인 태도로 기존의 지식을 분석하는
④ inspiring scientists to publicize significant discoveries
과학자들이 중대한 발견을 발표하도록 고무하는
⑤ informing students of a new field of science
학생들에게 새로운 과학 분야를 알려주는

[본문 해석]

비록 명시적인 목표는 아니지만, 최고의 과학은 실제로 무지를 개선하는 것으로 여겨질 수 있다. 과학자들, 특히 젊은 과학자들은 결과에 너무 집착할 수 있다. 사회는 그들이 이런 무모한 추구를 계속하도록 돕는다. 큰 발견들이 언론에 보도되고, 대학의 홈페이지에 등장하고, 보조금을 얻는 데 도움을 주고, 승진을 위한 논거를 만든다. 그러나 이는 잘못된 것이다. 위대한 과학자들, 우리가 존경하는 선구자들은 결과가 아니라 그다음 문제에 관심이 있다. 아주 존경받는 물리학자인 Enrico Fermi는 자신의 학생들에게, 가설을 성공적으로 입증하는 실험은 측정이며, 그렇지 않은 것은 발견이라고 말했다. 여기서 발견이란 새로운 무지를 드러내는 것이다. 과학적인 성취의 정점인 노벨상은 평생의 과학적인 업적이 아니라 하나의 발견, 결과에 대해 수여된다. 노벨상 위원회조차도 이것이 실제로 과학의 진정한 의미 속에 있는 것이 아니라는 것을 어떤 면에서 인식하고 있으며, 그들의 표창장도 흔히 '한 분야를 열었거나,' '한 분야를 변화시켰거나,' 혹은 '한 분야를 새롭고 예상치 못한 방향으로 이끈' 발견을 기리고 있다.

Why? 왜 정답일까?

오늘날 많은 과학자들이 결과를 내는 데 주력하고 있지만 사실상 진정한 과학은 결과가 아니라 결과가 상기시키는 그다음 문제에 관심을 둘 때 이루어질 수 있다(Great scientists, the pioneers that we admire, are not concerned with results but with the next questions.)는 내용을 다룬 글이다. 글 중간의 '~ an experiment that successfully proves a hypothesis is a measurement; one that doesn't is a discovery. A discovery, an uncovering—of new ignorance.'에서 발견은 가설을 성공적으로 입증하지 못한 것으로 볼 수 있는데 그 이유는 발견이 오히려 새로운 무지를 드러내기 때문임을 설명하므로, 밑줄 친 부분이 의미하는 바로 가장 적절한 것은 ① '알려진 대상 너머로 모르는 채로 남겨져 있는 쪽을 보는'이다.

- **explicit** ⓐ 명시적인, 뚜렷한
- **obsessed with** ~에 사로잡힌
- **hypothesis** ⓝ 가설
- **uncovering** ⓝ 드러냄, 밝힘, 폭로
- **publicize** ⓥ 발표하다, 알리다, 홍보하다
- **refine** ⓥ 개선하다, 정제하다
- **promotion** ⓝ 승진, 진급, 승격
- **measurement** ⓝ 측정, 측량
- **citation** ⓝ 표창장, 감사장

구문 풀이

8행 The highly respected physicist Enrico Fermi told his students
                                        4형식 동사   간접 목적어
{that an experiment [that successfully proves a hypothesis] is
      주어1   주·관·대   동사1
a measurement; / one [that doesn't (prove a hypothesis)] is a
              주어2   생략(중복)   동사2
discovery}. 〔 〕: 직접 목적어

04 아이들이 수학적 개념을 익혀 가는 방식   정답률 78% | 정답 ②

다음 글의 주제로 가장 적절한 것은?

① difficulties of children in learning how to count
아이들이 수를 세는 법을 배우는 데 있어 어려움
✓ how children build mathematical understanding
아이들이 수학적 이해를 어떻게 쌓아나가는가
③ why fingers are used in counting objects
수를 셀 때 왜 손가락을 쓰는가
④ importance of early childhood education
아동 조기 교육의 중요성
⑤ advantages of singing number songs
숫자 노래 부르기의 이점

[본문 해석]

매일, 아이들은 사물 사이의 관계들을 탐구하고 구성한다. 빈번히, 이러한 관계들은 무언가가 얼마만큼 혹은 몇 개 존재하는지에 초점을 맞춘다. 따라서, 아이들은 센다. "쿠키 하나, 신발 두 개, 생일 케이크 위에 초 세 개, 모래놀이 통에 아이 네 명." 아이들은 비교한다. "무엇이 더 많지? 무엇이 더 적지? 충분할까?" 아이들은 계산한다. "몇 개가 알맞을까? 나는 지금 다섯 개가 있어. 하나 더 필요하네." 이 모든 예시에서, 아이들은 수량의 개념을 발달시키는 중이다. 아이들은 간식 시간에 몇 개의 크래커를 가져갈지 알아내거나 조개껍질들을 더미로 분류하는 것과 같은, 그들만의 활동이나 경험을 통해 수학적 개념을 밝히고 연구한다.

Why? 왜 정답일까?

아이들은 자기만의 활동이나 경험을 통해 수학적 개념을 익혀 간다(Children reveal and investigate mathematical concepts through their own activities or experiences ~)는 것이 핵심 내용이므로, 글의 주제로 가장 적절한 것은 ② '아이들은 수학적 이해를 어떻게 쌓아나가는가'이다.

● explore ⓥ 탐구하다
● sandbox ⓝ 모래놀이 통
● fit ⓥ 맞다, 적합하다
● notion ⓝ 개념
● investigate ⓥ 연구하다, 조사하다
● construct ⓥ 구성하다
● calculate ⓥ 계산하다
● instance ⓝ 예시, 사례
● quantity ⓝ (측정 가능한) 양, 수량
● sort A into B A를 B로 분류하다

구문 풀이

2행 Frequently, these relationships focus on {how much or how many of something exists}.　{ } : 「how + 형/부 + 주어 + 동사 : 얼마나 ~한지」

05 과학의 독특한 체계   정답률 60% | 정답 ④

다음 글의 밑줄 친 부분 중, 어법상 틀린 것은? [3점]

[본문 해석]

우주의 불가사의한 것들에 관한 답을 찾는 많은 방법이 있고, 과학은 이러한 것들 중 단지 하나이다. 그러나 과학은 독특하다. 추측하는 대신에 과학자들은 그들의 생각이 사실인지 거짓인지 증명하도록 고안된 체계를 따른다. 과학자들은 그들의 이론과 결론을 끊임없이 재검토하고 시험한다. 기존의 생각들은 과학자들이 설명할 수 없는 새로운 정보를 찾을 때 대체된다. 누군가가 발견을 하면, 다른 사람들은 그들 자신의 연구에서 그 정보를 사용하기 전에 그것을 주의 깊게 검토한다. 더 이전의 발견들에 새로운 지식을 쌓아가는 이러한 방법은 과학자들이 그들의 실수를 바로잡는 것을 보장한다. 과학적 지식으로 무장해서, 사람들은 우리가 사는 방식을 변화시키는 도구와 기기를 만들고, 그것은 우리의 삶을 훨씬 더 쉽고 나아지게 한다.

Why? 왜 정답일까?

주어가 단수 명사인 This way이므로 동사 또한 단수형으로 써야 한다. 따라서 ensure를 ensures로 고쳐야 한다. 어법상 틀린 것은 ④이다.

Why? 왜 오답일까?

① a system이 '고안되는' 대상이므로 과거분사 designed를 써서 꾸민 것은 적절하다.
② 선행사 new information를 꾸미며 뒤에 목적어가 없는 불완전한 절을 수반하는 관계대명사로서 that을 쓴 것은 어법상 맞다.
③ 뒤에 목적어인 the information이 나오므로 능동을 나타내는 using을 쓴 것은 맞다.
⑤ 비교급을 꾸미는 부사로서 much를 쓴 것은 맞다. much, a lot, far, still, even 등은 비교급 앞에서 비교급을 꾸밀 수 있다.

● unique ⓐ 독특한
● constantly ⓐⓓ 끊임없이
● prove ⓥ 입증하다
● reexamine ⓥ 재검토하다

● replace ⓥ 대체하다
● ensure ⓥ 보장하다
● armed with ~으로 무장한
● discovery ⓝ 발견
● correct ⓥ 바로잡다
● transform ⓥ 변화시키다

구문 풀이

3행 Instead of making guesses, scientists follow a system
전치사(~ 대신에)　동명사　　　　　　　　　목적어
designed to prove if their ideas are true or false.
과거분사　부사적 용법　　　~인지 아닌지
(~하도록)

06 사냥에서 기원한 인간의 상호 이타주의   정답률 51% | 정답 ④

다음 글의 밑줄 친 부분 중, 문맥상 낱말의 쓰임이 적절하지 않은 것은? [3점]

[본문 해석]

사냥은 인간이 어떻게 상호 이타주의와 사회적 교류를 발전시켰는지를 설명할 수 있다. 인간은 영장류 중에서 몇 년, 수십 년, 혹은 평생 지속될 수 있는 광범위한 상호 관계를 보여준다는 점에서 특별한 것 같다. 큰 사냥감의 고기는 사냥꾼 한 명과 그의 직계가족이 소비할 수 있을 만한 양을 ① 초과한다. 게다가, 사냥의 성공은 매우 ② 변동이 심하다. 어떤 주에는 성공한 사냥꾼이 다음 주에는 실패할 수도 있다. 이러한 조건들은 사냥으로 인한 음식 공유를 ③ 장려한다. 사냥꾼이 당장 먹을 수 없는 고기를 나눠 주는 데 드는 비용은 혼자서 고기를 다 먹을 수 없고 남은 고기는 곧 상하기 때문에 ④ 많이(→ 적게) 든다. 그러나 그 사람이 나중에 스스로 음식을 얻지 못했을 때 그 사람의 음식을 받은 다른 사람들이 관대한 호의에 보답한다면 그 혜택은 클 수 있다. 결국 사냥꾼들은 자신의 친구와 이웃의 몸에 여분의 고기를 ⑤ 저장할 수 있다.

Why? 왜 정답일까?

④ 뒤의 because가 이끄는 절에서, 사냥꾼이 나누어주는 고기는 당장은 자신이 다 먹을 수 없고 놔두면 곧 상할 고기라고 하였다. 즉 어차피 자신에게 남는 고기를 나누어준다는 뜻이므로, 이로 인해 치르는 비용이 크다고 볼 수 없기에 ④의 high를 low로 고쳐야 한다. 따라서 문맥상 낱말의 쓰임이 적절하지 않은 것은 ④이다.

● extensive ⓐ 광범위한, 폭넓은
● quantity ⓝ 양
● immediate ⓐ (가족이) 직계인
● variable ⓐ 변동이 심한, 가변적인
● leftover ⓝ (식사 후) 남은 음식
● game ⓝ 사냥감
● exceed ⓥ 넘어서다, 초과하다
● consume ⓥ 먹다, 마시다
● give away 나눠주다, 거저 주다
● in essence 결국, 본질적으로

구문 풀이

10행 The costs (to a hunter of giving away meat) [he cannot eat
주어　　　　　　　　　　　　　　　　선행사
immediately] are low because he cannot consume all the meat
동사(복수)　접속사(이유)
himself and leftovers will soon spoil.
재귀대명사(he 강조)

★★★ 1등급 대비 고난도 2점 문제

07 세밀한 묘사의 필요성   정답률 46% | 정답 ②

다음 빈칸에 들어갈 말로 가장 적절한 것을 고르시오.

① similarities – 유사점
✓ particulars – 세부 사항
③ fantasies – 환상
④ boredom – 지루함
⑤ wisdom – 지혜

[본문 해석]

글을 인간미 있게 하는 구체적인 사례가 없는 일반화는 듣는 사람에게도 읽는 사람에게도 지루하다. 누가 상투적인 말을 온종일 읽고 싶어 하겠는가? 구체적인 사례가 없이 위대한, 더 위대한, 최고의, 제일 똑똑한, 가장 훌륭한, 인도주의적인, 이런 말들을 누가 계속해서 끊임없이 듣고 싶어 하겠는가? 이런 '공허한 말들'을 사용하는 대신에, 그것들을 완전히 빼고 세부 사항만을 서술하라. 주인공을 대놓고 영웅적이다, 용감하다, 비극적이다, 혹은 웃긴다고 묘사한 후 작가가 다른 것으로 빠르게 넘어가는 소설 속 장면을 읽는 것보다 더 끔찍한 것은 없다. 그건 좋지 않으며, 전혀 좋지 않다. 어떤 것을 실감 나는 것으로 만들고 싶다면, 한 단어 짜리 묘사는 덜 사용하고, 세밀하고 마음을 끄는 묘사를 더 많이 사용해야 한다.

Why? 왜 정답일까?

마지막 문장에서 장면을 실감 나게 만들려면 세밀하고 마음을 끄는 묘사를 사용해야 한다(You have to use less one word descriptions and more detailed, engaging descriptions if you want to make something real.)고 언급하는 것으로 보아, 빈칸에 들어갈 말로 가장 적절한 것은 ② '세부 사항'이다. 이는 빈칸 앞의 specific examples을 재진술한 말이기도 하다.

- **specific** ⓐ 구체적인
- **platitude** ⓝ 진부한 말, 상투적인 문구
- **humanitarian** ⓐ 인도주의적인
- **heroic** ⓐ 대담한, 영웅적인
- **engaging** ⓐ 마음을 끄는, 몰입시키는
- **humanize** ⓥ 인간적으로 만들다
- **finest** ⓐ 가장 훌륭한
- **leave out** ~을 빼다
- **tragic** ⓐ 비극적인
- **boredom** ⓝ 지루함

구문 풀이

7행 「nothing + 비교급 + than : ~보다 더 …한 것은 없다(최상급 의미)」

There is nothing worse than reading a scene in a novel 선행사
[in which a main character is described up front as heroic or brave
= where
or tragic or funny, while thereafter, the writer quickly moves on to
something else].

★★ 문제 해결 꿀~팁 ★★

▶ 많이 틀린 이유는?
첫 문장의 Generalization만 보고 ①을 고르면 안 된다. '특별한' 사례의 공통점을 찾아 '일반화'하라는 내용은 글 어디에도 없기 때문이다.

▶ 문제 해결 방법은?
빈칸이 주제문인 명령문에 있으므로, 마찬가지로 '~해야 한다'라는 당위의 의미를 나타내는 마지막 문장을 잘 읽어야 한다. more detailed, engaging와 같은 의미의 단어를 빈칸에 넣으면 된다.

---

08 식당 선택에 영향을 미치는 손님 수 정답률 60% | 정답 ⑤

다음 빈칸에 들어갈 말로 가장 적절한 것을 고르시오.

① both restaurants are getting busier
두 식당 모두 더 붐비게 된다
② you and your friend start hesitating
당신과 친구가 망설이기 시작한다
③ your decision has no impact on others'
당신의 결정은 다른 사람들의 결정에 영향이 없다
④ they reject what lots of other people do
그들은 많은 다른 사람들이 하는 일을 거부한다
✔ they decide to do the same as the other eight
그들도 다른 여덟 명과 같은 행동을 하기로 결정한다

[본문 해석]

어떤 식당이 대체로 붐빈다는 것을 알게 되면 우리가 그 식당에서 식사할 가능성이 더 크다. 아무도 우리에게 어떤 식당이 좋다고 말하지 않을 때조차도, 우리의 무리 행동은 우리의 의사를 결정한다. 당신이 두 개의 텅 빈 식당 쪽으로 걸어가고 있다고 가정하자. 당신은 어느 곳에 들어가야 할지 모른다. 하지만, 갑자기 당신은 여섯 명의 무리가 둘 중 하나의 식당으로 들어가는 것을 보게 된다. 당신은 텅 빈 식당 혹은 나머지 식당 중 어느 식당에 들어갈 가능성이 더 높겠는가? 대부분의 사람들은 사람들이 있는 식당에 들어갈 것이다. 당신과 친구가 그 식당에 들어간다고 가정하자. 이제, 그 식당 안에는 여덟 명이 있다. 다른 사람들은 한 식당은 텅 비어 있고 다른 식당은 여덟 명이 있는 것을 보게 된다. 그래서, 그들도 다른 여덟 명과 같은 행동을 하기로 결정한다.

Why? 왜 정답일까?

첫 문장인 'We are more likely to eat in a restaurant if we know that it is usually busy.'에서 우리는 붐비는 식당에서 식사할 가능성이 더 높다는 주제를 제시하고 이를 예를 들어 설명하는 글이다. 주제에 비추어볼 때, 빈칸 앞의 문장과 같이 텅 빈 식당과 여덟 명의 손님이 있는 식당을 각각 발견할 경우 사람들은 조금 더 붐비는 후자의 식당에서 식사를 하게 될 것임을 유추할 수 있다. 따라서 빈칸에 들어갈 말로 가장 적절한 것은 ⑤ '그들도 다른 여덟 명과 같은 행동을 하기로 결정한다'이다.

- **behavior** ⓝ 행동
- **decision-making** 의사 결정
- **suddenly** ⓐⓓ 갑자기
- **impact** ⓝ 영향, 충격
- **determine** ⓥ 결정하다
- **suppose** ⓥ 가정하다
- **hesitate** ⓥ 망설이다
- **reject** ⓥ 거부하다

구문 풀이

2행 Even when nobody tells us (that) a restaurant is good, /
심지어 ~할 때에도   생략
our herd behavior determines our decision-making.
주어   동사

---

09 기술과 생산성의 관계 정답률 58% | 정답 ④

다음 글에서 전체 흐름과 관계 없는 문장은?

[본문 해석]

기술은 생산성을 높일 수 있는 잠재력을 가지고 있지만, 또한 생산성에 부정적인 영향을 미칠 수 있다. 예를 들어, 많은 사무실 환경에서 직원들은 컴퓨터가 있는 책상에 앉아 인터넷에 접속한다. ① 그들은 원할 때마다 개인 이메일을 확인하고 소셜 미디어를 사용할 수 있다. ② 이것은 그들이 일을 하는 것을 방해하고 생산성이 떨어지게 할 수 있다. ③ 또한 새로운 기술을 도입하는 것은 생산 공정에 변화를 야기하거나 직원들에게 새로운 시스템을 배우도록 요구할 때 생산에 부정적인 영향을 미칠 수 있다. ④ 기술을 사용하는 것은 기업이 더 많은 제품을 생산하고 다른 생산 요소들로부터 더 많은 것을 얻게 할 수 있다. ⑤ 새로운 기술 사용법을 배우는 것은 직원들에게 시간이 많이 드는 일이고 스트레스를 줄 수 있으며, 이것은 생산성 저하를 야기할 수 있다.

Why? 왜 정답일까?

기술이 생산성을 떨어뜨릴 수 있다는 내용인데, ④는 기술 사용이 더 많은 제품 생산에 도움이 되고 생산 요소로부터 더 많은 것을 얻게 한다는 긍정적 내용이다. 따라서 전체 흐름과 관계 없는 문장은 ④이다.

- **impact** ⓝ 영향, 충격
- **production** ⓝ 생산, 제조
- **require** ⓥ 요구하다
- **time-consuming** ⓐ 시간이 많이 걸리는
- **have access to** ~에 접근하다
- **cause** ⓥ 야기하다
- **factor** ⓝ 요인, 요소

구문 풀이

7행 This can stop them from doing their work and make them
「stop + A + from + B : A가 B하지 못하게 하다」 5형식 동사 목적어
less productive.
형용사·보어

★★★ 1등급 대비 고난도 3점 문제

10 생산성이 최악일 때 오히려 더 발휘되는 창의성 정답률 44% | 정답 ⑤

주어진 글 다음에 이어질 글의 순서로 가장 적절한 것을 고르시오. [3점]

① (A) – (C) – (B)
② (B) – (A) – (C)
③ (B) – (C) – (A)
④ (C) – (A) – (B)
✔ (C) – (B) – (A)

[본문 해석]

대부분의 사람들은 아침이든 저녁이든 혹은 오후든, 하루 중 그들이 최고의 상태에 있다고 느끼는 완벽한 시간을 갖는다.

(C) 우리 중 몇몇은 저녁형 인간이고, 몇몇은 아침형 인간이며, 그 사이에 있는 누군가는 오후의 시간 동안 가장 활력을 느낄지도 모른다. 여러분이 하루를 계획하고 업무를 분배할 수 있다면, 집중을 요구하는 과업을 하루 중 최적의 시간에 처리하기로 정하라.

(B) 그러나, 만약 여러분이 직면한 과업이 창의성과 새로운 아이디어를 요구한다면, 하루 중 '최악의' 시간에 처리하는 것이 최선이다! 그래서 만약 여러분이 아침형 인간이라면 반드시 저녁에 창의적인 작업에 착수하고, 저녁형 인간이라면 반대로 하라.

(A) 여러분의 정신과 신체가 '정점' 시간보다 주의력이 덜할 때, 창의성의 영감이 깨어나 더 자유롭게 거니는 것이 허용된다. 다시 말해서, 여러분의 정신 기제가 차렷 자세로 있을 때보다(힘과 긴장이 바짝 들어가 있을 때보다) 느슨하게 풀려있을 때 창의성이 샘솟는다.

Why? 왜 정답일까?

사람들에게는 자기 신체와 잘 맞는 시간이 있다고 언급하는 주어진 글 뒤로, 집중력이 필요한 과업은 최적의 시간대에 처리해야 한다는 (C), '반면에' 창의성이 필요한 과업은 최악의 시간대에 처리하는 것이 좋다는 (B), 그 이유를 보충 설명하는 (A)가 연결되어야 자연스럽다. 따라서 글의 순서로 가장 적절한 것은 ⑤ '(C) – (B) – (A)'이다.

- **whether A or B** A이든 B이든
- **stand at attention** 차렷 자세를 취하다
- **tackle** ⓥ 해결하다, 처리하다, 다루다
- **vice versa** 그 반대도 같다
- **make it a point to** ~하기로 정하다, 으레 ~하다
- **loose** ⓐ 느슨한
- **novel** ⓐ 새로운, 신기한
- **early bird** 아침형 인간
- **night owl** 저녁형 인간

구문 풀이

14행 Some of us are night owls, some (are) early birds, and others
주어1 　　주어2(여럿 중 일부)↵ 생략(중복) 　　주어3(또 다른 일부)
in between may feel most active during the afternoon hours.

★★ 문제 해결 꿀~팁 ★★

▶ 많이 틀린 이유는?

(C) – (A)를 잘못 연결하기 쉽지만, (C)는 '정점' 시간에 수행할 과업(= 집중력이 필요한 일)을 언급하는 반면 (A)는 정점 시간이 '아닐' 때 수행할 과업(= 창의력이 필요한 일)을 언급한다. 즉 두 단락은 다루는 소재가 다르므로 적절한 흐름 전환의 연결어가 없으면 연결될 수 없다.

▶ 문제 해결 방법은?

하루 중 최적의 시간대가 개인마다 다르다는 주어진 글 뒤로, 누구는 아침이 좋고, 또 누구는 밤이 좋으니 각자 정점의 시간마다 집중력이 필요한 일을 처리하는 것이 좋다는 (C)가 먼저 연결된다. 즉 주어진 글과 (C)는 '일반적 내용 – 구체적 사례'의 흐름으로 자연스럽게 연결된다. 이어서 (A), (B)는 모두 (C)와는 달리 '창의력 과업을 수행하기 좋은 시간대'에 관한 내용인데, 이렇듯 흐름이나 소재가 달라질 때는 역접어가 있는 단락을 먼저 연결해야 한다. 따라서 (B) – (A)의 순서가 적합하다.

11-12 　언어의 근원이자 목적인 대화

[본문 해석]

모든 인간처럼, 맨 처음부터 언어를 구성하는 길고 힘든 과정을 시작한 최초의 호모 종은 거의 틀림없이 자신의 마음에 있는 것을 온전히 말하지 않았다. 동시에, 이 원시 호미닌(인간의 조상으로 분류되는 종족)들은 단순히 (a) 무작위적인 소리를 내거나 몸짓을 하지는 않았을 것이다. 대신, 그들은 남들이 이해할 것이라고 믿는 의사소통 수단을 사용했을 것이다. 그리고 그들은 또한 자신의 청자들이 '빈틈을 메울' 수 있고, 발화된 것을 해석하기 위해 그들의 문화와 세계에 대한 지식을 연결할 수 있다고 생각했다.

이러한 것들이 대화가 이해해야 할 것들의 목록 중 맨 위에 놓여지지 않는 한, 인간 언어의 (b) 기원이 효과적으로 논의될 수 없는 몇 가지 이유이다. 『인간의 뇌와 신체의 구성 요소들이 그래왔듯이, 인간 언어의 모든 측면은 대화와 사회 생활에 (c) 관여하도록 진화해 왔다.』 언어는 최초의 호미니드(사람과의 동물)가 최초의 단어나 문장을 발화했을 때 온전히 시작된 것은 아니었다. 그것은 최초의 대화와 함께 비로소 본격적으로 시작되었는데, 이는 언어의 근원이자 (d) 목적이다. 실제로, 언어는 삶을 변화시킨다. 그것은 사회를 세우고, 우리의 가장 높은 열망, 가장 기본적인 생각, 감정 그리고 삶의 철학을 표현한다. 『하지만 모든 언어는 궁극적으로 인간의 상호 작용을 위한 것이다.』 언어의 다른 요소들, 즉 문법과 이야기와 같은 것은 대화에 (e) 중요한(→ 부차적인) 것들이다.

- **construct** ⓥ 구성하다
- **primitive** ⓐ 원시의
- **utter** ⓥ 발화하다
- **aspect** ⓝ 측면, 양상
- **in earnest** 본격적으로
- **philosophy** ⓝ 철학
- **crucial** ⓐ 매우 중요한
- **from scratch** 맨 처음부터, 아무것도 없이
- **interpret** ⓥ 해석하다, 이해하다
- **effectively** ⓐ⃝ 효과적으로
- **engage in** ~에 관여하다, 참여하다
- **aspiration** ⓝ 열망
- **ultimately** ⓐ⃝ 궁극적으로
- **offend** ⓥ 마음을 상하게 하다

구문 풀이

1행 Like all humans, the first Homo species to begin the long
전치사(~처럼) 　　주어 　　형용사적 용법(~할, ~하는)
difficult process of constructing a language from scratch almost
certainly never said entirely what was on their minds.
동사 　　관계대명사(~것)

11 　제목 파악 　　　　정답률 64% | 정답 ②

윗글의 제목으로 가장 적절한 것은?

① Various Communication Strategies of Our Ancestors
조상들의 다양한 의사소통 전략
② Conversation: The Core of Language Development
대화: 언어 발달의 핵심
③ Ending Conversation Without Offending Others
타인을 기분 상하게 하지 않고 대화를 끝내기

④ How Language Shapes the Way You Think
언어는 어떻게 당신의 사고방식을 형성하는가
⑤ What Makes You a Good Communicator?
무엇이 의사소통을 잘하게 만드는가?

Why? 왜 정답일까?

두 번째 단락의 'Every aspect of human language has evolved, ~ to engage in conversation and social life.'를 통해 인간은 대화와 사회 상호작용에 참여하기 위해 언어를 발달시켜 왔다는 내용을 파악할 수 있다. 따라서 글의 제목으로 가장 적절한 것은 ② '대화: 언어 발달의 핵심'이다.

★★★ 1등급 대비 고난도 3점 문제

12 　어휘 추론 　　　　정답률 44% | 정답 ⑤

밑줄 친 (a) ~ (e) 중에서 문맥상 낱말의 쓰임이 적절하지 않은 것은? [3점]

① (a) 　② (b) 　③ (c) 　④ (d) 　✓ (e)

Why? 왜 정답일까?

'But all language is ultimately at the service of human interaction.'에서 모든 언어는 궁극적으로 인간의 상호 작용을 목적으로 한다고 언급한 것으로 보아, 상호 작용 외의 요소들, 즉 문법이나 이야기 등은 언어 발달 또는 대화의 '부수적' 요소임을 추론할 수 있다. 따라서 ⑤의 crucial은 secondary로 고쳐야 한다. 문맥상 낱말의 쓰임이 가장 적절하지 않은 것은 ⑤ '(e)'이다.

★★ 문제 해결 꿀~팁 ★★

▶ 많이 틀린 이유는?

최다 오답인 (d) goal이 포함된 문장 바로 앞에서 언어가 제대로 시작된 것은 말이 처음 이루어졌을 때가 아니라 '대화'가 처음 이루어졌을 때라고 한다. 이에 비추어 볼 때, 대화가 언어의 출발점이면서 '목적'이기도 했다는 의미의 goal은 맥락에 적합하다.

▶ 문제 해결 방법은?

두 번째 단락의 첫 문장에서 인간 언어의 기원을 효과적으로 논의하기 위해서는 대화를 가장 중요하게 고려해야 한다고 했다. 이를 근거로 볼 때, 문법 등 나머지 요소는 '아주 중요한' 요소라기보다는 '부차적인' 요소이다.

DAY 09

DAY 10 — 20분 미니 모의고사

01 ①	02 ①	03 ②	04 ③	05 ③
06 ②	07 ③	08 ⑤	09 ②	10 ④
11 ②	12 ④			

---

01 엄마와 시장에 간 Breaden
정답률 92% | 정답 ①

다음 글에 드러난 Breaden의 심경 변화로 가장 적절한 것은?

☑ excited → disappointed
　신이 난　　실망한

② embarrassed → satisfied
　당황한　　만족한

③ lonely → pleased
　외로운　　기쁜

④ annoyed → relieved
　짜증난　　안도한

⑤ delighted → jealous
　기쁜　　질투하는

[본문 해석]

귀여운 세 살짜리 소년인 Breaden은 간식, 바, 사탕이 있는 복도를 따라 환하게 미소를 지으며 걷고 있었다. Breaden에게 그곳은 여러 종류의 유혹을 하는 복도였다. "와!" 하고 그는 외쳤다. 그의 눈 바로 앞에 몇 줄로 늘어선 맛있어 보이는 초콜릿 바들이 손으로 건드려 주기를 기다리고 있었다. 그의 엄마는 그의 손을 쥐고 있었다. 그녀의 외아들인 Breaden은 항상 그녀의 관심 집중 대상이었고 그녀는 시장에서 아들을 잃어버리지 않으려고 조심했다. 갑자기, Breaden의 엄마는 그녀의 친구들에게 인사를 하려고 멈췄다. Breaden도 멈췄다. Breaden이 눈을 크게 뜨고 입에서 침을 흘리며, 팔을 뻗어 초콜릿 바를 움켜쥐려고 할 때, (누군가) 그의 손을 꽉 쥐는 것을 느꼈다. 그는 올려다보았다. "Breaden, 오늘은 안 돼!" 그는 그것이 무슨 뜻인지 알았다. "알았어요, 엄마."라고 말하며 그는 한숨을 쉬었다. 그의 어깨는 늘어졌다.

Why? 왜 정답일까?

시장에 간 어린 Breaden은 여러 물건을 보고 신이 나 소리를 지른다(It was the aisle of all kinds of temptation for him. "Wow!" he exclaimed.). 그런데 그가 사고 싶은 초콜릿을 어머니가 못 사게 하여, 마지막 문장에서 그는 한숨을 쉬고 그의 어깨는 늘어졌다(~ he sighed. His shoulders fell.). 따라서 Breaden의 심경 변화로 가장 적절한 것은 ① '신이 난 → 실망한'이다.

- along **prep** ~을 따라
- sweets ⑪ 사탕
- exclaim ⓥ 소리치다, 외치다
- cautious ⓐ 조심하는
- aisle ⑪ (물건이 쌓여 있는 사이의) 통로, 복도
- temptation ⑪ 유혹
- attention ⑪ 주의(집중), 주목, 관심, 흥미
- stretch out ~을 쭉 뻗다

구문 풀이

10행 With his eyes wide open and his mouth watering, Breaden
「with(전치사)+명사+형용사/분사 : 부대상황 분사구문」
stretched out his arm and was about to grab a bar / when he felt a
　　　　　　　막 ~하려고 하다　　　접속사
tight grip on his hand.

---

02 교실 장식이 적당할 필요성
정답률 82% | 정답 ①

다음 글의 요지로 가장 적절한 것은?

☑ 아이들의 집중을 돕기 위해 과도한 교실 장식을 지양할 필요가 있다.
② 아이들의 인성과 인지 능력을 균형 있게 발달시키는 것이 중요하다.
③ 아이들이 직접 교실을 장식하는 것은 창의력 발달에 도움이 된다.
④ 다양한 교실 활동은 아이들의 수업 참여도를 증진시킨다.
⑤ 풍부한 시각 자료는 아이들의 학습 동기를 높인다.

[본문 해석]

피츠버그시 Carnegie Mellon University에서 이루어진, '너무 많은 좋은 것이 나쁠 수도 있을 때'라고 불리는 최근 한 연구에 따르면, 너무 많은 장식이 있는 교실은 어린이들의 주의 산만의 원인이고 그들의 인지적인 수행에 직접적으로 영향을 미친다. 시각적으로 지나치게 자극되었을 때, 아이들은 집중하는 데 많이 어려워하고 결국 학습 결과가 더 나빠진다. 반면에, 교실 벽에 장식이 많지 않으면, 아이들은 덜 산만해지고, 수업 활동에 더 많은 시간을 사용하고, 더 많이 배운다. 그래서 이들의 집중을 도우려면 지나친 장식과 장식이 전혀 없는 것 사이의 적절한 균형을 찾는 것이 우리가 할 일이다.

Why? 왜 정답일까?

교실 장식이 과하면 아이들의 집중력이 떨어진다는 연구 내용을 토대로, 아이들의 집중력을 높여주려면 적당한 교실 장식의 균형을 찾아야 한다(~ in order to support their attention, to find the right balance between excessive decoration and the complete absence of it.)는 결론을 이끌어내고 있다. 따라서 글의 요지로 가장 적절한 것은 ① '아이들의 집중을 돕기 위해 과도한 교실 장식을 지양할 필요가 있다.'이다.

- decoration ⑪ 장식
- a great deal of 상당한, 큰, 많은
- excessive ⓐ 과도한
- overstimulate ⓥ 과도하게 자극하다
- end up with 결국 ~하다
- absence ⑪ 부재

구문 풀이

5행 Being visually overstimulated, the children have a great deal
분사구문　　　　　　「have difficulty + 동명사 : ~하는 데 어려움을 겪다」
of difficulty concentrating and end up with worse academic results.

---

03 성공적인 직업의 함정
정답률 67% | 정답 ②

다음 글의 제목으로 가장 적절한 것은?

① Don't Compete with Yourself – 자기 자신과 경쟁하지 말라
☑ A Trap of a Successful Career – 성공적인 직업의 함정
③ Create More Jobs for Young People – 젊은이들을 위해 더 많은 일자리를 창출하라
④ What Difficult Jobs Have in Common – 어려운 직업에는 어떤 공통점이 있는가
⑤ A Road Map for an Influential Employer – 영향력이 큰 고용주를 위한 지침

[본문 해석]

성공은 여러분이 의도한 길에서 벗어나 틀에 박힌 편안한 생활로 들어가도록 이끌 수 있다. 여러분이 어떤 일을 잘하고 그 일을 하는 데 대한 보상을 잘 받는다면, 그것을 즐기지 않게 되더라도 계속하고 싶을 수도 있다. 위험한 점은 어느 날 여러분이 주변을 둘러보고, 자신이 틀에 박힌 이 편안한 생활에 너무나 깊이 빠져 있어서 더는 태양을 보거나 신선한 공기를 호흡할 수 없으며, 그 틀에 박힌 생활의 양쪽 면이 너무나 미끄럽게 되어 기어올라 나오려면 초인적인 노력이 필요할 것이고, 사실상 자신이 꼼짝할 수 없다는 것을 깨닫게 된다는 것이다. 그리고 이는 많은 근로자가 현재 자신이 처해 있다고 걱정하는 상황이다. 열악한 고용 시장은 이들이 안정적이거나 심지어 보수가 좋을 수도 있지만 궁극적으로는 만족스럽지 못한 일자리에 갇혀 있다고 느끼게 했다.

Why? 왜 정답일까?

첫 두 문장을 통해, 직업에서 성공하고 높은 보상을 누리게 된다면 그 일을 즐기지 않게 되거나 일에서의 만족을 느끼지 못하게 되더라도 그 일을 고수하게 된다(If you are good at something and are well rewarded for doing it, you may want to keep doing it even if you stop enjoying it.)는 주제를 파악할 수 있다. 따라서 글의 제목으로 가장 적절한 것은 ② '성공적인 직업의 함정'이다.

- intended ⓐ 의도된
- be rewarded for ~에 대해 보상받다
- slippery ⓐ 미끄러운
- superhuman ⓐ 초인적인
- be stuck 꼼짝 못하다
- well-paying ⓐ 보수가 좋은
- unsatisfying ⓐ 불만족스러운
- have ~ in common ~을 공통적으로 지니다
- rut ⑪ 틀에 박힌 생활
- breathe ⓥ 호흡하다
- take effort to ~하는 데 (…한) 노력이 들다
- effectively **ad** 실질적으로, 사실상
- employment ⑪ 고용
- ultimately **ad** 궁극적으로
- compete with ~와 경쟁하다
- influential ⓐ 영향력 있는

구문 풀이

10행 The poor employment market has left them feeling locked
　　　　　　　　　　　　　동사　　목적어　목적격 보어(현재분사)
in [what may be a secure, or even well-paying — but ultimately
[ ] : in의 목적절　　　　　　　　　may be의 주격 보어
unsatisfying — job].

---

04 Margaret Knight의 생애
정답률 84% | 정답 ③

Margaret Knight에 관한 다음 글의 내용과 일치하지 않는 것은?

① 기자들이 '여자 Edison'이라는 별명을 지어 주었다.
② 가족을 위해 돈을 벌려고 학교를 그만두었다.
☑ 직물 장비에 쓰이는 안전장치를 발명하여 많은 돈을 벌었다.
④ 밑이 평평한 종이 가방을 자르고 접고 붙이는 기계를 발명했다.

⑤ 2006년에 국립 발명가 명예의 전당에 입성했다.

[본문 해석]

『Margaret Knight는 19세기 후반에 특출나게 다작한 발명가였고, 기자들은 가끔 '여자 Edison'이라는 별명을 지어주며 그녀를 Thomas Edison과 비교했다.』 어린 나이부터, 그녀는 오빠들을 위해 장난감을 만들었다. 아버지가 돌아가신 후, Knight의 가족은 Manchester로 이사했다. 『Knight는 가족을 위해 가까이에 있는 직물 공장에서 돈을 벌기 위해 1850년에 12세의 나이에 학교를 그만두었는데,』 그곳에서 그녀는 동료 노동자가 결함이 있는 장비에 부상 당하는 것을 목격했다. 『이로 인해 그녀는 첫 번째 발명품, 즉 직물 장비에 쓰이는 안전장치를 만들었지만, 그녀는 결코 그 발명품으로 돈을 벌지 않았다.』 『그녀는 또한 밑이 평평한 종이 가방을 자르고 접어 붙이는 기계를 발명해 1871년에 그것으로 첫 특허를 받았다.』 그것은 작업자들이 손으로 그것들을 천천히 조립할 필요가 없어지게 했다. 『Knight는 일생 동안 27개의 특허를 받았고, 2006년에 국립 발명가 명예의 전당에 입성했다.』 ──「」: ⑤의 근거 일치

Why? 왜 정답일까?

'~ a safety device for textile equipment, but she never earned money from the invention.'에서 Margaret Knight는 동료가 직물 장비에 부상당하는 것을 본 후 장비에 적용할 안전장치를 만들었지만 이것으로 돈을 벌지는 않았다고 한다. 따라서 내용과 일치하지 않는 것은 ③ '직물 장비에 쓰이는 안전장치를 발명하여 많은 돈을 벌었다.'이다.

Why? 왜 오답일까?

① '~ journalists occasionally compared her to Thomas Edison by nicknaming her "a woman Edison."'의 내용과 일치한다.
② 'Knight left school in 1850, at age 12, to earn money for her family ~'의 내용과 일치한다.
④ 'She also invented a machine that cut, folded and glued flat-bottomed paper bags ~'의 내용과 일치한다.
⑤ '~ entered the National Inventors Hall of Fame in 2006.'의 내용과 일치한다.

- **exceptionally** ad 이례적으로, 특출나게
- **journalist** n 기자
- **witness** v 목격하다
- **faulty** a 결함이 있는
- **glue** v 접착하다
- **assemble** v 조립하다
- **prolific** a 다작한
- **occasionally** ad 가끔, 때때로
- **fellow** n 동료
- **fold** v 접다
- **flat-bottomed** a 밑이 평평한
- **hall of fame** 명예의 전당

구문 풀이

2행 ~ journalists occasionally compared her to Thomas Edison by nicknaming her "a woman Edison."
'by + 동명사 : ~함으로써'

★★★ 1등급 대비 고난도 3점 문제

05 플라스틱의 특성 정답률 32% | 정답 ③

다음 글의 밑줄 친 부분 중, 어법상 틀린 것은? [3점]

[본문 해석]

플라스틱은 매우 느리게 분해되고 물에 떠다니는 경향이 있는데, 이는 플라스틱이 해류를 따라 수천 마일을 돌아다니게 한다. 대부분의 플라스틱은 자외선에 노출될 때 점점 더 작은 조각으로 분해되어 미세 플라스틱을 형성한다. 이러한 미세 플라스틱은 일단 그것들을 수거하는 데 일반적으로 사용되는 그물망을 통과할 만큼 충분히 작아지면 측정하기가 매우 어렵다. 미세 플라스틱이 해양 환경과 먹이 그물에 미치는 영향은 아직도 제대로 이해되고 있지 않다. 이 작은 조각들은 다양한 동물에게 먹혀 먹이 사슬 속으로 들어간다고 알려져 있다. 바다 속에 있는 대부분의 플라스틱 조각들은 매우 작기 때문에 바다를 청소할 실질적인 방법은 없다. 비교적 적은 양의 플라스틱을 수거하기 위해 엄청난 양의 물을 여과해야 할 수도 있다.

Why? 왜 정답일까?

'to collect'의 의미상 주어가 the nets인데 목적어는 microplastics이므로, 재귀대명사 themselves는 them으로 고쳐야 한다. 재귀대명사는 어떤 행위의 주어와 목적어가 같을 때 목적어 자리에 쓰이는 대명사임에 유의한다. 따라서 어법상 틀린 것은 ③이다.

Why? 왜 오답일까?

① 앞 문장의 내용을 받는 계속적 용법의 관계대명사로서 which를 쓴 것은 어법상 맞다.
② 앞에 나온 완전한 절 뒤로 주절의 의미를 보충 설명하는 분사구문으로서 의미상 능동을 나타내는 현재분사 forming을 쓴 것은 어법상 맞다.
④ 주어인 'most of the plastic particles'가 'most of + 복수명사' 형태이므로, 복수동사 are를 쓴 것은 어법상 맞다.
⑤ 뒤에 나온 형용사 small을 꾸미는 말로서 부사인 relatively를 쓴 것은 어법상 맞다.

- **extremely** ad 매우, 극도로
- **float** v (물 위나 공중에) 떠가다, 뜨다
- **break down into** ~로 분해되다
- **ultraviolet** a 자외선의 n 자외선
- **measure** v 측정하다, 재다
- **marine** a 해양의, 바다의
- **food web** 먹이 그물
- **practical** a 실질적인, 실용적인
- **enormous** a 엄청난, 거대한
- **tend** v 경향이 있다
- **current** n 해류, 흐름, 기류
- **exposed to** ~에 노출된
- **form** v 형성하다, 형성되다
- **typically** ad 일반적으로, 보통, 전형적으로
- **tiny** a (매우) 작은
- **food chain** 먹이 사슬
- **filter** v 여과하다
- **relatively** ad 비교적, 상대적으로

구문 풀이

3행 Most plastics break down into smaller and smaller pieces
          　　　　　　　동사
when (they are) exposed to ultraviolet (UV) light, forming microplastics.
접속사　생략　　과거분사　　　　　　　　　　　　　　　분사구문(그리고 ~하다)

★★ 문제 해결 꿀~팁 ★★

▶ 많이 틀린 이유는?
재귀대명사의 용법을 정확히 알아야 답을 찾을 수 있는 문제이다. 재귀대명사는 '행위'를 기준으로 그 주체와 대상을 따져야 한다. 여기서는 중심 되는 행위가 'to collect'이므로 '수거하는' 주체가 누구이고 대상은 무엇인지, 그것이 서로 일치하는지 여부를 파악해야 한다.

▶ 문제 해결 방법은?
어법 문제는 빈출되는 포인트를 미리 정리하고 답을 판단하는 기준을 명확히 잡도록 한다. 최다 오답인 ②의 경우, 현재분사에 밑줄이 있으므로 비교 대상은 과거분사이다.

06 경쟁과 협력 둘 다를 통해 형성되는 사회적 유대 정답률 56% | 정답 ②

(A), (B), (C)의 각 네모 안에서 문맥에 맞는 낱말로 가장 적절한 것은? [3점]

	(A)	(B)	(C)
①	creating 만들어내는	harmony 조화	prevent 막다
✓②	creating 만들어내는	tension 긴장	generate 만들어내다
③	creating 만들어내는	tension 긴장	prevent 막다
④	forgiving 용서하는	tension 긴장	prevent 막다
⑤	forgiving 용서하는	harmony 조화	generate 만들어내다

[본문 해석]

사회적 관계는 우리의 생존과 행복을 위해 매우 필수적이어서 우리는 관계를 형성하기 위해 다른 사람과 협력할 뿐만 아니라, 친구를 얻기 위해 다른 사람과 경쟁하기도 한다. 그리고 우리는 흔히 둘 다를 동시에 한다. 가십을 생각해 보자. 가십을 통해 우리는 친구들과 흥미로운 세부사항을 공유하면서 유대를 형성한다. 그러나 동시에 우리는 가십의 대상들 중에서 잠재적인 적을 (A) 만들어내고 있다. 또는 누가 그들의 파티에 참석할 것인지를 알아보기 위해 경쟁하는 라이벌 관계의 휴일 파티를 생각해 보라. 우리는 심지어 소셜 미디어에서도 사람들이 가장 많은 친구들과 팔로워들을 얻기 위해 경쟁할 때 이러한 (B) 긴장을 볼 수 있다. 동시에 경쟁적 배제는 또한 협력도 (C) 만들어낼 수 있다. 고등학교 친목 동아리와 컨트리클럽(전원생활을 즐기려는 도시 사람을 위하여 테니스장, 수영장 등의 시설을 교외에 갖춘 단체)은 이러한 공식을 사용하여 큰 효과를 발휘한다. 그들이 충성심과 지속적인 사회적 유대를 형성하는 것은 바로 선택적인 포함과 배제를 통해서이다.

Why? 왜 정답일까?

(A) But 앞에서 우리는 가십을 통해 친구들과 유대를 형성할 수 있다고 하므로, But 뒤에는 이와 상반된 내용이 이어져야 한다. 따라서 (A)에는 가십을 하는 도중에 적도 '만들어질 수 있다'는 의미를 완성하는 creating이 들어가야 한다.
(B) 앞 문장에서 누가 서로의 파티에 참석할지 의식하는 라이벌 관계의 파티를 예로 들고 있다. 이와 같은 맥락에서 (B)가 포함된 문장은 사람들이 소셜 미디어에서도 서로 더

DAY 10

많은 친구나 팔로워를 얻기 위해 경쟁한다는 의미를 나타내야 한다. 따라서 (B)에는 tension이 들어가야 적절하다.
(C) 마지막 두 문장에서 고등학교 친목 동아리와 컨트리클럽을 예로 들어 이들은 선택적인 포함뿐 아니라 배제를 통해 지속적인 유대감과 충성심을 만들어낸다고 한다. 따라서 (C)에는 협력을 '만들어낸다'는 의미를 완성하는 generate가 들어가야 한다. (A), (B), (C)의 각 네모 안에서 문맥에 맞는 낱말로 가장 적절한 것은 ② '(A) creating(만들어내는) – (B) tension(긴장) – (C) generate(만들어내다)'이다.

- essential ⓐ 필수적인, 본질적인
- forgive ⓥ 용서하다
- exclusion ⓝ 배제
- prevent ⓥ 막다, 예방하다, 방지하다
- selective ⓐ 선택적인
- loyalty ⓝ 충성심
- gossip ⓝ 가십, 뒷담화, 험담 ⓥ 뒷담화하다
- tension ⓝ 긴장
- generate ⓥ 만들어내다
- formula ⓝ 공식, 제조식
- inclusion ⓝ 포함

구문 풀이

8행 Or consider rival holiday parties [where people compete
선행사(공간) 관계부사
to see who will attend *their* party].
~하기 위해 └▸의문사(누가)

★★★ 1등급 대비 고난도 2점 문제

07 정보 공유에 있어 대면 상호작용의 중요성 정답률 49% | 정답 ③

다음 빈칸에 들어갈 말로 가장 적절한 것을 고르시오.

① natural talent – 천부적 재능
② regular practice – 규칙적인 연습
✓③ personal contact – 개인적인 접촉
④ complex knowledge – 복잡한 지식
⑤ powerful motivation – 강력한 동기

[본문 해석]

대면 상호 작용은 가장 간단한 것부터 가장 복잡한 것까지 많은 종류의 지식을 공유하는 유례 없이 강력한―때로는 유일한―방법이다. 그것은 새로운 생각과 아이디어를 자극하는 최고의 방법 중 하나이기도 하다. 우리 대부분이 그림으로만 신발 끈 묶는 법을 배웠거나, 책으로 셈법을 배웠다면 어려움을 겪었을 것이다. 심리학자 Mihàly Csikszentmihàlyi는 높은 성취도를 보이는 사람들을 연구하면서 다수의 노벨상 수상자가 이전 (노벨상) 수상자들의 학생들이라는 것을 발견했다. 그들은 다른 모든 사람들과 똑같은 (연구) 문헌에 접근할 수 있었지만, 개인적인 접촉이 이들의 창의성에 결정적인 차이를 만들었다. 이로 인해 조직 내에서 대화는 고급 전문 기술을 위한 매우 중요한 요소이자 일상 정보를 공유하는 가장 중요한 방식이 된다.

Why? 왜 정답일까?

첫 문장과 마지막 문장에서 정보를 공유하는 가장 중요한 방법으로 대면 상호 작용(Face-to-face interaction) 또는 대화(conversation)를 언급하고 있다. 따라서 빈칸에 들어갈 말로 가장 적절한 것은 ③ '개인적인 접촉'이다.

- interaction ⓝ 상호 작용
- simplest ⓐ 가장 간단한
- stimulate ⓥ 자극하다
- achiever ⓝ 성취도를 보이는 사람
- conversation ⓝ 대화
- uniquely ⓐ 유례없이
- complex ⓐ 복잡한
- arithmetic ⓝ 산수
- crucial ⓐ 아주 중요한, 중대한
- factor ⓝ 요소

구문 풀이

5행 Most of us would have had difficulty learning {how to tie a
「have difficulty + 동명사 : ~하는 데 어려움을 겪다」
shoelace} only from pictures, or {how to do arithmetic} from a book.
{ } : 명사구(how + to부정사 : ~하는 방법)

★★ 문제 해결 꿀~팁 ★★

▶ 많이 틀린 이유는?
글 처음과 마지막에 many kinds of knowledge, from the simplest to the most complex 또는 high-level professional skills와 같은 표현이 등장하므로 얼핏 보면 ④가 적절해 보인다. 하지만 빈칸은 이러한 정보 공유나 전문 능력 개발에 '무엇이 영향을 미치는지' 그 요인을 밝히는 것이므로 ④를 빈칸에 넣기는 부적절하다.
▶ 문제 해결 방법은?
첫 문장의 Face-to-face interaction과 마지막 문장의 conversation이 키워드이다. 이 둘을 일반화할 수 있는 표현이 바로 '빈칸'이다.

★★★ 1등급 대비 고난도 3점 문제

08 나이가 들면서 호기심이 줄어드는 까닭 정답률 31% | 정답 ⑤

글의 흐름으로 보아, 주어진 문장이 들어가기에 가장 적절한 곳을 고르시오. [3점]

[본문 해석]

교육 심리학자 Susan Engel에 따르면, 호기심은 네 살 정도라는 어린 나이에 줄어들기 시작한다. 우리가 어른이 될 무렵, 질문은 더 적어지고 기본값은 더 많아진다. Henry James가 말했듯이, '무관심한 호기심은 없어지고, 정신의 고랑과 경로가 자리잡는다.' ① 호기심의 감소는 유년 시절 동안의 뇌의 발달에서 원인을 찾을 수 있다. ② 비록 성인의 뇌보다 작지만, 유아의 뇌는 수백만 개 더 많은 신경 연결을 가지고 있다. ③ 그러나 연결 상태는 엉망인데, 유아의 뉴런 간의 전달은 성인 뇌 속 뉴런끼리의 전달보다 훨씬 덜 효율적이다. ④ 결과적으로 세상에 대한 아기의 인식은 매우 풍부하면서도 상당히 무질서하다. ⑤ 아이들이 그들 주변의 세상으로부터 더 많은 증거를 흡수함에 따라, 특정한 가능성들이 훨씬 더 커지게 되고 더 유용하게 되며 지식이나 믿음으로 굳어진다. 그러한 믿음을 가능하게 하는 신경 경로는 더 빠르고 자동적으로 이루어지게 되고, 반면에 아이가 주기적으로 사용하지 않는 경로는 제거된다.

Why? 왜 정답일까?

⑤ 앞은 아기의 인식이 성인에 비해 무질서하다는 내용인데, ⑤ 뒤에서는 갑자기 '믿음'을 언급하며, 신경 경로의 자동화와 제거를 설명한다. 이때 주어진 문장을 보면, 아이들이 주변 세상에서 더 많은 근거를 얻고 더 유용한 가능성들을 취하면서 '믿음'이 굳어지기 시작한다고 한다. 이 '믿음'이 ⑤ 뒤와 연결되는 것이므로, 주어진 문장이 들어가기에 가장 적절한 곳은 ⑤이다.

- absorb ⓥ (정보를) 받아들이다
- educational ⓐ 교육의
- decrease ⓥ 감소하다
- disinterested ⓐ 무관심한
- channel ⓝ 경로
- childhood ⓝ 어린 시절
- neural ⓐ 신경의
- perception ⓝ 지각, 인식
- intensely ⓐ 대단히, 강렬하게
- pathway ⓝ 경로
- prune ⓥ 가지치기하다
- harden ⓥ 굳어지다
- curiosity ⓝ 호기심
- default setting 기본값
- groove ⓝ 고랑
- development ⓝ 발달
- infant ⓝ 유아
- mess ⓝ 엉망
- consequently ⓐ 그 결과
- disordered ⓐ 무질서한
- automatic ⓐ 자동적인

구문 풀이

1행 As children absorb more evidence from the world around
접속사(~함에 따라)
them, certain possibilities become much more likely and more useful
=children 동사1 주격 보어(비교급 형용사구)
and harden into knowledge or beliefs.
동사2

★★ 문제 해결 꿀~팁 ★★

▶ 많이 틀린 이유는?
① 뒤의 문장 이후, ②~⑤ 사이의 내용은 모두 부연 설명이다. 호기심이 감소하는 까닭은 뇌 발달에 있다는 일반적인 내용 뒤로, 아이들의 뇌가 성인의 뇌보다 작지만 연결고리가 훨씬 더 많다는 설명, 그렇지만 그 연결고리가 엉망이라는 설명, 그렇기에 아이의 세상 인식은 어른보다 풍부할지언정 무질서하다는 설명이 모두 자연스럽게 이어지고 있다. 주어진 문장은 이 모든 설명이 마무리된 후 '어쩌다' 호기심이 떨어지는 것인지 마침내 언급하는 문장이다.
▶ 문제 해결 방법은?
연결어 힌트가 없어서 난해하게 느껴질 수 있지만, 지시어 힌트를 활용하면 아주 쉽다. ⑤ 뒤에는 '그러한 믿음(those beliefs)'이라는 표현이 나오는데, 이는 앞에서 '믿음'을 언급했어야만 쓸 수 있는 표현이다. 하지만 ⑤ 앞까지는 beliefs가 전혀 등장하지 않고, 오로지 주어진 문장에만 knowledge or beliefs가 등장한다.

09 건강에 관한 과학 연구가 단순하게 소개되는 이유 정답률 48% | 정답 ②

다음 글의 내용을 한 문장으로 요약하고자 한다. 빈칸 (A), (B)에 들어갈 말로 가장 적절한 것은?

	(A)		(B)
①	satisfy 만족시키지	……	simple 간단한
✓②	satisfy 만족시키지	……	complicated 복잡한

③ ignore ······ difficult
　무시하지　　　　어려운
④ ignore ······ simple
　무시하지　　　　간단한
⑤ reject ······ complicated
　거부하지　　　　복잡한

[본문 해석]

과학의 영역에는 종종 많은 불확실성이 존재하며 일반 대중은 그것을 불편하다고 느낀다. 그들은 '정보에 근거한 측측'을 원하지 않으며 자신의 삶을 더 편하게 만들어 주는 확실성을 원하는데, 과학은 종종 이러한 요구를 만족시키도록 갖춰져 있지 않다. 특히 인간의 신체는 굉장히 복잡하며 어떤 과학적인 답변은 흑백 양자택일의 말로는 절대 제공될 수 없다. 이 모든 것 때문에 미디어는 과학적 연구를 대중에게 제시할 때 그것을 지나치게 단순화하는 경향이 있다. 그들의 시각에서는, 그들은 극소수의 사람들만이 읽거나 이해할 더 정확하지만 복잡한 정보를 제공하는 것과는 반대로, 단지 '사람들에게 그들이 원하는 것을 제공하고' 있는 것이다. 이것의 완벽한 하나의 예시는 어떤 음식이 '좋은'지 '나쁜'지에 관해 사람들이 확정적인 답변을 원하는 방식이다. 과학적으로 말하자면 '좋고' '나쁜' 음식은 없으며, 오히려 음식의 질은 연속체상에 존재하는데 이는 어떤 음식들이 다른 것들보다 일반 건강과 웰빙 면에서 *더 낫다*는 것을 의미한다.

➡ 일반 건강과 관련하여 과학은 본질적으로 확실성에 대한 대중의 요구를 (A) 만족시키지 않으며, 이것은 미디어가 대중에게 덜 (B) 복잡한 답변을 제공하게 만든다.

Why? 왜 정답일까?

첫 두 문장에서 대중은 과학에 확실성을 기대하지만 과학은 이러한 요구를 흔히 만족시키지 못한다(~ science is often unequipped to meet these demands.)고 언급하는데, 'All this is why the media tends to oversimplify scientific research ~'에서는 이 때문에 미디어가 연구 내용을 지나치게 단순화하여 대중이 원할 만한 답을 주려 하는 상황이 생긴다고 언급한다. 따라서 요약문의 빈칸 (A), (B)에 들어갈 말로 가장 적절한 것은 ② '(A) satisfy(만족시키지), (B) complicated (복잡한)'이다.

● uncertainty ⓝ 불확실성
● informed ⓐ 정보에 입각한
● black-or-white ⓐ 흑백논리의, 양자택일의
● with regard to ~에 관하여
● realm ⓝ 영역
● fantastically ⓐⓓ 환상적으로, 엄청나게
● as opposed to ~와는 반대로, ~이 아니라

구문 풀이

1행 There is often a lot of uncertainty in the realm of science,
ᐧ계속적 용법(목적격 관·대)　　선행사
which the general public finds uncomfortable.
　　　　　주어　　　동사　　목적격 보어

10-12 한 소년의 도움으로 잃어버린 시계를 찾은 농부

[본문 해석]

(A)
어느 날, 한 농부가 헛간에서 일하는 동안 그의 귀중한 시계를 잃어버렸다. 그것은 다른 이들에게는 평범한 시계로 보일 수도 있었지만 「그것은 그에게 어린 시절의 많은 행복한 기억을 불러일으켰다.」 그것은 (a) 그에게 가장 중요한 것들 중 하나였다. 오랜 시간 동안 그것을 찾아본 뒤에 그 나이 든 농부는 지쳐버렸다.

(D)
그러나, 그 지친 농부는 자기 시계를 찾는 것을 포기하고 싶지 않았기에 밖에서 놀던 한 무리의 아이들에게 도와 달라고 요청했다. (e) 그는 자기 시계를 찾는 사람에게 매력적인 보상을 약속했다. 「보상에 대해 듣고 난 뒤, 그 아이들은 헛간 안으로 서둘러 들어갔고 시계를 찾으러 전체 건초 더미 사이와 주변을 다녔다.」 「시계를 찾느라 오랜 시간을 보낸 후, 아이들 중 일부는 지쳐서 포기했다.」

(B)
시계를 찾는 아이들의 숫자가 천천히 줄어들었고 지친 아이들 몇 명만이 남았다. 그 농부는 시계를 찾을 거라는 모든 희망을 포기하고 찾는 것을 멈추었다. 「농부가 막 헛간 문을 닫고 있었을 때 한 어린 소년이 그에게 다가와서 자신에게 또 한 번의 기회를 달라고 요청했다.」 농부는 시계를 찾을 어떤 가능성도 놓치고 싶지 않아서 (b) 그를 헛간 안으로 들어오게 해주었다.

(C)
「잠시 후 그 소년이 한 손에 농부의 시계를 들고 나왔다.」 (c) 그는 행복에 겨워 놀랐고 다른 모두가 실패했던 반면 소년이 어떻게 시계를 찾는 데 성공했는지를 물었다. 그는 "저는 거기에 앉아서 시계의 소리를 들으려고 했어요. 침묵 속에서, 그것을 듣고 소리의 방향을 따라가는 것이 훨씬 쉬웠어요."라고 답했다. (d) 그는 시계를 되찾아 기뻤고 그 어린 소년에게 약속했던 대로 보상해 주었다.

● precious ⓐ 소중한, 귀중한
● lose out on ~을 놓치다, ~에게 지다
● pile ⓝ 더미
● call off ~을 중단하다, 멈추다
● attractive ⓐ 매력적인
● hay ⓝ 건초

구문 풀이

(B) 1행 The number of children looking for the watch slowly
주어1(the number of+복수명사 : ~의 수)　　현재분사
decreased and only a few tired children were left.
동사1　　　　　　　주어2　　　　　　동사2

(C) 6행 In silence, it was much easier to hear it and follow the direction
가주어　비교급 강조(훨씬)　　　　　　　　진주어
of the sound.

10 글의 순서 파악　　　　　　정답률 77% | 정답 ④

주어진 글 (A)에 이어질 내용을 순서에 맞게 배열한 것으로 가장 적절한 것은?
① (B) - (D) - (C)
② (C) - (B) - (D)
③ (C) - (D) - (B)
④ (D) - (B) - (C)
⑤ (D) - (C) - (B)

Why? 왜 정답일까?

아끼던 시계를 잃어버린 농부를 소개하는 (A) 뒤로, 농부가 아이들에게 시계 찾기를 맡겼다는 내용의 (D), 모두가 실패한 가운데 한 소년이 다시 자원했다는 내용의 (B), 소년이 시계를 찾아냈다는 내용의 (C)가 차례로 이어져야 자연스럽다. 따라서 글의 순서로 가장 적절한 것은 ④ '(D) - (B) - (C)'이다.

11 지칭 추론　　　　　　정답률 73% | 정답 ②

밑줄 친 (a) ~ (e) 중에서 가리키는 대상이 나머지 넷과 *다른* 것은?
① (a)　　② (b)　　③ (c)　　④ (d)　　⑤ (e)

Why? 왜 정답일까?

(a), (c), (d), (e)는 the farmer, (b)는 a little boy이므로, (a) ~ (e) 중에서 가리키는 대상이 다른 하나는 ② '(b)'이다.

12 세부 내용 파악　　　　　　정답률 76% | 정답 ④

윗글에 관한 내용으로 적절하지 <u>않은</u> 것은?
① 농부의 시계는 어린 시절의 행복한 기억을 불러일으켰다.
② 한 어린 소년이 농부에게 또 한 번의 기회를 달라고 요청했다.
③ 소년이 한 손에 농부의 시계를 들고 나왔다.
④ 아이들은 시계를 찾기 위해 헛간을 뛰쳐나왔다.
⑤ 아이들 중 일부는 지쳐서 시계 찾기를 포기했다.

Why? 왜 정답일까?

(D) 'After hearing about the reward, the children hurried inside the barn ~'에서 아이들은 농부가 잃어버린 시계를 찾기 위해 헛간을 나온 것이 아니라 들어갔다고 하므로, 내용과 일치하지 않는 것은 ④ '아이들은 시계를 찾기 위해 헛간을 뛰쳐나왔다.'이다.

Why? 왜 오답일까?

① (A) '~ it brought a lot of happy childhood memories to him.'의 내용과 일치한다.
② (B) 'a little boy came up to him and asked the farmer to give him another chance.'의 내용과 일치한다.
③ (C) 'After a little while the boy came out with the farmer's watch in his hand.'의 내용과 일치한다.
⑤ (D) 'After a long time searching for it, some of the children got tired and gave up.'의 내용과 일치한다.

DAY 10

DAY 11 — 20분 미니 모의고사

01 ⑤	02 ③	03 ④	04 ④	05 ⑤
06 ①	07 ①	08 ④	09 ⑤	10 ①
11 ②	12 ③			

---

01 작은 일부터 잘 처리하기
정답률 87% | 정답 ⑤

다음 글에서 필자가 주장하는 바로 가장 적절한 것은?

① 숙면을 위해서는 침대를 깔끔하게 관리해야 한다.
② 일의 효율성을 높이려면 협동심을 발휘해야 한다.
③ 올바른 습관을 기르려면 정해진 규칙을 따라야 한다.
④ 건강을 유지하기 위해서는 기상 시간이 일정해야 한다.
⑤ 큰일을 잘 이루려면 작은 일부터 제대로 수행해야 한다.

[본문 해석]

내가 군대에 있을 때, 교관들이 나의 병영 생활관에 모습을 드러내곤 했는데, 그들이 맨 먼저 검사하곤 했던 것은 우리의 침대였다. 단순한 일이었지만, 매일 아침 우리는 침대를 완벽하게 정돈하도록 요구받았다. 그 당시에는 약간 우스꽝스럽게 보였지만, 이 단순한 행위의 지혜는 여러 차례 거듭하여 나에게 증명되었다. 여러분이 매일 아침 침대를 정돈한다면, 여러분은 하루의 첫 번째 과업을 성취한 것이 된다. 그것은 여러분에게 작은 자존감을 주고, 또 다른 과업을 잇따라 이어가도록 용기를 줄 것이다. 하루가 끝날 때쯤에는, 완수된 그 하나의 과업이 여러 개의 완수된 과업으로 변해 있을 것이다. 작은 일들을 제대로 할 수 없으면, 여러분은 결코 큰일들을 제대로 할 수 없을 것이다.

Why? 왜 정답일까?

매일 잠자리 정돈부터 잘해야 했던 군대 시절 이야기를 토대로 작은 일부터 잘 해내야 큰일을 처리할 수 있다(If you can't do little things right, you will never do the big things right.)는 결론을 이끌어내는 글이다. 따라서 필자의 주장으로 가장 적절한 것은 ⑤ '큰일을 잘 이루려면 작은 일부터 제대로 수행해야 한다.'이다.

- instructor ⓝ 교사, 교관, 강사
- inspect ⓥ 조사하다
- require ⓥ 필요하다
- perfection ⓝ 완벽, 완전
- wisdom ⓝ 지혜
- turn into ~로 바뀌다
- barrack ⓝ 막사, 병영
- task ⓝ 일, 과업, 과제
- make the bed 잠자리를 정돈하다
- ridiculous ⓐ 우스꽝스러운
- complete ⓥ 완수하다

구문 풀이

7행 If you make your bed every morning, you will have accomplished
접속사(조건) 동사(현재) 동사(미래완료)
the first task of the day.

---

02 컴퓨터된 사회에서 오히려 일이 늘어난 소비자들
정답률 54% | 정답 ③

다음 글의 요지로 가장 적절한 것은?

① 컴퓨터 기반 사회에서는 여가 시간이 더 늘어난다.
② 회사 업무의 전산화는 업무 능률을 향상시킨다.
③ 컴퓨터화된 사회에서 소비자는 더 많은 일을 하게 된다.
④ 온라인 거래가 모든 소비자들을 만족시키기에는 한계가 있다.
⑤ 산업의 발전으로 인해 기계가 인간의 일자리를 대신하고 있다.

[본문 해석]

우리가 듣기로, 컴퓨터된 사회의 약속은 그것이 모든 반복적인 고된 일을 기계에 넘겨 우리 인간들이 더 높은 목적을 추구하고 더 많은 여가 시간을 가질 수 있게 해준다는 것이었다. 일은 이런 식으로 되지는 않았다. 더 많은 시간 대신에, 우리 대부분은 더 적은 시간을 가지고 있다. 크고 작은 회사들은 일을 소비자들의 등에 떠넘겼다. 우리는 회사에 맡겨 해결하던 부가가치 서비스의 일환으로 우리를 위해 행해지던 일들을 이제 스스로 하도록 기대받는다. 항공 여행의 경우, 항공사 직원이나 여행사 직원들이 하던 일인 예약과 체크인을 이제는 우리가 직접 완수하도록 기대된다. 식료품점에서는, 우리가 우리 자신의 식료품을 직접 봉지에 넣도록, 그리고 일부 슈퍼마켓에서는 우리가 직접 구매한 물건을 스캔하도록 기대받는다.

Why? 왜 정답일까?

컴퓨터된 사회가 도래하면 개인은 더 많은 여가 시간을 누릴 것으로 기대되었지만, 실상은 반대로 더 많은 일을 하게 되었다(Instead of more time, most of us have less. Companies large and small have off-loaded work onto the backs of consumers.)는 내용이다. 따라서 글의 요지로 가장 적절한 것은 ③ '컴퓨터된 사회에서 소비자는 더 많은 일을 하게 된다.'이다.

- repetitive ⓐ 반복되는
- pursue ⓥ 추구하다
- as part of ~의 일환으로
- drudgery ⓝ 고된 일
- off-load ⓥ 짐을 내리다, 떠넘기다
- grocery store 슈퍼, 식료품 가게

구문 풀이

7행 Things [that used to be done for us], (as part of the value-
to do의 목적어 ~하곤 했다 ( ): 삽입구
added service of working with a company), we are now expected
주어 「be expected +
to do ourselves.
to부정사 : ~하도록 기대되다」

---

03 음식의 다양성이 음식 섭취량에 미치는 영향
정답률 80% | 정답 ④

다음 글의 주제로 가장 적절한 것은?

① necessity of consuming a varied diet in daily life
일상에서 다양한 식단을 취할 필요성
② reasons for people's rejection of unfamiliar foods
사람들이 친숙하지 않은 음식을 거부하는 이유
③ changes in people's preference for basic food items
기초식품에 대한 사람들의 선호 변화
④ impact of food variety on the amount of food people consume
음식의 다양성이 사람들이 소비하는 음식의 양에 미치는 영향
⑤ importance of maintaining food diversity to prevent overeating
과식을 예방하기 위해 음식의 다양성을 유지하는 것의 중요성

[본문 해석]

감각 특정적 포만이란 먹지 않은 음식이 주는 쾌락에는 변화가 거의 없는 가운데 식욕, 즉 먹고 있는 음식에 대한 주관적 애호가 감소하는 것으로 정의된다. 감각 특정적 포만의 결과로, 사람들은 다양한 종류의 음식을 먹을 때 과식하는 경향이 있다. 더 다양한 종류의 음식은 사람들로 하여금 그렇지 않을 경우에 먹는 것보다 더 많이 먹게 한다. 그러므로 배가 부르다는 것과 충분한 만족감을 느낀다는 것은 별개의 문제이다. 식욕, 즉 먹고자 하는 욕구가 회복된다는 것은, 많은 양의 식사 후 배가 아주 불러서 매일의 요구를 충족시킬 추가적인 에너지나 영양소가 필요하지는 않지만, 디저트 카트를 보고 나서 추가적인 칼로리를 더 섭취하기로 결심하는 사람이면 누구에게나 분명하다. 음식의 감각적 특성에 대한 작은 변화라도 음식의 섭취를 증가시키기에 충분하다. 예컨대 서로 다른 모양의 파스타를 제공받은 피실험자들은, 단 한 가지 형태의 파스타만을 먹는 피실험자들에 비할 때 쾌락 평점 증가와 에너지 섭취량 증가를 보였다.

Why? 왜 정답일까?

감각 특정적 포만의 개념을 들어 사람들은 한 가지 종류의 음식만 있을 때보다 다양한 종류의 음식이 있을 때 더 많이 먹게 된다(As a result of sensory-specific satiety, when people consume a variety of foods, they tend to overeat.)는 내용을 설명하는 글이다. 따라서 글의 주제로 가장 적절한 것은 ④ '음식의 다양성이 사람들이 소비하는 음식의 양에 미치는 영향'이다.

- sensory ⓐ 감각의
- liking ⓝ 선호
- separate ⓐ 별개의, 구별되는
- sufficient ⓐ 충분한
- specific ⓐ 특정적인
- overeat ⓥ 과식하다
- nutrient ⓝ 영양소
- intake ⓝ 섭취(량)

구문 풀이

6행 A greater variety of food leads people to eat more than they
「lead + 목적어 + to부정사 : ~이 …하도록 이끌다」
would otherwise.
부사(그렇지 않으면)

---

04 더 많은 것을 소비하게 하는 첨단 생활방식
정답률 59% | 정답 ④

다음 글의 밑줄 친 부분 중, 어법상 틀린 것은?

[본문 해석]

종이의 필요성을 부정하는 것처럼 보이는 모든 첨단 기기들에도 불구하고, 미국에서 종이 사용은 최근 거의 두 배로 증가했다. 우리는 현재 그 어느 때보다도

더 많은 종이를 소비하고 있어서, 전 세계에서 4억 톤을 쓰고 있으며 그 양은 증가하고 있다. 우리가 더 많이 사용하고 있는 자원은 종이만이 아니다. 기술의 발전은 흔히 더 적은 재료의 사용 가능성을 수반한다. 그러나, 현실은 그것들이 역사적으로 더 많은 재료 사용을 야기해 우리가 더 많은 천연자원에 의존하게 한다는 것이다. 세계는 이제 그 어느 때보다도 훨씬 더 많은 '재료'를 소비한다. 우리는 금, 구리, 희귀 금속과 같은 산업 광물을 고작 1세기 이전보다 27배 더 많이 사용한다. 우리는 또한 각자 더 많은 자원을 사용한다. 그중 많은 부분은 우리의 첨단 생활방식 때문이다.

Why? 왜 정답일까?

make는 형용사를 목적격 보어로 취하는 5형식 동사이므로, 부사 dependently를 형용사 dependent로 고쳐 making의 보어 자리를 채워야 한다. 따라서 어법상 틀린 것은 ④이다.

Why? 왜 오답일까?

① 주어 paper use가 불가산명사이므로 단수 동사 has가 어법상 적절하다.
② 선행사 the only resource 뒤로 목적어가 없는 불완전한 절을 이끌고자 관계대명사 that이 알맞게 쓰였다. 참고로 선행사에 the only가 있으면 관계대명사 that이 주로 쓰인다.
③ 전치사 of 뒤에 목적어인 동명사 using이 알맞게 쓰였다.
⑤ 앞에 나온 일반동사 use를 대신하는데 시제가 과거이므로(over a century ago) 대동사 did가 알맞게 쓰였다.

- **high-tech** ⓐ 첨단 기술의
- **recently** [ad] 최근에
- **material** ⓝ 물질, 자재, 재료
- **dependently** [ad] 의존적으로
- **mineral** ⓝ 광물
- **rare** ⓐ 희귀한
- **deny** ⓥ 부인[부정]하다
- **consume** ⓥ 소비하다
- **historically** [ad] 역사적으로
- **industrial** ⓐ 산업의
- **copper** ⓝ 구리

구문 풀이

7행 However, the reality is {that they have historically caused more materials use, making us dependently on more natural resources}.
분사구문(= and they make ~)　　　{ } : 명사절(주격 보어)

---

05 허브의 건강상 효과　　정답률 58% | 정답 ⑤

다음 글의 밑줄 친 부분 중, 문맥상 낱말의 쓰임이 적절하지 <u>않은</u> 것은? [3점]

[본문 해석]

어떤 허브는 왜인지는 몰라도 마법처럼 특정 장기의 기능을 향상시키고, 그 결과 특정한 질병을 '치유한다'고 널리 알려져 있다. 그러한 진술은 비과학적이고 근거가 없다. 때때로 허브는 효과가 있는 것처럼 보이는데, 이는 당신 몸이 신체로부터 그것을 제거하려고 적극 시도하는 과정에서 그것이 혈액 순환을 ① 증가시키는 경향이 있기 때문이다. 이는 ② 일시적으로 좋은 기분을 만들어 줄 수 있고, 마치 당신의 건강 상태가 향상된 것처럼 보이게 만든다. 또한 여느 다른 방법과 마찬가지로, 허브는 위약 효과를 가지고 있어서, 당신이 더 나아졌다고 느끼도록 도와준다. 어떠한 경우든, 건강을 ③ 되찾게 하는 지성을 가진 것은 허브가 아니라 바로 당신의 몸이다. 허브가 어떻게 당신의 몸을 더 건강해지는 방향으로 인도하는 데 필요한 지성을 가질 수 있겠는가? 그것은 불가능하다. 어떻게 허브가 당신의 몸 안으로 들어가 영리하게 당신의 문제를 ④ 해결할 수 있는지 상상해 보라. 만약 그렇게 해 본다면 당신은 그것이 얼마나 불가능하게 보이는지를 알게 될 것이다. 그렇지 않다면, 그것은 허브가 인간의 몸보다 ⑤ 덜(→더) 지적이라는 것을 의미할 텐데, 이는 정말로 믿기 어렵다.

Why? 왜 정답일까?

허브가 몸 안에서 어떻게 건강 문제를 해결해줄 수 있는지 상상해보면 얼마나 어려운지 깨닫게 될 것이라는 내용 뒤에는 허브가 인간의 몸보다 '더 똑똑하다'는 생각은 믿기 어렵다는 결론이 이어져야 하므로, ⑤의 less를 more로 고쳐야 한다. 따라서 문맥상 낱말의 쓰임이 적절하지 않은 것은 ⑤이다.

- **groundless** ⓐ 근거가 없는
- **eliminate** ⓥ 제거하다, 없애다
- **high** ⓝ 도취감
- **aggressive** ⓐ 적극적인, 공격적인
- **temporary** ⓐ 일시적인
- **whatever the case** 어떤 경우이든지

구문 풀이

11행 Whatever the case, it is your body that has the intelligence
어느 경우이든 간에　　「it is ~ that … : …한 것은 바로 ~이다」
to regain health, and not the herbs.

[문제편 p.066]

★★★ 1등급 대비 고난도 3점 문제

06 창의력의 위기　　정답률 31% | 정답 ①

다음 빈칸에 들어갈 말로 가장 적절한 것을 고르시오. [3점]

✓ ① unrivaled – 경쟁할 상대가 없지
② learned – 학습되지
③ universal – 보편적이지
④ ignored – 무시되지
⑤ challenged – 도전받지

[본문 해석]

창의력은 우리가 일반적으로 인간만이 고유하게 가지고 있다고 간주하는 능력이다. 인류 역사를 통틀어, 우리는 지구상에서 가장 창의적인 존재였다. 새는 둥지를 틀 수 있고, 개미는 개미탑을 쌓을 수 있지만, 지구상의 어떤 다른 종도 우리 인간이 보여주는 창의력 수준에 가까이 도달하지는 못한다. 하지만, 불과 지난 10년 만에 우리는 로봇 개발처럼 컴퓨터로 놀라운 것을 할 수 있는 능력을 습득하였다. 2010년대의 인공 지능의 급속한 발전으로 컴퓨터는, 몇 가지를 언급하자면, 이제 얼굴을 인식하고, 언어를 번역하고, 여러분을 대신해 전화를 받고, 시를 쓸 수 있으며 세계에서 가장 복잡한 보드게임에서 선수들을 이길 수 있다. 갑작스럽게, 우리는 우리의 창의력이 경쟁할 상대가 없지 않게 되는 가능성에 직면해야 할 것이다.

Why? 왜 정답일까?

빈칸 앞의 문장에서 컴퓨터는 얼굴 인식, 언어 번역, 전화 응대, 시 창작, 보드게임 경기 등 기존에 인간만의 영역으로 여겨졌던 다양한 활동을 할 수 있게 되었다고 언급하는 것으로 보아, 빈칸이 포함된 문장은 그간 인간만의 능력으로 간주되어 왔던 창의력도 컴퓨터의 능력에 포함될지도 모른다는 의미를 나타내야 한다. 따라서 빈칸에 들어갈 말로 가장 적절한 것은 ① '경쟁할 상대가 없지'이다.

- **creativity** ⓝ 창조성, 독창성
- **nest** ⓝ 둥지
- **display** ⓥ 드러내다, 내보이다
- **translate** ⓥ 번역하다
- **unrivaled** ⓐ 경쟁할 상대가 없는
- **uniquely** [ad] 고유하게
- **come close to** ~에 근접하다
- **artificial intelligence** 인공 지능
- **complicated** ⓐ 복잡한
- **universal** ⓐ 일반적인, 보편적인

구문 풀이

3행 Birds can make their nests, ants can make their hills, but
no other species on Earth comes close to the level of creativity [(that)
부정 주어　　　　　동사(단수)　　　　　생략(목적격 관계대명사)
we humans display].

★★ 문제 해결 꿀~팁 ★★

▶ 많이 틀린 이유는?
빈칸에 직접 대응시킬 주제문이 없고 추상적인 내용을 다루어 까다로운 지문이다. 최다 오답인 ④는 인공 지능의 발달로 인해 인간의 창의력이 '무시되지' 않을 가능성이 있다는 뜻인데, 이 글은 컴퓨터가 인간의 창의력을 따라잡을 수도 있다는 내용을 주로 다루고 있어 주제와 무관한 선택지이다. ⑤는 주제와 상충한다.

▶ 문제 해결 방법은?
글 중간에 역접의 연결어가 나오므로 전반부보다는 후반부에 무게를 실어 독해한다. 특히 빈칸이 마지막 문장에 있으므로 바로 앞의 예문을 읽고 이를 토대로 일반화된 결론을 추론해야 한다.

---

07 수생 생물의 특성을 유지하며 발달한 개구리　　정답률 60% | 정답 ①

다음 빈칸에 들어갈 말로 가장 적절한 것을 고르시오. [3점]

✓ ① still kept many ties to the water
여전히 물과의 여러 인연을 유지했다
② had almost all the necessary organs
필요한 신체 기관을 거의 모두 갖추고 있었다
③ had to develop an appetite for new foods
새로운 음식에 대한 식욕을 발달시켜야 했다
④ often competed with land-dwelling species
땅에 사는 생물 종들과 종종 경쟁했다
⑤ suffered from rapid changes in temperature
기온의 급격한 변화로 고생했다

[본문 해석]

과학자들은 개구리의 조상이 물에 사는, 물고기 같은 동물이었다고 믿는다. 최초의 개구리와 그들의 친척은 육지로 나와 그곳에서 먹을 것과 살 곳에 대한 기회를 누릴 수 있는 능력을 얻었다. 하지만 개구리는 여전히 물과의 여러 인연을 유지했다. 개구리의 폐는 그다지 기능을 잘하지 않고, 개구리는 피부를

통해 호흡함으로써 산소를 일부 얻는다. 하지만 이런 종류의 '호흡'이 제대로 이뤄지기 위해서는, 개구리의 피부가 촉촉하게 유지되어야 한다. 그래서 개구리는 건조해지는 것을 막기 위해 이따금 몸을 잠깐 담글 수 있는 물의 근처에 있어야 한다. 물고기 같은 조상들이 그랬던 것처럼, 개구리 역시 물속에 알을 낳아야 한다. 그리고 물속에 낳은 알이 살아남으려면, 물에 사는 생물로 발달해야 한다. 따라서, 개구리에게 있어서 탈바꿈은 물에 사는 어린 형체와 육지에 사는 성체를 이어주는 다리를 제공한다.

Why? 왜 정답일까?

개구리는 당초 물고기 같은 동물로 기원하여 육지에서 생활하도록 진화했지만 여전히 '물에 사는' 생물로서의 특징을 지니고 있다는 내용의 글이다. 빈칸 뒤에서 개구리는 폐가 그다지 발달해 있지 않아 피부를 이용해 호흡하는데, 호흡이 원활하기 위해서는 피부가 늘 젖어 있어야 하고, 따라서 물을 가까이 해야 하며, 알 또한 물속에 낳아 번식해야 하기에 '물에 살기 적합한' 생물로 발달할 수밖에 없는 운명임을 설명하고 있다. 이러한 흐름을 근거로 볼 때, 빈칸에 들어갈 말로 가장 적절한 것은 개구리가 '물고기다운' 특성을 완전히 포기하지 않았다는 의미의 ① '여전히 물과의 여러 인연을 유지했다'이다.

- **ancestor** ⓝ 조상
- **relative** ⓝ 친척
- **properly** ad 적절히
- **take a dip** 잠깐 수영을 하다
- **lay** ⓥ (알을) 낳다
- **creature** ⓝ 생물
- **organ** ⓝ (신체) 기관
- **compete with** ~와 경쟁하다
- **dwell** ⓥ 거주하다, 살다
- **shelter** ⓝ 살 곳, 쉼터, 은신처
- **moist** ⓐ 촉촉한
- **dry out** 건조하다, 바짝 마르다
- **tie** ⓝ 관계, 연결
- **adult** ⓝ 성체
- **appetite** ⓝ 식욕

구문 풀이

7행 But for this kind of "breathing" to work properly, the frog's
의미상 주어 / 부사적 용법(~하려면)
skin must stay moist.
2형식 동사 / 보어

---

08 서술자에 따라 다르게 이해되는 이야기 　　정답률 61% | 정답 ④

다음 글에서 전체 흐름과 관계 없는 문장은?

[본문 해석]

누구의 이야기인지가 무슨 이야기인지에 영향을 미친다. 주인공을 바꾸면, 이야기의 초점도 틀림없이 바뀐다. 만약 우리가 다른 등장인물의 눈을 통해 사건을 본다면, 우리는 그것을 다르게 해석할 것이다. ① 우리는 새로운 누군가에게 공감할 것이다. ② 이야기의 핵심인 갈등이 발생할 때, 우리는 다른 결과를 간절히 바랄 것이다. ③ 예컨대, 신데렐라 이야기가 사악한 의붓자매의 관점에서 이야기된다면 어떻게 바뀔지 생각해 보라. ④ 우리는 신데렐라의 왕국이 존재하지 않는다는 것을 알지만, 어쨌든 기꺼이 그곳에 간다. ⑤ *Gone with the Wind*는 Scarlett O'Hara의 이야기이지만, 만약 같은 사건이 Rhett Butler나 Melanie Wilkes의 관점에서 우리에게 제시된다면 어떠할 것인가?

Why? 왜 정답일까?

이야기의 주인공이 누구인가에 따라 이야기 내용이 다르게 받아들여진다는 내용인데, ④는 Cinderella의 왕국에 관해서만 지엽적으로 언급하고 있다. 따라서 전체 흐름과 관계 없는 문장은 ④이다.

- **affect** ⓥ 영향을 미치다
- **sympathy** ⓝ 공감
- **arise** ⓥ 발생하다
- **outcome** ⓝ 결과
- **shift** ⓥ 바꾸다
- **evil** ⓐ 사악한 ⓝ 악
- **kingdom** ⓝ 왕국
- **interpret** ⓥ 해석하다, 이해하다
- **conflict** ⓝ 갈등
- **pray for** ~을 위해 기도하다
- **tale** ⓝ 이야기
- **viewpoint** ⓝ 관점
- **stepsister** ⓝ 의붓자매
- **willingly** ad 기꺼이

구문 풀이

7행 Consider, for example, [how the tale of Cinderella would shift
명령문(~하라) 　　　　　　　　[ ]: 목적어
if told from the viewpoint of an evil stepsister].
접속사+과거분사(~한다면)

★★★ 1등급 대비 고난도 3점 문제

09 문학 텍스트의 이해 　　정답률 43% | 정답 ⑤

주어진 글 다음에 이어질 글의 순서로 가장 적절한 것을 고르시오. [3점]

① (A) – (C) – (B)
② (B) – (A) – (C)
③ (B) – (C) – (A)
④ (C) – (A) – (B)
✓⑤ (C) – (B) – (A)

[본문 해석]

문학 작품들은 그 본질상 설명하기보다는 암시하는데, 그들은 주장을 뚜렷하게 직접적으로 진술하기보다는 함축한다.

(C) 그러나 이 넓은 일반화는 문학 작품들이 직접적인 진술을 포함하지 않는다는 뜻은 아니다. 그들이 언제 누구에 의해 쓰였는지에 따라, 문학 작품들은 많은 양의 직접적 말하기와 더 적은 양의 암시와 함축을 포함할 수도 있다.

(B) 하지만 작품에서 말하기 대 보여 주기의 비율이 어떻든 간에 독자가 해석해야 하는 무언가가 항상 존재한다. 그러므로 우리는 문학적 해석에 접근하는 방법이자 텍스트의 함축에 대해 생각하기 시작하는 방법으로 "그 텍스트가 무엇을 암시하는가?"라는 질문을 한다.

(A) 텍스트가 무엇을 함축하는지는 종종 우리에게 매우 흥미롭다. 그리고 텍스트의 함축을 알아내는 작업은 우리의 분석적 능력을 시험한다. 텍스트가 무엇을 암시하는지를 고려하는 과정에서 우리는 텍스트를 이해하는 기량을 얻게 된다.

Why? 왜 정답일까?

주어진 글은 문학 작품의 특징으로 함축적 진술을 언급한다. 이어서 (C)는 however로 주의를 환기하며 문학 작품 안에 직접적 진술이 전혀 없지는 않다는 점을 상기시킨다. 한편 But으로 시작하는 (B)는 직접적 진술과 함축적 진술의 비율이 어떻든 간에 문학 텍스트에는 항상 독자가 해석해야 하는 부분이 있으며, 이 때문에 우리가 '그 텍스트가 무엇을 암시하는지' 자문하게 된다고 언급한다. (A)는 (B)의 "What does the text suggest?"를 What a text implies로 바꾸어 표현하며, 텍스트가 함축하는 바를 알아내는 과정에서 우리가 텍스트를 이해하는 능력을 기르게 된다고 설명한다. 따라서 글의 순서로 가장 적절한 것은 ⑤ '(C) – (B) – (A)'이다.

- **literary** ⓐ 문학의
- **boldly** ad 뚜렷하게, 대담하게
- **analytical** ⓐ 분석적인
- **generalization** ⓝ 일반화
- **nature** ⓝ 본질, 본성
- **implication** ⓝ 함축, 암시
- **interpret** ⓥ 해석하다

구문 풀이

4행 What a text implies is often of great interest to us.
주어(명사절) / 동사(단수) / 보어(= greatly interesting)

★★ 문제 해결 꿀~팁 ★★

▶ 많이 틀린 이유는?

(B)와 (C)의 순서를 잘 파악하는 것이 관건이다. 얼핏 보면 주어진 글의 imply rather than state가 (B)의 showing과 telling으로 바로 연결되는 것 같지만, (B)의 핵심은 '독자의 해석과 이해'에 관한 것이다. 이에 반해 (C)는 주어진 글과 마찬가지로 문학적인 글의 말하기 방식에 관해서 다루고 있으므로, 화제의 흐름상 (C)가 먼저 나온 뒤 (B)로 전환되는 것이 자연스럽다.

▶ 문제 해결 방법은?

주어진 글의 'Literary works ~ imply rather than state their claims boldly and directly.'가 (C)의 This broad generalization으로 이어지고, (C)의 literary works may contain large amounts of direct telling and lesser amounts of suggestion and implication이 (B)의 the proportion of a work's showing to telling으로 연결된다. 즉 (C)까지 문학 작품 속의 말하기와 보여주기(의 비중)에 관해 설명한 뒤, (B)에서 '그 비중에 상관없이' 독자가 해석할 부분이 있다는 내용으로 넘어가는 흐름임을 파악하도록 한다.

---

10 공공재의 비극을 막을 방법 　　정답률 63% | 정답 ①

다음 글의 내용을 한 문장으로 요약하고자 한다. 빈칸 (A), (B)에 들어갈 말로 가장 적절한 것은?

	(A)		(B)
✓①	reminder (상기물)	······	shared (공유)
②	reminder (상기물)	······	recycled (재활용된)
③	mistake (실수)	······	stored (저장된)
④	mistake (실수)	······	borrowed (빌려온)
⑤	fortune (행운)	······	limited (제한된)

[본문 해석]

Berkeley에 있는 California 대학에 다니는 Rhonda라는 여자에게는 한 가지 문제 상황이 있었다. 그녀는 여러 사람들과 함께 캠퍼스 근처에 살고 있었는데 그들 중 누구도 서로를 알지 못했다. 청소부가 주말마다 왔을 때 화장실 두 칸 각각에 몇 개의 두루마리 화장지를 두고 갔다. 그러나 월요일 즈음 모든 화장지가 없어지곤 했다. 그것은 전형적인 공유지의 비극 상황이었다. 일부 사람들이 자신들이 사용할 수 있는 몫보다 더 많은 휴지를 가져갔기 때문에 그 외 모두를 위한 공공재가 파괴됐다. 행동 변화에 대한 한 연구논문을 읽고 나서, Rhonda는 화장실 화장지는 공유재이므로 사람들에게 가져가지 말라고 요청하는 쪽지를 화장실 한 곳에 두었다. 아주 만족스럽게도, 몇 시간 후에 화장지 한 개가 다시 나타났고 그다음 날에는 또 하나가 다시 나타났다. 하지만 쪽지가 없는 화장실에서는 청소부가 돌아오는 그다음 주말까지 화장지가 없었다.

➡ 자그마한 (A) 상기물은 필요한 것보다 더 많은 (B) 공유 재화를 가져갔던 사람의 행동에 변화를 일으켰다.

Why? 왜 정답일까?

실험을 소개한 글이므로 결과 부분에 주목한다. 마지막 세 문장에 따르면, 화장실 휴지가 공유재임을 상기시키는 쪽지를 붙인 화장실에는 없어졌던 휴지가 다시 돌아온 반면, 쪽지를 붙이지 않은 화장실에는 휴지가 돌아오지 않았다고 한다. 이를 토대로, 어떤 것이 공유재임을 '환기시켜 주는' 장치가 있을 때 '공유재'를 가져갔던 이들의 행동에 변화가 일어날 수 있다는 결론을 도출할 수 있다. 따라서 요약문의 빈칸 (A), (B)에 들어갈 말로 가장 적절한 것은 ① '(A) reminder(상기물), (B) shared(공유)'이다.

- **classic** ⓐ 고전적인
- **destroy** ⓥ 파괴하다
- **bring about** ~을 야기하다
- **tragedy of the commons** 공유지의 비극
- **reappear** ⓥ 다시 나타나다
- **reminder** ⓝ 상기시켜주는 것

구문 풀이

3행 She was living near campus with several other people —
　　　　　　　　　　　　　　　　　　　　　선행사(사람)
none of whom knew one another.
계속적 용법

11-12 　배경 소음이 공부에 미치는 영향에 대한 논란

[본문 해석]

많은 고등학생은 TV를 보거나 시끄러운 음악을 들으면서 숙제를 하겠다고 고집하기 때문에 비효율적으로 공부하고 학습한다. 이 학생들은 또한 반복적인 전화 통화, 부엌에 들르기, 비디오 게임, 인터넷 서핑으로 보통 자신의 공부를 (a) 방해한다. 모순적이게도, 공부할 때 집중할 필요가 가장 큰 학생들은 흔히 주의를 산만하게 하는 것들로 가장 많이 자신을 에워싸는 학생들이다. 「이런 십 대들은 TV나 라디오를 (b) 켜 둔 채로 공부를 *더 잘 할 수* 있다고 주장한다.」 일부 전문가는 실제로 그들의 견해에 (c) 반대한다(→ 지지한다). 「그들은 많은 십 대들이 어린 시절부터 '배경 소음'에 반복적으로 노출되어 왔기 때문에 전혀 이상적이지 않은 상황에서 실제로 생산적으로 공부할 수 있다고 주장한다.」 이 교육 전문가들은 아이들이 TV, 비디오 게임, 그리고 시끄러운 음악 소리에 (d) 익숙해졌다고 주장한다. 그들은 또한 숙제를 할 때 학생들이 TV나 라디오를 꺼야 한다고 주장하는 것이 반드시 그들의 학업 성적을 높이는 것은 아니라고 주장한다. 그러나 이 견해는 분명히 일반적으로 공유되는 것은 아니다. 「많은 교사와 학습 전문가는 시끄러운 환경에서 공부하는 학생들이 흔히 비효율적으로 학습한다는 것을 스스로의 경험으로 (e) 확신한다.」
(11번의 근거)

- **inefficiently** ⓐd 비효율적으로
- **interrupt** ⓥ 방해하다
- **concentrate** ⓥ 집중하다
- **distraction** ⓝ 주의를 산만하게 하는 것
- **productively** ⓐd 생산적으로
- **repeatedly** ⓐd 반복적으로
- **improve** ⓥ 높이다, 향상시키다
- **insist on** ⓥ ~을 고집하다, 주장하다
- **ironically** ⓐd 모순적이게도
- **surround** ⓥ 에워싸다
- **professional** ⓝ 전문가 ⓐ 전문적인
- **less-than-ideal** ⓐ 결코 이상적이지 않은
- **not necessarily** 반드시 ~인 것은 아니다
- **convinced** ⓐ 확신하는

구문 풀이

22행 Many teachers and learning experts are convinced by their
　　　　주어　　　　　　　　　　　　　　　　　　동사
own experiences that students [who study in a noisy environment]
　　　　　　　접속사(~것)↙　주어(선행사)
often learn inefficiently.
　동사

11　제목 파악　　　　정답률 70% | 정답 ②

윗글의 제목으로 가장 적절한 것은?

① Successful Students Plan Ahead
성공하는 학생은 미리 계획한다
② Studying with Distractions: Is It Okay?
주의를 산만하게 만드는 것과 함께 공부하기: 괜찮을까?
③ Smart Devices as Good Learning Tools
좋은 학습 도구로서의 스마트 기기
④ Parents & Teachers: Partners in Education
부모와 교사: 교육에서의 파트너
⑤ Good Habits: Hard to Form, Easy to Break
좋은 습관: 형성하기는 어렵고 버리기는 쉽다

Why? 왜 정답일까?

학생들은 음악, TV 소리 등 각종 배경 소음이나 공부에 방해가 되는 활동들이 학습에 별 방해가 되지 않는다고 주장하지만, 실상 많은 교사와 학습 전문가들의 경험에 따르면 이 주장은 반박될 수 있다(~ students who study in a noisy environment often learn inefficiently.)는 내용을 다룬 글이다. 따라서 글의 제목으로 가장 적절한 것은 ② '주의를 산만하게 만드는 것과 함께 공부하기: 괜찮을까?'이다.

★★★ 1등급 대비 고난도 3점 문제

12　어휘 추론　　　　정답률 44% | 정답 ③

밑줄 친 (a) ~ (e) 중에서 문맥상 낱말의 쓰임이 적절하지 않은 것은? [3점]
① (a)　　② (b)　　③ (c)　　④ (d)　　⑤ (e)

Why? 왜 정답일까?

③이 포함된 문장 뒤에서 일부 전문가들은 십 대들이 어렸을 때부터 배경 소음이 있는 환경에 익숙해져 왔기 때문에 소음이 있어도 능률적으로 공부할 수 있다(They argue that many teenagers can actually study productively under less-than-ideal conditions because they've been exposed repeatedly to "background noise" since early childhood.)고 주장한다는 내용이 나온다. 이는 전문가들이 TV나 라디오를 켜 놓고도 공부를 더 잘 할 수 있다고 주장하는 십 대들을 지지 또는 옹호하는 것으로 볼 수 있으므로, ③의 oppose는 support로 고쳐야 한다. 따라서 문맥상 낱말의 쓰임이 적절하지 않은 것은 ③ '(c)'이다.

★★ 문제 해결 꿀~팁 ★★

▶ 많이 틀린 이유는?
(b)의 playing은 TV나 라디오가 자동사인 play의 행위 주체임을 나타내는 현재분사로 '재생되고 있는, 켜져 있는'이라는 의미를 나타낸다. 한편 (d)의 used는 become used to(~에 익숙해지다)라는 의미의 관용 표현으로 바르게 쓰였다.
▶ 문제 해결 방법은?
상식이나 배경지식에 기초해서 풀면 (c)의 oppose가 적절해 보이지만, 바로 뒤의 'They argue ~'를 근거로 보면 Some professionals가 '배경 소음이 있어도 공부를 잘할 수 있다'는 입장을 옹호하는 이들임을 알 수 있다.

DAY 12 ▶ 20분 미니 모의고사

01 ③	02 ⑤	03 ④	04 ④	05 ③
06 ③	07 ①	08 ②	09 ①	10 ②
11 ④	12 ⑤			

01　아파트 놀이터 시설 수리 요청　　정답률 93% | 정답 ③

다음 글의 목적으로 가장 적절한 것은?

① 아파트의 첨단 보안 설비를 홍보하려고
② 아파트 놀이터의 임시 폐쇄를 공지하려고
✓③ 아파트 놀이터 시설의 수리를 요청하려고
④ 아파트 놀이터 사고의 피해 보상을 촉구하려고
⑤ 아파트 공용 시설 사용 시 유의 사항을 안내하려고

[본문 해석]

관계자분께

저는 Blue Sky 아파트의 거주자입니다. 최근에 저는 아이들을 위한 구역이 수리가 필요하다는 것을 알게 되었습니다. 저는 귀하께서 그 구역 놀이터 설비의 열악한 상태에 관심을 기울여 주시기를 바랍니다. 그네가 손상되었고, 페인트가 떨어져 나가고 있고, 미끄럼틀의 볼트 몇 개가 빠져 있습니다. 시설들은 우리가 이곳으로 이사 온 이후로 이렇게 형편없는 상태였습니다. 이것들은 거기서 노는 아이들에게 위험합니다. 이것들을 수리해 주시겠습니까? 이 문제를 해결하기 위한 즉각적인 관심을 보여주시면 감사하겠습니다.

Nina Davis 드림

Why? 왜 정답일까?

'I want you to pay attention to the poor condition of the playground equipment in the zone.'와 'Would you please have them repaired?'에 놀이터 시설 수리를 요청하는 필자의 목적이 잘 드러나 있다. 따라서 글의 목적으로 가장 적절한 것은 ③ '아파트 놀이터 시설의 수리를 요청하려고'이다.

- **to whom it may concern** 관계자 귀하
- **pay attention to** ~에 주의를 기울이다
- **damaged** ⓐ 손상된
- **facility** ⓝ 시설
- **in need of** ~이 필요한
- **equipment** ⓝ 장비
- **fall off** 벗겨지다, 떨어져 나가다
- **immediate** ⓐ 즉각적인

구문 풀이

8행 The facilities have been in this terrible condition since we (현재완료) (접속사(~ 이후로))
moved here. (과거)

02　독자가 이해해야 비로소 완성되는 과학 연구　　정답률 45% | 정답 ⑤

밑줄 친 fall silently in the woods가 다음 글에서 의미하는 바로 가장 적절한 것은? [3점]

① fail to include the previous study
이전 연구를 포함하지 못한다
② end up being considered completely false
결국 완전히 틀렸다고 간주된다
③ become useless because they are not published
출판되지 않아서 쓸모없게 되어버린다
④ focus on communication to meet public demands
대중의 요구를 맞추기 위해 커뮤니케이션에 집중한다
✓⑤ are published yet readers don't understand them
출판되지만 독자가 그것을 이해하지 못한다

[본문 해석]

대부분의 사람들은 틀림없이 이 질문을 들어 봤을 것이다. 만약 숲에서 나무가 쓰러지고 그것이 쓰러지는 것을 들을 사람이 거기 없다면, 그것은 소리를 낼까? 정답은 '아니요'이다. 소리는 압력파 이상이며, 정말로 듣는 사람 없이는 소리가 있을 수 없다. 마찬가지로, 과학적 커뮤니케이션은 양방향 프로세스이다. 어떠한 종류의 신호든 감지되지 않으면 쓸모가 없는 것처럼, 출판된 과학 논문(신호)은 그것이 목표 독자에게 수신되고 *나아가 이해까지 되지* 않으면 쓸모가 없다. 따라서 우리는 과학의 자명한 이치를 다음과 같이 풀어 말할 수 있다.

과학 실험은 결과가 출판되고 *나아가 이해될* 때 비로소 완성된다. 출판된 논문이 이해되지 않으면 출판은 압력파에 지나지 않는다. 너무 많은 과학 논문이 소리 없이 숲속에서 쓰러진다.

Why? 왜 정답일까?

글에 따르면, 소리가 청자가 있을 때 비로소 만들어지듯이, 과학 논문 또한 출판되고 독자에게 '이해될' 때 비로소 완성된다고 한다. 밑줄 부분 또한 독자의 이해를 강조하는 비유로, 독자에게 '이해되지' 않으면 논문은 '진정한 소리'가 되어 나오지 못하고 그저 사라져버린다는 뜻이다. 따라서 밑줄 친 부분의 의미로 가장 적절한 것은 ⑤ '출판되지만 독자가 그것을 이해하지 못한다'이다.

- **no doubt** 분명히, 틀림없이
- **similarly** ⓐⓓ 비슷하게, 마찬가지로
- **signal** ⓝ 신호 ⓥ 알리다
- **publish** ⓥ 출판하다, 게재하다
- **intend** ⓥ 목표로 하다, 의도하다
- **as follows** 다음과 같이
- **publication** ⓝ 출판, 게재
- **previous** ⓐ 이전의
- **meet the demand** 요구에 맞추다
- **pressure wave** 압력파
- **scientific** ⓐ 과학적인
- **useless** ⓐ 쓸모없는
- **paper** ⓝ 논문, 서류
- **restate** ⓥ (더 분명하게) 고쳐 말하다
- **complete** ⓐ 완성된
- **no more than** 단지 ~일 뿐인
- **false** ⓐ 틀린

구문 풀이

10행 Thus we can restate the axiom of science as follows: A scientific experiment is not complete until the results have been 「not + A + until + B : B하고 나서야 비로소 A하다」
published *and understood*.

03　다양하게 이해할 수 있는 언어　　정답률 74% | 정답 ④

다음 글의 제목으로 가장 적절한 것을 고르시오.

① Erase Ambiguity in Language Production!
언어를 만들 때 애매함을 제거하라!
② Not Creative but Simple: The Way Language Works
창의적이지 않고 단순함: 언어가 작동하는 방식
③ Communication as a Universal Goal in Language Use
언어를 사용하는 데 일반적인 목표인 의사소통
✓④ What in Language Creates Varied Understanding?
무엇이 언어에서 다양한 이해를 하게 하는가?
⑤ Language: A Crystal-Clear Looking Glass
언어: 아주 분명하게 보이는 유리

[본문 해석]

구체적이고 사실적인 정보를 어떤 왜곡이나 모호함이 없이 전달하는 체계로서, 꿀벌의 신호 체계는 인간의 언어를 항상 쉽게 이길 것이다. 그러나, 언어는 단순히 정보를 교환하는 것보다 좀 더 가치 있는 어떤 것을 제공한다. 단어의 뜻은 바뀌기 때문이고 이해는 항상 해석을 포함하기 때문에 의사소통을 하는 행위는 언제나 공동의 창의적인 노력이다. 단어는 화자나 필자가 의식적으로 의도한 것을 넘는 의미를 전달하는데 청자나 독자는 자신이 접하는 언어에 자신만의 관점을 가져오기 때문이다. 부정확하게 표현된 생각은 단순한 사실보다 청자나 독자에게 더 지적으로 자극이 될 수 있다. 언어가 어떤 이의 마음 속에 명확한 의미가 생기도록 하는 데 있어 항상 믿을 만하지 않다는 사실은 새로운 이해를 창출하기 위한 수단인 언어의 강력한 힘을 반영하는 것이다. 언어와 사고 사이의 관계를 그렇게 특별하게 하는 것은 의미를 만들어내는 체계인 언어에 내재하는 애매함과 융통성이다.

Why? 왜 정답일까?

'Ideas expressed imprecisely may be more intellectually stimulating for listeners or readers than simple facts.'에서 불명확하게 표현된 생각은 도리어 청자나 독자에게 지적인 자극을 불러일으킨다고 말한 데 이어, 'It is the inherent ambiguity and adaptability of language as a meaning-making system that makes the relationship between language and thinking so special.'에서는 언어에 내재한 애매함과 융통성이야말로 언어와 사고 사이의 관계를 특별하게 만드는 요소라고 이야기한다. 이는 결국 언어에서 다양한 해석과 이해를 가능하게 하는 것이 '무엇(언어의 불명확성, 모호성)'인지 밝히는 것으로 볼 수 있어, 글의 제목으로 가장 적절한 것은 ④ '무엇이 언어에서 다양한 이해를 하게 하는가?'이다.

- **transmit** ⓥ 전달하다
- **ambiguity** ⓝ 모호성, 애매함
- **invariable** ⓐ 불변의
- **consciously** ⓐⓓ 의식하여, 의식적으로
- **encounter** ⓥ 접하다
- **stimulating** ⓐ 자극이 되는
- **adaptability** ⓝ 적응성
- **specific** ⓐ 구체적인, 명확한, 분명한
- **valuable** ⓐ 가치가 큰
- **joint** ⓐ 공동의
- **perspective** ⓝ 관점
- **imprecisely** ⓐⓓ 부정확하게, 애매하게
- **inherent** ⓐ 고유한

구문 풀이

8행 Words can carry meanings beyond those consciously
　　주어　　　동사　　　　　　　　　=meanings
intended by speakers or writers / because listeners or readers bring
과거분사　　　　　　　　　　　　　　이기 때문에
their own perspectives to the language [they encounter].
　　　　　　　　　　　　　　　　└ 목적격 관계대명사 that 생략

---

04 열기구 탑승 안내　　　　정답률 91% | 정답 ④

Willow Valley Hot Air Balloon Ride에 관한 다음 안내문의 내용과 일치하는 것은?

① 조종사를 제외하고 8인까지 탈 수 있다.
② 여름에는 오전 6시에 시작한다.
③ 요금에 보험이 포함되어 있다.
✓ 예약은 온라인으로 해야 한다.
⑤ 환불은 예외 없이 불가능하다.

[본문 해석]

Willow Valley 열기구 탑승

우리의 열기구를 타고 하늘에서 Willow Valley의 최고의 풍경을 즐겨보세요!

- **정원**: 조종사 포함 8인까지 ── 「」: ①의 근거 불일치
- **일정표**

봄과 여름 (4월부터 9월까지)	오전 5시 – 오전 7시 ── 「」: ②의 근거 불일치
가을과 겨울 (10월부터 3월까지)	오전 6시 – 오전 8시

※ 비행 시간: 약 1시간

- **요금**: 인당 150달러 (「보험은 포함되지 않음」) ── 「」: ③의 근거 불일치
- **공지사항**
  - 「예약은 필수이며 온라인으로 해야 합니다.」 ── 「」: ④의 근거 일치
  - 「24시간 전까지는 전액 환불을 받을 수 있습니다.」 ── 「」: ⑤의 근거 불일치
  - 더 많은 정보를 위해서 www.willowvalleyballoon.com을 방문해 주십시오.

Why? 왜 정답일까?

'Reservations are required and must be made online.'에서 예약은 필수이며 온라인으로 해야 한다고 하므로, 안내문의 내용과 일치하는 것은 ④ '예약은 온라인으로 해야 한다.'이다.

Why? 왜 오답일까?

① 'Capacity: up to 8 people including a pilot'에서 8인이라는 정원에 조종사가 포함된다고 하였다.
② 'Spring & Summer / (from April to September) / 5:00 a.m. – 7:00 a.m.'에서 봄과 여름에는 오전 5시부터 시작된다고 하였다.
③ '(insurance not included)'에서 보험은 요금에 포함되지 않는다고 하였다.
⑤ 'You can get a full refund up to 24 hours in advance.'에서 탑승 24시간 전까지는 전액 환불이 가능하다고 하였다.

- **get a refund** 환불을 받다
- **in advance** 미리, 사전에

---

05 악기 연주를 배우기 전 악기를 탐구할 시간 주기　　정답률 61% | 정답 ③

다음 글의 밑줄 친 부분 중, 어법상 틀린 것은? [3점]

[본문 해석]

비록 악기를 잡고 연주하는 정확한 방법이 대체로 있다고 해도 우선적으로 가장 중요한 가르침은 악기가 장난감이 아니라는 것과 악기를 관리해야 한다는 것이다. 아이들에게 (악기를 다루고 연주하는) 방법을 알려 주기 전에 직접 악기를 다루고 연주하는 방법을 탐구할 시간을 주어라. 소리를 만들어 내는 여러 가지 방법을 찾는 것은 음악적 탐구의 중요한 단계이다. 정확한 연주는 가장 알맞은 음질을 찾고 오랜 시간 동안 잘 다루면서 연주할 수 있도록 가장 편안한 연주 자세를 찾으려는 욕구에서 나온다. 악기와 음악이 더 복잡해짐에 따라, 알맞은 연주 기술을 알게 되는 것은 점점 더 유의미해진다.

Why? 왜 정답일까?

'Finding different ways ~'는 동명사구 주어이므로 단수 취급한다. 따라서 are 대신 is를 써야 한다. 어법상 틀린 것은 ③이다.

Why? 왜 오답일까?

① 뒤에 'they are not toys'라는 완전한 2형식 문장이 나오므로 앞에 접속사 that을 쓴 것은 적절하다. 참고로 that절은 동사 is의 주격 보어이다.
② 앞에 주어 You가 생략된 명령문으로 동사 Allow가 원형으로 바르게 쓰였다.
④ the desire를 꾸미는 말로 to부정사가 바르게 쓰였다. ability, attempt, chance, desire, opportunity 등은 to부정사의 꾸밈을 받는 명사임을 기억해 둔다.
⑤ 2형식 동사 becomes의 보어인 형용사 relevant를 꾸미기 위해 앞에 부사인 increasingly가 적절하게 쓰였다.

- **instrument** ⓝ 악기, 도구
- **look after** ~을 관리하다, 돌보다
- **appropriate** ⓐ 적절한
- **increasingly** ⓐⓓ 점점 더
- **instruction** ⓝ 지침, 가르침
- **explore** ⓥ 탐구하다
- **complex** ⓐ 복잡한
- **relevant** ⓐ 유의미한, 적절한, 관련 있는

구문 풀이

1행 Although there is usually a correct way of holding and playing
접속사(~에도 불구하고) 동사(단수)　　　　　　　　　주어
musical instruments, the most important instruction to begin with is
　　　　　　　　　　　　　　주어　　　　　　　　　　동사
{that they are not toys} and {that they must be looked after}.
접속사1　　　　　　　　　접속사2　　　　　　　　{ }: is의 보어

---

06 뇌의 에너지 소모　　　　정답률 67% | 정답 ③

(A), (B), (C)의 각 네모 안에서 문맥에 맞는 낱말로 가장 적절한 것은?

	(A)	(B)	(C)
①	warn 경고하다	less 더 적은	efficient 효율적인
②	warn 경고하다	more 더 많은	efficient 효율적인
✓	exhaust 지치게 하다	more 더 많은	efficient 효율적인
④	exhaust 지치게 하다	more 더 많은	creative 창의적인
⑤	exhaust 지치게 하다	less 더 적은	creative 창의적인

[본문 해석]

뇌는 몸무게의 2퍼센트만을 차지하지만 우리 에너지의 20퍼센트를 사용한다. 갓 태어난 아기의 경우, 그 비율은 자그마치 65퍼센트이다. 그것은 부분적으로 아기들이 항상 잠을 자고 — 뇌의 성장이 그들을 (A) 지치게 하고 — 많은 체지방을 보유하는 이유인데, 필요할 때 보유한 에너지를 사용하려는 것이다. 근육은 약 4분의 1 정도로 훨씬 더 많은 에너지를 사용하지만, 우리에게는 (워낙) 근육이 많다. 실제로, 물질 단위당, 뇌는 다른 기관보다 훨씬 (B) 더 많은 에너지를 사용한다. 그것은 우리 장기 중 뇌가 단연 가장 비용(에너지) 소모가 많다는 것을 의미한다. 하지만 그것은 또한 놀랍도록 (C) 효율적이다. 뇌는 하루에 약 400칼로리의 에너지만 필요로 하는데, 블루베리 머핀에서 얻는 것과 거의 같다. 머핀으로 24시간 동안 노트북을 작동시켜서 얼마나 가는지 보라.

Why? 왜 정답일까?

(A) 두 번째 문장에서 갓 태어난 아기들은 에너지의 65퍼센트를 뇌에서 소비한다고 언급하는 것으로 보아, 아이들의 뇌가 에너지를 '소모시켜서' 아기들이 항상 잠을 자는 것이라는 설명이 뒤따라야 한다. 따라서 (A)에는 exhaust가 들어가야 한다.
(B) 뒤따르는 문장 '~ the brain is the most expensive of our organs.'에서 우리 몸에서 가장 에너지 소모가 많은 기관은 뇌라고 언급하는 것으로 보아, (B)에는 more가 들어가야 한다.
(C) 바로 앞 문장에서 뇌는 우리 몸에서 단연 가장 많은 에너지를 쓰는 기관임을 언급한 후, But으로 흐름이 반전되고 있다. 뒤에 나온 설명을 함께 읽어볼 때, 뇌는 블루베리 머핀 하나에서 얻는 에너지만 있으면 우리 몸을 위해 그 모든 기능을 수행할 만큼 '효율적'이라는 사실을 상기시키는 맥락임을 알 수 있다. 따라서 (C)에는 efficient가 들어가야 한다. 따라서 각 네모 안에서 문맥에 맞는 낱말로 가장 적절한 것은 ③ '(A) exhaust (지치게 하다) – (B) more(더 많은) – (C) efficient(효율적인)'이다.

- **make up** ⓥ ~을 구성하다
- **no less than** 자그마치 ~이다
- **reserve** ⓝ 보유량
- **marvelously** ⓐⓓ 놀랍도록
- **efficient** ⓐ 효율적인
- **newborn** ⓝ 신생아
- **exhaust** ⓥ 지치게 하다, 소진시키다
- **organ** ⓝ (신체의) 기관
- **creative** ⓐ 창의적인

구문 풀이

3행 That's partly why babies sleep all the time — their growing
관계부사 주어 동사1 삽입(babies sleep 부연 설명)
brains exhaust them — and have a lot of body fat, to use as an energy
동사2 ~하기 위해
reserve when needed.
「접속사+분사구문 : ~할 때」

★★★ **1등급 대비 고난도 2점 문제**

07 혁신 지속에 도움이 되는 가상 환경의 특징   정답률 49% | 정답 ①

다음 빈칸에 들어갈 말로 가장 적절한 것을 고르시오.

☑ restrictions – 제한점
② responsibilities – 책임감
③ memories – 기억
④ coincidences – 우연의 일치
⑤ traditions – 전통

[본문 해석]

작년에 직면한 가장 큰 질문 중 하나는 사람들이 완전히 가상 공간에서 작업할 때 어떻게 혁신을 지속할 것인가 하는 것이었다. 그러나 전문가들은 디지털 작업이 혁신과 창의성에 부정적인 영향을 미치지 않았다고 말한다. 한계 내에서 일하는 것은 우리에게 문제를 해결하도록 독려한다. 전반적으로, 가상 미팅 플랫폼은 대면 환경보다 의사소통과 협업에 더 많은 제약들을 가한다. 예를 들어, 버튼을 누르면, 가상 회의 진행자는 소모임 그룹의 크기를 제어하고 시간 제한을 시행할 수 있다. 한 번에 한 사람만이 말할 수 있다. 비언어적 신호, 특히 어깨 아래의 신호는 줄어든다. '좌석 배치'는 개인이 아닌 플랫폼에 의해 할당된다. 그리고 다른 사람에 대한 시각적 접근은 각 참가자의 화면 크기에 따라 제한될 수 있다. 이러한 제한점은 참가자들을 일반적인 사고방식 너머까지 확장시켜 창의력을 증진시킬 가능성이 높다.

Why? 왜 정답일까?

'Working within limits pushes us to solve problems.'에서 한계 내에서 작업하는 것이 문제 해결을 독려한다고 언급하는 것으로 보아, 빈칸에 들어갈 말로 가장 적절한 것은 ① '제한점'이다.

● virtually [ad] (컴퓨터를 이용해) 가상으로
● have a negative effect on ~에 부정적 영향을 미치다
● constraint ⓝ 제한, 한계
● enforce ⓥ 시행하다
● seating arrangement 좌석 배치
● stretch ⓥ 늘이다, 확장하다
● breakout group 소집단
● diminish ⓥ 줄이다
● assign ⓥ 배정하다, 할당하다
● coincidence ⓝ 우연의 일치, 동시 발생

구문 풀이

1행 One of the big questions faced this past year was {how to
주어(one of the+복수명사) 과거분사 동사(단수)
keep innovation rolling when people were working entirely virtually}.
{ } : 주격 보어(how+to부정사 : ~하는 방법)

★★ **문제 해결 꿀~팁** ★★

▶ 많이 틀린 이유는?
Working within limits가 핵심 표현으로, 제약이나 제한이 혁신과 업무 수행에 도움이 된다는 것이 글의 주제다. 최다 오답인 ②의 responsibilities는 '책임, (맡은) 책무'라는 뜻이므로 글 내용과 관련이 없다.

▶ 문제 해결 방법은?
핵심어인 limits, constraints와 동의어를 찾으면 된다. 빈칸 앞에 not 등 부정어도 없어, 복잡하게 사고할 필요가 없는 비교적 단순한 빈칸 문제이다.

★★★ **1등급 대비 고난도 2점 문제**

08 느리게라도 계속 진행되는 변화   정답률 39% | 정답 ②

글의 흐름으로 보아, 주어진 문장이 들어가기에 가장 적절한 곳을 고르시오.

[본문 해석]

때때로 변화의 속도는 훨씬 더 느리다. ① 오늘 아침 당신이 거울에 비춰진 것을 본 얼굴은 아마도 당신이 그 전날 또는 일주일이나 한 달 전에 본 얼굴과 다르지 않게 보였을 것이다. ② 그러나 우리는 거울에서 우리를 마주보는 얼굴이 10분 전과 같지 않고, 같을 수 없다는 것을 안다. 증거는 당신의 사진 앨범에 있다. 5년 또는 10년 전에 찍은 당신의 사진을 보면 당신은 스냅사진 속의 얼굴

과 거울 속 얼굴 사이의 명확한 차이를 보게 될 것이다. ③ 만약 당신이 일 년간 거울이 없는 세상에 살고 그 이후 (거울에) 비친 당신의 모습을 본다면, 당신은 그 변화 때문에 깜짝 놀랄지도 모른다. ④ 스스로를 보지 않고 10년의 기간이 지난 후, 당신은 거울에서 쳐다보고 있는 사람을 처음에는 알아보지 못할지도 모른다. ⑤ 심지어 우리 자신의 얼굴같이 아주 기본적인 것조차도 순간순간 변한다.

Why? 왜 정답일까?

② 앞은 오늘 아침 거울로 본 얼굴이 전날, 일주일 전, 또는 한 달 전에 본 얼굴과 다르지 않았을 것이라는 내용인데, ② 뒤는 얼굴이 명확히 '달라졌다'는 것을 알 수 있는 증거에 관한 내용이다. 즉 ② 앞뒤로 상반된 내용이 제시되어 흐름이 어색하게 끊기므로, 주어진 문장이 들어가기에 가장 적절한 곳은 ②이다.

● reflect ⓥ 반사하다
● snapshot ⓝ 스냅사진, 짧은 묘사
● surprised ⓐ 놀란
● peer ⓥ 응시하다
● clear ⓐ 명확한
● reflection ⓝ (물이나 거울에 비친) 그림자
● interval ⓝ 간격
● from moment to moment 시시각각

구문 풀이

16행 Even something as basic as our own face changes from moment
to moment.
「as+원급+as : ~만큼 …한」

★★ **문제 해결 꿀~팁** ★★

▶ 많이 틀린 이유는?
가장 헷갈리는 ③ 앞을 보면, 우리가 5~10년 전 찍은 사진을 보면 지금 거울로 보는 얼굴과 다르다는 것을 알 수 있다는 내용이며, 주어진 문장 또한 우리 얼굴이 단 10분 사이에도 '달라진다'는 내용이다. 하지만 주어진 문장은 Yet(그럼에도 불구하고)으로 시작하므로, 이 앞에는 '다르지 않다'라는 반대되는 내용이 나와야 한다. 따라서 주어진 문장 내용과 똑같은 내용이 앞에 나오는 ③ 자리에 주어진 문장을 넣을 수는 없다.

▶ 문제 해결 방법은?
② 앞뒤로 발생하는 논리적 공백에 주목하자. ②는 거울로 보는 우리 얼굴이 '별 차이가 없어보인다'는 내용인데, ②는 사진 앨범 속 우리 얼굴이 '명확한 차이'를 보인다는 내용이다. 즉 ② 앞뒤의 의미가 '다르지 않다 ↔ 다르다'로 상반되는 상황인데, 이 경우 반드시 역접 연결어(주어진 문장의 Yet)가 있어야만 한다.

★★★ **1등급 대비 고난도 2점 문제**

09 기부하도록 설득하기   정답률 43% | 정답 ①

다음 글의 내용을 한 문장으로 요약하고자 한다. 빈칸 (A), (B)에 들어갈 말로 가장 적절한 것은?

(A)		(B)
☑ simultaneously 동시에	······	convinced 설득될
② separately 따로	······	confused 혼란을 느낄
③ frequently 자주	······	annoyed 짜증을 낼
④ separately 따로	······	satisfied 만족할
⑤ simultaneously 동시에	······	offended 기분 상할

[본문 해석]

내 동료들과 나는 (기부에) 저항하는 졸업생 수천 명이 기부하도록 설득할 의도로 작성된 두 개의 다른 메시지들을 실험하는 한 연구를 진행했다. 하나의 메시지는 좋은 일을 할 기회를 강조했다. '기부하는 것은 학생들, 교직원, 그리고 직원들에게 이익을 줄 것이다.' 다른 하나는 좋은 기분을 느끼는 기회를 강조했다. '기부자들은 기부의 따뜻한 온기를 즐길 것이다.' 두 메시지들은 똑같이 효과적이었다. 두 경우 모두에서, 마음 내키지 않아했던 졸업생 6.5%가 결국에는 기부했다. 그러고 나서 우리는 그것들을 결합했는데, 두 개 이유가 한 개보다 더 낫기 때문이었다. 안 그럴 경우를 제외한다면 말이다. 우리가 두 이유를 합쳤을 때, 기부율은 3% 아래로 떨어졌다. 각각의 이유를 따로 봤을 때 둘을 합친 것보다 두 배 이상 효과적이었다. 청중은 이미 회의적이었다. 우리가 그들에게 기부해야 할 다양한 이유를 주었을 때, 우리는 그들이 누군가가 그들을 설득하려고 하는 중이라고 인식하게 했고 — 그리고 그들은 그것에 맞서 스스로를 보호했다.

➡ 위에 언급된 실험에서, 기부할 이유 두 가지가 (A) 동시에 주어졌을 때, 청중

들은 (B) 설득될 가능성이 더 적었는데, 그들을 설득하려는 의도를 인식했기 때문이었다.

Why? 왜 정답일까?

실험 결과를 제시하는 마지막 문장에서, 기부해야 할 여러 이유를 한꺼번에 주면 청중들은 이미 기부를 해달라고 설득하려는 화자의 의도를 알아차리기 때문에 더 방어적이 된다고 한다. 따라서 요약문의 빈칸 (A), (B)에 들어갈 말로 가장 적절한 것은 ① '(A) simultaneously(동시에), (B) convinced(설득될)'이다.

- **make a donation** 기부하다
- **faculty** ⓝ 교직원
- **end up ~ing** 결국 ~하다
- **trigger** ⓥ 유발하다
- **benefit** ⓥ ~에게 이득이 되다
- **glow** ⓝ 빛, (기쁨이나 만족감을 동반한) 감정
- **put together** 합치다
- **simultaneously** ⓐⓓ 동시에

구문 풀이

13행 Each reason alone was more than twice as effective as the
「배수사 + as + 원급 + as : 몇 배 더 ~한」
two combined.

★★ 문제 해결 꿀~팁 ★★

▶ 많이 틀린 이유는?
마지막 문장에서 두 가지 다른 이유를 '한꺼번에' 주었을 때 사람들은 기부를 권유한다는 이면의 의도를 더 잘 읽었기 때문에 오히려 기부에 더 회의적인 태도를 보였다고 한다. ②와 ④는 공통적으로 (A)에 separately가 있는데, 이는 이유를 '따로' 주었다는 의미를 완성하므로, 실험의 핵심 결과와 모순된다.

▶ 문제 해결 방법은?
①의 (A)는 본문의 combined와 together를, (B)는 마지막 문장의 persuade를 재진술한 표현이다.

10-12 여행자들과 수도승의 대화

[본문 해석]

(A)
어느 날 한 젊은이가 한 마을로부터 다른 마을로 여행하며 길을 따라 걷고 있었다. 「그는 걷다가 들판에서 일하는 한 수도승을 보게 되었다.」 그 젊은이는 그 수도승을 향해 돌아보며 "실례합니다. 제가 (a) 스님께 질문을 하나 드려도 되겠습니까?"라고 말했다. "물론입니다."라고 그 수도승은 대답했다.
└「」: 12번 ①의 근거 일치

(C)
"저는 산속의 마을로부터 골짜기의 마을로 가고 있는데 (c) 스님께서 골짜기의 마을은 어떤지 아시는지 궁금합니다." 수도승은 "저에게 말해 보십시오. 산속의 마을에서의 경험은 어땠습니까?"라고 말했다. 그 젊은이는 "끔찍했습니다."라고 대답했다. "그곳을 벗어나게 되어 기쁩니다. 그곳 사람들이 정말로 불친절하다고 생각했습니다. 그러니 (d) 저에게 말씀해 주십시오, 제가 골짜기의 마을에서 무엇을 기대할 수 있을까요?" "말씀드리기에 유감이지만, 제 생각에 선생님의 경험은 그곳에서도 거의 같을 것 같다고 생각합니다." 수도승이 말했다. 「그 젊은이는 힘없이 고개를 숙이고 계속 걸어갔다.」—「」: 12번 ④의 근거 일치

(B)
잠시 후 한 중년 남자가 같은 길을 걸어와서 그 수도승을 만났다. 그 남자는 「"저는 골짜기의 마을로 가고 있습니다.」 「그곳이 어떤지 아십니까?"」라고 말했다. "알고 있습니다만, 먼저 (b) 저에게 선생님께서 떠나오신 마을에 관해 말해 주십시오."라고 그 수도승은 대답했다. 그 남자는 "저는 산속의 마을로부터 왔습니다. 그것은 멋진 경험이었습니다. 저는 마치 그 마을의 가족의 일원인 것처럼 느꼈습니다."라고 말했다.
└「」: 12번 ②의 근거 일치 └「」: 12번 ③의 근거 일치

(D)
그 수도승은 "왜 그렇게 느끼셨습니까?"라고 물었다. "어르신들은 저에게 많은 조언을 해 주셨고, 사람들은 친절하고 너그러웠습니다. 「그곳을 떠나서 슬픕니다.」 그런데 골짜기의 마을은 어떻습니까?"라고 그는 다시 물었다. "(e) 저는 선생님은 그곳이 (산속 마을과) 거의 같다고 여기실 거로 생각합니다."라고 수도승은 대답했다. "그 말씀을 들으니 기쁩니다."라고 그 중년 남자는 미소를 지으며 말하고서 여행을 계속했다.
└「」: 12번 ⑤의 근거 불일치

- **come upon** ~을 우연히 만나다
- **valley** ⓝ 골짜기

- **unwelcoming** ⓐ 불친절한, 환영하지 않는 ● **helplessly** ⓐⓓ 힘없이, 무기력하게
- **generous** ⓐ 관대한

구문 풀이

(B) 8행 I felt as though I was a member of the family in the village.
접속사(마치 ~인 것처럼)

(C) 7행 I found the people most unwelcoming.
5형식 동사 목적어 목적격 보어(형용사)

(D) 3행 I am sad to have left there.
완료부정사(am보다 과거에 일어난 일 묘사)

10 글의 순서 파악   정답률 66% | 정답 ②

주어진 글 (A)에 이어질 내용을 순서에 맞게 배열한 것으로 가장 적절한 것은?
① (B) − (D) − (C)   ✓② (C) − (B) − (D)
③ (C) − (D) − (B)   ④ (D) − (B) − (C)
⑤ (D) − (C) − (B)

Why? 왜 정답일까?

여행 중이던 젊은이가 수도승을 만나 물어볼 것이 있다고 말했다는 (A) 뒤에는, 젊은이가 산속 마을에 대한 자신의 부정적 감상을 말하며 골짜기의 마을이 어떤지 묻자 수도승이 산속 마을과 차이가 없을 것이라고 답했다는 내용의 (C)가 연결된다. 이어서 (B)에서는 똑같이 산속 마을에서 출발한 중년 남자가 수도승과 비슷한 대화를 나누며 산속 마을에 관해 좋은 감상을 이야기했다는 내용이 나오고, (D)에서는 수도승이 그렇다면 골짜기 마을도 좋게 느껴질 것이라 답해주었다고 한다. 따라서 글의 순서로 가장 적절한 것은 ② '(C) − (B) − (D)'이다.

11 지칭 추론   정답률 64% | 정답 ④

밑줄 친 (a) ~ (e) 중에서 가리키는 대상이 나머지 넷과 다른 것은?
① (a)   ② (b)   ③ (c)   ✓④ (d)   ⑤ (e)

Why? 왜 정답일까?

(a), (b), (c), (e)는 the monk, (d)는 the young man이므로, (a) ~ (e) 중에서 가리키는 대상이 다른 하나는 ④ '(d)'이다.

12 세부 내용 파악   정답률 72% | 정답 ⑤

윗글에 관한 내용으로 적절하지 않은 것은?
① 한 수도승이 들판에서 일하고 있었다.
② 중년 남자는 골짜기에 있는 마을로 가는 중이었다.
③ 수도승은 골짜기에 있는 마을에 대해 질문받았다.
④ 수도승의 말을 듣고 젊은이는 고개를 숙였다.
✓⑤ 중년 남자는 산속에 있는 마을을 떠나서 기쁘다고 말했다.

Why? 왜 정답일까?

(D) 'I am sad to have left there.'에 따르면 중년 남자는 산속 마을을 떠나서 슬펐다고 말했으므로, 내용과 일치하지 않는 것은 ⑤ '중년 남자는 산속에 있는 마을을 떠나서 기쁘다고 말했다.'이다.

Why? 왜 오답일까?

① (A) 'As he walked he noticed a monk working in the fields.'의 내용과 일치한다.
② (B) '"I am going to the village in the valley," said the man.'의 내용과 일치한다.
③ (B) '"Do you know what it is like?"'의 내용과 일치한다.
④ (C) 'The young man lowered his head helplessly and walked on.'의 내용과 일치한다.

DAY 13 | 20분 미니 모의고사

01 ①	02 ④	03 ①	04 ③	05 ④
06 ②	07 ⑤	08 ①	09 ④	10 ⑤
11 ③	12 ⑤			

---

01 남편과 딸이 없어진 줄 알았다가 찾고 안도함 ｜ 정답률 88% ｜ 정답 ①

다음 글에 드러난 'I'의 심경 변화로 가장 적절한 것은?

✔ ① anxious → relieved
　 불안한　　 안도한
② delighted → unhappy
　 기쁜　　　 불행한
③ indifferent → excited
　 무관심한　 신난
④ relaxed → upset
　 안도한　　 언짢은
⑤ embarrassed → proud
　 당황한　　　 자랑스러운

[본문 해석]

내가 호텔 방에서 깨어났을 때는 거의 자정이었다. 남편과 딸이 보이지 않았다. 나는 그들에게 전화를 걸었지만, 나는 그들의 전화가 방에서 울리는 것을 들었다. 걱정이 되어, 나는 밖으로 나가 거리를 걸어 내려갔지만, 그들을 어디에서도 찾을 수 없었다. 내가 누군가에게 도움을 요청하려고 했을 때, 근처에 있던 군중이 내 주의를 끌었다. 나는 남편과 딸을 찾으려는 희망을 안고 다가갔고, 갑자기 낯익은 두 얼굴이 보였다. 나는 안도하며 웃었다. 바로 그때, 딸이 나를 보고 "엄마!"라고 외쳤다. 그들은 마술 쇼를 보고 있는 중이었다. 마침내, 나는 내 모든 걱정이 사라지는 것을 느꼈다.

Why? 왜 정답일까?

호텔 방에서 잠을 자다가 깬 필자가 남편과 딸이 없어져 걱정했다가(Feeling worried, ~) 둘이 마술 쇼를 보고 있었다는 것을 알고 안도했다(I smiled, feeling calm. / Finally, I felt all my worries disappear.)는 글이다. 따라서 'I'의 심경 변화로 가장 적절한 것은 ① '불안한 → 안도한'이다.

- midnight ⓝ 자정
- worried ⓐ 걱정한
- ask for help 도움을 요청하다
- approach ⓥ 다가가다
- familiar ⓐ 익숙한
- anxious ⓐ 불안한
- embarrassed ⓐ 당황한
- ring ⓥ 울리다
- decide ⓥ 결심하다, 정하다
- catch one's attention 관심을 끌다
- suddenly ⓐⓓ 문득, 갑자기
- disappear ⓥ 사라지다
- delighted ⓐ 기쁜

구문 풀이

4행 Feeling worried, I went outside and walked down the street,
　　　 분사구문(~하면서)
but they were nowhere to be found.
　　　　　　　 수동 부정사(they 보충 설명)

---

02 글보다 많은 단어를 필요로 하는 말하기 ｜ 정답률 70% ｜ 정답 ④

다음 글에서 필자가 주장하는 바로 가장 적절한 것은?
① 연설 시 중요한 정보는 천천히 말해야 한다.
② 좋은 글을 쓰려면 간결한 문장을 사용해야 한다.
③ 말하기 전에 신중히 생각하는 습관을 길러야 한다.
✔ ④ 글을 쓸 때보다 말할 때 더 많은 단어를 사용해야 한다.
⑤ 청중의 이해를 돕기 위해 미리 연설문을 제공해야 한다.

[본문 해석]

글쓰기 전문가들은 '가능한 한 많은 단어를 삭제하라'고 말한다. 각 단어는 무언가 중요한 일을 해야 한다. 만일 그렇지 않다면 그것을 삭제하라. 자, 이 방법은 말하기에서는 통하지 않는다. 말을 할 때는 아이디어를 소개하고, 표현하며, 적절히 부연 설명하는 데 글을 쓸 때보다 더 많은 단어가 필요하다. 이것은 왜 그러한가? 독자는 글을 다시 읽을 수 있으나 청자는 다시 들을 수 없다. 화자는 반복 재생 버튼을 갖추고 있지 않다. 청자들은 쉽게 주의력이 흐려지기 때문에 화자가 말하는 것 중 많은 부분을 놓칠 것이다. 그들이 중요한 문장을 놓친다면, 절대로 따라잡을 수 없을 것이다. 이것은 화자들이 글을 쓸 때 같은 아이디어를 표현하기 위해 사용할 단어 수보다 더 많은 단어를 사용하여 요점을 더 길게 말할 필요가 있게 한다.

Why? 왜 정답일까?

'It takes more words to introduce, express, and adequately elaborate an idea in speech than it takes in writing.'에서 글보다 말에서 더 많은 단어가 필요하다고 언급하고, 그 이유를 부연 설명한 뒤 다시 논지를 반복하고 있다. 따라서 필자가 주장하는 바로 가장 적절한 것은 ④ '글을 쓸 때보다 말할 때 더 많은 단어를 사용해야 한다.'이다.

- get rid of ~을 제거하다
- express ⓥ 표현하다
- elaborate ⓥ 부연 설명하다, 자세히 말하다
- reread ⓥ 다시 읽다
- crucial ⓐ 아주 중요한
- work for ~에 효과가 있다
- adequately ⓐⓓ 적절하게
- speech ⓝ 연설, 말하기
- distract ⓥ 주의를 분산시키다
- catch up 따라잡다

구문 풀이

　　　　　　　　　　　　　 가목적어
11행 This makes it necessary for speakers to talk longer about
　　　　　　　　 목적격 보어　　의미상 주어　　진목적어
their points, using more words on them than would be used to
　　　　　　　 분사구문　 선행사　 　 유사관계대명사(비교급 선행사 뒤에 불완전한 절 연결)
express the same idea in writing.

---

03 두려움을 주는 뉴스의 부작용 ｜ 정답률 70% ｜ 정답 ①

다음 글의 요지로 가장 적절한 것은?
✔ ① 두려움을 주는 뉴스는 사람들이 문제에 덜 대처하게 할 수 있다.
② 정보를 전달하는 시기에 따라 뉴스의 영향력이 달라질 수 있다.
③ 지속적인 환경 문제 보도가 사람들의 인식 변화를 가져온다.
④ 정보 제공의 지연은 정확한 문제 인식에 방해가 될 수 있다.
⑤ 출처가 불분명한 건강 정보는 사람들에게 유익하지 않다.

[본문 해석]

오래된 격언에 따르면 '아는 것이 힘이다'라고 하지만, 무섭고 위협적인 뉴스에 관해서는 연구에서 정반대를 시사한다. 두려움을 주는 뉴스는 실제로 사람들로부터 내면의 통제력을 빼앗을 수 있어서, 그들이 스스로와 다른 사람들을 돌볼 가능성을 더 낮아지게 한다. 공중 보건 연구는 뉴스가 건강과 관련된 정보를 비관적인 방식으로 제시할 때, 결과적으로 사람들이 질병으로부터 자신을 보호하기 위한 조치를 취할 가능성이 실제로 더 낮다는 것을 보여준다. 예를 들어, 증가하는 암 발생률에 대해 사람들에게 경고하려는 뉴스 기사는 사람들이 발견될지도 모르는 것을 너무 두려워하기 때문에 병에 대해 검사받기로 선택하는 이들이 더 적어지는 결과를 가져올 수 있다. 이것은 기후 변화와 같은 문제에도 해당된다. 뉴스가 온통 파멸과 암울한 상황일 때, 사람들은 우울한 기분을 느끼고 생태학적 붕괴와 싸우기 위한 작고 개인적인 조치를 취하는 데 흥미를 덜 느끼게 된다.

Why? 왜 정답일까?

두려움을 주는 뉴스는 사람들의 문제 대처 능력을 약화시킨다는 내용의 글로, 'Frightening news can actually rob people of their inner sense of control, making them less likely to take care of themselves and other people.'에 주제가 잘 제시된다. 따라서 글의 요지로 가장 적절한 것은 ① '두려움을 주는 뉴스는 사람들이 문제에 덜 대처하게 할 수 있다.'이다.

- threatening ⓐ 겁을 주는
- public health 공공 보건
- take steps to ~하기 위해 조치를 취하다
- article ⓝ 기사
- screen ⓥ (어떤 질병이 있는지) 검진하다
- doom ⓝ 불운, 파멸
- collapse ⓝ 붕괴 ⓥ 쓰러지다
- rob A of B A에게서 B를 빼앗다
- pessimistic ⓐ 염세적인, 비관적인
- illness ⓝ 질병
- be intended to ~할 의도이다
- terrified ⓐ 겁에 질린
- gloom ⓝ 우울, 어둠

구문 풀이

10행 A news article [that's intended to warn people about
　　　　　　　　　　 주어
increasing cancer rates], for example, can result in fewer people
　　　　　　　　　　　　　　　　　　　　　 동사구　　 의미상 주어
choosing to get screened for the disease because they're so terrified
동명사(in의 목적어)
of what they might find.

---

04 검색 엔진을 사용한 정보의 정확성과 신뢰성 ｜ 정답률 93% ｜ 정답 ③

다음 도표의 내용과 일치하지 <u>않는</u> 것은?

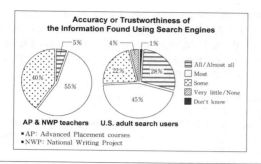

Accuracy or Trustworthiness of the Information Found Using Search Engines

AP & NWP teachers: 5%, 55%, 40%
U.S. adult search users: 4%, 1%, 28%, 22%, 45%

- All / Almost all
- Most
- Some
- Very little / None
- Don't know

AP & NWP teachers
U.S. adult search users
- AP: Advanced Placement courses
- NWP: National Writing Project

③ 주어인 The historical tendency에 이어지는 단수 동사로서 is의 쓰임은 어법상 맞다.
⑤ 뒤에 수동태가 쓰인 완전한 절이 연결되므로 의문부사 how의 쓰임은 어법상 맞다. 이는 '어떻게'라는 의미를 나타내며, 전치사 on의 목적어 역할을 하는 명사절을 이끈다.

- morality ⓝ 도덕성
- assumption ⓝ 가정
- cave in to ~에 굴복하다
- outdated ⓐ 시대에 뒤처진, 구식의
- allow for ~을 허용하다, 참작하다
- cognitive ⓐ 인지적인
- acceptance ⓝ 수용, 받아들임
- longstanding ⓐ 오래된, 오랜 세월에 걸친
- extremely ⓐⓓ 극도로, 몹시
- deny ⓥ 부정하다, 부인하다
- cling to ~을 고수하다
- stereotype ⓝ 고정관념
- capacity ⓝ 능력, 수용력
- have (an) influence on ~에 영향을 미치다

구문 풀이

1행 The belief [that humans have morality and animals don't] is
주어1   동격 접속사   동사1
such a longstanding assumption that it could well be called a habit
「such ~ that … : 너무 ~해서 …하다」
of mind, / and bad habits, as we all know, are extremely hard to break.
주어2   동사2

06 새로운 환경을 상상하기 어려워하는 어린 아이들   정답률 58% | 정답 ②
다음 글의 밑줄 친 부분 중, 문맥상 낱말의 쓰임이 적절하지 않은 것은? [3점]

[본문 해석]

이사는 모두에게 힘들지만, 아이들에게 특히 스트레스가 된다. 그들은 안정감을 잃고, 그들의 일상이 무너지고 ① 익숙한 모든 것이 사라질 때 혼란스러움을 느낄 수도 있다. 3세에서 6세 사이의 어린아이들은 이사에 특히 영향을 받는다. 이 시기에 그들의 이해력은 꽤 융통성이 없어서, 그들이 새로운 집과 자신의 새로운 방을 미리 상상하기란 ② 쉽다(→ 어렵다). 어린아이들은 "내가 새로운 곳에서도 여전히 나야?"와 "내 장난감과 침대는 우리랑 같이 가?"와 같은 걱정들을 가질지도 모른다. 아이들의 과거 경험을 인정하는 것, 그리고 그들이 새로운 곳에 ③ 적응하도록 돕는 데 집중하는 것 사이에 균형을 잡는 것이 중요하다. 아이들은 자신의 존재에 대한 중요한 부분으로서 자기 과거를 ④ 존중하는 방식으로 자신의 배경을 나눌 기회를 가져봐야 한다. 이것은 공동체 의식을 형성하는 데 기여하고, 이는 모든 아이들, 특히 ⑤ 변화를 겪는 아이들에게 몹시 중요하다.

Why? 왜 정답일까?

② 뒤로 아이들은 새로운 곳에 가도 자기 존재가 그대로일지, 물건도 그대로 있을지 잘 상상하지 못한다는 예시가 나오는 것으로 보아, 아이들은 새로운 환경에 처하기 전에 미리 그 환경을 상상해보는 것을 '어려워한다'는 설명이 적합하다. 즉 easy를 hard로 바꾸어야 하므로, 문맥상 쓰임이 적절하지 않은 단어는 ②이다.

- particularly ⓐⓓ 특히
- disoriented ⓐ 혼란스러워 하는
- disrupt ⓥ 무너뜨리다, 지장을 주다
- take away 없애다, 빼앗다
- literal ⓐ 융통성 없는, 문자 그대로의
- establish ⓥ 설정하다, 쌓다
- adjust to ~에 적응하다
- contribute to ~에 기여하다
- security ⓝ 안정
- routine ⓝ 일상, 루틴
- familiar ⓐ 익숙한
- understanding ⓝ 이해(력)
- beforehand ⓐⓓ 미리
- validate ⓥ 인정하다, 승인하다, 입증하다
- share ⓥ 나누다, 공유하다
- transition ⓝ 변화

구문 풀이

15행 This contributes to building a sense of community, which is
선행사   계속적 용법
essential for all children, especially those in transition.
= children

★★★ 1등급 대비 고난도 2점 문제

07 동물을 잘 보살피기 위한 환경의 조건   정답률 51% | 정답 ⑤
다음 빈칸에 들어갈 말로 가장 적절한 것을 고르시오.

① silent – 고요하도록
② natural – 자연스럽도록
③ isolated – 고립되도록
④ dynamic – 역동적이도록
✓ predictable – 예측 가능하도록

[본문 해석]

좋은 보살핌을 제공하는 것의 가장 중요한 측면 중에 한 가지는 반드시 동물의

[본문 해석]

위의 두 원 도표는 2012년에 두 응답자 집단(AP & NWP 교사와 미국 성인 검색 사용자들)이 검색 엔진을 사용해서 찾은 정보가 얼마나 정확하고 신뢰할 만하다고 여기는지를 보여준다. ① AP & NWP 교사들은 5퍼센트가 검색 엔진을 사용해서 찾은 정보의 "모든 / 거의 대부분"이 정확하거나 신뢰할 만하다고 한 반면, 미국 성인 검색 사용자들의 28%나 똑같이 말한다. ② AP & NWP 교사들과 미국 성인 검색 사용자들 중 가장 큰 비율이 정보의 "대부분"이 정확하고 신뢰할 만하다고 대답한다. ③ 게다가, AP & NWP 교사의 40%가 정보의 "일부"가 정확하며 신뢰할 만하다고 말하고, 미국 성인 검색 사용자들 중 30% 이상이 동일하게 대답한다. ④ 검색 엔진을 사용해서 찾은 정보의 "아주 적은 / 아무것도 없는" 정보가 정확하거나 신뢰할 만하다고 말하는 미국 성인 검색 사용자들은 5퍼센트가 되지 않는다. ⑤ "알지 못한다"고 대답한 미국 성인 검색 사용자들은 1퍼센트만 차지한다.

Why? 왜 정답일까?

도표에 따르면 미국 성인 검색 사용자들 중 정보의 "일부"가 정확하며 신뢰할 만하다고 답한 비율은 22%인데 이는 30%보다 적다. 따라서 도표의 내용과 일치하지 않는 것은 ③이다.

- accurate ⓐ 정확한
- respondent ⓝ 응답자
- search engine 검색 엔진
- trustworthy ⓐ 신뢰할만한
- as for ~에 관해 말하면
- account for ~을 차지하다

구문 풀이

15행 U.S. adult search users saying [that "Very little / None" of
문장 주어   접속사   주어
the information [found using search engines] is accurate or
동사
trustworthy] account for less than five percent.
문장 동사

05 동물의 도덕성에 관한 습관적 사고와 고정관념   정답률 44% | 정답 ④
다음 글의 밑줄 친 부분 중, 어법상 틀린 것은? [3점]

[본문 해석]

인간들은 도덕성을 가지고 있고 동물들은 그렇지 않다는 믿음은 너무나 오래된 가정이기에 이는 충분히 습관적 사고로 불릴 수 있고, 우리 모두 알다시피 나쁜 습관은 고치기가 극도로 어렵다. 많은 사람이 이러한 가정에 굴복해 왔는데, 왜냐하면 동물들이 도덕적 태도를 지닌다는 가능성의 복잡한 영향들을 다루는 것보다 동물에게서 도덕성을 부정하는 것이 더 쉽기 때문이다. 우리 대 그들이라는 시대에 뒤처진 이원론의 틀에 갇힌 역사적 경향은 많은 사람이 현재 상태를 고수하게 만들기에 충분히 강력하다. 동물들이 누구인가에 대한 부정은 동물들의 인지적, 감정적 능력에 대한 잘못된 고정관념을 유지하는 것을 편의대로 허용한다. 분명히 중대한 패러다임의 전환이 요구되는데, 왜냐하면 습관적 사고에 대한 안일한 수용이 동물들이 어떻게 이해되고 다루어지는지에 강한 영향을 미치기 때문이다.

Why? 왜 정답일까?

동사인 allows for를 꾸미기 위해서는 부사가 필요하므로, 형용사인 convenient는 conveniently로 고쳐야 한다. 따라서 어법상 틀린 것은 ④이다.

Why? 왜 오답일까?

① 형용사 hard를 꾸미는 부사적 용법의 to부정사구로서 to break의 쓰임은 어법상 맞다.
② the possibility와 동격을 이루는 완전한 명사절을 이끄는 접속사로서 that의 쓰임은 어법상 맞다.

욕구가 일관되고도 예측 가능하게 충족되도록 하는 것이다. 사람과 마찬가지로, 동물은 통제감이 필요하다. 그러므로 충분한 음식을 제공받고 있을지라도 음식이 언제 눈에 보일지 모르고 일관된 일정을 알 수 없는 동물은 괴로움을 겪지도 모른다. 우리 동물의 환경이 예측 가능하도록 보장함으로써 우리는 통제감을 줄 수 있다. 즉, 마실 수 있는 물이 늘 있고, 늘 같은 곳에 있다. 아침에 일어날 때 그리고 저녁 산책을 한 후에 늘 음식이 있다. 불편할 정도로 참을 필요 없이 변을 배설할 수 있는 시간과 장소가 늘 있을 것이다. 사람 친구는 한 순간에는 애정을 주다가 그다음에는 애정을 주지 않기보다는 일관된 정서적 지지를 보이는 것이 좋다. 기대할 수 있는 것이 무엇인지 알고 있을 때, 동물은 자신감과 차분함을 더 많이 느낄 수 있다.

Why? 왜 정답일까?

첫 문장인 'One of the most important aspects of providing good care is making sure that an animal's needs are being met consistently and predictably.'에서 동물을 잘 보살피기 위해서는 동물의 욕구가 일관적이고도 예측 가능한 방식으로 충족되게 해줄 필요가 있다고 언급하고 있다. 따라서 빈칸에 들어갈 말로 가장 적절한 것은 동물의 환경을 '예측 가능하게' 만들어 주어야 한다는 의미를 완성하는 ⑤ '예측 가능하도록'이다.

- aspect ⓝ 측면
- consistently [ad] 일관적으로
- sense of control 통제감
- ensure ⓥ 반드시 ~하다, 보장하다
- discomfort ⓝ 불편함
- confident ⓐ 자신감 있는
- make sure 반드시 ~하다
- predictably [ad] 예측 가능하게
- distress ⓝ 괴로움
- to the point of ~할 수 있을 정도로
- withhold ⓥ 주지 않다
- isolated ⓐ 고립된

구문 풀이

4행 So an animal [who may get enough food but doesn't know
주어(선행사) ┌주격 관·대
동사구1   동사구2
when the food will appear and can see no consistent schedule]
의문사(언제 ~할지)   동사구3
may experience distress.
동사

★★ 문제 해결 꿀~팁 ★★

▶ 많이 틀린 이유는?

빈칸 뒤에서 반려동물에게 정해진 장소와 시간에 따라 어떤 것을 기대할 수 있는 안정적인 환경을 제공할 필요가 있다는 내용이 주를 이루고 있다. 이 안정된 환경이 꼭 '자연스러운' 것이라고 볼 수는 없으므로 ②는 답으로 부적절하다.

▶ 문제 해결 방법은?

첫 문장에서 '일관되고 예측 가능한' 환경의 중요성을 언급한 데 이어, 마지막 문장에서도 동물에게 '무엇을 기대할 수 있는지'가 분명한 환경을 주는 것이 좋다는 내용을 제시하고 있으므로 ⑤가 답으로 가장 적절하다.

08 0부터 숫자 세기의 문제점   정답률 73% | 정답 ①

다음 빈칸에 들어갈 말로 가장 적절한 것을 고르시오. [3점]

☑ counting from 0 – 0부터 숫자를 세는 것
② numbering in reverse order – 수를 거꾸로 매기는 것
③ adding up the numbers given – 주어진 수를 더하는 것
④ learning words through games – 게임을 통해 단어를 익히는 것
⑤ saying numbers in a loud voice – 큰 소리로 수를 말하는 것

[본문 해석]

0부터 숫자를 세는 것에는 중대한 문제가 있다. 탁자에 몇 개의 사과가 있는지를 판단하는 것처럼, 수를 세어 대상의 수를 판단하기 위해, 많은 아이들은 첫 번째 사과를 만지거나 가리킨 후 "하나"라고 말하고, 그러고 나서 두 번째 사과로 옮겨가서 "둘"이라고 말하며, 모든 사과를 셀 때까지 이런 방식으로 계속할 것이다. 만약 우리가 0부터 시작하면 아무것도 만지지 않고 "영"이라고 말해야 하지만, 그 이후로는 사과를 만지기 시작하며 "하나, 둘, 셋" 등으로 말해야 할 것이다. 이것은 매우 혼란스러울 수 있는데 그 이유는 언제 만지고 언제 만지지 않아야 하는지를 강조할 필요가 있을 것이기 때문이다. 만약 한 아이가 실수로 "영"이라고 말하며 사과 하나를 만진다면, 사과의 총 개수는 한 개만큼 부족할 것이다.

Why? 왜 정답일까?

첫 문장에 빈칸이 있으므로 주제문을 완성하는 문제이며, 두 번째 문장부터 사과를 직접 만지며 수를 세는 경우를 예로 들고 있다. 특히 'This can be very confusing ~'

이후로 0부터 사과를 세어가는 방식이 수를 세고 있는 아이들로 하여금 혼동을 유발할 수 있음이 지적되고 있다. 0부터 수를 세면 언제 사과를 만지고 만지지 말아야 하는지를 따로 가르쳐야 할 수도 있기에 헷갈린다는 것이다(~ there would be a need to stress when to touch and when not to touch.). 따라서 빈칸에 들어갈 말로 가장 적절한 것은 ① '0부터 숫자를 세는 것'이다.

- determine ⓥ 알아내다
- move on to ~로 넘어가다
- call out ~을 부르다, 호출하다
- stress ⓥ 강조하다
- reverse ⓐ 거꾸로의
- point to ~을 가리키다
- manner ⓝ 방식
- confusing ⓐ 혼란을 유발하는
- accidentally [ad] 실수로, 우연히

구문 풀이

10행 This can be very confusing / because there would be a need
이유 접속사   동사   주어
to stress {when to touch} and {when not to touch}.
형용사적 용법   { } : 목적어('의문사 + to부정사')

09 패션의 의미   정답률 66% | 정답 ④

다음 글에서 전체 흐름과 관계 <u>없는</u> 문장은?

[본문 해석]

Marguerite La Caze에 따르면, 패션은 우리의 삶에 기여하고, 우리가 중요한 사회적 가치를 개발하고 나타낼 수단을 제공한다. ① 패션은 어쩌면 아름다울 수 있고, 혁신적일 수 있으며, 유용할 수 있다. 우리는 패션을 선택하는 데 있어서 창의성과 좋은 취향을 드러낼 수 있다. ② 그리고 취향과 관심에 따라 옷을 입을 때, 우리는 자아존중과 타인의 즐거움에 대한 관심 모두를 보여준다. ③ 의심의 여지없이, 패션은 우리를 서로 연결해 주는 흥미와 즐거움의 원천이 될 수 있다. ④ 패션 산업은 유럽과 미국에서 처음 발달했지만, 오늘날에는 국제적이고 매우 세계화된 산업이 되었다. ⑤ 다시 말해, 패션은 자신을 다르게 상상하는, 즉 다른 정체성을 시도하는 기회와 더불어 친교적인 측면을 제공한다.

Why? 왜 정답일까?

패션이 삶에서 갖는 의미를 설명한 글로, 개인의 삶과 타인과의 상호작용에서 어떤 의미를 갖는지가 주로 언급된다. 하지만 ④는 패션 사업의 발달에 관해 언급하며 글의 흐름에서 벗어나므로, 전체 흐름과 관계 없는 문장은 ④이다.

- contribute to ~에 기여하다
- exhibit ⓥ 보여주다, 드러내다
- represent ⓥ 나타내다, 표현하다
- link A to B A와 B를 연결하다
- sociable ⓐ 사교적인
- medium ⓝ 수단, 매체
- taste ⓝ 취향
- concern ⓝ 관심, 우려
- highly [ad] 매우
- along with ~와 더불어

구문 풀이

7행 There is no doubt {that fashion can be a source of interest
부정 주어   { } : doubt의 동격절   선행사
and pleasure [which links us to each other]}.
주격 관·대

★★★ 1등급 대비 고난도 2점 문제

10 반사면을 활용하여 암호 메시지 작성하기   정답률 40% | 정답 ⑤

주어진 글 다음에 이어질 글의 순서로 가장 적절한 것을 고르시오.

① (A) – (C) – (B)
② (B) – (A) – (C)
③ (B) – (C) – (A)
④ (C) – (A) – (B)
☑ (C) – (B) – (A)

[본문 해석]

거울과 부드럽고 광택이 나는 다른 표면들은 빛을 반사한다. 광선이 우리 눈의 망막에 이미지를 형성하기 때문에 우리는 그런 표면들로부터 반사된 것을 본다.

(C) 그런 이미지들은 항상 거꾸로 되어 있다. 거울에 비친 여러분의 모습을 보며 오른쪽 눈을 깜박여 보아라. 그러면 왼쪽 눈이 여러분에게 눈을 깜박이는 것처럼 보일 것이다. 여러분은 거울을 사용하여 친구에게 암호로 된 메시지를 보낼 수 있다.

(B) 탁자 위에 놓인 한 장의 종이가 거울 속에 명확하게 보일 수 있도록 거울을 탁자 위에 수직으로 세워라. 이제 거울을 볼 때 정상적으로 보이는 메시지를 적어라.

(A) 쓰는 동안 종이가 아니라 반사되는 이미지를 계속 보아라. 조금 연습을 하고 나면, '거꾸로' 쓰는 것이 더 쉬울 것이다. 여러분의 친구가 그런 메시지를 받으면, 그는 그 종이를 거울에 비춰 봄으로써 그것을 읽을 수 있을 것이다.

Why? 왜 정답일까?

거울 등 반짝이는 표면은 빛을 반사한다는 것을 언급하는 주어진 글 뒤에는, 반사된 이미지는 늘 거꾸로 되어 있기에 이를 활용하면 친구에게 암호 메시지를 보낼 수 있다는 내용의 (C), 거울을 이용하여 암호 메시지를 쓰는 방법을 설명하는 내용의 (B), 쓰는 동안 주의할 점을 언급한 후 몇 번의 연습을 거치면 친구에게 메시지를 잘 전달할 수 있다는 결론으로 이어지는 (A)가 차례로 이어져야 한다. 따라서 글의 순서로 가장 적절한 것은 ⑤ '(C) – (B) – (A)'이다.

- **smooth** ⓐ 부드러운
- **reflection** ⓝ (거울 등에) 반사된 것
- **form** ⓥ 형성하다
- **practice** ⓥ 연습하다
- **receive** ⓥ 받다, 받아들이다
- **reverse** ⓥ 뒤집다
- **surface** ⓝ (사물의)표면
- **ray** ⓝ 광선, 선, 빛살
- **retina** ⓝ (눈의) 망막
- **backwards** ⓐⓓ 거꾸로, 뒤로
- **upright** ⓐⓓ 똑바로
- **coded** ⓐ 암호화된, 부호화된

구문 풀이

7행 When your friend receives such a message he will be able
접속사(~할 때) 『such a + (형) + 명 : 그러한 (~한) …』
to read it by holding the paper up to a mirror.
~함으로써

★★ 문제 해결 꿀~팁 ★★

▶ 많이 틀린 이유는?
주어진 글의 Mirrors만 보고 기계적으로 (B)를 연결해서는 안 된다. 주어진 글에 '메시지'에 관한 언급이 없는데 (B)에서는 갑자기 거울을 세워놓고 종이를 꺼내 '메시지'를 써 볼 것을 지시하고 있다. 더구나 주어진 글의 특정 표현이나 어구가 (B)에서 재진술되거나 반복되지 않는 것으로 보아, 주어진 글 뒤에 (B)가 나올 수 없다.
▶ 문제 해결 방법은?
주어진 글 후반부의 an image를 (C)의 Such images와 대응시킨 후, 나머지 두 단락은 전체적으로 가볍게 훑으며 논리적인 흐름에 맞게 순서를 연결시키도록 한다.

11-12 그룹 간의 경계심을 사라지게 하는 협동

[본문 해석]

연구자들은 두 그룹의 11세 소년들을 Oklahoma에 있는 Robbers Cave 주립 공원의 여름 캠프에 데려왔다. 그 소년들은 서로 몰랐고 캠프에 도착하자마자 무작위로 두 그룹으로 나뉘었다. 그 그룹들은 약 1주일 동안 서로 떨어져 있었다. 그들은 수영하고, 야영하고, 하이킹을 했다. 각 그룹은 자기 그룹의 이름을 지었고, 소년들은 자신의 그룹 이름을 모자와 티셔츠에 새겼다. 그 후 두 그룹이 만났다. 그들 사이에 일련의 운동 시합이 마련되었다. 곧, 각 그룹은 서로를 (a) 적으로 여겼다. 각 그룹은 서로를 얕잡아 보게 되었다. 소년들은 먹을 것을 가지고 싸우기 시작했고 상대 그룹 구성원의 여러 물건을 훔쳤다. 그래서 경쟁적인 환경에서 소년들은 재빨리 뚜렷한 그룹 경계를 (b) 그었다.
그런 다음, 연구자들은 운동 시합을 멈추고, 해결에 두 그룹 사이의 협력이 (c) 필요한, 몇 가지 비상사태로 보이는 상황을 만들었다. 그러한 비상사태 중 하나는 캠프에 물을 공급하는 파이프가 새는 경우를 포함했다. 연구자들은 소년들을 두 그룹 모두의 일원들로 구성된 팀에 배정했다. 그들의 임무는 파이프를 조사하고 새는 곳을 고치는 것이었다. 그러한 (d) 협력적인 활동을 몇 차례 한 후에, 소년들은 싸우지 않고 함께 놀기 시작했다. 『일단 협력이 경쟁을 대체하고 그룹들이 서로를 얕잡아 보기를 (e) 시작하자(→ 중단하자), 그룹 경계가 형성되었던 것만큼 빠르게 사라져 갔다.』 : 11번의 근거

- **randomly** ⓐⓓ 무작위로
- **apart** ⓐⓓ 떨어져, 따로
- **look down on** ~을 얕잡아보다, 깔보다
- **boundary** ⓝ 경계
- **leak** ⓝ 새는 곳, 구멍 ⓥ (물이나 기체가) 새다
- **replace** ⓥ 대체하다
- **separate** ⓥ 나누다, 분리하다
- **athletic** ⓐ 운동의, 육상의
- **competitive** ⓐ 경쟁적인
- **emergency** ⓝ 비상사태
- **assign** ⓥ 배정하다
- **melt away** 차츰 사라지다

구문 풀이

16행 The researchers next stopped the athletic competitions and
동사1
created several apparent emergencies [whose solution required
동사2   선행사   소유격 관계대명사
cooperation between the two groups].

---

11 제목 파악 정답률 49% | 정답 ③

윗글의 제목으로 가장 적절한 것은?
① How Are Athletic Competitions Helpful for Teens?
운동 시합은 어떻게 십 대에게 도움이 되는가?
② Preparation: The Key to Preventing Emergencies
대비: 비상사태 예방의 비결
③ What Makes Group Boundaries Disappear?
무엇이 그룹 경계를 사라지게 하는가?
④ Respect Individual Differences in Teams
팀 내 개인차를 존중하라
⑤ Free Riders: Headaches in Teams
무임승차자: 팀의 골칫거리

Why? 왜 정답일까?

소년들을 두 그룹으로 나누어 일련의 경쟁을 하도록 했을 때에는 그룹 간에 적개심과 경계가 형성되었지만, 그룹 간의 협력이 필요한 활동에 참여하게 하자 그 경계가 쉽게 사라졌다(Once cooperation replaced competition ~, group boundaries melted away as quickly as they had formed.)는 내용의 실험을 소개한 글이다. 따라서 글의 제목으로 가장 적절한 것은 ③ '무엇이 그룹 경계를 사라지게 하는가?'이다.

★★★ 1등급 대비 고난도 2점 문제

12 어휘 추론 정답률 35% | 정답 ⑤

밑줄 친 (a) ~ (e) 중에서 문맥상 낱말의 쓰임이 적절하지 않은 것은?
① (a) ② (b) ③ (c) ④ (d) ⑤ (e)

Why? 왜 정답일까?

마지막 문장의 and 앞에서 협력이 경쟁을 대체하였다(cooperation replaced competition)는 내용이 언급되는 것으로 보아, and 뒤에는 그룹들이 경쟁 관계에서 벗어나 서로를 얕잡아 보기를 '그만두었다'는 내용이 이어지는 것이 적절하므로, (e)의 started는 반의어인 ceased로 고쳐야 한다. 따라서 문맥상 낱말의 쓰임이 적절하지 않은 것은 ⑤ '(e)'이다.

★★ 문제 해결 꿀~팁 ★★

▶ 많이 틀린 이유는?
문장이 어렵지는 않지만 길이로 인한 압박이 있어 전체 맥락을 파악하는 데 부담이 따르는 지문이다. 최다 오답인 ②는 앞에서 소년들이 팀 별로 경계심을 키웠음을 보여 주는 사례가 나오는 것으로 볼 때 맥락상 적절하다. (b) 바로 앞의 문장을 주의 깊게 읽도록 한다.
▶ 문제 해결 방법은?
첫 단락과 두 번째 단락이 '소년들 간 반목 vs. 협동'이라는 키워드로 대조를 이루므로, 이 점에 주의하여 선택지 문장의 맥락을 파악해야 한다.

DAY 14 — 20분 미니 모의고사

01 ②	02 ②	03 ④	04 ③	05 ③
06 ③	07 ③	08 ⑤	09 ①	10 ②
11 ⑤	12 ②			

---

01 분실물 확인 요청

정답률 96% | 정답 ②

다음 글의 목적으로 가장 적절한 것은?

① 제품의 고장 원인을 문의하려고
✓ ② 분실물 발견 시 연락을 부탁하려고
③ 시설물의 철저한 관리를 당부하려고
④ 여행자 보험 가입 절차를 확인하려고
⑤ 분실물 센터 확장의 필요성을 건의하려고

[본문 해석]

보트 투어 담당자께

3월 15일에 저희 가족은 귀사의 Glass Bottom Boat Tours 중 하나에 참여했습니다. 호텔에 돌아왔을 때, 제가 휴대 전화 케이스를 놓고 왔다는 것을 발견했습니다. 케이스를 닦기 위해 휴대 전화에서 분리했을 때 케이스가 제 무릎에서 바닥으로 떨어졌던 것이 틀림없습니다. 그것이 보트에 있는지 확인해 주시길 부탁드립니다. 그것의 색깔은 검은색이며 안쪽에 제 이름이 있습니다. 만약 케이스가 발견된다면, 저에게 알려주시면 감사하겠습니다.

Sam Roberts 드림

Why? 왜 정답일까?

보트 투어 중 잃어버린 휴대 전화 케이스가 보트에 있는지 확인해줄 것을 부탁하는(I would like to ask you to check if it is on your boat.) 글이다. 따라서 글의 목적으로 가장 적절한 것은 ② '분실물 발견 시 연락을 부탁하려고'이다.

- **leave behind** ~을 남겨놓고 오다
- **lap** ⑩ 무릎
- **fall** ⓥ 떨어지다
- **appreciate** ⓥ 감사하다

구문 풀이

5행 The case must have fallen off my lap and onto the floor when
「must have+과거분사 : ~했음에 틀림없다」
I took it off my phone to clean it.
부사적 용법(~하기 위해)

---

02 환경 친화적인 행동으로의 변화를 촉구할 필요성

정답률 55% | 정답 ②

밑줄 친 the role of the 'lion's historians'가 다음 글에서 의미하는 바로 가장 적절한 것은?

① uncovering the history of a species' biological evolution
한 종의 생물학적 진화의 역사를 밝혀내는 것
✓ ② urging a shift to sustainable human behaviour for nature
자연을 위해 지속 가능한 인간 행동으로의 변화를 촉구하는 것
③ fighting against widespread violations of human rights
만연한 인권 침해에 맞서 싸우는 것
④ rewriting history for more underrepresented people
더 드러나지 않은 사람들을 위해서 역사를 다시 쓰는 것
⑤ restricting the power of environmental lawmakers
환경법 제정자들의 권한을 제한하는 것

[본문 해석]

'사자가 자신의 역사가를 둘 때까지, 사냥 이야기는 항상 사냥꾼을 미화한다'라는 아프리카 속담이 있다. 이 속담은 권력과 통제와 법 제정에 관한 것이다. 환경 저널리스트들은 '사자의 역사가' 역할을 해야 한다. 그들은 법을 만드는 사람들에게 환경의 관점을 이해시켜야 한다. 그들은 야생 인도의 목소리가 되어야 한다. 현재 인간 소비의 비율은 완전히 지속 불가하다. 숲, 습지, 황무지, 해안 지대, 환경 민감 지역, 이것들은 모두 인구의 가속화되는 필요를 위해 마음대로 쓰일 수 있다고 여겨진다. 하지만 소비를 줄이는 것이든, 생활 방식을 바꾸는 것이든, 인구 증가를 줄이는 것이든, 인간의 행동에 그 어떤 변화라도 요구하는 것은 인권 침해로 간주된다. 그러나 어느 지점에 이르면 인권은 '잘못된 것'이 된다. 인간의 권리와 나머지 환경의 권리 사이에 차이가 없도록 우리가 우리 생각을 바꿔야 할 때이다.

Why? 왜 정답일까?

밑줄 친 문장 뒤로 인간의 자원 소비는 환경을 지속 불가하게 만드는 수준에 이르고 있으므로, 인간들이 환경의 권리를 생각하며 행동할 수 있도록 변화를 촉구해야 한다는 내용이 이어지고 있다. 이를 근거로 볼 때, 밑줄 앞의 아프리카 속담에 나오는 사자는 여태까지 그 입장이 무시되어 온 환경을 나타낸다고 볼 수 있다. 사자의 역사가란 밑줄 문장의 환경 저널리스트들을 나타내며, 이들은 밑줄 뒤 문장에 따르면 환경의 입장을 입법자들에게 이해시킬 의무를 지는 사람들이다(They have to put across the point of view of the environment to people who make the laws.). 따라서 사자의 역사가가 수행하는 역할이라는 뜻의 밑줄 친 부분이 진정 의미하는 바로 가장 적절한 것은 ② '자연을 위해 지속 가능한 인간 행동으로의 변화를 촉구하는 것'이다.

- **proverb** ⑩ 속담
- **tale** ⑩ 이야기, 소설
- **put across ~ to …** ~을 …에게 이해시키다
- **unsustainable** ⓐ 지속 불가능한
- **wastelands** ⑩ 황무지
- **sensitive** ⓐ 세심한, 민감한
- **accelerating** ⓐ 가속화되고 있는
- **violation** ⑩ 침해, 위반
- **uncover** ⓥ 밝히다, 드러내다
- **underrepresented** ⓐ 불충분하게 표시된
- **lawmaker** ⑩ 입법자, 제정자
- **historian** ⑩ 사학자
- **glorify** ⓥ 미화하다, 기리다
- **consumption** ⑩ 소비[소모](량)
- **wetland** ⑩ 습지(대)
- **coastal** ⓐ 해안의
- **disposable** ⓐ 마음대로 이용할 수 있는
- **cut down on** ~을 줄이다
- **wrong** ⑩ 잘못, 부정
- **urge** ⓥ 강력히 권고하다
- **restrict** ⓥ 제한하다

구문 풀이

11행 But to ask for any change in human behaviour —
부정사구 주어(단수 취급)
whether it be to cut down on consumption, alter lifestyles or decrease
「whether A, B, or C : A이든 B이든 C이든」
population growth — is seen as a violation of human rights.
동사구(be seen as : ~로 간주되다)

---

03 문제와 갈등에서 나오는 창의성

정답률 50% | 정답 ④

다음 글의 제목으로 가장 적절한 것은?

① Technology: A Lens to the Future
기술: 미래를 보는 렌즈
② Diversity: A Key to Social Unification
다양성: 사회적 통합의 핵심
③ Simple Ways to Avoid Conflicts with Others
다른 사람들과의 갈등을 피하는 간단한 방법
✓ ④ Creativity Doesn't Come from Playing It Safe
창의성은 위험을 피하는 것에서 근원하지 않는다
⑤ There Are No Challenges That Can't Be Overcome
극복되지 못할 어려움은 없다

[본문 해석]

다양성, 어려움, 그리고 갈등은 우리의 상상력을 유지하게 도와준다. 대부분의 사람들은 갈등은 나쁜 것이고 '편안한 구역'에 머무는 것이 좋은 것이라고 생각한다. 그것은 정확히는 사실이 아니다. 물론, 우리는 직장 또는 의료보험이 없거나, 배우자, 가족, 직장 상사, 직장 동료들과의 다툼에 빠진 자신의 모습을 보고 싶어 하지 않는다. 하나의 나쁜 경험이 우리에게 평생 지속되는 데 충분할 수 있다. 하지만 가족과 친구들과의 작은 의견 충돌, 기술적 또는 재정적 문제, 직장과 가정에서의 어려움이 우리의 능력에 대해 충분히 생각해보는 데 도움이 된다. 해결책이 필요한 문제들은 창의적인 해답들을 개발하기 위해 우리의 뇌를 사용하도록 강요한다. 시련과 갈등을 주는, 변화무쌍한 지역을 걸어가는 것은 우리 감각과 마음에 아무런 어려움을 주지 않는 지역을 다니는 것보다 창의성에 더 도움을 준다. 우리의 2백만년 역사는 어려움과 갈등으로 가득 차 있다.

Why? 왜 정답일까?

첫 문장에 이어 But 뒤로 우리가 문제를 해결하고 창의성을 발현하도록 돕는 것은 우리 삶의 시련과 각종 문제(But small disagreements ~, trouble ~, or challenges ~ can help us think through our own capabilities.)라는 내용이 제시된다. 따라서 글의 제목으로 가장 적절한 것은 ④ '창의성은 위험을 피하는 것에서 근원하지 않는다'이다.

- **conflict** ⑩ 갈등
- **medical insurance** 의료 보험
- **disagreement** ⑩ 불화, 불일치
- **capability** ⑩ 능력
- **varied** ⓐ 다양한
- **pose a challenge to** ~에 어려움을 주다
- **play safe** 위험을 피하다, 신중을 기하다
- **assume** ⓥ 가정하다, 추정하다
- **sufficient** ⓐ 충분한
- **think through** ~에 대해 충분히 생각하다
- **landscape** ⑩ 풍경, 지역
- **occasional** ⓐ 이따금씩 일어나는
- **be packed with** ~로 가득 차다
- **overcome** ⓥ 극복하다

구문 풀이

13행 Navigating landscapes [that are varied], [that offer trials and
　　　주어(동명사구)　　　주격 관·대1　　　　주격 관·대2
occasional conflicts], is more helpful to creativity than hanging out
　　　　　　　　동사(단수)
in landscapes [that pose no challenge to our senses and our minds].
선행사　　　　주격 관·대

---

04 Gary Becker의 생애 　　　정답률 86% | 정답 ③

Gary Becker에 관한 다음 글의 내용과 일치하지 않는 것은?
① New York City의 Brooklyn에서 자랐다.
② 아버지는 금융과 정치 문제에 깊은 관심이 있었다.
☑ Princeton University에서의 경제학 교육에 만족했다.
④ 1955년에 경제학 박사 학위를 취득했다.
⑤ *Business Week*에 경제학 칼럼을 기고했다.

[본문 해석]
「Gary Becker는 1930년 Pennsylvania 주 Pottsville에서 태어났고 New York City의 Brooklyn에서 자랐다.」「교육을 제대로 받지 못한 그의 아버지는 금융과 정치 문제에 깊은 관심이 있었다.」고등학교를 졸업한 후, Becker는 Princeton University로 진학했고, 거기서 그는 경제학을 전공했다. 「'Princeton University에서의 경제학 교육이 현실적인 문제를 다루고 있는 것처럼 보이지 않았기' 때문에 그는 그것에 불만족했다.」「그는 1955년에 University of Chicago에서 경제학 박사 학위를 취득했다.」차별의 경제학에 대한 그의 박사 논문은 노벨상 위원회에 의해 경제학에 대한 중요한 기여로 언급되었다. 「1985년부터, Becker는 *Business Week*에 경제학적 분석과 아이디어를 일반 대중에게 설명하는 경제학 칼럼을 정기적으로 기고했다.」1992년에, 그는 노벨 경제학상을 수상했다.

Why? 왜 정답일까?
'He was dissatisfied with his economic education at Princeton University ~'에서 Gary Becker는 Princeton University에서의 경제학 교육에 불만족했다고 하므로, 내용과 일치하지 않는 것은 ③ 'Princeton University에서의 경제학 교육에 만족했다.'이다.

Why? 왜 오답일까?
① 'Gary Becker ~ grew up in Brooklyn, New York City.'의 내용과 일치한다.
② 'His father, who was not well educated, had a deep interest in financial and political issues.'의 내용과 일치한다.
④ 'He earned a doctor's degree in economics from the University of Chicago in 1955.'의 내용과 일치한다.
⑤ 'Since 1985, Becker had written a regular economics column in *Business Week*, ~'의 내용과 일치한다.

● **financial** ⓐ 재정적인
● **doctoral paper** 박사 논문
● **mention** ⓥ 언급하다
● **analysis** ⓝ 분석
● **handle** ⓥ 다루다, 대처하다
● **discrimination** ⓝ 차별
● **contribution** ⓝ 기여, 이바지
● **award** ⓥ 상을 주다, 수여하다

구문 풀이

15행 In 1992, he was awarded the Nobel Prize in economic science.
　　　　　　　4형식 수동태　　　　　　　　직접목적어

★★★ 1등급 대비 고난도 3점 문제

05 물을 절약하는 다양한 방법 　　　정답률 21% | 정답 ③

다음 글의 밑줄 친 부분 중, 어법상 틀린 것은? [3점]

[본문 해석]
물에 대한 소비자 의식 향상이 가장 많은 물을 절약하는 가장 저렴한 방법일지 모르지만, 그것이 소비자들이 물 보존에 기여할 수 있는 유일한 방법은 아니다. 기술이 이전보다 더 빠르게 진보하면서, 소비자들이 물을 더 절약하기 위해 가정에 설치할 수 있는 장치들이 많이 있다. 35개가 넘는 고효율 변기 모델이 오늘날 미국 시장에 있으며, 이 중 일부는 물을 내릴 때마다 1.3갤런 미만을 사용한다. 200달러에서 시작하는 이 변기들은 가격이 적당하고 일반 소비자가 일 년에 수백 갤런의 물을 절약하는 데 도움이 될 수 있다. 가장 효율이 높다고

공식적으로 승인된 기기들은 소비자가 알 수 있게 Energy Star 로고가 붙어 있다. 그런 등급의 세탁기들은 40갤런을 사용하는 구형 제품에 비해, 1회 세탁 시 18에서 25갤런의 물을 사용한다. 고효율 식기 세척기는 훨씬 더 많은 물을 절약한다. 이런 기계들은 구형 모델보다 물을 50퍼센트까지 덜 사용한다.

Why? 왜 정답일까?
③을 포함한 문장을 보면 문장이 두 개인데 접속사가 없으므로 접속사와 대명사, 두 가지 역할을 할 수 있는 관계대명사가 필요하다. 따라서 them 대신 which가 오는 것이 어법상 맞다. 어법상 틀린 것은 ③이다.

Why? 왜 오답일까?
① **to save**는 앞의 the cheapest way를 꾸미는 형용사적 용법으로 쓰였으므로 어법상 맞다.
② **plenty of devices**가 주어이므로 복수 동사 are이 온 것은 어법상 맞다.
④ 부사 **officially**는 뒤의 형용사 approved를 꾸미고 있으므로 어법상 맞다.
⑤ **even**은 뒤의 비교급 more을 강조하므로 어법상 맞다.

● **improve** ⓥ 개선되다, 향상시키다
● **contribute to** ~에 기여하다
● **plenty of** ~이 많은
● **flush** ⓝ 물을 내림
● **approve** ⓥ 승인(시인)하다, 증명하다
● **alert** ⓥ 알 수 있게 하다, 알려주다
● **consciousness** ⓝ 의식, 자각
● **progress** ⓥ 진보하다
● **efficiency** ⓝ 효율
● **appliance** ⓝ 기기, 가전제품
● **be tagged with** ~에 붙어 있다

구문 풀이

4행 With technology progressing faster than ever before, / there
　　　「with + 목적어 + 목적격 보어(현재분사)」
are plenty of devices [that consumers can install in their homes to
　　　　　　　　　　　　　목적격 관계대명사
save more].

★★ 문제 해결 꿀~팁 ★★

▶ 많이 틀린 이유는?
이 문항의 경우 정답인 ③보다 오답인 ④의 선택률이 더 높았다. '형용사 vs. 부사'라는 주제 자체는 빈출이지만 approved를 꾸미는 부사 officially가 명사 Appliances 뒤에 나왔기 때문에 자칫 명사만 보고서 형용사가 들어가야 한다고 오해하기 쉬운 문제였다.

▶ 문제 해결 방법은?
어법 문항은 '돌다리도 두들겨 보는' 심정으로 풀 필요가 있다. 일단 답을 골랐더라도 한 번쯤은 문장별로 구조를 가볍게 훑으며 답을 확인하는 습관을 들이자.

---

06 성공한 사람들의 취침 전 습관 　　　정답률 54% | 정답 ③

(A), (B), (C)의 각 네모 안에서 문맥에 맞는 낱말로 가장 적절한 것은? [3점]

	(A)	(B)	(C)
①	regretful 후회한	hardship 어려움	avoid 피한다
②	regretful 후회한	success 성공	employ 이용한다
☑	thankful 감사함을 느낀	hardship 어려움	avoid 피한다
④	thankful 감사함을 느낀	success 성공	avoid 피한다
⑤	thankful 감사함을 느낀	hardship 어려움	employ 이용한다

[본문 해석]
성공한 많은 사람들은 좋은 취침 시간 습관을 지키는 경향이 있다. 그들은 잠들기 바로 전 하루 동안 있었던 일 중 (A) 감사함을 느낀 3가지 일에 대해 반추하거나 글로 써 보는 시간을 갖는다. 감사한 일들에 대해 일기를 쓰는 것은 어느 분야에서건 그들이 그날 이룬 발전에 대해 상기시켜준다. 이는 특히 그들이 (B) 어려움을 겪을 때 동기가 부여된 상태를 유지하는 핵심적인 방법이다. (어려움을 겪는) 이런 경우에 많은 사람들은 힘든 날의 부정적인 상황을 되풀이해서 생각하는 덫에 빠져든다. 하지만 하루가 얼마나 힘들게 흘러갔는가에 상관없이, 성공한 사람들은 보통 그런 부정적인 자기 대화의 덫을 (C) 피한다. 그것은 오로지 더 많은 스트레스를 만들어낸다는 것을 알기 때문이다.

Why? 왜 정답일까?
(A) 'Keeping a diary of things that they appreciate reminds them of the progress they made that day in any aspect of their lives.'에서 성공한 사람

들은 감사한 일들에 대해 일기를 쓰고 자기가 당일 이룬 발전에 대해 상기할 기회를 갖게 된다고 이야기하므로, (A)에는 'thankful'이 들어가야 적절하다.

(B) 'In such case, many people fall easily into the trap of replaying negative situations from a hard day.'에서 '이러한 경우'는 맥락상 사람들이 어려움을 겪는 경우를 가리키는 말이다. (B)에서 '어려움'을 먼저 언급해야 such cases가 이러한 내용을 나타낼 수 있으므로, (B)에는 'hardship'이 들어가야 적절하다.

(C) 'That is because they know it will only create more stress.'에서 알수 있듯이 부정적인 자기 대화는 더 많은 스트레스를 불러오므로, 성공한 사람들은 이를 '피할' 것이다. 따라서 (C)에는 'avoid'가 들어가야 적절하다. 정답은 ③ '(A) thankful (감사함을 느낀) – (B) hardship(어려움) – (C) avoid(피한다)'이다.

- successful ⓐ 성공한
- reflect on ~에 대해 반추하다
- appreciate ⓥ 감사하다
- progress ⓝ 발전, 진보
- situation ⓝ 상황, 처지
- typically ⓐⓓ 보통, 대개, 전형적으로
- routine ⓝ 습관, 틀
- regretful ⓐ 후회하는
- remind ⓥ 상기시키다
- fall into ~에 빠지다
- regardless of ~에 상관없이
- create ⓥ 만들다, 창조하다

구문 풀이

4행 Keeping a diary of things [that they appreciate]
주어(동명사) 　　목적격 관계대명사(생략 가능)
reminds them of the progress [they made that day in any aspect of
「remind A of B : A에게 B를 상기시키다」　(목적격 관계대명사 생략)
their lives].

★★★ 1등급 대비 고난도 3점 문제

07 생물의 진화 방향을 이끄는 실내 공간과 생활　정답률 46% | 정답 ③

다음 빈칸에 들어갈 말로 가장 적절한 것을 고르시오. [3점]

① produce chemicals to protect themselves
　스스로를 보호하고자 화학 물질을 만들어낼
② become extinct with the destroyed habitats
　파괴된 서식지와 함께 멸종할
✓③ evolve the traits they need to thrive indoors
　실내에서 번성하기 위해 자신에게 필요한 특성들을 진화시킬
④ compete with outside organisms to find their prey
　먹잇감을 찾고자 야외 생물들과 경쟁할
⑤ break the boundaries between wildlife and humans
　야생 종과 인간 사이의 경계를 무너뜨릴

[본문 해석]

우리의 집은 단순한 생태계가 아니라 독특한 곳이며, 실내 환경에 적응된 종들을 수용하고 새로운 방향으로 진화를 밀어붙인다. 실내 미생물, 곤충, 그리고 쥐들은 모두 항균제, 살충제, 독에 대한 내성을 키우면서 우리의 화학적 공격에서 살아남을 수 있는 능력을 진화시켰다. 독일 바퀴벌레는 바퀴벌레 덫에서 미끼로 흔히 사용되는 포도당에 대한 혐오감을 발달시킨 것으로 알려져 있다. 야외에 있는 상대방에 비해 먹이를 잡아먹을 기회가 더 적은 일부 실내 곤충은 먹이가 제한적일 때 생존할 수 있는 능력을 발달시킨 것으로 보인다. Dunn과 다른 생태학자들은 지구가 점점 더 발전되고 도시화되면서, 더 많은 종들이 실내에서 번성하기 위해 자신에게 필요한 특성들을 진화시킬 것이라고 말했다. 충분히 긴 시간에 걸쳐, 실내 생활은 또한 우리의 진화를 이끌 수 있었다. 아마도 실내 생활을 좋아하는 나의 모습은 인류의 미래를 대변할 것이다.

Why? 왜 정답일까?

첫 문장과 빈칸 뒤의 문장에서 집, 즉 실내 공간이 우리 진화를 이끌어 간다(indoor living could drive our evolution)는 주제를 반복하여 제시한다. 따라서 빈칸에 들어갈 말로 가장 적절한 것은 우리가 실내 생활에 필요한 방향으로 발전해 간다는 의미의 ③ '실내에서 번성하기 위해 자신에게 필요한 특성들을 진화시킬'이다.

- host ⓥ 접대하다, 주최하다
- resistance ⓝ 내성, 저항력
- insecticide ⓝ 살충제
- distaste ⓝ 혐오
- bait ⓝ 미끼
- ecologist ⓝ 생태학자
- extinct ⓐ 멸종한
- prey ⓝ 먹잇감
- microbe ⓝ 미생물
- antibacterial ⓐ 항균성의 ⓝ 항균제
- cockroach ⓝ 바퀴벌레
- glucose ⓝ 포도당
- counterpart ⓝ 상대방, 대응물
- represent ⓥ 표현하다, 나타내다
- habitat ⓝ 서식지

구문 풀이

6행 German cockroaches are known to have developed a
　　　　　「be known + to have p.p. : ~했다고 알려지다(완료부정사)」
distaste for glucose, which is commonly used as bait in roach traps.
　　　　　　　선행사　　　계속적 용법(보충 설명)

★★ 문제 해결 꿀~팁 ★★

▶ 많이 틀린 이유는?
chemical attacks 등 지엽적 소재만 보면 ①을 답으로 고르기 쉽다. 하지만 풀이의 핵심은 생태계의 생명체들이 '어떤 방향으로' 진화하도록 유도되어 왔는지를 파악하는 데 있다.
▶ 문제 해결 방법은?
빈칸 뒤를 보면 '실내 생활이 우리 진화를 이끌 수 있었다(indoor living could drive our evolution)'는 결론이 나온다. 이 결론과 동일한 말이 빈칸에도 들어갈 것이다.

★★★ 1등급 대비 고난도 3점 문제

08 일과 가정의 경계　정답률 26% | 정답 ⑤

글의 흐름으로 보아, 주어진 문장이 들어가기에 가장 적절한 곳을 고르시오. [3점]

[본문 해석]

휴대용 디지털 기술이 언제 어디서든 작업하는 것을 점차 가능하게 하면서, 직장과 가정의 경계가 흐릿해지고 있다. 사람들은 직장과 외부의 책임을 수행하기 위해 자기 시간을 관리하기를 바라는 방식이 서로 다르다. ① 어떤 사람들은 경계 교차 지점이 최소화되도록 역할을 분리하거나 분할하기를 선호한다. ② 예를 들어, 이러한 사람들은 직장과 가정을 위한 별개의 이메일 계정을 유지하고 직장에서 일하려고 하며, 쉴 때나 일하지 않는 시간 중에만 집안일을 처리하려고 할지도 모른다. ③ 우리는 더 많은 이러한 '분할자들'이 하나는 업무용이고 다른 하나는 개인용인 전화기 두 대를 가지고 다니고 있음을 심지어 알게 되었다. ④ 유연근무제는 이런 사람들에게 잘 적용되는데, 직장에서의 시간과 다른 역할에서의 시간 간에 더 큰 구별을 가능하게 하기 때문이다. ⑤ 다른 사람들은 하루 종일 직장과 가정의 역할을 통합하기를 선호한다. 이것은 직장으로 돌아가서 받은 편지함에서 수백 개의 메시지를 발견하는 대신, 사무실에서 아이들과 문자 메시지를 계속 주고받거나, 집에 있을 때와 휴가 중에 이메일을 체크하는 것을 수반할 수도 있다.

Why? 왜 정답일까?

⑤ 앞까지 일과 가정을 '분리하는' 사람들을 언급하는데, ⑤ 뒤에는 직장에서도 가족과 연락하고, 집에 있을 때도 업무 처리를 하는 등 둘을 '통합하는' 사람들을 언급하고 있다. 따라서 '통합자들'에 관한 화제로 처음 넘어가는 주어진 문장이 들어가기에 가장 적절한 곳은 ⑤이다.

- integrate ⓥ 통합하다
- boundary ⓝ 경계
- outside ⓐ 외부의
- separate ⓥ 분리하다 ⓐ 분리된, 개별의
- minimize ⓥ 최소화하다
- conduct ⓥ 수행하다
- carry ⓥ 들고 다니다
- distinction ⓝ 구별
- constantly ⓐⓓ 계속
- on vacation 휴가 중인
- all day long 하루 종일
- portable ⓐ 휴대용의
- responsibility ⓝ 책무, 책임
- segment ⓥ 분할하다, 나누다
- account ⓝ 계정
- workplace ⓝ 직장
- flexible schedule 유연근무제
- entail ⓥ 수반하다
- monitor ⓥ 확인하다, 감독하다, 점검하다
- inbox ⓝ 수신함

구문 풀이

3행 Boundaries between work and home are blurring as portable
　　　　　　　　　　　　　　　　　　　　　　가목적어 접속사(~ 때문에)
digital technology makes it increasingly possible to work anywhere,
　　　　　　　　5형식 동사　　목적격 보어　　　　진목적어
anytime.

★★ 문제 해결 꿀~팁 ★★

▶ 많이 틀린 이유는?
주어진 문장이 Other로 시작하므로, 앞에 Some이 있는 ②를 고르기 쉽다. 「Some ~ Other …」의 대구가 자연스러워 보이기 때문이다. 하지만 ② 뒤의 these people이 문맥상 ② 앞의 Some people이므로, 주어진 문장을 ②에 넣어 대명사의 흐름을 끊으면 안 된다. 또한 뒤에 갑자기 '유연근무제'라는 새로운 소재가 등장하는 ④도 정답처럼 보이기 쉽지만, ④ 앞뒤가 여전히 '일과 가정을 분리하는' 사람들에 대해서 설명하고 있어서 흐름이 끊기지 않기 때문에 다른 문장이 필요하지 않다.
▶ 문제 해결 방법은?
⑤ 뒤의 'trading ~ or monitoring ~'이 주어진 문장의 'integrating ~'에 대한 예시임을 파악해야 한다.

09 내집단을 동일시하고 선호하는 인간의 선천적 경향　정답률 49% | 정답 ①

다음 글의 내용을 한 문장으로 요약하고자 한다. 빈칸 (A), (B)에 들어갈 말로 가장 적절한 것은?

	(A)		(B)		(A)		(B)
✓	familiar 친숙한	……	inborn 선천적인	②	familiar 친숙한	……	acquired 후천적인
③	foreign 이질적인	……	cultural 문화적인	④	foreign 이질적인	……	learned 학습된
⑤	formal 공식적인	……	innate 타고난				

[본문 해석]

2007년에 있었던 연구에서 Katherine Kinzler와 그녀의 하버드 동료들은 내(內)집단과 동일시하려는 우리의 경향이 상당 부분 유아기에 시작되고 선천적일 수 있음을 보여 주었다. Kinzler와 그녀의 팀은 가족들이 영어로만 말하는 한 무리의 5개월 된 아이들을 골라 두 개의 영상을 보여 주었다. 한 영상에서 한 여성이 영어를 말하고 있었다. 다른 영상에서는 한 여성이 스페인어로 말하고 있었다. 그러고 나서 그들에게 두 여성 모두 말없이 나란히 있는 화면을 보여 주었다. 유아 심리학 연구에서 애착이나 관심의 표준 척도는 주목인데, 아기들은 분명 그들이 더 좋아하는 대상을 더 오래 쳐다볼 것이다. Kinzler의 연구에서 아기들은 영어 사용자들을 더 오래 쳐다보았다. 다른 연구들에서 연구자들은 유아들이 자신들과 같은 언어를 사용하는 사람이 제공하는 장난감을 받을 가능성이 더 높다는 점을 발견했다. 심리학자들은 '우리와 같은 종류'에 대한 우리의 내재된 진화론적인 선호에 대한 증거로 이것들과 다른 실험들을 반복해서 인용한다.

➡ (A) 친숙한 언어를 사용하는 사람들에 대한 유아들의 더 호의적인 반응은 내집단 구성원들을 선호하는 (B) 선천적인 경향이 있을 수 있음을 보여 준다.

Why? 왜 정답일까?

첫 문장과 마지막 문장(~ our tendency to identify with an in-group to a large degree begins in infancy and may be innate. / ~ our built-in evolutionary preference for "our own kind.")을 통해 인간은 내집단, 즉 친숙하고 비슷한 집단을 거의 선천적이라 볼 수 있을 정도로 아주 이른 시기부터 선호한다는 것을 알 수 있다. 따라서 요약문의 빈칸 (A), (B)에 들어갈 말로 가장 적절한 것은 ① '(A) familiar(친숙한), (B) inborn(선천적인)'이다.

- **colleague** ⓝ 동료
- **in-group** ⓝ 내(內)집단
- **innate** ⓐ 타고난, 선천적인
- **measure** ⓝ 척도, 기준
- **apparently** ⓐⓓ 분명히, 명백히
- **infant** ⓝ 유아
- **cite** ⓥ 인용하다
- **preference** ⓝ 선호
- **inborn** ⓐ 타고난
- **tendency** ⓝ 경향
- **infancy** ⓝ 유아기
- **psychology** ⓝ 심리학
- **interest** ⓝ 관심
- **stare at** ~을 쳐다보다, 응시하다
- **routinely** ⓐⓓ 판에 박힌 듯, 관례대로
- **evolutionary** ⓐ 진화의
- **favorable** ⓐ 호의적인
- **acquired** ⓐ 후천적인, 습득된

구문 풀이

1행 In their study in 2007 Katherine Kinzler and her colleagues
　　　　접속사(~것) 주어
at Harvard showed that our tendency to identify with an in-group
　　　　　　　　　　　　　　　　　형용사적 용법
to a large degree begins in infancy and may be innate.
부사구(상당 부분)　　동사1　　　　　　동사2

10-12 동물도 상실의 고통을 느낀다는 것을 깨달은 사냥꾼 왕

[본문 해석]

(A)

옛날 옛적에 사냥에 대해 엄청난 열정을 가진 젊은 왕이 살았다. 그의 왕국은 히말라야 산기슭에 위치해 있었다. 『매년 한 번씩, 그는 근처의 숲으로 사냥하러 가고는 했다.』 (a) 그는 모든 필요한 준비를 하고 자신의 사냥 여행을 떠나고는 했다.
└─『』: 12번 ①의 근거 일치

(C)

여느 해처럼, 사냥철이 왔다. 궁궐에서 준비가 시작되었고 왕은 (c) 자신의 사냥 여행을 갈 준비를 했다. 숲속 깊은 곳에서 그는 아름다운 야생 사슴을 발견했다. 그것은 큰 수사슴이었다. 그의 겨냥은 완벽했다. 『단 한 발의 화살로 그 사슴을 잡고서 왕은 의기양양했다.』 (d) 그 의기양양한 사냥꾼은 그 사슴의 가죽으로 사냥용 북을 만들도록 명령했다.
└─『』: 12번 ③의 근거 일치

(B)

계절이 바뀌었다. 1년이 지나갔다. 그리고 또 다시 사냥하러 갈 때가 되었다. 왕은 작년과 같은 숲으로 갔다. (b) 그는 아름다운 사슴 가죽으로 만든 북을 사용하여 동물을 몰았다. 그러나 아무도 오지 않았다. 모든 동물이 안전한 곳으로 도망쳤는데, 암사슴 한 마리는 예외였다. 『암사슴은 북 치는 사람에게 점점 더 가까이 다가왔다.』 갑자기, 암사슴은 두려움 없이 사슴 가죽으로 만든 북을 핥기 시작했다.
└─『』: 12번 ②의 근거 불일치

(D)

이 광경을 보고 왕은 놀랐다. 『한 나이 든 신하가 이 이상한 행동의 이유를 알고 있었다.』 "이 북을 만드는 데 사용된 사슴 가죽은 암사슴의 짝의 것인데, 우리가 작년에 사냥한 그 사슴입니다. 이 암사슴은 짝의 죽음을 애도하고 있는 것입니다."라고 (e) 그 남자는 말했다. 이 말을 듣자마자, 왕의 마음이 바뀌었다. 그는 동물도 역시 상실의 고통을 느낀다는 것을 전혀 몰랐다. 『그는 그날 이후 다시는 결코 야생 동물을 사냥하지 않겠다고 약속했다.』
└─『』: 12번 ④의 근거 일치　└─『』: 12번 ⑤의 근거 일치

- **passion** ⓝ 열정
- **preparation** ⓝ 준비, 채비
- **previous** ⓐ 이전의
- **lick** ⓥ 핥다
- **aim** ⓝ 겨냥, 목표 ⓥ 겨누다
- **loss** ⓝ 상실
- **at the foot of** ~의 기슭에, 하단부에
- **set out for** ~을 향해 나서다
- **fearlessly** ⓐⓓ 겁 없이, 대담하게
- **spot** ⓥ 알아채다, 발견하다
- **have a change of heart** 마음을 바꾸다

구문 풀이

(A) 1행 Once upon a time, there lived a young king [who had a great
　　　　　　　　　　　　　　동사　　주어　　　　주격 관계대명사
passion for hunting].

(C) 7행 The proud hunter ordered a hunting drum to be made out of
　　　　　　　　　　　　　　『order + 목적어 + to부정사 : ~이 …하게 명령하다』
the skin of the deer.

(D) 2행 The deerskin used to make this drum belonged to her mate,
　　　　　주어　　　과거분사 부사적 용법(목적)　　　동사
the deer [who(m) we hunted last year].
동격(= her mate)

(D) 7행 He made a promise, from that day on, to never again hunt
　　　　　『to + 부사 + 동사원형 : 분리부정사(부정사를 수식하는 부사가 to와 동사원형 사이에 삽입된 형태)』
wild animals.

10 글의 순서 파악　정답률 82% | 정답 ②

주어진 글 (A)에 이어질 내용을 순서에 맞게 배열한 것으로 가장 적절한 것은?

① (B) – (D) – (C)　　　　✓ (C) – (B) – (D)
③ (C) – (D) – (B)　　　　④ (D) – (B) – (C)
⑤ (D) – (C) – (B)

Why? 왜 정답일까?

시간적 단서를 잘 활용해야 하는 순서 문제이다. 옛날에 어느 한 왕이 사냥에 대한 열정이 있어 매년 사냥 여행을 떠났다는 내용의 (A) 뒤에는, 다른 모든 해처럼 사냥철이 와서 왕이 사냥을 떠났고 아름다운 야생 사슴 한 마리를 잡아 그 기념으로 북을 만들었다는 내용의 (C)가 이어져야 한다. 이어서 (B)에서는 '1년 후' 다시 사냥하러 갈 때가 되어 길을 떠난 왕이 북소리에 피하지 않고 도리어 가까이 오는 암사슴 한 마리를 발견했다는 내용이 전개된다. 마지막으로 (D)는 '이 광경'에 왕이 놀라자, 한 신하가 상황을 설명해주었다는 내용으로 마무리된다. 따라서 글의 순서로 가장 적절한 것은 ② '(C) – (B) – (D)'이다.

11 지칭 추론　정답률 81% | 정답 ⑤

밑줄 친 (a) ~ (e) 중에서 가리키는 대상이 나머지 넷과 다른 것은?

① (a)　② (b)　③ (c)　④ (d)　✓ (e)

Why? 왜 정답일까?

(a), (b), (c), (d)는 the king을, (e)는 An old servant를 가리키므로, (a) ~ (e) 중에서 가리키는 대상이 다른 하나는 ⑤ '(e)'이다.

12 세부 내용 파악　정답률 80% | 정답 ②

윗글에 관한 내용으로 적절하지 않은 것은?

① 왕은 매년 근처의 숲으로 사냥 여행을 갔다.
✓ 암사슴은 북 치는 사람으로부터 도망갔다.
③ 왕은 화살로 단번에 수사슴을 맞혔다.
④ 한 나이 든 신하가 암사슴의 행동의 이유를 알고 있었다.
⑤ 왕은 다시는 야생 동물을 사냥하지 않겠다고 약속했다.

Why? 왜 정답일까?

(B) 'She came closer and closer to the drummer.'에서 모든 동물들이 북소리를 듣고는 안전한 곳으로 피신하는 가운데 암사슴 한 마리는 북 치는 사람에게 가까이 다가왔다고 하므로, 내용과 일치하지 않는 것은 ② '암사슴은 북 치는 사람으로부터 도망갔다.'이다.

Why? 왜 오답일까?

① (A) 'Once every year, he would go hunting in the nearby forests.'의 내용과 일치한다.
③ (C) 'When he killed the deer with just one shot of his arrow, ~'의 내용과 일치한다.
④ (D) 'An old servant had an answer to this strange behavior.'의 내용과 일치한다.
⑤ (D) 'He made a promise, from that day on, to never again hunt wild animals.'의 내용과 일치한다.

DAY 15 — 20분 미니 모의고사

01 ②	02 ⑤	03 ⑤	04 ③	05 ④
06 ②	07 ①	08 ①	09 ④	10 ②
11 ①	12 ⑤			

01 공원에서 얼마 못 놀고 돌아가게 된 Matthew 정답률 93% | 정답 ②

다음 글에 드러난 Matthew의 심경 변화로 가장 적절한 것은?
① embarrassed → indifferent (당황한 → 무관심한)
✓ excited → disappointed (신난 → 실망한)
③ cheerful → ashamed (즐거운 → 수치스러운)
④ nervous → touched (긴장한 → 감동한)
⑤ scared → relaxed (겁에 질린 → 느긋한)

[본문 해석]

어느 토요일 아침, Matthew의 어머니는 Matthew에게 공원으로 데리고 가겠다고 말했다. 그의 얼굴에 환한 미소가 드리워졌다. 그는 밖에 나가서 노는 것을 좋아했기 때문에, 나가기 위해 서둘러 아침을 먹고 옷을 입었다. 공원에 도착했을 때, Matthew는 그네를 향해 바로 뛰어갔다. 그것은 그가 공원에서 가장 좋아하는 것이었다. 하지만 그네는 이미 모두 이용되고 있었다. 그의 어머니는 그네를 이용할 수 있을 때까지 미끄럼틀을 탈 수 있다고 말했지만, 그것은 부서져 있었다. 갑자기 그의 어머니가 전화를 받고 Matthew에게 떠나야 한다고 말했다. 그는 가슴이 내려앉았다.

Why? 왜 정답일까?

아침에 어머니와 함께 공원으로 가게 되어 기뻐하던 Matthew가(A big smile came across his face.) 제대로 놀지도 못한 채 갑자기 떠나야 한다는 이야기를 듣고 실망했다(His heart sank.)는 내용의 글이다. 따라서 Matthew의 심경 변화로 가장 적절한 것은 ② '신난 → 실망한'이다.

- take ⓥ 데리고 가다
- dress ⓥ 옷을 입다
- swing ⓝ 그네
- slide ⓝ 미끄럼틀
- broken ⓐ 고장난, 부서진
- sink ⓥ 가라앉다
- embarrassed ⓐ 당황한
- touched ⓐ 감동한

구문 풀이

3행 As he loved to play outside, he ate his breakfast and (접속사(이유)) (동사1) got dressed quickly so (that) they could go. (동사2) (접속사(목적): ~하도록)

02 상업용 블로그를 성공시킬 방법 정답률 89% | 정답 ⑤

다음 글에서 필자가 주장하는 바로 가장 적절한 것은?
① 인터넷 게시물에 대한 윤리적 기준을 세워야 한다.
② 블로그를 전문적으로 관리할 인력을 마련해야 한다.
③ 신제품 개발을 위해 상업용 블로그를 적극 활용해야 한다.
④ 상품에 대한 고객들의 반응을 정기적으로 분석할 필요가 있다.
✓ 상업용 블로그는 사람들이 흥미 있어 할 정보를 제공해야 한다.

[본문 해석]

여러분은 이미 사업체를 가지고 있고 여러분의 제품을 팔 수 있도록 블로그를 시작하려는 참이다. 유감스럽게도, 이 지점에서 '비즈니스 정신'은 나쁜 것이 될 수 있다. 대부분의 사람들은 제품을 홍보하는 성공적인 상업용 블로그를 가지기 위해서 엄격하게 '그 주제에' 머물러야 한다고 믿는다. 만일 여러분이 그저 뻔뻔스럽게 제품을 홍보하는 일만 하면, 그렇다면 누가 여러분이 쓰고 있는 최신 글을 읽고 싶어할까? 대신에, 사람들이 계속해서 다시 방문할 이유를 가지도록 여러분은 어떤 유용하거나 재미있는 정보를 무료로 줄 필요가 있다. 이렇게 해야만 여러분은 다음번에 판매할 수 있게 될 관심 있는 독자를 만들 수 있다. 따라서, 상업용 블로그로 성공하기 위한 가장 좋은 방법은 여러분의 독자들이 관심을 가질 만한 것들에 대해 글을 쓰는 것이다.

Why? 왜 정답일까?

'Instead, you need to give some useful or entertaining information ~.'

과 'So, the best way to be successful with a business blog is to write about things that your audience will be interested in.'에서 상업용 블로그를 성공시키려면 제품이나 사업에 관한 홍보만 하지 말고 사람들이 관심을 보일 내용에 관해 글을 쓰라고 한다. 따라서 필자가 주장하는 바로 가장 적절한 것은 ⑤ '상업용 블로그는 사람들이 흥미 있어 할 정보를 제공해야 한다.'이다.

- launch ⓥ 시작하다, 출시하다
- promote ⓥ 홍보하다
- shamelessly 〖ad〗 뻔뻔하게
- give away 공짜로 주다, 거저 주다
- entertaining ⓐ 재미있는
- audience ⓝ 청중, 독자
- unfortunately 〖ad〗 안타깝게도
- strictly 〖ad〗 엄격하게
- latest ⓐ 최신의
- useful ⓐ 유용한
- interested ⓐ 흥미를 느끼는
- successful ⓐ 성공적인

구문 풀이

11행 Only by doing this can you create an interested audience
준부정어(오로지 ~밖에)　조동사 주어　동사원형(도치)
that you will then be able to sell to.

---

03 자신의 의견을 때때로 내려놓기 　정답률 60% | 정답 ⑤

다음 글의 요지로 가장 적절한 것은?
① 대부분의 사람들은 진리에 도달하지 못하고 고통을 받는다.
② 맹목적으로 다른 사람의 의견을 받아들이는 것은 위험하다.
③ 남을 설득하기 위해서는 타당한 증거로 주장을 뒷받침해야 한다.
④ 믿을만한 사람이 누구인지 판단하려면 열린 마음을 가져야 한다.
☑ 자신의 의견이 최선이 아닐 수 있다는 것을 인정하는 것이 필요하다.

[본문 해석]

독자적으로 생각하고 자신이 믿는 것을 위해 싸우는 것도 중요하지만, 자신의 생각을 위해 싸우기를 중단하고 신뢰할 수 있는 집단이 가장 좋다고 생각하는 것을 받아들이는 쪽으로 나아 가는 것이 더 현명한 때가 온다. 이것은 매우 어려울 수 있다. 하지만 여러분이 마음을 열고 신뢰할 수 있는 집단의 결론이 여러분이 생각하는 어떤 것보다 낫다는 믿음을 갖는 것이 더 영리하고 궁극적으로 더 좋다. 만약 여러분이 그들의 생각을 이해할 수 없다면, 여러분은 아마도 단지 그들이 생각하는 방식을 보지 못하는 것이다. 모든 증거와 신뢰할 수 있는 사람들이 당신에게 반대할 때 당신이 최선이라고 생각하는 것을 계속한다면, 당신은 위험할 정도로 자신감에 차 있는 것이다. 사실 대부분의 사람들은 놀랍도록 마음을 열게 되는 반면에, 어떤 사람들은 자신이 옳지 않았을 때 옳았다고 확신하는 것으로부터 여러 차례 많은 고통을 겪고 난 후에도 그러지 못한다.

Why? 왜 정답일까?

첫 문장과 세 번째 문장에서 때로는 자신의 의견보다 다른 의견이 더 낫다는 것을 받아들이는 것이 좋다(~ it's wiser to ~ move on to accepting what a trustworthy group of people think is best.)고 언급하는 것으로 볼 때, 글의 요지로 가장 적절한 것은 ⑤ '자신의 의견이 최선이 아닐 수 있다는 것을 인정하는 것이 필요하다.'이다.

- independently 〖ad〗 독자적으로
- trustworthy ⓐ 믿을 만한
- ultimately 〖ad〗 결국, 궁극적으로
- faith ⓝ 믿음
- whatever 〖pron〗 ~한 어떤 것
- evidence ⓝ 증거, 단서
- confident ⓐ 자신 있는
- repeatedly 〖ad〗 반복해서, 되풀이하여
- bet ⓥ ~이 틀림없다, 분명하다(무엇에 대해 거의 확신함을 나타냄)
- wiser ⓐ 지혜로운, 현명한
- extremely 〖ad〗 몹시, 극도로
- open-minded ⓐ 마음이 열린
- conclusion ⓝ 결론, (최종적인) 판단
- blind to ~을 보지 못하게 만들다
- against 〖prep〗 ~에 반대하여
- incredibly 〖ad〗 놀랍도록, 엄청나게
- encounter ⓥ 접하다, 마주하다

구문 풀이

5행 But it's smarter, and ultimately better for you to be open-
가주어　　　　　　　　　　　　의미상 주어　진주어구
minded and have faith {that the conclusions of a trustworthy group
주어(복수)
of people are better than whatever you think}.[ ]: 동격절(= faith)
동사　　　　　　복합관계대명사(~하는 무엇이든)

---

04 보트 투어 홍보 　정답률 97% | 정답 ③

Turtle Island Boat Tour에 관한 다음 안내문의 내용과 일치하지 않는 것은?
① 주말에는 하루에 두 번 운영된다.
② 17세 이상만 참가할 수 있다.

☑ 당일 예약이 가능하다.
④ 출발 시간 이후에는 환불이 불가능하다.
⑤ 전문 다이버와 함께 하는 스노클링 활동이 있다.

[본문 해석]

Turtle Island 보트 투어

환상적인 Turtle Island 보트 투어가 아름다운 바다 세계로 여러분을 초대합니다.

날짜: 2024년 6월 1일부터 8월 31일까지

투어 시간

주중	오후 1시 ~ 오후 5시
「주말	오전 9시 ~ 오후 1시
	오후 1시 ~ 오후 5시」

└「」: ①의 근거 일치

※ 각 투어는 네 시간 동안 진행됩니다.

표와 예약
- 투어별로 1인당 50달러 「(17세 이상만 참가할 수 있습니다.)」 ←「」: ②의 근거 일치
- 「예약은 늦어도 투어 당일 이틀 전에 완료되어야 합니다.」 ←「」: ③의 근거 불일치
- 「출발 시각 이후에는 환불 불가」 ←「」: ④의 근거 일치
- 각각의 투어 그룹 규모는 10명의 참가자로 제한됩니다.

활동
- 「전문 다이버와 함께 하는 스노클링」 ←「」: ⑤의 근거 일치
- 열대어에게 먹이 주기

※ 저희 웹사이트인 www.snorkelingti.com을 마음껏 둘러보세요.

Why? 왜 정답일까?

'Bookings must be completed no later than 2 days before the day of the tour.'에서 예약은 투어 이틀 전까지는 이뤄져야 한다고 하므로, 안내문의 내용과 일치하지 않는 것은 ③ '당일 예약이 가능하다.'이다.

Why? 왜 오답일까?

① 'Weekends / 9 a.m. – 1 p.m. / 1 p.m. – 5 p.m.'의 내용과 일치한다.
② '(Only those aged 17 and over can participate.)'의 내용과 일치한다.
④ 'No refunds after the departure time'의 내용과 일치한다.
⑤ 'Snorkeling with a professional diver'의 내용과 일치한다.

- fantastic ⓐ 환상적인
- booking ⓝ 예약
- refund ⓝ 환불
- snorkeling ⓝ 스노클링
- feel free to 편하게 ~하다
- weekday ⓝ 평일
- no later than 늦어도 ~까지
- departure ⓝ 출발
- feed ⓥ 먹이를 주다
- explore ⓥ 탐색하다

★★★ 1등급 대비 고난도 3점 문제

05 변화에 대한 잘못된 인식 　정답률 49% | 정답 ④

다음 글의 밑줄 친 부분 중, 어법상 틀린 것은? [3점]

[본문 해석]

변화를 인식할 때 우리는 가장 최근의 변화를 가장 혁신적인 것으로 여기는 경향이 있다. 이는 종종 사실과 일치하지 않는다. 통신기술에서 최근의 발전은 상대적인 관점으로 볼 때 19세기 말에 일어났던 발전보다 더 혁명적이지는 않다. 게다가, 그 결과로 일어난 경제 및 사회 변화의 측면에서, 인터넷 혁명은 세탁기 및 다른 가전제품들만큼 중요하지는 않았다. 이런 것들은 가사에 필요한 일의 양을 막대하게 줄여주어서 여성들이 노동시장에 진입하도록 하였고 사실상 가사 서비스 같은 직업을 없애 버렸다. 과거를 들여다보며 "망원경을 거꾸로 놓고서" 옛것을 과소평가하고 새것을 과대평가해서는 안 된다. 이는 우리가 국가 경제 정책, 기업 정책 및 자기 자신의 경력에 관한 모든 종류의 잘못된 결정을 내리도록 이끈다.

Why? 왜 정답일까?

④가 있는 문장에서 주어는 These things이고 'by vastly ~ household chores'가 콤마로 삽입된 구이다. 따라서 이 문장에 동사가 없으므로 allowing을 동사 allowed로 바꾸어야 한다. 어법상 틀린 것은 ④이다.

Why? 왜 오답일까?

① 앞에 'changes'라는 복수 명사가 나왔고 이를 받는 복수대명사로서 ones가 나왔다.

DAY 15

② 뒤에 주어가 없는 불완전한 절이 연결되므로 관계대명사 what을 쓴 것은 적절하다.
③ 현재완료 형태로 쓰인 'has not been'의 보어 역할을 할 형용사로서 important의 쓰임은 적절하다.
⑤ 「lead＋목적어＋to부정사」는 '～가 …하도록 이끌다'라는 뜻이다. 여기서 to부정사는 lead의 목적격 보어이다.

- perceive ⓥ 인식하다, 이해하다
- inconsistent ⓐ 일치하지 않는
- relative ⓐ 상대적인
- consequent ⓐ ～의 결과로 일어나는
- vastly ⓐⓓ 막대하게, 방대하게
- get rid of ～을 없애다, 제거하다
- overestimate ⓥ 과대평가하다
- revolutionary ⓐ 혁신적인, 혁명적인
- progress ⓝ 발전, 진보
- in terms of ～의 관점에서
- household appliance 가전제품
- virtually ⓐⓓ 사실상, 거의
- underestimate ⓥ 과소평가하다
- corporate ⓐ 기업의

구문 풀이

12행 We should not "put the telescope backward" (when we look 조동사＋not 동사원형1 (접속사(～할 때) into the past) / and underestimate the old and overestimate the new. 동사원형2 동사원형3

★★ 문제 해결 꿀~팁 ★★

▶ 많이 틀린 이유는?
대명사 one 개념이 익숙하지 않다면 ①을 오답으로 고르기 쉬운 문제였다.
one은 앞에 나온 명사를 그대로 받지 않고 종류가 같은 것을 폭넓게 가리킬 때 쓰는 대명사이다. 이때 앞에 나온 명사가 단수라면 one, 복수라면 ones의 형태로 쓰는데 여기서는 앞에 나온 명사가 changes라는 복수 명사이므로 ones가 나왔다.

▶ 문제 해결 방법은?
정답인 ④와 같이 '준동사 vs. 동사'를 묻는 문제에서는 주변에 서술어 역할을 하는 동사가 이미 있는지, 있다면 접속사가 있는지 없는지를 따져야 한다.
만일 서술어가 있는데 접속사도 함께 있다면 뒤에 추가로 동사가 나올 수 있지만, 접속사가 없다면 준동사가 나와야 한다. 여기서는 서술어가 없으므로 접속사 유무를 따질 필요 없이 밑줄 부분을 서술어로 바꾸면 된다.

06 광고주의 메시지 조절 　정답률 55% | 정답 ②

다음 글의 밑줄 친 부분 중, 문맥상 낱말의 쓰임이 적절하지 않은 것은?

[본문 해석]

광고주들은 그들이 홍보하는 상품의 시장 지위에 주장을 ① 맞추는 상당한 능력을 자주 보여주었다. 예를 들어, Fleischmann의 효모는 집에서 만든 빵을 요리하는 재료로 사용되었다. 하지만 20세기 초에 점점 더 많은 사람들이 가게나 빵집에서 빵을 사고 있었고, 그래서 효모에 대한 소비자 수요는 ② 증가했다 (→ 감소했다). Fleischmann의 효모의 생산자는 판매를 ③ 촉진하기 위해서 다른 마케팅 전략을 고안하려고 J. Walter Thompson 광고 대행사를 고용했다. 더 이상 "Soul of Bread"를 쓰지 않고, Thompson 광고 대행사는 먼저 효모를 상당한 건강상의 ④ 이점이 있는 중요한 비타민 공급원으로 바꾸었다. 그 이후 얼마 안 되어, 광고 대행사는 효모를 천연 완하제로 바꾸었다. 효모의 ⑤ 이미지 전환은 매출을 증가시키는 것을 도왔다.

Why? 왜 정답일까?

과거 효모는 집에서 굽는 빵의 재료로 쓰였지만, 20세기에 접어들어 사람들이 점점 가게에서 구운 빵을 사면서 효모에 대한 수요가 '떨어졌다'는 설명이 되도록 increased를 declined로 고쳐야 한다. 따라서 문맥상 낱말의 쓰임이 적절하지 않은 것은 ②이다.

- considerable ⓐ 상당한
- ingredient ⓝ 재료
- come up with 떠올리다, 고안하다
- significant ⓐ 상당한, 중요한
- laxative ⓝ 완하제, 변비약
- facility ⓝ 능력, 재능
- hire ⓥ 고용하다
- strategy ⓝ 전략
- transform ⓥ 변모시키다
- reposition ⓥ (제품의) 이미지를 바꾸다

구문 풀이

1행 Advertisers often displayed considerable facility in adapting ～하는 데 있어, ～할 때 their claims to the market status of the goods [(that) they promoted]. 선행사 ▶ 생략

07 오늘날의 뉴스 순환 　정답률 63% | 정답 ①

다음 빈칸에 들어갈 말로 가장 적절한 것을 고르시오.

☑ Mobility – 기동성
③ Creativity – 창의성
⑤ Responsibility – 책임감
② Sensitivity – 민감성
④ Accuracy – 정확성

[본문 해석]

기동성은 저널리스트들의 환경에 대한 변화를 제공한다. 신문 기사, 텔레비전 보도, 그리고 심지어 (태블릿과 스마트폰과 같은 통신 기술 이전의) 초기 온라인 보도는 기자가 인쇄, 방송, 또는 게시를 위해 자신의 뉴스 기사를 제출할 하나의 중심적인 장소를 필요로 했다. 그러나 이제 기자는 비디오를 촬영하고, 오디오를 녹음하며, 자신의 스마트폰이나 태블릿에 직접 타이핑해서 즉시 뉴스 기사를 게시할 수 있다. 저널리스트들은 모두가 정보의 원천과 접촉하거나, 타이핑하거나, 또는 비디오를 편집하는 중심 장소에 보고할 필요가 없다. 기사는 즉석에서 작성되고, 촬영되고, 전 세계에서 보는 것이 가능해질 수 있다. 뉴스의 순환과 결국 저널리스트의 일은 결코 멈추지 않는다. 그러므로 케이블 TV의 성장으로 나타난 '24시간'의 뉴스 순환은 이제 과거의 것이다. 뉴스 '순환'은 정말로 끊임없이 계속되는 것이다.

Why? 왜 정답일까?

글 중간의 'Now, though, ～' 앞뒤로 글의 흐름이 반전되는 글이다. 예전에는 기자들이 기사를 제출할 중심적인 장소가 필요했지만 이제는 스마트폰이나 태블릿을 활용하여 언제 어디서든 기사 작성이 이루어질 수 있기 때문에 멈추지 않는 뉴스의 순환이 가능해졌다(The news cycle, and thus the job of the journalist, never takes a break.)는 내용이 언급되고 있다. 따라서 빈칸에 들어갈 말로 가장 적절한 것은 장소에 구애받지 않고 이어질 수 있는 기자 업무의 특성을 설명하기에 적합한 ① '기동성'이다.

- prior to ～의 이전에
- central ⓐ 중심적인
- printing ⓝ 인쇄
- posting ⓝ 게시
- directly ⓐⓓ 곧장
- instantly ⓐⓓ 즉시
- source ⓝ 원천, 근원
- instantaneously ⓐⓓ 즉석에서
- emerge ⓥ 나타나다
- cable TV 유선방송
- require ⓥ 필요로 하다
- submit ⓥ 제출하다
- broadcast ⓝ 방송
- shoot ⓥ 촬영하다
- post ⓥ 게시하다
- location ⓝ 장소, 위치
- edit ⓥ 편집하다
- take a break 멈추다
- rise ⓝ 성장, 상승, 증가
- constant ⓐ 일정불변의 것

구문 풀이

2행 Newspaper stories, television reports, and even early online 주어(A, B, and C) reporting (prior to communication technology such as tablets and ～ 이전에 smartphones) required one central place [to which a reporter would 동사 목적어(선행사) ＝where submit his or her news story for printing, broadcast, or posting].

★★★ 1등급 대비 고난도 3점 문제

08 개인에게 넘어간 음악 선택권 　정답률 38% | 정답 ①

다음 빈칸에 들어갈 말로 가장 적절한 것을 고르시오. [3점]

☑ choose and determine his or her musical preferences
자신이 선호하는 음악을 선택하고 결정해야
② understand the technical aspects of recording sessions
녹음 세션의 기술적 측면을 이해해야
③ share unique and inspiring playlists on social media
독특하고 영감을 주는 재생 목록을 소셜 미디어에 공유해야
④ interpret lyrics with background knowledge of the songs
노래에 대한 배경지식으로 가사를 해석해야
⑤ seek the advice of a voice specialist for better performances
더 나은 공연을 위해 음성 전문가의 조언을 구해야

[본문 해석]

기술 혁신으로 인해, 음악은 이제 이전보다 더 많은 시간 동안 더 많은 사람에 의해 경험될 수 있다. 대중 이용 가능성은 개인들에게 각자의 음향 환경에 대한 전례 없는 통제권을 주었다. 하지만 그들은 무수한 장르의 음악을 동시에 이용할 수 있는 상황에 맞닥뜨리게 되었고 그 상황에 적응해야만 한다. 사람들은 이전에 물리적 형태를 지닌 음악을 수집했던 것처럼 자신들의 디지털 라이브러리를 걸러 내고 정리하기 시작한다. 하지만 선택권은 자신이 가진다는 차이가 있다. 음악 배급자의 제한된 컬렉션에 국한되지 않고, 또한 최신 히트곡의 '사전 선택자'인 지역 라디오 프로그램의 안내를 받지 않고, 개인은 적극적으로 자신이 선호하는 음악을 선택하고 결정해야 한다. 따라서 적절한 노래를 찾는 것은 상당한 노력과 관련이 있다.

Why? 왜 정답일까?

첫 두 문장에서 기술 혁신으로 인해 개인이 자신의 음향 환경을 통제할 수 있는 권한을 갖게 되었다고 한다. 특히 'However, there is the difference that the choice lies in their own hands.'에서는 무수한 장르의 음악 속에서 자신의 디지털 라이브러리를 어떻게 구성할 것인지에 대한 선택권이 개인 자신에게 있다고 언급한다. 따라서 빈칸에 들어갈 말로 가장 적절한 것은 ① '자신이 선호하는 음악을 선택하고 결정해야'이다.

- availability ⓝ 이용 가능성
- confront A with B A를 B와 대면시키다
- restrict ⓥ 국한시키다, 제한하다
- considerable ⓐ 상당한
- unheard-of ⓐ 전례 없는
- orient ⓥ 적응하다
- distributor ⓝ 배급 업자
- interpret ⓥ 해석하다

구문 풀이

5행 However, it has also confronted them with the simultaneous
「confront + A + with + B : A를 B와 대면시키다」
availability of countless genres of music, in which they have to orient
계속적 용법(= where)
themselves.

★★ 문제 해결 꿀~팁 ★★

▶ 많이 틀린 이유는?
기술 혁신으로 개인이 음악 선택권을 갖게 되었다는 내용의 글이다. 최다 오답인 ③은 개인이 소셜 미디어에 플레이리스트를 공유해야 한다는 의미인데, 개인이 직접 만든 플레이리스트를 공유해야 하는지는 글에서 언급되지 않았다. 특히 '소셜 미디어'라는 소재 자체가 글에서 아예 언급되지 않았다.

▶ 문제 해결 방법은?
주제가 드러나는 'However ~.' 문장을 잘 읽으면 쉽다. 'the choice lies in their own hands'가 문제 해결에 핵심적인 표현이다.

09 커피의 부정적 영향 주의하기 정답률 60% | 정답 ④

다음 글에서 전체 흐름과 관계 없는 문장은?

[본문 해석]

공부하는 동안 깨어 있는 것을 돕기 위해 커피 한 잔을 이용해 보지 않은 사람이 있을까? 차, 커피 또는 탄산음료에서 흔히 발견되는 가벼운 자극제는 아마도 여러분을 더 주의 깊게 만들고, 따라서 더 잘 기억할 수 있게 한다. ① 하지만, 자극제가 기억력에 이로울 수 있는 만큼 부정적인 영향을 미칠 수도 있다는 것을 알아야 한다. ② 비록 그것이 특정 수준에서 수행을 향상할 수 있다고 할지라도, (자극제의) 이상적인 복용량은 현재 알려지지 않았다. ③ 만약 여러분이 완전히 깨어 있고 잘 쉬었다면, 카페인으로부터의 가벼운 자극은 여러분의 기억력을 더욱 향상하는 데 거의 영향을 주지 못할 수 있다. ④ 반면에, 많은 연구에서 커피를 마시는 것보다 차를 마시는 것이 건강에 더 좋다는 것이 밝혀졌다. ⑤ 실제로 만약 여러분이 자극제를 너무 많이 섭취하면, 신경이 과민해지고, 잠을 자기 어려워지며, 기억력도 저하될 것이다.

Why? 왜 정답일까?

커피를 지나치게 많이 마시면 부정적 영향이 나타날 수 있다는 내용의 글인데, ④는 커피보다 차가 몸에 좋다는 무관한 설명을 제시하고 있다. 따라서 전체 흐름과 관계 없는 문장은 ④이다.

- attentive ⓐ 주의 깊은
- ideal ⓐ 이상적인
- have an effect on ~에 영향을 미치다
- suffer ⓥ 악화되다

구문 풀이

4행 However, you should know that stimulants are as likely to
접속사(~것) 「as + 원급 + as :
have negative effects on memory as they are to be beneficial.
be to 용법(~할 수 있다) ~만큼 …한」

★★★ 1등급 대비 고난도 3점 문제

10 광물의 형성 정답률 42% | 정답 ②

주어진 글 다음에 이어질 글의 순서로 가장 적절한 것을 고르시오. [3점]
① (A) - (C) - (B)
✓② (B) - (A) - (C)
③ (B) - (C) - (A)
④ (C) - (A) - (B)
⑤ (C) - (B) - (A)

[본문 해석]

자연 과정은 많은 방법으로 광물을 형성한다. 예를 들어, 마그마라고 불리는 뜨거운 용암 물질은 지구의 표면에 도달할 때, 또는 심지어 표면 아래에 갇혔을 때도 식는다. 마그마가 식으면서 마그마의 원자는 열에너지를 잃고, 서로 더 가까이 이동해 화합물로 결합하기 시작한다.

(B) 이 과정 동안, 서로 다른 화합물의 원자가 질서 있고 반복적인 패턴으로 배열된다. 마그마에 존재하는 원소의 종류와 양이 어떤 광물이 형성될지를 부분적으로 결정한다.

(A) 또한, 형성되는 결정의 크기는 부분적으로는 마그마가 얼마나 빨리 식나에 달려 있다. 마그마가 천천히 식으면, 형성되는 결정은 대개 육안으로 볼 수 있을 만큼 충분히 크다.

(C) 이것은 원자가 함께 이동해 더 큰 결정을 형성할 충분한 시간을 가지기 때문이다. 마그마가 빠르게 식으면, 형성되는 결정은 작을 것이다. 이런 경우에는 개별 광물 결정을 쉽게 볼 수 없다.

Why? 왜 정답일까?

마그마가 식을 때 광물이 형성될 수 있다는 내용의 주어진 글 뒤로, '이 식어가는 과정' 동안 마그마 속 원소의 종류와 양에 따라 어떤 종류의 광물이 형성될지 결정된다고 설명하는 (B)가 먼저 연결된다. 이어서 Also로 시작하는 (A)는 추가로 마그마가 식는 속도에 따라 광물의 크기가 결정된다고 언급한다. 마지막으로 (C)는 (A) 후반부에서 언급되었듯이 마그마가 천천히 식을 때 광물의 크기가 커지는 이유에 관해 보충 설명한다. 따라서 글의 순서로 가장 적절한 것은 ② '(B) - (A) - (C)'이다.

- form ⓥ 형성하다
- melt ⓥ 녹이다, 녹다
- trap ⓥ 가두다
- combine into ~로 결합되다
- partly ⓐd 부분적으로
- with the unaided eye 육안으로
- orderly ⓐ 질서 있는
- in such cases 이런 경우에
- mineral ⓝ 광물
- surface ⓝ 표면
- atom ⓝ 원자
- compound ⓝ 화합물
- rapidly ⓐd 빠르게
- arrange ⓥ 배열하다
- element ⓝ 원소, 구성요소

구문 풀이

7행 Also, the size of the crystals that form depends partly on how rapidly the magma cools.
「how + 형/부 + 주어 + 동사 : 얼마나 ~한지」

★★ 문제 해결 꿀~팁 ★★

▶ 많이 틀린 이유는?
(B)는 마그마가 식는 속도에 따라 그로 인해 만들어지는 결정의 종류가 달라질 수 있다는 내용으로 끝나는데, (C)를 보면 갑자기 결정의 크기가 커지는 이유를 언급한다. (C)에 앞서 '크기'를 처음 언급하는 단락은 Also로 시작하는 (A)이다. (A)에서 먼저 size를 언급해줘야 크기가 커지는 '이유'를 설명하는 (C)가 자연스럽게 연결된다.

▶ 문제 해결 방법은?
(A)와 (C)가 둘 다 '크기'를 언급하고 있지만, (B)에는 '크기'에 관한 언급이 없다. 따라서 Also가 있는 (A)를 먼저 연결해 '크기'에 관한 내용을 추가한다는 뜻을 밝히고, 뒤이어 (C)를 연결해야 논리적 흐름이 자연스러워진다.

11-12 반복의 중요성

[본문 해석]

아이였을 때, 우리는 열심히 자전거 타기를 배웠고, 넘어지면 다시 올라탔는데, 그것이 우리에게 제2의 천성이 될 때까지 그렇게 했다. 그러나 어른으로 살면서 새로운 것을 시도해 볼 때 우리는 대체로 단 한 번만 시도해 보고 나서 그것이 (a) 잘되었는지 판단하려 한다. 만일 우리가 처음에 성공하지 못하거나 혹은 약간 어색한 느낌이 들면, (b) 또 한번 시도해 보기보다는 그것이 성공이 아니었다고 스스로에게 말할 것이다. 「그것은 애석한 일인데, 우리 뇌를 재연결하는 과정에서 반복이 핵심적이기 때문이다.」(: 11번의 근거) 여러분의 뇌가 뉴런의 연결망을 가지고 있다는 개념을 생각해 보라. 여러분이 뇌 친화적인 피드백 기술을 잊지 않고 사용할 때마다 그것들은 서로 (c) 연결될 것이다. 그 연결은 처음에는 그리 (d) 신뢰할 만하지 않고, 여러분의 첫 번째 시도가 다소 마구잡이가 되도록 할 수도 있다. 여러분은 연관된 단계 중 하나를 기억하고, 다른 것들을 기억하지 못할 수도 있다. 「그러나 과학자들은

"함께 활성화되는 뉴런들은 함께 연결된다."라고 말한다. 다시 말하자면, 어떤 행동의 반복은 그 행동에 연관된 뉴런들 사이의 연결을 (e) 차단한다(→ 강화한다). 그것은 여러분이 그 새로운 피드백 기술을 더 여러 차례 사용해 볼수록, 필요할 때 그것이 더 쉽게 여러분에게 다가올 것을 의미한다.

- **work hard at** ~을 들이파다, 열심히 하다
- **nature** ⑩ 본성, 천성
- **awkward** ⓐ (기분이) 어색한, 불편한
- **shame** ⑩ 애석한 일, 딱한 일
- **central** ⓐ 핵심적인
- **hit-and-miss** ⓐ 마구잡이로 하는
- **curious** ⓐ 호기심이 많은
- **fall off** 넘어지다
- **make an attempt** 시도하다
- **give it a shot** 시도하다
- **repetition** ⑩ 반복
- **reliable** ⓐ 신뢰할 만한
- **block** ⓥ 차단하다

구문 풀이

12행 They will connect with each other whenever you
(복합관계부사(~할 때마다))
remember to use a brain-friendly feedback technique.
「remember + to부정사 : ~할 것을 기억하다」

21행 That means the more times you try using that new feedback
「the + 비교급 ~,」
technique, the more easily it will come to you when you need it.
「the + 비교급 … : ~할수록 더 …하다」

---

11 제목 파악 | 정답률 72% | 정답 ①

윗글의 제목으로 가장 적절한 것은?

① Repeat and You Will Succeed – 반복하면 성공할 것이다
② Be More Curious, Be Smarter – 더 호기심을 가지고, 더 똑똑해져라
③ Play Is What Makes Us Human – 놀이는 우리를 인간답게 만드는 것이다
④ Stop and Think Before You Act – 행동하기 전에 가만히 생각하라
⑤ Growth Is All About Keeping Balance – 성장은 전적으로 균형 유지에 관한 것이다

Why? 왜 정답일까?

두 번째 단락의 첫 문장과 마지막 문장인 '~ repetition is central to the process of rewiring our brains.', '~ the more times you try using that new feedback technique, the more easily it will come to you when you need it.'에서 어떤 것을 반복할수록 다음에 그것이 필요할 때 더 쉽게 되살아날 가능성이 높아진다고 언급하는 것으로 볼 때, 글의 제목으로 가장 적절한 것은 기술 습득에 있어 '반복'이 중요하다는 의미의 ① '반복하면 성공할 것이다'이다.

12 어휘 추론 | 정답률 60% | 정답 ⑤

밑줄 친 (a) ~ (e) 중에서 문맥상 낱말의 쓰임이 적절하지 않은 것은?

① (a) ② (b) ③ (c) ④ (d) ⑤ (e)

Why? 왜 정답일까?

'But scientists have a saying: "neurons that fire together, wire together."'에서 함께 활성화되는 뉴런은 함께 연결된다고 언급하는 것으로 볼 때, (e)가 포함된 문장은 어떠한 행동을 반복할 때 그 행동과 연관된 뉴런들 사이의 연결이 '강화된다'는 의미여야 한다. 따라서 (e)는 blocks 대신 strengthens로 고쳐야 한다. 문맥상 낱말의 쓰임이 적절하지 않은 것은 ⑤ '(e)'이다.

DAY 16 — 20분 미니 모의고사

01 ②	02 ⑤	03 ②	04 ④	05 ⑤
06 ⑤	07 ③	08 ⑤	09 ①	10 ②
11 ⑤	12 ⑤			

01 여름 휴가 패키지 홍보 | 정답률 93% | 정답 ②

다음 글의 목적으로 가장 적절한 것은?

① 여행 일정 변경을 안내하려고
② 패키지 여행 상품을 홍보하려고
③ 여행 상품 불만족에 대해 사과하려고
④ 여행 만족도 조사 참여를 부탁하려고
⑤ 패키지 여행 업무 담당자를 모집하려고

[본문 해석]

ACC 여행사 고객님께

자연 속에서 휴가를 즐기는 것을 원한 적이 있습니까? 이번 여름이 당신의 꿈을 현실로 바꿀 최고의 시간입니다. 우리에게는 당신을 위한 완벽한 패키지 여행 상품이 있습니다. 이 패키지 여행 상품은 당신이 편히 쉴 수 있도록 돕는 마사지와 명상뿐만 아니라 Lake Madison으로의 특별한 여행을 포함합니다. 또한, 우리는 숙련된 강사의 요가 강의도 제공합니다. 만약 당신이 이 패키지를 예약한다면, 당신은 이 모든 것을 합리적인 가격으로 즐길 것입니다. 우리는 그것이 당신에게 잊지 못할 경험이 될 것이라고 확신합니다. 우리에게 전화하시면, 우리는 당신에게 더 많은 세부 사항을 기꺼이 알려드리겠습니다.

Why? 왜 정답일까?

여름 휴가에 적합한 패키지 여행 상품이 있음을 홍보하는 글(We have a perfect travel package for you.)이므로, 글의 목적으로 가장 적절한 것은 ② '패키지 여행 상품을 홍보하려고'이다.

- **travel agency** 여행사
- **A as well as B** B뿐 아니라 A도
- **experienced** ⓐ 경험 많은, 숙련된
- **reasonable** ⓐ 적당한
- **turn A into B** A를 B로 바꾸다
- **meditation** ⑩ 명상
- **instructor** ⑩ 강사
- **unforgettable** ⓐ 잊지 못할

구문 풀이

5행 This travel package includes special trips to Lake Madison
「A + as well as + B : B뿐 아니라 A도」
as well as massage and meditation to help you relax.
「help + 목적어 + 원형부정사 : ~이 …하는 데 도움이 되다」

★★★ 1등급 대비 고난도 2점 문제

02 더러움의 정의 | 정답률 40% | 정답 ⑤

밑줄 친 "matter out of place"가 다음 글에서 의미하는 바로 가장 적절한 것은?

① something that is completely broken – 완전히 부서진 물건
② a tiny dust that nobody notices – 아무도 눈치채지 못하는 아주 작은 먼지
③ a dirty but renewable material – 더럽지만 복구할 수 있는 물체
④ what can be easily replaced – 쉽게 대체될 수 있는 것
⑤ a thing that is not in order – 정돈되지 않은 것

[본문 해석]

어떤 것도 본래부터 쓰레기인 것은 없다. 인류학자 Mary Douglas는 더러운 것은 "제자리에 놓여있지 않은 물체"라는 흔히 하는 말을 다시 가져와 해석했다. 그녀가 강조하기로, 더러운 것은 상대적이다. "신발은 그 자체로는 더럽지 않지만, 식탁 위에 놓여 있을 때 더러운 것이며, 음식은 그 자체로는 더럽지 않지만, 침실에 냄비와 팬을 놓아둔다면, 혹은 음식이 옷에 다 묻어 있을 때 더럽다. 마찬가지로 거실에 있는 욕실 용품, 의자 위에 놓여 있는 옷, 실내에 있는 실외 물품들, 아래층에 있는 위층 물건들 등등이 더럽다." 깨끗한 것과 더러운 것을 분류하는 것, 즉 식탁에서 신발을 치우는 것, 세탁기에 더러운 옷을 넣는 것은 체계적인 정리와 분류를 포함하는 것이다. 그러므로 더러운 것을 제거하는 것은 긍정적인 과정이다.

Why? 왜 정답일까?

세 번째 문장에서 더러운 것은 상대적(Dirt is relative, ~)이라고 언급한 후, 이어지는 예시를 통해 식탁 위에 놓여있는 신발, 침실에 놓여 있거나 옷에 묻어 있는 음식, 거실에 있는 욕실 용품 등 있어야 할 자리에 있지 않은 물건들이 더러운 것이라고 설명하고 있다. 따라서 밑줄 친 부분의 의미로 가장 적절한 것은 ⑤ '정돈되지 않은 것'이다.

- **by nature** 본래, 천성적으로
- **analyze** ⓥ 분석하다
- **relative** ⓐ 상대적인
- **in oneself** 그 자체로
- **eliminate** ⓥ 제거하다, 없애다
- **in order** 정돈된, 적절한
- **anthropologist** ⓝ 인류학자
- **out of place** 제자리에 있지 않은
- **emphasize** ⓥ 강조하다
- **sort** ⓥ 분류하다, 나누다
- **renewable** ⓐ 복구 가능한

구문 풀이

3행 **Dirt is relative, she emphasizes.**
목적어(강조를 위해 도치)　주어　동사

★★ 문제 해결 꿀~팁 ★★

▶ **많이 틀린 이유는?**

'더러운' 것이 무엇인지 정의하는 내용이므로 dirty를 포함한 ③이 오답으로 많이 나왔다. 하지만 글에서 더러움의 복구 가능성(renewable)에 관해서는 언급되지 않는다.

▶ **문제 해결 방법은?**

직접인용구의 예시에서 엉뚱한 자리에 있는 물건을 열거하고 있고, out of place와 not in order가 둘 다 '제자리에 있지 않은, 정돈되지 않은' 등의 의미를 나타내므로 ⑤가 답으로 가장 적절하다.

---

03 감정을 인식하고 명명할 수 있는 능력　정답률 64% | 정답 ②

다음 글의 제목으로 가장 적절한 것은?

① True Friendship Endures Emotional Arguments
　진정한 우정은 감정적인 다툼을 견뎌낸다
② Detailed Labeling of Emotions Is Beneficial
　감정에 상세하게 이름을 붙이는 것은 이롭다
③ Labeling Emotions: Easier Said Than Done
　감정에 이름 붙이기: 말하기는 쉬워도 행하기는 어렵다
④ Categorize and Label Tasks for Efficiency
　효율성을 위해 작업을 분류하고 이름 붙이라
⑤ Be Brave and Communicate Your Needs
　용기를 갖고 여러분의 요구를 전달하라

[본문 해석]

감정을 정확하게 인식하고 그것에 이름을 붙일 수 있는 우리의 능력은 흔히 *감정 입자도*라고 불린다. Harvard 대학의 심리학자인 Susan David의 말에 의하면, "감정에 더 미묘한 차이가 있는 어휘로 이름을 붙이는 법을 배우는 것은 절대적으로 (사람을) 변화시킬 수 있다." David는 우리가 풍부한 감정적인 어휘를 갖고 있지 않으면, 우리의 욕구를 전달하고 다른 사람들로부터 우리가 필요로 하는 지지를 얻는 것이 어렵다고 설명한다. 그러나 광범위한 다양한 감정을 구별할 수 있는 사람들은 "모든 것을 흑백 논리로 보는 사람들보다 평범한 존재로 사는 중에 겪는 좋은 일들과 궂은 일들을 다스리는 일을 훨씬, 훨씬 더 잘한다." 사실, 감정적인 경험에 이름을 붙이는 과정은 더 큰 감정 통제 및 심리 사회적인 행복과 관련되어 있다는 것을 연구 결과가 보여 준다.

Why? 왜 정답일까?

마지막 문장에 따르면 감정적인 경험에 이름을 붙이는 것은 감정을 더 잘 통제하고 심리 사회적으로 더 큰 행복감을 느끼는 것과 관련되어 있다(~ the process of labeling emotional experience is related to greater emotion regulation and psychosocial well-being.)고 하므로, 글의 제목으로 가장 적절한 것은 ② '감정에 상세하게 이름을 붙이는 것은 이롭다'이다.

- **accurately** ⓐⓓ 정확하게
- **absolutely** ⓐⓓ 절대적으로
- **communicate** ⓥ 전달하다
- **ups and downs** 좋은 일과 궂은 일
- **regulation** ⓝ 통제
- **endure** ⓥ 견디다, 참다, 인내하다
- **refer to A as B** A를 B라고 부르다
- **transformative** ⓐ 변화시키는
- **distinguish** ⓥ 구별하다
- **existence** ⓝ 존재
- **psychosocial** ⓐ 심리사회적인
- **categorize** ⓥ 분류하다

구문 풀이

1행 **Our ability to accurately recognize and label emotions**
주어　　　　　　　　　형용사적 용법
is often referred to as *emotional granularity*.
동사(refer to A as B의 수동태)

---

04 Marjorie Kinnan Rawlings의 생애　정답률 94% | 정답 ④

Marjorie Kinnan Rawlings에 관한 다음 글의 내용과 일치하지 않는 것은?

① Washington, D.C.에서 태어난 미국 작가이다.
② 그녀의 이야기 중 하나가 *The Washington Post*에 실렸다.
③ 대학교를 졸업한 후 저널리스트로 일했다.
☑ *The Yearling*이라는 소설은 다른 제목으로 영화화되었다.
⑤ Cross Creek에 소유했던 땅은 Florida 주립 공원이 되었다.

[본문 해석]

『1896년 Washington D.C.에서 태어난 미국 작가인 Marjorie Kinnan Rawlings는 시골적인 주제와 배경의 소설을 썼다.』『그녀가 어렸을 때, 그녀의 이야기 중 하나가 *The Washington Post*에 실렸다.』『대학교를 졸업한 후 Rawlings는 저널리스트로 일하면서 동시에 소설가로 자리잡으려고 애썼다.』 1928년에 그녀는 Florida 주 Cross Creek에 있는 오렌지 과수원을 구입했다. 이것은 *The Yearling*과 자전적인 책인 *Cross Creek*을 포함한 그녀의 작품 일부에 영감의 원천이 되었다. 한 소년과 부모 잃은 아기 사슴에 관한 이야기였던 *The Yearling*은 1939년에 퓰리처상 소설 부문 수상작이 되었다. 『이후 1946년에 *The Yearling*은 같은 제목으로 영화화되었다.』『Rawlings는 1953년에 세상을 떠났고, 그녀가 Cross Creek에 소유한 땅은 Florida 주립 공원이 되어 그녀의 업적을 기리고 있다.』

Why? 왜 정답일까?

'*The Yearling* was made into a film of the same name.'에서 소설과 영화의 제목은 동일했다고 하므로, 내용과 일치하지 않는 것은 ④ '*The Yearling*이라는 소설은 다른 제목으로 영화화되었다.'이다.

Why? 왜 오답일까?

① 'Marjorie Kinnan Rawlings, an American author born in Washington, D.C. in 1896, ~'의 내용과 일치한다.
② '~ one of her stories appeared in *The Washington Post*.'의 내용과 일치한다.
③ 'After graduating from university, Rawlings worked as a journalist ~'의 내용과 일치한다.
⑤ '~ the land she owned at Cross Creek has become a Florida State Park honoring her achievements.'의 내용과 일치한다.

- **rural** ⓐ 시골의, 지방의
- **grove** ⓝ (작은 규모의) 과수원
- **autobiographical** ⓐ 자전적인, 자서전의
- **pass away** 세상을 떠나다
- **simultaneously** ⓐⓓ 동시에, 일제히
- **inspiration** ⓝ 영감, 자극
- **orphaned** ⓐ 부모를 잃은, 고아가 된

구문 풀이

14행 **Rawlings passed away in 1953, / and the land [(that) she**
주어1　　　동사1　　　　　　　주어2　생략(목적격 관계대명사)
owned at Cross Creek] has become a Florida State Park honoring
　　　　　　　　동사2　　　　　　　　　　　분사 구문
her achievements.

---

05 진짜 미소와 가짜 미소의 차이　정답률 61% | 정답 ⑤

다음 글의 밑줄 친 부분 중, 어법상 틀린 것은? [3점]

[본문 해석]

당신이 미소를 관찰했는데 그것이 진짜가 아니라고 느낄 수 있는 경우가 있었다. 진짜 미소와 진실하지 못한 미소를 알아보는 가장 명확한 방법은 가짜 미소는 주로 얼굴의 아랫부분, 주로 입에만 영향을 미친다는 것이다. 눈은 별로 관련이 없다. 거울을 볼 기회를 잡아서 당신의 얼굴 아랫부분만을 사용하여 미소를 지어보라. 당신이 이렇게 할 때, 당신의 얼굴이 실제로 얼마나 행복해 보이는지를 판단해 보라. 그것은 진짜인가? 진짜 미소는 눈가 근육과 주름에 영향을 주며, 티가 좀 덜 나게 눈썹과 윗눈꺼풀 사이의 피부는 진정한 즐거움으로 살짝 내려온다. 진짜 미소는 얼굴 전체에 영향을 줄 수 있다.

Why? 왜 정답일까?

and 앞에 'A genuine smile will impact ~'라는 '주어＋동사' 한 쌍이 나온 뒤 and 뒤로 새로운 '주어＋동사'가 이어지고 있다. 이때 단수 명사 주어인 the skin에 맞추어 동사인 are를 is로 고쳐야 한다. 따라서 어법상 틀린 것은 ⑤이다.

DAY 16

Why? 왜 오답일까?

① 뒤에 and로 연결된 두 문장 'you have observed a smile and you could sense ~'가 모두 완전한 3형식 구조이다. 따라서 '전치사 + 관계대명사' 형태의 in which가 바르게 쓰였다.
② 앞에 나온 smile을 지칭하기 위해 단수 부정대명사 one이 바르게 쓰였다.
③ 분사 뒤에 목적어 the lower half your face only가 나오는 것으로 보아 현재분사 using이 바르게 쓰였다.
④ 뒤에 '형용사 + 주어 + 동사'가 이어지는 것으로 보아 의문부사 how가 바르게 쓰였다. 의문부사 how가 '얼마나'라는 뜻이면 주로 'how + 형/부 + 주어 + 동사' 어순으로 쓰인다.

● occasion ⓝ 경우
● obvious ⓐ 명백한, 분명한
● insincere ⓐ 진실하지 않은
● manufacture ⓥ 만들다
● noticeably ⓐⓓ 눈에 띄게, 두드러지게
● entire ⓐ 전체의
● genuine ⓐ 진짜인
● identify ⓥ 알아보다, 식별하다
● primarily ⓐⓓ 주로
● impact ⓥ 영향을 미치다
● slightly ⓐⓓ 살짝, 약간

구문 풀이

3행 The most obvious way of identifying a genuine smile from
　　　　　　　　　　　주어
an insincere one is that a fake smile primarily only affects the lower
　　　　　동사(단수)　　주어　　　　　　　　　　동사　　목적어
half of the face, mainly with the mouth alone.

06 좋은 지도자의 자질　　　정답률 65% | 정답 ⑤

(A), (B), (C)의 각 네모 안에서 문맥에 맞는 낱말로 가장 적절한 것은?

	(A)	(B)	(C)
①	silence 침묵시키다	improvement 향상	decrease 감소하다
②	silence 침묵시키다	loss 상실	increase 증가하다
③	voice 말하다	improvement 향상	decrease 감소하다
④	voice 말하다	loss 상실	decrease 감소하다
✓⑤	voice 말하다	loss 상실	increase 증가하다

[본문 해석]

지도자는 어떻게 사람들이 중요하다고 느끼게 하는가? 첫 번째로, 그들에게 귀 기울이는 것을 통해서이다. 여러분이 그들의 생각을 존중한다는 것을 알게 하고, 그들이 자신의 의견을 (A) 말하게 하라. 덤으로 여러분도 뭔가를 배울지도 모른다! 내 친구 중 한 명이 나에게 대기업의 최고 경영자에 대해 말해 준 적이 있는데, 그는 자신이 거느리고 있는 관리자 중 한 명에게, "당신이 나에게 말할 수 있는 것 중에 내가 전에 이미 생각해 본 적이 없는 것은 없어요. 내가 당신에게 묻지 않으면 당신 생각을 나에게 절대로 말하지 마세요. 내 말 알아듣겠어요?"라고 말했다고 한다. 그 관리자가 틀림없이 느꼈을 자존감의 (B) 상실을 상상해 보라. 그 일은 그를 낙담시켜서 그의 업무 수행에 부정적인 영향을 미쳤음에 틀림없다. 반면 여러분이 누군가를 아주 중요한 사람이라고 느끼게 한다면, 그 사람은 의기양양해질 것이고 활력의 수준이 빠르게 (C) 증가할 것이다.

Why? 왜 정답일까?

(A) 첫 두 문장에서 지도자는 남의 말을 들어주며 자존감을 높여준다는 내용이 나오므로, 상대방이 '말하게' 하라는 맥락이 되도록 voice를 넣는 것이 적절하다.
(B) 네모 앞의 두 문장에서 질문을 받는 경우가 아니면 자기 생각을 말하지 않도록 지시받은 관리자의 예가 언급되는데, 이는 자존감의 향상보다는 '상실'로 이어질 수 있는 맥락이므로 loss가 적절하다.
(C) On the other hand 앞의 문장에서 자존감의 상실을 경험한 사람은 업무 수행에 부정적인 영향을 받게 될 수 있다고 말하므로, On the other hand 뒤에 나오는 (C) 안에는 반대로 사람들에게 그들이 중요한 사람임을 느끼게 했을 때 활력이 '증가'한다는 맥락이 되도록 increase를 넣는 것이 적절하다. 따라서 각 네모 안에서 문맥에 맞는 낱말로 가장 적절한 것은 ⑤ '(A) voice(말하다) – (B) loss(상실) – (C) increase(증가하다)'이다.

● important ⓐ 중요한
● silence ⓥ 침묵시키다
● self-esteem 자존감
● affect ⓥ 영향을 미치다
● on top of the world 의기양양한, 세상이 발아래 있는 듯한
● respect ⓥ 존중하다, 존경하다
● unless ⓒⓞⓝⓙ ~하지 않는 한
● discourage ⓥ 낙담시키다, 실망시키다
● performance ⓝ 수행, 성과

구문 풀이

12행 On the other hand, when you make a person feel a great
　　　　　　　　　　　　　　　사역 동사　　　　　원형부정사
sense of importance, / he or she will feel on top of the world — and
　　　　　　　　　　　주어1　　동사1　　　　주격 보어
the level of energy will increase rapidly.
　　　주어2　　　　동사2(자동사)

★★★ 1등급 대비 고난도 3점 문제

07 지속적인 노력의 중요성　　　정답률 30% | 정답 ③

다음 빈칸에 들어갈 말로 가장 적절한 것을 고르시오. [3점]

① cooperative – 협동하는
② productive – 생산적인
✓③ fruitless – 결실 없는
④ dangerous – 위험한
⑤ irregular – 불규칙한

[본문 해석]

날마다 해야 하는 많은 학업이 지루하고 반복적이기 때문에, 그것을 계속하기 위해서는 동기부여가 잘 되어야 한다. 어느 수학자는 연필을 깎고, 어떤 증명을 해내려고 애쓰며, 몇 가지 접근법을 시도하고, 아무런 성과를 내지 못하고, 하루를 끝낸다. 어느 작가는 책상에 앉아 몇 백 단어의 글을 창작하고, 그것이 별로라고 판단하며, 쓰레기통에 그것을 던져 버리고, 내일 더 나은 영감을 기대한다. 가치 있는 것을 만들어 내는 것은, 행여나 그런 일이 일어난다면, 여러 해 동안의 그런 결실 없는 노동을 필요로 할지도 모른다. 노벨상을 수상한 생물학자 Peter Medawar는 그가 과학에 들인 시간 중 5분의 4 정도가 헛되었다고 말하면서, "거의 모든 과학적 연구가 성과를 내지 못한다."라고 애석해하며 덧붙였다. 상황이 악화되고 있을 때 이 모든 사람들을 계속하게 했던 것은 자신들의 주제에 대한 열정이었다. 그러한 열정이 없었더라면, 그들은 아무것도 이루지 못했을 것이다.

Why? 왜 정답일까?

'Since a great deal of day-to-day academic work is boring and repetitive, you need to be well motivated to keep doing it.'에서 매일의 과업이 지루하고 반복적일지라도 동기를 갖고 지속하는 것이 중요하다고 말한 데 이어, 마지막 세 문장에서는 실제로 많은 연구가 성과가 없음에도 불구하고("nearly all scientific research leads nowhere.") 주제에 대한 열정을 갖고 연구를 지속하여 성과를 거둔 과학자들에 관해 이야기한다. 따라서 빈칸에 들어갈 말로 가장 적절한 것은 ③ '결실 없는'이다.

● repetitive ⓐ 반복적인
● sharpen ⓥ 날카롭게 하다, 뾰족하게 하다
● approach ⓝ 접근법
● bin ⓝ 쓰레기통
● worthwhile ⓐ 가치 있는
● biologist ⓝ 생물학자
● mathematician ⓝ 수학자
● work on ~을 연구하다, 작업하다
● get nowhere 아무런 성과를 내지 못하다
● inspiration ⓝ 영감
● require ⓥ 필요하다
● passion ⓝ 열정

구문 풀이

8행 To produce something worthwhile / — if it ever happens — /
　　to부정사구 주어　　　　　　　　　「if ever : 설령 ~한다 할지라도」
may require years of such fruitless labor.
　　동사

★★ 문제 해결 꿀~팁 ★★

▶ 많이 틀린 이유는?
비록 평소의 과업이 '성과가 없고 지루한' 일일지라도 열정과 동기를 다해 노력할 필요가 있다는 내용이 글의 주제이므로 ③이 답으로 가장 적절하다. 특히 글 후반부의 인용구 "nearly all scientific research leads nowhere."에서 nowhere가 빈칸에 들어갈 말과 같은 의미를 나타낸다는 점을 기억해 둔다. 최다 오답인 ②는 '생산적인'이라는 뜻으로 정답인 ③과 의미가 상반된다.

▶ 문제 해결 방법은?
주제문과 더불어 예시도 꼼꼼히 읽어야 답을 알 수 있는 문제이므로, 시간을 들여 글을 통독하도록 한다.

★★★ 1등급 대비 고난도 3점 문제

08 언어와 사고의 관계　　　정답률 42% | 정답 ⑤

글의 흐름으로 보아, 주어진 문장이 들어가기에 가장 적절한 곳을 고르시오. [3점]

[본문 해석]

우리는 사고를 이해하기 위해 언어를 사용해야 할까, 아니면 언어를 이해하기 위해 사고를 사용해야 할까? ① 분석 철학은 언어가 기본이고 적절한 언어 사용이 제대로 인식된다면 그 사고가 이치에 맞을 것이라고 역사적으로 가정한다. ② 그러나 현대 인지 과학은 언어가 인간에게 매우 중요한 사고의 한 측면일 뿐 모든 종류의 사고에 근본적이지는 않다고 당연히 판단한다. ③ 수많은 종의 동물들이 인간의 사고 속에 대체로 보존된 두뇌의 메커니즘을 통해 언어를 사용하지 않고 세계를 항해하고, 문제를 해결하고, 학습해낸다. ④ 언어가 정신 작용의 기본이라고 가정할 이유는 없다. ⑤ 그럼에도 불구하고, 언어는 인간의 삶에서 매우 중요하며 세계를 다루는 데 있어서 서로 협력하는 우리의 능력에 상당히 기여한다. 우리 종족인 호모 사피엔스는 놀라운 성공을 거두어 왔는데, 이것은 처음에는 협력적인 문제 해결에 효과적인 기여 요소로서, 그리고 훨씬 나중에는 글로 쓰인 기록을 통한 집단 기억으로서의 언어에 부분적으로 의존했다.

Why? 왜 정답일까?

언어가 먼저인지 사고가 먼저인지 논하는 글로, 분석 철학과 현대 인지 과학의 시각이 대비되고 있다. ⑤ 앞까지는 주로 현대 인지 과학의 관점에서 언어가 중요하기는 해도 근간은 사고력에 있다는 내용이 제시된다. 하지만 주어진 문장은 언어가 매우 중요함을 강조하며 특히 인간의 협업 능력에 크게 기여한다는 내용으로 흐름의 반전을 이끈다. 이어서 ⑤ 뒤의 문장은 주어진 문장에서 언급한 '협력'과 관련해 언어가 중요했다는 내용을 다시금 설명한다. 따라서 주어진 문장이 들어가기에 가장 적절한 곳은 ⑤이다.

- **enormously** [ad] 대단히, 거대하게
- **deal with** ~을 다루다, ~에 대처하다
- **philosophy** [n] 철학
- **make sense** 이치에 맞다
- **fundamental** [a] 근본적인
- **navigate** [v] 항해하다
- **contribute to** ~에 기여하다
- **analytic** [a] 분석적인
- **historically** [ad] 역사적으로
- **appreciate** [v] 제대로 인식하다
- **countless** [a] 무수히 많은
- **astonishingly** [ad] 놀랍도록

구문 풀이

16행 There is no reason to assume [that language is fundamental to mental operations]. [ ] : to assume의 목적어

★★ 문제 해결 꿀~팁 ★★

▶ 많이 틀린 이유는?
④ 앞뒤로 논리적 공백이 발생하는지 점검해 보면, 먼저 ④ 앞은 언어가 없는 동물도 세계를 항해하고 문제를 해결하는 데 문제가 없다는 내용이다. 한편 ④ 뒤는 그렇기에 언어가 정신 작용의 근간이라고 추정할 근거가 없다는 내용이다. 즉 ④ 앞을 근거로 ④ 뒤와 같은 결론을 내릴 수 있는 것이므로, ④의 위치에서 논리적 공백은 발생하지 않는다.

▶ 문제 해결 방법은?
⑤ 앞은 언어가 정신 작용에 근본적이라고 추정할 필요는 없다는 내용인데, ⑤ 뒤는 호모 사피엔스의 성공에 언어가 부분적으로는 중요한 기여를 했다는 내용이다. 즉 ⑤ 앞뒤가 서로 반대되는 내용이므로, 사이에 적절한 역접어(Nevertheless)가 있어야 흐름이 자연스러워진다.

---

09 사회적 증거의 위력   정답률 49% | 정답 ①

다음 글의 내용을 한 문장으로 요약하고자 한다. 빈칸 (A), (B)에 들어갈 말로 가장 적절한 것은?

	(A)	(B)		(A)	(B)
✓	numbers 숫자	uncertain 불확실한	②	numbers 숫자	unrealistic 비현실적인
③	experiences 경험	unrealistic 비현실적인	④	rules 규칙	uncertain 불확실한
⑤	rules 규칙	unpleasant 불쾌한			

[본문 해석]

무엇이 위험하고 무엇이 안전하며, 누구를 신뢰할 수 있고 없는지를 결정하는 것을 돕고자, 우리는 *사회적* 증거를 찾는다. 진화의 관점에서 볼 때, 집단을 따르는 것은 거의 항상 우리의 생존 전망에 긍정적이다. "모든 사람이 그것을 하고 있다면, 그것은 분별 있는 행동임에 틀림없다."라고 저명한 심리학자이자 *Influence*를 쓴 베스트셀러 작가인 Robert Cialdini는 설명한다. 오늘날 상품평에서 이를 자주 볼 수 있지만, 환경 내의 훨씬 더 미묘한 신호가 신뢰성을 나타낼 수 있다. 다음을 생각해보라. 여러분이 어느 현지 음식점을 방문할 때, 그들(식당 사람들)이 바쁜가? 밖에 줄이 있는가, 아니면 (사람들이 없어서) 자리를 찾

기 쉬운가? 기다리기는 성가시지만, 줄이라는 것은 음식이 맛있고 이곳의 좌석이 수요가 많다는 강력한 신호일 수 있다. 대개는 주변 사람들의 행동을 따르는 것이 좋다.

➡ 우리는 어떻게 행동할지 결정할 때 특히 (B) 불확실한 상황에 직면해 있다면 (A) 숫자에서 안전함과 안도감을 느끼는 경향이 있다.

Why? 왜 정답일까?

불확실한 상황에서 결정을 내려야 할 때 우리는 주변 집단의 행동을 따라 안전하게 선택하려 한다(~ following the group is almost always positive for our prospects of survival. / More often than not, it's good to adopt the practices of those around you.)는 내용의 글이다. 따라서 요약문의 빈칸 (A), (B)에 들어갈 말로 가장 적절한 것은 ① '(A) numbers(숫자), (B) uncertain(불확실한)'이다.

- **risky** [a] 위험한
- **evidence** [n] 근거, 증거
- **sensible** [a] 분별 있는, 현명한
- **subtle** [a] 미묘한
- **tasty** [a] 맛있는
- **more often than not** 대개
- **faced with** ~와 직면한
- **unrealistic** [a] 비현실적인
- **trustworthy** [a] 신뢰할 만한
- **prospect** [n] 예상, 가망성
- **frequently** [ad] 자주, 빈번히
- **hassle** [n] 성가신 일
- **in demand** 수요가 많은
- **practice** [n] 관례, 실행
- **uncertain** [a] 불확실한
- **unpleasant** [a] 불쾌한

구문 풀이

1행 To help decide what's risky and what's safe, who's trustworthy
목적(~하려면) 원형부정사   의문사절1   의문사절2
and who's not, we look for *social evidence*.

10-12 지폐가 부른 오해로 20년간 단절된 채 지냈던 쌍둥이 형제

[본문 해석]

(A)
어느 작은 마을의 한 상인에게 일란성 쌍둥이 아들들이 있었다. 『그 아들들은 아버지가 소유했던 가게에서 일했고 아버지가 죽었을 때, 그들은 그 가게를 물려받았다.』 20달러 지폐가 사라졌던 날까지는 모든 일이 잘 풀렸다. 형제 중 한 명이 카운터에 지폐를 두고 친구와 밖으로 나갔다. 『그가 돌아왔을 때, 돈은 사라졌다.』 (a) 그가 그의 형에게 "카운터에 있던 그 20달러 지폐 봤어?"라고 물었다.
(└ : 12번 ①의 근거 일치 / └ : 12번 ②의 근거 일치)

(C)
그의 형은 보지 못했다고 대답했다. 그러나 (c) 그 동생은 계속해서 그에게 물었다. "20달러 지폐가 일어나서 걸어 나갈 리 없잖아! 분명히 형은 그것을 봤을 거야!" (d) 그의 목소리에는 미묘한 비난이 담겨 있었다. 화가 나기 시작했다. 증오가 자리 잡았다. 머지않아 적대감이 쌍둥이 형제를 갈라놓았다. 그들은 말하는 것을 거부했다. 『그들은 마침내 더 이상 함께 일하지 않기로 결심했고 가게를 나누는 벽이 가게 중앙에 세워졌다.』 20년 동안 증오심이 자랐고, 그들의 가족과 지역사회에 전해졌다.
(└ : 12번 ④의 근거 일치)

(B)
그러던 어느 날 다른 주의 한 남자가 가게에 들렀다. 그가 들어와서 동생에게 "당신은 얼마나 여기에 있었나요?"라고 물었다. (b) 그는 평생 그곳에 있었다고 대답했다. 『손님은 "20년 전에 저는 이 마을에 유개화차를 타고 왔어요. 3일 동안 음식을 먹지 못했죠. 저는 이 가게에 들어와 카운터 위의 20달러 지폐 한 장을 봤어요. 저는 그것을 주머니에 넣고 나갔죠. 지금까지 저는 제 자신을 용서할 수 없었어요. 그래서 저는 그것을 돌려주러 돌아와야 했어요."라고 말했다.』
(└ : 12번 ③의 근거 일치)

(D)
손님은 그 남자의 눈에 눈물이 샘솟는 것을 보고 놀랐다. 동생은 "당신은 옆 가게로 가서 안에 있는 (e) 남자에게 똑같은 이야기를 해줄 수 있나요?"라고 말했다. 그런 다음 손님은 두 중년의 남자가 가게 앞에서 서로 안고 흐느껴 우는 것을 보고 훨씬 더 놀랐다. 『20년 후에, 단절된 관계가 회복되었다.』 그들을 갈라놓았던 분노의 벽은 무너졌다.
(└ : 12번 ⑤의 근거 불일치)

- **merchant** [n] 상인
- **disappear** [v] 사라지다
- **subtle** [a] 미묘한
- **hatred** [n] 증오
- **bitterness** [n] 냉소, 쓰라림, (맛이) 씀
- **identical twin** [n] 일란성 쌍둥이
- **boxcar** [n] (기차의) 유개화차
- **accusation** [n] 비난, 기소
- **set in** 시작되다
- **hostility** [n] 적대감

DAY 16

● spread ⓥ 퍼지다
● weep ⓥ 울다
● brokenness ⓝ 깨짐, 단절

구문 풀이

(A) 4행 One of the brothers had left the bill on the counter and
　　　　　　주어　　　　　　동사1(과거완료)
walked outside with a friend.
동사2(과거)

(C) 2행 "Twenty-dollar bills just don't get up and walk away! Surely
　　　　　　　　　　　　　　　　　　　　　　　　　　　문장 수식 부사
you must have seen it!"
「must have + 과거분사」: ~했음에 틀림없다

(D) 3행 Then the customer was even more amazed to see
　　　　　　　　　　　　　　비교급 수식 부사　감정 형용사　　부사적 용법(~해서)
the two middle-aged men hugging each other and weeping together
　　　to see의 목적어　　　 to see의 목·보1　　　to see의 목·보2
in the front of the store.

10　글의 순서 파악　　　정답률 77% | 정답 ②

주어진 글 (A)에 이어질 내용을 순서에 맞게 배열한 것으로 가장 적절한 것은?
① (B) – (D) – (C)　　　☑ (C) – (B) – (D)
③ (C) – (D) – (B)　　　④ (D) – (B) – (C)
⑤ (D) – (C) – (B)

Why? 왜 정답일까?

사이가 좋았던 쌍둥이 형제의 가게에서 어느 날 20달러짜리 지폐가 없어졌다는 내용의 (A) 뒤에는, 20달러를 보았냐는 동생의 물음에 형이 모른다고 답하자 동생이 비난조로 응수했고 형제가 서로를 미워하게 된 채로 20년을 보내게 되었다는 내용의 (C)가 먼저 연결된다. 이어서 (B)는 '그러던 어느 날' 한 남자가 동생의 가게로 찾아와 20달러짜리 지폐를 자신이 가져갔었다고 고백하는 내용을, (D)는 오해를 푼 형제가 서로 화해했다는 내용을 제시한다. 따라서 글의 순서로 가장 적절한 것은 ② '(C) – (B) – (D)'이다.

11　지칭 추론　　　정답률 71% | 정답 ⑤

밑줄 친 (a) ~ (e) 중에서 가리키는 대상이 나머지 넷과 다른 것은?
① (a)　② (b)　③ (c)　④ (d)　☑ (e)

Why? 왜 정답일까?

(a), (b), (c), (d)는 모두 쌍둥이 동생을, (e)는 쌍둥이 형을 가리키므로, (a) ~ (e) 중에서 가리키는 대상이 다른 하나는 ⑤ '(e)'이다.

12　세부 내용 파악　　　정답률 85% | 정답 ⑤

윗글에 관한 내용으로 적절하지 않은 것은?
① 쌍둥이 형제는 아버지의 가게를 물려받았다.
② 카운터 위에 놓여진 20달러 지폐가 없어졌다.
③ 손님은 20년 만에 가게에 다시 방문했다.
④ 쌍둥이 형제의 가게 중앙에 벽이 세워졌다.
☑ 쌍둥이 형제는 끝까지 화해하지 못했다.

Why? 왜 정답일까?

(D) 'After twenty years, the brokenness was repaired.'에 따르면 지폐의 행방에 관해 20년 만에 밝혀진 진실 덕분에 쌍둥이 형제는 마침내 관계를 회복했다. 따라서 내용과 일치하지 않는 것은 ⑤ '쌍둥이 형제는 끝까지 화해하지 못했다.'이다.

Why? 왜 오답일까?

① (A) 'The boys worked for their father in the store he owned and when he died, they took over the store.'의 내용과 일치한다.
② (A) 'One of the brothers had left the bill on the counter ~. When he returned, the money was gone.'의 내용과 일치한다.
③ (B) 'The customer said, "Twenty years ago ~ I came into this store and saw a twenty-dollar bill on the counter. I put it in my pocket and walked out. ~ I had to come back to return it."'의 내용과 일치한다.
④ (C) '~ a dividing wall was built down the center of the store.'의 내용과 일치한다.

---

01 ①	02 ④	03 ①	04 ⑤	05 ③
06 ⑤	07 ②	08 ④	09 ④	10 ②
11 ②	12 ④			

01　어른으로서 진정한 놀이 즐기기　　　정답률 88% | 정답 ①

다음 글에서 필자가 주장하는 바로 가장 적절한 것은?
☑ 어른도 규범에 얽매이지 말고 자유롭게 놀이를 즐겨야 한다.
② 아동에게 사회 규범을 내면화할 수 있는 놀이를 제공해야 한다.
③ 개인의 창의성을 극대화할 수 있는 놀이 문화를 조성해야 한다.
④ 타인의 시선을 의식하지 않고 자신의 목표 달성에 매진해야 한다.
⑤ 어른을 위한 잠재력 계발 프로그램에서 놀이의 비중을 늘려야 한다.

[본문 해석]

아마도 어른에게 놀이에 대한 가장 큰 장애물은 그들이 진정으로 논다면 그들 자신이 어리석거나, 부적절하거나, 혹은 바보같이 보일 것이라는 걱정일 것이다. 아니면 노는 것에 자신을 아주 송두리째 맡기는 것은 무책임하고, 미숙하며, 유치하다고 그들은 생각한다. 당찮음과 어리석음이 아이들에게는 자연스럽게 다가오지만, '경박함'을 경시하는 규범이 그들을 계속 두들겨 댄다. 이것은 부모나 교육제도에 의해 정해졌거나, 내면화되어 더 이상 의문시 되지 않는 다른 문화 규범에 의해 측정되어 온 성과 기준으로 평가되어 온 사람들에게 있어 특히 그러하다. 만약 누군가가 항상 존경할 만하고, 유능하며, 박식해 보이는 것에 대해 걱정하며 성년기를 보냈다면, 때때로 다 내려놓고 육체적이고 감정적으로 자유로워지는 것은 어려울 수 있다. 중요한 것은 즉흥적으로 하고, 흉내 내고, 오랫동안 숨겨져 있던 정체성을 나타낼 수 있도록 스스로에게 허락해야 한다는 것이다.

Why? 왜 정답일까?

서두에서 어른이 진정으로 놀이를 즐기기 어려운 까닭은 규범에 얽매여 생각하는 걱정 때문임을 지적한 후, 마지막 문장에서 즉흥적으로 하고 흉내를 내는 등 자유롭게 놀이를 즐길 필요가 있다(The thing is this: You have to give yourself permission to improvise, to mimic, to take on a long-hidden identity.)는 결론을 제시한 글이다. 따라서 필자가 주장하는 바로 가장 적절한 것은 ① '어른도 규범에 얽매이지 말고 자유롭게 놀이를 즐겨야 한다.'이다.

● dumb ⓐ 멍청한
● norm ⓝ 표준, 규범
● mimic ⓥ 흉내를 내다
● irresponsible ⓐ 신뢰할 수 없는
● internalize ⓥ 내면화하다

구문 풀이

1행 Probably the biggest roadblock to play for adults is the worry
　　　　　　　　　주어　　　　　　　　　　　　　　　동사　보어
[that they will look silly, improper, or dumb / if they allow themselves
동격 접속사　2형식 동사　　　　형용사 보어　　　　　　　「allow + 목적어 +
to truly play].
to부정사 : ~이 …하도록 허락하다」

02　결정을 미루는 것에 수반되는 대가　　　정답률 61% | 정답 ④

다음 글의 요지로 가장 적절한 것은?
① 적당한 수준의 불안감은 업무 수행에 도움이 된다.
② 성급한 의사 결정은 의도하지 않은 결과를 초래한다.
③ 반복되는 실수를 줄이기 위해서는 신중함이 요구된다.
☑ 더 나은 선택을 위해 결정을 미루는 것은 결국 해가 된다.
⑤ 규칙적인 생활 습관은 직장에서의 성공 가능성을 높인다.

[본문 해석]

FOBO, 즉 더 나은 선택에 대한 두려움은 더 나은 어떤 것이 생길 것이라는 불안감인데, 이것은 결정을 내릴 때 기존의 선택지에 전념하는 것을 탐탁지 않게 한다. 그것은 여러분이 모든 선택지를 열어 두고 위험을 피하도록 만드는 풍족함의 고통이다. 여러분의 선택지들을 평가하고, 하나를 선택하고 여러분의 하루를 살아가기보다는, 여러분은 꼭 해야 할 것을 미룬다. 그것은 알람시계의 스누즈 버튼을 누르고는 결국 이불을 머리 위로 뒤집어 쓰고 다시 잠들어 버리는 것과 다르지 않다. 아마도 여러분이 고생하여 알게 되었듯이 스누즈 버튼을 많이 누르면, 결국 늦어서 사무실로 달리게 되고, 여러분의 하루와 기분을 망치게 된다. 스누즈 버튼을 누르는 것이 그때는 기분이 아주 좋겠지만, 그것은 결국 대가를 요구한다.

Why? 왜 정답일까?

더 나은 선택이 생길지도 모른다는 생각으로 결정하기를 미루다 보면 결국 대가가 따를 수 있다(~ it ultimately demands a price.)는 내용의 글로, 특히 글 후반부에서 '결정을 미루는' 행위를 '아침 알람이 울릴 때 스누즈 버튼을 누르는' 행위에 비유하고 있다. 따라서 글의 요지로 가장 적절한 것은 ④ '더 나은 선택을 위해 결정을 미루는 것은 결국 해가 된다.'이다.

- anxiety ⓝ 불안
- commit to ~에 전념하다
- assess ⓥ 평가하다
- snooze button 스누즈 버튼(아침에 잠이 깬 뒤 조금 더 자기 위해 누르는 타이머 버튼)
- end up 결국 ~하게 되다
- ultimately ⓐⓓ 결국, 궁극적으로
- undesirable ⓐ 탐탁지 않은, 원하지 않는
- abundance ⓝ 풍족함
- inevitable ⓐ 피할 수 없는, 반드시 있는
- ruin ⓥ 망치다

구문 풀이

10행 As you probably found out the hard way, if you hit snooze
접속사(~대로, ~듯이) 조건 접속사 현재시제
enough times, you'll end up being late and racing for the office,
미래시제 동명사1 동명사2
your day and mood ruined.
의미상 주어 분사구문(그리고 ~하다)

★★★ 1등급 대비 고난도 2점 문제

03 관광 산업이 성장한 배경 정답률 39% | 정답 ①

다음 글의 주제로 가장 적절한 것은?

✓ factors that caused tourism expansion
관광 산업의 확장을 일으킨 요인
② discomfort at a popular tourist destination
유명한 여행지에서의 불편
③ importance of tourism in society and economy
사회와 경제에서 관광 산업이 갖는 중요성
④ negative impacts of tourism on the environment
관광 산업이 환경에 미치는 부정적 영향
⑤ various types of tourism and their characteristics
다양한 유형의 관광 산업과 그 특징

[본문 해석]
국가들의 사회적 및 경제적 상황이 더 나아지면서, 임금 수준과 근로 여건이 개선되었다. 점차 사람들은 더 많은 휴가를 받게 되었다. 동시에, 운송 형태가 개선되었고 장소를 이동하는 것이 더 빠르고 더 저렴해졌다. 영국의 산업 혁명이 이러한 변화 중 많은 것을 일으켰다. 19세기에, 철도로 인해 Blackpool과 Brighton 같은 현재 유명한 해안가 리조트가 들어서게 되었다. 철도가 생기면서 많은 대형 호텔이 생겨났다. 예를 들어, 캐나다에서는 새로운 대륙 횡단 철도 시스템이 로키산맥의 Banff Springs와 Chateau Lake Louise 같은 유명한 호텔 건설을 가능하게 했다. 이후에 항공 운송의 출현은 세계의 더 많은 곳(으로 가는 길)을 열어 주었고 관광 산업의 성장을 이끌었다.

Why? 왜 정답일까?

관광 산업의 성장(tourism growth)을 이끈 원인을 흐름에 따라 열거하는 글이다. 가장 먼저 사회경제적 상황이 개선되면서 임금 수준과 근로 조건이 개선되고, 이에 따라 여가가 늘어나고, 운송 사업이 발달하여 이동을 편하게 했다는 것이다. 따라서 글의 주제로 가장 적절한 것은 ① '관광 산업의 확장을 일으킨 요인'이다.

- wage ⓝ 임금
- improve ⓥ 향상되다
- time off 휴가
- industrial revolution 산업 혁명
- tourism ⓝ 관광(업)
- expansion ⓝ 확장
- tourist destination 관광지
- working condition 근무 조건
- gradually ⓐⓓ 점차, 점점
- transport ⓝ 운송, 이동
- lead to ~을 초래하다
- factor ⓝ 요인
- discomfort ⓝ 불편
- characteristic ⓝ 특징

구문 풀이

9행 In Canada, for example, the new coast-to-coast railway
system made possible the building of such famous hotels as Banff
동사 목적격 보어 목적어(길어져서 뒤로 빠짐)
Springs and Chateau Lake Louise in the Rockies.

---

04 국가별 GDP 대비 의료 지출 정답률 81% | 정답 ⑤

다음 도표의 내용과 일치하지 않는 것은?

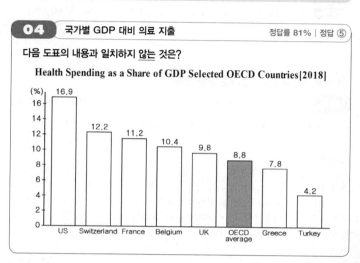

Health Spending as a Share of GDP Selected OECD Countries[2018]

[본문 해석]
위 그래프는 2018년 선택된 OECD 국가들의 의료 지출을 GDP 점유율로 보여 준다. ① 평균적으로, OECD 국가들은 GDP의 8.8%를 의료에 지출한 것으로 추정되었다. ② 위 국가들 중 미국은 GDP의 16.9%로 가장 높은 점유율을 보였고, 이어 스위스는 12.2%를 보였다. ③ 프랑스는 GDP의 11% 이상을 지출했던 반면, 터키는 GDP의 5% 이하를 의료에 지출했다. ④ GDP 점유율로서 벨기에의 의료 지출은 프랑스와 영국 사이였다. ⑤ 영국과 그리스 사이에는 의료에 지출된 GDP의 점유율에 있어 3%p의 차이가 있었다.

Why? 왜 정답일까?

도표에 따르면 GDP를 기준으로 영국의 의료 지출은 9.8%, 그리스의 의료 지출은 7.8%였다. 즉 두 국가 간 비율의 차이는 2%p이므로, 도표와 일치하지 않는 것은 ⑤이다.

- on average 평균적으로
- estimate ⓥ 추정하다, 추산하다

---

05 비슷한 대상과 어울리기를 선호하는 경향 정답률 63% | 정답 ③

다음 글의 밑줄 친 부분 중, 어법상 틀린 것은?

[본문 해석]
우리는 보통 우리와 같다고 생각하는 사람들과 가장 잘 지낸다. 사실, 우리는 그들을 찾아낸다. 이 이유로 리틀 이탈리아, 차이나타운, 코리아타운과 같은 장소들이 존재한다. 하지만 나는 인종, 피부색, 또는 종교만을 말하는 것이 아니다. 우리의 가치관을 공유하고 우리와 같은 방식으로 세상을 바라보는 사람들을 말하는 것이다. 속담에서처럼, 같은 깃털을 가진 새가 함께 무리 짓는다(유유상종이다). 이것은 우리 종이 발전한 방식에 깊게 뿌리박혀 있는 매우 흔한 인간의 경향이다. 여러분이 숲에 나가 걷는다고 상상해 보라. 친숙하지 않거나 낯선 것은 여러분을 죽이는 데 관심이 있을 가능성이 커 여러분은 그런 것을 피하도록 조건화되어 있을 것이다. 유사점(을 갖고 있는 것)은 우리가 다른 사람들과 마음이 더 잘 통할 수 있도록 하는데, 그들이 우리를 다른 사람들보다 더 깊이 있는 수준으로 이해할 것으로 생각하기 때문이다.

Why? 왜 정답일까?

관계대명사 what은 선행사를 포함하고 있는데, ③ 앞에는 선행사 a very common human tendency가 있으므로 what을 that 또는 which로 고쳐야 한다. 따라서 어법상 틀린 것은 ③이다.

Why? 왜 오답일까?

① 주어가 복수 명사인 places이므로 복수 동사 exist가 바르게 쓰였다. like Little Italy, Chinatown, and Koreatown은 주어 places를 꾸미는 전명구이다.

★★ 문제 해결 꿀~팁 ★★

▶ 많이 틀린 이유는?
사회경제적 변화 상황이 결국 '관광업의 성장'을 이끌었다는 결론이 글의 핵심이다. 따라서 첫 문장에 언급된 '사회와 경제'만 다소 두루뭉술하게 언급하는 ③은 답으로 부적합하다.

▶ 문제 해결 방법은?
시간 흐름에 따라 관광업의 성장을 이끈 배경 요인을 열거하는 글로, '그래서 결론이 무엇인지'를 파악하는 것이 중요하다.

[문제편 p.102]

② 앞의 일반동사구 look at을 가리키는 대동사 do가 바르게 쓰였다.
④ something unfamiliar or foreign을 받는 단수 대명사로 it이 바르게 쓰였다.
⑤ 사역동사 make의 목적격 보어로 원형부정사 relate가 바르게 쓰였다.

- get along with ~와 잘 지내다, 어울리다
- race ⓝ 인종
- be rooted in ~에 뿌리박고 있다
- avoid ⓥ 피하다
- likelihood ⓝ 가능성
- seek out (오랫동안 공들여) 찾아다니다
- as the saying goes 속담에서 말하듯이
- condition ⓥ 조건화하다
- unfamiliar ⓐ 친숙하지 않은
- relate to ~을 이해하다, ~에 공감하다

구문 풀이

1행 We usually get along best with people [who (we think) are like us].
선행사 주격 관·대 ( ) : 삽입절

★★★ 1등급 대비 고난도 2점 문제

06 인과관계 추론에 오류가 생기는 이유 정답률 44% | 정답 ⑤

다음 글의 밑줄 친 부분 중, 문맥상 낱말의 쓰임이 적절하지 않은 것은?

[본문 해석]

사람들은 선천적으로 사건의 원인을 찾는, 즉, 설명과 이야기를 구성하려는 경향이 있다. 그것이 스토리텔링이 그토록 ① 설득력 있는 수단인 한 가지 이유이다. 이야기는 우리의 경험을 떠올리게 하고 새로운 경우의 사례를 제공한다. 우리의 경험과 다른 이들의 이야기로부터 우리는 사람들이 행동하고 상황이 돌아가는 방식에 관해 ② 일반화하는 경향이 있다. 우리는 사건에 원인을 귀착시키고 이러한 원인과 결과 ③ 쌍이 이치에 맞는 한, 그것을 미래의 사건을 이해하는 데 사용한다. 하지만 이러한 인과관계의 귀착은 종종 잘못되기도 한다. 때때로 그것은 ④ 잘못된 원인을 연관시키기도 하고, 발생하는 어떤 일에 대해서는 단 하나의 원인만 있지 않기도 하다. 오히려 그 결과에 모두가 원인이 되는 복잡한 일련들의 사건들이 있는데, 만일 사건들 중에 어느 하나라도 발생하지 않았었다면, 결과는 ⑤ 유사했을(→ 달랐을) 것이다. 하지만 원인이 되는 행동이 단 하나만 있지 않을 때조차도, 그것이 사람들로 하여금 어떤 하나를 귀착시키는 것을 막지는 못한다.

Why? 왜 정답일까?

'Sometimes they implicate the wrong causes, and for some things that happen, there is no single cause. Rather, there is a complex chain of events that all contribute to the result; ~'에 따르면 한 가지 결과가 여러 원인과 연관될 수 있기에 인과관계의 귀착은 잘못될 수 있는데, 원인이 되는 여러 사건 중 하나라도 발생하지 않았으면 결과는 '달랐을' 수도 있으므로 ⑤의 similar는 different로 고쳐야 한다. 따라서 문맥상 낱말의 쓰임이 적절하지 않은 것은 ⑤이다.

- innately ad 선천적으로
- persuasive ⓐ 설득력이 있는
- generalization ⓝ 일반화
- make sense 이치에 맞다, 일리가 있다
- assign ⓥ (원인을) ~에 돌리다, ~의 탓으로 보다
- inclined to ~하는 경향이 있는
- instance ⓝ 경우, 사례
- attribute A to B A를 B의 결과로 보다
- contribute to ~의 원인이 되다

구문 풀이

12행 Rather, there is a complex chain of events [that all contribute to the result]; / if any one of the events would not have occurred, the result would be similar.
선행사 주격 관·대 동사(복수)
「if+주어+과거 조동사+have+과거분사 ~, 주어+과거 조동사+동사원형 : 혼합 가정법」

★★ 문제 해결 꿀~팁 ★★

▶ 많이 틀린 이유는?
사람들은 알맞은 원인과 결과를 서로 연결(pairing)시켜 사건의 앞뒤를 이해하려 하는 경향이 있음을 소개한 글로, ③은 주제에 부합하는 선택지이다. 이어서 'Yet these causal attributions are often mistaken.'에서는 인과관계의 연결이 때때로 '잘못될' 수도 있음을 지적하므로, mistaken을 wrong으로 바꾼 ④ 또한 주제에 부합한다.

▶ 문제 해결 방법은?
⑤가 포함된 문장의 가정법 구문을 정확히 이해해야 한다. 한 가지 결과에도 여러 원인이 관여한다는 것은 원인들 중 하나라도 발생하지 않았더라면 '똑같은 결과가 일어나지 않았을 수도 있다는' 뜻이며, 이는 결과가 '달라질' 수도 있었다는 말과 같다.

07 사전 통보로 변화에 적응할 시간을 주기 정답률 61% | 정답 ②

다음 빈칸에 들어갈 말로 가장 적절한 것을 고르시오.

① unite – 연합할
② adapt – 적응할
③ object – 반대할
④ compete – 경쟁할
⑤ recover – 회복할

[본문 해석]

우리는 소통하기 위해 더 이상 전보를 보내지 않지만 이것은 사전 통보를 하는 것에 대한 훌륭한 비유이다. 때때로 여러분은 중요한 정보를 미리 잘 전달함으로써 다가오는 변화를 자신에게 가까운 사람들에게 알려야 한다. 사람들에게 그 변화를 이해하고 받아들일 충분한 시간을 주지 않고 "지금부터 우리는 일을 다르게 할 겁니다."라고 말하는 것과 "다음 달부터 우리는 일에 다르게 접근할 겁니다." 같은 말을 하는 것 사이에는 큰 차이가 있다. 전보를 보내는 것은 사람들이 적응할 수 있도록 해 준다. 전보를 보내는 것은 다가오는 사건이나 상황을 보고 다른 사람들에게 그 변화를 처리하고 받아들일 충분한 시간을 주는 기술을 포함한다. 사람들을 익숙하고 편안한 것에서 벗어나게 할 무엇이든 전보로 보내라. 이것은 그들이 그 상황을 받아들이고 일어나고 있는 일을 최대한으로 활용할 수 있는 처리 시간을 허락할 것이다.

Why? 왜 정답일까?

빈칸이 포함된 문장 뒤에서 비유적 의미의 전보는 사람들이 다가오는 변화를 처리하고 받아들일 시간을 충분히 준다(Telegraphing involves the art of seeing an upcoming event or circumstance and giving others enough time to process and accept the change. / This will allow processing time for them to accept the circumstances and make the most of what's happening.)고 설명하므로, 빈칸에 들어갈 말로 가장 적절한 것은 ② '적응할'이다.

- telegraph ⓝ 전보
- metaphor ⓝ 은유
- notice ⓝ 통지, 통보
- convey ⓥ 전달하다
- accept ⓥ 받아들이다
- circumstance ⓝ 상황
- comfortable ⓐ 편안한
- anymore ad 더 이상
- advance ⓐ 사전의
- upcoming ⓐ 다가오는
- from now on 이제부터, 지금부터
- involve ⓥ 포함하다
- familiar ⓐ 익숙한
- make the most of ~을 최대한 활용하다

구문 풀이

3행 Sometimes, you must inform those close to you of upcoming change by conveying important information well in advance.
「inform+A of+B : A에게 B를 알리다」
「by+동명사 : ~함으로써」

★★★ 1등급 대비 고난도 3점 문제

08 의뢰인의 속마음을 드러내준 의뢰인의 발 정답률 40% | 정답 ④

다음 빈칸에 들어갈 말로 가장 적절한 것을 고르시오. [3점]

① a signal of his politeness – 그의 공손함의 표시
② the subject of the conversation – 대화의 주제
③ expressing interest in my words – 내 말에 관심을 나타내고 있는
④ the most honest communicators – 가장 정직한 의사 전달자
⑤ stepping excitedly onto the ground – 발을 경쾌하게 내딛고 있는

[본문 해석]

최근에 나는 나와 거의 5시간을 보낸 고객과 함께 있었다. 저녁을 위해 헤어지면서, 우리는 그날 다룬 내용을 되새겼다. 비록 우리의 대화가 매우 평등했음에도 불구하고, 나는 나의 고객이 한쪽 다리를 몸과 직각으로 두고 있다는 것을 알아챘는데, 외견상 (한쪽 다리가) 혼자서 떠나고 싶어 하는 것 같았다. 그때 나는 "지금 정말 가셔야 하죠, 그렇지 않나요?"라고 말했다. "네."라고 그는 인정했다. "정말 미안합니다. 무례하게 굴고 싶지는 않았지만 런던에 전화해야 하는데 시간이 5분밖에 없어요!" 여기서 내 의뢰인의 언어와 그의 몸의 대부분은 긍정적인 감정만을 드러내고 있었다. 그러나 그의 발은 가장 정직한 의사 전달자였고 그것들은 그가 남아있고 싶어 하지만 해야 할 일이 있다는 것을 분명히 나타냈다.

Why? 왜 정답일까?

'~ I noticed that my client was holding one leg at a right angle to his body, seemingly wanting to take off on its own.'에서 필자는 의뢰인이 한쪽 발을 몸과 직각으로 위치하게 빼둔 것을 보고 의뢰인이 빨리 가야 한다고 생각하고 있음

을 눈치챘다고 하므로, 빈칸에 들어갈 말로 가장 적절한 것은 발이 의뢰인의 속마음을 드러내 주었다는 의미를 나타내는 ④ '가장 정직한 의사 전달자'이다.

- **reflect on** ⓥ ~을 되새기다, 반추하다
- **right angle** ⓝ 직각
- **rude** ⓐ 무례한
- **communicator** ⓝ 의사 전달자
- **cover** ⓥ (기사 등에서) 다루다
- **take off** ⓥ 떠나다
- **politeness** ⓝ 공손함
- **excitedly** ⓐⓓ 신나게, 들떠서

구문 풀이

12행 His feet, however, were the most honest communicators,
주어1　　　　　　　　　　　　　동사1
and they clearly told me that as much as he wanted to stay, duty
주어2　　　　동사2　　　　　'(문두의) as + 원급 + as : ~하기는 하지만',　　주어
　　　　　　　　　　　　　　　└→ 접속사(~것)
was calling.
동사

★★ 문제 해결 꿀~팁 ★★

▶ 많이 틀린 이유는?
일화가 나오면 부분적인 표현에 집중하기보다 이야기의 전체적인 흐름을 파악해야 한다. ①은 본문의 'I didn't want to be rude ~'만, ⑤는 '~ seemingly wanting to take off on its own.'만 보았을 때 각각 고르기 쉬운 오답이다.
▶ 문제 해결 방법은?
이 일화의 핵심은 필자의 고객이 말이나 몸 자세로 대체로 긍정적인 신호를 나타내고 있었음에도 불구하고 유일하게 '몸과 직각을 이루며 떠나고 싶어 하는 것처럼 보였던' 그의 발이 그의 진심을 대변해주고 있었다는 것이다. 이렇듯 이야기 흐름의 큰 줄기를 파악한 후 이를 토대로 추론할 수 있는 논리적인 결론을 선택지에서 찾도록 한다.

09　기술 진보로 가능해진 새로운 서비스 제공　정답률 49% | 정답 ④

다음 글에서 전체 흐름과 관계 없는 문장은?

[본문 해석]
정보와 의사소통 기술(ICTs)의 빠른 진화는 관광업과 서비스업의 역학과 비즈니스 모델을 급격하게 변화시켰다. ① 이것은 서비스 제공자 간 새로운 수준/형식의 경쟁으로 이어지고, 새로운 서비스를 통해 고객 경험을 변화시킨다. ② 독특한 경험을 만드는 것과 고객에게 편리한 서비스를 제공하는 것은 만족감을 낳고, 종국에는 서비스 제공자나 브랜드(즉, 호텔)에 대한 고객 충성도로 이어진다. ③ 특히, 관광업 분야에서 받아들여진 가장 최근의 *기술적* 부상은 모바일 애플리케이션으로 대표된다. ④ 서비스 제공자 간의 경쟁을 증가시키는 것이 반드시 고객 서비스의 질을 증진시키는 것을 의미하지는 않는다. ⑤ 사실, 관광객에게 호텔 예약, 항공권 발권, 그리고 지역 관광지 추천과 같은 서비스에 대한 모바일 접근 권한을 주는 것은 강력한 흥미와 상당한 수익을 만들어 낸다.

Why?　왜 정답일까?

빠른 기술적 진보로 소비자에게 새로운 경험과 서비스를 제공하는 것이 가능해졌고, 이것이 고객 만족이나 충성도, 수익 면에서 모두 좋은 결과를 이끌어낼 수 있다는 내용이다. ③과 ⑤는 특히 관광업의 모바일 애플리케이션을 예로 들고 있다. 한편 ④는 서비스 제공자 간 경쟁의 증가가 고객 서비스 질을 반드시 높이지는 않는다는 내용이어서 흐름상 무관하다. 따라서 전체 흐름과 관계 없는 문장은 ④이다.

- **fast-paced** ⓐ 빠른
- **dynamics** ⓝ 역학, 역동성
- **loyalty** ⓝ 충성도
- **profit** ⓝ 수익
- **radically** ⓐⓓ 급진적으로
- **competitiveness** ⓝ 경쟁력, 경쟁적인 것
- **empower** ⓥ 권한을 부여하다

구문 풀이

10행 In particular, the most recent technological boost
　　　　　　　　　　　주어(최상급)
received by the tourism sector is represented by mobile applications.
과거분사　　　　　　　　　동사(수동태)

10　결정의 형성　정답률 72% | 정답 ②

주어진 글 다음에 이어질 글의 순서로 가장 적절한 것을 고르시오. [3점]

① (A) – (C) – (B)
② (B) – (A) – (C) ✓
③ (B) – (C) – (A)
④ (C) – (A) – (B)
⑤ (C) – (B) – (A)

[본문 해석]
아마 여러분은 이 농담을 들어본 적이 있을 것이다. "코끼리를 어떻게 먹지?" 정답은 '한 번에 한 입'이다.

(B) 그렇다면, 여러분은 어떻게 지구를 '건설'하는가? 이것도 간단하다. 한 번에 하나의 원자이다. 원자는 결정의 기본 구성 요소이고, 모든 암석은 결정으로 이루어져 있기 때문에, 여러분은 원자에 대해 더 많이 알수록 더 좋다. 결정은 과학자들이 습성이라고 부르는 다양한 모양으로 나온다.

(A) 일반적인 결정 습성은 사각형, 삼각형, 육면의 육각형을 포함한다. 보통 여러분이 얼음을 만들 때와 같이 액체가 차가워질 때 결정이 형성된다. 많은 경우, 결정은 완벽한 모양을 허용하지 않는 방식으로 형성된다. 조건이 너무 차갑거나, 너무 뜨겁거나, 혹은 원천 물질이 충분하지 않으면 이상하고 뒤틀린 모양을 형성할 수 있다.

(C) 하지만 조건이 맞을 때, 우리는 아름다운 배열을 본다. 보통, 이것은 개별적인 원자들이 충분한 시간을 들여 결합해서 *결정격자*라고 알려진 것에 완벽하게 들어맞게 되는 느리고 안정적인 환경을 수반한다. 이것은 반복하여 보이는 원자의 기본적인 구조이다.

Why?　왜 정답일까?

주어진 글에서 '코끼리를 어떻게 먹나'라는 물음에 '한 번에 한 입씩' 먹으면 된다는 농담이 있다고 하는데, (B)는 이것이 지구가 만들어진 과정에도 적용될 수 있다면서 결정의 습성을 언급한다. (A)는 이 결정의 습성을 설명하면서, 많은 경우 결정이 뒤틀린 모양으로 형성된다고 언급하는데, (C)는 But으로 흐름을 반전시키며 아름다운 배열을 지닌 결정도 만들어진다고 설명한다. 따라서 글의 순서로 가장 적절한 것은 ② '(B) – (A) – (C)'이다.

- **bite** ⓝ 한 입 (베어문 조각) ⓥ 베어 물다
- **hexagon** ⓝ 육각형
- **ice cube** 얼음 조각
- **twisted** ⓐ 뒤틀린
- **be made up of** ~로 구성되다
- **plenty of** 많은
- **lattice** ⓝ 격자 (모양)
- **crystal** ⓝ 결정
- **liquid** ⓝ 액체
- **allow for** ~을 허용하다
- **atom** ⓝ 원자
- **steady** ⓐ 안정된, 꾸준한
- **fit into** ~에 들어 맞다
- **time after time** 자주, 매번, 되풀이해서

구문 풀이

17행 Usually, this involves a slow, steady environment [where the
　　　　　　　　　　　　　　선행사(상황)　　　　　　관계부사
individual atoms have plenty of time to join and fit perfectly into
　　　　　　　　　　　　　　　　　형용사적 용법　　　　　　　전치사
{what's known as the *crystal lattice*}].
　명사절

11-12　양질의 수면을 위한 적정한 침실 온도

[본문 해석]
표준적인 침구와 복장을 가정할 때 대략 화씨 65도(섭씨 18.3도)의 침실 온도가 대부분의 사람들의 수면에 이상적이다. 이것은 안락함을 위해서는 다소 너무 추운 것처럼 들리기 때문에 많은 사람을 (a) 놀라게 한다. 물론, 이 특정 온도는 해당하는 사람과 그들의 성별 그리고 나이에 따라 다를 것이다. 하지만, 권장 칼로리처럼, 그것은 평균적인 사람에게 좋은 목표이다. 『우리 대부분은 좋은 수면을 위해 침실 온도를 이상적인 것보다 높게 설정하는데, 이는 그렇게 하지 않는다면 당신이 얻을 수 있는 것보다 (b) 더 낮은 수면의 양과 질을 초래할 것이다.』따뜻한 침구와 잠옷이 사용되지 않는다면 화씨 55도보다 더 낮은 온도는 잠을 자는 데 도움이 되기보다 오히려 해로울 수 있다. 『하지만, 우리 대부분은 70도 또는 72도라는 너무 높은 침실 온도를 설정하는 (c) 정반대의 범주에 속한다.』밤에 잠을 못 자는 환자를 치료하는 수면 임상의는 종종 침실 온도를 묻고, 환자들에게 온도 조절 장치의 현재 설정값을 그들이 지금 사용하는 설정값보다 3도에서 5도 가량 (d) 올리라고(→ 낮추라고) 조언할 것이다. 온도가 수면에 미치는 영향에 대해 불신하는 사람은 누구든지 주제에 관한 몇몇 관련 실험들을 살펴볼 수 있다. 예를 들어, 과학자들은 혈액을 피부의 표면으로 올라가게 하고 열을 방출시키기 위해 쥐의 발이나 몸을 서서히 따뜻하게 했고, 그럼으로써 심부 체온을 낮추었다. 그 쥐들은 그렇지 않았던 평상시보다 훨씬 (e) 더 빨리 잠들었다.

- **specific** ⓐ 특정한, 구체적인
- **depending on** prep ~에 따라
- **vary** ⓥ 다르다
- **recommendation** ⓝ 권장, 충고

- ideal ⓐ 이상적인
- otherwise 〔ad〕 그렇지 않으면
- disbelieve of ⓥ ~을 불신하다
- quantity ⓝ 수
- clinician ⓝ 임상의
- surface ⓝ 표면

구문 풀이

> **9행** Most of us set bedroom temperatures higher than are ideal
> 　　　　 주어1　　　　　　　　　　　　　　　　　　 동사1
> for good sleep and this likely contributes to lower quantity and quality
> 　　　　　　　　　　주어2　　　　동사2(~의 원인이 되다)　　　　명사구(to의 목적어)
> of sleep than you are otherwise capable of getting.

---

11 제목 파악　　　　　　　　　　　　　정답률 66% | 정답 ②

윗글의 제목으로 가장 적절한 것은?

① Signs of Sleep Problems – 수면 문제의 징후
☑ Stay Cool for Better Sleep – 더 좋은 수면을 위해 시원하게 유지해라
③ Turn Up the Heat in Your Room – 당신의 방 온도를 높여라
④ How to Correct Bad Sleeping Posture – 나쁜 수면 자세를 고치는 방법
⑤ A Key to Quality Sleep: Clean Bedding – 양질의 수면을 위한 비결: 깨끗한 침구

Why? 왜 정답일까?

첫 두 문장에 따르면 일반 사람들에게 적합한 침실 온도는 얼핏 '춥다'고 느껴질 수 있는 섭씨 18.3도 정도이지만, 'Most of us set bedroom temperatures higher than are ideal for good sleep and this likely contributes to lower quantity and quality of sleep than you are otherwise capable of getting.'에서 언급하듯이 대부분의 사람들은 이상적인 수준보다 높게 침실 온도를 설정하므로 이에 따라 수면의 양과 질이 저하되는 문제를 겪을 수 있다. 따라서 글의 제목으로 가장 적절한 것은 ② '더 좋은 수면을 위해 시원하게 유지해라'이다.

---

12 어휘 추론　　　　　　　　　　　　정답률 51% | 정답 ④

밑줄 친 (a) ~ (e) 중에서 문맥상 낱말의 쓰임이 적절하지 않은 것은? [3점]

① (a)　　② (b)　　③ (c)　　☑ (d)　　⑤ (e)

Why? 왜 정답일까?

'However, most of us fall into the opposite category of setting a controlled bedroom temperature that is too high: ~'에서 너무 낮은 온도도 수면에 방해가 되지만, 대부분의 사람들은 이와 반대로 너무 높은 온도를 설정해 둔다고 언급한다. 이에 이어지는 (d)가 포함된 문장은 그리하여 수면 임상의들이 환자들을 볼 때면 종종 침실 온도를 물어보고 온도를 '낮추도록' 권유한다는 의미를 나타내야 한다. 따라서 (d)의 raise를 반의어인 drop으로 고쳐야 한다. 밑줄 친 (a) ~ (e) 중 문맥상 낱말의 쓰임이 적절하지 않은 것은 ④ '(d)'이다.

DAY 18　20분 미니 모의고사

01 ①	02 ⑤	03 ④	04 ③	05 ④
06 ①	07 ①	08 ⑤	09 ①	10 ④
11 ③	12 ④			

---

01 브랜드 로고 제작 요청　　　　　　정답률 89% | 정답 ①

다음 글의 목적으로 가장 적절한 것은?

☑ 회사 로고 제작을 의뢰하려고
② 변경된 회사 로고를 홍보하려고
③ 회사 비전에 대한 컨설팅을 요청하려고
④ 회사 창립 10주년 기념품을 주문하려고
⑤ 회사 로고 제작 일정 변경을 공지하려고

[본문 해석]

Jones씨에게,

저는 KHJ Corporation의 홍보부 이사 James Arkady입니다. 저희 회사의 창립 10주년을 기념하기 위해서 저희 회사 브랜드 정체성을 다시 설계하고 새로운 로고를 선보일 계획입니다. 저희 회사의 핵심 비전 '인류애를 고양하자'를 가장 잘 반영한 로고를 제작해 주시기를 요청합니다. 새로운 로고가 저희 회사 브랜드 메시지를 전달하고 KHJ의 가치를 담아내기를 바랍니다. 로고 디자인 제안서를 완성하는 대로 보내 주십시오. 감사합니다.

James Arkady 드림

Why? 왜 정답일까?

'We request you to create a logo that best suits our company's core vision, ~'에서 회사 핵심 비전을 잘 반영한 로고를 제작해줄 것을 요청한다고 하므로, 글의 목적으로 가장 적절한 것은 ① '회사 로고 제작을 의뢰하려고'이다.

- identity ⓝ 정체성
- celebrate ⓥ 기념하다
- suit ⓥ ~에 적합하다
- humanity ⓝ 인류애
- launch ⓥ 시작하다, 런칭하다
- anniversary ⓝ 기념일
- inspire ⓥ 고무시키다

구문 풀이

> **5행** We request you to create a logo [that best suits our
> 　　　　5형식 동사　목적어　목적격 보어　선행사　└→주격 관계대명사
> company's core vision, 'To inspire humanity.']

---

02 믿음보다는 사용의 대상인 패러다임　정답률 70% | 정답 ⑤

다음 글의 주제로 가장 적절한 것은? [3점]

① difficulty in drawing novel theories from existing paradigms
　기존의 패러다임으로부터 새로운 이론을 도출하는 것의 어려움
② significant influence of personal beliefs in scientific fields
　과학 분야에서 개인 신념의 상당한 영향력
③ key factors that promote the rise of innovative paradigms
　혁신적 패러다임의 출현을 촉진하는 핵심 요인
④ roles of a paradigm in grouping like-minded researchers
　생각이 비슷한 연구원들을 분류할 때 패러다임의 역할
☑ functional aspects of a paradigm in scientific research
　과학 연구에서 패러다임의 기능적 측면

[본문 해석]

과학자들은 패러다임을 믿기보다는 *사용한다*. 연구에서 패러다임의 사용은 일반적으로 공유된 개념, 상징적 표현, 실험 및 수학적 도구와 절차, 그리고 심지어 동일한 이론적 진술의 일부를 사용하여 관련된 문제들을 다룬다. 과학자들은 다른 사람들이 받아들일 방식으로 이러한 다양한 요소들을 사용하는 *방법*을 이해하기만 하면 된다. 따라서 이러한 공유된 실행의 요소들은 과학자들이 그것들을 사용할 때 그들이 하고 있는 것에 관한 그들의 믿음에서 그 어떤 비슷한 통일성을 전제로 할 필요는 없다. 실제로, 패러다임의 한 가지 역할은 과학자들이 자신이 무엇을 하고 있는지 또는 자신이 그것에 관해 무엇을 믿고 있는지에 대한 상세한 설명을 제공할 필요 없이 성공적으로 일할 수 있게 하는 것이다. Thomas Kuhn이 언급하기를, 과학자들은 "패러다임에 대한 완전한 *해석*이나 *이론적 설명*에 동의하거나, 심지어 그런 것을 만들어 내려고 시도조차 하지

않고도 그것을 *식별*하는 데 있어서 일치를 보일 수 있다. 표준적인 해석이나 규칙으로 축약되어 합의된 것이 부족하다 해도 패러다임이 연구를 안내하는 것을 막지는 못할 것이다."

Why? 왜 정답일까?

첫 문장에서 과학자들에게 패러다임은 믿기보다는 사용하는 대상(Scientists *use* paradigms rather than believing them.)이라고 했다. 이어서 Indeed로 시작하는 문장에서는 패러다임은 과학자들이 패러다임에 관해 어떻게 생각하는가에 상관없이 연구를 진행할 수 있게 도와준다고 했다. 따라서 글의 주제로 가장 적절한 것은 패러다임의 역할 또는 유용성을 다른 말로 진술한 ⑤ '과학 연구에서 패러다임의 기능적 측면'이다.

- **address** ⓥ (문제를) 다루다, 처리하다
- **procedure** ⓝ 절차
- **comparable** ⓐ 비슷한
- **identification** ⓝ 식별
- **rationalization** ⓝ 이론적 설명, 합리화
- **like-minded** ⓐ 생각이 비슷한
- **employ** ⓥ 사용하다
- **presuppose** ⓥ 전제하다
- **account** ⓝ 설명
- **interpretation** ⓝ 해석
- **prevent A from B** A가 B하지 못하게 하다

구문 풀이

11행 Indeed, one role of a paradigm is to enable scientists to work successfully without having to provide a detailed account of {what they are doing} or {what they believe about it}.

---

03 새로운 관점에 마음 열기 정답률 50% | 정답 ④

다음 글의 제목으로 가장 적절한 것은?

① The Value of Being Honest
정직의 가치
② Filter Out Negative Points of View
부정적인 관점을 걸러라
③ Keeping Your Word: A Road to Success
약속 지키기: 성공으로 향하는 길
④ Being Right Can Block New Possibilities
옳다는 것은 새로운 가능성을 차단할 수 있다
⑤ Look Back When Everyone Looks Forward
모두가 앞을 볼 때 뒤를 봐라

[본문 해석]

누군가에게 아이디어나 제안을 내놨는데, 그들이 즉시 "아니, 그건 안 될 거야."라고 말한 것을 들은 적이 있는가? 여러분은 아마도 "그 사람은 기회조차 주지 않았는데. 어떻게 그것이 안 될 것이라고 알지?"라고 생각했을 것이다. 여러분이 어떤 일에 대해 옳다면, 여러분은 다른 관점이나 기회의 가능성을 닫아 버린다. 어떤 일에 대해 옳다는 것은 "그것은 원래 그런 거야, 끝."이라고 하는 것을 의미한다. 여러분이 맞을 수도 있다. 여러분이 그것을 보는 특정한 방법이 사실에 부합할 수도 있다. 하지만 다른 선택이나 다른 사람의 관점을 고려하는 것은 이로울 수 있다. 만약 여러분이 그들의 관점을 안다면, 여러분은 새로운 것을 알게 되거나 적어도 다른 사람이 삶을 바라보는 방식에 대한 무언가를 배울 것이다. 왜 모두가 여러분이 하는 방식대로 삶을 보거나 경험할 거라고 생각하는가? 그것이 얼마나 지루할지는 제외하고라도, 그것은 모든 새로운 기회, 아이디어, 발명, 그리고 창의성을 없앨 것이다.

Why? 왜 정답일까?

어떤 것에 대해 옳다는 것은 새로운 가능성을 차단할 수 있다(When you are right about something, you close off the possibility of another viewpoint or opportunity.)고 지적한 뒤, 새로운 관점을 고려해보려는 태도가 필요하다고 조언하는 글이다. 따라서 글의 제목으로 가장 적절한 것은 ④ '옳다는 것은 새로운 가능성을 차단할 수 있다'이다.

- **bring up** (화제를) 꺼내다, (아이디어를) 내놓다
- **close off** 차단하다
- **period** ⓐⓓ (문장 끝에서) 끝, 더 말하지 마라
- **at worse** 최소한, 적어도
- **eliminate** ⓥ 제거하다
- **filter out** ~을 걸러내다, 여과하다
- **block** 차단하다
- **suggestion** ⓝ 제안
- **viewpoint** ⓝ 관점, 견해
- **beneficial** ⓐ 이로운
- **besides** ⓟ rep ~을 제외하더라도
- **invention** ⓝ 발명
- **keep one's word** 약속을 지키다

구문 풀이

1행 Have you ever brought up an idea or suggestion to someone and heard them immediately say "No, that won't work."?

---

04 Claude Bolling의 생애 정답률 93% | 정답 ③

Claude Bolling에 관한 다음 글의 내용과 일치하지 <u>않는</u> 것은?

① 1930년에 프랑스에서 태어났다.
② 학교 친구를 통해 재즈를 소개받았다.
✓ 20대에 Best Piano Player 상을 받았다.
④ 성공적인 영화 음악 작곡가였다.
⑤ 1975년에 플루트 연주자와 협업했다.

[본문 해석]

『피아니스트, 작곡가, 그리고 빅 밴드 리더인 Claude Bolling은 1930년 4월 10일 프랑스 칸에서 태어났지만,』 삶의 대부분을 파리에서 보냈다. 그는 젊었을 때 클래식 음악을 공부하기 시작했다. 『그는 학교 친구를 통해 재즈의 세계를 소개받았다.』 후에 Bolling은 최고의 재즈 음악가들 중 한 명인 Fats Waller의 음악에 관심을 가졌다. 『그는 10대 때 프랑스의 아마추어 대회에서 Best Piano Player 상을 수상하며 유명해졌다.』 『그는 또한 성공적인 영화 음악 작곡가였고, 100편이 넘는 영화의 음악을 작곡했다.』 『1975년에, 그는 플루트 연주자 Rampal과 협업했고, *Suite for Flute and Jazz Piano Trio*를 발매했으며, 이것으로 가장 잘 알려지게 되었다.』 그는 두 아들 David와 Alexandre를 남기고 2020년 사망했다.

Why? 왜 정답일까?

'Bolling became famous as a teenager by winning the Best Piano Player prize at an amateur contest in France.'에서 Claude Bolling이 아마추어 재즈 연주자 대회에서 Best Piano Player 상을 받은 것은 10대 시절이었다고 하므로, 내용과 일치하지 않는 것은 ③ '20대에 Best Piano Player 상을 받았다.'이다.

Why? 왜 오답일까?

① 'Claude Bolling, was born on April 10, 1930, in Cannes, France, ~'의 내용과 일치한다.
② 'He was introduced to the world of jazz by a schoolmate.'의 내용과 일치한다.
④ 'He was also a successful film music composer, ~'의 내용과 일치한다.
⑤ 'In 1975, he collaborated with flutist Rampal ~'의 내용과 일치한다.

- **composer** ⓝ 작곡가
- **introduce** ⓥ 소개하다
- **flutist** ⓝ 플루티스트
- **well-known for** ~로 유명한
- **youth** ⓝ 젊은 시절, 청춘
- **collaborate with** ~와 협업하다
- **publish** ⓥ 발매하다, 출간하다

구문 풀이

1행 Pianist, composer, and big band leader, Claude Bolling, was born on April 10, 1930, in Cannes, France, but spent most of his life in Paris.

---

05 칭찬이 아이들의 자존감에 미치는 효과 정답률 55% | 정답 ④

다음 글의 밑줄 친 부분 중, 어법상 틀린 것은? [3점]

[본문 해석]

칭찬은 어린 아이들의 행동을 개선하는 데 사용할 수 있는 가장 강력한 도구 중 하나이지만, 그것은 아이의 자존감을 향상시키는 데에도 똑같이 강력하다. 미취학 아동들은 그들의 부모가 그들에게 하는 말을 매우 뜻 깊게 여긴다. 그들은 분석적으로 추론하고 잘못된 정보를 거부할 수 있는 인지적 정교함을 아직 가지고 있지 않다. 만약 미취학 소년이 그의 어머니로부터 그가 똑똑하고 좋은 조력자라는 것을 계속 듣는다면, 그는 그 정보를 자기 자아상으로 통합시킬 가능성이 높다. 스스로를 똑똑하고 일을 어떻게 하는지 아는 소년으로 생각하는 것은 그가 문제 해결 노력에 있어 더 오래 지속하게 하고, 새롭고 어려운 일을 시도할 때 그의 자신감을 높일 가능성이 높다. 마찬가지로, 자신을 좋은 조력자인 그런 부류의 소년으로 생각하는 것은 그가 집과 유치원에서 일을 자발적으로 도울 가능성이 더 커지게 할 것이다.

Why? 왜 정답일까?

주어인 동명사구(Thinking of himself as a boy ~) 뒤에 동사가 있어야 하므로, being을 is로 고쳐야 한다. 따라서 어법상 틀린 것은 ④이다.

DAY 18

Why? 왜 오답일까?

① tell의 주어는 their parents인데, 목적어는 문맥상 문장의 주어인 Preschoolers 이다. 따라서 재귀대명사를 쓰지 않고, 인칭대명사 them을 썼다.
② to부정사구 to reason을 수식하는 부사 analytically이다.
③ hears의 목적절을 이끄는 접속사로 that이 알맞다. from his mother가 동사 앞으로 들어간 구조이다.
⑤ volunteer는 to부정사를 목적어로 취하므로 to help가 알맞다.

- praise ⓝ 칭찬
- improve ⓥ 개선하다, 향상시키다
- preschooler ⓝ 미취학 아동
- cognitive ⓐ 인지적인
- reason ⓥ 추론하다
- reject ⓥ 거부하다
- be likely to ~할 가능성이 크다
- endure ⓥ 지속하다, 참다
- confidence ⓝ 자신감
- available ⓐ 이용할 수 있는
- self-esteem ⓝ 자존감
- profound ⓐ 뜻 깊은
- sophistication ⓝ 정교화(함)
- analytically ⓐⓓ 분석적으로
- consistently ⓐⓓ 지속적으로
- incorporate A into B A를 B로 통합시키다
- problem-solving ⓝ 문제 해결

구문 풀이

7행 If a preschool boy consistently **hears** from his mother
_____동사_____부사구_____
{that he is smart and a good helper}, he is likely to incorporate that
{ } : hears의 목적어
information into his self-image.

★★★ 1등급 대비 고난도 3점 문제

06 팀워크 기술을 요구하는 학교 과제의 필요성 | 정답률 45% | 정답 ①

(A), (B), (C)의 각 네모 안에서 문맥에 맞는 낱말로 가장 적절한 것은? [3점]

(A)	(B)	(C)
✔ individual 개인적	less 덜	adding 늘려주는
② collective 집단적	less 덜	decreasing 줄여주는
③ individual 개인적	less 덜	decreasing 줄여주는
④ collective 집단적	more 더	decreasing 줄여주는
⑤ individual 개인적	more 더	adding 늘려주는

[본문 해석]
학교 과제는 전형적으로 학생들이 혼자 공부하도록 요구해 왔다. 이러한 (A) 개인적 생산성의 강조는 독립성이 성공의 필수 요인이라는 의견을 반영했던 것이다. 타인에게 의존하지 않고 자신을 관리하는 능력을 가지는 것이 모든 사람에게 있어 필수 사항으로 간주되었다. 따라서, 과거의 교사들은 모둠 활동을 (B) 덜 자주 마련하거나 학생들이 팀워크 기술을 배우는 것을 덜 권장했다. 그러나 뉴 밀레니엄 시대 이후 기업들은 향상된 생산성을 요구하는 더 많은 국제적 경쟁을 경험하고 있다. 이러한 상황은 고용주들로 하여금 노동 시장의 신입들이 전통적인 독립성뿐만 아니라 팀워크 기술을 통해 드러나는 상호 의존성도 입증해야 한다고 요구하도록 만들었다. 교육자의 도전 과제는 기본적인 기술에서의 개별 능력을 보장하는 동시에 학생들이 팀에서도 잘 수행할 수 있도록 하는 학습 기회를 (C) 늘려주는 것이다.

Why? 왜 정답일까?

(A) 'School assignments have typically required that students work alone.'에서 학교 과제는 보통 학생들의 개별 작업을 요구해 왔다는 내용이 제시되므로, (A)에는 individual이 들어가야 적절하다.
(B) 'Having the ability to take care of oneself without depending on others was considered a requirement ~'에서 남에게 의존하지 않고 스스로 일을 잘 처리하는 능력이 요구되었다는 내용이 언급되므로, (B)에는 less가 들어가야 적절하다.
(C) 'This situation has led employers to insist that newcomers to the labor market provide evidence of ~ interdependence shown through teamwork skills.'에서 오늘날의 고용주들은 신입 지원자들이 독립성뿐 아니라 상호 의존성을 입증하기를 요구한다는 내용이 나오므로, 이 뒤에는 학교 현장에서부터 팀워크를 배워나갈 기회가 제공되어야 한다는 주장이 연결되어야 한다. 그러므로 (C)에는 adding이 적절하다. 따라서 문맥에 맞는 낱말로 가장 적절한 것은 ① '(A) individual(개인적) – (B) less(덜) – (C) adding(늘려주는)'이다.

- assignment ⓝ 과제, 할당
- emphasis ⓝ 강조
- productivity ⓝ 생산성
- requirement ⓝ 요건, 필수 사항
- acquire ⓥ 습득하다
- competition ⓝ 경쟁
- labor market 노동 시장
- interdependence ⓝ 상호 의존성
- individual ⓐ 개별적인
- typically ⓐⓓ 일반적으로
- collective ⓐ 집단의, 공동의
- independence ⓝ 독립
- consequently ⓐⓓ 결과적으로
- experience ⓥ ~을 경험하다
- insist ⓥ 요구하다, 주장하다, 고집하다
- evidence ⓝ 증거
- ensure ⓥ 보장하다, 확실히 하다
- perform ⓥ 행하다, 수행하다

구문 풀이

11행 This situation has led employers to **insist** that newcomers to
_____주장 동사 접속사__
the labor market **(should) provide** evidence of traditional independence
_____생략_____동사원형_____전치사_____목적어1_____
but also interdependence [**shown** through teamwork skills].
_____목적어2_____과거분사

★★ 문제 해결 꿀~팁 ★★

▶ 많이 틀린 이유는?
(B), (C)에 들어갈 말을 옳게 고르는 것이 풀이의 관건이다. 첫 문장으로 보아 과거에는 혼자 하는 과업이 강조되었으므로 모둠 활동이나 팀워크를 할 기회는 '덜했다'는 맥락이 되도록 (B)에는 less가 들어가는 것이 적절하다. 한편 However 뒤에 나오는 (C)의 경우 과거와는 상황이 달라진 오늘날의 경우를 묘사한다. 오늘날의 고용 시장에서는 독립성뿐만 아니라 상호 의존성 또한 강조되므로 교육자들은 미리 학생들이 팀워크의 기회를 더 많이 갖도록 그 기회를 '늘려줄' 필요가 있다. 따라서 (C)에는 However 앞과는 상반된 주제를 완성하는 adding을 넣어야 한다.
▶ 문제 해결 방법은?
'However, since the new millennium, ~' 앞뒤로 현재와 과거가 대비되므로, (A), (B)의 근거는 앞에서, (C)의 근거는 뒤에서 찾도록 한다.

★★★ 1등급 대비 고난도 2점 문제

07 실수를 통한 이익 | 정답률 36% | 정답 ①

다음 빈칸에 들어갈 말로 가장 적절한 것을 고르시오.

✔ share the benefits – 이익들을 공유해서
② overlook the insights – 통찰력을 간과해서
③ develop creative skills – 창의력을 발달시켜서
④ exaggerate the achievements – 성취를 과장해서
⑤ underestimate the knowledge – 지식을 과소평가해서

[본문 해석]
과학과 무대 마술 사이의 한 가지 큰 차이점은 마술사들이 실수를 관중에게 숨기는 반면, 과학에서는 공공연히 실수를 한다는 것이다. 당신은 모두가 실수로부터 배울 수 있도록 실수를 드러내 보여준다. 이런 식으로, 당신은 실수라는 영역을 거쳐 온 당신 자신만의 특유한 길(에서 얻은 이익)뿐만 아니라, 다른 모든 사람들의 경험이라는 이익을 얻는다. 한편, 이는 왜 우리 인간이 다른 모든 종보다 훨씬 더 영리한지에 대한 또 다른 이유이다. 그것은 우리의 뇌가 더 크거나 더 강력해서, 혹은 심지어 우리가 우리 자신의 과거 실수들을 반추하는 능력을 가져서가 아니라, 우리 개개인들의 뇌가 각자 자신의 시행착오의 역사로부터 얻어낸 이익들을 공유해서이다.

Why? 왜 정답일까?

'You show them off so that everybody can learn from them. This way, you get the advantage of everybody else's experience, ~'에서 서로 실수를 드러내 보여주면 실수를 통해 얻은 경험과 이익을 공유할 수 있다고 했다. 이를 근거로 볼 때, 인간이 똑똑한 이유를 설명하는 마지막 문장은 '실수로 인한 이익이 공유되기' 때문이라는 의미가 되어야 하므로, 빈칸에 들어갈 말로 가장 적절한 것은 ① '이익들을 공유해서'이다.

- magician ⓝ 마술사
- in public 공공연히
- idiosyncratic ⓐ 특이한, 특유의
- ability ⓝ (~을) 할 수 있음, 능력
- past ⓝ 과거, 지난날
- earn ⓥ (돈을) 벌다
- trial and error 시행착오
- overlook ⓥ 간과하다, 못 보고 넘어가다
- underestimate ⓥ 과소평가하다, 경시하다
- audience ⓝ 청중[관중]
- advantage ⓝ 이점
- species ⓝ (생물) 종
- reflect on ~을 반추하다
- individual ⓐ 각각[개개]의
- history ⓝ 역사
- benefit ⓝ 혜택, 이득
- exaggerate ⓥ 과장하다

구문 풀이

9행 It is not {that our brains are bigger or more powerful}, or even
↑not + A   ↑or A' +
{that we have the ability to reflect on our own past errors}, but {that
but + B : A나 A'가 아니라 B인 (A, A', B 자리에 모두 that절)
we share the benefits [that our individual brains have earned from
선행사   목적격 관·대
their individual histories of trial and error]}.

★★ 문제 해결 꿀~팁 ★★

▶ 많이 틀린 이유는?
첫 두 문장에서 모두 배울 수 있도록 실수를 드러내 보이는 것을 글의 주된 소재로
언급하고 있다. 창의력 발달에 관해서는 언급되지 않으므로 ③은 답으로 적절하지 않다.

▶ 문제 해결 방법은?
'You show them[your mistakes] off so that everybody can learn from
them. This way, you get the advantage of everybody else's experience.
~'에서 show off가 ①의 share로, advantage가 ①의 benefits로 재진술되었다.

★★★ 1등급 대비 고난도 3점 문제

08 정확한 온도 측정   정답률 42% | 정답 ⑤

글의 흐름으로 보아, 주어진 문장이 들어가기에 가장 적절한 곳을 고르시오. [3점]

[본문 해석]
우리는 흔히 물건을 만졌을 때 얼마나 뜨겁게 또는 차갑게 느껴지는지를 온도
개념과 연관 짓는다. 이런 식으로, 우리의 감각은 우리에게 온도의 정성적 지
표를 제공한다. ① 그러나, 우리의 감각은 신뢰할 수 없으며 종종 우리를 잘못
인도한다. ② 예를 들어, 여러분이 맨발로 한쪽 발은 카펫 위에, 다른 한쪽 발
은 타일 바닥 위에 놓고 서 있다면, 둘 다 같은 온도임에도 불구하고 카펫보다
타일이 더 차갑게 느껴질 것이다. ③ 타일이 카펫보다 더 높은 비율로 에너지
를 열의 형태로 전달하기 때문에 그 두 물체는 다르게 느껴진다. ④ 여러분의
피부는 실제 온도보다는 열에너지 전도율을 '측정한다'. ⑤ 우리가 필요로 하는
것은 에너지 전도율보다는 물체의 상대적 뜨거움과 차가움을 측정하기 위한
신뢰할 수 있고 재현 가능한 수단이다. 과학자들은 그런 정량적인 측정을 하기
위해 다양한 온도계를 개발해 왔다.

Why? 왜 정답일까?
우리의 감각은 온도에 대한 정성적 지표를 제공하기는 하지만 완전히 정확한 정보를 주
지는 못한다는 내용의 글로, ⑤ 앞의 문장은 이것이 피부가 실제 온도보다는 열에너지 전
도율을 측정하기 때문이라고 설명한다. 한편 주어진 문장에서는 이 상황에서 우리에게
필요한 것이 상대적 온도를 신뢰도 높게 측정할 수 있는 도구라고 언급하고, ⑤ 뒤에서는
이 도구가 바로 정량적 측정이 가능한 온도계라고 밝힌다. 따라서 주어진 문장이 들어가
기에 가장 적절한 곳은 ⑤이다.

- **reproducible** ⓐ 재현 가능한
- **qualitative** ⓐ 정성적, 질적인
- **bare** ⓐ 맨, 벌거벗은
- **energy transfer** 에너지 전도
- **mislead** ⓥ 잘못 이끌다
- **quantitative** ⓐ 정량적인

구문 풀이

12행 The two objects feel different because tile transfers energy
감각동사   형용사 보어
by heat at a higher rate than carpet does.
대동사(= transfers)

★★ 문제 해결 꿀~팁 ★★

▶ 많이 틀린 이유는?
③, ④가 헷갈리므로 하나씩 살펴보자. 먼저 ③ 앞은 서로 온도가 같은 타일과 카펫
이 '다르게' 느껴진다는 예를 드는데, ③ 뒤는 그것이 '열에너지 전도율의 차이' 때문
이라고 설명한다. 이어서 ④ 뒤도 우리 피부가 실제 온도보다는 '열에너지 전도율'에
집중한다고 한다. 즉, ③ ~ ④ 앞뒤 문장들은 지시어나 연결어의 공백 없이 모두 자
연스럽게 연결된다.

▶ 문제 해결 방법은?
⑤ 앞에서 우리가 측정하는 것이 '열에너지 전도율'이라고 언급한 데 이어서, 주어진
문장은 '이것 말고 우리에게 실제 필요한 것'이 무엇인지 언급하고 있다. 그것이 바로
주어진 문장에서 언급한, '물체의 상대적 온도를 신뢰성 있게 측정할 수 있는 수단'인
데, ⑤ 뒤에서는 '그래서' 온도계가 개발되었다는 결론을 제시하고 있다.

09 경쟁자 제거에 망가니즈를 활용하는 식물   정답률 55% | 정답 ①

다음 글의 내용을 한 문장으로 요약하고자 한다. 빈칸 (A), (B)에 들어갈 말로 가장
적절한 것은?

	(A)	(B)		(A)	(B)
✔①	increase 증가시키다	deadly 치명적인	②	increase 증가시키다	advantageous 이로운
③	indicate 보여주다	nutritious 영양가 있는	④	reduce 줄이다	dry 건조한
⑤	reduce 줄이다	warm 따뜻한			

[본문 해석]
common blackberry(*Rubus alleghaniensis*)는 뿌리를 이용하여 토양의 한 층에서
다른 층으로 망가니즈를 옮기는 놀라운 능력이 있다. 이것은 식물이 가지기에
는 기이한 재능처럼 보일 수도 있지만, 그것이 근처의 식물에 미치는 영향을
깨닫고 나면 전부 명확해진다. 망가니즈는 식물에 매우 해로울 수 있으며, 특
히 고농도일 때 그렇다. common blackberry는 이 금속 원소의 해로운 효과에
영향을 받지 않으며, 망가니즈를 자신에게 유리하게 사용하는 두 가지 다른 방
법을 발달시켰다. 첫째로, 그것은 뿌리를 작은 관으로 사용하여 망가니즈를 깊
은 토양층으로부터 얕은 토양층으로 재분배한다. 둘째로, 그것은 성장하면서
망가니즈를 흡수하여 그 금속 원소를 잎에 농축한다. 잎이 떨어지고 부패할
때, 그것의 농축된 망가니즈 축적물은 그 식물 주변의 토양을 독성 물질로 더
욱 오염시킨다. 망가니즈의 유독한 영향에 면역이 없는 식물에게 이것은 매우
나쁜 소식이다. 본질적으로, common blackberry는 중금속으로 그것의 이웃을
중독시켜 경쟁자를 제거한다.

➡ common blackberry는 주변 위쪽 토양에 있는 망가니즈의 양을 (A) 증가시
키는 능력이 있는데, 그것은 근처의 토양이 다른 식물에게 상당히 (B) 치명적
이게 만든다.

Why? 왜 정답일까?
첫 문장과 마지막 세 문장에 따르면 common blackberry는 뿌리를 이용해 망가니즈
를 끌어올리거나 이동시킬 수 있어서 주변 토양에 망가니즈가 더 많아지게 할 수 있는데,
이것은 경쟁자 제거에 도움이 된다고 한다. 따라서 요약문의 빈칸 (A), (B)에 들어갈 말
로 가장 적절한 것은 ① '(A) increase(증가시키다), (B) deadly(치명적인)'이다.

- **concentration** ⓝ 농도, 농축
- **absorb** ⓥ 흡수하다
- **eliminate** ⓥ 제거하다
- **shallow** ⓐ 얕은
- **be immune to** ~에 면역이 있다

구문 풀이

3행 This may seem like a funny talent for a plant to have, but
주어1   동사1   주격 보어   의미상 주어   형용사적 용법
it all becomes clear when you realize the effect [it has on nearby
주어2   동사2   주격 보어2   선행사
plants].

10-12 사원 관리자의 자격 요건

[본문 해석]

(A)
「옛날, 한 노인이 마을 중심부에 큰 사원을 지었다.」 사람들이 사원에서 예배를
└─『 』: 12번 ①의 근거 일치
드리기 위해 멀리서 왔다. 그래서 노인은 사원 안에 음식과 숙소를 준비했다.
그는 사원을 관리할 수 있는 사람이 필요했고, 그래서 (a) 그는 '관리자 구함'이
라는 공고를 붙였다.

(D)
「공고를 보고, 많은 사람들이 노인을 찾아갔다.」 그러나 그는 "이 일에는 자격을
└─『 』: 12번 ⑤의 근거 일치
갖춘 사람이 필요합니다."라고 말하며 면접 후 모든 지원자들을 돌려보냈다.
노인은 사람들이 사원의 문을 통과하는 것을 지켜보며 매일 아침 (d) 자기 집
지붕에 앉아 있곤 했다. 어느 날 (e) 그는 한 젊은이가 사원으로 오는 것을 보
았다.

(B)
「젊은이가 사원을 나설 때, 노인이 그를 불러 "이 사원의 관리를 맡아 주겠소?"
└─『 』: 12번 ②의 근거 일치
라고 질문했다.」 「젊은이는 그 제안에 놀라서 "저는 사원을 관리한 경험이 없고,
└─『 』: 12번 ④의 근거 일치
심지어 교육도 받지 못했습니다."라고 대답했다.」 노인은 웃으며 "나는 교육을
└─『 』: 12번 ③의 근거 일치
받은 사람이 필요한 게 아니오. 나는 자격 있는 사람을 원하오."라고 말했다.

혼란스러워하며, 젊은이는 "그런데 (b) <u>당신</u>은 왜 제가 자격이 있는 사람이라고 여기시나요?"라고 물었다.

(C)
「노인은 대답했다. "나는 사원으로 통하는 길에 벽돌 한 개를 묻었소. 나는 여러 날 동안 사람들이 그 벽돌에 발이 걸려 넘어지는 것을 지켜보았소. 아무도 그것을 치울 생각을 하지 않았소. 하지만 당신은 그 벽돌을 파냈소.」라고 말했소." 젊은이는
└ : 12번 ④의 근거 불일치
"저는 대단한 일을 한 것이 아닙니다. 타인을 생각하는 것은 모든 사람의 의무인 걸요. (c) <u>전</u> 제 의무를 다했을 뿐입니다."라고 말했다. 노인은 미소를 지으며 "자신의 의무를 알고 그 의무를 수행하는 사람만이 자격이 있는 사람이오." 라고 말했다.

- **grand** ⓐ 큰, 위대한
- **worship** ⓥ 예배하다
- **accommodation** ⓝ 숙소
- **bury** ⓥ 묻다
- **trip over** ~에 걸려 넘어지다
- **duty** ⓝ 의무
- **temple** ⓝ 사원, 절
- **make arrangements for** ~을 준비하다
- **care for** ~을 관리하다, 돌보다
- **brick** ⓝ 벽돌
- **dig up** 파내다
- **applicant** ⓝ 지원자

구문 풀이

(B) 7행 Confused, the young man asked, "But why do you consider
→목적어 분사구문(Being 생략) 5형식 동사
me a qualified person?"
목적격 보어

(D) 4행 The old man would sit on the roof of his house every morning,
조동사(과거 습관)
watching people go through the temple doors.
지각동사 목적어 원형부정사

---

10 글의 순서 파악 정답률 83% | 정답 ④

주어진 글 (A)에 이어질 내용을 순서에 맞게 배열한 것으로 가장 적절한 것은?
① (B) − (D) − (C) ② (C) − (B) − (D)
③ (C) − (D) − (B) ☑ (D) − (B) − (C)
⑤ (D) − (C) − (B)

Why? 왜 정답일까?

한 노인이 사원을 짓고 관리자 모집에 나섰다는 **(A)** 뒤로, 지원자들이 몰려들었지만 노인은 계속 자격 있는 사람을 기다렸다는 **(D)**, 어떤 젊은이가 다녀가는 것을 보고 노인이 관리자 직을 제안했다는 **(B)**, 왜 자신을 채용하려 하는지 묻는 젊은이에게 노인이 답을 주었다는 **(C)**가 차례로 연결된다. 따라서 글의 순서로 가장 적절한 것은 ④ '(D) − (B) − (C)'이다.

---

11 지칭 추론 정답률 84% | 정답 ③

밑줄 친 (a) ~ (e) 중에서 가리키는 대상이 나머지 넷과 다른 것은?
① (a) ② (b) ☑ (c) ④ (d) ⑤ (e)

Why? 왜 정답일까?

(a), (b), (d), (e)는 the old man을, (c)는 the young man을 가리키므로, (a) ~ (e) 중에서 가리키는 대상이 다른 하나는 ③ '(c)'이다.

---

12 세부 내용 파악 정답률 79% | 정답 ④

윗글에 관한 내용으로 적절하지 <u>않은</u> 것은?
① 노인은 마을 중심부에 사원을 지었다.
② 젊은이가 사원을 나설 때 노인이 그를 불렀다.
③ 젊은이는 노인의 제안에 놀랐다.
☑ 노인은 사원으로 통하는 길에 묻혀있던 벽돌을 파냈다.
⑤ 공고를 보고 많은 사람들이 노인을 찾아갔다.

Why? 왜 정답일까?

(C) "I buried a brick on the path to the temple. I watched for many days as people tripped over that brick. No one thought to remove it. But you dug up that brick."에서 노인은 자신이 묻어뒀던 벽돌을 파낸 사람이 젊은이라

고 말하고 있으므로, 내용과 일치하지 않는 것은 ④ '노인은 사원으로 통하는 길에 묻혀 있던 벽돌을 파냈다.'이다.

Why? 왜 오답일까?

① (A) 'Long ago, an old man built a grand temple at the center of his village.'의 내용과 일치한다.
② (B) 'When that young man left the temple, the old man called him ~' 의 내용과 일치한다.
③ (B) 'The young man was surprised by the offer ~'의 내용과 일치한다.
⑤ (D) 'Seeing the notice, many people went to the old man.'의 내용과 일치한다.

DAY 19 · 20분 미니 모의고사

01 ③	02 ①	03 ②	04 ⑤	05 ③
06 ⑤	07 ①	08 ②	09 ④	10 ①
11 ②	12 ④			

---

01 독자들을 능동적으로 생각하게 하며 글쓰기
정답률 81% | 정답 ③

다음 글에서 필자가 주장하는 바로 가장 적절한 것은?

① 저자의 독창적인 견해를 드러내야 한다.
② 다양한 표현으로 독자에게 감동을 주어야 한다.
☑ 독자가 능동적으로 사고할 수 있도록 글을 써야 한다.
④ 독자에게 가치판단의 기준점을 명확히 제시해야 한다.
⑤ 주관적 관점을 배제하고 사실을 바탕으로 글을 써야 한다.

[본문 해석]

당신이 글을 쓰려고 할 때, 당신의 관점을 가져야 하는 한편, 독자에게 무엇을 생각할지 말하는 것을 피해야 한다고 스스로 상기할 가치가 있다. (논점) 전체에 물음표를 달기 위해 노력해라. 이런 방식으로 당신은 독자들이 당신의 요점과 주장들에 대해 스스로 생각할 수 있게 만든다. 결과적으로 독자들은 당신만큼이나 당신이 한 주장과 당신이 드러내는 통찰력에 몰입되는 자신을 발견하면서, 좀 더 열중하는 느낌을 받게 될 것이다. 당신은 독자들의 수동성을 피하면서도 흥미롭고 사람들을 생각하게 만드는 글을 쓰게 될 것이다.

Why? 왜 정답일까?

명령문인 'Try to hang a question mark over it all.' 이후로 논점을 물음 형태로 제시하면 독자들이 필자의 견해에 관해 스스로 생각해 보게 유도할 수 있다고 한다. 따라서 필자가 주장하는 바로 가장 적절한 것은 ③ '독자가 능동적으로 사고할 수 있도록 글을 써야 한다.'이다.

- be worth ~ing ~할 가치가 있다
- argument ⓝ 논점, 주장
- insight ⓝ 통찰력
- remind ⓥ 상기시키다
- committed to ~에 몰입하는, 열중하는
- passivity ⓝ 수동성

구문 풀이

1행 As you set about to write, it is worth reminding yourself
　　　　　　　　　　　　　　　　「be worth + 동명사」 ~할 가치가 있다
{that (while you ought to have a point of view), you should avoid
( ) : 부사절
telling your readers what to think}.( ) : 명사절

---

02 인터넷 시대 이후 음악 비평에 야기된 변화
정답률 85% | 정답 ①

다음 글의 요지로 가장 적절한 것은?

☑ 미디어 환경의 변화로 음악 비평이 대중의 영향을 받게 되었다.
② 인터넷의 발달로 다양한 장르의 음악을 접하는 것이 가능해졌다.
③ 비평가의 음악 비평은 자신의 주관적인 경험을 기반으로 한다.
④ 오늘날 새로운 음악은 대중의 기호를 확인한 후에 공개된다.
⑤ 온라인 환경의 대두로 음악 비평의 질이 전반적으로 상승하였다.

[본문 해석]

파일 공유 서비스 이전에, 음악 앨범은 발매 전에 음악 비평가들의 손에 독점적으로 들어갔다. 이런 비평가들은 일반 대중들이 들을 수 있기 훨씬 전에 그것을 듣고 나머지 세상 사람들을 위해 자신의 비평에서 시사평을 쓰곤 했다. 인터넷을 통해 음악을 쉽게 접할 수 있게 되고, 미리 공개된 곡들까지 온라인 소셜 네트워크를 통해 퍼질 수 있게 되자, 신곡을 접할 수 있는 것이 민주화되었고, 이는 비평가들이 더 이상 고유한 접근 권한을 갖지 않는다는 것을 의미했다. 즉, 비평가와 비전문가가 똑같이 동시에 신곡을 얻을 수 있었다. 소셜 미디어 서비스는 또한 사람들이 신곡에 대한 자신의 견해를 알리고, 자신의 소셜 미디어 약력에 자신이 좋아하는 새로운 밴드의 리스트를 작성하고, 메시지 게시판에서 신곡을 놓고 끝없이 논쟁할 수 있게 했다. 그 결과 비평가들은 이제 자신의 비평을 쓰기 전에 특정 앨범에 관한 대중의 의견을 접할 수 있었다. 그리하여 (인터넷 이전 시대에 했던 것처럼) 예술에 관한 여론을 인도하는 대신에, 음악 비평은 의식적이든 무의식적이든 여론을 반영하기 시작했다.

Why? 왜 정답일까?

Thus로 시작하는 마지막 문장에서 인터넷 시대에 접어들면서 음악이 비평가와 대중에 동시에 도달하게 됨에 따라 음악 비평이 여론을 반영하기 시작했다(Thus, instead of music reviews guiding popular opinion toward art (as they did in preinternet times), music reviews began to reflect—consciously or subconsciously—public opinion.)는 결론을 제시하고 있다. 따라서 글의 요지로 가장 적절한 것은 ① '미디어 환경의 변화로 음악 비평이 대중의 영향을 받게 되었다.'이다.

- prior to ~ 이전에
- exclusively ⓐⓓ 독점적으로
- accessible ⓐ 접할 수 있는
- simultaneously ⓐⓓ 동시에
- bio ⓝ 약력
- file-sharing service 파일 공유 서비스
- preview ⓥ 시사평을 쓰다
- democratize ⓥ 민주화하다
- publicize ⓥ 알리다
- subconsciously ⓐⓓ 무의식적으로

구문 풀이

5행 Once the internet made music easily accessible and allowed
　　　접속사(일단 ~하자)　5형식 동사1 목적어1 목적격 보어1 5형식 동사2
even advanced releases to spread through online social networks,
　목적어2　　　　　목적격 보어2
availability of new music became democratized, which meant critics
주어(불가산 명사)　　　2형식 동사　　보어　　계속적 용법(주절 받음)
no longer had unique access.

---

03 문화적 다양성이 너무 클 때의 문제점
정답률 58% | 정답 ②

다음 글의 주제로 가장 적절한 것은?

① roles of culture in ethnic groups
　민족 집단에서 문화의 역할
☑ contrastive aspects of cultural diversity
　문화적 다양성의 대립적 양상
③ negative perspectives of national identity
　국가 정체성에 대한 부정적인 시각
④ factors of productivity differences across countries
　국가 간 생산성 차이의 요인
⑤ policies to protect minorities and prevent discrimination
　소수자를 보호하고 차별을 방지하려는 정책들

[본문 해석]

다른 문화적 배경을 가진 노동자들과 현지 주민의 상호 작용은 지식의 확산과 같은 긍정적인 외부 효과로 인해 생산성을 증가시킬 수 있다. 이것은 어느 정도까지만 장점이다. 배경의 다양성이 너무 크면, 분열은 의사소통에 대한 과도한 거래 비용을 초래하고, 이는 생산성을 저하시킬 수 있다. 다양성은 노동 시장에 영향을 줄 뿐만 아니라 한 지역의 삶의 질에도 영향을 미칠 수 있다. 관용적인 원주민은 이용 가능한 재화와 용역 범위의 증가로 인해 다문화 도시나 지역을 가치 있게 여길 수 있다. 반면에, 원주민들이 다양성을 국가 정체성이라고 여겨지는 것에 대한 왜곡으로 인식한다면 그것(다양성)은 매력적이지 않은 특징으로 인지될 수 있다. 그들은 심지어 다른 민족 집단을 차별할 수도 있고, 다양한 외국 국적들 간의 사회적 갈등이 그들 인근으로 유입되는 것을 두려워할 수도 있다.

Why? 왜 정답일까?

한 지역 사회 내에서 외지 출신 노동자들의 문화적 다양성이 일정 수준을 넘어가면 생산성 또는 삶의 질 저하나 갈등을 겪게 될 수 있다는 내용이다. 따라서 글의 주제로 가장 적절한 것은 ② '문화적 다양성의 대립적 양상'이다.

- cultural ⓐ 문화적인
- productivity ⓝ 생산성
- knowledge spillover 지식의 확산
- excessive ⓐ 과도한
- lower ⓥ 떨어뜨리다
- labo(u)r market 노동 시장
- tolerant ⓐ 관용적인
- on the other hand 반면에
- distortion ⓝ 왜곡
- discriminate against ~을 차별하다
- conflict ⓝ 갈등
- contrastive ⓐ 대비되는, 대립적인
- policy ⓝ 정책
- population ⓝ 인구
- externality ⓝ 외부 효과
- fractionalization ⓝ 분열
- cost ⓝ 비용, 대가
- impact ⓥ 영향을 주다, 충격을 주다
- quality of life 삶의 질
- multicultural ⓐ 다문화의
- perceive A as B A를 B로 인식하다
- identity ⓝ 정체성
- ethnic ⓐ 민족의
- import ⓥ 유입하다, 수입하다
- factor ⓝ 요인

구문 풀이

12행 On the other hand, diversity could be perceived as an
　　　　　　　　　　　　　　　　　　～로 인식되다
unattractive feature if natives perceive it as a distortion of [what
　　　　　　　　　　　　　　　　　　　　　　전치사 관계대명사(~것)
they consider to be their national identity].

04 미국에서 반려동물을 키우는 가정의 비율 정답률 88% | 정답 ⑤

다음 도표의 내용과 일치하지 않는 것은?

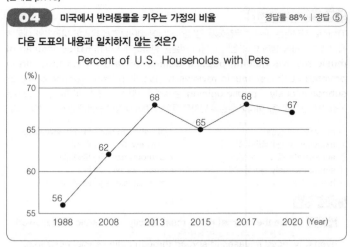

Percent of U.S. Households with Pets

[본문 해석]

위 그래프는 1988년부터 2020년까지 반려동물을 기르는 미국 가정의 비율을 보여준다. ① 1988년에는 절반 이상의 미국 가정이 반려동물을 길렀고, 2008년에서 2020년까지 10개 중 6개 이상의 미국 가정이 반려동물을 길렀다. ② 1988년과 2008년 사이, 반려동물 보유는 미국 가정들에서 6퍼센트포인트 증가했다. ③ 2008년과 2013년 사이, 반려동물 보유는 6퍼센트포인트가 추가적으로 올랐다. ④ 2013년의 반려동물을 기르는 미국 가정의 비율은 2017년의 비율과 같고, 68퍼센트였다. ⑤ 2015년에는, 반려동물을 기르는 미국 가정의 비율이 2020년보다 3퍼센트포인트 더 낮았다.

Why? 왜 정답일까?

도표에 따르면 미국에서 반려동물을 기르는 가정의 비율은 **2015년 65%, 2020년 67%**로, 두 해 간 비율은 **2퍼센트포인트**의 격차를 보인다. 따라서 도표와 일치하지 않는 것은 ⑤이다.

- household ⓝ 가정, 가구
- ownership ⓝ 보유, 소유
- rise ⓥ 오르다

05 인간의 뇌 크기 감소 정답률 67% | 정답 ③

다음 글의 밑줄 친 부분 중, 어법상 틀린 것은? [3점]

[본문 해석]

인간의 뇌는 15,000년에서 30,000년 전 크기가 정점에 도달한 이래 부피가 약 10퍼센트 줄어들었다는 것이 밝혀졌다. 한 가지 가능한 이유는 수천 년 전에 인간은 죽임을 당하는 것을 피하기 위해 그들이 늘 기지를 발휘해야 했던 위험한 포식자의 세계에서 살았다는 것이다. 오늘날, 우리는 우리 자신을 효율적으로 길들여 왔고 생존의 많은 과업이 — 즉각적인 죽음을 피하는 것부터 쉴 곳을 짓고 음식을 얻어 내는 일까지 — 더 넓은 사회로 위탁되어 왔다. 우리는 우리의 조상보다 더 작기도 한데, 가축이 그들의 야생 사촌보다 일반적으로 더 작다는 것은 이들의 특징 중 하나이다. 이중 어떤 것도 우리가 더 어리석다는 뜻은 아니지만 — 뇌 크기가 반드시 인간의 지능의 지표는 아니다 — 그것은 오늘날 우리의 뇌가 다른 식으로, 그리고 우리 조상보다 아마도 더 효율적으로 장착되어 있음을 뜻할 수도 있다.

Why? 왜 정답일까?

and 뒤에 새로 나온 주어가 **many of the tasks of survival**이라는 복수 명사구이므로, 단수형 **has**를 복수형 **have**로 고쳐야 한다. 따라서 어법상 틀린 것은 ③이다.

Why? 왜 오답일까?

① '주어 + 현재완료 동사 ~, since + 주어 + 과거 동사 ~' 형태가 알맞게 쓰였다.
② 선행사가 바로 앞의 **predators**가 아닌 **a world**이므로, 장소의 관계부사 **where**가 알맞게 쓰였다.
④ **it**이 가주어이고, 'they are generally smaller ~'가 진주어이므로 명사절을 이끄는 접속사 **that**을 알맞게 썼다.
⑤ **than** 앞의 복수 명사 **brains**를 가리키기 위해 복수 대명사 **those**를 썼다.

- shrink ⓥ 줄어들다
- mass ⓝ 부피, 질량
- have one's wits about one ~의 기지를 발휘하다
- domesticate ⓥ 길들이다
- indicator ⓝ 지표
- wire ⓥ 연결하다, 장착하다

구문 풀이

3행 One possible reason is that many thousands of years ago humans lived in a world of dangerous predators where they had to (장소 선행사) (관계부사) have their wits about them at all times to avoid being killed.
(= predators) (수동 동명사(~되는 것))

★★★ 1등급 대비 고난도 3점 문제

06 거절에 대한 두려움 극복하기 정답률 45% | 정답 ⑤

다음 글의 밑줄 친 부분 중, 문맥상 낱말의 쓰임이 적절하지 않은 것은? [3점]

[본문 해석]

거절은 우리 삶의 일상적인 부분이지만, 대부분의 사람은 그것을 잘 감당하지 못한다. 많은 사람에게 거절이 너무 고통스러워서, 그들은 요청하고 거절의 ① 위험을 감수하기보다는 아예 무언가를 요청하지 않으려 한다. 하지만 옛말처럼, 요청하지 않으면 대답은 항상 '아니오'이다. 거절을 피하는 것은 여러분의 삶의 많은 측면에 ② 부정적으로 영향을 준다. 이 모든 것은 단지 여러분이 거절을 감당할 만큼 ③ 강하지 않기 때문에 일어난다. 이러한 이유로 거절 요법을 (시도하는 것을) 고려해 보라. 일반적으로 거절당할 만한 ④ 요청이나 활동을 생각해 내라. 판매 분야에서 일하는 것이 그러한 사례 중 하나이다. 매장에서 할인을 요청하는 것 또한 효과가 있을 것이다. 의도적으로 스스로를 ⑤ 환영받는(→ 거절당하는) 상황에 놓이게 함으로써 여러분은 더 둔감해지고, 인생에서 훨씬 더 많은 것을 떠맡을 수 있게 되며, 그리하여 호의적이지 않은 상황에 더 성공적으로 대처할 수 있게 될 것이다.

Why? 왜 정답일까?

⑤ 앞에서 판매 분야에서 일하는 등 거절을 경험할 법한 요청이나 활동에 참여해보라고 언급하는데, 이는 거절을 부르는 상황의 예시이므로 ⑤의 welcomed는 rejected로 바뀌어야 적절하다. 따라서 문맥상 낱말의 쓰임이 적절하지 않은 것은 ⑤이다.

- rejection ⓝ 거절
- handle ⓥ 감당하다
- painful ⓐ 고통스러운
- rather ⓐⓓ 오히려, 차라리
- negative ⓐ 부정적인
- reason ⓝ 이유
- therapy ⓝ 요법
- come up with ~을 생각해내다, 떠올리다
- deliberately ⓐⓓ 고의로, 의도적으로
- grow a thick skin 무덤덤해지다
- unfavorable ⓐ 호의적이지 않은
- circumstance ⓝ 상황, 환경

구문 풀이

2행 For many, it's so painful that they'd rather not
「so ~ that ... : 너무 ~해서 ...하다」 차라리 ~ 않다
ask for something at all than ask and risk rejection.
동사원형1 동사원형2

★★ 문제 해결 꿀~팁 ★★

▶ 많이 틀린 이유는?
오답 중 ③이 포함된 문장은 우리가 거절을 왜 피하려 하는지 그 이유를 설명하는 문장이다. 우리가 거절에 잘 대처할 만큼 '충분히 강하지' 않기 때문이라는 것이다. 그렇기에 훈련이 필요하다는 결론까지 자연스럽게 연결되므로, ③은 문맥상 어색하지 않다.
▶ 문제 해결 방법은?
정답인 ⑤가 포함된 문장은 예시 앞의 'Come up with a request or an activity that usually results in a rejection.'과 같은 의미이다. '일부러 거절이라는 결과를 초래할' 수 있는 상황은 '환영받는' 상황이 아니라 그야말로 '거부당하는' 상황이다.

07 비행 방향에 따른 시차 피로 차이 정답률 55% | 정답 ①

다음 빈칸에 들어갈 말로 가장 적절한 것을 고르시오.

✓ direction - 방향
② purpose - 목적
③ season - 계절
④ length - 길이
⑤ cost - 비용

[본문 해석]

시차로 인한 피로감을 극복하기 위해서 체내 시계를 얼마나 빨리 재설정할 수 있는지는 사람마다 서로 다르며, 그 회복 속도는 이동의 방향에 달려 있다. 일반

적으로 동쪽으로 비행하여 하루를 단축하는 것보다 서쪽으로 비행해 하루를 연장하는 것이 더 쉽다. 시차로 인한 피로감에서 이러한 동서의 차이는 스포츠 팀의 경기력에 영향을 미칠 만큼 충분히 크다. 연구에 따르면 서쪽으로 비행하는 팀이 동쪽으로 비행하는 팀보다 프로 야구와 대학 미식 축구에서 상당히 더 잘한다. 46,000건 이상의 메이저 리그 야구 경기에 관한 더 최근의 연구에서는 동쪽으로 이동하는 것이 서쪽으로 이동하는 것보다 더 힘들다는 추가적인 증거를 발견했다.

Why? 왜 정답일까?

빈칸 뒤에서 동쪽으로 이동해 하루를 줄이게 되는 경우보다 서쪽으로 이동해 하루를 연장하게 되는 경우 시차 회복이 더 쉽다고 한다(Generally, it's easier to fly westward and lengthen your day than it is to fly eastward and shorten it.). 즉, 이동의 '방향'이 중요하다는 글이므로, 빈칸에 들어갈 말로 가장 적절한 것은 ① '방향'이다.

- differ in ~에 관해 다르다
- biological clock 체내 시계
- jet lag 시차로 인한 피로감
- depend on ~에 좌우되다
- lengthen ⓥ 연장하다
- shorten ⓥ 단축하다
- have an impact on ~에 영향을 주다
- significantly ⓐ 상당히, 현저히
- tough ⓐ 어려운, 힘든
- reset ⓥ 재설정하다
- overcome ⓥ 극복하다
- recovery ⓝ 회복
- westward ⓐ 서쪽으로
- eastward ⓐ 동쪽으로
- sizable ⓐ 꽤 큰, 상당한
- performance ⓝ 경기력, 수행, 성과
- additional ⓐ 추가적인

구문 풀이

> **5행** This east-west difference in jet lag is sizable enough to have
> 「형/부 + enough + to부정사: ~할 만큼 충분히 …한」
> an impact on the performance of sports teams.

★★★ 1등급 대비 고난도 3점 문제

08 아기의 언어 습득에 바탕이 되는 통계 분석 능력   정답률 41% | 정답 ②

다음 빈칸에 들어갈 말로 가장 적절한 것을 고르시오. [3점]

① lack of social pressures - 사회적 압력의 부족
☑ ability to calculate statistics - 통계를 계산하는 능력
③ desire to interact with others - 타인과 상호작용하려는 욕구
④ preference for simpler sounds - 더 간단한 소리에 대한 선호
⑤ tendency to imitate caregivers - 양육자를 모방하려는 경향

[본문 해석]

시간이 지나면서 아기는 자신이 어떤 소리를 언제 들을지에 대한 기대를 형성한다. 그들은 규칙적으로 발생하는 소리 패턴을 기억한다. 그들은 '내가 이 소리를 먼저 들으면 아마도 저 소리가 따라올 것이다'와 같은 가설을 세운다. 과학자들은 아기의 언어 학습 능력의 상당 부분이 통계를 계산하는 능력 때문이라고 결론짓는다. 아기에게 있어 이것은 그들이 언어에서 반복되는 패턴에 세심한 주의를 기울이는 것처럼 보인다는 것을 의미한다. 그들은 소리가 얼마나 자주, 어떤 순서로, 어떤 간격으로, 어떤 음조의 변화로 발생하는지를 체계적인 방식으로 기억한다. 이 기억 저장소는 그들이 뇌의 신경 회로 내에서 소리 패턴의 빈도를 추적하고, 이 지식을 사용해 소리 패턴의 의미에 대해 예측하게 해준다.

Why? 왜 정답일까?

마지막 두 문장에서 아기들은 패턴이 어떻게 반복되는지에 관한 세부 사항을 기억하고, 패턴의 빈도를 추적하여 후에 의미를 예측할 때 그러한 정보를 사용한다고 설명하고 있다. 빈칸에는 이러한 일련의 인지 작용을 일반화하는 말이 필요하므로, 빈칸에 들어갈 말로 가장 적절한 것은 ② '통계를 계산하는 능력'이다.

- construct ⓥ 형성하다, 구성하다
- hypothesis ⓝ 가설
- interval ⓝ 간격
- calculate ⓥ 계산하다
- on a regular basis 규칙적으로
- systematic ⓐ 체계적인
- make a prediction 예측하다
- statistics ⓝ 통계

구문 풀이

> **12행** This memory store allows them to track, (within the neural
> 5형식 동사   목적어   목적격 보어1
> circuits of their brains), the frequency of sound patterns and to use
> ( ): 삽입구   to track 목적어   목적격 보어2
> this knowledge to make predictions about the meaning in patterns
> 부사적 용법(목적)
> of sounds.

▶ 많이 틀린 이유는?
아기들의 언어 소리 습득에 관한 글이다. 빈칸 뒤로, 아기들이 언어에서 반복되는 소리에 주의를 기울이고, 소리의 빈도나 순서, 고저를 분석하여 언어 패턴을 익혀 나간다는 설명이 이어지고 있다. '더 간단한' 소리를 선호한다는 내용은 언급되지 않기에 ④는 답으로 적절하지 않다.

▶ 문제 해결 방법은?
아기들이 주변에서 들은 소리 데이터를 바탕으로 그 패턴을 분석하여 추후 예측에 활용한다는 설명을 '통계 자료 계산(calculate statistics)'이라는 비유적 표현으로 일반화할 수 있어야 한다.

09 바넘 효과   정답률 62% | 정답 ④

다음 글에서 전체 흐름과 관계 없는 문장은?

[본문 해석]

바넘 효과는 누군가가 매우 일반적인 것을 읽거나 듣지만 그것이 자신에게 적용된다고 믿는 현상이다. ① 이러한 진술들은 표면적으로는 매우 개인적인 것처럼 보이지만 실제로는 많은 사람에게 적용된다. ② 인간 심리는 우리가 개인적 차원에서 동일시할 수 있는 것들을 믿고, 정보가 반드시 존재하지는 않는 경우에도 나머지에 대해서는 우리의 상상으로 공백을 채우면서 정보를 심지어 찾고 싶어 하게 한다. ③ 이것은 개인적인 것처럼 보이지만 수많은 사람에게 대개 들어맞는 정보를 제공하는 별자리 운세가 의존하는 원리이다. ④ 아침에 매일 별자리 운세를 읽는 것은 그것들이 남은 하루에 대한 예측을 제공하기 때문에 유익하다. ⑤ 그것들을 읽는 사람들이 그 정보를 너무나도 믿고 싶어 하기 때문에 그들은 그것을 사실로 만드는 삶에서 의미를 찾을 것이다.

Why? 왜 정답일까?

일반적인 진술을 개인적인 것으로 믿고 받아들이게 하는 바넘 효과에 관해 설명한 글이다. ①, ②, ③, ⑤는 흐름에 적합하지만, ④는 ③에서 예로 언급된 별자리 운세에 초점을 맞추어 사람들이 아침마다 별자리 운세를 읽으면 좋은 이유에 관해 언급하므로 흐름상 적절하지 않다. 따라서 글의 흐름과 관계 없는 문장은 ④이다.

- phenomenon ⓝ 현상
- statement ⓝ 진술
- identify with ~와 동일시하다
- rest ⓝ 나머지
- offer ⓥ 제공하다
- countless ⓐ 수많은
- prediction ⓝ 예측
- apply to ~에 적용되다
- on the surface 표면적으로
- fill in the blank 공백을 메우다
- principle ⓝ 원리
- make sense 일리가 있다
- beneficial ⓐ 이로운

구문 풀이

> **5행** Human psychology allows us to want to believe things
> 5형식 동사   목적어   목적격 보어1   선행사
> [that we can identify with on a personal level] and even seek
> 목적격 관계대명사   목적격 보어2
> information where it doesn't necessarily exist, filling in the blanks
> 접속사(~한 곳에서)   분사구문
> with our imagination for the rest.

10 더 나은 것을 위한 지속된 추구   정답률 50% | 정답 ①

주어진 글 다음에 이어질 글의 순서로 가장 적절한 것을 고르시오.

☑ (A) - (C) - (B)
② (B) - (A) - (C)
③ (B) - (C) - (A)
④ (C) - (A) - (B)
⑤ (C) - (B) - (A)

[본문 해석]

학생들은 심지어 공부에 관심이 없을 때에도 좋은 성적을 얻기 위해 공부한다. 사람들은 심지어 이미 가지고 있는 직업에 만족할 때에도 승진을 추구한다.

(A) 그것은 마치 사람들로 붐비는 축구 경기장에서 중요한 경기를 관람하는 것과 같다. 몇 줄 앞에 있는 한 관중이 더 잘 보기 위해 일어서고, 뒤이어 연쇄 반응이 일어난다.

(C) 단지 이전처럼 잘 보기 위해 곧 모든 사람들이 일어서게 된다. 모두가 앉기보다는 일어서지만, 그 누구의 위치도 나아지지 않았다.

(B) 그리고 만약 누군가가 일어서기를 거부한다면, 그는 경기에 있지 않은 편이

나을 것이다. 사람들이 위치상의 이익을 추구할 때, 그들은 치열하고 무의미한 경쟁을 하지 않을 수 없다. 뛰지 않기로 선택하는 것은 지는 것이다.

Why? 왜 정답일까?

주어진 글에서 학생들과 직장인들의 예를 들어 사람들은 계속 더 나은 것을 추구한다는 점을 언급한 데 이어, **(A)**는 축구 경기장의 비유를 소개하고 있다. **(A)**의 마지막 부분은 한 사람이 더 잘 보려고 일어서면 연쇄 반응이 일어난다는 내용으로 끝나고, **(C)**는 결국 모든 사람이 일어나게 된다고 설명한다. **(B)**는 일어서기를 거부하는 누군가가 있다면 그 사람은 경기장에 없는 편이 나을 것임을 언급하며 비유를 마무리한다. 따라서 글의 순서로 가장 적절한 것은 ① '(A) – (C) – (B)'이다.

- **job advancement** ⓝ 승진
- **crucial** ⓐ 중요한
- **improve** ⓥ 나아지다, 개선되다
- **crowded** ⓐ 붐비는
- **positional** ⓐ 위치상의

구문 풀이

9행 And if someone refuses to stand, he might just as well not be at the game at all.

→ 「refuse + to부정사 : ~하기를 거부하다」
조건 접속사
「might as well not + 동사원형 : ~하지 않는 것이 낫다」

11-12 광고 속 통계 수치의 신뢰도

[본문 해석]

『많은 광고는 통계 조사를 인용한다. 하지만 우리는 보통 이러한 조사들이 어떻게 실시되는지를 모르기 때문에 (a) 신중해야 한다.』 예를 들면, 한 치약 제조업체가 예전에 "80%가 넘는 치과의사들이 *Smiley Toothpaste*를 추천합니다." 라고 적혀 있는 포스터를 올렸다. 이것은 대부분의 치과의사들이 다른 브랜드보다 *Smiley Toothpaste*를 (b) 선호한다고 말하는 것처럼 보인다. 하지만 그 조사 항목이 치과의사들에게 한 가지 이상의 브랜드를 추천할 수 있게 했다는 것과, 실제로 또 다른 경쟁업체의 브랜드도 *Smiley Toothpaste*만큼 많이 추천되었다는 것이 드러난다! 당연히도 2007년에 영국 Advertising Standards Authority는 그 포스터가 (c) 잘못된 정보를 준다고 결정을 내렸고 그것은 더 이상 게시될 수 없었다.

주름을 빠른 속도로 줄여 준다는 크림을 판매하는 유명 화장품 회사의 경우도 유사하다. 그러나 주어진 유일한 증거라고는 "50명의 여성 중 76%가 동의했다." 라는 것뿐이다. 『하지만 이것이 의미하는 것은 그 증거가 피부 상태에 대한 객관적인 측정이 없었던 소수의 표본에서 얻은 개인적 의견에만 근거한다는 것이다.』 게다가, 우리는 이 여성들이 어떻게 선별되었는지 알 수 없다. 그런 정보 없이 있는 주어진 "증거"는 아주 (d) 유용하다(→ 쓸모가 없다). 불행하게도, 『그러한 광고들은 아주 전형적이고, 소비자인 우리가 스스로 판단해야 하며 광고의 주장을 너무 진지하게 받아들이는 것을 (e) 피해야 한다.』

- **cite** ⓥ 들다, 인용하다
- **cautious** ⓐ 조심스러운, 신중한
- **toothpaste** ⓝ 치약
- **recommend** ⓥ 추천하다
- **turn out** 판명되다, 밝혀지다
- **misleading** ⓐ 오해의 소지가 있는
- **similar** ⓐ 비슷한, 유사한
- **rapidly** ⓐⓓ 빨리, 급속히
- **evidence** ⓝ 증거
- **quite** ⓐⓓ 꽤, 상당히
- **avoid** ⓥ 회피하다, 모면하다
- **seriously** ⓐⓓ 심각하게, 진심으로
- **statistical** ⓐ 통계적인
- **conduct** ⓥ 수행하다, 행동을 하다
- **manufacturer** ⓝ 제조 회사
- **prefer** ⓥ 선호하다
- **rule** ⓥ 결정하다, 판결하다
- **display** ⓥ 진열하다, 전시하다
- **concern** ⓥ ~에 관련되다
- **wrinkle** ⓝ 주름
- **objective** ⓐ 객관적인
- **typical** ⓐ 전형적인
- **claim** ⓝ 주장
- **reliable** ⓐ 믿을만한, 신뢰할만한

구문 풀이

7행 But it turns out that the survey questions allowed the dentists to recommend more than one brand, and in fact another competitor's brand was recommended just as often as *Smiley Toothpaste*!

~임이 판명되다 접속사 / 주어1 / 동사1
목적격 보어 / 주어2
동사2 / 원급 비교(~만큼 …한)

11 제목 파악

정답률 57% | 정답 ②

윗글의 제목으로 가장 적절한 것은?

① The Link between Advertisements and the Economy
   광고와 경제의 연관성
② Are Statistical Data in Advertisements Reliable?
   광고 속 통계 데이터가 신뢰할 만한가?
③ Statistics in Advertisements Are Objective!
   광고 속 통계 자료들은 객관적이다!
④ The Bright Side of Public Advertisements
   대중 광고의 긍정적인 면
⑤ Quality or Price, Which Matters More?
   질과 가격, 무엇이 더 중요한가?

Why? 왜 정답일까?

첫 두 문장인 'Many advertisements cite statistical surveys. But we should be cautious because we usually do not know how these surveys are conducted.'에서 많은 광고가 통계 조사를 인용하지만 그 조사가 진행된 과정에 대해 소비자는 보통 잘 모르고 있기 때문에 정보의 신빙성을 판단함에 있어 주의가 필요하다는 내용을 주제로 제시하므로, 글의 제목으로 가장 적절한 것은 ② '광고 속 통계 데이터가 신뢰할 만한가?'이다.

★★★ *1등급 대비 고난도 3점 문제*

12 어휘 추론

정답률 43% | 정답 ④

밑줄 친 (a)~(e) 중에서 문맥상 낱말의 쓰임이 적절하지 않은 것은? [3점]

① (a) ② (b) ③ (c) ✔ (d) ⑤ (e)

Why? 왜 정답일까?

'But what this means is that the evidence is based on just the personal opinions from a small sample with no objective measurement of their skin's condition. Furthermore, we are not told how these women were selected.'에서 화장품 광고에서 통계 수치를 제시할 때 보통 소비자인 우리는 표본의 객관성이나 선별 과정 등에 관해 자세히 알 수 없다는 내용이 언급되고 있다. 이에 비추어 볼 때, 이 광고에서 제시된 통계 데이터는 '믿을 만하지 않다'는 것이 예시의 결론임을 알 수 있다. 따라서 문맥상 낱말의 쓰임이 적절하지 않은 것은 ④ '(d)'이다.

★★ 문제 해결 꿀~팁 ★★

▶ 많이 틀린 이유는?

최다 오답인 (c)를 제치는 데 있어서는 '~ it could no longer be displayed.' 가 가장 큰 힌트이다. 포스터가 더 이상 게시되지 못한 까닭은 포스터에 포함된 정보가 부적절했기 때문임을 유추할 수 있으므로, (c)의 misleading은 맥락상 적절하다.

▶ 문제 해결 방법은?

장문 어휘 문제에서는 밑줄 문장의 전후 맥락 파악이 가장 중요하다. (d) 또한 앞의 두 문장을 주의 깊게 읽어 맥락을 파악하면 쉽게 답임을 알 수 있다.

DAY 20 · 20분 미니 모의고사

01 ⑤	02 ③	03 ①	04 ②	05 ④
06 ③	07 ②	08 ②	09 ①	10 ④
11 ③	12 ③			

---

01 신문 이용에 관한 허락 구하기
정답률 93% | 정답 ⑤

다음 글의 목적으로 가장 적절한 것은?
① 도서관 이용 시간 연장을 건의하려고
② 신청한 도서의 대출 가능 여부를 문의하려고
③ 도서관에 보관 중인 자료 현황을 조사하려고
④ 글쓰기 동아리 신문의 도서관 비치를 부탁하려고
☑ 도서관에 있는 오래된 신문의 사용 허락을 요청하려고

[본문 해석]

학교 사서 선생님께,

저는 학교 영어 글쓰기 동아리 회장인 Kyle Thomas입니다. 저는 저희 동아리 회원들의 글쓰기 실력을 증진할 활동들을 계획해 왔습니다. 이러한 활동들의 목표 중 하나는 저희가 뉴스 미디어의 다양한 유형과 인쇄된 신문 기사에 사용된 언어를 인식하게 만드는 것입니다. 그러나 일부 오래된 신문은 온라인으로 접근하는 것이 쉽지 않습니다. 그러므로 학교 도서관에 보관되어 온 오래된 신문을 저희가 사용할 수 있도록 허락해 달라는 것이 선생님께 드리는 저의 겸허한 요청입니다. 만약 선생님께서 저희에게 허락해 주시면 정말 감사하겠습니다.

Kyle Thomas 드림

Why? 왜 정답일까?

'It is, therefore, my humble request to you to allow us to use old newspapers that have been stored in the school library.'에서 도서관에 보관된 오래된 신문을 이용할 수 있게 해달라고 요청하므로, 글의 목적으로 가장 적절한 것은 ⑤ '도서관에 있는 오래된 신문의 사용 허락을 요청하려고'이다.

- aim ⓝ 목표, 목적
- appreciate ⓥ 감사하다
- humble ⓐ 겸손한
- grant ⓥ (공식적으로) 주다

구문 풀이

5행 주어(one of the + 복수명사: ~ 중 하나)
One of the aims of these activities is to make us aware of
동사(단수) / 보어(~것)
various types of news media and the language used in printed
of의 목적어1 / of의 목적어2 / 과거분사
newspaper articles.

★★★ 1등급 대비 고난도 3점 문제

02 노력만이 가치 있다는 믿음에 대한 반박
정답률 45% | 정답 ③

밑줄 친 challenge this sacred cow가 다음 글에서 의미하는 바로 가장 적절한 것은? [3점]
① resist the tendency to avoid any hardship
그 어떤 난관이든 피하려는 경향에 저항한다
② escape from the pressure of using formal language
공식적인 언어를 사용해야 한다는 압박에서 벗어난다
☑ doubt the solid belief that only hard work is worthy
오로지 노력만이 가치 있다는 확고한 믿음을 의심한다
④ abandon the old notion that money always comes first
돈이 항상 먼저라는 오래된 관념을 버린다
⑤ break the superstition that holy animals bring good luck
신성한 동물은 행운을 가져다 준다는 미신을 깬다

[본문 해석]

우리의 언어는 우리의 더 깊은 전제를 드러내는 것을 돕는다. 이것을 잘 드러내는 다음과 같은 문구들을 생각해 보라. 우리는 중요한 무언가를 성취할 때 그것이 '피, 땀, 그리고 눈물'을 필요로 했다고 말한다. 우리는 중요한 성과는 '힘들게 얻은' 것이라고 말한다. 우리는 '하루 동안의 일'이라는 말로도 충분할 때 '하루 동안의 고생'이라는 말을 권한다. 우리가 '쉬운 돈'이라는 말을 할 때, 우리는 그것이 불법적이거나 의심스러운 수단을 통해 얻어졌다는 것을 넌지시 드러낸다. 우리는 보통 누군가의 의견이 틀렸음을 입증하려고 할 때, 우리는

'말은 쉽지'라는 문구를 비판으로 사용한다. 이는 마치 우리 모두가 '올바른' 방법은 반드시 더 어려운 방법이라는 것을 저절로 받아들이는 것과 같다. 나의 경험상 여기에는 거의 한 번도 의문이 제기되지 않는다. 만약 여러분이 정말로 이 신성한 소에 맞선다면 무슨 일이 일어날까? 우리는 중요하고 가치 있는 무언가가 쉬워질 수 있다고 잠시 멈춰 생각해 보지도 않는다. 만약 우리가 중요한 일을 하지 못하게 하는 가장 큰 것이 중요한 일은 엄청난 노력이 들어야 한다는 잘못된 전제라면 어떨까?

Why? 왜 정답일까?

밑줄 친 부분 앞까지 우리는 성과가 힘들게 얻어진다는 믿음을 우리 언어를 통해 드러내는 경향이 있다는 내용이 주를 이룬다. 이어서 밑줄 친 부분은 이러한 우리의 믿음을 '신성한 소'에 비유하며, 이 믿음에 '맞선다면' 무슨 일이 생길 것인지 묻고 있다. 즉, '노력과 수고만이 가치롭다'는 믿음에 '의문을 품는다'는 것이 밑줄 친 부분의 의미이므로, 답으로 가장 적절한 것은 ③ '오로지 노력만이 가치 있다는 확고한 믿음을 의심한다'이다.

- assumption ⓝ 가정, 추정
- achievement ⓝ 성취, 성과
- imply ⓥ 암시하다
- questionable ⓐ 의심스러운
- invalidate ⓥ 틀렸음을 입증하다
- inevitably ⓐd 불가피하게, 필연적으로
- sacred ⓐ 성스러운
- hardship ⓝ 고난, 난관, 어려움
- solid ⓐ 확고한
- superstition ⓝ 미신
- sweat ⓝ 땀
- hard-earned ⓐ 힘들게 얻은
- illegal ⓐ 불법적인
- criticism ⓝ 비판
- automatically ⓐd 저절로
- challenge ⓥ 도전하다, 이의를 제기하다
- huge ⓐ 거대한
- formal ⓐ 공식적인
- abandon ⓥ 버리다

구문 풀이

15행 What if the biggest thing (keeping us from doing what matters)
~라면 어떨까? / 주어 / ( ): 주어 수식(현재분사구)
is the false assumption [that it has to take huge effort]?
동사(단수) / [ ]: 동격절(= the false assumption)

★★ 문제 해결 꿀~팁 ★★

▶ 많이 틀린 이유는?
첫 문장의 주어가 '언어'이므로 얼핏 보면 언어를 언급하는 ②가 정답일 것 같지만, '공식적인 언어' 사용은 전혀 글과 관련이 없다. 이 글은 쉬운 성공을 경시하고 힘든 노력만이 가치 있게 말하는 언어 습관이 우리에게 어떤 영향을 미치는지에 관한 글이다.

▶ 문제 해결 방법은?
this sacred cow가 가리키는 것은 문맥상 'the "right" way is, inevitably, the harder one'이다. 이는 '힘든 노력만을 옳게' 여기는 사고방식인데, 밑줄 부분은 여기에 '반박을 제기한다'는 의미이다.

---

03 인간의 생활방식에 깊은 영향을 주는 건물과 개발
정답률 60% | 정답 ①

다음 글의 제목으로 가장 적절한 것은?
☑ Buildings Transform How We Live!
건물이 우리의 삶의 방식을 바꾼다!
② Why Do We Build More Than We Need?
우리는 왜 필요 이상으로 건물을 지을까?
③ Copying Ancient Buildings for Creativity
창의성을 위해 고대 건물을 베끼라
④ Was Life Better in Hunter-gatherer Times?
수렵 채집인 시대에는 삶이 더 괜찮았을까?
⑤ Innovate Your Farm with New Constructions
새로운 건축물로 농장을 혁신하라

[본문 해석]

우리는 우리가 건물을 형성하고 있다고 생각한다. 그러나 실제로 우리의 건물과 개발도 또한 우리를 형성하고 있다. 이것의 가장 좋은 예 중 하나는 가장 오래된 것으로 알려진 건축물인, 튀르키예의 Göbekli Tepe에 있는 화려하게 조각된 입석의 고리이다. 이 조상들이 약 12,000년 전에 입석을 세우는 아이디어를 얻기 전에, 그들은 수렵 채집인이었다. 거석으로 된 여러 개의 고리를 세우는 데 오랜 시간이 걸리고 많은 잇따른 세대를 거쳐야 했기에, 이 혁신가들은 건설 작업을 완료하기 위해 정착해야만 했던 것으로 보인다. 그 과정에서, 그들은 지구상 최초의 농업 사회가 되었다. 이것은 결국 사회 자체를 근본적으로 재구성하는 무언가를 건설하는 사회의 초기 예이다. 우리 시대에도 상황이 그렇게 다르지 않다.

Why? 왜 정답일까?

튀르키예의 초기 인류가 입석을 건설하며 수렵 채집인에서 농경인으로 정착하게 된 예시를 들어, 건물이나 개발이 인간 (사회)를 형성한다(~ our buildings and development are also shaping us.)는 점을 설명하는 글이다. 따라서 글의 제목으로 가장 적절한 것은 ① '건물이 우리의 삶의 방식을 바꾼다'이다.

- shape ⓥ 형성하다
- ornately ⓐ 화려하게
- erect ⓥ 세우다
- multiple ⓐ 여럿의
- successive ⓐ 연속된, 잇따른
- settle down 정착하다
- transform ⓥ 바꾸다, 변모시키다
- construction ⓝ 건설, 구성
- carve ⓥ 새기다
- hunter-gatherer ⓝ 수렵 채집인
- megalithic ⓐ 거석의
- be forced to 어쩔 수 없이 ~하다
- radically ⓐ 근본적으로, 급진적으로

구문 풀이

7행 It appears that the erection of the multiple rings of megalithic
~한 것으로 보인다
stones took so long, and so many successive generations, that these
┌→ 「so ~ that : 너무 ~해서 …하다」←┐
innovators were forced to settle down to complete the construction
어쩔 수 없이 ~했다
works.

---

04 리조트 보수 공사 공지   정답률 97% | 정답 ②

다음 Renovation Notice의 내용과 일치하지 않는 것은?
① 보수 공사는 2022년 11월 21일에 시작된다.
☑ 보수 공사는 주말에만 진행될 것이다.
③ 체육관과 실내 수영장은 폐쇄될 것이다.
④ 모든 야외 레저 활동은 평소와 같이 가능할 것이다.
⑤ 손님은 무료로 테니스장을 이용할 수 있다.

[본문 해석]

보수 공사 공지

Natural Jade 리조트는 투숙객들에게 더 나은 서비스를 제공하기 위해 지속적으로 시설을 개선하고 있습니다. 그래서 우리는 아래 일정에 따라 리조트의 몇몇 구역을 보수 공사하려고 합니다.

「보수 공사 기간: 2022년 11월 21일부터 12월 18일까지」──「」: ①의 근거 일치
• 「보수 공사는 매일 오전 9시부터 오후 5시까지 진행됩니다.」──「」: 「」: ②의 근거 불일치

「폐쇄 예정 구역: 체육관과 실내 수영장」──「」: ③의 근거 일치

추가 정보
• 「모든 야외 여가 활동은 평소와 같이 가능할 것입니다.」──「」: ④의 근거 일치
• 투숙객들은 식당의 모든 식사에 대해 15%의 할인을 받을 것입니다.
• 「투숙객들은 테니스장을 무료로 이용할 수 있습니다.」──「」: ⑤의 근거 일치

저희는 소음과 다른 어떤 불편함이든 최소화하기 위해 최대한 조치를 취할 것입니다. 이해해 주셔서 진심으로 감사합니다.

Why? 왜 정답일까?

'Renovations will take place every day from 9:00 a.m. to 5:00 p.m.'에서 공사는 매일 진행된다고 하므로, 안내문의 내용과 일치하지 않는 것은 ② '보수 공사는 주말에만 진행될 것이다.'이다.

Why? 왜 오답일까?

① 'Renovation Period: November 21 to December 18, 2022'의 내용과 일치한다.
③ 'Areas to be Closed: Gym and indoor swimming pool'의 내용과 일치한다.
④ 'All outdoor leisure activities will be available as usual.'의 내용과 일치한다.
⑤ 'Guests may use the tennis courts for free.'의 내용과 일치한다.

- renovation ⓝ 보수, 개조, 수리
- facility ⓝ 시설
- according to ~에 따라
- period ⓝ 기간
- leisure activity 여가 활동
- as usual 평소대로
- continually ⓐ 지속적으로
- serve ⓥ (상점 등에서 손님의) 시중을 들다
- below ⓐ 아래에
- take place 발생하다
- available ⓐ 이용 가능한
- inconvenience ⓝ 불편, 폐

---

05 비언어적 의사소통의 역할   정답률 52% | 정답 ④

다음 글의 밑줄 친 부분 중, 어법상 틀린 것은? [3점]

[본문 해석]

비언어적 의사소통은 언어적 의사소통의 대체물이 아니다. 오히려 그것은 전달되고 있는 메시지 내용의 풍부함을 강화시키도록 도와주면서 보충으로서 기능해야 한다. 비언어적 의사소통은 말하기가 불가능하거나 부적절할지도 모르는 상황에서 유용할 수 있다. 여러분이 어떤 개인과 이야기하는 동안 불편한 입장에 있다고 상상해 보라. 비언어적 의사소통은 여러분이 그 사람에게 다시 편안해지도록 대화에서 잠깐 벗어날 시간을 달라는 메시지를 전하게 도와줄 것이다. 비언어적 의사소통의 또 다른 장점은 그것이 여러분에게 감정과 태도를 적절하게 표현할 기회를 제공한다는 것이다. 비언어적 의사소통의 도움이 없다면 적절하게 표현되지 못할 여러분의 본성과 성격의 여러 측면들이 있다. 따라서 다시 말하면, 그것은 언어적 의사소통을 대체하는 것이 아니라 오히려 그것을 보완한다.

Why? 왜 정답일까?

뒤에 나오는 'it offers you the opportunity ~'가 완전한 4형식 구조임을 미루어볼 때, 뒤에 불완전한 문장을 수반하는 관계대명사 what을 쓰기에는 부적절하다. 따라서 what을 명사절 접속사인 that으로 고쳐야 한다. 어법상 틀린 것은 ④이다.

Why? 왜 오답일까?

① 완전한 주절 뒤로 '~하면서'라는 뜻의 분사구문이 적절히 연결되고 있다. 뒤에 나오는 to부정사는 serving의 목적어로, 'serve + to부정사(~하는 것을 돕다)'를 기억해 둔다.
② 앞에 추상적 공간의 선행사 situations가 나온 후 뒤에 may be가 동사인 완전한 2형식 구조가 나오는 것으로 보아 관계부사 where의 쓰임은 적절하다.
③ 준사역동사 help는 목적어와 목적격 보어가 능동 관계일 때 원형부정사 또는 to부정사를 목적격 보어로 취한다. 따라서 get의 쓰임이 적절하다.
⑤ 「not A but (rather) B(A가 아니라 B인)」 구문에서 A 자리에 주어 it에 연결되는 단수 동사 does not substitute가 나오므로, B 자리에도 단수 동사 complements가 적절하게 나왔다.

- substitute ⓝ 대체물 ⓥ 대체하다
- pass across ⓥ 전달하다
- get A across to B ⓥ A를 B에게 전하다
- aid ⓝ 도움
- complement ⓥ 보완하다
- enhance ⓥ 강화하다
- inappropriate ⓐ 부적절한
- properly ⓐ 적절히
- adequately ⓐ 적절하게

구문 풀이

2행 Rather, it should function as a supplement, serving to enhance
자동사(기능하다)   분사구문(~하면서)
the richness of the content of the message [that is being passed
선행사 ↰   현재진행 수동태(~되고 있다)
across].

---

06 인간과 개의 뇌 크기가 줄어든 이유   정답률 49% | 정답 ③

(A), (B), (C)의 각 네모 안에서 문맥에 맞는 낱말로 가장 적절한 것은? [3점]

	(A)	(B)	(C)
①	physical 신체적인	developed 발달시켰다	expanded 커졌다
②	physical 신체적인	lost 잃어버렸다	expanded 커졌다
☑	physical 신체적인	lost 잃어버렸다	shrank 줄어들었다
④	psychological 심리적인	developed 발달시켰다	shrank 줄어들었다
⑤	psychological 심리적인	lost 잃어버렸다	shrank 줄어들었다

[본문 해석]

최근의 연구는 인간과 개의 관계 진화가 두 종 모두의 뇌 구조를 바꿨다는 것을 시사한다. 사육으로 인해 야기된 다양한 (A) 신체적 변화들 중 하나는 뇌 크기의 감소인데, 말은 16%, 돼지는 34%, 그리고 개는 10에서 30% 감소했다. 이는 일단 인간이 이 동물들을 돌보기 시작하면서 그것들이 생존하기 위해 다양한 뇌 기능을 더는 필요로 하지 않았기 때문이다. 인간이 먹이를 주고 보호해 주는 동물들은 야생 조상들에 의해 요구된 기술 중 많은 것들을 필요로 하지 않았고 그러한 능력들과 관련된 뇌의 부분들을 (B) 잃어버렸다. 유사한 과정이 인간에게 나타났는데, 이들은 늑대에 의해 길들여진 것으로 보인다. 약 1만 년 전, 개의 역할이 대부분의 인간 사회에서 확실하게 정해졌을 때, 인간의 뇌도 약 10% (C) 줄어들었다.

Why? 왜 정답일까?

(A) 네모 뒤에서 신체적 변화로 볼 수 있는 뇌 크기 감소가 언급되므로, physical이 적절하다.

(B) 'This is because ~' 문장에서 개를 포함한 동물들의 뇌가 줄어든 까닭은 인간에 의해 길러지면서 생존에 필요했던 기능이 더 이상 필요하지 않게 되었기 때문임을 언급한다. 이를 근거로 할 때, 한때 필요했으나 더는 필요 없어진 능력과 관련된 뇌 부분이 실제로 '손실되면서' 뇌 크기가 줄어들었을 것임을 유추할 수 있다. 따라서 (B)에는 lost가 적절하다.

(C) 'A similar process occurred for humans, ~'에서 인간 또한 한때는 위협적이었던 늑대를 개로 키우게 되면서 늑대에 '길들게' 되었고, 이로 인해 '유사한 과정', 즉 뇌 크기가 줄어드는 일을 겪게 되었음을 시사하고 있다. 따라서 (C)에는 shrank가 적절하다.

(A), (B), (C)의 각 네모 안에서 문맥에 맞는 낱말로 가장 적절한 것은 ③ '(A) physical (신체적인) – (B) lost(잃어버렸다) – (C) shrank(줄어들었다)'이다.

- **physical** ⓐ 신체적인
- **domestication** ⓝ 사육, 길들이기
- **ancestor** ⓝ 조상
- **firmly** ⓐⓓ 확실히, 단호히
- **expand** ⓥ 커지다, 확장하다
- **psychological** ⓐ 심리적인
- **reduction** ⓝ 감소
- **capacity** ⓝ 능력
- **established** ⓐ 자리를 잡은
- **shrink** ⓥ 줄어들다

구문 풀이

9행 Animals [who were fed and protected by humans] did not need
주어 주격 관계대명사 동사1
many of the skills required by their wild ancestors and lost the parts
목적어1 과거분사 동사2 목적어2
of the brain related to those capacities.
과거분사(the parts 수식)

★★★ 1등급 대비 고난도 3점 문제

07 전통적 수요 법칙의 예외인 기펜재 | 정답률 56% | 정답 ②

다음 빈칸에 들어갈 말로 가장 적절한 것을 고르시오. [3점]

① order more meat – 더 많은 고기를 주문한다
✓ consume more rice – 더 많은 쌀을 소비한다
③ try to get new jobs – 새로운 일자리를 구하려 한다
④ increase their savings – 저축액을 늘린다
⑤ start to invest overseas – 해외에 투자하기 시작한다

[본문 해석]

수요의 법칙은 가격이 하락할수록 상품과 서비스에 대한 수요가 증가하고, 가격이 상승할수록 수요가 감소하는 것이다. *기펜재*는 전통적인 수요 법칙이 적용되지 않는 특별한 유형의 상품이다. 저렴한 대체품으로 바꾸는 대신 소비자들은 가격이 상승할 때 기펜재를 더 많이, 가격이 하락할 때 덜 필요로 한다. 예를 들어, 중국의 쌀은 가격이 하락할 때 사람들이 덜 구매하는 경향이 있기 때문에 기펜재이다. 그 이유는, 쌀값이 하락하면, 사람들이 고기나 유제품 같은 다른 종류의 상품에 쓸 돈이 많아지고, 그 결과 소비 패턴을 바꾸기 때문이다. 반면에, 쌀값이 상승하면, 사람들은 더 많은 쌀을 소비한다.

Why? 왜 정답일까?

전통적인 수요 법칙에 따르면 가격과 수요는 반비례하지만, 이 법칙의 예외에 있는 기펜재는 가격과 상승 및 하락 흐름을 같이한다(Instead of switching to cheaper replacements, consumers demand more of giffen goods when the price increases and less of them when the price decreases.)는 내용의 글이다. 중반부 이후로 중국의 쌀이 기펜재의 예시로 언급되므로, 쌀 가격이 오를 때 오히려 사람들은 '쌀을 더 산다'는 내용이 결론이어야 한다. 따라서 빈칸에 들어갈 말로 가장 적절한 것은 ② '더 많은 쌀을 소비한다'이다.

- **demand** ⓝ 수요 ⓥ 필요로 하다, 요구하다
- **switch to** ~로 바꾸다
- **dairy** ⓝ 유제품
- **apply for** ~에 적용되다
- **replacement** ⓝ 대체(품)
- **overseas** ⓐⓓ 해외에

구문 풀이

3행 *Giffen goods* are special types of products [for which the
선행사 「전치사+관계대명사」
traditional law of demand does not apply].

★★ 문제 해결 꿀~팁 ★★

▶ 많이 틀린 이유는?
기펜재의 개념을 잘 이해하고 사례에 적용해야 하는 빈칸 문제이다. 최다 오답 ④는 '저축액을 늘린다'는 의미인데, 글에서 기펜재와 저축액을 연결짓는 내용은 언급되지 않았다.

▶ 문제 해결 방법은?
글에 따르면 기펜재는 일반적 재화와 달리 가격이 오를 때 수요도 오르고, 가격이 떨어질 때 수요도 떨어지는 재화이다. 빈칸 문장에서는 '쌀 가격이 오르는' 상황을 상정하고 있으므로, '쌀에 대한 수요도 덩달아 오른다'는 결과를 예측할 수 있다.

★★★ 1등급 대비 고난도 2점 문제

08 우리 생활의 다방면에 연관된 밤하늘 | 정답률 34% | 정답 ②

글의 흐름으로 보아, 주어진 문장이 들어가기에 가장 적절한 곳을 고르시오.

[본문 해석]

우리는 많은 방식으로 밤하늘과 연결되어 있다. ① 그것은 항상 사람들이 궁금해하고 상상하도록 영감을 주었다. ② 문명의 시작부터, 우리 선조들은 밤하늘에 대해 신화를 만들었고 전설적 이야기를 했다. 그러한 이야기들의 요소들은 여러 세대의 사회 · 문화적 정체성에 깊이 새겨졌다. ③ 실용적인 수준에서, 밤하늘은 과거 세대들이 시간을 기록하고 달력을 만들도록 도왔고 이는 농업과 계절에 따른 수확의 보조 도구로서 사회를 발전시키는 데 필수적이었다. ④ 수 세기 동안, 그것은 또한 무역과 새로운 세계를 탐험하는 데 필수적인 유용한 항해 도구를 제공하였다. ⑤ 심지어 현대에도, 지구의 외딴 지역에 있는 많은 사람이 그러한 실용적인 목적을 위해 밤하늘을 관찰한다.

Why? 왜 정답일까?

② 앞에서 인류는 밤하늘을 궁금해했다고 언급한 후, 주어진 문장은 인류가 거의 문명이 시작되던 시기부터 밤하늘에 대한 다양한 전설과 신화를 만들어냈다고 설명한다. 그리고 ② 뒤의 문장은 주어진 문장의 myths and legendary stories를 those narratives로 가리킨다. 따라서 주어진 문장이 들어가기에 가장 적절한 곳은 ②이다.

- **civilization** ⓝ 문명
- **legendary** ⓐ 전설의
- **wonder** ⓥ 궁금하다
- **embed** ⓥ ~ 을 깊이 새겨 두다
- **practical** ⓐ 실용적인
- **calendar** ⓝ 달력
- **farming** ⓝ 농업
- **gathering** ⓝ 수집, 수확
- **commerce** ⓝ 무역, 상업
- **ancestor** ⓝ 선조
- **inspire** ⓥ 영감을 주다
- **element** ⓝ 요소
- **identity** ⓝ 정체성
- **keep track of** ~을 기록하다
- **aid** ⓝ 보조 도구
- **seasonal** ⓐ 계절에 따른
- **navigation** ⓝ 항해
- **planet** ⓝ 지구

구문 풀이

7행 On a practical level, the night sky helped past generations
동사 목적어
to keep track of time and (to) create calendars — (which are) essential
목적격 보어1 목적격 보어2 선행사 생략
to developing societies as aids to farming and seasonal gathering.

★★ 문제 해결 꿀~팁 ★★

▶ 많이 틀린 이유는?
③ 앞에서 밤하늘에 대한 이야기는 '사회문화적 정체성에 깊이 새겨졌다'고 하는데, ③ 뒤에서는 '실용적으로 살펴보면' 밤하늘 연구가 달력 제작 등에 영향을 미쳤다고 한다. 즉 On a practical level 앞뒤로 일반적 논의에서 더 구체적 논의로 나아가는 내용이 자연스럽게 연결된다.

▶ 문제 해결 방법은?
② 앞에서는 '이야기'로 볼 만한 내용이 없는데, ② 뒤에서는 갑자기 those narratives를 언급하므로 논리적 공백이 발생한다. 이때 주어진 문장을 보면 myths와 legendary stories가 있으므로, 이것을 ② 뒤에서 those narratives로 연결했다는 것을 알 수 있다.

09 음악과 감정 표현에 관한 두 가지 견해 | 정답률 63% | 정답 ①

다음 글의 내용을 한 문장으로 요약하고자 한다. 빈칸 (A), (B)에 들어갈 말로 가장 적절한 것은?

	(A)		(B)		(A)		(B)
✓	culturally 문화적으로	……	similarity 유사성	②	culturally 문화적으로	……	balance 균형
③	socially 사회적으로	……	difference 차이	④	incorrectly 부정확하게	……	connection 연결성
⑤	incorrectly 부정확하게	……	contrast 대조				

DAY 20

[본문 해석]

음악이 감정을 표현할 수 있는 한 방법은 단지 학습된 연관을 통해서이다. 단조나 낮은 음으로 느리게 연주된 악곡에 대해 본질적으로 슬픈 무언가가 있는 것은 아마 아닐 것이다. 어쩌면 우리는 우리의 문화 속에서 어떤 종류의 음악을 장례식과 같은 슬픈 일과 연관시키는 것을 학습해 왔기 때문에 그것을 슬프게 듣게 된다. 만약 이 관점이 옳다면, 우리는 문화적으로 친숙하지 않은 음악에 표현된 감정을 이해하는 데 분명 어려움이 있을 것이다. 이 관점과 완전히 반대되는 입장은 음악과 감정 사이의 연결고리는 유사함이라는 것이다. 예컨대, 슬프다고 느낄 때 우리는 느리게 움직이고 낮은 음의 목소리로 느리게 말한다. 따라서 우리가 느리고 낮은 음의 음악을 들을 때, 우리는 그것을 슬프게 듣는다. 만약 이 관점이 옳다면, 우리는 문화적으로 친숙하지 않은 음악에 표현된 감정을 이해하는 데 분명 어려움이 거의 없을 것이다.

➡ 음악에 표현된 감정은 (A) 문화적으로 학습된 연관을 통해서 이해될 수 있다고 믿어지거나, 혹은 음악과 감정 사이의 (B) 유사성 때문에 이해될 수 있다고 믿어진다.

Why? 왜 정답일까?

음악을 통한 감정 표현에 대한 두 가지 상반된 시각이 존재한다는 내용의 글이다. 첫 문장에서는 음악이 특정한 감정과 연관지어 이해되는 까닭이 문화적인 학습(a learned association)에 기인한다고 설명한다. 즉, 단조로 된 음악을 우리가 슬프게 듣는 까닭은 단조가 본질적으로 슬픈 까닭이 아니라 우리가 단조를 슬픔과 연관시켜 듣도록 학습해 왔기 때문이라는 것이다. 이와는 반대로 'Totally opposed to this view ~'에서는 특정한 음악 형식이 특정한 감정과 본질적으로 유사한 까닭에 그 감정을 나타낼 수 있다고 보는 견해를 소개한다. 따라서 요약문의 빈칸 (A), (B)에 들어갈 말로 가장 적절한 것은 각 견해의 핵심어를 반영한 ① '(A) culturally(문화적으로), similarity(유사성)'이다.

- **association** ⓝ 연관
- **culturally** ⓐⓓ 문화적으로
- **opposed to** ~에 반대되는
- **low-pitched** ⓐ 저음의
- **funeral** ⓝ 장례식
- **unfamiliar** ⓐ 친숙하지 않은
- **resemblance** ⓝ 유사성

구문 풀이

10행 Totally opposed to this view is the position that the link
「주격 보어 + 동사 + 주어 : 도치 구문」 동격(= 주어)
between music and emotion is one of resemblance.

10-12 손자에게 최고의 학교를 찾아주려 한 할아버지

[본문 해석]

(A)

한 소년이 마을에 있는 가장 좋은 학교에 한 자리를 얻었다. 아침에 그의 할아버지는 그를 학교에 데리고 갔다. (a) 그가 손자와 함께 운동장으로 들어갔을 때, 아이들이 그들을 둘러쌌다. "진짜 우스꽝스러운 할아버지다."라며 한 소년이 히죽히죽 웃었다. 「갈색 머리 소녀가 그 둘에게 손가락질하며 위아래로 뛰었다.」 갑자기 종이 울렸고, 아이들이 첫 수업에 급히 뛰어갔다.

(D)

노인은 손자의 손을 꽉 잡고, 그를 교문 밖으로 데리고 나갔다. 「"굉장한걸, 나 학교에 가지 않아도 되네!"라고 소년이 소리쳤다.」 "가긴 가야지, 그렇지만 이 학교는 아니야."라고 할아버지가 대답했다. "내가 직접 네게 학교를 찾아주마." 할아버지는 손자를 집으로 데리고 돌아가 할머니에게 그를 돌봐달라고 하고 나서, (e) 자신이 선생님을 찾아 나섰다. 학교를 발견할 때마다, 노인은 운동장으로 들어가서 아이들이 쉬는 시간에 나오기를 기다렸다.

(B)

몇몇 학교에서는 아이들이 노인을 완전히 무시했고, 다른 학교들에서는 아이들이 (b) 그를 놀렸다. 이런 일이 일어났을 때, 그는 슬프게 돌아서서 집으로 가곤 했다. 「마침내, 그는 매우 작은 한 학교의 아주 작은 운동장으로 들어섰고, 지쳐서 울타리에 기댔다.」 종이 울렸고, 아이들 무리가 운동장으로 달려 나왔다. "할아버지, 괜찮으세요? 물 한 잔 가져다드릴까요?" 누군가가 말했다. "우리 운동장에 벤치가 있어요, 오셔서 앉으세요." 또 다른 누군가가 말했다. 곧 한 젊은 선생님이 운동장으로 나왔다.

(C)

노인은 (c) 그에게 인사하면서 이렇게 말했다. "마침내, 제가 손자에게 마을 최고의 학교를 찾아주었네요." "잘못 아신 겁니다, 어르신. 우리 학교는 최고가

아니에요. 작고 비좁은걸요." 「노인은 선생님과 논쟁을 벌이지 않았다.」 대신, 노인은 손자가 그 학교에 다닐 수 있도록 준비해주고, 그런 다음에 떠났다. 그날 저녁, 소년의 어머니는 (d) 그에게 말했다. "아버지, 글을 읽을 줄도 모르시잖아요. 최고의 선생님을 찾았다는 것을 어떻게 아세요?" "선생님은 그 제자를 보고 판단해야 해."라고 노인이 대답했다.

- **surround** ⓥ 둘러싸다, 에워싸다
- **ignore** ⓥ 무시하다
- **tiny** ⓐ 아주 작은
- **exhausted** ⓐ 지친, 소진된
- **make arrangements for** ~을 준비하다
- **firmly** ⓐⓓ 단단히, 꽉
- **look after** ~을 돌보다
- **run off to** ~로 뛰어가다, 달아나다
- **make fun of** ~을 조롱하다
- **lean against** ~에 기대다
- **You are mistaken.** 잘못 생각하고 계세요.
- **pupil** ⓝ 학생, 제자
- **exclaim** ⓥ 소리치다, 외치다
- **spot** ⓥ 찾다, 발견하다

구문 풀이

(D) 2행 "Brilliant, I don't have to go to school!" the boy exclaimed. "You do, but not this one," his granddad replied. "I'll find you a school
대동사(= go to school) └ 대명사(= school)
myself."
강조 용법(주어 | 강조)

10 글의 순서 파악   정답률 69% | 정답 ④

주어진 글 (A)에 이어질 내용을 순서에 맞게 배열한 것으로 가장 적절한 것은?

① (B) − (D) − (C)
② (C) − (B) − (D)
③ (C) − (D) − (B)
④ (D) − (B) − (C)
⑤ (D) − (C) − (B)

Why? 왜 정답일까?

한 할아버지가 손자를 데리고 마을 최고의 학교로 갔다가 아이들에게 놀림을 받았다는 내용의 (A) 뒤에는, 할아버지가 손자를 집에 데려다 놓고 직접 다른 학교를 찾아나섰다는 내용의 (D), 할아버지가 어느 예의 바른 아이들 무리와 선생님을 만나게 되었다는 내용의 (B), 할아버지가 학교를 결정했고, 그 결정이 어떻게 내려진 것인지 결론 짓는 내용의 (C)가 차례로 연결되어야 한다. 따라서 글의 순서로 가장 적절한 것은 ④ '(D) − (B) − (C)'이다.

11 지칭 추론   정답률 69% | 정답 ③

밑줄 친 (a) ~ (e) 중에서 가리키는 대상이 나머지 넷과 다른 것은?

① (a)   ② (b)   ③ (c)   ④ (d)   ⑤ (e)

Why? 왜 정답일까?

(a), (b), (d), (e)는 the old man[grandad], (c)는 a young teacher를 가리키므로, (a) ~ (e) 중에서 가리키는 대상이 다른 하나는 ③ '(c)'이다.

12 세부 내용 파악   정답률 73% | 정답 ③

윗글에 관한 내용으로 적절하지 않은 것은?

① 갈색 머리 소녀가 노인과 소년을 향해 손가락질했다.
② 노인은 지쳐서 울타리에 기댔다.
③ 노인은 선생님과 논쟁을 벌였다.
④ 노인은 글을 읽을 줄 몰랐다.
⑤ 소년은 학교에 가지 않아도 된다고 소리쳤다.

Why? 왜 정답일까?

(C) 'The old man didn't argue with the teacher.'에서 노인은 선생님과 논쟁을 벌이지 않았다고 하므로, 내용과 일치하지 않는 것은 ③ '노인은 선생님과 논쟁을 벌였다.'이다.

Why? 왜 오답일까?

① (A) 'A girl with brown hair pointed at the pair and jumped up and down.'의 내용과 일치한다.
② (B) '~ leant against the fence, exhausted.'의 내용과 일치한다.
④ (C) 'Dad, you can't even read.'의 내용과 일치한다.
⑤ (D) '"Brilliant, I don't have to go to school!" the boy exclaimed.'의 내용과 일치한다.

DAY 21 · 20분 미니 모의고사

01 ③	02 ①	03 ⑤	04 ④	05 ③
06 ③	07 ④	08 ④	09 ③	10 ④
11 ①	12 ④			

---

01 · 미래에 관한 구체적인 분석과 계획의 필요성
정답률 74% | 정답 ③

다음 글에서 필자가 주장하는 바로 가장 적절한 것은?

① 성공적인 삶을 위해 미래에 대한 구체적인 계획을 세워야 한다.
② 중요한 결정을 내릴 때에는 자신의 직관에 따라 판단해야 한다.
☑ 더 나은 선택을 위해 성공 가능성을 확률적으로 분석해야 한다.
④ 빠른 목표 달성을 위해 지름길로 가고자 할 때 신중해야 한다.
⑤ 인생의 여정에서 선택에 따른 결과를 스스로 책임져야 한다.

[본문 해석]

평생에 걸친 우리 여정의 모든 단계에서 우리는 먼 곳으로 이어지는 여러 다른 길이 있는 분기점을 만난다. 각각의 선택은 어떤 길이 여러분의 목적지로 데려다줄지에 대한 불확실성을 포함한다. 선택을 하기 위해 우리의 직관을 믿으면 흔히 우리가 결국 차선의 선택을 하게 되는 것으로 끝난다. 불확실성을 숫자로 바꾸는 것은 여러분의 목적지로 가는 길을 분석하고 지름길을 찾는 강력한 방법으로 입증되었다. 확률에 대한 수학적 이론은 위험을 제거하지는 않았지만, 우리가 그 위험을 더 효과적으로 관리할 수 있게 해준다. 미래가 안고 있는 모든 가능한 시나리오를 분석한 다음, 그것들이 성공이나 실패로 이어질 비율이 얼마나 되는지를 살펴보는 것이 전략이다. 이것은 여러분이 어떤 길을 선택할 것인지에 관한 결정을 내릴 때 그 근거로 삼을 수 있는 미래에 대한 훨씬 더 좋은 지도를 여러분에게 제공한다.

Why? 왜 정답일까?

글 후반부에서 '불확실성을 숫자로 바꾸어' 모든 가능한 시나리오의 성공 및 실패 확률을 따져볼 것을 조언하고 있다(~ analyze all the possible scenarios that the future holds and then to see what proportion of them lead to success or failure.). 따라서 필자가 주장하는 바로 가장 적절한 것은 ③ '더 나은 선택을 위해 성공 가능성을 확률적으로 분석해야 한다.'이다.

- **journey** ⓝ 여정, 여행
- **junction** ⓝ 분기점
- **uncertainty** ⓝ 불확실성
- **intuition** ⓝ 직관
- **suboptimal** ⓐ 차선의
- **potent** ⓐ 강력한
- **shortcut** ⓝ 지름길
- **eliminate** ⓥ 제거하다
- **proportion** ⓝ 비율
- **encounter** ⓥ 만나다, 조우하다
- **pathway** ⓝ 경로
- **destination** ⓝ 행선지, 목적지
- **end up with** 결국 ~하다
- **turn A into B** A를 B로 바꾸다
- **analyze** ⓥ 분석하다
- **probability** ⓝ 확률, 가능성
- **effectively** ⓐⓓ 효과적으로
- **base A on B** A의 근거를 B에 두다

구문 풀이

11행 The strategy is {to analyze all the possible scenarios that 【목적격 관계대명사】【선행사】 the future holds} and then {to see what proportion of them lead to 【의문형용사(어떤)】 success or failure}.
[ ] : 주격 보어(~것)

---

02 · 수면의 중요한 기능
정답률 92% | 정답 ①

다음 글의 요지로 가장 적절한 것은?

☑ 수면은 건강 유지와 최상의 기능 발휘에 도움이 된다.
② 업무량이 증가하면 필요한 수면 시간도 증가한다.
③ 균형 잡힌 식단을 유지하면 뇌 기능이 향상된다.
④ 불면증은 주위 사람들에게 부정적인 영향을 미친다.
⑤ 꿈의 내용은 깨어 있는 시간 동안의 경험을 반영한다.

[본문 해석]

많은 사람이 수면을 그저 뇌는 멈추고 신체는 쉬는 '가동되지 않는 시간'으로 본다. 일, 학교, 가족, 또는 가정의 책임을 다하기 위해 서두르는 와중에, 사람들은 수면 시간을 줄이고, 그것이 문제가 되지 않을 것으로 생각하는데, 왜냐하면 이러한 모든 다른 활동들이 훨씬 더 중요해 보이기 때문이다. 하지만 연구는 수면 중에 수행되는 매우 중요한 여러 과업이 건강을 유지하는 데 도움이 되고 사람들이 최상의 수준으로 기능할 수 있게 해 준다는 것을 밝히고 있다. 잠을 자는 동안, 여러분의 뇌는 학습하고 기억과 새로운 통찰을 만드는 데 필요한 경로를 형성하느라 열심히 일하고 있다. 충분한 수면이 없다면, 여러분은 정신을 집중하고 주의를 기울이거나 빠르게 반응할 수 없다. 수면이 부족하면 심지어 감정 (조절) 문제를 일으킬 수도 있다. 게다가, 계속된 수면 부족이 심각한 질병의 발생 위험을 증가시킨다는 것을 점점 더 많은 증거가 보여 준다.

Why? 왜 정답일까?

주제를 제시하는 'But ~ a number of vital tasks carried out during sleep help to maintain good health and enable people to function at their best.'에서 수면 중 이루어지는 많은 일이 건강 및 기능 유지에 도움이 된다고 하므로, 글의 요지로 가장 적절한 것은 ① '수면은 건강 유지와 최상의 기능 발휘에 도움이 된다.'이다.

- **view A as B** A를 B로 보다
- **down time** 정지 시간, 휴식 시간
- **carry out** ~을 수행하다
- **lack** ⓝ 부족
- **develop a disease** 병을 키우다
- **merely** ⓐⓓ 그저, 단순히
- **cut back on** ~을 줄이다
- **insight** ⓝ 통찰력
- **evidence** ⓝ 증거

구문 풀이

6행 But research reveals that a number of vital tasks carried out 【접속사(~것)】【주어(a number of + 복수 명사: 많은 ~)】【과거분사구】 during sleep help to maintain good health and enable people 【동사1】【목적어】【동사2】【목적어】 to function at their best. 【목적격 보어】

---

03 · 해수면 상승의 결과
정답률 70% | 정답 ⑤

다음 글의 주제로 가장 적절한 것은?

① cause of rising temperatures on the Earth
지구의 온도가 상승하는 원인
② principles of planets maintaining their shapes
행성들이 모양을 유지하는 원리
③ implications of melting ice on marine biodiversity
녹는 얼음이 해양 생물 다양성에 미치는 영향
④ way to keep track of time without using any device
어떤 장치도 쓰지 않고 시간을 아는 방법
☑ impact of melting ice and rising seas on the length of a day
녹는 얼음과 해수면 상승이 하루의 시간 길이에 미치는 영향

[본문 해석]

녹는 얼음과 상승하는 바다의 가장 놀랍고 믿을 수 없는 결과는 그것들이 함께 일종의 타임머신이 된다는 것인데, 이것은 너무도 현실적이어서 우리 하루의 지속시간을 바꾸고 있다. 그것은 다음과 같이 작동한다. 빙하가 녹고 바다가 높아지면서 중력이 적도를 향해 더 많은 물을 밀어 넣는다. 이것은 지구의 모양을 아주 약간 변화시켜 가운데 주변으로 더 불룩해지게 만들고, 이것은 결과적으로 발레 무용수가 양팔을 뻗어서 회전을 늦추는 방식과 유사하게 행성의 회전을 늦춘다. 이 감속이 매년 단지 몇천 분의 1초로 크지는 않지만, 해마다 상승하는 바다의 거의 드러나지 않는 증가와 마찬가지로 그것은 쌓인다. 공룡들이 지구에 살았을 때, 하루는 약 23시간만 지속되었다.

Why? 왜 정답일까?

지구 온난화로 인한 해수면 상승이 지구의 가운데를 더 불룩해지게 만들어 지구의 하루가 지속되는 시간을 연장할 수 있다(The most remarkable and unbelievable consequence of melting ice and rising seas ~ so real that they are altering the duration of our day.)는 내용의 글이다. 따라서 글의 주제로 가장 적절한 것은 ⑤ '녹는 얼음과 해수면 상승이 하루의 시간 길이에 미치는 영향'이다.

- **remarkable** ⓐ 현저한, 두드러지는
- **alter** ⓥ 바꾸다
- **glacier** ⓝ 빙하
- **equator** ⓝ 적도
- **rotation** ⓝ 회전
- **spread out** 벌리다, 펴지다
- **barely** ⓐⓓ 거의 ~않다, 가까스로
- **last** ⓥ 지속되다
- **implication** ⓝ 영향
- **keep track of** ~을 추적하다
- **consequence** ⓝ 결과, 영향
- **duration** ⓝ 지속 시간
- **gravity** ⓝ 중력
- **slightly** ⓐⓓ 약간
- **spin** ⓝ 회전
- **slowdown** ⓝ 둔화, 지연
- **noticeable** ⓐ 분명한, 뚜렷한
- **principle** ⓝ 원리
- **biodiversity** ⓝ 생물 다양성

구문 풀이

1행 The most remarkable and unbelievable consequence (of
　　　　　주어(최상급)
melting ice and rising seas) is that together they are a kind of time
　　　　　　　　　　　　　동사(단수)
machine, so real that they are altering the duration of our day.
　　　　　　　「so ~ that … : 너무 ~해서 …하다」

---

04 수질 오염 대책 아이디어 공모전　　정답률 86% | 정답 ④

Kenner High School's Water Challenge에 관한 다음 안내문의 내용과
일치하는 것은?
① 제안서는 직접 방문하여 제출해야 한다.
② 9월 23일부터 제안서를 제출할 수 있다.
③ 제안서는 한 팀당 4개까지 제출할 수 있다.
✓ 제공된 제안서 양식을 사용해야 한다.
⑤ 2등은 10달러의 상품권을 받는다.

[본문 해석]

Kenner High School's Water Challenge
(Kenner 고등학교 물 챌린지)

Kenner 고등학교 물 챌린지는 수질 오염에 대한 대책을 제안하는 새로운 대회
입니다. 수질 오염에 대처하기 위한 여러분의 아이디어를 공유해 주세요!

제출
– **방법:** 여러분의 제안서를 이메일 admin@khswater.edu로 제출해 주세요.」
　　　　　　　　　　　　　　　　　　　　「└: ①의 근거 불일치
– **일시:** 2022년 9월 5일부터 2022년 9월 23일까지」
　　　　　　　　　　　　　　└「: ②의 근거 불일치

세부 사항
– 참가자들은 반드시 4인으로 구성된 팀으로 참가해야 하며, 오직 한 팀에
　만 참여할 수 있습니다.
– 한 팀당 한 개의 제안서만 제출할 수 있습니다.」──「: ③의 근거 불일치
– 참가자들은 웹사이트에 제공된 제안서 양식을 사용해야 합니다.」
　　　　　　　　　　　　　　　　　　　　「」: ④의 근거 일치

상품
– 1등: 50달러 상품권
– 2등: 30달러 상품권」──「: ⑤의 근거 불일치
– 3등: 10달러 상품권

대회에 대해 더 알고 싶으면, www.khswater.edu를 방문해 주세요.

Why? 왜 정답일까?

'Participants must use the proposal form provided on the website.'에서
제안서는 제공된 양식을 사용해 작성되어야 한다고 공지하므로, 안내문의 내용과 일치하
는 것은 ④ '제공된 제안서 양식을 사용해야 한다.'이다.

Why? 왜 오답일까?

① 'Submit your proposal by email to admin@khswater.edu.'에서 제안서
는 이메일로 제출하면 된다고 하였다.
② 'When: September 5, 2022 to September 23, 2022'에서 9월 23일은 제출
시작일이 아니라 마감일이라고 하였다.
③ 'Submission is limited to one proposal per team.'에서 팀별로 제안서는
하나만 제출할 수 있다고 하였다.
⑤ '2nd: $30 gift certificate'에서 2등은 30달러짜리 상품권을 받는다고 하였다.

● measure ⓝ 대책, 조치　　　● water pollution 수질 오염
● gift certificate 상품권

★★★ 1등급 대비 고난도 3점 문제

05 만화란 읽기 권유　　정답률 39% | 정답 ③

다음 글의 밑줄 친 부분 중, 어법상 틀린 것은? [3점]

[본문 해석]

시간을 내어 만화란을 읽어라. 만화는 당신을 웃게 할 뿐 아니라 삶의 본질에
대한 지혜를 담고 있기 때문에 가치가 있다. *Charlie Brown*과 *Blondie*는 내 아
침 일과의 일부분이고 내가 하루를 미소로 시작하도록 도와준다. 신문의 만화
란을 읽을 때, 당신을 웃게 하는 만화를 잘라두어라. 그것을 볼 때마다 웃음을
띠고 기분이 좋아지는 것을 느낄 수 있도록, 냉장고나 직장처럼 당신이 가장

필요로 하는 곳에 그 만화를 붙여두어라. 모두가 함께 웃을 수 있도록 당신이
가장 좋아하는 만화를 친구들 및 가족들과 공유하라. 큰 웃음을 진정 잘 활용
할 수 있는 아픈 친구들을 방문할 때 당신의 만화를 가지고 가라.

Why? 왜 정답일까?

When이 이끄는 부사절 뒤에 주절의 서술어 역할을 할 동사가 없으므로, 동명사 cutting
을 원형인 cut으로 바꾸어 명령문 형태의 문장을 완성해야 한다. 따라서 어법상 틀린 것은
③이다.

Why? 왜 오답일까?

① 'not only[just] A but (also) B' 구문이다. A와 B 자리에 모두 because절이 나와
병렬을 이룬다.
② 준사역동사 help는 목적격 보어 자리에 원형부정사 또는 to부정사가 나온다. 여기서
는 to start라는 to부정사가 나왔다.
④ feel의 목적어인 your spirit이 '고양되는, 좋아지는' 대상이므로 이를 보충 설명하
는 목적격 보어 자리에 수동을 나타내는 과거분사 lifted를 쓴 것은 적절하다.
⑤ 선행사가 sick friends라는 사람 명사이므로 who를 쓴 것은 적절하다. 이는 주격
관계대명사이므로 뒤에 주어 없이 'can ~ use'라는 동사로 시작하는 불완전한 절이 나
온다.

● worthwhile ⓐ 가치가 있는　　● contain ⓥ 담다, 포함하다
● wisdom ⓝ 지혜　　　　　　　● nature ⓝ 본질
● routine ⓝ 일과, 일상, 틀　　　● cut out ~을 잘라 내다
● post ⓥ 붙이다, 게시하다　　　● spirit ⓝ 기분, 기운

구문 풀이

7행 Post it wherever you need it most, (such as on your
　　　　명령문　　　　복합관계부사(어디 ~이든)
refrigerator or at work) / — so that (every time you see it), you will
　　　　　　　　　　　　　　　　~하도록　　　　　~할 때마다
smile and feel your spirit lifted.
　동사1　　동사2　　목적어　　목적격 보어(과거분사)

★★ 문제 해결 꿀~팁 ★★

▶ 많이 틀린 이유는?
① 'not only A but (also) B', ③ '동명사 vs. 동사', ④ '현재분사 vs. 과거분사' 등
빈출 포인트 중심으로 구성된 문법 문항이다. 정답인 ③에서 동명사는 문장의 주어
기능을 할 수 있기에 문장 맨 앞에 나오는 동명사에 밑줄이 있으면 맞다고 생각하기
쉽지만, 문장의 나머지 부분에 동사가 없다면 이 부분이 동사로 바뀌어 명령문이 되어
야 문장이 성립한다.
▶ 문제 해결 방법은?
평소 문제를 풀면서 눈에 자주 띄는 문법 개념은 기본서를 참고하여 반드시 정리해
두도록 한다. 특히 ④와 같이 5형식 문장의 목적격 보어에서 '능동(현재분사) vs. 수동
(과거분사)'를 묻는 유형은 매우 흔하다. 이 경우에는 목적어가 '하는' 주체인지, '당하는'
객체인지에 주목하여 문제를 푼다.

---

06 인공 조명의 가격 하락에 따른 결과　　정답률 59% | 정답 ③

다음 글의 밑줄 친 부분 중, 문맥상 낱말의 쓰임이 적절하지 않은 것은? [3점]

[본문 해석]

기본적인 어떤 것의 가격이 크게 하락할 때, 온 세상이 바뀔 수 있다. 조명을
생각해 보자. 아마 여러분은 어떤 유형의 인공조명 아래에서 이 문장을 읽고
있을 것이다. 또한, 여러분은 독서를 위해 인공조명을 이용하는 것이 그럴 만한
가치가 있는지에 대해 아마 생각해 본 적이 없을 것이다. 조명이 너무 ① 싸서
여러분은 생각 없이 그것을 이용한다. 하지만 1800년대 초반에는, 같은 양의
조명에 대해 오늘날 지불하고 있는 것의 400배만큼의 비용이 들었을 것이다.
그 가격이면, 여러분은 비용을 ② 의식할 것이고 책을 읽기 위해 인공조명을
이용하기 전에 다시 한 번 생각할 것이다. 조명 가격의 ③ 증가(→ 하락)는 세상
을 밝혔다. 그것은 밤을 낮으로 바꾸었을 뿐 아니라, ④ 자연의 빛(자연광)이
들어올 수 없는 큰 건물에서 우리가 살고 일할 수 있게 해 주었다. 만약 인공조
명의 비용이 거의 공짜 수준으로 하락하지 않았더라면 우리가 오늘날 누리는
것 중에 ⑤ 가능한 것은 거의 아무것도 없을 것이다.

Why? 왜 정답일까?

마지막 두 문장에서 인공조명의 비용이 거의 공짜 수준으로 떨어졌기 때문에 오늘날 우리
는 자연광이 들어올 수 없는 건물에서도 살고 일하며 많은 것들을 누릴 수 있게 되었다고
언급하고 있다. 이를 근거로 볼 때, ③이 포함된 문장은 한때는 몹시 높았던 인공조명의

가격이 '떨어지면서' 세상이 밝아졌다는 의미가 되어야 한다. 따라서 **increase**를 **drop**으로 고쳐야 한다. 문맥상 낱말의 쓰임이 적절하지 않은 것은 ③이다.

- **fundamental** ⓐ 기본적인
- **artificial** ⓐ 인공의
- **cost** ⓥ (~에게 …의 비용을) 요하다, 치르게 하다 ⓝ 비용
- **drop** ⓥ 하락하다, 떨어지다 ⓝ 하락
- **worth** ⓐ ~의 가치가 있는

구문 풀이

12행 Not only did it turn night into day, but it allowed us to live
「조동사＋주어＋동사원형 : 도치 구문」　「allow＋목적어＋to부정사 :
and work in big buildings [that natural light could not enter].
~이 …하게 해 주다」　선행사　「not only＋A＋but (also)＋B : A뿐 아니라 B도(A, B 자리에 문장)」

---

07 일반화된 호혜성에 기반한 동물의 협동　정답률 69% | 정답 ④

다음 빈칸에 들어갈 말로 가장 적절한 것을 고르시오.

① friction – 마찰
② diversity – 다양성
③ hierarchy – 계층
✓ cooperation – 협동
⑤ independence – 독립성

[본문 해석]

만약 여러분이 과학 뉴스에 관심을 가진다면, 여러분은 동물들 사이의 협동이 대중 매체에서 뜨거운 화제가 되어 왔다는 것을 알아차리게 될 것이다. 예를 들어, 2007년 후반에 과학 매체는 Claudia Rutte와 Michael Taborsky가 '일반화된 호혜성'이라고 부르는 것을 쥐들이 보여 준다고 시사하는, 그들에 의한 연구를 널리 보도했다. 쥐들 각각이 낯선 쥐에 의해 도움을 받았던 자신의 이전 경험에 근거하여 낯설고 무관한 개체에게 도움을 제공했다. Rutte와 Taborsky는 쥐들에게 파트너를 위한 음식을 얻기 위해 막대기를 잡아당기는 협동적 과업을 훈련시켰다. 이전에 모르는 파트너에게 도움을 받은 적이 있는 쥐는 다른 쥐들을 돕는 경향이 더 컸다. 이 연구가 수행되기 전에는, 일반화된 호혜성은 인간들에게 고유한 것으로 여겨졌다.

Why? 왜 정답일까?

인간뿐 아니라 동물 또한 일반화된 호혜성(generalized reciprocity)에 근거하여 협력한다는 내용을 설명한 글로, For example 이하에서 쥐들이 낯설고 무관한 개체끼리도 서로 돕는다는 결론을 밝혀낸 실험을 소개하고 있다. 따라서 빈칸에 들어갈 말로 가장 적절한 것은 ④ '협동'이다.

- **generalize** ⓥ 일반화하다
- **unfamiliar** ⓐ 낯선, 익숙하지 않은
- **cooperative** ⓐ 협동적인
- **previously** ⓐ 이전에, 사전에, 미리
- **reciprocity** ⓝ 호혜성, 이익 교환
- **unrelated** ⓐ 무관한, 관계없는, 친족이 아닌
- **obtain** ⓥ 얻다
- **conduct** ⓥ 수행하다

구문 풀이

6행 They each provided help to an unfamiliar and unrelated
individual, based on their own previous experience of having been
분사구문(~에 기반을 두어)　전치사←　완료 수동 동명사 :
helped by an unfamiliar rat.　주절보다 먼저 일어남

★★★ 1등급 대비 고난도 3점 문제

08 문제 해결에서 가정이 필요한 이유　정답률 43% | 정답 ④

다음 빈칸에 들어갈 말로 가장 적절한 것을 고르시오. [3점]

① prevent violations of consumer rights
　소비자 권리 침해를 방지할
② understand the value of cultural diversity
　문화적 다양성의 가치를 이해할
③ guarantee the safety of experimenters in labs
　실험실에 있는 실험자의 안전을 보장할
✓ focus our thinking on the essence of the problem
　문제의 본질에 우리의 사고를 집중할
⑤ realize the differences between physics and economics
　물리학과 경제학의 차이를 깨달을

[본문 해석]

만약 당신이 10층 건물 꼭대기에서 구슬이 떨어지는 데 시간이 얼마나 걸리는지 물리학자에게 묻는다면, 그는 진공상태에서 구슬이 떨어진다고 가정하고 그 질문에 답할 것 같다. 실제로 건물은 공기로 둘러싸여 있는데, 그것이 떨어지는 구슬에 마찰을 가하며 속도를 떨어뜨린다. 그러나 그 물리학자는 구슬에 가해지는 마찰이 너무 작아서 그것의 영향은 무시할 수 있다는 점을 지적할 것이다. 구슬이 진공상태에서 떨어진다고 가정하는 것은 그 답에 큰 영향을 주지

않고 그 문제를 단순화한다. 경제학자들도 같은 이유로 가정을 한다. 가정은 복잡한 세상을 단순화하고 이해하는 것을 더 쉽게 만들 수 있다. 예를 들어, 국제 무역의 효과를 연구하기 위해 우리는 세상이 단 두 국가로만 구성되었고, 각 국가가 두 가지 상품만을 생산한다고 가정할 수 있다. 그렇게 함으로써, 우리는 문제의 본질에 우리의 사고를 집중할 수 있다. 따라서 우리는 복잡한 세상에서 국제 무역을 이해하는 더 나은 위치에 있게 된다.

Why? 왜 정답일까?

가정은 세상을 이해하기 쉽도록 더 단순하게 만들어주기 때문에(Assumptions can simplify the complex world and make it easier to understand.) 문제 해결에 도움이 된다는 내용을 다룬 글이므로, 빈칸에 들어갈 말로 가장 적절한 것은 ④ '문제의 본질에 우리의 사고를 집중할'이다.

- **physicist** ⓝ 물리학자
- **assume** ⓥ 가정하다, 추정하다
- **friction** ⓝ 마찰
- **substantially** ⓐ 상당히, 많이
- **diversity** ⓝ 다양성
- **marble** ⓝ 구슬, 대리석
- **vacuum** ⓝ 진공, 공백
- **simplify** ⓥ 단순화하다
- **violation** ⓝ 침해, 위반, 위배
- **guarantee** ⓥ 보장하다

구문 풀이

12행 To study the effects of international trade, for example, /
~하기 위해
we might assume {that the world consists of only two countries} and
~로 구성되다　{ } : might assume의 목적어
{that each country produces only two goods}.

★★ 문제 해결 꿀~팁 ★★

▶ 많이 틀린 이유는?
과학이나 경제학 등에서 문제를 해결하기 위해 특정한 상황을 '가정'하는 것이 왜 필요한지를 설명한 글이다. 오답 중 ②에는 '문화적 다양성'이라는 표현이 나오는데 이는 본문의 다른 부분에서 한 번도 쓰이지 않은 표현이다. ⑤의 경우에는, 본문에 언급된 '물리학', '경제학' 등의 단어를 포함하고 있지만, 본문의 내용은 두 학문 간 차이를 설명하는 것과는 관련이 없다.

▶ 문제 해결 방법은?
본문에서 '가정'의 기능을 설명한 표현은 'simplify', 'makes it easier to understand'이고, 이를 ④에서는 'focus ~ on the essence of the problem'이라는 말로 바꾸었다.

---

09 인간의 편향을 강화하도록 작용하는 검색 알고리즘　정답률 62% | 정답 ③

다음 글에서 전체 흐름과 관계 없는 문장은?

[본문 해석]

인터넷 활동가인 Eli Pariser는 온라인 검색 알고리즘이 우리가 이미 지닌 신념이 옳음을 확인해 주는 모든 것을 움켜쥐고, 반면에 그러한 신념과 맞지 않는 정보는 조용히 무시하는 인간의 경향을 어떻게 조장하는지에 주목했다. ① 우리는 자신의 주변에 소위 '필터 버블'을 설치하는데 그곳에서 우리는 자신이 동의하는 그런 자료에만 끊임없이 노출된다. ② 우리는 결코 이의를 제기 받지 않으며 스스로에게 다양성과 차이의 존재를 인정할 기회를 주지 않는다. ③ 다른 사람이 갖지 못한 차이를 만들어 내는 것이 자신의 분야에서 성공하는 방법이며 혁신의 창조를 이끈다. ④ 최상의 경우 우리는 세상을 모르고 보호 받으며, 최악의 경우 우리는 극단적인 시각으로 과격화되어 우리의 특정 버블 밖의 삶을 상상할 수 없게 된다. ⑤ 그 결과는 참담하여, 예를 들면 지적 고립과 우리가 스스로 만드는 작은 세계가 전 세계라고 믿게 되어 따라오는 진정한 왜곡이 있다.

Why? 왜 정답일까?

첫 문장에서 온라인 검색 알고리즘은 이미 믿고 있는 신념을 확인해주는 정보를 주로 보려 하는 인간의 편향을 강화한다고 언급한다. 이어서 ①과 ②는 우리가 '필터 버블' 안에 갇혀 다양성과 차이를 인정할 기회를 갖지 못한다고 설명하고, ④와 ⑤는 그로 인한 부정적 결과를 설명한다. 하지만 ③은 다른 사람이 갖지 못한 차이를 만들어낼 때 자기 분야에서 성공할 수 있다는 내용이므로 흐름에서 벗어난다. 따라서 전체 흐름과 관계 없는 문장은 ③이다.

- **grab hold of** ~을 (갑자기) 움켜잡다
- **acknowledge** ⓥ 인정하다
- **innovation** ⓝ 혁신
- **isolation** ⓝ 고립
- **filter-bubble** ⓝ 필터 버블
- **existence** ⓝ 존재
- **disastrous** ⓐ 참담한

구문 풀이

5행 We set up a so-called "filter-bubble" around ourselves, where
장소 선행사 / *계속적 용법*
we are constantly exposed only to that material [that we agree with].
선행사 / *목적격 관·대*

★★★ 1등급 대비 고난도 3점 문제

10 | AI 로봇과 일반 로봇의 차이 | 정답률 40% | 정답 ④

주어진 글 다음에 이어질 글의 순서로 가장 적절한 것을 고르시오. [3점]

① (A) – (C) – (B) 　　② (B) – (A) – (C)
③ (B) – (C) – (A) 　　✔ (C) – (A) – (B)
⑤ (C) – (B) – (A)

[본문 해석]

AI 로봇과 일반 로봇의 근본적 차이는 센서로부터 얻는 데이터에 기반하여 결정을 내리고 학습하여 환경에 적응하는 로봇과 그것의 소프트웨어의 능력이다.

(C) 좀 더 구체적으로 말해서 일반 로봇은 결정론적인 행동을 보인다. 즉, 일련의 입력에 대해 그 로봇은 항상 똑같은 결과를 만들 것이다.

(A) 예를 들어, 장애물을 우연히 마주치는 것과 같이 동일한 상황에 직면한다면 그 로봇은 그 장애물을 왼쪽으로 돌아서 가는 것과 같이 항상 똑같은 행동을 할 것이다. 하지만 AI 로봇은 일반 로봇이 할 수 없는 두 가지, 즉, 결정을 내리는 것과 경험으로부터 학습하는 것을 할 수 있다.

(B) 그것은 환경에 적응할 것이고, 어떤 상황에 직면할 때마다 다른 행동을 할 수 있다. AI 로봇은 경로에서 장애물을 밀어내거나 새로운 경로를 만들거나 아니면 목표를 바꾸려 할 수 있다.

Why? 왜 정답일까?

AI 로봇과 일반 로봇의 차이를 화두로 제시하는 주어진 글 다음에는, 차이를 구체적으로 언급하겠다고 말하며 먼저 일반 로봇의 특징을 설명한 (C), 일반 로봇의 활동에 대한 예를 제시한 뒤 **however**를 통해 AI 로봇으로 화제를 전환하는 (A), 문단 첫 머리의 **It**으로 AI 로봇을 받아 그 특징을 설명하는 (B)가 차례로 이어지는 것이 자연스럽다. 따라서 글의 순서로 가장 적절한 것은 ④ '(C) – (A) – (B)'이다.

- **difference** ⓝ 차이점
- **adapt to** ~에 적응하다
- **run into** ~을 우연히 마주치다
- **circumstances** ⓝ 사정, 상황
- **push ~ out of the way** ~을 밀어내다, 물리치다
- **specific** ⓐ 구체적인
- **produce** ⓥ 생산하다
- **decision** ⓝ 결정, 판단
- **faced with** ~에 직면한
- **obstacle** ⓝ 장애물, 방해물
- **input** ⓝ 입력, 투입
- **output** ⓝ 산출, 결과

구문 풀이

1행 The basic difference between an AI robot and a normal robot
주어
is the ability of the robot and its software to make decisions, and
동사 / *주격 보어* / *형용사적 용법1*
(to) learn and (to) adapt to its environment based on data from its
형용사적 용법2 / *형용사적 용법3* / *~에 기반하여*
sensors.

★★ 문제 해결 꿀~팁 ★★

▶ 많이 틀린 이유는?
주어진 글 뒤에 가장 먼저 이어지는 단락을 찾는 것이 풀이의 관건이다. 주어진 글에서 AI 로봇과 일반 로봇이라는 두 가지 소재를 모두 제시하므로, (B)와 같이 단수대명사 **It**이 뒤에 이어질 경우 이 **It**이 무엇을 가리키는지가 불분명해진다.

▶ 문제 해결 방법은?
'To be a bit more specific'은 주어진 글에서 언급된 AI 로봇과 일반 로봇 중 어느 한 대상을 특정하여 언급할 것임을 알리는 신호어이다. 신호어의 기능을 잘 파악하면 순서 문제 풀이 시간을 단축하는 데 도움이 된다.

11-12 | 취침 시간과 심장 건강의 연관관계

[본문 해석]

「영국 연구원들은 밤 10시와 밤 11시 사이의 취침 시간이 가장 좋다고 이야기한다. 그들은 이 시간대 사이에 잠드는 사람들이 (a) 더 낮은 심장 질환의 위험

성을 가지고 있다고 이야기한다.」 6년 전, 그 연구원들은 8만 명의 자원자들의 수면 패턴 데이터를 수집했다.「:11번의 근거」 그 자원자들은 연구원들이 그들의 수면과 기상 시간에 대한 데이터를 수집할 수 있도록 7일간 특별한 시계를 착용해야만 했다. 그러고 나서 연구원들은 그 자원자들의 건강을 관찰했다. 약 3천 명의 자원자들이 이후에 심장 문제를 보였다.「그들은 밤 10시에서 밤 11시 사이라는 (b) 이상적인 시간대보다 더 이르거나 더 늦게 잠자리에 들었다.」 「:12번의 근거」 그 연구 저자 중 한 명인 Dr. David Plans는 자신의 연구와 취침 시간이 우리의 심장 건강에 끼치는 (c) 영향에 대해 언급했다. 그는 그 연구가 결과의 특정한 원인을 시사하지는 못하지만, 이르거나 늦은 취침 시간이 심혈관 건강에 (d) 긍정적인(→ 부정적인) 결과와 함께 체내 시계를 혼란케 할 가능성이 더 높을 수 있다는 것을 제시한다고 이야기했다. 그는 우리의 몸이 아침 빛에 맞추어 일어나는 것이 중요하고, 잠자리에 드는 가장 나쁜 시간이 자정 이후인데, 우리의 체내 시계를 재설정하는 아침 빛을 볼 가능성을 (e) 낮출 수도 있기 때문이라고 말했다. 그는 만약 우리의 체내 시계가 적절하게 재설정되지 않으면 우리가 심혈관 질환의 위험을 안게 된다고 덧붙였다.

- **author** ⓝ 저자
- **consequence** ⓝ 결과, 영향
- **likelihood** ⓝ 가능성, 공산
- **sound** ⓐ 좋은, 건전한
- **body clock** 생체 시계
- **reduce** ⓥ 낮추다, 줄이다
- **properly** ⓐⓓ 적절하게

구문 풀이

15행 He said {that it was important for our body to wake up to
가주어 / *동사1* / *의미상 주어* / *진주어(주어1)*
the morning light,} and {that the worst time to go to bed was after
주어2 / *형용사적 용법* / *동사2*
midnight because it may reduce the likelihood of seeing morning light
접속사(이유) / *선행사*
[which resets the body clock]}.
주격 관·대

11 | 제목 파악 | 정답률 67% | 정답 ①

윗글의 제목으로 가장 적절한 것은?

✔ The Best Bedtime for Your Heart – 당신의 심장을 위한 최적의 취침 시간
② Late Bedtimes Are a Matter of Age – 늦은 취침 시간은 나이 문제이다
③ For Sound Sleep: Turn Off the Light – 숙면을 위해: 불을 끄세요
④ Sleeping Patterns Reflect Personalities – 수면 패턴은 성격을 반영한다
⑤ Regular Exercise: A Miracle for Good Sleep – 규칙적인 운동: 숙면을 위한 기적

Why? 왜 정답일까?

취침 시간이 심혈관 건강에 미치는 영향에 관한 연구 내용을 들어 적절한 취침 시간의 중요성을 설명하는 글로, 첫 두 문장에 화제가 잘 제시된다(~ a bedtime of between 10 p.m. and 11 p.m. is best. ~ people who go to sleep between these times have a lower risk of heart disease.)이다. 따라서 글의 제목으로 가장 적절한 것은 ① '당신의 심장을 위한 최적의 취침 시간'이다.

12 | 어휘 추론 | 정답률 68% | 정답 ④

밑줄 친 (a) ~ (e) 중에서 문맥상 낱말의 쓰임이 적절하지 않은 것은?

① (a)　　② (b)　　③ (c)　　✔ (d)　　⑤ (e)

Why? 왜 정답일까?

연구 결과를 언급하는 첫 문단의 마지막 두 문장에 따르면, 이상적인 취침 시간보단 이르거나 늦게 잠드는 사람들은 이후 심장 문제가 생길 가능성이 높았다(Around 3,000 volunteers later showed heart problems. They went to bed earlier or later than the ideal 10 p.m. to 11 p.m. timeframe.)고 한다. 즉 이상적인 취침 시간보다 빨리 자든 늦게 자든, 그로 인해 '부정적인' 영향을 입을 수 있다는 것이므로, (d)의 **positive**를 **negative**로 고쳐야 한다. 따라서 문맥상 낱말의 쓰임이 적절하지 않은 것은 ④ '(d)'이다.

DAY 22 — 20분 미니 모의고사

DAY 22

01 ⑤	02 ①	03 ②	04 ④	05 ②
06 ⑤	07 ①	08 ②	09 ③	10 ④
11 ③	12 ④			

01 학급 파티에 가져올 음식에 관한 유의 사항

정답률 93% | 정답 ⑤

다음 글의 목적으로 가장 적절한 것은?

① 학급 파티 일정 변경을 공지하려고
② 학교 식당의 새로운 메뉴를 소개하려고
③ 학생의 특정 음식 알레르기 여부를 조사하려고
④ 학부모의 적극적인 학급 파티 참여를 독려하려고
⑤ 학급 파티에 가져올 음식에 대한 유의 사항을 안내하려고

[본문 해석]

부모님들 / 보호자들께,

학급 파티가 2022년 12월 16일 금요일 오후에 열릴 것입니다. 아이들은 사탕류, 포테이토 칩, 비스킷, 케이크, 그리고 음료를 가져올 수 있습니다. 우리는 아이들이 집에서 만들거나 준비한 음식을 가져오지 않기를 요청합니다. 모든 음식은 성분을 명확하게 목록으로 작성하여 밀봉된 꾸러미로 가져와야 합니다. 과일과 채소는 가게에서 밀봉된 꾸러미로 사전 포장된 것이라면 환영합니다. 심각한 견과류 알레르기가 있는 학생들이 많이 있기 때문에 견과류가 포함된 음식은 어떤 것도 학교에 보내지 마십시오. 아이들이 가져오는 모든 음식의 성분을 주의 깊게 확인해 주십시오. 여러분의 지속적인 지원과 협조에 감사드립니다.

교장 Lisa Brown 드림

Why? 왜 정답일까?

두 번째 문장부터 학급 파티에 어떤 음식을 가져올 수 있는지 열거한 뒤, 음식의 성분을 꼭 확인해달라고 요청하고 있다(Please check the ingredients of all food ~). 따라서 글의 목적으로 가장 적절한 것은 ⑤ '학급 파티에 가져올 음식에 대한 유의 사항을 안내하려고'이다.

- **guardian** ⓝ 보호자
- **sealed** ⓐ 밀봉한
- **pre-packed** ⓐ 사전 포장된
- **headteacher** ⓝ (공립학교) 교장
- **home-cooked** ⓐ 집에서 요리한
- **ingredient** ⓝ 성분, 재료
- **severe** ⓐ 심각한

구문 풀이

4행 We are requesting that children do not bring in homecooked or prepared food.
(현재진행 / 접속사(~것))

02 젊은이들이 채식을 선택하는 이유

정답률 74% | 정답 ①

다음 글의 주제로 가장 적절한 것은?

① reasons why young people go for vegetarian diets
  젊은 사람들이 채식주의 식단을 선택하는 이유
② ways to build healthy eating habits for teenagers
  십 대들이 건강한 식습관을 기르는 방법
③ vegetables that help lower your risk of cancer
  암 위험을 낮추는 데 도움이 되는 채소
④ importance of maintaining a balanced diet
  균형 잡힌 식습관 유지의 중요성
⑤ disadvantages of plant-based diets
  식물 중심 식단의 단점

[본문 해석]

채식은 점점 더 많은 젊은이들이 고기, 가금류, 생선에 반대함에 따라 주류가 되어가고 있다. American Dietetic Asociation에 따르면, '대략적으로 계획된 채식 식단이 건강에 좋고, 영양학적으로도 적당하고, 특정 질병을 예방하고 치료하는 데 건강상의 이점을 제공한다.' 그러나 건강에 대한 염려만이 젊은이들이 식단을 바꾸려고 하는 유일한 이유는 아니다. 몇몇은 동물의 권리에 대한 관심 때문에 선택한다. 음식으로 길러지는 대다수의 동물들이 갇혀서 산다는 것을 보여주는 통계자료를 볼 때, 많은 십 대들은 그러한 상황에 저항하기 위해

고기를 포기한다. 다른 사람들은 환경을 지지하기 위해 채식주의자가 된다. 고기를 생산하는 것은 거대한 양의 물, 땅, 곡식과 에너지를 사용하고 가축에서 나오는 쓰레기와 그에 따른 오염과 같은 문제들을 만들어낸다.

Why? 왜 정답일까?

글 초반부에서 젊은이들은 건강상의 이유로 채식주의 식단을 선택한다는 내용이 제시된 후, 'But health concerns are not the only reason ~'부터는 환경적인 이유 또한 이러한 선택의 근거라는 내용이 제시된다. 따라서 글의 주제로 가장 적절한 것은 ① '젊은 사람들이 채식주의 식단을 선택하는 이유'이다.

- **vegetarian** ⓐ 채식의
- **healthful** ⓐ 건강에 좋은
- **adequate** ⓐ 적절한, 충분한
- **treatment** ⓝ 치료
- **statistics** ⓝ 통계 자료, 통계학
- **protest** ⓥ 항의하다
- **vast** ⓐ 방대한
- **approximately** ⓐⓓ 대략적으로
- **nutritionally** ⓐⓓ 영양적으로
- **prevention** ⓝ 예방
- **concern** ⓝ 관심, 우려
- **confinement** ⓝ 가둠, 감금
- **turn to** ~로 바뀌다, ~에 의지하다
- **disadvantage** ⓝ 불리한 점, 단점

구문 풀이

9행 When faced with the statistics [that show (that) the majority of animals (raised as food) live in confinement], many teens give up meat to protest those conditions.
(접속사 / 분사구문 / 선행사 / 주격 관·대 / (생략) / 주어 / 과거분사 / 동사 / 주어 / 동사 / 부사적 용법(목적))

03 현대 사회에서의 정체성

정답률 57% | 정답 ②

다음 글의 제목으로 가장 적절한 것은?

① What Makes Our Modern Society So Competitive?
  무엇이 우리 현대 사회를 이토록 경쟁적으로 만드는가?
② How Modern Society Drives Us to Discover Our Identities
  현대 사회는 어떻게 우리가 정체성을 발견하는가?
③ Social Masks: A Means to Build Trustworthy Relationships
  사회적 가면: 믿을 만한 관계를 구축하는 수단
④ The More Social Roles We Have, the Less Choice We Have
  더 많은 사회적 역할을 가질수록, 선택권은 더 적어진다
⑤ Increasing Social Mobility Leads Us to a More Equal Society
  사회적 유동성의 증가가 더 평등한 사회로 이끈다

[본문 해석]

현대에는 사회가 더욱 역동적이 되었다. 사회적 유동성이 증가하였고, 사람들은 가령 자신의 직업, 결혼 혹은 종교와 관련하여 더 높은 정도의 선택권을 행사하기 시작했다. 이것은 사회의 전통적인 역할에 이의를 제기했다. 대안이 실현될 수 있을 때 개인이 타고난 역할에 전념할 필요가 있다는 것은 덜 분명해졌다. 자신의 삶의 선택에 대한 통제력을 늘리는 것이 가능해졌을 뿐만 아니라 바람직하게 되었다. 그러자 정체성이 문제가 되었다. 그것은 더 이상 태어날 때 대체로 주어진 것이 아닌, 발견되어야 할 것이었다. 사회에 의해 규정된 전통적인 역할 정체성은 사람들에게 부여된 가면처럼 보이기 시작해서, 진정한 자아는 그 뒤 어딘가에서 발견되어야 하는 것처럼 여겨지기 시작했다.

Why? 왜 정답일까?

역동적인 현대 사회에서 우리의 정체성은 태어날 때 주어진 것보다는 사회적으로 발견되어야 하는 것이 되었다(Identity then became a problem. It was no longer almost ready-made at birth but something to be discovered.)는 내용의 글이다. 따라서 글의 제목으로 가장 적절한 것은 ② '현대 사회는 어떻게 우리가 정체성을 발견하도록 부추기는가'이다.

- **mobility** ⓝ 유동성
- **pose a challenge** 이의를 제기하다
- **commit to** ~에 전념하다
- **prescribe** ⓥ 규정하다, 처방하다
- **profession** ⓝ 직업
- **evident** ⓐ 명백한
- **ready-made** ⓐ 이미 주어진, 기성품의

구문 풀이

11행 Traditional role identities prescribed by society began to appear as masks imposed on people [whose real self was to be found somewhere underneath].
(주어 / 과거분사 / 동사 / 전치사(~로서) / 명사 / 과거분사 / 소유격 관·대 / be to 용법: ~해야 한다(의무))

04 선사 시대 예술

정답률 51% | 정답 ④

다음 글의 밑줄 친 부분 중, 어법상 틀린 것은?

[본문 해석]

선사 시대 예술의 의미와 목적에 대한 고찰은 현대의 수렵 채집 사회와의 사이에서 끌어낸 유사점에 많은 것을 의존한다. Steven Mithen이 *The Prehistory of the Modern Mind*에서 강조하듯이, 그런 원시 사회는 인간과 짐승, 동물과 식물, 생물체의 영역과 무생물체의 영역을 통합적이고 살아 있는 총체에 대한 참여자로 여기는 경향이 있다. 이런 경향이 표현된 두 가지가 *의인화*(동물을 인간으로 간주하는 관행)와 *토테미즘*(인간을 동물로 간주하는 관행)인데, 이 두 가지는 원시 문화의 시각 예술과 신화에 널리 퍼져 있다. 따라서 자연의 세계는 인간의 사회적 관계 측면에서 개념화된다. 이런 측면에서 고려될 때, 초기 인류가 자신들의 세계에 살고 있는 인간 이외의 생명체들에 대하여 시각적으로 집착한 것은 깊은 의미를 띠게 된다. 인류학자인 Claude Lévi-Strauss가 말했듯이 수렵 채집인들에게 동물은 먹기 좋은 대상일 뿐만 아니라, *생각해 보기에도 좋은* 대상이다. 토템 신앙의 풍습에서 문맹의 인류는 "자연 속에서의 자신과 자신의 위치에 대해 곰곰이 생각한다."라고 그는 말했다.

Why? 왜 정답일까?

뒤에 거주지에 해당하는 their world가 목적어로 나오는 것으로 볼 때, 수동을 나타내는 과거분사 inhabited를 능동의 현재분사 inhabiting으로 고쳐야 한다. 따라서 어법상 틀린 것은 ④이다.

Why? 왜 오답일까?

① 주어가 복수 명사인 Speculations이므로 동사 또한 rely라는 복수형으로 쓴 것은 어법상 맞다.
② '~듯이'의 의미를 나타내고자 부사절 접속사 as를 쓴 것은 어법상 맞다.
③ 선행사 *anthropomorphism*와 *totemism*을 보충 설명하기 위해 계속적 용법의 관계대명사 which를 쓴 것은 어법상 맞다. 관계절의 주어는 both of which이며 동사 spread가 뒤따르고 있다.
⑤ 동사 broods upon의 주어인 an unlettered humanity가 목적어와 일치하므로 재귀대명사 itself를 목적어 자리에 쓴 것은 어법상 맞다.

- **rely** ⓥ 의지하다, 신뢰하다
- **tend** ⓥ 경향이 있다
- **spread** ⓥ 널리 퍼지다
- **preoccupation** ⓝ 집착
- **unlettered** ⓐ 문맹의
- **primitive** ⓐ 원시의
- **integrated** ⓐ 통합적인
- **conceptualize** ⓥ 개념화하다
- **profoundly** ⓐⓓ 깊이

구문 풀이

3행 Such primitive societies, (as Steven Mithen emphasizes in *The Prehistory of the Modern Mind*), tend to view man and beast, animal and plant, organic and inorganic spheres, as participants in an integrated, animated totality.
주어 / 접속사 / ( ): 부사절(~듯이) / 동사「view+A+as+B : A를 B로 여기다」

---

05 완전한 규칙성과 완전한 무질서의 특징 정답률 53% | 정답 ②

(A), (B), (C)의 각 네모 안에서 문맥에 맞는 낱말로 가장 적절한 것은? [3점]

(A)	(B)	(C)
① predictability 예측 가능성	excited 흥분한	denies 부정한다
✓② predictability 예측 가능성	frustrated 좌절한	implies 내포한다
③ predictability 예측 가능성	frustrated 좌절한	denies 부정한다
④ unpredictability 예측 불가능성	excited 흥분한	implies 내포한다
⑤ unpredictability 예측 불가능성	frustrated 좌절한	implies 내포한다

[본문 해석]

우리는 혼돈 속에서 반복을 알아차리고 그 반대, 즉 반복적인 패턴에서의 단절을 알아차린다. 그러나 이러한 배열들이 우리로 하여금 어떻게 느끼도록 만들까? 그리고 '완전한' 규칙성과 '완전한' 무질서는 어떨까? 어느 정도의 반복은 우리가 다음에 무엇이 올지 안다는 점에서 우리에게 안정감을 준다. 우리는 어느 정도의 (A) 예측 가능성을 좋아한다. 우리는 대체로 반복적인 스케줄 속에 생활을 배열한다. 조직이나 행사에서 무작위성은 우리 대부분에게 더 힘들고 더 무섭다. '완전한' 무질서로 인해 우리는 몇 번이고 적응하고 대응해야만 하는 것에 (B) 좌절한다. 그러나 '완전한' 규칙성은 아마도 그 단조로움에 있어서 임의성보다 훨씬 더 끔찍할 것이다. 그것은 차갑고 냉혹하며 기계 같은 특성을 (C) 내포한다. 그러한 완전한 질서는 자연에 존재하지 않으며 서로 대항하여 작용하는 힘이 너무 많다. 그러므로 어느 한쪽의 극단은 위협적으로 느껴진다.

Why? 왜 정답일까?

(A) 'Some repetition gives us a sense of security, in that we know what is coming next.'에서 어느 정도의 반복은 다음에 어떤 일이 생길지를 예측하게 한다는 내용이 나오므로, (A)에는 이 내용을 요약한 predictability가 적절하다.
(B) 'Randomness, in organization or in events, is more challenging and more frightening for most of us.'에서 무질서가 갖는 무작위성은 대체로 힘들고 무섭게 느껴진다는 내용이 나오므로, (B)에는 역시 부정적인 의미로서 frustrated가 적절하다.
(C) 'But "perfect" regularity is perhaps even more horrifying in its monotony ~'에서 완전한 질서는 단조로움을 갖는다는 내용을 제시하고 (C)가 있는 문장에서는 이 '단조로움'을 '차갑고 냉혹하며 기계 같은 특성'이라는 말로 풀어 쓰고 있다. 따라서 (C)에는 implies가 적절하다. 따라서 (A), (B), (C)의 각 네모 안에서 문맥에 맞는 낱말로 가장 적절한 것은 ② '(A) predictability(예측 가능성) – (B) frustrated(좌절한) – (C) implies(내포한다)'이다.

- **repetition** ⓝ 반복
- **arrangement** ⓝ 배열, 정리
- **predictability** ⓝ 예측 가능성
- **frightening** ⓐ 무서운, 겁에 질리게 하는
- **adapt** ⓥ 적응하다
- **monotony** ⓝ 단조로움
- **extreme** ⓝ 극단
- **confusion** ⓝ 혼돈, 혼란
- **regularity** ⓝ 규칙성
- **randomness** ⓝ 무작위성, 임의성
- **frustrated** ⓐ 좌절감을 느끼는
- **horrifying** ⓐ 끔찍한, 몸서리쳐지는
- **unfeeling** ⓐ 냉정한, 무정한
- **threatening** ⓐ 위협적인

구문 풀이

4행 Some repetition gives us a sense of security, / in that we know what is coming next.
4형식 동사 / 간접목적어 / 직접 목적어 / ~라는 점에서 / 의문사

★★★ **1등급 대비 고난도 2점 문제**

06 선수의 인성과 도덕성에 양면적으로 작용하는 승리 정답률 43% | 정답 ⑤

다음 빈칸에 들어갈 말로 가장 적절한 것을 고르시오.
① a piece of cake – 식은 죽 먹기(아주 쉬운 일)
② a one-way street – 일방통행로
③ a bird in the hand – 수중에 든 새(확실한 일)
④ a fish out of water – 물 밖에 나온 고기(낯선 환경에서 불편해하는 사람)
✓⑤ a double-edged sword – 양날의 검(양면성을 가진 상황)

[본문 해석]

연구에 따르면 운동선수는 선수가 아닌 사람들보다 (사회적으로) 받아들여지지 않는 행동을 덜 할 것이라고 한다. 그러나 운동선수가 더 높은 경쟁적 수준까지 올라감에 따라 부분적으로 승리에 대한 강조가 커지기 때문에 도덕적 분별력과 바람직한 스포츠 행위가 감소하는 것 같다. 그래서 승리라는 것은 인성 함양을 가르치는 데 있어서 양날의 검이 될 수 있다. 어떤 선수는 너무나 이기려고 하다 보니 그 결과 거짓말하고 속이고 팀 규칙을 위반한다. 그들은 단시간에 이길 수 있는 자신의 능력을 강화할 수 있는 바람직하지 못한 인격 특성을 계발할지 모른다. 그러나 선수가 부정직한 방법으로 이기고자 하는 유혹에 저항할 때 그들은 일생동안 지속되는 긍정적인 인격 특성을 계발할 수 있다. 인성이라는 것은 학습되는 행동이며 코치가 그러한 교훈을 체계적으로 가르치고자 계획할 때 비로소 페어플레이 정신이 발달한다.

Why? 왜 정답일까?

첫 두 문장에 따르면 운동선수는 선수가 아닌 사람들에 비할 때 사회적으로 용인되지 않는 행동을 덜 하는 경향이 있지만, 승리가 강조되는 환경에 살기 때문에 경쟁이 심해질수록 도덕적 분별력이 떨어질 수 있다고 한다(~ athletes are less likely to participate in unacceptable behavior ~. However, moral reasoning and good sporting behavior seem to decline ~.). 따라서 빈칸에 들어갈 말로 가장 적절한 것은 승리라는 것이 선수의 인격 또는 도덕성 함양에 양면적으로 작용할 수 있다는 의미의 ⑤ '양날의 검'이다.

- **confirm** ⓥ (맞다고) 확인하다
- **reasoning** ⓝ 추론(능력)
- **competitive** ⓐ 경쟁하는, 경쟁력 있는
- **undesirable** ⓐ 바람직하지 않은
- **resist** ⓥ 저항하다
- **dishonest** ⓐ 부정직한
- **systematically** ⓐⓓ 체계적으로
- **unacceptable** ⓐ 받아들여지지 않는
- **decline** ⓥ 감소하다
- **emphasis** ⓝ 강조
- **enhance** ⓥ 강화하다
- **temptation** ⓝ 유혹
- **learned** ⓐ 학습된, 후천적인

구문 풀이

1행 Research has confirmed that athletes are less likely
　　　　　　　　　　　　　　접속사(~것)　　　　　　　　　「be less likely +
to participate in unacceptable behavior than are non-athletes.
to부정사 : 덜 ~하는 경향이 있다」　　　　　　「than + 동사 + 주어 : 도치 구문」

★★ 문제 해결 꿀~팁 ★★

▶ 많이 틀린 이유는?
빈칸 뒤에 따르면 선수들은 승리를 위해 부도덕한 행동을 저지르면서 바람직하지 못한 인격 특성을 키우게 될 수 있지만, 한편으로 부정직한 승리의 유혹에 저항하는 과정에서 좋은 인격 특성을 함양하게 될 수도 있다고 한다. 이는 결국 승리가 선수에게 좋은 쪽과 나쁜 쪽 둘 다로 작용할 수 있다는 의미이므로, ② 'a one-way street (일방통행로)'은 빈칸에 적합하지 않다. 또한 ① 'a piece of cake(식은 죽 먹기)'는 글의 내용과 전혀 관련이 없다.

▶ 문제 해결 방법은?
빈칸 뒤의 세부 진술을 읽고 일반적인 결론을 도출한 뒤, 이를 다시 비유적으로 잘 나타낸 선택지를 찾아야 하는 문제이다. 핵심은 승리의 '양면성'에 있음을 염두에 둔다.

★★★ 1등급 대비 고난도 3점 문제

07 도시처럼 상호작용으로 작동하는 뇌　　정답률 43% | 정답 ①

다음 빈칸에 들어갈 말로 가장 적절한 것을 고르시오. [3점]

☑ operates in isolation – 독립적으로 작동하지
② suffers from rapid changes – 급속한 변화로 고생하지
③ resembles economic elements – 경제적 요소를 닮지
④ works in a systematic way – 체계적으로 작동하지
⑤ interacts with another – 서로 상호 작용하지

[본문 해석]

뇌를 도시라고 생각해보라. 만약 당신이 도시를 내다보며 "경제는 어디에 위치해 있나요?"라고 묻는다면 그 질문에 좋은 답이 없다는 것을 알게 될 것이다. 대신, 경제는 상점과 은행에서 상인과 고객에 이르기까지 모든 요소의 상호 작용으로부터 나타난다. 뇌의 작용도 그렇다. 즉 그것은 한 곳에서 일어나지 않는다. 도시에서처럼, 뇌의 어떤 지역도 독립적으로 작동하지 않는다. 뇌와 도시 안에서, 모든 것은 모든 규모로, 근거리든 원거리든, 거주자들 간의 상호 작용으로부터 나타난다. 기차가 자재와 직물을 도시로 들여오고, 그것이 경제 속으로 처리되는 것처럼, 감각 기관으로부터의 가공되지 않은 전기화학적 신호는 뉴런의 초고속도로를 따라서 전해진다. 거기서 신호는 처리와 우리의 의식적인 현실로의 변형을 겪는다.

Why? 왜 정답일까?

경제가 모든 요소의 상호 작용으로 작동하는 것처럼 뇌 또한 그렇다(And so it is with the brain's operation: it doesn't happen in one spot. / ~ everything emerges from the interaction ~)는 내용이므로, 빈칸에 들어갈 말로 가장 적절한 것은 ① '독립적으로 작동하지'이다.

● think of A as B A를 B로 여기다
● element ⓝ 요소
● operation ⓝ 작동, 작용
● distantly [ad] 멀리, 원거리로
● process ⓥ 가공하다, 처리하다
● electrochemical ⓐ 전기화학의
● transport ⓥ 수송하다, 실어 나르다
● transformation ⓝ 변화, 변모
● in isolation 고립되어
● emerge ⓥ 나타나다, 생겨나다
● merchant ⓝ 상인
● locally [ad] 국지적으로
● textile ⓝ 직물
● raw ⓐ 원재료의, 날것의
● sensory organ 감각 기관
● undergo ⓥ 거치다, 겪다
● conscious ⓐ 의식적인

구문 풀이

1행 If you were to look out over a city and ask "where is the
「if + 주어 + were to + ~ + 동사원형1 ~　　　　　　동사원형2 ~
economy located?" you'd see there's no good answer to the question.
주어 + 조동사 과거형 + 동사원형 : 가정법 미래(거의 불가능한 상황에 대한 가정)」

★★ 문제 해결 꿀~팁 ★★

▶ 많이 틀린 이유는?
도시가 많은 경제 주체의 상호 작용을 통해 돌아가듯이 뇌 또한 수많은 요소의 상호 작용으로 돌아간다는 내용이다. 주어가 「no + 명사」 형태이므로, 빈칸에는 주제와

반대되는 말을 넣어야 문장 전체가 주제를 나타내게 된다. 하지만 ③은 '경제 주체와 비슷하다'는 주제를 직접 제시하므로, 이를 빈칸에 넣어서 읽으면 '뇌의 그 어느 구역도 경제 주체와 비슷하지 않다'는 의미가 되어버린다. 즉 ③은 주제와 정반대되는 의미를 완성한다.

▶ 문제 해결 방법은?
'뇌 = 도시'라는 비유를 확인하고, 둘의 공통점이 무엇인지 파악한 후, 선택지를 하나씩 대입하며 빈칸 문장의 의미를 주의 깊게 이해해 보자.

★★★ 1등급 대비 고난도 2점 문제

08 철자 맞히기 대회에서 정직함을 보여준 한 소년　　정답률 44% | 정답 ②

글의 흐름으로 보아, 주어진 문장이 들어가기에 가장 적절한 곳을 고르시오.

[본문 해석]

몇 년 전 Washington D.C.에서 있었던 전국 단어 철자 맞히기 대회에서, 한 13세 소년이 '들은 것은 무엇이든 반복하는 경향'을 의미하는 단어인 echolalia의 철자를 말하도록 요구받았다. ① 그는 철자를 잘못 말했지만 심판은 잘못 듣고 철자를 맞혔다고 말했고 그가 (다음 단계로) 진출하도록 허락했다. ② 그 소년은 자신이 단어 철자를 잘못 말했다는 것을 알았을 때 심판에게 가서 말했다. 그래서 그는 결국 대회에서 탈락했다. ③ 다음 날 신문기사 헤드라인이 그 정직한 소년을 "단어 철자 맞히기 대회 영웅"으로 알렸고, 그의 사진이 The New York Times에 실렸다. ④ "심판이 내가 아주 정직하다고 말했어요."라고 그 소년은 기자들에게 말했다. ⑤ 그는 그렇게 했던 이유 중 하나를 덧붙여 말했다. "저는 거짓말쟁이가 되고 싶지 않았어요."

Why? 왜 정답일까?

② 앞에서 철자 대회에 참가한 소년이 답을 잘못 말했음에도 불구하고 심판이 이를 잘못 듣고 그를 다음 단계로 진출시켰다는 이야기가 나오는데, 주어진 문장에서는 그 소년이 자신이 틀렸다는 것을 알았을 때 심판에게 가서 이를 털어놓았다는 내용을 이어서 언급한다. ② 뒤에서는 그리하여 소년이 결국 탈락했다는 내용이 이어진다. 따라서 주어진 문장이 들어가기에 가장 적절한 곳은 ②이다.

● misspell ⓥ 철자를 잘못 말하다
● tendency ⓝ 경향
● mishear ⓥ 잘못 듣다
● eliminate ⓥ 탈락시키다, 제거하다
● headline ⓝ 표제
● honesty ⓝ 정직, 솔직함
● judge ⓝ 심판, 심사위원
● repeat ⓥ 반복하다
● advance ⓥ 진출하다, 나아가다
● competition ⓝ 경쟁
● appear ⓥ 발간되다
● motive ⓝ 동기

구문 풀이

6행 Although he misspelled the word, / the judges misheard
양보 접속사(비록 ~일지라도)　　　　　　　　　　　　　　동사1
him, told him (that) he had spelled the word right, and allowed him
동사2　　생략(접속사)　　　　　　　　　　　　　　　　　　　　동사3
to advance.
목적격 보어(~하도록)

★★ 문제 해결 꿀~팁 ★★

▶ 많이 틀린 이유는?
문장 삽입 문제는 논리적 공백 찾기에 주력해야 한다. 최다 오답인 ① 앞뒤는 '철자 경연 대회에 나간 소년이 제시어를 받고 → 철자를 잘못 말했는데 심판이 제대로 듣지 못하고 통과시켰다'는 내용이므로 서로 자연스럽게 이어진다.

▶ 문제 해결 방법은?
만일 ②에 주어진 문장이 들어가지 않으면 ② 앞뒤는 '심판이 통과시켰다 → 그래서 소년은 탈락했다'는 뜻이 되므로, 중간에 논리적 공백이 발생한다.

09 유능한 코치와 그렇지 않은 코치의 차이　　정답률 52% | 정답 ③

다음 글의 내용을 한 문장으로 요약하고자 한다. 빈칸 (A), (B)에 들어갈 말로 가장 적절한 것은? [3점]

	(A)		(B)
①	scores 점수	……	complete 완수하다
②	scores 점수	……	remember 기억하다
☑	mistakes 실수	……	picture 상상하다

④ mistakes ······ ignore
  실수   무시하다
⑤ strengths ······ achieve
  강점   성취하다

[본문 해석]

어떤 코치들은 선수들에게서 최상의 결과를 이끌어 내는 반면 다른 코치들은 그렇지 않다는 것을 알아챘는가? 서투른 코치는 당신이 무엇을 잘못했는지 알려주고 나서 다시는 그러지 말라고 말할 것이다. "공을 떨어뜨리지 마라!" 그 다음 무슨 일이 일어날까? 당신이 머릿속에서 보게 되는 이미지는 당신이 공을 떨어뜨리는 이미지이다! 당연히, 당신의 마음은 그것이 들은 것을 바탕으로 방금 '본' 것을 재현한다. 놀랄 것도 없이, 당신은 코트에 걸어가서 공을 떨어뜨린다. 좋은 코치는 무엇을 하는가? 그 사람은 개선될 수 있는 것을 지적하지만, 그 후에 어떻게 할 수 있는지 또는 어떻게 해야 하는지에 대해 말할 것이다. "이번에는 네가 공을 완벽하게 잡을 거라는 걸 알아." 아니나 다를까, 다음으로 당신의 마음속에 떠오르는 이미지는 당신이 공을 잡고 골에 넣는 것이다. 다시 한 번, 당신의 마음은 당신의 마지막 생각을 현실의 일부로 만들지만, 이번에는, 그 '현실'이 부정적이지 않고, 긍정적이다.

➡ 선수의 (A) 실수에 초점을 맞추는 유능하지 않은 코치와 달리, 유능한 코치는 선수들이 성공적인 경기를 (B) 상상하도록 격려함으로써 그들이 향상되도록 돕는다.

Why? 왜 정답일까?

유능한 코치와 서투른 코치의 특성을 대조한 글이다. 본문에 따르면 서투른 코치는 선수가 무엇을 잘못했는가에 집중하지만(A poor coach will tell you what you did wrong and then tell you not to do it again: ~) 유능한 코치는 선수가 보완해야 할 점을 지적하면서도 선수로 하여금 성공적인 모습을 상상하게 만들어 실제로 선수의 경기력이 향상되도록 돕는다(He or she ~ will then tell you how you could or should perform: ~)고 한다. 이를 근거로 할 때, 요약문의 빈칸 (A), (B)에 들어갈 말로 가장 적절한 것은 ③ '(A) mistakes(실수), (B) picture(상상하다)'이다.

- get the most out of ⓥ ~을 최대한으로 활용하다
- recreate ⓥ 재현하다
- unlike prep ~와는 달리
- encourage ⓥ 격려하다
- perfectly ad 완벽하게
- ineffective ⓐ 무능한, 효과가 없는

구문 풀이

5행 The images [you see in your head] are images of you
주어   동사 보어 전치사→ 의미상 주어
dropping the ball!
동명사

10-12 생일 선물로 받은 곰 인형을 다시 선물한 Marie

[본문 해석]

(A)

우리 딸 Marie의 8번째 생일에, 그녀는 학교에서 친구들에게 많은 선물을 받았다. 『그날 저녁, 그녀가 가장 좋아하는 선물인 테디 베어를 팔에 안고 우리는 그녀의 생일을 축하하러 식당에 갔다.』 다정한 여성이었던 종업원은 우리 딸이 테디 베어를 안고 있다는 것을 알아차렸고, "제 딸도 테디 베어를 좋아해요." 라고 말했다. 그러고 나서 우리는 (a) 그녀의 가족에 대해 이야기를 나누기 시작했다.

(D)

『대화 도중 그 종업원은 자신의 딸이 다리가 부러져 병원에 있다고 말했다.』 또한 (e) 그녀는 Marie가 자기 딸과 거의 또래 같아 보인다고 말했다. 『그녀는 저녁 내내 매우 친절하고 세심했고 심지어 Marie에게 쿠키를 무료로 주었다.』 우리는 식사를 마친 후 값을 지불하고 차로 걸어가기 시작했는데 그때 갑자기 Marie가 내게 기다려 달라고 부탁하고 식당으로 다시 뛰어 들어갔다.

(B)

Marie가 돌아왔을 때 나는 그녀에게 뭘 하고 왔는지 물었다. 그녀는 자신의 테디 베어를 종업원에게 주어 그녀가 (b) 자기 딸에게 그것을 갖다 줄 수 있게 했다고 말했다. 『나는 딸아이가 이미 그 곰인형을 얼마나 좋아하는지 알 수 있었기에 딸의 갑작스러운 행동에 놀랐다.』 (c) 딸(Marie)은 내 얼굴 표정을 분명히 봤을 것인데, 왜냐하면 "저는 병원 침대에 갇혀 있는 것을 상상할 수 없어요. 그저 그 애가 빨리 나았으면 좋겠어요."라고 말했기 때문이다.

(C)

차를 향해 걸어가면서 나는 그녀의 말에 감동받았다. 『그때 우리의 종업원이 우리 차로 달려 나와 Marie의 관대함에 고마워했다.』 종업원은 전에는 (d) 그녀에게 그녀 가족을 위해 그런 일을 해준 사람이 한 명도 없었다고 했다. 후에 Marie는 그날이 최고의 생일이었다고 말했다. 나는 그녀의 공감과 따뜻함이 너무 자랑스러웠고, 이것은 우리 가족에게 잊을 수 없는 경험이었다.

- server ⓝ 종업원
- get well (병 등이) 낫다
- generosity ⓝ 관대함
- attentive ⓐ 주의 깊은, 세심한
- chat about ~에 관해 이야기하다
- moved ⓐ 감동한
- unforgettable ⓐ 잊을 수 없는

구문 풀이

(B) 6행 She must have seen the look on my face, because she said,
                과거에 대한 강한 추측(~했음에 틀림없다)
"I can't imagine being stuck in a hospital bed. I just want her to get
                        목적어(수동 동명사)
better soon."

---

10 글의 순서 파악   정답률 73% | 정답 ④

주어진 글 (A)에 이어질 내용을 순서에 맞게 배열한 것으로 가장 적절한 것은?

① (B) – (D) – (C)   ② (C) – (B) – (D)
③ (C) – (D) – (B)   ④ (D) – (B) – (C)
⑤ (D) – (C) – (B)

Why? 왜 정답일까?

필자가 딸인 Marie의 생일을 기념해 가족끼리 저녁 식사를 하러 갔다가 식당 종업원과 이야기를 나누었다는 내용의 (A) 뒤로, 종업원이 병원에 입원해 있는 Marie 또래의 딸에 관해 이야기했다는 내용의 (D), Marie가 그 딸을 위해 자신이 선물받은 테디 베어를 전해주었다는 내용의 (B), 필자와 종업원이 모두 감동했다는 결말의 (C)가 이어져야 자연스럽다. 따라서 글의 순서로 가장 적절한 것은 ④ '(D) – (B) – (C)'이다.

---

11 지칭 추론   정답률 62% | 정답 ③

밑줄 친 (a) ~ (e) 중에서 가리키는 대상이 나머지 넷과 다른 것은?

① (a)   ② (b)   ③ (c)   ④ (d)   ⑤ (e)

Why? 왜 정답일까?

(a), (b), (d), (e)는 the server, (c)는 Marie를 가리키므로, (a) ~ (e) 중에서 가리키는 대상이 다른 하나는 ③ '(c)'이다.

---

12 세부 내용 파악   정답률 69% | 정답 ④

윗글에 관한 내용으로 적절하지 않은 것은?

① Marie는 테디 베어를 팔에 안고 식당에 갔다.
② 'I'는 Marie의 갑작스러운 행동에 놀랐다.
③ 종업원은 Marie의 관대함에 고마워했다.
④ 종업원은 자신의 딸이 팔이 부러져서 병원에 있다고 말했다.
⑤ 종업원은 Marie에게 쿠키를 무료로 주었다.

Why? 왜 정답일까?

(D) 'The server mentioned during the conversation that her daughter was in the hospital with a broken leg.'에서 종업원의 딸은 팔이 아니라 다리가 부러져서 병원에 입원했음을 알 수 있다. 따라서 내용과 일치하지 않는 것은 ④ '종업원은 자신의 딸이 팔이 부러져서 병원에 있다고 말했다.'이다.

Why? 왜 오답일까?

① (A) 'That evening, with her favorite present, a teddy bear, in her arms, we went to a restaurant ~'의 내용과 일치한다.
② (B) 'I was surprised at her sudden action ~'의 내용과 일치한다.
③ (C) 'Then, our server ~ thanked Marie for her generosity.'의 내용과 일치한다.
⑤ (D) 'She ~ even gave Marie cookies for free.'의 내용과 일치한다.

DAY 23 · 20분 미니 모의고사

01 ②	02 ③	03 ②	04 ④	05 ③
06 ④	07 ①	08 ③	09 ③	10 ②
11 ⑤	12 ④			

01 야생에서 회색곰을 만난 필자   정답률 82% | 정답 ②

다음 글에 드러난 'I'의 심경 변화로 가장 적절한 것은?

① sad → angry
　슬픈　　화난
✔ delighted → scared
　기쁜　　겁에 질린
③ satisfied → jealous
　만족한　　질투하는
④ worried → relieved
　걱정하는　　안도한
⑤ frustrated → excited
　좌절한　　신난

[본문 해석]

로키산맥에서 2주간의 여행 중, 나는 자연 서식지에서 회색곰 한 마리를 보았다. 처음에 나는 그 곰이 땅을 가로질러 걸어가는 모습을 보았을 때 기분이 좋았다. 그것은 이따금 멈춰 서서 고개를 돌려 깊게 코를 킁킁거렸다. 그것은 무언가의 냄새를 따라가고 있었고, 나는 서서히 거대한 이 동물이 내 냄새를 맡고 있다는 것을 깨닫기 시작했다! 나는 얼어붙었다. 이것은 더는 멋진 경험이 아니었고, 이제 생존의 문제였다. 그 곰의 동기는 먹을 고기를 찾는 것이었고, 나는 분명히 그의 메뉴에 올라 있었다.

Why? 왜 정답일까?

처음에 회색곰을 발견하고 기분이 좋았던(At first, I felt joy as I watched the bear walk across the land.) 필자가 곰이 자신을 노린다는 것을 알고 겁에 질렸다(I froze.)는 내용이다. 따라서 'I'의 심경 변화로 가장 적절한 것은 ② '기쁜 → 겁에 질린'이다.

● grizzly bear 회색곰
● habitat ⑪ 서식지
● walk across ~을 횡단하다
● turn about 뒤돌아보다, 방향을 바꾸다
● deeply [ad] 깊게
● slowly [ad] 천천히
● freeze ⓥ 얼어붙다
● issue ⑪ 문제, 이슈
● motivation ⑪ (행동의) 이유, 동기 (부여)
● jealous ⓐ 질투하는
● native ⓐ 토착의, 토종의
● at first 처음에
● every once in a while 이따금
● sniff ⓥ 킁킁거리다
● scent ⑪ 냄새
● smell ⓥ 냄새 맡다
● no longer 더 이상 ~않다
● survival ⑪ 생존
● clearly [ad] 분명히
● frustrated ⓐ 좌절한

구문 풀이

3행 He stopped every once in a while to turn his head about,
　　　　　　　　　　　　　　　　　　　　목적(~하려고)
sniffing deeply.
분사구문(~하면서)

02 교사와 학생의 관계에서 비언어적 표현의 중요성   정답률 87% | 정답 ③

다음 글에서 필자가 주장하는 바로 가장 적절한 것은?

① 교사는 학생 간의 상호 작용을 주의 깊게 관찰해야 한다.
② 수업 시 교사는 학생의 수준에 맞는 언어를 사용해야 한다.
✔ 학생과의 관계에서 교사는 비언어적 표현에 유의해야 한다.
④ 학교는 학생에게 다양한 역할 경험의 기회를 제공해야 한다.
⑤ 교사는 학생 안전을 위해 교실의 물리적 환경을 개선해야 한다.

[본문 해석]

일부 전문가들은 우리가 전달하는 것의 절반 정도는 우리가 몸을 움직이는 방식을 통해 행해진다고 추정한다. 여러분이 보내는 비언어적인 메시지에 주의를 기울이는 것은 학생들과 여러분의 관계에 중요한 차이를 만들 수 있다. 일반적으로 대부분의 학생들은 선생님의 몸짓 언어에 종종 관심이 면밀하게 맞춰져 있다. 예를 들어, 여러분의 학생들이 처음 교실에 들어갈 때 처음 하는 행동은 선생님을 찾는 것이다. 선생님이 친근하게 인사하고 환영하는 미소를 지어줄 때 학생에게 얼마나 격려와 힘이 되는지 생각해 보자. 학생들에게 미소 짓는 것, 즉 그들에게 여러분이 그들을 알게 돼서 기쁘다는 것을 알려 주는 것이 많은 시간이나 노력을 요구하지는 않지만, 그것은 수업의 바로 시작부터 교실 분위기를 크게 달라지게 할 수 있다.

Why? 왜 정답일까?

'Paying attention to the nonverbal messages you send can make a significant difference in your relationship with students.'에서 교사는 학생과의 관계에서 자신이 사용하는 비언어적 표현에 주의를 기울일 필요가 있음을 시사하는 것으로 보아, 필자의 주장으로 가장 적절한 것은 ③ '학생과의 관계에서 교사는 비언어적 표현에 유의해야 한다.'이다.

● expert ⑪ 전문가
● as much as ~ 정도
● attention ⑪ 주의, 주목
● significant ⓐ 상당한, 유의미한, 중요한
● in general 보통, 대개, 일반적으로
● closely [ad] 면밀하게, 밀접하게
● body language 몸짓 언어, 보디랭귀지
● initial ⓐ 초기의
● look for 찾다
● empower ⓥ 능력을 주다, 힘을 주다
● greeting ⑪ 인사
● a great deal of (양이) 많은
● climate ⑪ 분위기
● estimate ⓥ 추정하다
● way ⑪ 방법, 방식
● nonverbal ⓐ 비언어적인
● difference ⑪ 차이
● often [ad] 자주, 종종
● tune in to ~에 맞추다
● enter ⓥ 들어가다
● action ⑪ 행동
● encourage ⓥ 격려하다
● friendly ⓐ 친근한, 다정한
● require ⓥ 요구하다
● effort ⑪ 노력

구문 풀이

1행 Some experts estimate that as much as half of what we
　　　　　　　　　　　접속사(~것)←　　　　　　주어(half of + 전체)
communicate is done through the way [we move our bodies].
　　　　　　동사(단수)　　　　　　　선행사

03 개인의 문화적 경험에 영향을 받는 학습   정답률 76% | 정답 ②

다음 글의 요지로 가장 적절한 것은?

① 문화 다양성에 대한 체계적 연구가 필요하다.
✔ 개인의 문화적 경험이 학습에 영향을 끼친다.
③ 인간의 뇌 구조는 학습을 통해 복잡하게 진화했다.
④ 원만한 대인관계 형성은 건강한 성장의 토대가 된다.
⑤ 학습 발달 단계에 적합한 자극을 제공하는 것이 좋다.

[본문 해석]

학습자들은 복잡한 발달적, 인지적, 신체적, 사회적, 그리고 문화적 체계 안에서 기능한다. 다양한 분야에서의 연구와 이론은 모든 학습자들이 문화적으로 정의된 맥락 안에서 문화적으로 정의된 방식으로 성장하고 배운다는 이해의 발전에 기여해 왔다. 인간은 가족 관계, 연령대별 단계, 기타 등등 기본적인 경험뿐만 아니라 기본적인 뇌 구조와 처리 과정을 공유하지만, 각각의 이러한 현상은 개인의 정확한 경험에 의해 형성된다. 문화적 영향은 인생의 시작부터 영향력이 있기 때문에 학습은 모든 사람들에게 똑같은 방식으로 일어나지는 않는다. 학습과 문화의 뒤얽힘에 관한 이러한 생각은 학습과 발달의 많은 측면에 대한 연구에 의해 지지되어 왔다.

Why? 왜 정답일까?

'Learning does not happen in the same way for all people because cultural influences are influential from the beginning of life.'에서 문화적 영향이 인생의 처음부터 영향을 미치기 때문에 학습은 개인마다 다르게 일어나게 된다는 핵심 내용을 제시한다. 따라서 글의 요지로 가장 적절한 것은 ② '개인의 문화적 경험이 학습에 영향을 끼친다.'이다.

● developmental ⓐ 발달에 관련된
● diverse ⓐ 다양한
● evolving ⓐ 발전하는
● structure ⑪ 구조
● age-related ⓐ 나이와 관련된
● shape ⓥ 형성하다
● precise ⓐ 정확한
● cognitive ⓐ 인지적인
● contribute to ~에 기여하다
● define ⓥ 정의하다, 규정하다
● fundamental ⓐ 기본적인
● phenomenon ⑪ 현상
● individual ⑪ 개인
● influential ⓐ 영향력 있는

구문 풀이

6행 While humans share basic brain structures and processes,
　　　　~한 반면
as well as fundamental experiences such as relationships with family,
「A + as well as + B : B뿐만 아니라 A도」
age-related stages, and many more, each of these phenomena
　　　　　　　　　　　　　　　　　주어(each of + 복수명사)
is shaped by an individual's precise experiences.
동사(단수)

04 고기를 덜 먹거나 먹지 않는 사람들의 이유
정답률 74% | 정답 ④

다음 도표의 내용과 일치하지 <u>않는</u> 것은?

Reasons for People Interested in Eating Less Meat and Non-meat Eaters in the UK (2018)

- Health: 49 / 31
- Weight management: 29 / 9
- Animal welfare: 22 / 52
- Environment: 22 / 32
- Taste: 10 / 30

□ People interested in eating less meat ■ Non-meat eaters

※ allowed to choose multiple reasons

[본문 해석]

위 그래프는 고기를 덜 먹는 것에 관심 있는 사람들과 고기를 먹지 않는 사람들의 이유에 대한 2018년 영국에서의 조사 결과를 보여 준다. ① 고기를 덜 먹는 것에 관심 있는 집단 사람들에게 그렇게 하려는 가장 강력한 동기는 건강이다. ② 고기를 먹지 않는 집단 사람들의 경우, 모든 이유 중 동물 복지가 가장 큰 비율을 차지하고, 환경, 건강, 그리고 맛이 그 뒤를 따른다. ③ 두 집단 간 퍼센트포인트 격차가 가장 큰 것은 동물 복지인 반면, 가장 작은 격차는 환경이다. ④ 고기를 먹지 않는 사람들 중 맛을 언급한 비율은 고기 섭취를 줄이는 데 관심이 있는 사람들 중 맛을 언급한 비율보다 4배 높다. ⑤ 체중 관리는 고기를 먹지 않는 사람들에게 10퍼센트 미만으로 가장 낮은 순위를 차지한다.

Why? 왜 정답일까?

도표에 따르면 고기를 먹지 않는 사람들 중 맛 때문이라고 언급한 사람은 **30%**인데, 이는 고기를 덜 먹으려는 사람들 중 맛을 이유로 언급한 비율(**10%**)의 3배이다. 따라서 도표와 일치하지 않는 것은 ④이다.

- **survey** ⓝ 설문 조사
- **motivator** ⓝ 동기 요인
- **account for** ～을 차지하다
- **cite** ⓥ 언급하다, 인용하다
- **weight** ⓝ 체중, 무게
- **reason** ⓝ 이유
- **welfare** ⓝ 복지
- **followed by** ～이 뒤를 잇다
- **consumption** ⓝ 소비

구문 풀이

11행 The percentage of non-meat eaters citing taste is
┌→ '배수사 + 비교급 + than : ～보다 몇 배 더 …한'
four times higher than that of people (interested in reducing their
　　　　　　　　　　　 = the percentage　 (　) : people 수식
meat consumption) (citing taste).

★★★ 1등급 대비 고난도 3점 문제

05 인상주의 예술의 특징
정답률 41% | 정답 ③

다음 글의 밑줄 친 부분 중, 어법상 틀린 것은? [3점]

[본문 해석]

인상주의 화가의 그림은 아마도 가장 인기가 있는데, 그것은 보는 사람이 그 형상을 이해하기 위해 열심히 노력할 것을 요구하지 않는, 쉽게 이해되는 예술이다. 인상주의는 보기에 '편하고', 여름의 장면과 밝은 색깔은 눈길을 끈다. 그러나 이 새로운 그림 방식은 그것이 만들어지는 방법뿐 아니라, 보이는 것에 있어서도 대중들에게 도전적이었다는 것을 기억하는 것이 중요하다. 그들은 이전에 그렇게 '형식에 구애받지 않는' 그림을 본 적이 결코 없었다. 캔버스의 가장자리는 마치 카메라로 스냅사진을 찍는 것처럼, 임의적으로 장면을 잘라 냈다. 그 소재는 기찻길과 공장과 같은 현대화된 풍경을 포함했다. 이전에는 이러한 대상이 결코 화가들에게 적절하다고 여겨지지 않았다.

Why? 왜 정답일까?

전치사 in의 목적어 역할을 할 명사가 없고 'was shown'이 주어가 없는 불완전한 절이므로, ③의 that은 what으로 고쳐야 한다. 어법상 틀린 것은 ③이다.

Why? 왜 오답일까?

① 5형식 동사 ask는 to부정사를 목적격 보어로 취한다.

---

② 'with + 명사 + 분사' 구문이다. 'appeal to the eye'는 '눈길을 끌다'라는 뜻의 동사구로서 여기서는 현재분사 형태로 쓰였다.

④ such는 'such + a/an + 형용사 + 단수 명사' 또는 'such + 형용사 + 복수 명사' 형태로 쓰인다.

⑤ 5형식 동사 consider는 뒤에 목적어와 형용사 보어를 취할 수 있는데, 여기서는 'had ~ been considered'가 수동태이므로 뒤에 형용사 보어(appropriate)가 바로 이어진다.

- **impressionist** ⓝ 인상파 화가
- **informal** ⓐ 격식에 얽매이지 않는
- **modernization** ⓝ 현대화
- **appropriate** ⓐ 적절한, 알맞은
- **imagery** ⓝ 형상(화), 이미지
- **arbitrary** ⓐ 임의적인, 자의적인
- **landscape** ⓝ 풍경

구문 풀이

9행 The edge of the canvas cut off the scene in an arbitrary way,
　　　　주어　　　　　　 동사　　　　　　 임의적 방식으로
/ as if (it was) snapped with a camera.
　　 생략　　 과거분사

★★ 문제 해결 꿀~팁 ★★

▶ **많이 틀린 이유는?**
형용사 appropriate 대신 부사 appropriately가 나와 수동태 동사인 had been considered를 꾸민다고 생각했다면 ⑤를 고르기 쉬웠을 것이다. 하지만 consider는 5형식 동사로서 능동태로 쓰일 때 뒤에 목적어와 목적격 보어를 취하며, 수동태로 쓰일 때에도 반드시 뒤에 보어가 나와야 한다. 보어 역할을 할 수 있는 품사는 명사 또는 형용사뿐이므로 ⑤에서 appropriate를 쓴 것은 어법상 맞다.

▶ **문제 해결 방법은?**
'that vs. what', '형용사 vs. 부사' 등은 수능에 빈출되는 개념이다. 평소 시험에 자주 나오는 어법을 테마별로 정리해 두고 문제를 풀 때마다 한 번씩 체크하는 습관을 들이도록 한다.

06 상점가 경제의 특성
정답률 62% | 정답 ④

다음 글의 밑줄 친 부분 중, 문맥상 낱말의 쓰임이 적절하지 <u>않은</u> 것은? [3점]

[본문 해석]

상점가 경제는 공유되는 문화라는 더 지속적인 유대 위에 자리 잡은, 겉으로 보기에 유연한 가격 설정 메커니즘을 특징으로 한다. 구매자와 판매자 둘 다 서로의 ① 제약을 알고 있다. 델리의 상점가에서, 구매자와 판매자는 대체로 다른 행위자들이 그들의 일상생활에서 가지는 재정적 압박을 ② 가늠할 수 있다. 특정 경제 계층에 속하는 각 행위자는 상대방이 무엇을 필수품으로 여기고 무엇을 사치품으로 여기는지를 이해한다. 비디오 게임과 같은 전자 제품의 경우, 그것들은 식품과 같은 다른 가정 구매품과 동일한 수준의 ③ 필수품이 아니다. 따라서 델리의 상점가에서 판매자는 비디오 게임에 대해 직접적으로 매우 ④ 낮은(→ 높은) 가격을 요구하지 않으려 주의하는데, 구매자가 비디오 게임의 소유를 절대적인 필수 사항으로 볼 이유가 전혀 없기 때문이다. 이러한 유형의 지식에 대한 접근은 ⑤ 비슷한 문화경제적 세계에 속하여 비롯되는 서로의 선호와 한계를 관련지어 가격 일치를 형성한다.

Why? 왜 정답일까?

③이 포함된 문장에서 식품과 동등한 수준의 필수품으로 여겨지지 않는 비디오 게임을 언급하고 있다. 판매자와 구매자가 서로의 선호와 제약을 알고 있는 상점가 경제의 특성상, 판매자는 절대적 필수품이 '아닌' 비디오 게임에 대해 '높은' 가격을 불러 구매자의 구매욕을 더욱 떨어뜨리는 선택을 하지 않으려 노력할 것이다. 즉 ④에 low 대신 high를 써야 자연스러우므로, 문맥상 낱말의 쓰임이 적절하지 않은 것은 ④이다.

- **bazaar** ⓝ 상점가, 시장 거리
- **apparently** ⓐⓓ 겉으로 보기에
- **atop** ⓟⓡⓔⓟ 위에, 맨 꼭대기에
- **aware of** ～을 아는
- **assess** ⓥ 가늠하다, 평가하다
- **constraint** ⓝ 압박
- **necessity** ⓝ 필수품, 필요
- **food item** 식품
- **at no point** 전혀 ～않는
- **absolute** ⓐ 절대적인
- **establish** ⓥ 형성하다, 세우다
- **relate to** ～을 관련 짓다, 이해하다
- **universe** ⓝ 세계, 우주, 세상
- **feature** ⓥ 특징으로 하다
- **flexible** ⓐ 유연한
- **enduring** ⓐ 오래가는, 지속적인
- **restriction** ⓝ 제약
- **to a large extent** 대체로, 많은 부분
- **economic class** 경제 계층
- **luxury** ⓝ 사치품
- **be careful not to** ～하지 않도록 주의하다
- **possession** ⓝ 소유
- **access** ⓝ 접근, 이용
- **consensus** ⓝ 일치
- **limitation** ⓝ 한계

07 대도시의 분업
정답률 48% | 정답 ①

다음 빈칸에 들어갈 말로 가장 적절한 것을 고르시오. [3점]

✓ ① specialization – 전문화
② criticism – 비판
③ competition – 경쟁
④ diligence – 근면
⑤ imagination – 상상

[본문 해석]

작은 마을에서는 똑같은 일꾼이 의자와 문, 탁자를 만들고, 바로 같은 사람이 종종 집도 짓는다. 그리고 물론 많은 직업을 가진 한 사람이 그 모든 데 능하기는 불가능하다. 반면에 대도시에서는, 많은 사람들이 각 직종을 필요로 하기에, 아주 흔하게 전체 직종에 훨씬 못 미치는 한 가지 직종만으로도, 한 사람이 먹고 사는 데 충분하다. 예를 들어, 한 사람은 남자 신발을 만들고, 다른 사람은 여자 신발을 만든다. 그리고 어떤 사람은 신발을 깁기만 하고, 다른 사람은 자르기만 하고, 또 다른 사람은 신발 위창을 꿰매기만 하여 생계를 꾸려가는 경우까지도 있다. 그런 숙련된 노동자들은 간단한 도구만을 썼을지도 모르지만, 그들의 전문화는 정말로 더 효율적이고 생산적인 작업으로 이어졌다.

Why? 왜 정답일까?

작은 마을과 대도시의 업무 방식을 대조한 글이다. 작은 마을에서는 한 사람이 여러 가지 일을 하게 되지만, 대도시에서는 한 사람이 한 가지 직종만 갖고서도 먹고 사는 데 충분하여 분업이 이루어진다(In large cities, ~, because many people make demands on each trade, one trade alone — very often even less than a whole trade — is enough to support a man.)고 이야기하므로, 빈칸에 들어갈 말로 적절한 것은 '분업'과 대응될 수 있는 ① '전문화'이다.

- **workman** ⓝ 일꾼, 노동자, 직공
- **skilled** ⓐ 숙련된
- **stitch** ⓥ 깁다, 꿰매다, 바느질하다
- **result in** ~로 이어지다, ~을 초래하다
- **productive** ⓐ 생산적인
- **diligence** ⓝ 근면
- **impossible** ⓐ 불가능한
- **place** ⓝ 경우
- **sew** ⓥ 꿰매다, 깁다
- **efficient** ⓐ 효율적인
- **criticism** ⓝ 비판

구문 풀이

12행 Such skilled workers may have used simple tools, / but their
　　　　　　　　　　　　　　　　「may have + 과거분사 : ~했을지도 모른다」
specialization did result in more efficient and productive work.
동사 강조(과거) 　　원형

★★★ 1등급 대비 고난도 3점 문제

08 차이점에 집중할 때 가려지는 유사점
정답률 32% | 정답 ③

다음 빈칸에 들어갈 말로 가장 적절한 것을 고르시오. [3점]

① prove the uniqueness of each society
　각 사회의 고유함을 입증하게
② prevent cross-cultural understanding
　다문화적 이해를 막게
✓ ③ mask the more overwhelming similarities
　더 압도적인 유사점을 가리게
④ change their perspective on what diversity is
　다양성이 무엇인가에 대한 그들의 견해를 바꾸게
⑤ encourage them to step out of their mental frame
　그들이 정신적 틀을 벗어나도록 장려하게

[본문 해석]

사회들 사이의 차이점에 집중하는 것은 더 깊은 실체를 숨기는데, 그것들의 유사점은 차이점보다 더 크고 더 심오하다. 1만 피트 높이의 고원에 서서 두 개의 언덕을 유심히 본다고 상상해 보라. 여러분의 관점에서 보면, 한 언덕이 300피트 높이인 것처럼 보이고 다른 언덕이 900피트 높이인 것처럼 보인다. 이 차이가 커 보일 수 있고 여러분은 침식과 같은 어떤 국부적인 힘이 크기의 차이를 설명하는지에 관심을 집중할지도 모른다. 그러나 이 좁은 관점은 다른 관점, 즉 하나는 10,300피트 높이이고 다른 하나는 10,900피트 높이로 사실상 아주 비슷한 두 개의 산을 만들어 낸 더 중대한 지질학적 힘을 연구할 기회를 놓치고 있다. 그리고 인간 사회에 관한 한, 사람들은 1만 피트의 고원에 서서 사회들 사이의 차이점이 더 압도적인 유사점을 가리게 두고 있다.

Why? 왜 정답일까?

첫 문장에서 사회들 사이의 차이점에 주목하면 그들간의 유사점이라는 더 깊은 실체를 놓치게 된다(Focusing on the differences among societies conceals a deeper reality: their similarities are greater and more profound than

their dissimilarities.)고 언급하고 있다. 따라서 빈칸에 들어갈 말로 가장 적절한 것은 ③ '더 압도적인 유사점을 가리게'이다.

- **conceal** ⓥ 숨기다
- **dissimilarity** ⓝ 차이점
- **account for** ⓥ ~을 설명하다
- **significant** ⓐ 중대한, 유의미한
- **when it comes to** ~에 관한 한
- **overwhelming** ⓐ 압도적인
- **profound** ⓐ 심오한
- **plateau** ⓝ 고원
- **narrow** ⓐ 좁은
- **geological** ⓐ 지질학적인
- **uniqueness** ⓝ 고유성
- **step out of** ⓥ ~에서 나오다

구문 풀이

7행 This difference may seem large, and you might **focus** your
　　　 의문형용사(어떤) 　　　2형식 동사 형용사 보어 「focus + A + on + B :
attention on what local forces, such as erosion, account for the
　　　　　　　명사(주어) 　　　삽입구 　　 동사
difference in size.

★★ 문제 해결 꿀~팁 ★★

▶ **많이 틀린 이유는?**
첫 문장에서 제시하듯 이 글의 주제는 차이점에 집중하다보면 훨씬 더 두드러지는 유사성을 놓치기 쉽다는 것이다. ④에서 언급하는 '다양성에 관한 시각'은 주제와 무관한 소재이다.

▶ **문제 해결 방법은?**
첫 문장과 마지막 문장이 결국 같은 내용을 말하는 일관된 흐름의 글이다. 예시 부분은 가볍게 넘어가고 'conceals a deeper reality: ~'을 'mask ~'로 재진술한 ③을 바로 답으로 고를 수 있도록 한다.

09 뮤지션들이 홀로 설 수 있게 된 음악 시장
정답률 65% | 정답 ③

다음 글에서 전체 흐름과 관계 없는 문장은?

[본문 해석]

오늘날의 음악 사업은 뮤지션들이 스스로 일을 처리할 수 있게 해 주었다. ① 뮤지션들이 음반사나 TV 프로그램의 문지기(권력을 쥐고 사람들이 들어가는 것을 막는 사람)가 그들이 스포트라이트를 받을 만하다고 말해주기를 기다리던 시대는 지났다. ② 오늘날의 음악 사업에서는 팬층을 만들기 위해 허락을 요청할 필요가 없으며, 그렇게 하려고 회사에 수천 달러를 지불할 필요도 더 이상 없다. ③ TV 오디션을 이용하여 나이 어린 뮤지션들을 마케팅하는 데에 대한 우려가 증가하고 있다. ④ 매일 뮤지션들은 어떤 외부의 도움도 없이 수천 명의 청취자에게 자신들의 음악을 내놓고 있다. ⑤ 그들은 노출을 얻거나 수천 명의 청취자와 관계를 형성하기 위해 허락이나 외부의 도움을 요청하지 않고, 그저 자신들의 음악을 팬들에게 직접 전달한다.

Why? 왜 정답일까?

오늘날 뮤지션들은 음반사 등에 크게 의지할 필요 없이 직접 대중에게 음악을 전달하고 스스로 마케팅할 수 있는 시장 환경에서 활동한다는 내용을 다룬 글이다. ①, ②, ④, ⑤는 주제에 부합하지만, ③은 TV 오디션을 통한 어린 뮤지션들의 마케팅에 관해 언급하고 있어 흐름에서 벗어난다. 따라서 전체 흐름과 관계없는 문장은 ③이다.

- **take matters into one's own hands** 스스로 일을 추진하다, 일을 독자적으로 하다
- **gatekeeper** ⓝ 문지기, 수위
- **permission** ⓝ 허락
- **deliver** ⓥ 전달하다
- **be worthy of** ~을 받을 만하다
- **concern** ⓝ 우려

구문 풀이

2행 Gone are the days of musicians waiting for a gatekeeper
　　　 「보어 + 동사 + 주어 : 도치 구문」 　현재분사 「wait + 의미상 주어 +
(someone [who holds power and prevents you from being let in]) at
　　　　　　　　　　　동사1 　　　　동사2
a label or TV show to say they are worthy of the spotlight.
└ 동격(= a gatekeeper) to부정사 : ~이 …하도록 기다리다」

10 식량 문제와 그 해결
정답률 64% | 정답 ②

주어진 글 다음에 이어질 글의 순서로 가장 적절한 것을 고르시오.

① (A) – (C) – (B)
✓ ② (B) – (A) – (C)
③ (B) – (C) – (A)
④ (C) – (A) – (B)
⑤ (C) – (B) – (A)

[본문 해석]

전 세계에 거의 10억 명의 굶주리는 사람들이 있는데, 분명 원인이 단 하나만 있는 것은 아니다.

(B) 그렇지만, 가장 큰 원인은 단연 빈곤이다. 세계의 굶주리는 사람들의 79퍼센트가 식량 순 수출국에 살고 있다. 어떻게 이럴 수가 있을까?

(A) 그러한 국가에서 사람들이 굶주리는 이유는 그곳에서 생산된 산물들이 현지 시민들이 그것들에 지불할 수 있는 것보다 더 비싸게 세계 시장에서 팔릴 수 있기 때문이다. 현대에는 여러분이 식량이 없어서 굶주리는 것이 아니라, 돈이 없어서 굶주리는 것이다.

(C) 그래서 진짜 문제는 거대한 체계로 볼 때 식량이 너무 비싸고 많은 사람들은 너무 가난하여 그것을 구매할 수 없다는 것이다. 해답은 식량의 가격을 낮추는 추세를 지속하는 데 있을 것이다.

Why? 왜 정답일까?

식량 문제의 원인이 다양함을 언급하는 주어진 글 뒤로, 빈곤이 가장 큰 원인임을 제시하는 (B), 빈곤한 국가의 굶주리는 사람들은 말 그대로 돈이 없어서 굶주린다는 설명을 이어가는 (A), 해결책을 언급하며 글을 맺는 (C)가 차례로 이어져야 한다. 따라서 글의 순서로 가장 적절한 것은 ② '(B) – (A) – (C)'이다.

- billion ⓝ 10억
- afford to ~할 여유가 되다
- poverty ⓝ 가난, 빈곤
- obviously ㏛ 분명히
- starve ⓥ 굶주리다

구문 풀이

3행 The reason (that) people are hungry in those countries is that the products produced there can be sold on the world market for more than the local citizens can afford to pay for them.

11-12 사회적 두려움을 극복하는 방법

[본문 해석]

발코니에 서 있는 것을 두려워한다면, 당신은 더 낮은 층에서 시작해서 천천히 더 높은 층으로 올라갈 것이다. 완전히 통제된 방식으로 높은 발코니에 서 있는 두려움을 직면하기는 쉬울 것이다. 사람을 사귄다는 것은 (a) 더 까다롭다. 사람은 그저 주변에 있어서 익숙해지는 건물과 같은 무생물이 아니다. 당신은 그들과 상호 작용을 해야 하며 그들의 반응을 예측하기가 힘들 수 있다. 그들에 대한 당신의 느낌도 역시 더 복잡하다. 대부분의 사람들의 자존감은 그들이 발코니를 좋아하지 않는다고 해도 그렇게 많이 영향을 받지 않을 것이지만, 당신이 효과적으로 사람들을 사귈 수 없다면 당신의 자신감은 (b) 상처받을 수 있다. 점차적으로 마주할 여러 사교적 두려움을 깔끔한 방법을 설계하는 것 또한 더 어렵다. 「당신을 드러낼 필요가 있는 사교적 상황이 당신이 원할 때 (c) 형성되지 않을 수 있고, 또는 그것들은 상황이 통제 가능하다고 감지할 만큼 충분히 잘 진행되지 않을지도 모른다.」 한 단계에서 다음 단계로의 진행은 분명하지 않을 수 있으며, 한 단계에서 다음 단계로 진행할 때 피할 수 없이 어려움이 크게 (d) 줄어들게(→ 늘어나게) 된다. 당신 주변의 사람들은 당신 자신의 목적을 위해서 끊임없이 실험해 볼 수 있는 로봇이 아니다. 이것은 사람을 사귈 때 당신의 두려움을 직면하는 것이 의미가 없다는 말이 아니다. 「점진적인 노출의 원칙은 여전히 매우 (e) 유용하다. 그것들을 적용하는 과정은 더 복잡하지만, 시작하기 전에 그것을 아는 것은 도움이 된다.」

（「」 : 12번의 근거 / 「」 : 11번의 근거）

- socialize ⓥ (사람과) 사귀다, 사회화하다
- inanimate ⓐ 무생물의
- unpredictable ⓐ 예측 불가한
- confidence ⓝ 자신감
- under control 통제되는
- unavoidable ⓐ 피할 수 없는
- pointless ⓐ 의미 없는
- tricky ⓐ 까다로운, 다루기 힘든
- get used to ~에 익숙해지다
- self-esteem ⓝ 자존감
- gradually ㏛ 점차적으로
- progression ⓝ 진전
- endlessly ㏛ 끝없이
- principle ⓝ 원칙, 원리

구문 풀이

1행 If you were afraid of standing on balconies, you would start on some lower floors and slowly work your way up to higher ones.

---

11 제목 파악   정답률 39% | 정답 ⑤

윗글의 제목으로 가장 적절한 것은?

① How to Improve Your Self-Esteem
  자존감을 높이는 방법
② Socializing with Someone You Fear: Good or Bad?
  당신이 두려워하는 사람과 어울리는 것: 좋을까, 나쁠까?
③ Relaxation May Lead to Getting Over Social Fears
  휴식은 사회적 두려움을 극복하게 해줄 수 있다
④ Are Social Exposures Related with Fear of Heights?
  사회적 노출은 고소공포증과 연관이 있을까?
✓⑤ Overcoming Social Anxiety Is Difficult; Try Gradually!
  사회적 불안을 극복하기는 어렵지만, 점진적으로 시도하라!

Why? 왜 정답일까?

마지막 두 문장에 따르면 사교적으로 불안을 느끼는 상황에 점진적 노출 기법을 적용하기는 어렵지만 그래도 여전히 이 기법은 유용하다고 한다. 따라서 글의 제목으로 가장 적절한 것은 ⑤ '사회적 불안을 극복하기는 어렵지만, 점진적으로 시도하라!'이다.

★★ 문제 해결 꿀~팁 ★★

▶ 많이 틀린 이유는?
사교에 대한 두려움을 고소공포증 극복처럼 점진적 노출 기법, 즉 두려운 상황의 강도를 조금씩 높여가며 노출되는 방식으로 극복해나갈 수 있는지 논한 글이다. 무서워하는 사람과 상호작용을 하는 것이 좋은지 나쁜지 판단하는 내용은 없으므로 ②는 답으로 부적절하다.

▶ 문제 해결 방법은?
명확한 주제문 없이 '사교적 두려움 극복'이라는 소재에 관해 설명하고 마지막 부분에서 결론을 내리는 구조의 글이므로, 전체적으로 글을 다 읽되 필자의 의견이 가장 잘 드러난 부분을 찾아 답으로 연결시켜야 한다.

---

12 어휘 추론   정답률 57% | 정답 ④

밑줄 친 (a) ~ (e) 중에서 문맥상 낱말의 쓰임이 적절하지 않은 것은?

① (a)   ② (b)   ③ (c)   ✓④ (d)   ⑤ (e)

Why? 왜 정답일까?

두 번째 단락의 첫 두 문장에서 사회적 불안을 점진적으로 직면할 수 있는 상황을 형성하거나 통제하는 것은 어렵다고 설명하고 있다. 이를 근거로 볼 때, (d)가 포함된 문장은 상황의 단계가 진행할수록 어려움이 '커진다'는 내용이어야 하므로, (d)의 decreases를 increases로 고쳐야 한다. 따라서 문맥상 낱말의 쓰임이 적절하지 않은 것은 ④ '(d)'이다.

DAY 24 · 20분 미니 모의고사

01 ③	02 ②	03 ④	04 ⑤	05 ⑤
06 ③	07 ②	08 ⑤	09 ①	10 ②
11 ②	12 ④			

---

01 이메일을 보내기 전 꼭 최종 검토하기   정답률 91% | 정답 ③

다음 글에서 필자가 주장하는 바로 가장 적절한 것은?

① 중요한 이메일은 출력하여 보관해야 한다.
② 글을 쓸 때에는 개요 작성부터 시작해야 한다.
☑ 이메일을 전송하기 전에 반드시 검토해야 한다.
④ 업무와 관련된 컴퓨터 기능을 우선 익혀야 한다.
⑤ 업무상 중요한 내용은 이메일보다는 직접 전달해야 한다.

[본문 해석]

출판사와 신문사에서 다음과 같이 알게 된다. 결국 인쇄물로 나오지 않으면 그것은 실수가 아니다. 그것은 이메일에서도 마찬가지다. 전송 버튼을 눌러 버리기 전까지는 어떤 나쁜 일도 일어날 수 없다. 여러분이 쓴 글에는 잘못 쓴 철자, 사실의 오류, 무례한 말, 명백한 거짓말이 있을 수 있지만, 그것은 문제가 되지 않는다. 그것을 전송하지 않았다면, 아직 그것을 고칠 시간이 있다. 어떤 실수라도 수정할 수 있고 누구도 결코 그 변화를 모를 것이다. 물론, 이것은 말은 쉽지만 행하기는 어렵다. 전송은 여러분 컴퓨터의 가장 매력적인 명령어이다. 그러나 그 전송 버튼을 누르기 전에, 반드시 문서를 마지막으로 한 번 주의 깊게 읽어 보라.

Why? 왜 정답일까?

마지막 문장인 '~ before you hit the Send key, make sure that you read your document carefully one last time.'에서 이메일의 전송 버튼을 누르기 전 꼭 마지막으로 주의 깊게 읽어보라고 언급하는 것으로 볼 때, 필자가 주장하는 바로 가장 적절한 것은 ③ '이메일을 전송하기 전에 반드시 검토해야 한다.'이다.

- in print 출간되는, 발표되는
- rude ⓐ 무례한
- fix ⓥ 고치다
- command ⓝ 명령(어) ⓥ 명령하다
- misspelling ⓝ 오탈자
- obvious ⓐ 명백한
- easier said than done 행동보다 말이 쉽다

구문 풀이

10행 But before you hit the Send key, make sure that you read your document carefully one last time.
접속사(~ 전에)   명령문(~하라)   접속사(~것)

---

02 긍정적 재구성에 도움이 되는 호기심   정답률 60% | 정답 ②

다음 글의 주제로 가장 적절한 것은?

① importance of defensive reactions in a tough situation
  힘든 상황에서 방어적인 반응의 중요성
☑ curiosity as the hidden force of positive reframes
  긍정적인 재구성의 숨은 동력인 호기심
③ difficulties of coping with stress at work
  직장에서의 스트레스에 대처하는 것의 어려움
④ potential threats caused by curiosity
  호기심으로 인한 잠재적 위험
⑤ factors that reduce human curiosity
  인간의 호기심을 떨어뜨리는 요인

[본문 해석]

호기심은 우리가 어려운 문제를 맡아야 할 흥미로운 도전으로 더 여기게 한다. 상사와의 스트레스를 받는 회의는 배울 수 있는 기회가 된다. 긴장이 되는 첫 데이트는 새로운 사람과의 멋진 밤이 된다. 주방용 체는 모자가 된다. 일반적으로, 호기심은 우리가 스트레스를 받는 상황을 위험보다는 도전으로 여기게 하고, 어려움을 더 터놓고 말하게 하고, 문제 해결에 있어 새로운 접근을 시도하도록 동기를 부여해 준다. 실제로 호기심은 스트레스에 대한 방어적인 반응이 줄어들고, 그 결과 짜증에 반응할 때 공격성이 줄어드는 것과 관련이 있다.

Why? 왜 정답일까?

'Curiosity makes us much more likely to view a tough problem as an interesting challenge to take on.'에서 호기심은 우리가 어려운 문제를 흥미로운 도전처럼 여길 수 있게 해준다고 언급한 데 이어, 'In general, curiosity motivates us to view stressful situations as challenges ~'에서도 같은 내용을 제시한다. 따라서 글의 주제로 가장 적절한 것은 ② '긍정적인 재구성의 숨은 동력인 호기심'이다.

- curiosity ⓝ 호기심
- defensive ⓐ 방어적인
- irritation ⓝ 짜증
- threat ⓝ 위험
- aggression ⓝ 공격
- cope with ~에 대처하다

구문 풀이

1행 Curiosity makes us much more likely to view a tough problem
5형식 동사 | 목적어   목적어 보어
as an interesting challenge to take on.
as+B : A를 B로 여기다

---

03 가끔 혹은 자주 뉴스를 회피한 사람들의 비율   정답률 93% | 정답 ④

다음 도표의 내용과 일치하지 않는 것은?

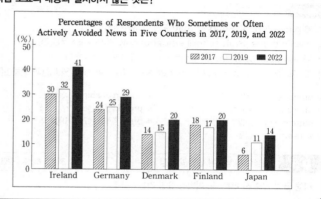

Percentages of Respondents Who Sometimes or Often Actively Avoided News in Five Countries in 2017, 2019, and 2022

[본문 해석]

위 도표는 2017년, 2019년 및 2022년에 가끔 또는 자주 적극적으로 뉴스를 회피한 다섯 개 국가의 응답자 비율을 보여준다. ① 세 연도에서 각각, 아일랜드가 도표의 국가 중, 가끔 또는 자주 적극적으로 뉴스를 회피한 응답자의 가장 높은 비율을 보여주었다. ② 독일의 경우, 가끔 또는 자주 적극적으로 뉴스를 회피한 응답자 비율이 세 연도 각각 30%보다 낮았다. ③ 덴마크의 경우, 2019년에 가끔 또는 자주 적극적으로 뉴스를 회피한 응답자 비율이 2017년보다 더 높았으나 2022년보다는 더 낮았다. ④ 핀란드의 경우, 2019년에 가끔 또는 자주 적극적으로 뉴스를 회피한 응답자 비율이 2017년보다 더 낮았으며, 이는 일본도 마찬가지였다. ⑤ 일본의 경우, 가끔 또는 자주 적극적으로 뉴스를 회피한 응답자 비율이 세 연도 각각 15%를 넘지 않았다.

Why? 왜 정답일까?

일본에서 뉴스를 가끔 또는 자주 적극 회피했던 사람들 비율은 2017년(6%)에 비해 2019년(11%)에 오히려 증가했으므로, 도표와 일치하지 않는 것은 ④이다.

- actively ⓐⓓ 적극적으로
- true for ~에도 해당되는
- less than ~보다 적은

---

04 드론 레이싱 선수권   정답률 94% | 정답 ⑤

2023 Drone Racing Championship에 관한 다음 안내문의 내용과 일치하지 않는 것은?

① 7월 9일 일요일에 개최된다.
② 고등학생만 참가할 수 있다.
③ 자신의 드론을 가져와야 한다.
④ 상금과 메달이 우승자에게 수여될 것이다.
☑ 20명의 참가자가 기념품을 받을 것이다.

[본문 해석]

2023 Drone Racing Championship(2023 드론 레이싱 선수권)

여러분은 최고의 드론 레이서인가요? 그렇다면 여러분이 바로 그 사람이라는 것을 증명할 기회를 잡으세요!

일시 & 장소
• 7월 9일 일요일 오후 6시부터 오후 8시까지 ─ ①의 근거 일치

• Lakeside 주민센터

필수 조건
• 『참가자: 고등학생만』── 『』: ②의 근거 일치
• 『레이스를 위해 당신의 드론을 가져 오세요.』── 『』: ③의 근거 일치

부상
• 『500달러와 메달이 우승자에게 수여될 것입니다.』── 『』: ④의 근거 일치

참고 사항
• 『선착순 10명의 참가자들은 기념품을 받게 될 것입니다.』── 『』: ⑤의 근거 불일치

더 많은 세부 정보를 원하시면, www.droneracing.com을 방문하거나 313-6745-1189로 전화하세요.

Why? 왜 정답일까?

'The first 10 participants will get souvenirs.'에서 선착순 **10**명의 참가자에게 기념품을 준다고 하므로, 안내문의 내용과 일치하지 않는 것은 ⑤ '**20**명의 참가자가 기념품을 받을 것이다.'이다.

Why? 왜 오답일까?

① '6 p.m. – 8 p.m., Sunday, July 9'의 내용과 일치한다.
② 'Participants: High school students only'의 내용과 일치한다.
③ 'Bring your own drone for the race.'의 내용과 일치한다.
④ '$500 and a medal will be awarded to the winner.'의 내용과 일치한다.

• drone ⓝ 드론, 무인 항공기
• take an opportunity 기회를 잡다
• requirement ⓝ 필수 요건
• souvenir ⓝ 기념품
• championship ⓝ 선수권
• prove ⓥ 증명하다
• bring ⓥ 가져오다, 지참하다

---

05 동물에게 투영된 인간의 특징 　정답률 62% | 정답 ⑤

다음 글의 밑줄 친 부분 중, 어법상 틀린 것은? [3점]

[본문 해석]

동물에게 투영된 가장 눈에 띄는 인간의 특징은 동물이 인간의 언어로 대화할 수 있다는 점이다. 신체적으로도, 동물 만화 캐릭터와 동물을 본떠 만든 장난감은 또한 인간을 닮도록 변형되는 경우가 아주 많다. 이것은 그들이 인간과 같은 얼굴 특징과 사람의 손을 닮게 변형된 앞다리를 갖고 있는 모습을 보여줌으로써 이뤄진다. 더 최근의 만화 영화에서 추세는 동물을 더 '자연스러운' 방식으로 묘사하는 것이었다. 그러나 이 동물들은 여전히 사람 손처럼 (가령 사자가 한 발로 작은 물체를 집어들 수 있는 것처럼) 앞다리를 사용하고, 여전히 적절한 표정을 지으며 이야기한다. 동물 캐릭터를 아이와 어른 모두에게 더 감정적으로 매력적이게 만들기 위해 이용하는 일반적인 전략은 그것들에 확대되고 변형된 어린이 같은 특징을 부여하는 것이다.

Why? 왜 정답일까?

핵심 주어가 단수 명사인 **A general strategy**이므로, 동사 또한 복수형인 **are** 대신 단수형인 **is**를 쓰는 것이 적합하다. 따라서 어법상 틀린 것은 ⑤이다.

Why? 왜 오답일까?

① 주격 보어 역할의 명사절을 이끌기 위해 접속사 that을 썼다.
② animal cartoon characters and toys가 '만들어지는' 대상이므로 과거분사 made를 사용해 꾸몄다.
③ 전치사 by 뒤에 목적어로 동명사 showing을 썼다.
④ 뒤에 명사구 human hands가 나오는 것으로 보아 전치사 like(~처럼)가 적절하게 쓰였다.

• noticeable ⓐ 눈에 띄는, 두드러지는
• project onto ~에게 투영시키다
• deform ⓥ 변형하다
• resemble ⓥ ~와 닮다
• natural ⓐ 자연스러운
• emotionally ⓐⓓ 정서적으로
• enlarge ⓥ 확대하다
• characteristic ⓝ 특징
• cartoon character 만화 캐릭터
• in such a way as to ~한 방식으로
• humanlike ⓐ 인간 같은
• paw ⓝ (동물의) 발
• appealing ⓐ 매력적인
• feature ⓝ 특징, 이목구비

구문 풀이

[3행] Physically, animal cartoon characters and toys made after
　　　　　　　　　　주어　　　　　　　　　　　　과거분사구
animals are also most often deformed in such a way as to resemble
　　　　　　동사구(수동태)　　　　　　　　　　　~하는 (그런) 식으로
humans.

---

06 소셜 텔레비전 시스템이 만들어낸 상호작용 방식 　정답률 70% | 정답 ③

(A), (B), (C)의 각 네모 안에서 문맥에 맞는 낱말로 가장 적절한 것은?

	(A)	(B)	(C)
①	connectedness 유대감	allowed 허용했다	disliking 싫어하는
②	connectedness 유대감	forbade 금지하다	disliking 싫어하는
✓③	connectedness 유대감	allowed 허용했다	favoring 선호하는
④	isolation 고립	forbade 금지하다	favoring 선호하는
⑤	isolation 고립	allowed 허용했다	disliking 싫어하는

[본문 해석]

새로운 기술은 새로운 상호작용과 문화적 규칙을 만든다. TV 시청을 장려할 방법으로, 소셜 텔레비전 시스템은 현재 다른 장소에 있는 TV 시청자들 간의 사회적 상호작용을 가능하게 한다. 이러한 시스템은 TV를 이용하는 친구들 사이의 더 큰 (A) 유대감을 만들어내는 것으로 알려져 있다. 한 현장 연구에서는 나이가 30 ~ 36세인 다섯 명의 친구들이 각자 집에서 TV를 보는 동안 어떻게 의사소통을 하는지에 초점을 두었다. (소셜 텔레비전) 기술은 그들이 어떤 친구가 TV를 보고 있으며 무엇을 보고 있는지를 알도록 (B) 허용했다. 그들은 소셜 텔레비전을 통해 어떤 방식으로 의사소통을 할 것인지, 즉 음성 채팅을 할 것인지 문자 채팅을 할 것인지를 선택했다. 연구에서는 음성보다 문자에 대한 강력한 선호가 있음을 보여주었다. 이용자들은 문자 채팅을 (C) 선호하는 두 가지 주된 이유를 제시했다. 첫째로, 문자 채팅은 노력과 주의력을 덜 요구하며, 음성 채팅보다 더 재미있었다. 둘째로, 연구 참여자들은 문자 채팅이 더 공손하다고 여겼다.

Why? 왜 정답일까?

(A) 'As a way to encourage TV viewing, social television systems now enable social interaction among TV viewers in different locations.'에서 소셜 텔레비전 시스템은 시청자 간의 상호작용을 가능하게 한다고 했으므로 이를 통해 시청자들 사이에는 유대감이 생겨날 것임을 알 수 있다. 따라서 (A)에 적절한 말은 'connectedness (유대감)'이다.
(B) 주어 The technology는 소셜 텔레비전 기술을 가리키는 것인데 이 기술은 시청자 간의 상호작용이 일어나도록 돕는 기술이다. 따라서 이 기술을 통해 다른 친구가 TV를 보고 있는지, 본다면 무엇을 보고 있는지를 아는 것이 '가능해진다'라는 뜻이 되도록 (B)에는 'allowed(허용했다)'를 넣는 것이 적절하다.
(C) 'The study showed a strong preference for text over voice.'에서 실험 참여자들은 음성보다 문자에 대한 '선호'가 있었다고 이야기하므로 (C)에 적절한 말은 'favoring(선호하는)'이다. 정답은 ③ '(A) connectedness(유대감) – (B) allowed(허용했다) – (C) favoring(선호하는)'이다.

• interaction ⓝ 상호작용
• encourage ⓥ 장려하다, 고무하다
• interaction ⓝ 상호작용
• communicate ⓥ 의사소통하다
• preference ⓝ 선호
• participant ⓝ 참여자, 참가자
• cultural ⓐ 문화적인, 문화의
• enable ⓥ 가능하게 하다
• location ⓝ 장소, 위치
• forbid ⓥ 금지하다
• require ⓥ 요구하다, 필요로 하다
• polite ⓐ 공손한

구문 풀이

[8행] The technology allowed them to see which of the friends were
　　　　　　　　　　　동사　목적어　　목적격 보어(to부정사)　　간접의문문1
watching TV and what they were watching.
　　　　　　　　　간접의문문2

★★★ 1등급 대비 고난도 2점 문제

07 인간이 쉽게 과열되지 않는 이유 　정답률 44% | 정답 ②

다음 빈칸에 들어갈 말로 가장 적절한 것을 고르시오.

① hot weather – 더운 날씨
✓② a lack of fur – 털의 부족
③ muscle strength – 근력
④ excessive exercise – 과도한 운동
⑤ a diversity of species – 다양한 종들

[본문 해석]

인간들은 최고의 장거리 달리기 선수들이다. 한 사람과 침팬지가 달리기를 시작하자마자 그들은 둘 다 더위를 느낀다. 침팬지는 빠르게 체온이 오르지만, 인간들은 그렇지 않은데, 그들은 신체 열을 떨어뜨리는 것을 훨씬 잘하기 때문

이다. 유력한 한 이론에 따르면, 털이 더 적으면 더 시원하고 장거리 달리기에 더 효과적인 것을 의미하기 때문에 선조들은 잇따른 세대에 걸쳐서 털을 잃었다. 그런 능력은 우리 조상들이 먹잇감을 이기고 앞질러서 달리게 했다. 덥고 습한 날에 여분의 재킷 두 개를 — 혹은 더 좋게는, 털 코트를 — 입는 것을 시도하고 1마일을 뛰어라. 이제, 그 재킷을 벗고 다시 시도하라. 당신은 <u>털의 부족</u>이 만드는 차이점이 무엇인지 알 것이다.

Why? 왜 정답일까?

'According to one leading theory, ancestral humans lost their hair over successive generations because less hair meant cooler, more effective long-distance running.'에서 털이 더 적으면 더 시원해지고 장거리 달리기를 더 잘하게 되므로 인간의 연이은 세대에 걸쳐 계속 털이 적어지게 되었다고 설명하고 있다. 따라서 빈칸에 들어갈 말로 가장 적절한 것은 ② '털의 부족'이다.

- **overheat** ⓥ 과열되다
- **ancestral** ⓐ 선조의, 조상의
- **generation** ⓝ 세대
- **outrun** ⓥ ~보다 빨리 달리다
- **lack** ⓝ 부족, 결여
- **leading** ⓐ 선도적인
- **successive** ⓐ 잇따른, 연속적인
- **effective** ⓐ 효과적인
- **humid** ⓐ 습한
- **excessive** ⓐ 과도한

구문 풀이

3행 Chimps quickly overheat; humans do not, because they are much better at shedding body heat.
주어1 / 동사1 / 주어2 / 동사2(= do not overheat) / 이유 접속사
「be good at + 동명사」: ~을 잘하다

★★ 문제 해결 꿀~팁 ★★

▶ 많이 틀린 이유는?
인간이 침팬지와 다르게 장시간을 달려도 크게 과열되지 않는 근본적인 이유를 파악해야 한다. ①의 '더운 날씨'는 원인으로 지적되지 않았고, ④의 '과도한 운동' 또한 '장거리 달리기'를 비약시킨 표현에 불과하다.
▶ 문제 해결 방법은?
글 중간에서 조상들이 '털을 잃어왔다'는 내용이 등장한 이유를 생각해 본다. 이는 인간이 다른 동물에 비해 '털이 적기 때문에' 체온 조절에 능하다는 내용을 보충하기 위한 것이다.

★★★ 1등급 대비 고난도 3점 문제

08 운동 에너지와 위치 에너지 　　정답률 35% | 정답 ⑤

글의 흐름으로 보아, 주어진 문장이 들어가기에 가장 적절한 곳을 고르시오. [3점]

[본문 해석]
일반적으로 운동 에너지는 운동과 관련 있는 에너지인 반면에, 위치 에너지는 물리계에 '저장되는' 에너지를 나타낸다. 게다가 총 에너지는 항상 보존된다. ① 그러나 총 에너지가 변하지 않는 채로 있는 반면 총 에너지의 운동과 위치 에너지 비율은 항상 변할 수 있다. ② 예를 들어 앞뒤로 흔들리는 추를 상상해 보자. ③ 그것은 흔들릴 때 호 모양으로 쓸어내리듯 움직이다가, 그러고 나서 최고점에 가까워지면서 속도가 줄어드는데, 이 지점에서 추는 더 이상 움직이지 않는다. ④ 그래서 이 지점에서 에너지는 완전히 위치 에너지로 주어지게 된다. ⑤ 하지만 이 짧은 순간의 멈춤 이후에 그 추는 다시 뒤로 흔들리게 되며, 따라서 총 에너지의 일부가 그때 운동 에너지의 형태로 주어진다. 그래서 그 추가 흔들리면서 운동과 위치 에너지는 끊임없이 서로 바뀐다.

Why? 왜 정답일까?

위치 에너지와 운동 에너지는 같은 에너지 총량 안에서 계속 서로 바뀐다는 내용의 글로, ② 뒤의 문장부터 흔들리는 추를 예로 들어 이 변화를 설명하고 있다. ⑤ 앞의 두 문장에서 추의 높이가 최고점에 이르면 추는 더 이상 움직이지 않고, 모든 에너지가 위치 에너지로 바뀐다고 언급한다. 주어진 문장은 But으로 흐름을 전환하며, 이 짧은 멈춤(this brief moment of rest) 이후로 다시 추가 뒤로 흔들리면서 일부 에너지가 다시 운동 에너지로 바뀐다고 설명한다. ⑤ 뒤의 문장은 그리하여 운동 에너지와 위치 에너지는 서로 끊임없이 교환되는 관계라는 결론을 제시한다. 따라서 주어진 문장이 들어가기에 가장 적절한 곳은 ⑤이다.

- **brief** ⓐ 짧은
- **kinetic energy** 운동 에너지
- **conserve** ⓥ 보존하다
- **sweep out** 쓸어내리다
- **constantly** ⓐ𝚍 지속적으로, 끊임없이
- **pendulum** ⓝ (시계의) 추
- **potential energy** 위치 에너지
- **swing back and forth** 앞뒤로 흔들리다
- **arc** ⓝ 호(弧)

구문 풀이

11행 When it swings, it sweeps out an arc and then slows down as it comes closer to its highest point, where the pendulum does not move at all.
접속사(~하면서, ~함에 따라) / 동사1 / 선행사 / 관계부사(계속적 용법) / 동사2

★★ 문제 해결 꿀~팁 ★★

▶ 많이 틀린 이유는?
④ 앞의 does not move가 바로 주어진 문장의 this brief moment of rest로 연결되는 것처럼 보일 수 있지만, 사실 이 does not move는 ④ 뒤의 at this point로 연결된다. 이 '움직이지 않는' 지점에서 에너지는 모두 위치에너지로 전환되었음을 알 수 있다는 것이다.
▶ 문제 해결 방법은?
⑤ 앞뒤 문장에 모두 결론의 So가 나오므로, 이 So가 어느 내용에 이어져야 하는지에 주목하며 읽는다.

★★★ 1등급 대비 고난도 3점 문제

09 의견 불일치가 학생들에게 미치는 영향 　　정답률 38% | 정답 ①

다음 글의 내용을 한 문장으로 요약하고자 한다. 빈칸 (A), (B)에 들어갈 말로 가장 적절한 것은? [3점]

	(A)		(B)
✓①	increases 증가한다	……	differ 의견을 달리하도록
②	increases 증가한다	……	approve 동의하도록
③	increases 증가한다	……	cooperate 협력하도록
④	decreases 감소한다	……	participate 참여하도록
⑤	decreases 감소한다	……	argue 논쟁하도록

[본문 해석]
Nancy Lowry와 David Johnson은 교수환경을 연구하고자 5학년과 6학년 학생들이 한 주제에 대해 상호작용을 하게 하는 실험을 진행했다. 한 집단에서는 토론이 합의를 도출하는 방식으로 유도되었다. 두 번째 집단에서는 토론이 옳은 정답에 대해 불일치를 낳도록 설계되었다. 쉽게 합의에 도달한 학생들은 주제에 흥미를 덜 보이고 더 적게 공부했으며 부가적인 정보를 얻기 위해 도서관에 가는 경향이 더 적었다. 그러나 가장 눈에 띄는 차이는 교사가 학생들에게 점심시간 동안 토론 주제와 관련된 특별한 영화를 보여주었을 때 나타났다! 동의한 집단의 18퍼센트만이 영화를 보기 위해 점심시간을 놓쳤으나 동의하지 않은 집단의 45퍼센트는 그 영화를 보기 위해 남았다. 집단 내에서 누가 옳았는지 알기 위해 지식 격차를 메우려는 열망은 미끄럼틀과 정글짐을 향한 열망보다 더 강했던 것이다.

➡ 위 연구에 따르면 주제에 대한 학생들의 흥미는 학생들이 (B) <u>의견을 달리</u>하도록 장려될 때 (A) <u>증가한다</u>.

Why? 왜 정답일까?

실험 결과를 제시한 마지막 두 문장에서 토론 중 의견 불일치를 경험한 학생들은 점심시간에 토론 주제와 관련된 영화를 보여주었을 때 거의 절반 가까이 남아서 볼 정도로 그 주제에 대한 관심이 크게 증가해 있었다고 한다. 따라서 요약문의 빈칸 (A), (B)에 들어갈 말로 가장 적절한 것은 ① '(A) increases(증가한다), (B) differ(의견을 달리하도록)'이다.

- **experiment** ⓝ 실험
- **assign** ⓥ (과업 등을) 할당하다
- **noticeable** ⓐ 두드러지는, 눈에 띄는
- **reveal** ⓥ 드러내다, 밝히다
- **thirst** ⓝ 갈망, 갈증
- **approve** ⓥ 동의하다, 승인하다
- **environment** ⓝ 환경
- **disagreement** ⓝ 불일치, 불화
- **difference** ⓝ 차이
- **film** ⓝ 영화
- **fill a gap** 격차를 메우다

구문 풀이

16행 The thirst (to fill a knowledge gap) — (to find out who was right within the group) — can be more powerful than the thirst for slides and jungle gyms.
주어 / 형용사적 용법 / ( ): 삽입구('to fill ~' 보충 설명) / 동사

★★ 문제 해결 꿀~팁 ★★

▶ 많이 틀린 이유는?

'The most noticeable difference, ~' 이후로 제시되는 실험 결과를 잘 이해해야 한다. 결과에 따르면 토론 중 합의에 도달했던 그룹보다 합의에 이르지 못하고 의견이 서로 불일치했던 그룹에서 더 많은 수가 토론 주제와 관련된 영화를 추가로 보려 남았다고 한다.

②, ③은 서로의 의견에 '동의하거나' '협력할' 때 학생들의 흥미가 커질 수 있다는 내용을 완성하는데, 이는 주제와 반대된다.

▶ 문제 해결 방법은?

글의 disagreement가 ①의 differ로 재진술된 것임에 유의한다.

10-12 가난한 노인의 부탁에 따라 레슬링 시합에서 져 준 James

[본문 해석]

(A)

「James Walker는 유명한 레슬링 선수였고 레슬링으로 생계를 유지했다.」 그의 마을에는 마을의 지도자가 하루를 정해 James가 자신의 기술을 보여 주는 전통이 있었다. 지도자는 어느 날 James가 레슬링 선수로서 기술을 보여 줄 것임을 알렸고, 사람들에게 상금을 위해 (a) 그에게 도전할 사람이 있는지 물었다.

(C)

모두가 군중 속에서 주위를 둘러보던 중 한 노인이 일어나서 떨리는 목소리로 "내가 (c) 그와의 경기에 참가하겠소."라고 말했다. 모두가 그것이 농담이라고 여기며 웃음을 터뜨렸다. James는 그를 바로 뭉개버릴 것이었다. 「관례에 따라 지도자는 본인의 자유 의지로 경기에 참여하려는 사람을 막을 수가 없었기에 그 노인이 그 레슬링 선수에게 도전하는 것을 허용했다.」— 「」: 12번 ④의 근거 불일치

(B)

「James가 그 노인을 봤을 때, 그는 말문이 막혔다.」 다른 모든 사람과 마찬가지로 그는 그 노인이 죽기를 바란다고 생각했다. (b) 그(노인)가 James에게 할 말이 있었기 때문에 노인은 James에게 더 가까이 와줄 것을 청했다. James가 더 가까이 가자 노인은 "내가 이기는 게 불가능하다는 것은 알고 있지만 내 아이들이 집에서 굶주리고 있소.」 내가 상금으로 아이들에게 밥을 먹일 수 있게 나에게 이 시합을 져줄 수 있소?"라고 속삭였다.

(D)

James는 곤경에 처한 사람을 도울 아주 좋은 기회를 얻었다고 생각했다. (d) 그는 아무도 그 시합이 정해졌다고 의심하지 못하도록 몇 가지 동작을 했다. 「그러나 그는 전력을 다하지 않았고 그 노인이 이기게 했다.」 노인은 상금을 받고 매우 기뻤다. 그날 밤 James는 (e) 그가 이제껏 느껴보지 못한 가장 큰 승리감을 느꼈다.

- renowned ⓐ 유명한
- exhibit ⓥ 보여주다, 전시하다
- whisper ⓥ 속삭이다
- competition ⓝ 대회, 경쟁
- of one's own free will 자유 의지로
- suspect ⓥ 의심하다
- demonstrate ⓥ (시범을) 보이다
- speechless ⓐ 말문이 막힌
- starve ⓥ 굶주리다
- crush ⓥ 뭉개다, 진압하다, 눌러 부수다
- distress ⓝ 곤경, 괴로움
- overjoyed ⓐ 매우 기뻐하는

구문 풀이

(A) 2행 In his town, there was a tradition [in which the leader of the town chose a day [when James demonstrated his skills]].
（동사 / 주어(선행사) / = where / 선행사 / 관계부사）

(B) 7행 Can you lose this competition to me so (that) I can feed them with the prize money?
（~하기 위해, ~하도록）

(C) 5행 According to the law, the leader could not stop someone [who of his own free will entered the competition], so he allowed the old man to challenge the wrestler.
（주격 관계대명사 / 선행사 / 부사구 / 동사）
「allow+목적어+to부정사 : ~이 …하게 허락하다」

---

10 글의 순서 파악 정답률 74% | 정답 ②

주어진 글 (A)에 이어질 내용을 순서에 맞게 배열한 것으로 가장 적절한 것은?

① (B) – (D) – (C)
③ (C) – (D) – (B)
⑤ (D) – (C) – (B)
✓② (C) – (B) – (D)
④ (D) – (B) – (C)

Why? 왜 정답일까?

(A)에서 마을의 유명한 레슬링 선수였던 James가 레슬링 기술을 선보이는 날이 돌아왔고, 마을 지도자는 그에게 도전할 의사가 있는 사람이 있는지 물었다고 했다. 이어서 어떤 노인이 도전자로 나섰다는 내용의 (C)가 연결된다. 이 (C)는 지도자가 관례에 따라 노인의 도전을 허락해주었다는 내용으로 끝나는데, (B)는 James가 상대로 나선 노인을 보고 말문이 막혔다는 내용으로 시작한다. 이어서 (B)의 후반부는 노인이 James에게 자신의 궁핍한 사정을 설명하며 져줄 것을 부탁했다는 내용으로 마무리되고, (D)는 James가 이 부탁에 응하여 시합에서 전력을 다하지 않고 실제로 져 준 뒤 오히려 뿌듯해 했다는 결말을 제시한다. 따라서 글의 순서로 가장 적절한 것은 ② '(C) – (B) – (D)' 이다.

---

11 지칭 추론 정답률 73% | 정답 ②

밑줄 친 (a) ~ (e) 중에서 가리키는 대상이 나머지 넷과 다른 것은?

① (a) ✓② (b) ③ (c) ④ (d) ⑤ (e)

Why? 왜 정답일까?

(a), (c), (d), (e)는 James를, (b)는 The old man을 가리키므로, (a) ~ (e) 중에서 가리키는 대상이 다른 하나는 ② '(b)'이다.

---

12 세부 내용 파악 정답률 79% | 정답 ④

윗글에 관한 내용으로 적절하지 않은 것은?

① James는 레슬링으로 생계를 유지했다.
② James는 노인을 보고 말문이 막혔다.
③ 노인의 아이들은 집에서 굶주리고 있었다.
✓④ 지도자는 노인이 James와 겨루는 것을 말렸다.
⑤ James는 노인과의 시합에서 전력을 다하지 않았다.

Why? 왜 정답일까?

(C) 'According to the law, the leader could not stop someone who of his own free will entered the competition, so he allowed the old man to challenge the wrestler.'에서 관례상 지도자는 노인이 James와 겨루는 것을 말릴 수 없었기에 노인과 James의 겨루기를 허락했다고 하였다. 따라서 내용과 일치하지 않는 것은 ④ '지도자는 노인이 James와 겨루는 것을 말렸다.'이다.

Why? 왜 오답일까?

① (A) '~ he made his living through wrestling.'의 내용과 일치한다.
② (B) 'When James saw the old man, he was speechless.'의 내용과 일치한다.
③ (B) 'I know it is impossible for me to win but my children are starving at home.'의 내용과 일치한다.
⑤ (D) 'However, he did not use his full strength and allowed the old man to win.'의 내용과 일치한다.

DAY 25 | 20분 미니 모의고사

01 ③	02 ①	03 ④	04 ④	05 ④
06 ⑤	07 ④	08 ②	09 ⑤	10 ⑤
11 ②	12 ④			

01 산책로 조성 계획에 대한 재고 요청　정답률 65% | 정답 ③

다음 글의 목적으로 가장 적절한 것은?
① 환경 보호 캠페인 참여를 부탁하려고
② 지역 관광 프로그램에 대해 문의하려고
☑ 산책로 조성 계획의 재고를 요청하려고
④ 보행자 안전을 위해 인도 설치를 건의하려고
⑤ 야생 동물 보호구역 관리의 문제점을 지적하려고

[본문 해석]
담당자 귀하

저는 Boulder 시에서 태어나고 자랐으며 평생 동안 우리의 경치 좋은 자연 공간을 누려왔습니다. 제안된 Pine Hill 산책로가 지나가게 될 그 땅은 다양한 종들의 서식지입니다. 야생 동물은 개발의 압력에 직면해 있고, 이 동물들은 인간 활동으로부터 숨을 수 있는 공간이 필요합니다. 비록 산책로는 우리가 자연 세계에 접근하고 그 안의 야생 동물을 감상할 수 있는 훌륭한 원천의 역할을 하지만, 만약 우리가 계속해서 과도한 산책로들로 서식지를 파괴한다면 야생 동물은 이 지역들을 이용하는 것을 중단할 것입니다. 제안된 산책로가 정말로 필요한지 재고해 주시기 바랍니다.

Tyler Stuart 드림

Why? 왜 정답일까?
산책로가 지나갈 땅에 다양한 야생 동물 종이 서식하므로 산책로 조성 계획을 재고해줄 것을 요청하는 글이다(Please reconsider whether the proposed trail is absolutely necessary.). 따라서 글의 목적으로 가장 적절한 것은 ③ '산책로 조성 계획의 재고를 요청하려고'이다.

- scenic ⓐ 경치 좋은
- wildlife ⓝ 야생 동물
- appreciate ⓥ 감상하다, 제대로 이해하다
- absolutely ⓐⓓ 정말로, 전적으로
- propose ⓥ 제안하다
- serve as ~의 역할을 하다
- habitat ⓝ 서식지

구문 풀이

8행 Although trails serve as a wonderful source for us to access the natural world and appreciate the wildlife within it, if we continue to destroy habitats with excess trails, the wildlife will stop using these areas.

02 진정한 발전을 이끄는 사고방식　정답률 66% | 정답 ①

다음 글의 요지로 가장 적절한 것은?
☑ 발전은 한 번의 목표 성취가 아닌 지속적인 개선 과정에 의해 결정된다.
② 결승선을 통과하기 위해 장시간 노력해야 원하는 바를 얻을 수 있다.
③ 성공을 위해서는 구체적인 목표를 설정하는 것이 중요하다.
④ 지난 과정을 끊임없이 반복하는 것이 성공의 지름길이다.
⑤ 목표 지향적 성향이 강할수록 발전이 빠르게 이루어진다.

[본문 해석]
목표 지향적인 사고방식은 "요요" 효과를 낼 수 있다. 많은 달리기 선수들이 몇 달 동안 열심히 연습하지만, 결승선을 통과하는 순간 훈련을 중단한다. 그 경기는 더 이상 그들에게 동기를 주지 않는다. 당신의 모든 노력이 특정한 목표에 집중될 때, 당신이 그것을 성취한 후에 당신을 앞으로 밀고 나갈 수 있는 것 중에 무엇이 남았는가? 이것이 많은 사람들이 목표를 성취한 후 옛 습관으로 되돌아가는 자신을 발견하는 이유다. 목표를 설정하는 목적은 경기에서 이기기 위함이다. 시스템을 구축하는 목적은 게임을 계속하기 위한 것이다. 진정한 장기적 사고는 목표가 없는 사고이다. 그것은 어떤 하나의 성취에 관한 것이 아니다. 그것은 끝없는 정제와 지속적인 개선의 순환에 관한 것이다. 궁극적으로, 당신의 발전을 결정짓는 것은 그 과정에 당신이 몰두하는 것이다.

Why? 왜 정답일까?
마지막 세 문장인 'It's not about any single accomplishment. It is about the cycle of endless refinement and continuous improvement. Ultimately, it is your commitment to the process ~'에서 발전을 결정 짓는 것은 목표 또는 목표의 성취가 아니고 개선의 순환을 유지시키는 것, 즉 과정에 몰두하는 것임을 서술하고 있다. 따라서 글의 요지로 가장 적절한 것은 ① '발전은 한 번의 목표 성취가 아닌 지속적인 개선 과정에 의해 결정된다.'이다.

- goal-oriented ⓐ 목표 지향적인
- work hard 열심히 일하다
- particular ⓐ 특정한
- long-term ⓐ 장기적인
- improvement ⓝ 개선, 향상
- determine ⓥ 결정하다
- mind-set ⓝ 사고방식
- motivate ⓥ 동기를 부여하다
- accomplish ⓥ 성취하다
- refinement ⓝ 정제, 개선
- commitment ⓝ 몰두, 전념
- progress ⓝ 발전

구문 풀이

13행 Ultimately, it is your commitment to the process that will determine your progress.
「it is + 강조하는 말 + that + 나머지 문장 : 강조구문(~한 것은 바로 …이다)」

03 Bessie Coleman의 생애　정답률 85% | 정답 ④

Bessie Coleman에 관한 다음 글의 내용과 일치하지 않는 것은?
① 11살 때 Wright 형제의 첫 비행 소식을 들었다.
② 비행 수업을 듣기 위해 파리로 가야 했다.
③ 국제 조종사 면허를 딴 최초의 흑인 여성이 되었다.
☑ 유럽에서 에어쇼에 첫 출현을 했다.
⑤ 다음 세대가 비행의 꿈을 추구하도록 영감을 주었다.

[본문 해석]
Bessie Coleman은 1892년에 텍사스에서 태어났다. 『그녀가 11살이었을 때 그녀는 Wright 형제가 첫 비행을 했다는 것을 들었다.』그때부터 그녀는 자신이 하늘을 높이 날아오르는 그 날을 꿈꿨다. 23살 때 Coleman은 시카고로 이사했고 그곳에서 식당 일을 하여 비행 수업을 위한 돈을 모았다. 『그러나 그 당시 미국 비행 학교가 여성이나 흑인의 입학을 허가하지 않았기 때문에 그녀는 비행 수업을 듣기 위해 파리로 가야 했다.』『1921년에 그녀는 마침내 국제 조종사 면허를 딴 최초의 흑인 여성이 되었다.』『그녀는 또한 유럽에서 곡예 비행을 공부했고 1922년에 뉴욕의 에어쇼에 첫 출현을 했다.』『여성 비행 개척자로서 그녀는 다음 세대가 비행의 꿈을 추구하도록 영감을 주었다.』

Why? 왜 정답일까?
'She also studied flying acrobatics in Europe and made her first appearance in an airshow in New York in 1922.'에 따르면 Coleman은 유럽에서 곡예 비행을 공부한 후 첫 에어쇼를 뉴욕에서 치렀다. 따라서 내용과 일치하지 않는 것은 ④ '유럽에서 에어쇼에 첫 출현을 했다.'이다.

Why? 왜 오답일까?
① 'When she was eleven, she was told that the Wright brothers had flown their first plane.'의 내용과 일치한다.
② 'However, she had to travel to Paris to take flying lessons ~'의 내용과 일치한다.
③ 'In 1921, she finally became the first Black woman to earn an international pilot's license.'의 내용과 일치한다.
⑤ '~ she inspired the next generation to pursue their dreams of flying.'의 내용과 일치한다.

- soar ⓥ 솟아오르다
- inspire ⓥ 영감을 주다
- pioneer ⓝ 선구자

구문 풀이

1행 When she was eleven, she was told {that the Wright brothers had flown their first plane}. { } : 목적어

04 학교 축제 관련 온라인 회의
정답률 83% | 정답 ④

Virtual Idea Exchange에 관한 다음 안내문의 내용과 일치하는 것은?

① 동아리 회원이라면 누구나 참여 가능하다.
② 티켓 판매는 논의 대상에서 제외된다.
③ 회의는 3시간 동안 열린다.
☑ 접속 링크를 문자로 받는다.
⑤ 채팅방 입장 시 동아리명으로 참여해야 한다.

[본문 해석]

Virtual Idea Exchange

실시간으로 접속하여 다가오는 학교 축제에 관해 토론하세요.

□ 목표
• 학교 축제를 계획하고 아이디어를 공유하세요.

□ 『참가자 : 동아리장만』──『 』:①의 근거 불일치

□ 토론 내용
• 주제   • 『티켓 판매』 • 예산
          『 』:②의 근거 불일치

□ 『날짜 & 시간 : 2021년 6월 25일 금요일 오후 5시 ~ 7시』──『 』:③의 근거 불일치

□ 참고사항
• 『회의 10분 전에 문자 메시지로 전송되는 접속 링크를 받아서 클릭하세요.』──『 』:④의 근거 일치
• 『대화방에 들어올 때 실명을 입력하세요.』──『 』:⑤의 근거 불일치

Why? 왜 정답일까?

'Get the access link by text message 10 minutes before the meeting and click it.'에서 회의 10분 전에 회의 접속 링크가 문자 메시지로 전송된다고 하므로, 안내문의 내용과 일치하는 것은 ④ '접속 링크를 문자로 받는다.'이다.

Why? 왜 오답일까?

① 'Participants: Club leaders only'에서 동아리장들만 참여 가능하다고 하였다.
② 'What to Discuss / Ticket sales'에서 티켓 판매가 논의 대상에 포함된다고 하였다.
③ 'Date & Time: 5 to 7 p.m. on Friday, June 25th, 2021'에서 회의는 오후 5시부터 7시까지 2시간 동안 열린다고 하였다.
⑤ 'Type your real name when you enter the chatroom.'에서 채팅방에 들어올 때 실명을 입력해야 한다고 하였다.

● virtual ⓐ (컴퓨터를 이용한) 가상의
● upcoming ⓐ 다가오는
● real time 실시간
● budget ⓝ 예산

★★★ 1등급 대비 고난도 3점 문제

05 인공 지능의 핵심 특징
정답률 44% | 정답 ④

다음 글의 밑줄 친 부분 중, 어법상 틀린 것은? [3점]

[본문 해석]

여러분은 인공 지능으로 구동되는 기계가 할 수 있는 몇 가지 일에 대한 헤드라인들을 뉴스에서 본 적이 있을 것이다. 하지만, AI로 구동되는 기계가 실제로 수행할 수 있는 모든 작업을 고려한다면 꽤 놀라울 것이다! 인공 지능의 핵심 특징들 중 하나는 이것에 새로운 작업에 특화된 프로그래밍이 필요하다기보다는, 이것(인공 지능)이 기계가 새로운 것을 학습할 수 있게 한다는 것이다. 그러므로, 미래 컴퓨터와 과거 컴퓨터 사이의 핵심 차이점은 미래의 컴퓨터가 학습하고 스스로 개선할 수 있을 것이라는 점이다. 가까운 미래에, 스마트 가상 비서는 여러분의 가장 가까운 친구나 가족보다도 여러분에 관해 더 많이 알게 될 것이다. 그것이 우리의 삶을 어떻게 변화시킬지 상상할 수 있는가? 이러한 변화가 바로 새로운 기술들이 우리 세계에 미칠 영향을 인식하는 것이 아주 중요한 이유이다.

Why? 왜 정답일까?

비교급 구문의 than 앞에 일반동사인 will know가 나오므로, than 뒤에 일반동사의 대동사인 do를 써야 한다. 따라서 어법상 틀린 것은 ④이다.

Why? 왜 오답일까?

① 앞에 나온 all the tasks를 꾸미면서 뒤에 목적어가 없는 문장(AI-powered machines could actually perform)을 연결하는 목적격 관계대명사 that의 쓰임이 알맞다.

---

② 'one of the + 복수 명사'가 주어이므로 단수동사 is는 알맞게 쓰였다.
③ 앞의 복수 명사 computers를 가리키는 복수 대명사 those가 알맞게 쓰였다.
⑤ 가주어 it에 대응되는 진주어 역할의 to부정사구 to recognize가 알맞게 쓰였다.

● artificial intelligence 인공 지능
● mind-blowing ⓐ 너무도 감동적인
● self-improve ⓥ 자가 발전하다
● assistant ⓝ 조수, 비서
● recognize ⓥ 인식하다, 깨닫다
● perform ⓥ 수행하다
● feature ⓝ 특징
● virtual ⓐ 가상의
● exactly ⓐ 바로, 정확히

구문 풀이

11행 In the near future, smart virtual assistants will know more about you than your closest friends and family members do.
대동사(= know about you)

★★ 문제 해결 꿀~팁 ★★

▶ 많이 틀린 이유는?
③이 포함된 문장을 보면, 문맥상 미래의 컴퓨터와 과거의 '컴퓨터(computers)'를 비교한다는 의미를 나타내면서 컴퓨터라는 명사의 중복을 피하기 위해 those를 알맞게 썼다. 이렇듯 대명사에 밑줄이 있으면 가장 기본적으로 대명사의 수 일치를 집중적으로 살펴봐야 한다.
▶ 문제 해결 방법은?
정답인 ④ are는 대동사의 쓰임을 묻는 선택지이다. 대동사는 간단한 듯 싶어도 문맥을 전체적으로 살펴야 하기에 어렵게 나오면 한없이 어려워진다. 여기서는 비교구문의 than 앞뒤는 병렬구조를 이루므로 than 앞의 동사와 than 뒤의 동사가 서로 같은 종류여야 한다는 점에 집중하면 된다.

06 인류가 최초의 배를 만들게 된 이유
정답률 54% | 정답 ⑤

다음 글의 밑줄 친 부분 중, 문맥상 낱말의 쓰임이 적절하지 않은 것은?

[본문 해석]

유럽 최초의 호모 사피엔스는 주로 큰 사냥감, 특히 순록을 먹고 살았다. 심지어 이상적인 상황에서도, 이런 빠른 동물을 창이나 활과 화살로 사냥하는 것은 ① 불확실한 일이다. 그러나 순록에게는 인류가 인정사정없이 이용할 ② 약점이 있었는데, 그것은 순록이 수영을 잘 못한다는 것이었다. 순록은 물에 떠 있는 동안, 코를 물 위로 내놓으려고 애쓰면서 가지진 뿔을 높이 쳐들고 천천히 움직이기 때문에, 유례없이 ③ 공격받기 쉬운 상태가 된다. 어느 시점에선가, 석기 시대의 한 천재가 수면 위를 활주함으로써 자신이 얻을 엄청난 사냥의 ④ 이점을 깨닫고 최초의 배를 만들었다. ⑤ 힘들게(→ 쉽게) 따라잡아서 도살한 먹잇감을 일단 배 위로 끌어 올리면, 사체를 부족이 머무는 곳으로 가지고 가는 것은 육지보다는 배로 갈 때 훨씬 더 수월했을 것이다. 인류가 이런 장점을 다른 물품에 적용하는 데는 오랜 시간이 걸리지 않았을 것이다.

Why? 왜 정답일까?

현대 인류의 조상인 호모 사피엔스가 순록 사냥을 위해 배를 처음 만들게 되었음을 설명한 글이다. 'The reindeer, however, had a weakness that mankind would mercilessly exploit: it swam poorly. While afloat, it is uniquely vulnerable, ~'에서, 순록은 수영을 못하기에 물에서는 공격받기 쉬운 상태가 된다고 이야기하므로, 육지에서보다 물 위에서 순록을 사냥할 때 훨씬 '쉽게' 할 수 있었을 것이라는 내용을 추론할 수 있다. 따라서 문맥상 낱말의 쓰임이 적절하지 않은 것은 ⑤이다.

● primarily ⓐ 주로
● circumstances ⓝ 상황, 사정
● mercilessly ⓐ 인정사정없이, 무정하게
● antler ⓝ (사슴의) 가지진 뿔
● laboriously ⓐ 힘들게, 공을 들여서
● game ⓝ 사냥감, 먹이
● uncertain ⓐ 불확실한
● afloat ⓐ 물에 뜬
● glide over ~을 활주하다
● overtake ⓥ 따라잡다, 앞지르다, 추월하다

구문 풀이

6행 While afloat, it is uniquely vulnerable, moving slowly
『접속사 + 형용사 보어 : 생략 구문』   분사 구문
with its antlers held high as it struggles to keep its nose above water.
『with + 명사 + 분사 : ~한 채로』 ~하면서 ~하려고 분투하다   목적어 목적격 보어(전명구)

★★★ 1등급 대비 고난도 2점 문제

07 탁월함과 타인의 신뢰
정답률 50% | 정답 ④

다음 빈칸에 들어갈 말로 가장 적절한 것을 고르시오.

① Patience – 인내심　　② Sacrifice – 희생
③ Honesty – 정직함　　✓ Excellence – 탁월함
⑤ Creativity – 창의력

[본문 해석]

자기 직업에서 높은 수준으로 수행하는 사람들은 흔히 다른 사람들에게 즉각적인 신뢰를 얻는다. 사람들은 그들을 존경하고, 그들처럼 되고 싶어 하고, 그들과 연결되어 있다고 느낀다. 그들이 말할 때, 다른 사람들은 비록 그들의 기술 분야가 그들이 주는 조언과 전혀 관련이 없을지라도 경청한다. 세계적으로 유명한 농구 선수에 대해 생각해 보라. 그는 그가 농구를 하면서 그간 벌었던 것보다 광고로부터 더 많은 돈을 벌었다. 그것이 그가 광고하는 제품에 대한 그의 지식 때문일까? 아니다. 그것은 그가 농구로 할 수 있는 것 때문이다. 올림픽 메달리스트 수영 선수도 마찬가지이다. 사람들은 그가 수영장에서 할 수 있는 것 때문에 그의 말을 경청한다. 그리고 어떤 배우가 우리에게 특정 자동차를 운전해야 한다고 말할 때, 우리는 엔진에 대한 그의 전문 지식 때문에 경청하는 것은 아니다. 우리는 그의 재능을 존경하기 때문에 경청한다. 탁월함이 연결된다. 만약 당신이 어떤 분야에서 높은 수준의 능력을 갖고 있다면, 다른 사람들은 그것 때문에 당신과 연결되기를 원할 수도 있다.

Why? 왜 정답일까?

처음(Individuals who perform at a high level in their profession often have instant credibility with others.)과 마지막(If you possess a high level of ability in an area, others may desire to connect with you because of it.)에서 자기 분야에서 '높은 수준의 능력'을 가진 사람들은 다른 이들의 신뢰를 사기 쉽다고 언급하는 것으로 보아, 빈칸에 들어갈 말로 가장 적절한 것은 ④ '탁월함'이다.

- **profession** ⓝ 직업
- **credibility** ⓝ 신뢰
- **have nothing to do with** ~와 관련이 없다
- **endorsement** ⓝ 보증 선전
- **medalist** ⓝ 메달리스트
- **patience** ⓝ 인내심
- **instant** ⓐ 즉각적인
- **admire** ⓥ 존경하다
- **world-famous** ⓐ 세계적으로 유명한
- **endorse** ⓥ 보증하다, 홍보하다
- **expertise** ⓝ 전문 지식
- **sacrifice** ⓝ 희생

구문 풀이

7행 He has made more money from endorsements than he ever did playing basketball.
대동사(= made money)

★★ **문제 해결 꿀~팁** ★★

▶ 많이 틀린 이유는?
빈칸 바로 앞에서 '전문 지식' 때문이 아니라 '재능' 때문에 유명인들의 말을 듣게 된다고 하는데, 이것을 ② '희생'이나 ③ '정직함'의 사례로 볼 수는 없다.
▶ 문제 해결 방법은?
글 처음과 마지막에 요지가 반복 제시된다. 즉 주제문인 첫 문장을 보고 빈칸을 완성하면 간단하다.

08　머릿속 아이디어일 때 이미 완성된 미래　정답률 53% | 정답 ②

다음 빈칸에 들어갈 말로 가장 적절한 것을 고르시오. [3점]

① didn't even have the potential to accomplish
　성취할 잠재력조차 지니고 있지 않았던
✓ have mentally concluded about the future
　미래에 대해 머릿속에서 완성한
③ haven't been able to picture in our mind
　(전에는) 머릿속에 그릴 수 없었던
④ considered careless and irresponsible
　조심성 없고 무책임하다고 여겼던
⑤ have observed in some professionals
　몇몇 전문가에게서 관찰해 낸

[본문 해석]

우리 주변 세상의 모든 것은 시작되기 전에 그것을 만들어 낸 사람의 마음속에서 완성되었다. 우리가 사는 집, 우리가 운전하는 자동차, 우리 옷, 이 모든 것이 아이디어에서 시작했다. 각각의 아이디어는 그런 다음 첫 번째 못이 박히거나 첫 번째 천 조각이 재단되기에 앞서 연구되고, 다듬어지고, 완성되었다. 그 아이디어가 물리적 실체로 바뀌기 훨씬 전에 마음은 완제품을 분명하게 그렸다. 인간은 거의 똑같은 과정을 통해 자신의 미래를 설계한다. 우리는 미래가 어떤지에 대한 아이디어로 시작한다. 일정 기간에 걸쳐서 우리는 그 비전을 다듬어 완성한다. 머지않아, 우리의 모든 생각, 결정, 활동은 우리가 미래에 대해 머릿속에서 완성한 것을 생겨나게 하려고 모두 조화롭게 작용하게 된다.

Why? 왜 정답일까?

첫 문장에서 세상 모든 것은 실체가 있기 이전에 머릿속에서 이미 완성된 아이디어(finished in the mind of its creator)였다고 설명하는데, 글 중반부에서 우리 미래 역시 같은 식으로 설계된다고 말한다. 즉, 처음에 '이미 머릿속에서 만들어진' 아이디어가 다듬어지고 구현되는 과정이 똑같이 진행된다는 의미로, 빈칸에 들어갈 말로 가장 적절한 것은 ② '미래에 대해 머릿속에서 완성한'이다.

- **clothing** ⓝ 옷, 의복
- **perfect** ⓥ 완성하다, 완벽하게 하다
- **turn A into B** A를 B로 바꾸다
- **process** ⓝ 과정
- **before long** 머지않아
- **bring into existence** ~을 생겨나게 하다
- **careless** ⓐ 조심성 없는
- **professional** ⓝ 전문가 ⓐ 전문적인
- **refine** ⓥ 다듬다
- **nail** ⓝ 못
- **picture** ⓥ 상상하다, 그리다
- **over a period of time** 일정 기간에 걸쳐서
- **in harmony** 조화롭게
- **mentally** ⓐⓓ 머릿속에, 마음속으로
- **irresponsible** ⓐ 무책임한

구문 풀이

1행 Everything in the world around us was finished in the mind
주어(every-)　　　　　　　　동사(단수)
of its creator before it was started.

09　흡혈귀가 존재했을 수 없는 이유　정답률 62% | 정답 ⑤

주어진 글 다음에 이어질 글의 순서로 가장 적절한 것을 고르시오. [3점]

① (A) – (C) – (B)　　② (B) – (A) – (C)
③ (B) – (C) – (A)　　④ (C) – (A) – (B)
✓ (C) – (B) – (A)

[본문 해석]

전설에 따르면, 흡혈귀가 사람을 물면 그 사람은 다른 사람의 피를 갈구하는 흡혈귀로 변한다. 한 연구자는 이 대단히 잘 알려진 존재가 실존할 수 없다는 것을 증명하는 간단한 계산법을 생각해냈다.

(C) University of Central Florida의 물리학과 교수 Costas Efthimiou의 연구가 그 미신을 무너뜨렸다. 1600년 1월 1일에 인구가 막 5억 명을 넘겼다고 가정해 보자.

(B) 그날 최초의 흡혈귀가 생겨나서 한 달에 한 명을 물었다면, 1600년 2월 1일까지 흡혈귀가 둘 있었을 것이다. 한 달 뒤면 넷, 그다음 달은 여덟, 그리고 열여섯 등등으로 계속 늘어났을 것이다.

(A) 불과 2년 반 만에, 원래의 인류는 모두 흡혈귀가 되어 더 이상 남아 있지 않았을 것이다. 하지만 주위를 둘러보라. 흡혈귀가 세상을 정복하였는가? 아니다. 왜냐하면 흡혈귀는 존재하지 않으니까.

Why? 왜 정답일까?

흡혈귀가 존재했음을 부정하는 계산식을 생각해낸 사람이 있다는 내용의 주어진 글 뒤에는, 먼저 1600년 1월 1일에 인구가 5억 명이 넘었다고 가정해 보자며 계산식에 관해 설명하기 시작하는 (C)가 연결된다. 이어서 (B)는 (C)에서 언급한 날짜를 that day로 가리키며, 흡혈귀가 달마다 두 배씩 늘어가는 상황을 가정해 보자고 설명한다. 마지막으로 (A)는 (C) – (B)의 상황이 성립한다면 5억 명의 사람들이 불과 2년 반 만에 모두 흡혈귀로 변했을 것인데, 인류는 현재까지 지속되고 있으므로 흡혈귀가 존재할 수 없다는 결론을 제시하고 있다. 따라서 글의 순서로 가장 적절한 것은 ⑤ '(C) – (B) – (A)'이다.

- **legend** ⓝ 전설
- **come into existence** 생기다, 나타나다
- **myth** ⓝ 미신, (잘못된) 통념
- **take over** ~을 지배하다, 장악하다
- **break down** 무너뜨리다

구문 풀이

6행 In just two-and-a-half years, the original human population would all have become vampires with no humans left.
「would have + 과거분사 : ~했을 것이다」（가정법 과거완료 주절）　「with + 명사 + 과거분사 : ~이 …된 채로」

10　보완재의 개념　정답률 50% | 정답 ⑤

글의 흐름으로 보아, 주어진 문장이 들어가기에 가장 적절한 곳을 고르시오.

[본문 해석]

'보완재'는 종종 또 다른 제품과 함께 소비되는 제품이다. ① 예를 들어, 팝콘

DAY 25

은 영화에 대한 보완재인 한편, 여행 베개는 긴 비행기 여행에 대한 보완재이다. ② 한 제품의 인기가 높아지면 그것의 보완재 판매량도 늘어난다. ③ 여러분은 이미 인기가 있는 (또는 곧 있을) 다른 제품을 보완하는 제품을 생산해서 여러분의 제품에 대한 꾸준한 수요 흐름을 보장할 수 있다. ④ 일부 제품들은 완벽한 보완적 상태를 누리고 있고, 그것들은 램프와 전구와 같이 함께 소비되어야 한다. ⑤ 그러나 고객들이 그 제품에 완전히 고정되어 있지 않을 수 있으므로, 어떤 제품이 완벽하게 보완적이라고 가정하지 말라. 예를 들어, 비록 운전자들이 차를 운전하기 위해 휘발유를 구매할 필요가 있는 것처럼 보이기는 해도, 이들이 전기 자동차로 바꿀 수도 있다.

Why? 왜 정답일까?

보완재에 관해 설명하는 글이다. ⑤ 앞에서 일부 제품은 램프 – 전구의 예시처럼 완벽히 서로 보완 관계에 있다고 하는데, ⑤ 뒤에서는 자동차 – 기름의 예시를 들며, 운전자들이 전기 차로 넘어갈 수도 있기 때문에 둘을 완벽한 보완 관계로 볼 수 없다고 한다. 즉, ⑤ 앞뒤로 내용이 서로 반대된다. 이때 주어진 문장은 '보완재인 두 재화가 항상 보완 관계에 있을 거라고 가정하지 말라'는 내용으로, **However**가 있어 흐름 전환을 적절히 유도한다. 따라서 주어진 문장이 들어가기에 가장 적절한 곳은 ⑤이다.

- **assume** ⓥ 가정하다
- **locked in** 갇힌, 고정된
- **journey** ⓝ 여정
- **ensure** ⓥ 확실히 하다, 보장하다
- **status** ⓝ 지위, 입지
- **motorist** ⓝ 운전자
- **switch to** ～로 바꾸다

- **complementary** ⓐ 보완하는
- **alongside** prep ～와 함께
- **complement** ⓥ 보완하다, 보충하다
- **stream** ⓝ 흐름
- **lightbulb** ⓝ 전구
- **gasoline** ⓝ 휘발유
- **electric** ⓐ 전기의

구문 풀이

15행 For example, although motorists may seem required to
　　　　접속사(～에도 불구하고)　　　2형식 동사　　주격 보어
purchase gasoline to run their cars, they can switch to electric cars.
　～하기 위해

11-12 회사에 기회를 열어줄 수 있는 소비자 불평

[본문 해석]

회사에게 실패에 대해 말해주는 시장의 방식은 가혹하면서 간단하다. 『불평은 다루기에 비용이 덜 들뿐 아니라 판매자가 (a) 향상되도록 만들 수도 있다.』 판매자는 또한 뭔가를 배울지도 모른다. 나는 끈적거리는 선크림 로션에 대한 불평을 받은 한 화장품 회사를 기억한다. 그 당시에, 그러한 로션은 모두 다소 끈적거렸기에 고객들이 경쟁사의 제품을 사게 하는 위험은 (b) 크지 않았다. 하지만 이것은 또한 기회였다. 그 회사는 끈적거리지 않는 제품을 개발해냈고 첫 해에 시장의 20퍼센트를 점유했다. 또 다른 회사는 (c) 반대되는 문제를 가졌다. 그 회사의 상품은 충분히 끈적거리지 않았다. 그 회사는 유럽에 있는 Royal Post Office였고 상품은 우표였다. 문제는 우표가 편지 봉투에 붙지 않았다는 것이다. 경영진은 우표 제작자에게 연락했는데, 그는 만약 사람들이 우표를 적절히 적시기만 한다면, 우표가 어떤 종이에든 달라붙을 것이라는 점을 명확히 밝혔다. 어떻게 할까? 경영진은 오래지 않아 (우표에) 더 많은 풀을 첨가하는 것보다 고객에게 우표를 적시도록 교육하려 애쓰는 데 비용이 (d) 덜(→ 더) 들 것이라는 결론에 이르렀다. 『우표 제작자는 더 많은 풀을 첨가하라고 지시받았고 그 문제는 더 이상 일어나지 않았다.』——『: 12번의 근거

구매자가 다른 곳으로 가게 하는 것보다는 불평하게 하는 것이 회사에게는 더 나은 일이기 때문에, 불만족한 고객들이 불평하는 것을 (e) 더 쉽게 만드는 것이 중요하다.

- **market** ⓝ 시장
- **harsh** ⓐ 혹독한
- **complaint** ⓝ 불평
- **handle** ⓥ 다루다
- **cosmetics** ⓝ 화장품
- **sunblock lotion** 선크림 로션
- **manage to** 이럭저럭 ～하다
- **opposite** ⓐ 정반대의
- **stick to** ～에 달라붙다
- **management** ⓝ 경영진
- **properly** ad 적절하게, 제대로
- **costly** ⓐ 많은 비용이 드는
- **glue** ⓝ 풀

- **failure** ⓝ 실패
- **brief** ⓐ 간단한, 짧은
- **less expensive** 덜 비싼
- **seller** ⓝ 판매자
- **sticky** ⓐ 끈적거리는, 잘 달라붙는
- **rival** ⓝ 경쟁자, 경쟁 상대
- **capture** ⓥ 사로잡다
- **stamp** ⓝ 우표
- **envelope** ⓝ 봉투
- **moisten** ⓥ 적시다
- **come to the conclusion** 결론에 이르다
- **educate** ⓥ 교육하다, 가르치다
- **elsewhere** ad 다른 곳으로

- **dissatisfied** ⓐ 불만족한
- **unsolved** ⓐ 해결되지 않은
- **enemy** ⓝ 적

- **cheap** ⓐ (값이) 싼, 돈이 적게 드는
- **competitor** ⓝ 경쟁자, 경쟁 상대

구문 풀이

2행 Not only are complaints less expensive to handle but they also
「부정어구＋be동사＋주어 : 도치 구문」　「not only＋A＋but also＋B : A뿐만 아니라 B도」
can cause the seller to improve.
「cause＋목적어＋to부정사 : ～이 …하도록 야기하다」

---

11 제목 파악　　　　　　　　　　정답률 55% | 정답 ②

윗글의 제목으로 가장 적절한 것은?

① Designs That Matter the Most to Customers
　소비자들에게 가장 중요한 디자인
✓② Complaints: Why Firms Should Welcome Them
　불평: 왜 회사들은 이것을 환영해야 하는가
③ Cheap Prices Don't Necessarily Mean Low Quality
　싼 가격이 꼭 저품질을 뜻하는 것은 아니다
④ More Sticky or Less Sticky: An Unsolved Problem
　더 끈적거릴 것인가, 덜 끈적거릴 것인가: 해결되지 않은 문제
⑤ Treat Your Competitors Like Friends, Not Enemies
　경쟁자를 적이 아닌 친구처럼 대하라

Why? 왜 정답일까?

'Not only are complaints less expensive to handle but they also can cause the seller to improve.'에서 언급하듯이 소비자의 불평은 처리하는 데 돈도 덜 비싸게 들거니와 판매자에게 나아질 기회를 제공해 주기에 의미가 있다는 내용의 글이다. 따라서 글의 제목으로 가장 적절한 것은 ② '불평: 왜 회사들은 이것을 환영해야 하는가'이다.

★★★ **1등급 대비 고난도 3점 문제**

12 어휘 추론　　　　　　　　　　정답률 42% | 정답 ④

밑줄 친 (a) ~ (e) 중에서 문맥상 낱말의 쓰임이 적절하지 않은 것은? [3점]
① (a)　② (b)　③ (c)　✓④ (d)　⑤ (e)

Why? 왜 정답일까?

우표 제작에 관한 두 번째 예시를 마무리하는 'The stamp producer was told to add more glue and the problem didn't occur again.'에서, 우표 제작자는 결국 잘 달라붙지 않는 우표에 풀을 더 첨가할 것을 요청받았고 더 이상 같은 문제는 발생하지 않게 되었다고 한다. 이는 경영진에서 소비자에게 우표 사용법을 교육하는 것보다 제작 때 풀을 더 넣는 것이 비용상 이득이라고 판단했기에 이행된 대처로 볼 수 있다. 다시 말해, 소비자를 교육하는 것이 제작 과정을 수정하는 것보다 비용이 '더' 드는 일이었다는 의미가 되도록 (d)의 less를 more로 고쳐야 한다. 따라서 문맥상 낱말의 쓰임이 적절하지 않은 것은 ④ '(d)'이다.

★★ **문제 해결 꿀~팁** ★★

▶ 많이 틀린 이유는?
최다 오답인 ③의 (c) 앞에서 끈적거리는 선크림(sticky sunblock lotion)에 관해 불평을 받았던 화장품 회사를 언급한 후, (c) 뒤에서는 충분히 끈적거리지 않는(not sticky enough) 우표 때문에 문제가 있었던 회사를 언급하고 있다. 즉 (c) 앞뒤로 '반대되는' 예가 제시되므로 (c)에 opposite를 쓴 것은 맥락상 맞다.

▶ 문제 해결 방법은?
(d)의 구문이 다소 복잡하므로 (d) 뒤의 'The stamp producer was told ~' 문장을 먼저 잘 이해한 뒤 (d)가 포함된 문장을 다시 읽도록 한다. (d) 뒤에 따르면 우표 제작자가 결국 우표에 풀을 더 첨가하라는 지시를 받았다고 하는데, 이는 '소비자들에게 우표를 적시라고 교육하는 것'과 '우표에 풀을 더 발라 제작하는 것' 사이에서 경영진이 후자를 선택했기 때문이다. (d)는 경영진이 이와 같은 결정을 내린 까닭으로 제작 과정을 수정하는 것보다 소비자를 교육하는 데 돈이 오히려 '더 들기' 때문임을 설명하는 것이다. 따라서 less 대신 more를 쓸 때 문맥이 자연스럽다.

DAY 26 20분 미니 모의고사

01 ②	02 ④	03 ①	04 ④	05 ⑤
06 ①	07 ⑤	08 ④	09 ③	10 ⑤
11 ④	12 ②			

---

01 피아노 대회에서 친구에게 진 후의 심경 변화
정답률 91% | 정답 ②

다음 글에 드러난 'I'의 심경 변화로 가장 적절한 것은?

① grateful → sorrowful
고마워하는   슬픈
✔ upset → calm
불쾌한   차분한
③ envious → doubtful
부러워하는   의심하는
④ surprised → disappointed
놀란   실망한
⑤ bored → relieved
따분한   안도한

[본문 해석]

또다시 나는 피아노 경연대회에서 내 친구에게 졌다. Linda가 우승했다는 것을 알게 되었을 때, 나는 매우 괴롭고 우울했다. 내 몸은 불쾌감으로 떨리고 있었다. 내 심장은 빠르게 뛰었고, 내 얼굴은 불그스레해졌다. 나는 마음을 가라앉히기 위해 콘서트홀에서 뛰쳐나와야 했다. 홀로 계단에 앉아, 나는 선생님께서 하신 말씀을 떠올렸다. "인생은 이기는 것과 관련이 있는데, 반드시 다른 사람들과 싸워서 이기는 것이 아니라 자기 자신이 되는 것에서 이기는 것과 관련이 있단다. 그리고 이기는 방법은 자기 자신이 누구인가를 알고 최선을 다하는 거란다." 선생님 말씀은 절대적으로 옳았다. 나는 내 친구를 적대할 이유가 없었다. 대신, 나는 나 자신과 나 자신의 발전에 중점을 두어야 한다. 나는 천천히 숨을 내쉬었다. 내 손은 이제 떨리지 않았다. 마침내 내 마음이 편해졌다.

Why? 왜 정답일까?

'~ I was deeply troubled and unhappy. My body was shaking with uneasiness.'을 통해 피아노 대회에서 친구 Linda보다 성적이 좋지 않았던 필자가 괴로움과 우울감, 불쾌감 등을 느꼈다는 것을 알 수 있고, 'My hands were steady now. At last, my mind was at peace.'에서 피아노 선생님의 말을 상기하며 마음을 다스린 필자가 평정심을 되찾았다는 것을 알 수 있다. 따라서 'I'의 심경 변화로 가장 적절한 것은 ② '불쾌한 → 차분한'이다.

- **uneasiness** ⓝ 불쾌감
- **settle down** (마음을) 가라앉히다
- **steady** ⓐ 안정된, 꾸준한
- **reddish** ⓐ 불그스레한
- **oppose** ⓥ 적대하다

구문 풀이

6행 Sitting on the stairs alone, I recalled what my teacher
분사구문(~하면서)   과거   관계대명사(~것)
had said.
과거완료(recalled보다 먼저 일어남)

★★★ 1등급 대비 고난도 3점 문제

02 몸짓 언어의 이해
정답률 27% | 정답 ④

밑줄 친 by reading a body language dictionary가 의미하는 바로 가장 적절한 것은? [3점]

① by learning body language within social context
사회적 맥락 안에서 언어를 배움으로써
② by comparing body language and French
몸짓 언어와 프랑스어를 비교함으로써
③ with a body language expert's help
몸짓 언어 전문가의 도움을 받아
✔ without understanding the social aspects
사회적 측면을 이해하지 못한 채로
⑤ in a way people learn their native language
사람들이 자기 모국어를 배우는 방식으로

[본문 해석]

실용성 있고 효과적인 몸짓 언어는 개별 전달 신호의 합계 이상이다. 사람들이 이러한 암기식의 사전식 접근법으로부터 의사전달을 할 때, 그들은 더 큰 그림, 즉 사회적 인식의 모든 다양한 측면을 보지 못하게 된다. 대신, 그들은 팔짱을 낀 사람을 보고 '과묵하고 화가 난' 것으로 생각한다. 그들은 미소를 보고 '행복한' 것으로 생각한다. 그들은 다른 사람들에게 '누가 윗사람인가'를 보여 주기 위해 세게 악수를 한다. 몸짓 언어 사전을 읽어서 몸짓 언어를 사용하려고 하는

것은 프랑스어 사전을 읽어서 프랑스어를 말하려고 하는 것과 같다. (의미 구성의) 요소들은 실용성 없는 상태로 분리되어 버리는 경향이 있다. 당신의 행동은 로봇처럼 어색해 보이고, 당신의 몸짓 언어 신호는 서로 단절된다. 당신의 몸짓 언어가 그야말로 잘못 전달되었기 때문에 결국에는 당신이 마음을 끌려고 하는 바로 그 사람들을 혼란스럽게 하고 만다.

Why? 왜 정답일까?

'When people work from this rote-memory, dictionary approach, they stop seeing the bigger picture, all the diverse aspects of social perception.'에서 사전식으로 몸짓 언어를 바라보면 사회적 인식의 다양한 면을 보지 못한다고 하므로, 다시금 몸짓 언어 사전을 언급하는 밑줄 친 부분의 의미로 가장 적절한 것은 ④ '사회적 측면을 이해하지 못한 채로'이다.

- **authentic** ⓐ 실용성 있는, 진짜의
- **rote-memory** ⓐ 기계적 암기의
- **disconnect** ⓥ 단절시키다
- **attract** ⓥ (마음을) 끌다, 매혹시키다
- **sum** ⓝ 합계
- **fall apart** ⓥ 분리되다
- **end up** ⓥ 결국 ~하게 되다

구문 풀이

13행 You end up confusing the very people [you're trying to
결국 ~하게 되다   바로 그   선행사
attract] because your body language just rings false.
이유 접속사

★★ 문제 해결 꿀~팁 ★★

▶ 많이 틀린 이유는?

서두에서 사전식으로 몸짓 언어에 접근하면 큰 그림, 즉 사회적 맥락에 관한 정보를 놓치게 된다고 언급한다. 이를 근거로 볼 때, '몸짓 언어 사전을 읽으려는' 행위가 '맥락 속에서 몸짓 언어를 배우려는' 행위라고 설명한 ①은 아예 틀린 진술이다.

▶ 문제 해결 방법은?

a body language dictionary라는 비유적 표현을 이해하려면 dictionary approach라는 표현이 포함된 두 번째 문장을 주의 깊게 읽어야 한다. 여기서 말하는 '사전식 접근'이란 '사회적 인식의 면을 파악하는 것과 동떨어진 것'임을 이해한 후 답을 찾도록 한다.

---

03 부유한 국가의 스트레스 요소
정답률 64% | 정답 ①

다음 글의 제목으로 가장 적절한 것은?

✔ Why Are Even Wealthy Countries Not Free from Stress?
왜 심지어 부유한 국가들도 스트레스에서 자유롭지 못한 걸까?
② In Search of the Path to Escaping the Poverty Trap
가난의 덫을 벗어나기 위한 길을 찾아서
③ Time Management: Everything You Need to Know
시간 관리: 당신이 알아야 할 모든 것
④ How Does Stress Affect Human Bodies?
스트레스는 우리 몸에 어떤 영향을 미칠까?
⑤ Sound Mind Wins the Game of Life!
건전한 정신이 인생이란 게임에서 이긴다!

[본문 해석]

가난이 스트레스를 유발하는 경향이 있다는 것을 듣고 놀랄 사람은 거의 없을 것이다. 예를 들어, 미국의 저널 *Psychosomatic Medicine*에 발표된 2006년 연구는 더 낮은 사회 경제적 지위가 체내의 더 높은 수치의 스트레스 호르몬과 관련이 있다고 언급했다. 하지만, 더 부유한 국가는 그들 특유의 스트레스를 가지고 있다. 핵심 쟁점은 시간 압박이다. 미국 심리학자 Robert Levine과 캐나다 심리학자 Ara Norenzayan이 31개국을 대상으로 한 1999년 연구는 더 부유하고 더 산업화된 국가들이 더 빠른 삶의 속도를 가지고 있다는 것, 그리고 이것이 더 높은 생활 수준으로 이어졌지만, 동시에 사람들이 심장병에 걸리기 더 쉽게 했을 뿐 아니라 지속적인 촉박함을 느끼게 했다는 것을 알아냈다. 사실, 빠른 속도의 생산력은 부를 창출하지만, 이는 또한 사람들이 긴장을 풀고 즐겁게 지낼 시간이 없을 때 시간이 부족하다고 느끼게 한다.

Why? 왜 정답일까?

부유한 국가에 사는 사람들이 시간 압박이라는 스트레스에 시달린다(However, richer economies have their own distinct stresses. The key issue is time pressure.)는 내용이므로, 글의 제목으로 가장 적절한 것은 ① '왜 심지어 부유한 국가들도 스트레스에서 자유롭지 못한 걸까?'이다.

- **poverty** ⓝ 가난
- **status** ⓝ 지위
- **psychologist** ⓝ 심리학자
- **socioeconomic** ⓐ 사회경제적인
- **distinct** ⓐ 특유의, 독특한, 뚜렷한
- **wealthy** ⓐ 부유한

DAY 26

● industrialize ⓥ 산업화하다
● constant ⓐ 지속적인
● urgency ⓝ 다급함
● prone to ~에 걸리기 쉬운
● productivity ⓝ 생산성

구문 풀이

1행 Few people will be surprised to hear that poverty tends to
감정 형용사   원인(~해서)
create stress: ~

★★★ 1등급 대비 고난도 3점 문제

04 음식 평가에 지대한 영향을 끼치는 시각적 정보   정답률 42% | 정답 ④

다음 글의 밑줄 친 부분 중, 어법상 틀린 것은? [3점]

[본문 해석]

비록 음식에 대한 우리 평가의 일부가 음식의 시각적 외관인 것은 분명하지만, 어떻게 시각적인 입력 정보가 맛과 냄새에 우선할 수 있는가는 놀라울 것이다. 만약 예를 들어 색이 초록색인 오렌지 음료의 경우처럼 색깔이 잘못되어 있다면, 사람들은 과일 맛이 나는 음료를 정확하게 식별하기가 매우 어렵다는 것을 알게 된다. 포도주 맛을 감정하는 사람들의 경험은 어쩌면 훨씬 더 놀랍다. 포도주와 포도주 제조에 관해 공부하는 Bordeaux University 학생들을 대상으로 한 연구는 그들이 붉은색 색소로 물들인 백포도주를 받았을 때, '자두와 초콜릿'과 같은 적포도주에 적합한 시음표를 선택했다는 것을 보여주었다. 숙련된 뉴질랜드 포도주 전문가들도 마찬가지로 백포도주 Chardonnay를 붉은색 색소로 물들였을 때 속아서 그것이 실제로 적포도주라고 생각하게 되었다.

Why? 왜 정답일까?

4형식 동사 give는 능동태로 쓰일 때 목적어를 2개 취하며, 이 중 주로 사람에 해당하는 간접 목적어를 주어로 삼아 수동태를 쓰더라도 뒤에 '~을'에 해당하는 목적어 1개가 남는다. 여기서도 '~을'에 해당하는 목적어 white wine이 뒤에 나오고, 주어인 they가 이것을 '받는' 입장임을 고려할 때, gave를 were given으로 고쳐야 한다. 어법상 틀린 것은 ④이다.

Why? 왜 오답일까?

① 뒤에 주어, 동사, 목적어를 모두 갖춘 완전한 문장이 나오는 것으로 보아 how(어떻게)의 쓰임은 적절하다.
② find 동사를 포함한 5형식 가목적어 구문이므로, 가목적어 it과 진목적어인 to부정사 사이에 보어 역할을 하는 형용사 difficult가 적절하게 쓰였다.
③ 형용사 보어가 문장 맨 앞에 나오고 주어와 동사가 서로 위치를 바꾼 도치 구문이다. 즉 뒤에 나오는 단수 명사 the experience가 주어이므로 is가 앞에 바르게 쓰였다.
⑤ 'trick A into B(A를 속여 B하게 하다)'의 수동태인 'A be tricked into B(A가 속아서 B하다)' 구문에서, B에 해당하는 동명사 thinking 뒤로 목적어인 완전한 명사절이 이어지고 있다. 따라서 접속사 that이 바르게 쓰였다.

● assessment ⓝ 평가
● visual ⓐ 시각의, 눈으로 보는
● appearance ⓝ 외관, 겉모습
● perhaps ⓐⓓ 아마, 어쩌면
● override ⓥ ~보다 더 중요하다, 우선하다
● identify ⓥ 식별하다, 알아보다
● striking ⓐ 놀라운, 두드러진, 눈에 띄는
● appropriate for ~에 적합한
● dye ⓝ 색소, 염료
● trick A into B ⓥ A를 속여 B하게 하다

구문 풀이

1행 Although it is obvious {that part of our assessment of food
양보 접속사(~일지라도) ↳가주어   접속사(~것)
is its visual appearance}, it is perhaps surprising {how visual input
가주어   의문부사(어떻게)↳ 주어
can override taste and smell}. { }: 진주어
동사   목적어

★★ 문제 해결 꿀~팁 ★★

▶ 많이 틀린 이유는?
최다 오답인 ③은 도치 구문의 수 일치를 묻고 있다. 주어 역할을 할 수 있는 것은 명사(구)뿐인데 is 앞의 even more striking은 형용사이다. 이는 강조되기 위해 앞에 나온 보어일 수밖에 없고, 뒤에는 '동사+주어'의 어순이 이어지므로 the experience를 근거로 is가 적절한지를 판단해야 한다.
▶ 문제 해결 방법은?
④의 '능동 vs. 수동' 문제를 해결하기 위해서는 원칙적으로 주어를 잘 살펴야 한다. 주어가 '행하는' 주체이면 능동태를, 주어가 '당하는' 대상이면 수동태를 쓴다는 점을 명심하자.

★★★ 1등급 대비 고난도 2점 문제

05 동물원의 포획 사육 프로그램   정답률 24% | 정답 ⑤

다음 글의 밑줄 친 부분 중, 문맥상 낱말의 쓰임이 적절하지 않은 것은?

[본문 해석]

멸종에 이르고 있는 종에게 동물원은 생존을 위한 마지막 기회로 작용할 수 있다. 현장 환경 보호 활동가와 야생 동물 당국의 노력을 통합하기 위해 ① 회복 프로그램이 수립된다. 그 종의 개체수가 ② 감소하면서 동물원이 포획 사육 프로그램을 시작하는 것은 드물지 않다. 포획 사육은 멸종을 막기 위해 작용한다. 어떤 경우에는 포획 사육된 개체가 다시 야생으로 방생되어 야생 개체수를 보충할 수도 있다. 이는 개체가 ③ 특정한 생애 주기 동안에 가장 큰 위협에 놓여 있는 상황에서 가장 성공적이다. 예를 들어 거북이 알은 부화한 이후까지 고위험 장소로부터 제거될 수도 있다. 이는 성체까지 생존하는 거북이 수를 ④ 증가시킬 수 있다. 악어 프로그램 역시 알과 부화한 유생을 보호하는 데 있어서 성공적이었으며, 일단 그것이 스스로를 보호할 준비를 더 잘 갖추면 부화한 유생을 ⑤ 포획한다(→ 방생한다).

Why? 왜 정답일까?

멸종 위기 종의 개체수를 회복하는 데 동물원이 도움을 줄 수 있다는 내용의 글로, '~ it is not unusual for zoos to start captive breeding programs.' 뒤로 포획 사육 프로그램의 내용이 소개되고 있다. 이 포획 사육 프로그램에서는 멸종 위기 동물이나 그 알을 잡아두었다가 위험한 시기가 지나고 동물이 스스로를 보호할 준비가 되면 그 동물을 다시 야생으로 '돌려보낸다'. 이러한 흐름으로 볼 때, ⑤의 capturing을 releasing으로 고쳐야 한다. 따라서 문맥상 낱말의 쓰임이 가장 적절하지 않은 것은 ⑤이다.

● extinction ⓝ 멸종
● conservationist ⓝ 환경 보호 활동가
● authority ⓝ 당국
● diminish ⓥ 감소하다, 줄어들다
● supplement ⓥ 보충하다
● hatchling ⓝ (갓 부화한) 유생
● be equipped to ~할 준비를 갖추다

구문 풀이

9행 This is most successful in situations [where individuals are
선행사(추상적 공간)←   관계부사
at greatest threat during a particular life stage].

★★ 문제 해결 꿀~팁 ★★

▶ 많이 틀린 이유는?
동물원의 포획 사육이라는 생소한 소재를 다루어 이해하기 까다로운 지문이다. 가장 헷갈리는 ④ 주변의 문맥을 살펴보면, 포획 사육이 생존에 큰 위험이 있는 시기를 지나는 동물에게 도움이 된다는 일반적인 내용 뒤로 바다거북의 사례가 언급된다. 바다거북의 알은 부화하기 전까지 고위험 지역으로부터 다른 곳으로 옮겨진다고 했다. 이는 바다거북이 무사히 부화해 성체까지 생존할 수 있도록 돕는 절차이므로, 실제로 이 조치를 통해 살아남는 바다거북의 수가 '증가할' 수 있다는 뜻의 ④ increase는 문맥상 적절하다.
▶ 문제 해결 방법은?
정답인 ⑤의 capturing은 핵심 소재인 captive (breeding programs)와 비슷한 형태의 단어이지만, 문맥적 의미는 정반대이다. 포획 사육 기간에 악어가 스스로를 보호할 준비를 갖추고 나면 '계속 잡아두는' 것이 아니라 '방생해야' 야생 동물의 보호와 생존에 도움이 된다.

06 사실보다 감정에 기반한 우리의 선택   정답률 54% | 정답 ①

다음 빈칸에 들어갈 말로 가장 적절한 것을 고르시오.

✓ anxiety - 불안감
② boredom - 지루함
③ confidence - 자신감
④ satisfaction - 만족감
⑤ responsibility - 책임감

[본문 해석]

많은 사람들은 비행기를 타는 것을 두려워한다. 종종, 이 두려움은 통제력의 부족에서 비롯된다. 조종사는 통제를 하지만 승객은 그렇지 않으며, 이러한 통제력의 부족은 두려움을 스며들게 한다. 많은 잠재적인 승객들은 너무 두려운 나머지 비행기를 타는 대신 먼 거리를 운전해 목적지에 도착하기를 선택한다. 그러나 운전을 하기로 한 그들의 결정은 논리가 아닌 오직 감정에 근거한다. 논리에 따르면, 통계적으로 자동차 사고로 사망할 확률은 약 5,000분의 1인 반면, 비행기 사고로 사망할 확률은 1,100만분의 1에 가깝다고 한다. 만약 여러

분이 위험을 감수할 것이라면, 특히 여러분의 안녕을 혹시 포함할 수 있는 위험을 감수할 것이라면, 여러분에게 유리한 확률을 원하지 않겠는가? 그러나 사람들 대부분은 그들에게 최소한의 불안감을 야기할 선택을 한다. 여러분이 위험을 감수하는 데 관해 하고 있는 생각에 주의를 기울여보고, 단지 감정이 아니고 사실에 기반하여 결정을 내리고 있는지 확인하라.

Why? 왜 정답일까?

글에서 사람들이 비행기를 타는 대신 장거리 운전을 하기로 결심하는 것은 사실상 사고의 실질적 확률을 고려하지 않은, 감정 중심의 선택(their decision to drive is based solely on emotion)이라고 지적하고 있다. 즉, 사람들은 실제 통계적으로 교통사고 확률이 비행기 사고 확률보다 높은데도 오로지 '불안'을 피하려고 운전을 선택한다는 것이므로, 빈칸에 들어갈 말로 가장 적절한 것은 ① '불안감'이다.

- terrified ⓐ 겁에 질린
- lack ⓝ 부족, 결여
- potential ⓐ 잠재적인
- solely ⓐ 오로지
- statistically ⓐ 통계적으로
- in one's favor ~에 유리한
- anxiety ⓝ 불안
- stem from ~에서 기원하다
- instill ⓥ 스며들게 하다, 주입하다
- destination ⓝ 목적지
- logic ⓝ 논리
- odds ⓝ 공산, 가능성
- make sure 반드시 ~하다
- boredom ⓝ 지루함

구문 풀이

3행 Many potential passengers are so afraid (that) they choose
「so ~ that : 너무 ~해서 …하다」
to drive great distances to get to a destination instead of flying.
목적어(~것)   부사적 용법(~하기 위해)

---

07 두 가지 다른 정보를 동시에 처리할 수 없는 인간 정답률 51% | 정답 ⑤

다음 빈칸에 들어갈 말로 가장 적절한 것을 고르시오. [3점]

① decide what they should do in the moment
그들이 그 순간 뭘 해야 하는지를 판단할
② remember a message with too many words
너무 긴 메시지를 기억할
③ analyze which information was more accurate
어떤 정보가 더 정확한지 분석할
④ speak their own ideas while listening to others
다른 사람들의 말을 들으면서 자기 생각을 말할
✓⑤ process two pieces of information at the same time
두 개의 정보를 동시에 처리할

[본문 해석]

1950년대 메사추세츠 공과대학 소속이었던 Colin Cherry의 연구에서, 우리가 두 사람이 이야기하는 것을 동시에 들을 수 있는지 판단하기 위해 참가자들은 한 번은 한쪽 귀로만 목소리를 듣고, 그다음에는 양쪽 귀로 들었다. 한쪽 귀로는 듣는 사람이 다시 반복해야 하는('섀도잉'이라 불림) 메시지를 계속 들려주었고 다른 한쪽 귀로는 사람들이 말하는 것을 들려주었다. 속임수는 사람들이 주된 메시지에 완전히 집중하면서 다른 귀로는 다른 사람이 말하는 것 또한 들을 수 있는지를 알아보기 위한 것이었다. 영리하게도, Cherry는 참가자들이 다른 한쪽 귀로 들리는 메시지가 남자가 말한 것인지 혹은 여자가 말한 것인지, 영어인지 다른 외국어인지, 심지어 실제 단어로 구성된 것인지조차 전혀 알아차리지 못했다는 것을 발견했다! 다시 말해서, 사람들은 두 개의 정보를 동시에 처리할 수 없었다.

Why? 왜 정답일까?

실험 결과를 제시하는 '~ it was impossible for his participants to know whether the message in the other ear was spoken by a man or woman, in English or another language, or was even comprised of real words at all!'에서 사람들은 양쪽 귀에 각기 다른 정보가 들어올 때 이를 동시에 처리하지 못하여, 화자가 남자였는지 여자였는지, 사용된 언어가 영어였는지 다른 언어였는지 등등을 제대로 판별하지 못했다고 한다. 따라서 빈칸에 들어갈 말로 가장 적절한 것은 ⑤ '두 개의 정보를 동시에 처리할'이다.

- at a time 한 번에
- shadowing ⓝ 섀도잉(남의 말을 듣는 동시에 따라서 하는 것)
- trick ⓝ 속임수, 요령
- accurate ⓐ 정확한
- in an effort to ~하기 위해서
- comprise ⓥ ~을 구성하다

구문 풀이

8행 The trick was to see if you could totally focus on the main
주격 보어(~것)   접속사(~인지 아닌지)
message and also hear someone talking in your other ear.
지각동사 목적어 목적격 보어

---

08 대중 연설 시 청중의 피드백 정답률 70% | 정답 ④

다음 글에서 전체 흐름과 관계 없는 문장은?

[본문 해석]

연사들은 연설하는 동안 청중에게 "귀를 기울이기" 때문에 대중 연설은 청중 중심이다. 그들은 청중의 피드백, 즉 청중이 연사에게 주는 언어적, 비언어적 신호를 주시한다. ① 청중의 피드백은 흔히 청중들이 연사의 생각을 이해하고, 그것에 관심을 갖고, 그것을 받아들일 준비가 되었는지를 보여 준다. ② 이 피드백은 연사를 여러모로 도와준다. ③ 그것은 연사가 언제 속도를 늦출지, 언제 무언가를 더 주의해서 설명할지, 혹은 언제 연설의 끝에 있는 질의응답 시간에 어떤 주제로 되돌아 갈 것이라고 청중에게 말할지까지도 파악하는 데 도움이 된다. ④ 무대 불안을 줄이기 위해 연사가 자신의 원고를 암기하는 것이 중요하다. ⑤ 청중의 피드백은 연사가 청중과 존중하는 관계를 만드는 것을 도와준다.

Why? 왜 정답일까?

대중 연설에 있어 청중의 피드백은 연사에게 연설 진행에 관련된 여러 요소를 파악하는 데 도움을 주며 청중과의 좋은 관계를 형성하는 데에도 참고가 된다는 내용을 다룬 글인데, ④의 경우 '무대 불안'이라는 무관한 소재를 언급하고 있어 흐름에서 벗어난다. 따라서 전체 흐름과 관계 없는 문장은 ④이다.

- audience ⓝ 청중, 관객
- monitor ⓥ 추적 관찰하다
- accept ⓥ 받아들이다, 수용하다
- session ⓝ 시간
- memorize ⓥ 외우다, 암기하다
- anxiety ⓝ 불안, 염려
- centered ⓐ 중심의, 위주의
- indicate ⓥ 보여주다, 나타내다, 시사하다
- explain ⓥ 설명하다
- at the close of ~의 끝에 있는
- on-stage 무대 위에서의, 관객 앞에서의
- respectful ⓐ 경의를 표하는

구문 풀이

7행 It helps the speaker know when to slow down, (to) explain
준사역동사   원형부정사 「의문사+to부정사1 +   to부정사2 +
something more carefully, or even (to) tell the audience {that she or
                                    to부정사3 : 언제 ~할지」   접속사
he will return to an issue in a question-and-answer session at the
close of the speech}.

---

09 권위가 있는 부모 밑에서 자란 자녀들의 학업 성취 정답률 65% | 정답 ③

다음 글의 내용을 한 문장으로 요약하고자 한다. 빈칸 (A), (B)에 들어갈 말로 가장 적절한 것은? [3점]

	(A)	(B)		(A)	(B)
①	likely 가능성이 크며	random 무작위적인	②	willing 자발적이며	minimal 최소한의
✓③	willing 자발적이며	active 적극적인	④	hesitant 망설이며	unwanted 원치 않는
⑤	hesitant 망설이며	constant 지속적인			

[본문 해석]

스웨덴 청소년들에 대한 연구에 따르면, 청소년들의 학업 성공의 중요한 요인은 그들이 어려움에 반응하는 방식이다. 이 연구는 어려움에 직면했을 때 권위가 있는 양육 방식에 노출된 청소년들은 덜 수동적이고, 덜 무기력하며, 실패를 덜 두려워한다고 보고하고 있다. Wisconsin과 northern California의 9개 고교에서 진행된 또 다른 연구는 권위가 있는 부모들의 아이들이 학습을 잘하는데, 그 이유는 이러한 부모들이 아이들의 학교 활동에 관여하고자 많은 노력을 기울이기 때문이라고 밝히고 있다. 즉, 권위가 있는 부모들은 아이들의 숙제를 도와주고, 학교 프로그램에 참여하며, 스포츠에 참여하는 아이들을 지켜보고, 아이들의 과목 선택을 도와줄 가능성이 훨씬 더 크다. 게다가, 이러한 부모들은 아이들이 학교에서 무엇을 하는지, 어떤 성과를 내는지 더 잘 인지하고 있다. 마지막으로, 권위가 있는 부모들은 다른 부모들에 비해 학문적 탁월함과 근면함의 중요성을 더 많이 칭찬한다.

➡ 위 연구는 권위가 있는 부모의 아이들이 어려움에 대처하는 데 더 (A) 자발적이며, 그 부모들의 (B) 적극적인 관여에 영향을 받기 때문에 학업 성취가 좋다는 것을 보여준다.

Why? 왜 정답일까?

두 번째 문장인 '~ when facing difficulties, adolescents exposed to an authoritative parenting style are less likely to be passive ~'에서 권위적인 양육 방식에 노출된 자녀는 어려움 앞에서 덜 수동적이라고 한다. 이어서 '~ children of authoritative parents do well in school, because these parents put a lot of effort into getting involved in their children's school activities.'에서 권위가 있는 부모는 자녀의 학습에 더 적극 관여하기 때문에, 이들 자녀의 학업 성취가 실제로 더 좋다는 연구 결과를 언급하고 있다. 따라서 요약문의 빈칸 **(A)**, **(B)**에 들어갈 말로 가장 적절한 것은 ③ '**(A)** willing(자발적이며), **(B)** active(적극적인)'이다.

- adolescent ⓝ 청소년
- authoritative ⓐ 권위적인
- put effort into ~에 노력을 쏟다
- hesitant ⓐ 망설이는
- factor ⓝ 요인
- helpless ⓐ 무기력한
- significantly ⓐⓓ 상당히

구문 풀이

3행 The study reports that when facing difficulties, adolescents
　　　　　　　　　　　분사구문(~할 때)　　　　　　　　주어
exposed to an authoritative parenting style are less likely to be
과거분사　　　　　　　　　　　　　　　　동사구(~할 가능성이 적다)
passive, helpless, and afraid to fail.
주격 보어1　주격 보어2　　　주격 보어3

10-12 적이 될 뻔한 사냥꾼 이웃과 친구가 된 농부

[본문 해석]

(A)

오래전 작은 마을의 한 농부가 사냥꾼인 이웃을 두었다. 사냥꾼은 사납고 훈련이 잘되지 않은 사냥개 몇 마리를 소유하고 있었다. 그들은 울타리를 자주 뛰어넘어 농부의 새끼 양들을 쫓아 다녔다. 농부는 그 이웃에게 (a) 그의 개들을 제지해 달라고 요청했지만, 이 말은 무시되었다. 『그 개들이 울타리를 뛰어넘은 어느 날, 그들은 새끼 양 중 몇 마리를 공격해서 심하게 다치게 했다.』
　　　　　　　　　　　　　　　　　└『』: 12번 ①의 근거 일치

(D)

농부는 이쯤 되자 진절머리가 났다. 『그는 재판관에게 조언을 구하기 위해 가장 가까운 도시로 갔다.』 그의 이야기를 주의 깊게 들은 후 그 재판관이 말했다.
└『』: 12번 ⑤의 근거 일치
"저는 사냥꾼을 벌하고 (e) 그에게 개들을 사슬로 묶거나 가두라고 지시할 수 있습니다. 하지만 당신은 친구를 잃고 적을 얻게 될 것입니다. 당신은 이웃을 친구 아니면 적, 어느 쪽으로 두고 싶습니까?" 농부는 친구가 더 좋다고 대답했다.

(C)

"좋습니다. 저는 당신에게 새끼 양들을 안전하게 지키고 당신의 이웃 또한 좋은 친구로 바꿀 수 있는 해결책을 제안하겠습니다." 『재판관의 해결책을 듣고, 농부는 동의했다.』 농부가 집에 도착하자마자, 그는 즉시 재판관의 제안을 시험
└『』: 12번 ③의 근거 일치
해 보았다. (d) 그(the farmer)는 자신의 농장에서 가장 귀여운 새끼 양들 중 세 마리를 골랐다. 『그러고 나서 그는 자기 이웃의 어린 세 아들들에게 그것들을 선물했다.』 아이들은 기뻐하며 받고 새끼 양들과 함께 놀기 시작했다.
└『』: 12번 ④의 근거 일치

(B)

자기 아들들의 새로 얻은 놀이 친구들을 보호하기 위해서, 사냥꾼은 자기 개들을 위해 튼튼한 개집을 지었다. 그 개들은 농부의 새끼 양들을 다시는 괴롭히지 않았다. (b) 자기 아이들에 대한 농부의 관대함에 감사한 마음에서, 사냥꾼은 농부를 진수성찬에 자주 초대했다. 『그 답례로 농부는 양고기와 자신이 만든 치즈를 제공했다.』 농부는 금세 (c) 그와 진한 우정을 키우게 되었다.
└『』: 12번 ②의 근거 불일치

- poorly-trained ⓐ 훈련이 잘되지 않은
- fall on deaf ears 무시되다
- severely ⓐⓓ 심하게
- generosity ⓝ 관대함
- put ~ to the test ~을 시험해보다
- punish ⓥ 벌하다
- frequently ⓐⓓ 자주
- keep in check 제지하다, 감독하다
- gratitude ⓝ 감사
- feast ⓝ 진수성찬, 연회
- suggestion ⓝ 제안

구문 풀이

(A) 6행 One day [when the dogs jumped the fence], they attacked
　　　　　　 시간 선행사　관계부사　　　　　　　　　　 동사1
and severely injured several of the lambs.
　　　　　　　　　　 동사2

(C) 3행 Having heard the judge's solution, the farmer agreed.
　　　　 완료분사구문(agreed보다 먼저 일어남)

---

10 글의 순서 파악　　　정답률 68% | 정답 ⑤

주어진 글 **(A)**에 이어질 내용을 순서에 맞게 배열한 것으로 가장 적절한 것은?

① (B) – (D) – (C)
② (C) – (B) – (D)
③ (C) – (D) – (B)
④ (D) – (B) – (C)
☑ (D) – (C) – (B)

Why? 왜 정답일까?

사냥개를 키우는 이웃 때문에 피해를 본 농부를 소개하는 **(A)** 뒤에는, 농부가 재판관에게 해결책을 구했다는 내용의 **(D)**, 재판관이 준 해결책을 농부가 실천에 옮겼다는 내용의 **(C)**, 해결책이 잘 통하여 사냥꾼 이웃과 농부가 친구가 되었다는 내용의 **(B)**가 차례로 이어져야 자연스럽다. 따라서 글의 순서로 가장 적절한 것은 ⑤ '**(D)** – **(C)** – **(B)**'이다.

11 지칭 추론　　　정답률 59% | 정답 ④

밑줄 친 (a) ~ (e) 중에서 가리키는 대상이 나머지 넷과 다른 것은?

① (a)　② (b)　③ (c)　☑ (d)　⑤ (e)

Why? 왜 정답일까?

(a), (b), (c), (e)는 the hunter를, (d)는 바로 앞 문장의 the farmer를 가리키므로, (a) ~ (e) 중에서 가리키는 대상이 다른 하나는 ④ '(d)'이다.

12 세부 내용 파악　　　정답률 60% | 정답 ②

윗글의 농부에 관한 내용으로 적절하지 않은 것은?

① 그의 양이 사냥개의 공격을 받았다.
☑ 사냥꾼에게 양고기와 치즈를 받았다.
③ 재판관의 해결책에 동의했다.
④ 세 명의 아들을 둔 이웃이 있었다.
⑤ 도시로 조언을 구하러 갔다.

Why? 왜 정답일까?

(B) 'In turn, the farmer offered him lamb meat and cheese he had made.'에서 농부는 친구가 된 사냥꾼에게 양고기와 치즈를 주었다고 하므로, 내용과 일치하지 않는 것은 ② '사냥꾼에게 양고기와 치즈를 받았다.'이다.

Why? 왜 오답일까?

① **(A)** 'One day when the dogs jumped the fence, they attacked and severely injured several of the lambs.'의 내용과 일치한다.
③ **(C)** 'Having heard the judge's solution, the farmer agreed.'의 내용과 일치한다.
④ **(C)** 'He then presented them to his neighbor's three small sons.'에서 이웃인 사냥꾼에게 세 명의 아들이 있었음을 알 수 있다.
⑤ **(D)** 'He went to the nearest city to consult a judge.'의 내용과 일치한다.

DAY 27 · 20분 미니 모의고사

01 ①	02 ①	03 ④	04 ④	05 ④
06 ①	07 ③	08 ④	09 ⑤	10 ③
11 ②	12 ⑤			

---

01 전쟁에서 적에 대한 개념화
정답률 87% | 정답 ①

다음 글에서 필자가 주장하는 바로 가장 적절한 것은?

☑ 전쟁과 적을 추상적이고 획일적으로 개념화하는 것을 경계해야 한다.
② 적에 따라 다양한 전략과 전술을 수립하고 적용해야 한다.
③ 보편적 윤리관에 기초하여 적의 개념을 정의해야 한다.
④ 전쟁 예방에 도움이 되는 정치적 결정을 해야 한다.
⑤ 어떠한 경우에도 전쟁을 정당화하지 말아야 한다.

[본문 해석]

전쟁은 적에 대한 어떤 이미지, 즉 개념 없이는 생각할 수 없다. 전쟁에 의미와 정당화를 제공하는 것은 바로 적의 존재이다. Carl Schmitt는 이렇게 썼다. '전쟁은 증오감을 따라 나온다.' '전쟁은 그 나름의 전략적, 전술적, 그리고 여타의 규칙과 관점을 가지고 있지만, 그 모든 것은 모두 적이 누구냐에 대해 정치적인 결정이 이미 내려졌다는 것을 상정하고 있다.' 적의 개념은 전쟁의 도덕적 평가에 핵심적이다. 즉 '적의 이미지를 확립하는 데 있어서 전쟁을 하고 있는 국가의 기본적인 목표는 죽이는 행위와 살인 행위를 가능한 한 뚜렷이 구별하는 것이다.' 하지만, 우리는 전쟁과 그것에 영향을 미치는 적의 이미지를 추상적이고 획일적인 방식으로 생각하는 데 주의할 필요가 있다. 오히려 둘은 그것들 본연의 문화적이고 불확정적인 현상으로 간주되어야 한다.

Why? 왜 정답일까?

전쟁에서 적이 정의되는 방식에 관해 설명한 글로, 적이 어떻게 개념화되는가에 따라 전쟁에 대한 도덕적 평가에 영향이 미칠 수 있다는 내용을 다루고 있다. 특히 당위의 의미를 나타내는 **need to**가 쓰인 'However, we need to be cautious about thinking of war and the image of the enemy that informs it in an abstract and uniform way.'에서, 전쟁과 적의 개념을 추상적이고 획일적으로 생각하는 데 주의가 필요하다고 이야기하므로, 필자가 주장하는 바로 가장 적절한 것은 ① '전쟁과 적을 추상적이고 획일적으로 개념화하는 것을 경계해야 한다.'이다.

- **inconceivable** ⓐ 생각할 수 없는
- **hatred** ⓝ 증오
- **tactical** ⓐ 전술적인
- **assessment** ⓝ 평가
- **phenomenon** ⓝ 현상
- **presence** ⓝ 존재, 있음
- **strategic** ⓐ 전략적인
- **presuppose** ⓥ 상정하다, 추정하다
- **abstract** ⓐ 추상적인

구문 풀이

7행 The concept of the enemy is fundamental to the moral
　　　　주어1　　　　　　　　동사구1(~에 핵심적인)
assessment of war: / 'The basic aim of a nation at war
　　　　　　　　　　　　　　주어2
in establishing an image of the enemy is to distinguish as sharply as
~하는 데 있어　　　　　　　　　　　동사2 주격 보어「distinguish +
possible the act of killing from the act of murder'.
A+from+B : A를 B와 구별하다」

---

02 행복한 뇌를 위한 습관 만들기
정답률 75% | 정답 ①

다음 글의 주제로 가장 적절한 것은?

☑ possibility of forming brain habits for well-being
행복을 위한 뇌 습관을 만들어낼 수 있는 가능성
② role of brain circuits in improving body movements
신체 움직임을 향상시키는 데 있어 뇌 회로의 역할
③ importance of practice in playing musical instruments
악기 연주에서 연습의 중요성
④ effect of taking a break on enhancing memory capacity
휴식이 기억력 향상에 미치는 영향
⑤ difficulty of discovering how neurons in the brain work
뇌 속 뉴런의 작동 방식을 발견하는 것의 어려움

[본문 해석]

우리는 뇌가 절대 변하지 않는다고 생각했지만, 신경과학자 Richard Davidson

에 따르면 우리는 이제 이것이 사실이 아님을, 즉, 특정한 뇌 회로가 규칙적인 연습을 통해 더 강해진다는 것을 안다. 그는 "행복은 첼로 연주를 배우는 것과 기본적으로 다르지 않다. 만약 어떤 이가 행복의 기술을 연습한다면 그 사람은 그것을 더 잘하게 된다."라고 설명한다. 이것이 의미하는 바는 여러분이 감사, 휴식 또는 자신감을 불러일으키는 경험을 반복함으로써 더 감사하거나 편안하거나 자신감을 갖도록 여러분의 뇌를 실제로 훈련시킬 수 있다는 것이다. 뇌는 여러분이 반복하는 생각에 의해 형성된다. 뉴런은 반복된 생각과 활동에 의해 활성화되면서 더 많이 점화할수록 신경 경로로 더 빠르게 발달하게 되고, 이는 뇌에 지속적인 변화를 야기한다. 혹은 Donald Hebb의 말을 빌리면 "함께 점화하는 뉴런은 함께 연결된다." 이는 대단히 고무적인 전제이다. 즉, 결론은 뇌가 더 행복해지도록 우리가 습관을 의도적으로 만들 수 있다는 것이다.

Why? 왜 정답일까?

마지막 문장(~ we can intentionally create the habits for the brain to be happier.)에서 우리는 뇌를 더 행복하게 할 습관을 만들어 갈 수 있다는 결론을 제시하므로, 글의 주제로 가장 적절한 것은 ① '행복을 위한 뇌 습관을 만들어낼 수 있는 가능성'이다.

- **neuroscientist** ⓝ 신경과학자
- **grateful** ⓐ 감사하는
- **bottom line** 핵심, 요점, 결론
- **enhance** ⓥ 향상시키다
- **fundamentally** ⓐ 기본적으로
- **activate** ⓥ 활성화하다
- **intentionally** ⓐ 의도적으로

구문 풀이

11행 The more neurons fire as they are activated by repeated
「the + 비교급 ~
thoughts and activities, the faster they develop into neural pathways,
the + 비교급 … : …할수록 더 …하다」
which cause lasting changes in the brain.
계속적 용법(주절 보충)

---

03 지역별 산림 면적 점유율 비교
정답률 80% | 정답 ④

다음 도표의 내용과 일치하지 않는 것은?

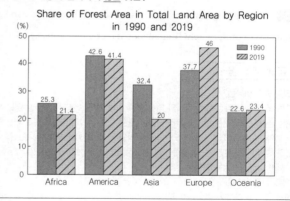

Share of Forest Area in Total Land Area by Region in 1990 and 2019

[본문 해석]

위 도표는 1990년과 2019년의 지역별 총 토지 면적에서 산림 면적의 점유율을 보여준다. ① 아프리카의 전체 토지 면적에서 산림 면적의 점유율이 1990년과 2019년 둘 다 20%를 넘었다. ② 1990년 아메리카의 산림 면적 점유율은 42.6% 였고, 이는 2019년보다 더 컸다. ③ 아시아의 산림 면적 점유율은 1990년부터 2019년까지, 10퍼센트포인트 이상 감소했다. ④ 2019년 유럽의 산림 면적 점유율은 다섯 개 지역 중 가장 컸고, 같은 해 아시아의 세 배가 넘었다. ⑤ 오세아니아는 1990년과 2019년 사이에 총 토지 면적에서 산림 면적의 점유율에 있어 가장 작은 차이를 보였다.

Why? 왜 정답일까?

도표에 따르면 2019년 아시아의 산림 면적 점유율은 20%인데, 유럽의 점유율은 46% 이므로 두 비율은 3배 이상 차이 나지 않는다. 따라서 도표와 일치하지 않는 것은 ④이다.

- **region** ⓝ 지역
- **decline** ⓥ 감소하다, 줄어들다

★★★ 1등급 대비 고난도 2점 문제

04 정서에 영향을 미치는 조명
정답률 49% | 정답 ④

다음 글의 밑줄 친 부분 중, 어법상 틀린 것은?

[본문 해석]

너무 밝은 빛이나 눈에 직선으로 들어오는 빛과 마찬가지로 좋지 못한 조명은 여러분의 눈에 스트레스를 증가시킬 수 있다. 형광등 또한 피로감을 줄 수 있다. 여러분이 모를 수도 있는 것은 빛의 질 또한 중요할 수 있다는 것이다. 대부분의 사람들은 밝은 햇빛 속에서 가장 행복하다 — 이것은 아마 정서적인 행복감을 주는 체내 화학물질을 분비시킬지도 모른다. 전형적으로 몇 개 안 되는 빛 파장만 포함하는 인공 조명이 기분에 미치는 효과는 햇빛과 똑같지 않을 수 있다. 창가에서 작업하거나 책상 전등에 있는 모든 파장이 있는 전구를 사용하여 실험해 보아라. 이것이 여러분의 작업 환경의 질을 향상시킨다는 것을 아마도 알게 될 것이다.

Why? 왜 정답일까?

주어가 불가산명사인 Artificial light이므로 동사는 단수인 does로 쓰는 것이 적절하다. 따라서 어법상 틀린 것은 ④이다.

Why? 왜 오답일까?

① 동사 shines를 꾸미는 말로서 부사 directly의 쓰임은 어법상 맞다.
② 주어인 Fluorescent lighting이 피로감을 주는 주체이므로 능동의 현재분사 tiring의 쓰임은 어법상 맞다.
③ 선행사 chemicals를 꾸미고 뒤에 복수 동사 bring를 연결하는 말로서 주격 관계대명사 that의 쓰임은 어법상 맞다.
⑤ 등위접속사 or 앞에 동명사 experimenting이 나오므로, 이와 병렬을 이루도록 동명사인 using을 쓴 것은 어법상 맞다. 두 동명사는 명령문 동사 Try의 목적어이다.

- **lighting** ⓝ 조명, 빛
- **bright** ⓐ 밝은
- **appreciate** ⓥ 이해하다
- **chemical** ⓝ 화학 물질
- **artificial** ⓐ 인공의
- **contain** ⓥ …이 들어 있다
- **experiment** ⓥ 실험하다 ⓝ 실험
- **improve** ⓥ 향상시키다, 개선하다
- **shine** ⓥ 비추다
- **directly** ⓐⓓ 곧장, 똑바로
- **release** ⓝ 분비, 방출
- **emotional** ⓐ 정서적인
- **typically** ⓐⓓ 일반적으로
- **wavelength** ⓝ 파장, 주파수
- **bulb** ⓝ 전구

구문 풀이

1행 Bad lighting can increase stress on your eyes, / as can light
「as + 동사 + 주어 : ~이 …하듯이(도치 구문)」
[that is too bright], or light [that shines directly into your eyes].

★★ 문제 해결 꿀~팁 ★★

▶ 많이 틀린 이유는?
최다 오답인 ②는 감정 유발 동사의 태를 묻고 있다. 감정 유발 동사를 분사로 바꿀 때에는 분사가 설명하는 명사에 따라 태를 결정한다. 즉 명사가 감정을 유발하는 주체라면 현재분사를, 감정을 느끼게 되는 대상이라면 과거분사를 쓴다. 여기서는 분사가 주어인 '형광등'을 설명하는데 이는 피로감을 유발하는 주체로 보는 것이 타당하다. 따라서 tiring의 쓰임은 어법상 맞다.
▶ 문제 해결 방법은?
④에서 묻는 수 일치 개념은 어법 최빈출 포인트 중 하나이다. 뒤에 관계절을 수반하는 긴 주어가 나오면 관계절이 어디에서 시작되고 끝나는지, 주어의 핵심부는 무엇인지 눈여겨보고 동사의 단복수 여부를 결정하도록 한다.

★★★ 1등급 대비 고난도 3점 문제

05 다양한 수요를 충족시켜야 하는 현대 사회 정답률 39% | 정답 ④

다음 글의 밑줄 친 부분 중, 문맥상 낱말의 쓰임이 적절하지 <u>않은</u> 것은? [3점]

[본문 해석]

산업 사회가 1940년대와 1950년대 동안 더 부유해지고, 더 경쟁적이 되고, 지리적으로 더 확산되면서 판매 개념에 주요한 철학적 변화가 일어났다. 이로 인해 기업은 구매자 및 고객과 ① 더 긴밀한 관계를 발전시켜야 했고, 이것은 결과적으로 기업이 합리적인 가격에 양질의 제품을 생산하는 것으로는 충분하지 않다는 것을 깨닫게 했다. 사실, 고객이 실제로 원하는 제품을 내놓는 것이 마찬가지로 ② 매우 중요했다. 1908년에 Henry Ford는 가장 많이 팔렸던 T-모델 Ford를 한 가지 색상(검은색)으로만 생산했지만, 현대 사회에서는 이것이 더 이상 ③ 가능하지 않다. 사회의 현대화는 생산이 그 자체의 수요를 창출할 것이라는 견해로 ④ 강화한(→ 파괴한) 마케팅 혁명으로 이어졌다. 고객과 이들의 다양하고 흔히 복잡한 욕구를 ⑤ 충족하고자 하는 욕망이 기업의 초점이 되었다.

Why? 왜 정답일까?

현대 사회에 이르러 사람들이 전체적으로 풍족해지고 기업 간 경쟁이 치열해지면서, 합리적인 비용의 대량 생산으로 이득을 보던 시대는 지나고 고객마다의 다양한 수요에 부응할 필요성이 커졌다는 내용이다. ④가 포함된 문장 앞에서, 과거에는 Ford 사처럼 한 가지 색상만으로 제품을 생산해도 괜찮았지만 현대 사회에서는 이것이 '가능하지' 않다고 한다. 이 뒤에는 생산만으로 수요가 창출되리라는 기대가 '무너졌다'가 설명이 이어져야 적합하므로, ④의 strengthened를 destroyed로 고쳐야 한다. 따라서 문맥상 낱말의 쓰임이 적절하지 않은 것은 ④이다.

- **philosophical** ⓐ 철학적인
- **industrial** ⓐ 산업의
- **geographically** ⓐⓓ 지리적으로
- **in turn** 결과적으로
- **best-selling** ⓐ 가장 많이 팔리는
- **revolution** ⓝ 혁명
- **complex** ⓐ 복잡한
- **shift** ⓝ 변화, 전환 ⓥ 바뀌다
- **affluent** ⓐ 부유한
- **spread** ⓥ 퍼지다
- **essential** ⓐ 매우 중요한
- **modernization** ⓝ 현대화
- **strengthen** ⓥ 강화하다

구문 풀이

4행 [This forced business to develop closer relations with buyers and clients], which in turn made business realize that it was not
[ ] : 선행사 계속적 용법   사역동사   원형부정사   가주어
enough to produce a quality product at a reasonable price.
진주어

★★ 문제 해결 꿀~팁 ★★

▶ 많이 틀린 이유는?
T-model Ford가 한 가지 색상으로 출시된 것이 어떤 예시인지 파악해야 한다. 색상을 한 가지로만 출시해도 차가 잘 팔렸다는 것은, 과거에는 '그저 질 좋은 제품을 합리적인 가격에 제공하는 것으로 족했다'는 의미와 같다. 하지만 지금은 상황이 달라져서, 이러한 전략이 더 이상(no longer) '가능하지' 않다는 의미로 ③은 자연스럽다.
▶ 문제 해결 방법은?
Ford 차의 예시를 일반화한 표현이 바로 'production would create its own demand'이다. 즉 '생산만으로 수요가 만들어지고 제품이 팔리는' 상황을 가리키는 것이다. 오늘날에는 이런 상황이나 견해가 '강화되는' 것이 아니라 점점 '깨지고' 있다는 것이 글의 주제이다.

06 생존 기술의 일종인 편향 정답률 65% | 정답 ①

다음 빈칸에 들어갈 말로 가장 적절한 것을 고르시오.

✓① necessary survival skill – 필수적인 생존 기술
② origin of imagination – 상상력의 근원
③ undesirable mental capacity – 바람직하지 않은 정신적 능력
④ barrier to relationships – 관계에 대한 장애물
⑤ challenge to moral judgment – 도덕적 판단에 대한 도전 과제

[본문 해석]

여기 불편한 진실이 있는데, 우리는 모두 편향되어 있다. 모든 인간은 다른 사람들에 대해 부정확한 추측을 하도록 이끄는 무의식적인 편견에 영향을 받는다. 모두가 그렇다. 어느 정도, 편견은 필수적인 생존 기술이다. 만약에 당신이, 가령 호모 에렉투스처럼, 정글을 돌아다니는 초기 인류라면, 당신은 어떤 동물이 다가오는 것을 볼지 모른다. 당신은 그 동물의 외양에만 기초하여 그 동물이 안전한지 아닌지에 대해서 매우 빨리 추측해야 한다. 이것은 다른 인류에게도 똑같이 적용된다. 당신은 만약 필요하다면 도망갈 시간이 충분하도록 위험에 대해서 순간적인 결정을 내려야 한다. 이것이 타인의 외모와 옷으로 그들을 범주화하고 분류하려는 성향의 한 근간일 수도 있다.

Why? 왜 정답일까?

빈칸 뒤를 통해 우리는 초기 인류 시절 동물을 보고 위험한지 아닌지를 빨리 판단해야 도망갈 시간을 벌 수 있었기에 편향을 발달시켜 왔고, 이것을 오늘날까지 유지해온 것임을 알 수 있다. 따라서 빈칸에 들어갈 말로 가장 적절한 것은 편향이 우리의 '생존'을 위해 발달되어 온 것이라는 의미를 완성하는 ① '필수적인 생존 기술'이다.

- **unpleasant** ⓐ 불쾌한
- **unconscious** ⓐ 무의식적인
- **assumption** ⓝ 가정
- **approach** ⓥ 다가오다, 접근하다
- **The same is true of** ~에도 해당하다
- **categorize** ⓥ 범주화하다
- **bias** ⓥ 편견을 갖게 하다 ⓝ 편견, 편향
- **incorrect** ⓐ 부정확한
- **to a certain extent** 어느 정도
- **solely** ⓐⓓ 단지, 오로지
- **split-second** ⓐ 찰나의, 순식간의
- **undesirable** ⓐ 바람직하지 않은

구문 풀이

10행 You make split-second decisions about threats in order to
~하기 위해
have plenty of time to escape, if (it is) necessary.
형용사적 용법   생략   보어(형용사)
접속사

---

07   유혹을 극복하는 방법
정답률 51% | 정답 ③

다음 빈칸에 들어갈 말로 가장 적절한 것을 고르시오.

① letting go of all-or-nothing mindset
양자택일의 사고방식을 버림
② finding reasons why you want to change
왜 변하고 싶은지 이유를 찾음
③ locking yourself out of your temptations
여러분 자신을 유혹으로부터 차단함
④ building a plan and tracking your progress
계획을 세워 진행 상황을 추적함
⑤ focusing on breaking one bad habit at a time
한 번에 하나의 나쁜 습관을 깨는 데 집중함

[본문 해석]

여러분이 한 번이라도 좋지 못한 선택을 한 적이 있다면, 그런 습관을 깨는 방법을 배우는 데 관심이 있을지도 모른다. 여러분의 뇌를 속여 그렇게 하는 한 가지 좋은 방법은 'Ulysses 계약'에 서명하는 것이다. 이 인생에 대한 조언의 이름은 Ulysses에 관한 그리스 신화에서 유래되었는데, 그는 저항할 수 없는 노래를 통해 희생자들을 죽음으로 유혹한 위험한 여성 부족인 사이렌의 섬을 지나던 배의 선장이었다. Ulysses는 그렇게 하지 않으면 저항할 수 없다는 것을 알고, 선원들에게 귀를 솜으로 막고 자신을 배의 돛대에 묶게 시켜 자신이 사이렌 쪽으로 배를 돌리지 못하게 했다. 그것은 그에게 효과가 있었고, 여러분은 여러분 자신을 유혹으로부터 차단함으로써 똑같은 일을 할 수 있다. 예를 들어, 만약 여러분이 휴대폰을 멀리하고 일에 집중하고 싶다면, 여러분의 주의를 산만하게 하는 앱들을 삭제하거나, 친구에게 여러분의 비밀번호를 바꿔달라고 요청하라!

Why? 왜 정답일까?

빈칸 앞에서 신화 속 인물 **Ulysses**는 선원들을 시켜 자기 몸을 돛대에 묶게 해서 사이렌의 노래에 유혹되려는 자기 자신을 막았다고 한다. 빈칸에는 이러한 **Ulysses**의 조치를 일반화할 수 있는 표현이 필요하므로, 답으로 가장 적절한 것은 ③ '여러분 자신을 유혹으로부터 차단함'이다. 일에 집중하기 위해 일에 도움이 안 되는 앱을 지우거나 친구를 통해 비밀번호를 바꾸게 하라는 내용 또한 '유혹에 넘어가지 않기' 위한 예시에 해당한다.

- **break a habit** 습관을 깨다
- **sign a contract** 계약서에 서명하다
- **myth** ⓝ 신화
- **lure** ⓥ 유혹하다
- **instruct** ⓥ 지시하다, 가르치다
- **tie** ⓥ 묶다
- **prevent** ⓥ 예방하다, 막다
- **let go of** ~을 놔두다, 내려놓다
- **temptation** ⓝ 유혹
- **trick A into B** A를 속여 B하게 하다
- **come from** ~에서 기원하다
- **sail** ⓥ 항해하다
- **irresistible** ⓐ 저항할 수 없는
- **stuff** ⓥ (속을) 채우다, 막다
- **mast** ⓝ 돛대
- **distract** ⓥ 산만하게 하다
- **all-or-nothing** ⓐ 양자택일의

구문 풀이

4행 The name of this life tip comes from the Greek myth about Ulysses, (a captain whose ship sailed past the island of the Sirens), { a tribe of dangerous women who lured victims to their death with their irresistible songs}.   ( ) : Ulysses와 동격   { } : the Sirens와 동격

---

08   전염병의 확산과 이에 대한 도시 환경의 대응력
정답률 58% | 정답 ④

다음 글에서 전체 흐름과 관계 없는 문장은? [3점]

[본문 해석]

건강과 질병의 확산은 우리가 어떻게 살고 우리의 도시가 어떻게 작동하느냐와 매우 밀접하게 연관되어 있다. 좋은 소식은 도시가 믿을 수 없을 정도로 회복력이 있다는 것이다. 많은 도시는 과거에 전염병을 경험했고 살아남았을 뿐만 아니라 발전했다. ① 19세기와 20세기 초 유럽의 도시들은 콜레라, 장티푸스, 독감의 파괴적인 창궐을 목격했다. ② 영국 출신의 Jon Snow와 독일의 Rudolf Virchow와 같은 의사들은 열악한 주거 환경, 인구 과밀, 위생과 질병의 연관성을 알게 되었다. ③ 이 연관성에 대한 인식은 전염병의 확산을 막기 위한 도시 재계획과 재건축으로 이어졌다. ④ 재건 노력에도 불구하고 많은 지역에서 도시는 쇠퇴하였고 많은 사람이 떠나기 시작했다. ⑤ 19세기 중반에 지어진,

---

오늘날까지도 사용되고 있는 런던의 선구적인 하수 처리 시스템은 깨끗한 물이 콜레라의 확산을 막는 데 중요하다는 이해의 결과로 만들어졌다.

Why? 왜 정답일까?

첫 문장에서 전염병의 확산은 우리의 생활방식 및 도시 환경과 밀접하게 연관되어 있다는 주제를 제시한 뒤, ①, ②, ③, ⑤는 19~20세기 초 각종 전염병의 창궐을 경험한 유럽 도시들이 도시 환경의 개선을 통해 전염병을 극복했다는 예시를 든다. 하지만 ④는 도시가 재건 노력에도 불구하고 쇠퇴했다는 무관한 내용을 제시한다. 따라서 전체 흐름과 관계 없는 문장은 ④이다.

- **spread** ⓝ 확산 ⓥ 퍼지다
- **epidemic** ⓝ 전염병
- **outbreak** ⓝ 발발, 창궐
- **sanitation** ⓝ 위생 (관리)
- **incredibly** ⓐⓓ 놀라울 정도로
- **destructive** ⓐ 파괴적인
- **overcrowding** ⓝ 과밀 거주, 초만원
- **reconstruction** ⓝ 재건

구문 풀이

1행 Health and the spread of disease are very closely linked to
주어   동사구(복수)
how we live and how our cities operate.
간접의문문1   간접의문문2

---

09   대접받고 싶은 대로 상대를 대접한다는 규칙의 맹점
정답률 58% | 정답 ⑤

주어진 글 다음에 이어질 글의 순서로 가장 적절한 것을 고르시오. [3점]

① (A) - (C) - (B)
② (B) - (A) - (C)
③ (B) - (C) - (A)
④ (C) - (A) - (B)
⑤ (C) - (B) - (A)

[본문 해석]

다른 문화에 대한 존중과 지식을 발달시키는 방법을 이해하는 것은 다음의 황금률을 재점검해보는 일에서 시작된다. "나는 상대를 내가 대접받고 싶은 대로 대접한다."

(C) 이 법칙은 어느 수준에서는 일리가 있다. 만약 다른 사람들을 우리가 대접받고 싶은 만큼 대접한다면 우리는 보답으로 잘 대접받게 될 것이다. 이 법칙은 모든 사람이 같은 문화적 틀 안에서 일하는 단일 문화 환경에서는 잘 통한다.

(B) 그러나 단어, 제스처, 신념과 관점이 다른 의미를 지닐지도 모르는 다문화 환경에서는 이 법칙이 의도치 않은 결과를 낳는다. 그것은 나의 문화가 상대의 것보다 낫다는 메시지를 줄 수 있다.

(A) 그것은 또한 우리가 하는 것이 옳다고 믿지만, 그것이 의도된 방식으로 해석되지 않는 답답한 상황을 낳을 수도 있다. 이러한 의사소통 오류는 문제를 야기할 수 있다.

Why? 왜 정답일까?

자신이 대접받기를 원하는 대로 상대를 대접한다는 황금률을 다시 살펴봐야 한다는 주어진 글 뒤로, 이 법칙(This rule)이 단일 문화 환경에서는 잘 통한다는 내용의 (C), 하지만 (however) 다문화 환경에서는 잘 안 통할 수 있다는 내용의 (B), 안 통할 때 생기는 문제에 관해 부연하는 (A)가 차례로 이어져야 자연스럽다. 따라서 글의 순서로 가장 적절한 것은 ⑤ '(C) - (B) - (A)'이다.

- **reexamine** ⓥ 재점검하다
- **frustrating** ⓐ 답답한, 좌절스러운
- **miscommunication** ⓝ 의사소통 오류
- **unintended** ⓐ 의도되지 않은
- **in return** 보답으로, 반응으로
- **golden rule** 황금률
- **interpret** ⓥ 해석하다, 이해하다
- **multicultural** ⓐ 다문화의
- **make sense** 일리가 있다, 의미가 통하다
- **monocultural** ⓐ 단일 문화의

구문 풀이

5행 It can also create a frustrating situation [where we believe
선행사   관계부사
(that) we are doing what is right, but what we are doing is not being
생략   주어1   동사1   주어2(관계대명사절: ~것) 동사2(현재진행 수동태)
interpreted in the way [in which it was meant]].
선행사

---

10   문제 해결로서의 언어 학습
정답률 51% | 정답 ③

글의 흐름으로 보아, 주어진 문장이 들어가기에 가장 적절한 곳을 고르시오. [3점]

DAY 27

[본문 해석]

우리의 뇌는 끊임없이 문제를 해결하고 있다. ① 우리가 무언가를 배우거나, 기억하거나, 이해할 때마다, 우리는 문제를 해결한다. ② 일부 심리학자들은 모든 유아 언어 학습을 문제 해결이라고 특정지었고, 이를 어린이에게 확장하여 그러한 과학적 절차들을 '실험을 통한 학습' 혹은 '가설 검증'으로 보았다. ③ 어른들은 아이들에게 문법적인 규칙이 어떻게 작용하는지는 말할 것도 없고, 새로운 단어의 의미를 거의 설명하지 않는다. 대신에 그들은 대화에서 단어나 규칙을 사용하고, 무슨 상황인지 알아내는 일을 아이들에게 맡긴다. ④ 언어를 배우기 위해서는, 유아는 언어를 사용하는 맥락을 파악해야 하는데, 즉 문제는 반드시 해결돼야 한다는 것이다. ⑤ 우리 모두는 우리가 무엇을 하고 있는지 인식하지 못한 채 이 어린 시절부터 이런 종류의 문제들을 해결해왔다.

Why? 왜 정답일까?

③ 앞에서 일부 심리학자들은 유아 언어 학습을 문제 해결로 규정하였다고 언급한 후, ③ 뒤의 문장에 **they**가 나오는데, 이 **they**는 앞에 이어서 **Some psychologists**를 가리키지 않는다. 즉 심리학자들이 언어 학습을 문제 해결의 과정으로 보았다는 내용 뒤로, 실제로 어른들이 언어를 배우는 아이들에게 문법 규칙이나 단어에 관해 설명하는 경우는 드물다는 주어진 문장이 연결된 후, '대신에' 이 어른들은 아이들이 스스로 파악하고 해결할 수 있도록 내버려둔다는 설명이 이어지는 맥락인 것이다. 따라서 주어진 문장이 들어가기에 가장 적절한 곳은 ③이다.

- **grown-up** ⓐ 다 큰, 어른이 된
- **let alone** ~은 말할 것도 없고
- **constantly** [ad] 끊임없이
- **characterize** ⓥ ~의 특징을 기술하다
- **extend** ⓥ 확장시키다
- **hypothesis** ⓝ 가설
- **explain** ⓥ 설명하다
- **grammatical** ⓐ 문법적인
- **make sense of** ⓥ ~을 이해하다
- **infant** ⓝ 유아
- **procedure** ⓝ 절차
- **awareness** ⓝ 인식, 앎

구문 풀이

11행 In order to learn language, an infant must make sense of
목적(~하기 위해)
the contexts [in which language occurs]; problems must be solved.
선행사   = where   조동사 수동태

11-12 식품 수송의 탄소 발자국을 줄이기 위해 거리보다 중요한 요소들

[본문 해석]

『로컬푸드 생산이 운송 연료의 연소를 줄여서 온실가스 배출을 줄였다는 주장들은 대개 근거가 충분하지 않다.』 운송은 식품 부문 내에서 온실가스 배출의 11퍼센트만을 차지하는 원천이기에, 식품이 농장을 떠난 후 이동하는 거리를 줄이는 것은 농장에서 낭비되는 에너지 사용을 줄이는 것보다 훨씬 (a) 덜 중요하다. 먼 곳에서 오는 식품은 그것이 어떻게 재배되었느냐에 따라 실제로 (b) 기후에 더 좋을 수 있다. 예를 들어, 겨울에 멕시코로부터 수송된 밭에서 재배된 토마토는 온실에서 재배된 (c) 현지의 겨울 토마토보다 탄소 발자국이 더 적을 것이다. 영국에서는, 뉴질랜드에서 11,000마일을 이동하는 양고기는 영국의 양고기에 비해 파운드당 탄소 배출량의 4분의 1만 발생시키는데, 영국의 농부들은 클로버 목초지에서가 아닌 (화석 연료를 사용하여 생산되어야 하는) 사료로 자신의 동물들을 기르기 때문이다. 식품이 이동할 때, 가장 중요한 것은 이동 (d) 거리가 아니고, 이동 방식(지상 대 공중)과 무엇보다도 적재량의 규모이다. 대량의 적재된 식품은 단거리만 이동하지만 적재량이 훨씬 (e) 더 많은(→ 더 적은) 식품에 비해, 해상 화물 운송으로 배달된 파운드당 탄소 발자국을 더 적게 들여 세계 절반을 이동할 수 있다. 『예를 들어, 18륜 대형트럭은 픽업트럭보다 훨씬 더 많은 적재량을 운반하므로, 배달된 식품 파운드당 3분의 1의 연료만 연소하면서 100배 멀리 식품을 이동시킬 수 있다.』 ─『』:12번의 근거

- **greenhouse gas** 온실가스
- **well founded** 근거가 충분한
- **wasteful** ⓐ 낭비하는
- **ship** ⓥ 운송하다, 수송하다
- **lamb** ⓝ 어린 양
- **raise** ⓥ 기르다, 키우다
- **fossil fuel** 화석 연료
- **travel mode** 이동 수단
- **load** ⓝ 적재(량) ⓥ (짐을) 싣다
- **freight** ⓝ 화물 운송
- **shorten** ⓥ 짧게 줄이다
- **agriculture** ⓝ 농업
- **emission** ⓝ 배출(량)
- **sector** ⓝ 부문
- **depending on** ~에 따라
- **carbon footprint** 탄소 발자국
- **generate** ⓥ 발생시키다, 생성하다
- **feed** ⓝ 사료, 먹이
- **pastureland** ⓝ 목초지
- **surface** ⓝ 지면
- **bulk** ⓝ 대량 ⓐ 대량의
- **pickup truck** 픽업트럭, 소형 오픈 트럭
- **ruin** ⓥ 파괴하다, 망치다

구문 풀이

20행 When food does travel, what matters most is **not** {the distance
동사 강조   not + {A} +
traveled} but {the travel mode (surface versus air), and most of all the
but + {B} : A가 아니라 B인
load size}.

11 제목 파악   정답률 56% | 정답 ②

윗글의 제목으로 가장 적절한 것은?

① Shorten the Route, Cut the Cost
   거리를 줄여서 비용을 줄이라
☑ Is Local Food Always Better for the Earth?
   로컬푸드가 지구를 위해 항상 더 좋을까?
③ Why Mass Production Ruins the Environment
   왜 대량 생산이 환경을 망치나
④ New Technologies: What Matters in Agriculture
   신기술: 농업에서 중요한 것
⑤ Reduce Food Waste for a Smaller Carbon Footprint
   더 적은 탄소 발자국을 위해 음식물 쓰레기를 줄이라

Why? 왜 정답일까?

로컬푸드로 식품 수송의 거리를 줄여 탄소 발자국을 줄일 수 있다는 주장에 대한 반박으로, 거리보다는 수송 수단이나 적재량 등 다른 요소가 더 중요하다(**When food does travel, what matters most is not the distance traveled but the travel mode ~ and most of all the load size.**)고 주장하는 글이다. 따라서 글의 제목으로 가장 적절한 것은 ② '로컬푸드가 지구를 위해 항상 더 좋을까?'이다.

★★★ 1등급 대비 고난도 2점 문제

12 어휘 추론   정답률 38% | 정답 ⑤

밑줄 친 (a) ~ (e) 중에서 문맥상 낱말의 쓰임이 적절하지 않은 것은?

① (a)   ② (b)   ③ (c)   ④ (d)   ☑ (e)

Why? 왜 정답일까?

마지막 문장에서 적재량이 더 많을 때 탄소 발자국을 훨씬 줄여 이동할 수 있다(~ 18-wheelers carry much larger loads than pickup trucks so they can move food 100 times as far while burning only one-third as much gas per pound of food delivered.)는 예를 드는 것으로 보아, 적재량이 '더 적을' 때보다 많을 때가 낫다는 설명이 적합하다. 즉 (e)의 **larger**를 **smaller**로 고쳐야 하므로, 문맥상 낱말의 쓰임이 적절하지 않은 것은 ⑤ '(e)'이다.

★★ 문제 해결 꿀~팁 ★★

▶ 많이 틀린 이유는?
첫 문장 내용을 잘 이해하지 못하면 ①이 어색해 보일 수 있다. 하지만 식품 수송 거리를 줄인다고 해서 탄소 발자국을 줄일 수 있다는 주장에 '근거가 부족하다'는 말은 결국 거리 단축이 비교적 '덜 중요하다'는 뜻이 맞다.

▶ 문제 해결 방법은?
마지막 문장의 예시는 더 가까운 거리를 가더라도 적재량이 '더 적은' 경우보다, 더 먼 거리를 가도 양이 많은 편이 더 낫다는 핵심 내용으로 귀결된다. (e)가 than 뒤에 나온다는 점에 주의해야 한다.

DAY 28 — 20분 미니 모의고사

01 ②	02 ①	03 ⑤	04 ④	05 ②
06 ⑤	07 ②	08 ③	09 ②	10 ③
11 ②	12 ⑤			

---

01 휴가 도중 아버지의 부상 소식을 들은 필자   정답률 83% | 정답 ②

다음 글에 드러난 'I'의 심경 변화로 가장 적절한 것은?

① nervous → confident
긴장한   자신 있는
☑ relaxed → worried
여유로운   걱정하는
③ excited → indifferent
신난   무관심한
④ pleased → jealous
즐거운   질투하는
⑤ annoyed → grateful
짜증 난   고마워하는

[본문 해석]

어느 아름다운 봄날, 나는 휴가를 충분히 즐기고 있었다. 나는 네일 숍에 도착해서 내 휴대폰을 음소거하고 그 시간 동안 단절되어 차분하고 평화로운 기분을 느끼고자 했다. 나는 매니큐어를 받는 동안 아주 편안했다. 그곳을 떠나면서, 나는 나의 휴대폰을 확인했고 낯선 번호에서 걸려 온 네 통의 부재중 전화를 봤다. 나는 뭔가 나쁜 일이 생겼다는 것을 즉시 알고 다시 전화했다. 한 젊은 여성이 전화를 받아 우리 아버지가 돌에 걸려 넘어져 다쳤고 지금 벤치에 앉아 있다고 말했다. 아버지는 무릎 수술에서 회복한 직후라서 나는 정말 걱정되었다. 나는 아버지를 보러 가기 위해 급히 차에 올랐다.

Why? 왜 정답일까?

네일숍에 들러 휴가를 여유롭게(feel calm and peaceful, comfortable) 즐기고 있던 필자가 아버지가 넘어져 다쳤다는 소식에 몹시 걱정했다(concerned)는 내용이다. 따라서 'I'의 심경 변화로 가장 적절한 것은 ② '여유로운 → 걱정하는'이다.

- **day off** 휴가
- **disconnected** ⓐ 단절된
- **comfortable** ⓐ 편안한
- **fall over** ~에 걸려 넘어지다
- **recover from** ~로부터 회복하다
- **rush** ⓥ 서두르다
- **relaxed** ⓐ 느긋한, 여유로운
- **jealous** ⓐ 질투하는
- **mute** ⓥ 음소거하다
- **calm** ⓐ 차분한
- **call back** 전화를 회신하다
- **concerned** ⓐ 걱정되는
- **surgery** ⓝ 수술
- **nervous** ⓐ 긴장한
- **indifferent** ⓐ 무관심한
- **grateful** ⓐ 고마워하는

구문 풀이

2행 I arrived at the nail salon, and muted my cellphone so that
            접속사(~하기 위해)
I would be disconnected for the hour and (would) feel calm and
  동사1   동사2
peaceful.

---

02 위험을 감수할 필요성   정답률 89% | 정답 ①

다음 글의 요지로 가장 적절한 것은?

☑ 위험을 무릅쓰지 않으면 아무 것도 얻지 못한다.
② 자신이 잘하는 일에 집중하는 것이 효율적이다.
③ 잦은 실패 경험은 도전할 의지를 잃게 한다.
④ 위험 요소가 있으면 미리 피하는 것이 좋다.
⑤ 부탁을 자주 거절하면 신뢰를 잃는다.

[본문 해석]

사실상 모든 가치 있는 것은 우리가 실패나 거절당할 위험을 무릅쓸 것을 요구한다. 이것은 우리 앞에 놓인 더 큰 보상을 성취하기 위해 우리 모두가 지불해야 하는 대가이다. 위험을 무릅쓴다는 것은 언젠가 성공할 것이라는 것을 의미하지만 위험을 전혀 무릅쓰지 않는 것은 결코 성공하지 못할 것임을 의미한다. 인생은 많은 위험과 도전으로 가득 차 있으며, 이 모든 것에서 벗어나기를 원하면 인생이라는 경주에서 뒤처지게 될 것이다. 결코 위험을 무릅쓰지 못하는 사람은 아무것도 배울 수 없다. 예를 들어, 만약 차를 운전하기 위해 위험을 무릅쓰지 않는다면, 여러분은 결코 운전을 배울 수 없다. 거절당할 위험을 무릅쓰지 않는다면 친구나 파트너를 절대 얻을 수 없다. 마찬가지로 면접에 참석하는 위험을 무릅쓰지 않음으로써, 여러분은 결코 일자리를 얻지 못할 것이다.

Why? 왜 정답일까?

예시 앞에 나와 주제를 제시하는 'A person who can never take a risk can't learn anything.'에서 위험을 감수하지 않는 사람은 그 어떤 것도 배울 수 없다는 논지를 말하고 있다. 따라서 글의 요지로 가장 적절한 것은 ① '위험을 무릅쓰지 않으면 아무 것도 얻지 못한다.'이다.

- **practically** ⓐⓓ 사실상, 거의
- **reject** ⓥ 거절하다
- **filled with** ~로 가득 찬
- **take a risk** ⓥ 위험을 무릅쓰다
- **reward** ⓝ 보상
- **be left behind** 뒤처지다

구문 풀이

1행 Practically anything of value requires that we (should) take
          주어   ⌐= valuable   동사(요구)   생략
a risk of failure or being rejected.
전치사⌐ 목적어1   목적어2(수동 동명사)

---

03 뇌 시각 체계의 독립성   정답률 70% | 정답 ⑤

다음 글의 제목으로 가장 적절한 것은?

① Visual Systems Never Betray Our Trust!
시각 체계는 결코 우리의 신뢰를 저버리지 않는다!
② Secret Missions of Color-Sensitive Brain Cells
색에 예민한 뇌세포의 비밀 임무
③ Blind Spots: What Is Still Unknown About the Brain
맹점: 뇌에 관해 아직 알려지지 않은 것
④ Why Brain Cells Exemplify Nature's Recovery Process
뇌세포가 자연의 회복 과정의 전형적 예가 되는 이유
☑ Separate and Independent: Brain Cells' Visual Perceptions
분리되어 있고 독립적이다: 뇌세포의 시각적 인식

[본문 해석]

뇌 시각 시스템의 다양한 부분들은 필요할 때 필요한 것만 알려주는 방식으로 정보를 얻는다. 여러분의 손 근육이 어떤 물체에 닿을 수 있도록 돕는 세포들은 그 물체의 크기와 위치를 알아야 하지만 색깔에 대해 알 필요는 없다. 그것들은 모양에 대해 약간 알아야 하지만, 매우 자세히는 아니다. 여러분이 사람의 얼굴을 인식하도록 돕는 세포는 모양의 세부 사항에 극도로 예민해야 할 필요가 있지만, 위치에는 신경을 덜 쓸 수 있다. 어떤 물체를 보는 사람이라면 모양, 색깔, 위치, 움직임 등 그것에 관한 모든 것을 보고 있다고 추정하는 것은 당연하다. 하지만, 여러분 뇌의 한 부분은 그것의 모양을 보고, 다른 한 부분은 색깔을 보며, 또 다른 한 부분은 위치를 감지하고, 또 다른 한 부분은 움직임을 인식한다. 따라서 국부적 뇌 손상 후 물체의 특정한 측면은 볼 수 있으면서 다른 측면은 보지 못하는 것이 가능하다. 수 세기 전, 사람들은 어떻게 누군가가 색깔이 무엇인지 못 보면서 그 물체를 볼 수 있는지 상상하기가 어려웠다. 심지어 오늘날에도, 여러분은 물체가 어디에 있는지 못 보면서 그 물체를 보거나, 또는 물체가 움직이고 있는지 보지 못하면서 물체를 보는 사람들에 대해 알게 되면 놀라워할 수 있다.

Why? 왜 정답일까?

첫 문장에서 뇌의 시각적 시스템은 각 부분별로 필요할 때 필요한 것만 아는 방식으로 정보를 얻는다(Different parts of the brain's visual system get information on a need-to-know basis.)는 주제를 제시하고 있다. 이어서 However 뒤를 보면, 뇌의 부분별로 어떤 물체의 모양, 색깔, 위치 등 정해진 면만 보기 때문에, 예컨대 이중 어느 한 가지 측면을 못 보면서도 물체를 '보는' 상황이 가능하다고 설명하고 있다. 따라서 글의 제목으로 가장 적절한 것은 ⑤ '분리되어 있고 독립적이다: 뇌세포의 시각적 인식(Separate and Independent: Brain Cells' Visual Perceptions)'이다.

- **on a need-to-know basis** 필요할 때 필요한 것만 알려주는 방식으로
- **muscle** ⓝ 근육
- **location** ⓝ 위치
- **recognize** ⓥ 알아보다, 인식하다
- **sensitive to** ~에 민감한, 예민한
- **detect** ⓥ 감지하다
- **consequently** ⓐⓓ 그 결과
- **certain** ⓐ 특정한
- **unknown** ⓐ 미지의
- **separate** ⓐ 분리된, 개별의
- **reach out to** (손을 뻗어) ~에 닿다
- **shape** ⓝ 모양 ⓥ 형성하다
- **extremely** ⓐⓓ 몹시, 매우
- **assume** ⓥ 가정하다
- **perceive** ⓥ 인식하다
- **localized** ⓐ 국소적인, 국부적인
- **betray** ⓥ 배신하다
- **exemplify** ⓥ ~의 전형적 예가 되다
- **independent** ⓐ 독립된

구문 풀이

15행 Centuries ago, people found it difficult to imagine
                         가목적어   진목적어
how someone could see an object without seeing what color it is.
간접의문문(how + 주어 + 동사)   ~하지 않은 채

DAY 28

04 보석 만들기 수업
정답률 95% | 정답 ④

Silversmithing Class에 관한 다음 안내문의 내용과 일치하지 <u>않는</u> 것은?
① 두 시간 동안 진행된다.
② 10월 1일부터 등록할 수 있다.
③ 등록 인원은 6명으로 제한된다.
☑ 참가 연령에 제한이 없다.
⑤ 수업 당일 취소 시 환불이 불가하다.

[본문 해석]

Silversmithing Class(은세공 수업)

Kingston Club은 정교한 보석 만들기 수업을 제공합니다. 여러분만의 보석을 만들어볼 이런 좋은 기회를 놓치지 마세요!

시간 & 장소
• 「2023년 10월 21일 토요일(오후 2시부터 오후 4시까지)」—「」: ①의 근거 일치
• Kingston Club 스튜디오

등록
• 온라인으로만 가능
• 「일자: 2023년 10월 1 ~ 14일」—「」: ②의 근거 일치
• 비용: 40달러(이것은 모든 도구와 재료를 포함합니다.)
• 「등록은 6명으로 제한됩니다.」—「」: ③의 근거 일치

유의 사항
• 「참가자는 16세 이상이어야 합니다.」—「」: ④의 근거 불일치
• 「수업 당일 취소 시 환불 불가」—「」: ⑤의 근거 일치

Why? 왜 정답일까?

'Participants must be at least 16 years old.'에서 참가자는 16세 이상이어야 한다고 하므로, 안내문의 내용과 일치하지 않는 것은 ④ '참가 연령에 제한이 없다.'이다.

Why? 왜 오답일까?

① 'Saturday, October 21, 2023 (2 p.m. to 4 p.m.)'의 내용과 일치한다.
② 'Dates: October 1–14, 2023'의 내용과 일치한다.
③ 'Registration is limited to 6 people.'의 내용과 일치한다.
⑤ 'No refund for cancellation on the day of the class'의 내용과 일치한다.

● silversmith ⓝ 은세공하는 사람
● jewelry ⓝ 보석
● registration ⓝ 등록
● refund ⓝ 환불
● on the day of ~의 당일에
● fine ⓐ 정교한, 미세한
● miss a chance 기회를 놓치다
● material ⓝ 재료
● cancellation ⓝ 취소

★★★ 1등급 대비 고난도 3점 문제

05 지적 잠재력을 충분히 발굴하지 못하는 학교
정답률 30% | 정답 ②

(A), (B), (C)의 각 네모 안에서 문맥에 맞는 낱말로 가장 적절한 것은? [3점]

	(A)		(B)		(C)
①	intelligent 똑똑한	……	accept 받아들이다	……	widely 넓게
☑	intelligent 똑똑한	……	overlook 간과하다	……	narrowly 좁게
③	unintelligent 영리하지 못한	……	overlook 간과하다	……	widely 넓게
④	unintelligent 영리하지 못한	……	overlook 간과하다	……	narrowly 좁게
⑤	unintelligent 영리하지 못한	……	accept 받아들이다	……	widely 넓게

[본문 해석]

세상 물정에 인상적일만큼 밝아도 학교에서는 부진한 어떤 젊은이를 모두가 알고 있다. 우리는 인생의 많은 것에 대해 그토록 (A) 똑똑한 사람이 그 똑똑함을 학업에 적용할 수 없는 것처럼 보이는 것이 낭비라고 생각한다. 우리가 깨닫지 못하는 것은 학교나 대학이 그러한 세상 물정에 밝은 사람들을 끌어들여 그들을 뛰어난 학업으로 안내해 줄 기회를 놓치는 잘못을 하고 있을지도 모른다는 것이다. 또한 우리는 왜 학교와 대학이 세상 물정에 밝은 사람들의 지적 잠재력을 (B) 간과하는지에 대한 주요한 이유 중 하나를 고려하지 않는데, 즉 우리는 이러한 세상 물정에 밝은 사람들을 반지성적인 근심거리와 연관시킨다는 사실이다. 우리는 교육받은 삶, 지성인의 삶을 우리가 본질적으로 중요하고 학문적이라고 여기는 교과와 교과서에 지나치게 (C) 좁게 연관시킨다.

Why? 왜 정답일까?

(A) 앞 문장의 'street smart'를 풀어 쓴 말이 'so intelligent about so many things in life'이므로, (A)에는 intelligent가 적절하다.
(B) 앞 문장에서 학교나 대학은 세상 물정에 밝은 사람들을 끌어들여 그들을 학업으로 안내할 기회를 '놓치고' 있다(missing the opportunity to draw such street smarts and guide them toward good academic work)고 하므로, (B)에는 학교가 이들의 지적 잠재력을 '간과한다'는 의미의 overlook을 쓰는 것이 적절하다.
(C) 'the fact that we associate those street smarts with anti-intellectual concerns.'에서 세상 물정에 밝은 사람들은 '반지성적인', 즉 교과서적이고 학문적이지 '않다'고 여겨지는 근심거리들과 연관지어진다고 말하므로, (C)에는 narrowly가 적절하다. 따라서 각 네모 안에서 문맥에 맞는 낱말로 가장 적절한 것은 ② '(A) intelligent(똑똑한) – (B) overlook(간과하다) – (C) narrowly(좁게)'이다.

● impressively ⓐⓓ 인상적으로, 인상 깊게
● intelligent ⓐ 똑똑한, 지적인
● miss an opportunity 기회를 놓치다
● associate ⓥ 연관시키다
● educated ⓐ 교양 있는, 교육받은
● weighty ⓐ 중대한, 무거운
● street smart 세상 물정에 밝은
● at fault 잘못한, 책임이 있는
● overlook ⓥ 간과하다
● concern ⓝ 우려, 걱정거리 ⓥ 걱정시키다
● inherently ⓐⓓ 본질적으로, 내재적으로

구문 풀이

8행 Nor do we consider one of the major reasons [why schools
「nor + 조동사 + 주어 + 동사원형 : 부정어구의 도치」
and colleges overlook the intellectual potential of street smarts]:
동격
the fact [that we associate those street smarts with anti-intellectual
「associate + A + with + B : A를 B와 연관시키다」
concerns]. [ ] : the fact와 동격

★★ 문제 해결 꿀~팁 ★★

▶ 많이 틀린 이유는?
(B)보다는 (A), (C)에서 오답이 많이 나온 문제였다. (A)는 해설에서 언급하였듯이 'street smart'를 다시 풀어쓰는 부분이므로 intelligent를 써야 하며, (C)의 경우에는 학교가 세상 물정에 밝은 사람들의 학문적 가능성을 충분히 포용하지 못하고 있다는 의미로서 narrowly를 써야 한다.

▶ 문제 해결 방법은?
단순히 단어의 의미를 묻기보다는 주제에 비추어 글의 문맥적 흐름을 이해할 수 있는지를 묻는 문제이다. 마치 빈칸이 여러 개 있는 문제를 푸는 느낌으로 접근하도록 한다.

★★★ 1등급 대비 고난도 2점 문제

06 과학기술이 종종 거부되는 이유
정답률 36% | 정답 ⑤

다음 글의 밑줄 친 부분 중, 문맥상 낱말의 쓰임이 적절하지 <u>않은</u> 것은?

[본문 해석]

과학기술의 발전은 흔히 변화를 강요하는데, 변화는 불편하다. 이것은 과학기술이 흔히 저항을 받고 일부 사람들이 그것을 ① 위협으로 인식하는 주된 이유 중 하나이다. 과학기술이 우리 삶에 끼치는 영향력을 고려할 때 우리는 불편함에 대한 우리의 본능적인 ② 질색을 이해하는 것이 중요하다. 사실, 우리 대부분은 ③ 최소한의 저항의 길을 선호한다. 이 경향은 많은 사람들에게 새로운 무엇인가를 시작하는 것이 그저 너무 힘든 일이기 때문에 새로운 과학기술의 진정한 잠재력이 ④ 실현되지 않은 채로 남아 있을 수 있다는 것을 의미한다. 심지어 새로운 과학기술이 어떻게 우리의 삶을 향상시킬 수 있는가에 관한 우리의 생각은 편안함을 향한 이런 욕구에 의해 ⑤ 장려될(→ 제한될) 수 있다.

Why? 왜 정답일까?

첫 두 문장에 주제가 제시된 글로, 과학기술은 변화를 야기하여 우리에게 불편감을 주고 이로 인해 거부감을 사기도 한다는 내용을 다루고 있다. 앞에서 우리는 불편감을 본능적으로 싫어하며(our natural hate of being uncomfortable) 저항이 최소화되는 길을 선호한다(~ prefer the path of least resistance.)고 언급하는 것으로 볼 때, 과학기술이 설령 우리의 삶을 향상시킬 수 있다고 하더라도 이는 편안함을 추구하고자 하는 우리의 욕구로 인해 방해를 받을 수 있다는 내용이 이어지는 것이 적절하다. 따라서 ⑤의 encouraged를 limited로 고쳐야 한다. 문맥상 낱말의 쓰임이 적절하지 않은 것은 ⑤이다.

● resist ⓥ 저항하다
● threat ⓝ 위협
● as a matter of fact 사실, 실상은
● perceive ⓥ 감지하다
● impact ⓝ 영향
● prefer ⓥ 선호하다

- **tendency** ⓝ 경향
- **struggle** ⓝ 힘든 일, 투쟁
- **unrealized** ⓐ 실현되지 않은
- **enhance** ⓥ 향상시키다

구문 풀이

11행 Even our ideas about {how new technology can enhance our
　　　　　　주어　　　전치사　　{ } : 간접의문문(about의 목적어)
lives} may be limited by this natural desire for comfort.
　　　　조동사 수동태

★★ 문제 해결 꿀~팁 ★★

▶ 많이 틀린 이유는?
많은 수험생들이 어려워하는 과학기술을 소재로 다룬 글이다. 앞에서 우리는 저항과 불편감이 최소이기를 추구한다고 언급한 것으로 볼 때, 새로운 시작 자체를 버거워해서 새로운 기술의 잠재력 또한 종종 실현하지 못한 채로 남겨둔다는 의미의 ④는 적절하다.

▶ 문제 해결 방법은?
글에 따르면 새로운 기술의 잠재력이 충분히 실현되지 않는 까닭은 편안함을 추구하고 변화와 새로운 시작을 꺼리는 인간의 욕구 때문이다. 따라서 편안함에 대한 욕구로 인해 새로운 기술에 대한 고려가 장려된다는 ⑤의 내용은 맥락상 부적절하다.

---

07 정기적인 회의를 통한 창의력 향상　　정답률 57% | 정답 ②

다음 빈칸에 들어갈 말로 가장 적절한 것을 고르시오. [3점]

① consumer complaints – 소비자 불만
✓ the regular meetings – 이 정기적인 회의들
③ traveling experiences – 여행 경험
④ flexible working hours – 유연한 근무 시간
⑤ the financial incentives – 재정적 인센티브

[본문 해석]
실리콘 밸리의 가장 혁신적인 회사들 중 한 회사의 최고 경영자는 지루하고 창의력을 해치는 듯 보이는 관례가 있다. 그는 일주일에 하루 오전 9시에 시작하는 세 시간짜리 회의를 연다. 그 회의에 빠지거나 다른 시간으로 일정이 변경되는 일은 결코 없다. 그것은 의무적인데 너무 그러하여 심지어 이 다국적 기업의 모든 경영자들은 그 회의와 시간이 겹치는 어떠한 이동 일정도 절대 잡지 않아야 한다는 것을 알고 있다. 언뜻 보아, 여기에 특별히 독특한 점은 없다. 그러나 정말로 독특한 것은 이 정기적인 회의들로부터 나오는 아이디어의 질이다. 최고경영자는 회의를 계획하거나 누가 회의에 참여하고 참여하지 않을지에 대해 생각하는 것과 관련된 정신적 비용을 없앴기 때문에, 사람들은 창의적인 문제 해결에 초점을 맞출 수 있다.

Why? 왜 정답일까?

시간을 바꾸거나 불참할 수 없는 '정기적인' 회의(He holds a three-hour meeting that starts at 9:00 A.M. one day a week. It is never missed or rescheduled at a different time.)를 통해 불필요한 정신적 비용을 해소하고(~ the CEO has eliminated the mental cost involved in planning the meeting ~) 창의력 증진에 시간을 투자하는 회사가 있음을 소개한 글이다. 따라서 빈칸에 들어갈 말로 가장 적절한 것은 ② '이 정기적인 회의들'이다.

- **innovative** ⓐ 혁신적인
- **executive** ⓝ 경영진, 중역
- **eliminate** ⓥ 없애다, 제거하다
- **flexible** ⓐ 유연한, 융통성 있는
- **mandatory** ⓐ 의무적인, 강제의
- **at first glance** 언뜻 보기에, 처음에는
- **involved in** ~와 관련된, ~에 연루된
- **incentive** ⓝ 인센티브, 상여금, 장려금

구문 풀이

5행 It is mandatory — so much so that even in this global firm all
　　　　　　　　　　　매우 그러하므로 ~하다
the executives know never to schedule any travel [that will conflict with
　　　　　　　　　　　　　　　　　　　　　주격 관계대명사 　~와 상충되다
the meeting].

---

08 야구 선수를 위한 운동의 일부가 된 근력 운동　　정답률 66% | 정답 ③

다음 글에서 전체 흐름과 관계 없는 문장은?

[본문 해석]
야구를 위한 훈련과 몸만들기는 체력, 힘, 속도, 신속함, 유연성을 발달시키는

데 초점을 둔다. ① 1980년대 이전에 근력 운동은 야구 선수를 위한 몸만들기의 중요한 부분이 아니었다. ② 사람들은 야구를 근력보다는 기술과 테크닉의 경기로 보았고, 대부분의 감독과 코치는 근력 운동을 야구 선수가 아닌 보디빌더를 위한 것으로 여겼다. ③ 더 분리된 보디빌딩 운동과는 달리 운동선수용 운동은 가능한 한 많은 근육군과 기능을 동시에 훈련시킨다. ④ 그들은 역도와 큰 근육을 키우는 것이 선수들로 하여금 유연성을 잃어버리게 하고 신속함과 적절한 테크닉을 방해할 것이라고 두려워했다. ⑤ 그렇지만 오늘날 전문가들은 근력 운동의 중요성을 이해하고 그것을 경기의 일부로 만들어 오고 있다.

Why? 왜 정답일까?

근력 운동은 본디 야구 선수를 위한 운동으로 여겨지지 않았지만 시간이 지나며 야구 선수를 위한 운동의 일부로 자리하게 되었다는 내용을 다룬 글이다. 하지만 ③은 보디빌딩 운동과 운동선수용 운동의 차이를 설명하는 데 중점을 두고 있다. 따라서 전체 흐름과 관계없는 문장은 ③이다.

- **conditioning** ⓝ 훈련, 조절
- **flexibility** ⓝ 유연성
- **athletic** ⓐ 운동선수의
- **fear** ⓥ (~을) 두려워하다
- **interfere with** ⓥ ~을 방해하다
- **quickness** ⓝ 신속함
- **isolated** ⓐ 분리된, 고립된
- **muscle** ⓝ 근육
- **weight lifting** ⓝ 역도
- **proper** ⓐ 적절한

구문 풀이

11행 They feared that weight lifting and building large muscles
　　　　　　　　　　접속사(~것)
would cause players to lose flexibility and (would) interfere with
「cause + 목적어 + to부정사 : ~이 …하게 야기하다」　　　　생략
quickness and proper technique.

★★★ 1등급 대비 고난도 2점 문제

09 존재만으로 관계를 상하게 하는 휴대폰　　정답률 52% | 정답 ②

다음 글의 내용을 한 문장으로 요약하고자 한다. 빈칸 (A), (B)에 들어갈 말로 가장 적절한 것은?

(A)	(B)		(A)	(B)
① weakens 약화시킨다	answered 응대되고		✓ weakens 약화시킨다	ignored 무시되고
③ renews 새롭게 한다	answered 응대되고		④ maintains 유지시킨다	ignored 무시되고
⑤ maintains 유지시킨다	updated 업데이트되고			

[본문 해석]
한 연구에서, 연구자들은 서로 모르는 사람들끼리 짝을 지어 한 방에 앉아서 이야기하도록 했다. 절반의 방에는 근처 탁자 위에 휴대폰이 놓여 있었고, 나머지 절반에는 휴대폰이 없었다. 대화가 끝난 후, 연구자들은 참가자들에게 서로에 대해 어떻게 생각하는지를 물었다. 여기에 그들이 알게 된 것이 있다. 방에 휴대폰이 있을 때 참가자들은 휴대폰이 없는 방에서 대화했던 참가자들에 비해 자신들의 관계의 질이 더 나빴다고 말했다. 휴대폰이 있는 방에서 대화한 짝들은 자신의 상대가 공감을 덜 보여 주었다고 생각했다. 친구와 점심을 먹기 위해 자리에 앉아 탁자 위에 휴대폰을 놓았던 모든 순간을 떠올려 보라. 메시지를 확인하려고 휴대폰을 집어 들지 않았으므로 잘했다고 느꼈을지 모르지만, 여러분의 확인하지 않은 메시지는 여전히 맞은편에 앉아 있는 사람과의 관계를 상하게 하고 있었다.

➡ 휴대폰의 존재는 심지어 휴대폰이 (B) 무시되고 있을 때조차 대화에 참여하는 사람들 간의 관계를 (A) 약화시킨다.

Why? 왜 정답일까?

'~ when a cell phone was present in the room, the participants reported the quality of their relationship was worse than those who'd talked in a cell phone-free room.'과 '~ your unchecked messages were still hurting your connection with the person sitting across from you.'에서 우리가 휴대폰을 확인하지 않고 내버려두는 상황일지라도 휴대폰이 '있다'는 사실 자체로 상대방과의 관계가 약해질 수 있다는 연구 결과가 제시된다. 이를 근거로 볼 때, 요약문의 빈칸에 들어갈 말로 가장 적절한 것은 ② '(A) weakens(약화시킨다), (B) ignored(무시되고)'이다.

- **study** ⓝ 공부, 학습, 학문
- **pair** ⓝ 짝
- **chat** ⓥ 이야기하다
- **place** ⓥ 놓다, 두다
- **researcher** ⓝ 연구원, 조사원, 탐색자
- **stranger** ⓝ 모르는 사람, 낯선 사람
- **cell phone** 휴대폰
- **nearby** ⓐ 근처의

DAY 28

[문제편 p.171]

- **present** ⓐ 존재하는
- **report** ⓥ 말하다, 전하다
- **partner** ⓝ 상대
- **unchecked** ⓐ 확인되지 않은
- **connection** ⓝ 관계, 연결
- **weaken** ⓥ 약화시키다
- **ignore** ⓥ 무시하다
- **maintain** ⓥ 유지하다
- **participant** ⓝ 참가자
- **relationship** ⓝ 관계
- **empathy** ⓝ 감정이입, 공감
- **hurt** ⓥ 손상시키다, 다치게 하다
- **involved** ⓐ 관여하는, 관련된, 연루된
- **answer** ⓥ 대답하다, 대응하다
- **renew** ⓥ 새롭게 하다, 갱신하다, 재개하다

구문 풀이

14행 You might have felt good about yourself because you didn't
「might have + p.p. : ~했을지도 모른다」　접속사(~ 때문에)
pick it up to check your messages, but your unchecked messages
　　　　　　　　　　　　　　　　　　　　　　주어
were still hurting your connection with the person sitting across
동사(과거진행)　　　　　　　　　　　　　　　　현재분사
from you.

★★ 문제 해결 꿀~팁 ★★

▶ 많이 틀린 이유는?
마지막 문장에서 '확인하지 않은(unchecked)' 휴대폰 메시지가 관계에 악영향을 미치고 있었다는 결론이 제시된다. 즉 요약문의 (B)에는 휴대전화에 '응답하고 있지 않은' 상황에조차 관계가 약화되고 있었다는 의미를 완성하는 말이 들어가야 한다. ①의 answered는 휴대전화에 '응답하는' 상황에조차 관계가 나빠지고 있었다는 의미를 나타내므로 부적절하다.

▶ 문제 해결 방법은?
요약문에서 '실험 – 결과' 구조의 글이 나오면 바로 결과가 제시되는 문장을 찾아 요약문을 그 문장과 일치시킨다는 느낌으로 문제를 풀면 된다. 이 문제에서도 실험의 결론을 제시하는 마지막 문장과 요약문의 내용이 서로 같아야 한다.

10-12　선물한 사람을 배려한 사려 깊은 왕자

[본문 해석]

(A)
「어느 날 한 가난한 남자가 포도 한 송이를 왕자에게 선물로 가져왔다.」 그는 너무 가난해서 그 이상의 여유가 없었기 때문에 (a) 그를 위한 선물을 가져올 수 있어서 매우 흥분했다. 그는 왕자의 옆에 포도를 놓고 "오, 왕자님, 저의 이 작은 선물을 부디 받아주세요."라고 말했다. 그의 얼굴은 작은 선물을 바치면서 행복으로 빛났다.

(C)
왕자는 그에게 정중하게 감사를 표했다. 그 남자가 기대에 부풀어 그를 바라보았을 때 왕자는 포도 한 알을 먹었다. 그러고 나서 (c) 그는 또 다른 하나를 먹었다. 천천히 왕자는 혼자서 포도 한 송이 전부를 다 먹었다. 「그는 자신의 곁에 있는 어떤 이에게도 포도를 권하지 않았다.」 그 포도를 (d) 그에게 가져온 남자는 매우 기뻐하고 떠났다. 왕자의 주변에 있던 그의 가까운 친구들은 매우 놀랐다.

(D)
「평소에 왕자는 자신이 가지고 있는 어떤 것이든 다른 사람들과 나눴다.」 그는 그들에게 자신이 받은 것은 무엇이든 권하고 그들은 그것을 함께 먹곤 했다. 이번에는 달랐다. 아무에게도 그것을 권하지 않고 (e) 그는 포도 한 송이를 혼자 다 먹었다. 그 친구들 중 한 명이 "왕자님! 어찌하여 혼자서 포도를 다 드시고 우리 중 그 누구에게도 그것을 권하지 않으셨나요?"라고 물었다. 「그는 웃으며 그 포도가 너무 시어서 혼자서 모든 포도를 다 먹었다고 말했다.」

(B)
만약 왕자가 그들에게 그 포도를 권했다면 그들은 우스꽝스러운 표정을 지으며 포도에 대한 불쾌감을 드러냈을 것이다. 그것은 그 가난한 남자의 감정을 상하게 했을 것이다. 그는 모든 포도를 기분 좋게 먹고 (b) 남자를 기쁘게 하는 것이 더 낫다고 속으로 생각했다. 「그는 그 가난한 남자의 감정을 상하게 하고 싶지 않았다.」 주위의 모든 사람들은 그의 사려 깊음에 감동 받았다.

- **bunch** ⓝ (포도 등의) 송이
- **beam with** ~으로 환히 웃다
- **distaste** ⓝ 불쾌감
- **expectantly** ⓐⓓ 기대하여
- **place** ⓥ 놓다, 두다
- **politely** ⓐⓓ 정중하게
- **thoughtfulness** ⓝ 사려 깊음

구문 풀이

(A) 2행 He was very excited to be able to bring a gift for him because
　　　　　　　　　　감정 형용사　　부사적 용법(~해서)
he was too poor to afford more.
「too ~ to … : 너무 ~해서 …하지 못하다」

(B) 1행 If the prince had offered the grapes to them, they might
「if + 주어 + had p.p. ~　　　　　　　　　　　주어 + 조동사 과거형 +
have made funny faces and shown their distaste for the grapes.
have p.p. ~ : 가정법 과거완료(과거 사실의 반대)」

(D) 1행 Usually the prince shared whatever he had with others.
　　　　　　　　　　　　　　　복합관계대명사(~하는 것은 무엇이든)

10　글의 순서 파악　　정답률 73% | 정답 ③

주어진 글 (A)에 이어질 내용을 순서에 맞게 배열한 것으로 가장 적절한 것은?

① (B) – (D) – (C)
② (C) – (B) – (D)
③✓ (C) – (D) – (B)
④ (D) – (B) – (C)
⑤ (D) – (C) – (B)

Why? 왜 정답일까?

왕자가 가난한 남자로부터 포도를 선물 받았다는 내용의 (A) 뒤로, 왕자가 주변 사람에게 권하지 않고 그 포도를 다 먹었다는 내용의 (C), 평소 왕자는 가진 것은 다른 사람들과 다 나누는 성품이었기에 주변 사람들이 의아해하며 이유를 물었다는 내용의 (D), 이유를 자세히 설명하는 (B)가 차례로 이어진다. 따라서 글의 순서로 가장 적절한 것은 ③ '(C) – (D) – (B)'이다.

11　지칭 추론　　정답률 71% | 정답 ②

밑줄 친 (a) ~ (e) 중에서 가리키는 대상이 나머지 넷과 다른 것은?

① (a)　②✓ (b)　③ (c)　④ (d)　⑤ (e)

Why? 왜 정답일까?

(a), (c), (d), (e)는 the prince, (b)는 that poor man을 가리키므로, (a) ~ (e) 중에서 가리키는 대상이 다른 하나는 ② '(b)'이다.

12　세부 내용 파악　　정답률 80% | 정답 ⑤

윗글의 왕자에 관한 내용으로 적절하지 않은 것은?

① 가난한 남자에게 포도 한 송이를 선물로 받았다.
② 가난한 남자의 감정을 상하게 하고 싶지 않았다.
③ 곁에 있던 어떤 이에게도 포도를 권하지 않았다.
④ 가지고 있는 어떤 것이든 평소에 다른 사람들과 나눴다.
⑤✓ 포도가 너무 시어서 혼자 다 먹지 못했다.

Why? 왜 정답일까?

(D) '~ he ate all the grapes by himself because the grapes were too sour.'에서 왕자는 가난한 남자가 가져온 포도가 너무 시어서 누구에게도 권하지 않고 혼자 다 먹었다고 하므로, 내용과 일치하지 않는 것은 ⑤ '포도가 너무 시어서 혼자 다 먹지 못했다.'이다.

Why? 왜 오답일까?

① (A) 'One day a poor man brought a bunch of grapes to a prince as a gift.'의 내용과 일치한다.
② (B) 'He did not want to hurt the feelings of that poor man.'의 내용과 일치한다.
③ (C) 'He did not offer grapes to anyone near him.'의 내용과 일치한다.
④ (D) 'Usually the prince shared whatever he had with others.'의 내용과 일치한다.

가 되는 것들은 어디에나 있지만, 목표를 달성하고 싶다면 여러분은 집중에 방해가 되는 것들에 대처하는 법을 배워야 한다. 집중에 방해가 되는 것들을 제거할 수는 없지만, 그것들이 여러분을 제한하지 않도록 하는 방식으로 그것들과 함께 살아가는 것을 배울 수 있다.

Why? 왜 정답일까?

'~ if you want to achieve your goals, you must learn how to tackle distractions.'에서 목표를 달성하려면 집중에 방해가 되는 요인에 대처하는 방법을 알아야 한다고 언급하는 것으로 보아, 필자가 주장하는 바로 가장 적절한 것은 ② '집중을 방해하는 요인에 대처할 줄 알아야 한다.'이다.

- distract ⓥ 집중이 안 되게 하다
- victim ⓝ 희생자
- tackle ⓥ (문제 등에) 대처하다, 맞서다
- ensure ⓥ 반드시 ~하게 하다
- complete ⓐ 완전한
- run away from ~로부터 도망치다
- eliminate ⓥ 제거하다

구문 풀이

7행 These students were victims of distractions [who found it very difficult to study anywhere except in their private bedrooms].

---

03 기후 변화에 관한 우리 자신의 책임 인식하기 정답률 54% | 정답 ④

밑줄 친 a slap in our own face가 다음 글에서 의미하는 바로 가장 적절한 것은? [3점]

① giving the future generation room for change
미래 세대에 변화의 여지를 주는 것
② warning ourselves about the lack of natural resources
우리 자신에게 천연자원 부족을 경고하는 것
③ refusing to admit the benefits of fossil fuel production
화석 연료 생산의 이점을 인정하기를 거부하는 것
④ failing to recognize our responsibility for climate change
기후 변화에 대한 우리의 책임을 인식하지 못하는 것
⑤ starting to deal with environmental problems individually
환경 문제를 따로 다루기 시작하는 것

[본문 해석]

기후 변화에 관해 많은 사람들은 온실가스를 배출하는 것에 대해 화석 연료 산업을, 열대 우림을 태우는 것에 대해 농업 분야를, 혹은 과다한 의복을 생산하는 것에 대해 패션 산업을 탓한다. 하지만 잠깐, 무엇이 이러한 산업 활동들을 가동시키는가? 우리의 소비이다. 기후 변화는 각 개인 행위의 합쳐진 산물이다. 예를 들어, 화석 연료 산업은 기후 위기에 있어서 일반적인 희생양이다. 하지만 왜 그들은 화석 연료를 시추하고 태울까? 우리가 그들에게 강력한 금전적인 동기를 제공한다. 예를 들어, 어떤 사람들은 화석 연료를 태우는 비행기와 차로 정기적으로 여행한다. 어떤 사람들은 발전소에서 연료를 태워 생산된 전기를 낭비한다. 어떤 사람들은 원유로부터 얻어진 플라스틱 제품을 매일 사용하고 버린다. 이러한 행위들에 참여하면서 화석 연료 산업을 탓하는 것은 자기 얼굴 때리기이다.

Why? 왜 정답일까?

For example 앞에서 기후 변화의 원인으로 지적되는 산업 활동을 촉발하는 것은 우리의 소비이고, 그러므로 기후 변화는 개인의 행위를 합친 산물로 볼 수 있다(Our consumption. Climate change is a summed product of each person's behavior.)고 언급한다. 이어서 'But why do they drill and burn fossil fuels? We provide them strong financial incentives: ~'에서도 애초에 화석 연료를 태우는 까닭이 우리가 그럴 동기를 제공하기 때문이라는 내용을 제시한다. 이러한 흐름으로 보아, 마지막 문장은 결국 기후 변화의 원인을 화석 연료 사용에 돌리는 것이 '자기 얼굴에 침 뱉기'와 같다는 뜻이다. 따라서 밑줄 친 부분이 의미하는 바로 가장 적절한 것은 ④ '기후 변화에 대한 우리의 책임을 인식하지 못하는 것'이다.

- blame A for B B에 대해 A를 탓하다
- excessive ⓐ 과다한
- crisis ⓝ 위기
- crude oil 원유
- agricultural ⓐ 농업의
- consumption ⓝ 소비
- drill ⓥ (자원, 연료 등을) 시추하다, 구멍을 뚫다
- slap ⓝ 철썩 때리기

구문 풀이

1행 When it comes to climate change, many blame {the fossil fuel industry} for {pumping greenhouse gases}, {the agricultural sector} for {burning rainforests}, or {the fashion industry} for {producing excessive clothes}.

DAY 29 20분 미니 모의고사

01 ②	02 ②	03 ④	04 ⑤	05 ⑤
06 ④	07 ③	08 ①	09 ②	10 ③
11 ②	12 ④			

01 식당 연례행사 초대 정답률 90% | 정답 ②

다음 글의 목적으로 가장 적절한 것은?

① 식당 개업을 홍보하려고
② 식당의 연례행사에 초대하려고
③ 신입 요리사 채용을 공고하려고
④ 매장 직원의 실수를 사과하려고
⑤ 식당 만족도 조사 참여를 부탁하려고

[본문 해석]

Dennis Brown씨께,

우리 G&D 식당은 우리의 연례행사인 Fall Dinner에 당신을 초대하게 되어 영광이고 기쁩니다. 그 연례행사는 2021년 10월 1일에 우리 식당에서 열릴 것입니다. 그 행사에서, 우리는 우리 식당이 곧 제공할 새로운 멋진 음식들을 소개할 것입니다. 이 맛있는 음식들은 우리의 뛰어난 요리사들의 멋진 재능을 보여줄 것입니다. 또한, 우리의 요리사들은 요리 비법들과 당신의 주방을 위해 무엇을 사야 할지에 대한 생각들, 그리고 특별한 요리법을 제공할 것입니다. 우리 G&D 식당은 만약에 당신이 이 특별한 행사에 와서 축하의 일원이 되어준다면 매우 감사할 것입니다. 우리는 당신을 곧 뵙기를 고대합니다. 매우 감사합니다.

G&D 식당 주인, Marcus Lee 드림

Why? 왜 정답일까?

'We at G&D Restaurant are honored and delighted to invite you to our annual Fall Dinner.'에서 식당 연례행사에 초대하게 되어 영광이라고 언급한 뒤, 후반부에서 행사의 일원이 되어주기를 거듭 당부하고 있다. 따라서 글의 목적으로 가장 적절한 것은 ② '식당의 연례행사에 초대하려고'이다.

- honored ⓐ 명예로운, 영광으로 생각하여
- annual ⓐ 연례의
- offer ⓥ 내놓다, 제공하다
- gifted ⓐ 재능 있는
- grateful ⓐ 고마워하는
- look forward to ~하기를 고대하다
- delighted ⓐ 기쁜
- dish ⓝ 요리
- showcase ⓥ 전시하다, 소개하다
- recipe ⓝ 조리법
- celebration ⓝ 기념, 축하

구문 풀이

8행 Also, our chefs will be providing cooking tips, ideas on what to buy for your kitchen, and special recipes.

02 집중을 방해하는 요인에 대한 적절한 대처법 정답률 82% | 정답 ②

다음 글에서 필자가 주장하는 바로 가장 적절한 것은?

① 자신에게 적합한 시간 관리법을 찾아야 한다.
② 집중을 방해하는 요인에 대처할 줄 알아야 한다.
③ 학습 공간과 휴식 공간을 명확하게 분리해야 한다.
④ 집중력 향상을 위해 정돈된 학습환경을 유지해야 한다.
⑤ 공공장소에서 타인에게 피해를 주는 행동을 삼가야 한다.

[본문 해석]

내가 고등학교에 다닐 때, 커피숍에서 공부하면서 소음이나 그들 주변에서 일어나는 모든 것에 방해를 받지 않을 수 있는 학생들이 있었다. 도서관이 아주 조용하지 않으면 공부할 수 없는 학생들도 있었다. 후자의 학생들은 도서관에서조차 그들이 추구하는 유형의 완전한 고요함을 얻는 것이 불가능했기 때문에 고통을 받았다. 이 학생들은 개인 침실을 제외하고 어디에서든 공부하는 것이 매우 어렵다는 것을 알게 된, 집중에 방해가 되는 것들의 희생자였다. 요즘 세상에서 집중에 방해가 되는 것들로부터 도망치는 것은 불가능하다. 집중에 방해

04 　형편없는 과제에 개선의 기회를 주기　정답률 71% | 정답 ⑤

다음 글의 요지로 가장 적절한 것은?
① 학생에게 평가 결과를 공개하는 것은 학습 동기를 떨어뜨린다.
② 학생에게 추가 과제를 부여하는 것은 학업 부담을 가중시킨다.
③ 지속적인 보상은 학업 성취도에 장기적으로 부정적인 영향을 준다.
④ 학생의 자기주도적 학습 능력은 정서적으로 안정된 학습 환경에서 향상된다.
☑ 학생의 과제가 일정 수준에 도달하도록 개선 기회를 주면 동기 부여에 도움이 된다.

[본문 해석]

낮은 성적이나 점수가 학생으로 하여금 미래에 더 노력을 기울이도록 독려할 것이라 희망하며 학생에게 그것으로 벌을 주는 대신, 교사는 그들의 과제를 미완성으로 보고 추가적인 노력을 요구함으로써 학생들에게 동기 부여를 더 잘 할 수 있다. 오하이오 주 Beachwood의 Beachwood 중학교 교사는 학생의 성적을 A, B, C 또는 I(미완성)로 기록한다. I 성적을 받은 학생은 자신의 과제 수행을 수용 가능한 수준까지 끌어올리기 위해서 추가적인 과제를 하도록 요구받는다. 이런 방침은 학생이 낙제 수준으로 수행하거나 낙제 과제를 제출하는 것이 대체로 교사가 그것을 받아들이기 때문이라는 믿음에 근거한다. Beachwood의 교사는 만약 그들이 더 이상 기준 이하의 과제를 받아들이지 않는다면, 학생이 그것을 제출하지 않을 것이라고 생각한다. 그리고 그들은 학생들이 적절한 도움을 받아서 자신의 과제 수행이 만족스러울 때까지 계속 노력할 것이라고 믿는다.

Why? 왜 정답일까?

첫 문장에서 학생들의 과제가 일정 수준 미만일 때 그저 점수를 낮게 주기보다는 '미완성된' 과제로 보고 더 노력을 들이도록 요구하는 것이 동기 부여에 좋다(~ teachers can better motivate students by considering their work as incomplete and then requiring additional effort.)고 하므로, 글의 요지로 가장 적절한 것은 ⑤ '학생의 과제가 일정 수준에 도달하도록 개선 기회를 주면 동기 부여에 도움이 된다.'이다.

- **punish** ⓥ 처벌하다
- **additional** ⓐ 추가적인
- **substandard** ⓐ 수준 이하의, 열악한
- **satisfactory** ⓐ 만족스러운
- **incomplete** ⓐ 미완성된
- **acceptable** ⓐ 수용 가능한
- **appropriate** ⓐ 적절한

구문 풀이

1행 Rather than attempting to punish students with a low grade or mark in the hope (that) it will encourage them to give greater effort in the future, teachers can better motivate students by considering their work as incomplete and then requiring additional effort.

`~라는 희망으로` / `encourage + 목적어 + to부정사 : ~이 …하도록 독려하다`
주어 / 동사구 / 전치사 / 동명사1 / 동명사2

05 　국내 출생자 수와 사망자 수의 변화 추이　정답률 74% | 정답 ⑤

다음 도표의 내용과 일치하지 않는 것은?

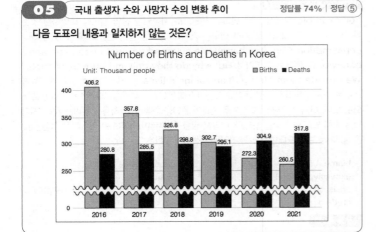

Number of Births and Deaths in Korea
Unit: Thousand people　☐ Births　■ Deaths

연도	2016	2017	2018	2019	2020	2021
Births	406.2	357.8	326.8	302.7	272.3	260.5
Deaths	280.8	285.5	298.8	295.1	304.9	317.8

[본문 해석]

위 그래프는 2016년부터 2021년까지 한국에서의 출생자 수와 사망자 수를 보여 준다. ① 출생자 수는 전체 기간 내내 계속 감소했다. ② 출생자 수와 사망자 수 사이의 차이는 2016년에 가장 컸다. ③ 2019년에는 출생자 수와 사망자 수 사이의 차이가 가장 작았는데, 출생자 수가 사망자 수보다 약간 더 컸다. ④ 사망자 수는 2018년과 2019년까지의 기간을 제외하고 전체 기간 동안 꾸준히 증가했다. ⑤ 2021년에는 처음으로 사망자 수가 출생자 수보다 더 컸다.

Why? 왜 정답일까?

도표에 따르면 한국의 사망자 수는 2020년에 이미 출생자 수를 추월했다. 따라서 도표와 일치하지 않는 것은 2021년에 사망자 수가 처음으로 출생자 수를 넘어섰다고 언급한 ⑤이다.

- **decrease** ⓥ 감소하다
- **slightly** ⓐ 약간
- **gap between A and B** A와 B 사이의 격차
- **steadily** ⓐ 꾸준히

구문 풀이

10행 In 2021, the number of deaths was larger than that of births for the first time.

`비교급 + than : ~보다 더 …한` ＝ the number

06 　세포의 탄생과 성장　정답률 50% | 정답 ④

다음 글의 밑줄 친 부분 중, 어법상 틀린 것은? [3점]

[본문 해석]

개체 전체와 마찬가지로, 세포도 수명이 있다. 생명 주기(세포 주기) 동안에, 세포의 크기, 모양, 물질대사 활동은 극적으로 변할 수 있다. 세포는 모세포가 분열하며 두 개의 딸세포를 만들 때 쌍둥이로 '탄생한다'. 각각의 딸세포는 모세포보다 더 작으며, 특이한 경우를 제외하고는 각각 모세포의 크기만큼 커질 때까지 자란다. 이 기간 중에, 세포는 물, 당, 아미노산, 그리고 다른 영양소들을 흡수하고 그것들을 새로운 살아있는 원형질로 조합한다. 세포는 적절한 크기로 성장한 후 분열할 준비를 하거나 혹은 성숙하여 특화 세포로 분화하면서 물질대사가 변화한다. 성장과 발달 둘 다 모든 세포 부분을 포함하는 일련의 복잡하고 역동적인 상호 작용을 필요로 한다. 세포의 물질대사와 구조가 복잡할 것임은 당연하지만, 실제로 그것들은 꽤 간단하고 논리적이다. 가장 복잡한 세포조차도 그저 몇몇 부분만을 가지고 있는데, 각각은 세포 생명의 뚜렷하고 명확한 측면을 맡고 있다.

Why? 왜 정답일까?

동사 would not be의 주어인 명사절 'cell metabolism and structure should be complex'가 완전한 2형식 구조이므로, 관계대명사 대신 명사절 접속사를 사용해야 한다. 즉 What을 That으로 고쳐야 적절하다. 따라서 어법상 틀린 것은 ④이다.

Why? 왜 오답일까?

① 콤마 앞의 완전한 주절 뒤에 목적어를 수반하는 능동의 분사구문 producing이 적절하게 쓰였다.
② 원래 be를 제외한 일반동사는 대동사 do로 대체되지만 become의 경우 be와 의미가 비슷하고 뒤에 보어를 취한다는 공통점이 있어 be로 대체되는 경우가 많다. 여기서도 becomes를 was가 대신했다. 분열 '이후' 생겨난 딸세포의 크기가 분열 '전' 모세포의 크기와 비슷해진다는 문맥으로 보아 시점의 차이가 있기 때문에 be동사의 시제를 과거로 썼다.
③ 「either A or B and B'」 구조로, A, B, B' 자리에 모두 it에 호응하는 단수 동사가 나온다. 따라서 differentiates가 적절하게 쓰였다.
⑤ 콤마 뒤는 원래 '~ and each is responsible ~'이다. 여기서 접속사 and를 생략하고, 문장의 주어와 다른 each는 그대로 두고, 동사 is를 being으로 바꾸어 분사구문을 만들었다가 being을 생략했다. 즉 여기서 형용사 responsible은 생략된 being의 보어 역할을 하는 품사로 적절히 쓰였다.

- **life span** 수명
- **absorb** ⓥ 흡수하다
- **assemble** ⓥ 조립하다
- **mature** ⓥ 성숙하다
- **specialized** ⓐ 특화된, 전문화된
- **well-defined** ⓐ 명확한
- **dramatically** ⓐ 극적으로
- **nutrient** ⓝ 영양소
- **proper** ⓐ 적절한
- **differentiate into** ~로 분화하다
- **responsible for** ~을 담당하는

07 　상처 받은 상대방에게 시간을 주며 기다려주기　정답률 56% | 정답 ③

다음 빈칸에 들어갈 말로 가장 적절한 것을 고르시오.
① curiosity - 호기심
☑ patience - 인내
⑤ honesty - 정직
② independence - 자립
④ creativity - 창의성

[본문 해석]

인내가 항상 가장 중요하다는 것을 기억해라. 사과가 받아들여지지 않으면, 그 사람이 여러분의 말을 끝까지 들어줬다는 것에 감사하고, 그 사람이 화해하고 싶을 경우와 시기를 위해 문(가능성)을 열어 두어라. 단지 누군가가 여러분의 사과를 받아들인다고 해서 그 사람이 여러분을 온전히 용서했다는 뜻이 아니라는 사실을 알고 있어라. 상처받은 당사자가 완전히 떨쳐 버리고 여러분을 온전히 다시 믿기까지 시간이 걸릴 수 있고, 어쩌면 오래 걸릴 수 있다. 이 과정을 빨라지게 하기 위해 여러분이 할 수 있는 것은 거의 없다. 그 사람이 여러분에게 진정으로 중요하다면, 그 사람에게 치유되는 데 필요한 시간과 공간을 주는 것이 가치가 있다. 그 사람이 즉시 평상시의 행동으로 바로 돌아갈 것이라고 기대하지 마라.

Why? 왜 정답일까?

마지막 세 문장에서 용서의 과정을 빨라지게 할 방법은 없고, 상대방에게 시간을 줄 필요가 있으므로 상대방이 곧바로 평상시대로 돌아갈 것이라는 기대를 하지 말라(~ it is worthwhile to give him or her the time and space needed to heal. Do not expect the person to go right back to acting normally immediately.)고 조언하고 있다. 이는 상대방을 기다려주며 인내심을 발휘하라는 내용으로 요약할 수 있으므로, 빈칸에 들어갈 말로 가장 적절한 것은 ③ '인내'이다.

- **be of the essence** 가장 중요하다
- **accept** ⓥ 받아들이다
- **conscious** ⓐ 알고 있는, 의식하는
- **injured** ⓐ 상처받은, 부상 당한
- **speed up** 빨라지게 하다
- **immediately** ⓐⓓ 즉시, 곧
- **independence** ⓝ 자립, 독립

- **apology** ⓝ 사과
- **hear ~ out** ~의 말을 끝까지 들어주다
- **take time** 시간이 걸리다
- **let go** (걱정·근심 등을) 떨쳐 버리다
- **normally** ⓐⓓ 정상적으로
- **curiosity** ⓝ 호기심
- **patience** ⓝ 인내

구문 풀이

4행 Be conscious of the fact that just because someone accepts
동격 접속사↵   주어(부사절이 명사절처럼 쓰임)
your apology does not mean she has fully forgiven you.
동사   목적어

★★★ 1등급 대비 고난도 3점 문제

08 수행으로 자기 자신의 가치를 매길 때   정답률 37% | 정답 ①

다음 빈칸에 들어갈 말로 가장 적절한 것을 고르시오. [3점]

☑ ① it is the sole determinant of one's self-worth
그것이 자신의 가치를 결정하는 유일한 요소일
② you are distracted by others' achievements
다른 사람의 성취에 의해 주의가 분산될
③ there is too much competition in one field
한 분야의 경쟁이 너무 심할
④ you ignore feedback about a performance
수행에 관한 피드백을 무시할
⑤ it is not accompanied by effort
그것에 노력이 따르지 않을

[본문 해석]

많은 사람들에게 능력은 지적 능력을 의미하기 때문에, 그들은 자신이 하는 모든 것이 자신이 얼마나 똑똑한지를 보여주기를 원한다. 예컨대, 훌륭한 소송 의견서를 작성하는 것, 시험에서 최고의 성적을 받는 것, 명쾌한 컴퓨터 코드를 작성하는 것, 대화 도중 탁월하게 현명하거나 재치 있는 말을 하는 것이다. 여러분은 또한 피아노를 얼마나 잘 치는지, 언어를 얼마나 잘 배우는지, 테니스 공을 얼마나 잘 서브하는지와 같은 특정한 기술이나 재능의 관점에서 능력을 정의할 수도 있다. 어떤 사람들은 매력적이고, 재미있고, 최신 유행에 맞추거나, 최신 기기를 가질 수 있는 능력에 초점을 맞춘다. 능력이 어떻게 정의되든지, 그것이 자신의 가치를 결정하는 유일한 요소일 때 문제가 발생한다. 수행이 그 사람의 유일한 척도가 되며, 다른 것은 고려되지 않는다. 뛰어난 수행은 뛰어난 사람을 의미하고, 평범한 수행은 평범한 사람을 의미한다. 끝.

Why? 왜 정답일까?

빈칸 뒤에서 수행을 자신의 가치에 대한 유일한 평가 척도로 삼는 경우(The performance becomes the *only* measure of the person; nothing else is taken into account.)의 부작용을 언급하는 것으로 보아, 빈칸에 들어갈 말로 가장 적절한 것은 ① '그것이 자신의 가치를 결정하는 유일한 요소일'이다.

- **competence** ⓝ 능력, 역량
- **brilliant** ⓐ 뛰어난
- **elegant** ⓐ 명쾌한, 멋있는
- **witty** ⓐ 재치 있는

- **reflect** ⓥ 반영하다
- **brief** ⓝ (법률) 취지서, 의견서, 보고서
- **exceptionally** ⓐⓓ 탁월하게
- **in terms of** ~의 면에서

- **serve a ball** 서브를 넣다
- **entertaining** ⓐ 재미있는, 즐거움을 주는
- **measure** ⓝ 척도
- **outstanding** ⓐ 뛰어난
- **determinant** ⓝ 결정 요소
- **distracted** ⓐ 정신이 팔린

- **attractive** ⓐ 매력적인
- **gadget** ⓝ 장비, 기기
- **take into account** ~을 고려하다
- **sole** ⓐ 유일한
- **self-worth** ⓝ 자존감, 자부심

구문 풀이

11행 However ability may be defined, a problem occurs when it
복합관계부사(어떻게 ~하든 간에 = no matter how)
is the sole determinant of one's self-worth.

★★ 문제 해결 꿀~팁 ★★

▶ 많이 틀린 이유는?
특정 분야의 재능이나 역량을 보여주려 한다는 내용 때문에, 빈칸 뒤를 제대로 읽지 않으면 남과의 비교를 언급하는 ②나 수행에 대한 피드백을 언급하는 ④가 빈칸에 적절해 보인다. 하지만 빈칸 문제를 풀 때는 해당 지문 자체의 내용에 충실해야 한다.

▶ 문제 해결 방법은?
빈칸 뒤에서 수행이 '한 사람을 평가하는 유일한 척도(the *only* measure of the person)'가 될 때를 언급하는데, 이 표현이 거의 그대로 ①에서 재진술되었다(the sole determinant of one's self-worth).

★★★ 1등급 대비 고난도 3점 문제

09 소수 집단과 다수 집단의 건강 지표 차이   정답률 38% | 정답 ②

주어진 글 다음에 이어질 글의 순서로 가장 적절한 것을 고르시오. [3점]

① (A) - (C) - (B)   ☑ ② (B) - (A) - (C)
③ (B) - (C) - (A)   ④ (C) - (A) - (B)
⑤ (C) - (B) - (A)

[본문 해석]

많은 연구들이 사람들의 건강과 주관적 웰빙이 민족 관계에 의해 영향을 받는다는 것을 보여주었다. 소수 집단의 구성원들이 일반적으로 다수 집단보다 더 좋지 않은 건강 결과를 보인다.

(B) 그러나 사회 계층과 의료 서비스에 대한 접근성 같은 명백한 요소들이 통제될 때조차도 그러한 차이가 남아 있다. 이것은 우세 관계가 사람들의 건강에 자체적인 영향을 미친다는 것을 보여 준다. 어떻게 그럴 수 있을까?

(A) 한 가지 가능한 답은 스트레스이다. 다수의 생리학적 연구를 통해 우리는 비교적 안전한 실험실 환경에서조차도 다른 민족적–인종적 범주의 구성원들과 마주치는 것이 스트레스 반응을 유발한다는 것을 안다.

(C) 소수 집단의 개인들은 다수 집단의 개인들과 많이 마주치며, 각각의 마주침은 이러한 반응을 유발할지도 모른다. 이러한 영향이 아무리 작을지라도 그것의 빈번한 발생이 총체적 스트레스를 증가시킬지도 모르며 이는 소수 집단 개인들의 건강상 불이익의 일부를 설명할 것이다.

Why? 왜 정답일까?

소수 집단의 구성원들이 대체로 다수 집단의 구성원보다 건강이 더 좋지 않다는 일반적인 내용을 제시하는 주어진 글 뒤에는, 심지어 사회 계층이나 의료 서비스에 대한 접근성 등 다른 요소들이 통제되었을 때조차 왜 이러한 결과가 나타나는지 자문하는 (B), 그 답이 스트레스에 있음을 제시하는 (A), 답을 보충 설명하는 (C)가 차례로 이어지는 것이 자연스럽다. 따라서 글의 순서로 가장 적절한 것은 ② '(B) - (A) - (C)'이다.

- **subjective** ⓐ 주관적인
- **relation** ⓝ 관계
- **poorer** ⓐ 더 좋지 못한, 더 부족한
- **physiological** ⓐ 생리학적인
- **category** ⓝ 범주
- **dominance** ⓝ 우세
- **frequency** ⓝ 빈도
- **disadvantage** ⓝ 불이익

- **ethnic** ⓐ 민족적인
- **minority** ⓝ 소수
- **majority** ⓝ 다수
- **encounter** ⓝ 마주침 ⓥ 마주치다
- **trigger** ⓥ 유발하다
- **have an effect on** ⓥ ~에 영향을 미치다
- **account for** ⓥ ~을 설명하다

구문 풀이

17행 However minimal these effects may be, / their frequency may
「however + 형용사/부사 + 주어 + 동사 : 아무리 ~하더라도」
increase total stress, which would account for part of the health
계속적 용법(주절 부연)
disadvantage of minority individuals.

★★ 문제 해결 꿀~팁 ★★

▶ 많이 틀린 이유는?
주어진 글의 Members of minority groups만 보고 바로 (C)를 연결시켜서는 안 된다. 주어진 글의 마지막 문장은 전체적으로 볼 때 소수 집단 사람들과 다수 집단 사람들의 건강 지표상 차이를 언급하는 내용이어서, 이를 (B)에서 that difference 로 요약하는 것이다.

▶ 문제 해결 방법은?
주어진 글의 마지막 문장이 (B)의 that difference로, (B)의 'How could that be the case?'라는 질문이 (A)의 'One possible answer'라는 답으로 연결된다는 것을 파악하면 쉽게 정답을 찾을 수 있다.

★★★ 1등급 대비 고난도 3점 문제

10 호혜주의가 침팬지 무리 서열 결정에 끼친 결과   정답률 28% | 정답 ③

글의 흐름으로 보아, 주어진 문장이 들어가기에 가장 적절한 곳을 고르시오. [3점]

[본문 해석]
호혜주의는 포획된 상황에서 침팬지 한 마리에게 수박이나 잎이 많은 가지처럼 많은 양의 먹이를 건네주고 뒤이어 일어나는 것을 관찰함으로써 탐구될 수 있다. ① 먹이 소유자가 주위의 다른 침팬지들에 둘러싸여 중심에 있게 되고, 모든 먹이가 다 분배될 때까지 꽤 큰 몫을 얻은 침팬지들 주변으로 새로이 형성된 무리들이 곧 뒤따르게 된다. ② 먹이를 구걸하는 침팬지들은 불평하고 울부짖을 수도 있지만 호전적인 충돌은 드물다. ③ 간혹 그러한 일이 정말 일어날 때, 누군가를 무리에서 떠나게 하려는 것은 먹이 소유자다. 먹이 소유자는 그들이 자신을 귀찮게 하지 않을 때까지 그들의 머리를 나뭇가지로 때리거나 그들에게 고음으로 울부짖는다. ④ 그들의 서열이 무엇이든 간에, 먹이 소유자가 먹이의 흐름을 제어한다. ⑤ 침팬지들이 호혜주의 상태에 접어들게 되면, 사회적 서열은 더 이상 중요한 것이 아니다.

Why? 왜 정답일까?

침팬지들이 호혜주의에 접어들면 서열보다도 먹이 소유자인지 아닌지가 중요해진다는 내용의 글이다. ③ 앞의 문장은 먹이 소유자에게 먹이를 구걸하는 침팬지들이 불평은 할 수 있지만 충돌은 피한다는 내용을 제시하는데, 주어진 문장은 '그런 상황', 즉 충돌의 상황이 빚어질 때 이를 통제하는 것이 먹이 소유자임을 언급한다. ③ 뒤의 문장은 먹이 소유자가 갈등 상황에서 취하는 행동을 열거한다. 따라서 주어진 문장이 들어가기에 가장 적절한 곳은 ③이다.

- **possessor** ⓝ 소유자
- **leafy** ⓐ 잎이 많은
- **sizable** ⓐ 상당한
- **distribute** ⓥ 분배하다
- **high-pitched** ⓐ 고음의
- **captivity** ⓝ 포획, 감금
- **obtain** ⓥ 얻다
- **share** ⓝ 몫 ⓥ 나누다
- **aggressive** ⓐ 공격적인
- **leave ~ alone** ~을 그대로 내버려 두다

구문 풀이

1행 The few times [that they do occur], it is the possessor who
(선행사) (동사 강조) 「it is ~ who[that] … : 강조 구문
tries to make someone leave the circle. (…한 것은 바로 ~이다)

★★ 문제 해결 꿀~팁 ★★

▶ 많이 틀린 이유는?
④ 앞의 문장에서 먹이 소유자가 다른 구성원들을 '때리며' 상황에 대한 자신의 의사를 표현할 수 있다고 언급한 것을 근거로, ④ 뒤에서는 서열보다도 먹이 소유자인지 아닌지가 먹이 흐름을 제어할 권한을 준다는 결론을 정리하고 있다. 따라서 ④ 앞뒤에는 논리적 공백이 없다.

▶ 문제 해결 방법은?
③ 앞뒤의 논리적 공백에 주목한다. ③ 앞에서 갈등은 '드물다'고 언급했는데 ③ 뒤에서는 갑자기 She, 즉 먹이 소유자가 구성원들을 때리며 불편함을 나타내는 상황이 제시된다. 이는 '드물게도 갈등이 일어났을 때' 먹이 소유자가 취할 행동으로 볼 수 있으므로, '갈등이 일어났을 때'라는 말로 시작하는 주어진 문장은 ③에 들어가야 한다.

11-12 곤충 섭취에 대한 태도 바꾸기

[본문 해석]
곤충 섭취를 거부하는 사회에서는 이러한 거부를 극복한 몇몇 개인들이 있지만,

대부분은 이러한 태도를 지속할 것이다. 곤충이 섭취에 완전히 적합하다는 것을 전체 사회에 납득시키기는 매우 (a) 어려울지도 모른다. 하지만, 특정 음식에 대한 이러한 태도의 (b) 역전이 전체 사회에 발생한 사례들이 있다. 지난 120년 간 유럽-아메리카 사회로부터의 몇몇 사례는 로브스터를 하인과 죄수용 음식 대신에 고급진 음식으로 여기는 것, 초밥을 안전하고 맛있는 음식으로 여기는 것, 그리고 피자를 단지 시칠리아 시골의 가난한 사람들이 먹는 음식으로 여기지 않는 것이다. 곤충이 이미 섭취되는 라틴 아메리카 국가들에서는 일부 인구는 곤충 섭취를 싫어하며, 이를 빈곤과 (c) 연관 짓는다. 또한 그것을 섭취하는 습관이 있었으나 수치심 때문에, 그리고 『가난하거나 미개하다고 분류되고 싶지 않아서』 그 습관을 (d) 권장한(→ 버린) 사람들의 사례들도 있다. 『인류학자인 Esther Katz에 따르면, 만약 호사스러운 음식으로서의 곤충 섭취가 장려된다면, 이러한 습관을 보이지 않는 몇몇 개인들이 자신이 교육받았던 생각을 극복할 가능성이 더 커질 것이다. 그리고 이것은 또한 이미 곤충을 먹고 있는 사람들에 의한 곤충 섭취를 (e) 재평가하는 데에도 도움을 줄 수 있다.』
「 : 12번의 근거」
「 : 11번의 근거」

- **consumption** ⓝ 섭취, 소비
- **convince** ⓥ 납득시키다, 설득하다
- **prisoner** ⓝ 죄수
- **associate A with B** A와 B를 연관 짓다
- **categorize A as B** A를 B라고 분류하다
- **promote** ⓥ 장려하다, 촉진하다, 홍보하다
- **shortage** ⓝ 부족
- **overcome** ⓥ 극복하다
- **suitable for** ~에 적합한
- **rural** ⓐ 시골의
- **shame** ⓝ 수치심
- **anthropologist** ⓝ 인류학자
- **edible** ⓐ 먹을 수 있는

구문 풀이

20행 According to Esther Katz, an anthropologist, if the
동격(= Esther Katz)
consumption of insects as a food luxury is to be promoted, there
be to 용법(~하려면)
would be more chances [that some individuals who do not present
this habit overcome ideas under which they were educated].
[ ] : chances 동격

11 제목 파악   정답률 56% | 정답 ②

윗글의 제목으로 가장 적절한 것은?
① The More Variety on the Table, The Healthier You Become
   식탁에 놓인 음식 종류가 다양할수록, 더 건강해진다
☑ Edible or Not? Change Your Perspectives on Insects
   먹을 수 있는가, 없는가? 곤충에 대한 당신의 관점을 바꾸라
③ Insects: A Key to Solve the World Food Shortage
   곤충: 세계 식량 부족을 해결하는 열쇠
④ Don't Let Uniqueness in Food Culture Disappear
   식문화의 고유성이 사라지게 내버려두지 말라
⑤ Experiencing Various Cultures by Food
   음식으로 다양한 문화 경험하기

Why? 왜 정답일까?

곤충 섭취에 대한 부정적 태도가 바뀐 사례나, 반대로 부정적 인식 때문에 곤충 섭취 습관을 포기했던 사례를 언급한 후, 이 부정적 태도를 전환할 방법을 제시하는 글이다. 따라서 글의 제목으로 가장 적절한 것은 ② '먹을 수 있는가, 없는가? 곤충에 대한 당신의 관점을 바꾸라'이다.

12 어휘 추론   정답률 56% | 정답 ④

밑줄 친 (a) ~ (e) 중에서 문맥상 낱말의 쓰임이 적절하지 않은 것은?
① (a)   ② (b)   ③ (c)   ☑ (d)   ⑤ (e)

Why? 왜 정답일까?

(d) 뒤의 '~ due to shame, and because they do not want to be categorized as poor or uncivilized.'는 곤충을 섭취하던 사람들이 수치감이나, 가난 또는 미개한 사람들로 분류되고 싶지 않은 마음 때문에 이 습관을 '포기했음'을 설명하는 것이므로, (d)의 encouraged를 abandoned로 고쳐야 한다. 따라서 문맥상 낱말의 쓰임이 적절하지 않은 것은 ④ '(d)'이다.

DAY 30 — 20분 미니 모의고사

01 ⑤	02 ①	03 ⑤	04 ②	05 ④
06 ②	07 ②	08 ④	09 ②	10 ②
11 ③	12 ③			

---

01 신체 리듬이 정점일 때를 파악해 활용하기 　정답률 81% | 정답 ⑤

다음 글에서 필자가 주장하는 바로 가장 적절한 것은?

① 부정적인 감정에 에너지를 낭비하지 말라.
② 자신의 신체 능력에 맞게 운동량을 조절하라.
③ 자기 성찰을 위한 아침 명상 시간을 확보하라.
④ 생산적인 하루를 보내려면 일을 균등하게 배분하라.
☑ 자신의 에너지가 가장 높은 시간을 파악하여 활용하라.

[본문 해석]

우리 중 누구라도 근무일 내내 일정한 수준의 주의 집중을 유지하기는 어렵다. 우리 모두 에너지와 기민함의 정점과 저점을 특징으로 하는 신체 리듬을 가지고 있다. 가장 힘든 작업을 가장 잘 처리할 수 있는 시간에 하도록 계획을 잡으면, 더 많은 것을 이루고, 이득으로 자신감을 느낄 것이다. 만약 전에 에너지 정점에 관해 생각해 본 적이 없다면, 며칠 동안 자신을 관찰하라. 상태가 제일 좋을 때를 알아차리도록 노력하라. 우리는 모두 다르다. 어떤 사람에게는 정점이 아침에 제일 먼저 오지만, 다른 사람에게는 준비되는 데 얼마간의 시간이 걸릴 수도 있다.

Why? 왜 정답일까?

힘든 작업을 분배할 수 있도록 하루 중 신체 리듬이 가장 좋은 시간을 찾아보라(**Try to note the times when you are at your best.**)고 조언하는 글이므로, 필자의 주장으로 가장 적절한 것은 ⑤ '자신의 에너지가 가장 높은 시간을 파악하여 활용하라.'이다.

- **constant** ⓐ 지속적인
- **peaks and valleys** 정점과 저점
- **confident** ⓐ 자신감 있는
- **demanding** ⓐ 까다로운, 힘든
- **throughout** prep ~ 내내
- **alertness** ⓝ 기민함
- **benefit** ⓝ 이득
- **cope with** ~을 처리하다

구문 풀이

8행 Try to note the times when you are at your best.
선행사(시간) 관계부사

---

02 재생 가능한 에너지원 이용에 따른 환경적 부작용 　정답률 74% | 정답 ①

다음 글의 주제로 가장 적절한 것은?

☑ environmental side effects of using renewable energy sources
　재생 가능한 에너지원을 사용하는 것의 환경적 부작용
② practical methods to meet increasing demand for electricity
　늘어나는 전기 수요를 맞추기 위한 현실적인 방법
③ negative impacts of the use of traditional energy sources
　전통적 에너지원 사용의 부정적 영향
④ numerous ways to obtain renewable sources of energy
　재생 가능한 에너지원을 얻기 위한 무수히 많은 방법
⑤ effective procedures to reduce greenhouse emissions
　온실가스 배출을 줄이기 위한 효과적 절차

[본문 해석]

전력 생산을 위한 재생 가능한 에너지원의 사용은 전력 공급 확보의 필요성과 환경 보호 목적을 일치시키기 위한 방법으로 점점 장려되어 왔다. 그러나 재생 가능한 자원의 이용 또한 그 자체의 결과가 수반되는데, 이는 고려할 필요가 있다. 재생 가능한 에너지원은 수력 발전과 해양 기반 기술처럼 다양한 자원을 포함한다. 게다가, 태양열, 풍력, 지열 그리고 바이오매스(에너지로 사용 가능한 생물체) 재생 에너지원 또한 환경에 저마다의 영향을 미친다. 예를 들어, 수력 발전 댐은 수생 생태계에 영향을 미치고, 더 최근에는 온실가스 배출의 중요한 원인으로 확인되었다. 풍력, 태양열 그리고 바이오매스 또한 시각 공해, 집약적인 토지 점유 그리고 조류 개체 수에 미치는 부정적인 영향과 같은 부정적인 환경 영향을 초래한다.

Why? 왜 정답일까?

'But the use of renewable sources also comes with its own consequences,

---

which require consideration.' 이후로 재생 가능한 에너지원을 쓰더라도 나름의 환경적 영향이 따르므로 이에 관한 고려가 필요하다는 내용이 이어지고 있다. 따라서 글의 주제로 가장 적절한 것은 ① '재생 가능한 에너지원을 사용하는 것의 환경적 부작용'이다.

- **renewable** ⓐ 재생 가능한
- **harmonize A with B** A와 B를 점점 더 조화시키다, 일치시키다
- **secure** ⓥ 확보하다
- **consequence** ⓝ 결과, 영향
- **hydropower** ⓝ 수력
- **identify** ⓥ 확인하다
- **intensive** ⓐ 집약적인, 집중적인
- **practical** ⓐ 현실적인, 실제적인
- **increasingly** ad 점점 더
- **objective** ⓝ 목적, 목표
- **consideration** ⓝ 고려
- **have an impact on** ~에 영향을 주다
- **significant** ⓐ 중요한, 유의미한
- **occupation** ⓝ 점유, 차지
- **numerous** ⓐ 무수히 많은

구문 풀이

1행 The use of renewable sources of energy to produce
주어 / 전치사(~로서) / ~하기 위한
electricity has increasingly been encouraged as a way to harmonize
현재완료 수동태(~되어 왔다) / 형용사적 용법
the need to secure electricity supply with environmental protection
형용사적 용법
objectives.

---

03 Paul Laurence Dunbar의 생애 　정답률 63% | 정답 ⑤

Paul Laurence Dunbar에 관한 다음 글의 내용과 일치하지 <u>않는</u> 것은?

① 14세쯤에 *Dayton Herald*에 시를 발표했다.
② 고등학교 재학 시 학교 신문을 편집했다.
③ 재정상의 이유로 대학에 진학하지 못했다.
④ 두 번째 출판한 책으로 국내외에서 인정받게 되었다.
☑ 표준 영어로 쓴 시들로 가장 큰 주목을 받았다.

[본문 해석]

아프리카계 미국인 시인인 Paul Laurence Dunbar는 1872년 6월 27일에 태어났다. 『14세 무렵 Dunbar는 *Dayton Herald*에 시를 발표했다.』 『그는 고등학교에 다닐 때 학교 신문을 편집했다.』 『훌륭한 학생이었음에도 Dunbar는 재정상 대학에 갈 수 없었고 엘리베이터 운전자라는 직업을 가졌다.』 1893년 Dunbar는 자신의 첫 번째 책인 *Oak and Ivy*를 자비로 출판했다. 『1895년, 그는 두 번째 책인 *Majors and Minors*를 출판했고, 이것은 그에게 국내외의 인정을 가져다 주었다.』 표준 영어로 쓴 시들은 'majors'라 불렸고, 방언으로 쓴 시는 'minors'라 불렸다. 『표준 영어로 쓴 'majors' 시들이 방언으로 쓴 시들보다 많지만, Dunbar가 가장 큰 주목을 받게 해 준 것은 방언으로 쓴 시들이었다.』 ─「」: ⑤의 근거 불일치

(근거 표시: ①의 근거 일치 / ②의 근거 일치 / ③의 근거 일치 / ④의 근거 일치)

Why? 왜 정답일까?

'~ it was the dialect poems that brought Dunbar the most attention.'에서 Dunbar는 표준 영어로 된 시(majors)보다 방언으로 된 시(minors)를 통해 가장 큰 주목을 받았다고 한다. 따라서 내용과 일치하지 않는 것은 ⑤ '표준 영어로 쓴 시들로 가장 큰 주목을 받았다.'이다.

Why? 왜 오답일까?

① 'By the age of fourteen, Dunbar had poems published in the *Dayton Herald*.'의 내용과 일치한다.
② 'While in high school he edited his high school newspaper.'의 내용과 일치한다.
③ 'Despite being a fine student, Dunbar was financially unable to attend college ~'의 내용과 일치한다.
④ 'In 1895, he published the second book, *Majors and Minors*, which brought him national and international recognition.'의 내용과 일치한다.

- **publish** ⓥ 출판하다
- **financially** ad 재정적으로
- **at one's own expense** 자비로, 사비로
- **recognition** ⓝ 인정
- **term** ⓥ 이름짓다, 칭하다
- **edit** ⓥ 편집하다
- **operator** ⓝ 기사, 운전자
- **international** ⓐ 국제적인
- **dialect** ⓝ 방언
- **A outnumber B** A의 수가 B보다 많다

구문 풀이

3행 While (he was) in high school he edited his high school
접속사 / 생략 / 전명구
newspaper.

★★★ 1등급 대비 고난도 3점 문제

04 의사 결정에 중요한 느낌과 감정   정답률 52% | 정답 ②

(A), (B), (C)의 각 네모 안에서 문맥에 맞는 낱말로 가장 적절한 것은? [3점]

(A)	(B)	(C)
① able 할 수 있는	contradicts 반하다	assistance 도움
✓② unable 할 수 없는	contradicts 반하다	assistance 도움
③ unable 할 수 없는	contradicts 반하다	interference 방해
④ unable 할 수 없는	supports 옹호하다	interference 방해
⑤ able 할 수 있는	supports 옹호하다	interference 방해

[본문 해석]

느낌과 감정은 매일 하는 의사 결정에 매우 중요하다. 신경과학자인 Antonio Damasio는 감정 체계에 손상을 입힌 뇌 부상을 제외하고 모든 면에서 완벽하게 정상인 사람들을 연구했다. 결과적으로, 그들은 세상 속에서 효과적으로 결정을 내리거나 기능 (A) 할 수 없었다. 그들은 자신들이 어떻게 기능하고 있어야 했는지 정확하게 설명할 수는 있었지만, 어디에 살고, 무엇을 먹고, 어떤 제품을 사서 사용할지는 결정할 수가 없었다. 이러한 연구 결과는 의사 결정이 이성적이고 논리적인 사고의 핵심이라는 보편적 믿음에 (B) 반한다. 그러나 최신 연구에서는 정서적 체계가 여러분이 좋고 나쁜 것 사이에서 빨리 선택하도록 돕고, 고려해야 할 것들의 수를 줄여주면서 의사 결정에 결정적인 (C) 도움을 준다는 것을 보여 준다.

Why? 왜 정답일까?

(A) 뒤를 보면 그들은 자신들이 어떻게 기능하고 있어야 했는지 정확하게 설명할 수는 있었지만 어디에 살고, 무엇을 먹고, 어떤 제품을 사서 사용할지는 결정할 수가 없었다고 한다. 따라서 (A)에 문맥에 맞는 낱말로 가장 적절한 것은 'unable(할 수 없는)'이다.

(B) 뒤에 나온 보편적인 믿음은 의사 결정이 이성적이고 논리적인 생각의 핵심이라는 것이다. 이는 감정 체계에 손상이 있는 사람들이 의사 결정을 할 수 없었다는 내용과 반대되므로 문맥에 맞는 낱말로 가장 적절한 것은 'contradicts(반하다)'이다.

(C) 문장이 But이라는 역접의 접속사로 시작하므로 앞에서 말한 보편적인 믿음에 반대되는 내용이 나올 것이다. 이 글에서 이성과 논리의 반대는 감정, 정서를 뜻하므로 정서적 체계가 의사 결정에 도움이 된다는 내용이 이어져야 한다. 따라서 문맥에 맞는 낱말로 가장 적절한 것은 'assistance(도움)'이다. 정답은 ② '(A) unable(할 수 없는) – (B) contradicts(반하다) – (C) assistance(도움)'이다.

- **crucial** ⓐ 중요한
- **effectively** ⓐⓓ 효과적으로, 사실상
- **rational** ⓐ 이성적인
- **critical** ⓐ 결정적인, 중요한
- **neuroscientist** ⓝ 신경과학자
- **finding** ⓝ 결정, 판결, 결론
- **affective** ⓐ 정서적인
- **rapid** ⓐ 빠른

구문 풀이

6행 While they could describe [exactly how they should have
접속사(반면에, ~이지만)   의문사
been functioning], / they couldn't determine [where to live, what to
[ ] : 간접의문문
eat, and what products to buy and use].
[ ] : determine의 목적어(의문사 + to부정사)

12행 But modern research shows [that the affective system provides
              접속사
critical assistance to your decision making by helping you make
                           「준사역 동사 + 목적어 + 목적격 보어」
rapid selections between good and bad, reducing the number of
                                    분사구문(~하면서)
things {to be considered}].
         형용사적 용법

★★ 문제 해결 꿀~팁 ★★

▶ 많이 틀린 이유는?

최다 오답으로 ③이 많이 나왔는데, (A)나 (B)보다는 (C)를 어렵게 느낀 수험생들이 많았다는 뜻으로 풀이된다.

'interference(방해)'가 다소 낯선 어휘였다는 점이 오답률을 높이는 데 기여한 것으로 보인다.

▶ 문제 해결 방법은?

'While they could describe exactly ~'에서 감정 체계에 손상을 입은 사람들은 일상의 결정을 빨리 내리지 못했다는 내용을 말하는데, (C)의 문장에서는 이를 뒤집어서 감정 체계가 일상의 빠른 판단을 '돕는다'고 이야기하고 있다.

---

05 판단과 선택의 오류를 막는 방법   정답률 52% | 정답 ④

다음 글의 밑줄 친 부분 중, 문맥상 낱말의 쓰임이 적절하지 않은 것은? [3점]

[본문 해석]

Paula가 극심한 공포증을 겪는다는 것을 우리가 안다고 가정해 보자. Paula가 뱀이나 거미 둘 중 하나를 두려워한다고 추론한 다음, 그녀가 뱀을 두려워하지 않는다는 것을 ① 규명한다면, 우리는 Paula가 거미를 두려워한다고 결론지을 것이다. 그러나 우리의 결론은 실제로 Paula의 두려움이 뱀이나 거미 둘 중 하나와 관계가 있는 경우에만 타당하다. 만약 우리가 Paula가 공포증이 있다는 것만 알고 있다면, 그녀가 뱀을 두려워하지 않는다는 사실은 그녀가 높은 곳, 물, 개, 또는 숫자 13을 두려워한다는 것과 전적으로 ② 양립한다. 더 일반적으로는 우리에게 어떤 현상에 대한 일련의 대안적 설명이 제공되고, 그런 다음 그 설명들 중 하나를 제외하고는 모든 것이 ③ 적절하지 않다는 것을 확신한다면, 우리는 멈춰서 심사숙고해야 한다. 남아 있는 그 설명이 옳은 것이라는 것을 ④ 부정하기(→ 인정하기) 전에, 타당해 보이는 다른 선택 사항들이 무시되거나 간과되고 있는지를 고려해 보라. 잘못된 선택의 오류는, 우리가 숨어 있는 중요한 가정에 불충분하게 주의를 기울일 때, 명백한 것으로 밝혀진 선택 사항들이 ⑤ 합리적인 대안을 고갈시키도록 오도한다.

Why? 왜 정답일까?

③이 포함된 문장에서 한 가지를 제외한 나머지 대안이 모두 적절치 않다고 확신할 때 숙고가 필요하다(~ when we are ~ persuaded that all but one of those explanations are unsatisfactory, we should pause to reflect.)고 언급하는 것으로 볼 때, ④가 포함된 문장은 이 남은 한 가지를 '인정하기' 앞서 다른 타당한 대안이 혹시 무시되거나 간과되지 않았는지 살펴봐야 한다는 내용을 나타내야 한다. 따라서 ④의 denying은 반의어인 conceding으로 고쳐야 한다. 문맥상 낱말의 쓰임이 적절하지 않은 것은 ④이다.

- **reason** ⓥ 추론하다
- **concern** ⓥ ~와 관계가 있다
- **alternative** ⓝ 대안
- **insufficiently** ⓐⓓ 불충분하게
- **explicit** ⓐ 명백한
- **reasonable** ⓐ 합리적인
- **present** ⓥ 제시하다
- **pause** ⓥ 잠시 멈추다
- **assumption** ⓝ 가정
- **exhaust** ⓥ 고갈시키다

구문 풀이

17행 The fallacy of false choice misleads (when we're insufficiently
         주어   동사   주격 관계대명사
attentive to an important hidden assumption), that the choices [which
  ( ) : 부사절   접속사   주어
have been made explicit] exhaust the sensible alternatives.
  동사(5형식 수동태)   보어   동사

★★★ 1등급 대비 고난도 2점 문제

06 역할의 상호 작용과 관계 내 상호 작용   정답률 32% | 정답 ②

다음 빈칸에 들어갈 말로 가장 적절한 것을 고르시오.

① careers – 직업   ✓② statuses – 지위
③ abilities – 능력   ④ motivations – 동기
⑤ perspectives – 관점

[본문 해석]

사람들은 자신의 역할과 다른 사람의 역할 사이의 관계에 근거하여 전형적인 양식의 상호 작용에 참여한다. 의사들이 환자들과 그러한 것처럼 고용주들은 직원들과 특정한 방식으로 상호 작용하도록 기대된다. 각각의 경우에 행동은 개인의 사회 내 지위와 관련된 역할 책임과 의무에 의해 제한된다. 예를 들어 부모와 자식은 특정한 권리, 특권, 의무에 의해 연결된다. 부모는 자기 자녀에게 의식주 등 기본적인 생필품을 제공할 책임이 있다. 이러한 기대가 너무 강해서 그것을 충족시키지 못하는 것은 부모를 태만이나 학대 혐의로 비난받기 쉽게 할지도 모른다. 역으로 아이들은 자신의 부모가 말하는 대로 하도록 기대된다. 그러므로 관계 내의 상호 작용은 연관된 사람들 개개의 성격의 작용일 뿐만 아니라 그들이 지닌 지위와 관련된 역할 요구의 작용이다.

Why? 왜 정답일까?

첫 문장에서 사람들은 역할 간의 관계에 근거한 전형적인 상호 작용에 참여하게 된다고 언급한 후, 다양한 예시가 이어지고 있다. 특히 '~ actions are restricted by the role responsibilities and obligations associated with individuals' positions within society.'에서 개인의 행동은 사회 내에서의 '지위'와 연관된 책임과

의무로 인해 제한을 받게 된다고 설명하는 것을 근거로 볼 때, 빈칸에 들어갈 말로 가장 적절한 것은 ② '지위'이다.

- **engage in** ⓥ ~에 참여하다, 관여하다
- **obligation** ⓝ 의무
- **privilege** ⓝ 특권
- **charge** ⓝ 혐의, 비난
- **status** ⓝ 지위
- **restrict** ⓥ 제한하다
- **associated with** ~와 관련된
- **necessity** ⓝ 필수품
- **abuse** ⓝ 학대, 남용
- **perspective** ⓝ 관점

11행 These expectations are <u>so</u> powerful <u>that</u> not meeting them
『so ~ that …: 너무 ~해서 …하다』   동명사구 주어
may make the parents vulnerable to charges of negligence or abuse.
5형식 동사   목적어   형용사 보어

★★ 문제 해결 꿀~팁 ★★

▶ 많이 틀린 이유는?
글은 상호작용의 주체가 각자의 '지위'에 따라 역할이나 책임을 부여받는다는 내용을 다루고 있다. ③의 '능력'은 언급되지 않았다.

▶ 문제 해결 방법은?
예시 앞에는 대체로 주제가 나오므로, 여기서도 For instance 앞의 'In each case ~' 에 답의 근거가 있음을 예상할 수 있다.

★★★ 1등급 대비 고난도 3점 문제

07 감각 신경의 작용   정답률 38% | 정답 ②

다음 글에서 전체 흐름과 관계 없는 문장은? [3점]

[본문 해석]
감각 신경은 특정 감각을 포착하는 특화된 말단을 조직에 가지고 있다. 예를 들어, 만약 여러분이 핀과 같이 날카로운 물체를 밟는다면, 피부의 신경 말단이 통증 감각을 여러분의 다리 위로, 그리고 척수를 따라 위로 뇌까지 전달할 것이다. ① 통증 자체는 불쾌하지만, 이것은 사실 발을 보호하는 메커니즘으로 작용하고 있다. ② 즉, 여러분은 그 통증에 익숙해져 통증을 피할 수 있는 능력이 감소한다. ③ 뇌 안에서, 신경은 언어를 통제하는 부분에 연결될 것이고, 그래서 여러분은 '아야' 또는 다소 덜 공손한 무언가를 외칠 것이다. ④ 그것들은 또한 척수를 타고 다시 내려오는 운동 신경에 연결될 것이고, 그리고 이제 재빨리 수축하여 고통을 주는 물체로부터 발을 떼서 들어 올리게 하는 여러분의 다리 근육에 연결될 것이다. ⑤ 감각 신경과 운동 신경은 심장의 박동에서부터 장 운동, 발한과 그 밖에 모든 것에 이르기까지 신체의 거의 모든 기능을 통제한다.

Why? 왜 정답일까?
통증이 위험을 피하는 보호 기제 역할을 한다는 예시를 들어 감각 신경의 작용을 설명하는 글인데, ②는 통증에 익숙해져 둔감해진다는 내용이다. 따라서 전체 흐름과 관계 없는 문장은 ②이다.

- **sensory** ⓐ 감각의
- **tissue** ⓝ (생체) 조직
- **transmit** ⓥ 전달하다
- **unpleasant** ⓐ 불쾌한
- **capacity** ⓝ 능력
- **painful** ⓐ 고통스러운
- **gut** ⓝ 내장, 소화관
- **nerve** ⓝ 신경
- **sensation** ⓝ 감각
- **spinal cord** 척수
- **protective mechanism** 보호 기제
- **lift** ⓥ 들어올리다
- **motor** ⓐ 운동 신경의
- **sweating** ⓝ 발한, 땀이 남

7행 That is, you get used to the pain so the capacity [with which
주어1 동사1(~에 익숙해지다)   주어2
you can avoid pain] decreases.
               『전치사 + 목적격 관·대』
               동사2

★★ 문제 해결 꿀~팁 ★★

▶ 많이 틀린 이유는?
③에서 갑자기 '언어(speech)'가 언급되어 글과 무관해 보이지만, '아야'라는 말이 결국에는 고통에서 비롯된 반응의 예시이므로 전체 흐름상 어색하지 않다.

▶ 문제 해결 방법은?
정답인 ②에도 핵심 소재(pain)가 그대로 등장하므로 자연스러워 보일 수 있지만, 큰 소재만 대충 읽지 말고 주제와 문장별 핵심 내용을 더 세부적으로 파악해야 한다.

---

08 먹이 사슬의 특징   정답률 58% | 정답 ④

글의 흐름으로 보아, 주어진 문장이 들어가기에 가장 적절한 곳을 고르시오. [3점]

[본문 해석]
먹이 사슬은 식물 안에 있는 에너지원으로부터 먹고 먹히는 반복되는 과정 속에서 일련의 유기체를 통해 식품 에너지가 이동하는 것을 의미한다. ① 초원에서 풀은 토끼에게 먹히지만 토끼는 이윽고 여우에게 먹힌다. ② 이것은 단순한 먹이 사슬의 예이다. ③ 이 먹이 사슬은 식품 에너지가 생산자로부터 소비자 또는 더 높은 영양 수준으로 전달되는 연쇄를 의미한다. ④ 각 이동 단계에서 잠재적 에너지의 상당한 부분인 80 ~ 90%가 열로 손실되는 것으로 관찰되어 왔다. 그래서 하나의 사슬 안에 있는 단계나 연결의 수는 보통 4 ~ 5개로 제한된다. ⑤ 먹이 사슬이 짧을수록 또는 유기체가 사슬의 시작 단계(하위 영양 단계)에 가까울수록 이용 가능한 에너지 섭취량이 더 커진다.

Why? 왜 정답일까?
④ 앞의 문장에서 먹이 사슬은 식품 에너지가 생산자에서 소비자로, 즉 더 높은 영양 수준으로 이동하는 연쇄적 과정을 의미하는 것이라고 한다. 이어서 주어진 문장은 먹이 사슬의 각 이동 단계(each level of transfer)에서 에너지의 80 ~ 90%가 열로 손실되어 버린다는 사실을 언급한다. ④ 뒤의 문장은 주어진 문장에서 언급된 이유로(Hence) 한 먹이 사슬 안의 단계 수가 4 ~ 5개로 제한된다고 설명한다. 따라서 주어진 문장이 들어가기에 가장 적절한 곳은 ④이다.

- **transfer** ⓝ 이동
- **in turn** 이윽고, 차례로
- **restrict** ⓥ 제한하다
- **proportion** ⓝ 비율
- **imply** ⓥ 암시하다
- **intake** ⓝ 섭취량

13행 The shorter the food chain or the nearer the organism is to
『the + 비교급1 ~   the + 비교급2 ~
the beginning of the chain, the greater the available energy intake is.
『the + 비교급 …: ~하거나 ~할수록 더 …하다』

---

09 성찰적 일기 쓰기의 긍정적 효과   정답률 52% | 정답 ②

다음 글의 내용을 한 문장으로 요약하고자 한다. 빈칸 (A), (B)에 들어갈 말로 가장 적절한 것은?

	(A)		(B)		(A)		(B)
①	factual 사실적인	……	rethinking 다시 생각하는 것	✔	worthwhile 가치 있는	……	rethinking 다시 생각하는 것
③	outdated 구식인	……	generalizing 일반화하는 것	④	objective 객관적인	……	generalizing 일반화하는 것
⑤	demanding 까다로운	……	describing 기술하는 것				

[본문 해석]
우리의 삶에서 의미를 찾기 위한 가장 강력한 도구 중 하나는 성찰적 일기 쓰기, 즉 우리에게 일어난 일을 돌아보고 그것에 관해 쓰는 것이다. 1990년대에 Stanford University 연구자들은 봄방학에 학부생들에게 가장 중요한 개인적인 가치와 하루 활동에 대해 써보라고 요청했다. 다른 사람들은 그날 있었던 좋은 일만 쓰도록 요청받았다. 3주 후에, 자신의 가치에 관해 썼던 학생들은 좋은 것에만 초점을 맞췄던 학생들보다 더 행복하고, 더 건강하고, 스트레스에 대처할 수 있는 능력에 더 자신 있었다. 어떻게 자신의 하루 일과가 자신의 가치관을 뒷받침하는지를 성찰하면서, 학생들은 그 활동들과 선택들에 대해 새로운 관점을 얻었다. 작은 스트레스와 귀찮은 일들은 이제 그들의 가치가 행해지고 있음을 보여주는 것이었다. 갑자기 그들의 삶은 의미 있는 활동으로 가득 찼다. 그리고 그들이 해야 했던 일이라고는 그들의 경험을 개인적인 가치로 긍정적으로 재구성하면서 그것에 대해 돌아보고 쓰는 것뿐이었다.

➡ 우리가 (A) 가치 있다고 믿는 것에 근거해 일과에 관해 일기를 쓰는 것은 우리가 새로운 방식으로 경험을 (B) 다시 생각하면서 삶이 의미 있다고 느끼게 만들 수 있다.

Why? 왜 정답일까?
연구 결과를 정리하는 마지막 문장에서, 삶의 의미를 느끼기 위해 필요했던 일은 일과 중 있었던 경험을 가치관에 근거해 다시 생각해보고 정리하는 일뿐이었다(~ positively reframing their experiences with their personal values.)고 한다. 따라서 요약문의 빈칸 (A), (B)에 들어갈 말로 가장 적절한 것은 ② '(A) worthwhile(가치 있는), (B) rethinking(다시 생각하는 것)'이다.

- **reflective** ⓐ 성찰적인
- **think back on** ~에 대해 되돌아보다
- **handle** ⓥ 대처하다, 다루다
- **perspective** ⓝ 관점, 시각
- **demonstration** ⓝ 입증, 시연
- **reframe** ⓥ 재구성하다
- **worthwhile** ⓐ 가치 있는
- **demanding** ⓐ 까다로운, 힘든
- **journaling** ⓝ 일기 쓰기
- **undergraduate** ⓐ 학부의
- **support** ⓥ 뒷받침하다
- **hassle** ⓝ 귀찮은 일
- **in action** 활동 중인, 작용 중인
- **factual** ⓐ 사실적인
- **outdated** ⓐ 구식의

구문 풀이

18행 And all they had to do was reflect and write about it —
주어 ｜ 동사 ｜ 주격 보어(원형부정사)
positively reframing their experiences with their personal values.

10-12 천사를 찾기 위한 Amy의 여정

[본문 해석]

(A)

"할머니, 천사는 정말 있어요?" Amy가 물었다. "몇몇 사람들은 그렇다고 하지," 할머니가 말했다. Amy는 할머니에게 그녀가 그림에서 천사들을 본 적이 있다고 말했다. 하지만 (a) 그녀는 또한 그녀의 할머니도 실제로 천사를 본 적이 있는지 알고 싶어 했다. 할머니는 천사를 본 적이 있다고 하였으나 그림에서 본 것과는 다르다고 말했다. 「그럼, 천사를 찾으러 가볼래요!」 Amy가 말했다. "그거 좋네! 하지만 나는 너와 함께 가야겠어. 네가 너무 어리잖니." 할머니가 말했다. "하지만 할머니는 너무 천천히 걷잖아요." Amy가 불평했다. "할머니는 네가 생각하는 것보다 더 빨리 걸을 수 있어." 할머니가 미소를 지으며 대답했다.

(C)

그래서 그들은 길을 나섰고 Amy는 뛰어다녔다. 그때, 그녀가 그들 쪽으로 다가오는 말을 보았다. 그 말에는 멋진 여자가 타고 있었다. Amy가 그녀를 보았을 때 그녀는 보석과 황금으로 반짝이고 있었고, 그녀의 눈은 다이아몬드보다 더욱더 밝게 빛났다. "당신은 천사인가요?" Amy가 물었다. 「그 여자는 대답하지 않고 (d) 그녀를 차갑게 바라보며 아무 말도 없이 자리를 떠났다.」
└─┐: 12번 ③의 근거 불일치

(B)

"저 사람은 천사가 아니야!" Amy가 말했다. "아니고 말고!" 할머니가 말했다. 그래서 Amy는 다시 앞장서서 길을 걷기 시작했다. 그때, (b) 그녀는 눈처럼 하얀 드레스를 입은 한 아름다운 여자를 만났다. "당신은 천사가 틀림없어요!" Amy가 외쳤다. "귀여운 아가씨, 내가 정말 천사처럼 보여?" (c) 그녀가 물었다. "당신은 천사예요!" Amy가 말했다. 「하지만 Amy가 실수로 그녀의 드레스를 밟았을 때 갑자기 그녀의 얼굴이 돌변했다.」 "저리 비켜, 집에나 가!" 그녀가 외쳤다.
└─┐: 12번 ②의 근거 일치

(D)

Amy가 그녀로부터 뒤로 물러나며 비틀거리다 바닥으로 넘어졌다. (e) 그녀는 더러운 길가에 넘어졌고 울음을 터뜨렸다. 「"저 피곤해요! 할머니, 저를 집으로 좀 데려다 주세요." 그녀는 부탁했다.」 "물론이지! 그래서 내가 여기 있는 거잖니." 할머니가 따뜻한 목소리로 말했다. 그들은 길을 따라 걷기 시작했다. 갑자기 그녀가 고개를 들어 말했다. "할머니, 할머닌 천사가 아니죠, 그렇죠?" "오, 아가, 난 천사가 아니야." 「"음, 할머니, 할머니는 저에게 천사가 맞으세요. 왜냐면 항상 제 곁에 있어 주시니까요."라고 Amy가 말했다.」 └─┐: 12번 ⑤의 근거 일치

- **different than** ~와는 다른
- **by mistake** 실수로
- **dusty** ⓐ 먼지투성이의
- **step on** ⓥ ~을 밟다
- **leap** ⓥ 뛰어오르다

구문 풀이

(A) 5행 Her grandmother said she had, but they looked different
= had seen an angel(앞 문장 동사)   2형식 동사 형용사 보어
than in pictures.

(B) 3행 Then, she met a beautiful woman [who wore a dress
선행사   주격 관·대
as white as snow].
「as + 원급 + as : ~만큼 …한」

(C) 1행 So they started, Amy leaping and running.
주어 ｜ 동사 ｜ 의미상 주어 ｜ 분사구문

---

10 글의 순서 파악   정답률 73% ｜ 정답 ②

주어진 글 (A)에 이어질 내용을 순서에 맞게 배열한 것으로 가장 적절한 것은?

① (B) - (D) - (C)
✓② (C) - (B) - (D)
③ (C) - (D) - (B)
④ (D) - (B) - (C)
⑤ (D) - (C) - (B)

Why? 왜 정답일까?

Amy가 천사에 관해 할머니와 대화를 나누다가 직접 천사를 찾으러 가겠다고 결심했다는 내용의 (A) 뒤에는, Amy가 길을 나서서 말을 탄 여자를 보고 말을 걸었지만 답을 듣지 못했다는 내용의 (C), Amy가 천사처럼 보이는 다른 여자를 만났지만 여자의 드레스를 밟아 여자가 화를 냈다는 내용의 (B), Amy가 여자로부터 물러나다가 바닥에 넘어졌고 할머니와 다시 집으로 돌아가다가 문득 할머니가 천사라고 생각하게 되었다는 내용의 (D)가 차례로 이어져야 한다. 따라서 글의 순서로 가장 적절한 것은 ② '(C) - (B) - (D)' 이다.

11 지칭 추론   정답률 68% ｜ 정답 ③

밑줄 친 (a) ~ (e) 중에서 가리키는 대상이 나머지 넷과 다른 것은?

① (a) ② (b) ✓③ (c) ④ (d) ⑤ (e)

Why? 왜 정답일까?

(a), (b), (d), (e)는 Amy를, (c)는 'a beautiful woman who wore a dress ~'를 가리키므로, (a) ~ (e) 중에서 가리키는 대상이 다른 하나는 ③ '(c)'이다.

12 세부 내용 파악   정답률 75% ｜ 정답 ③

윗글의 Amy에 관한 내용으로 적절하지 않은 것은?

① 천사를 찾고 싶어 했다.
② 한 여자의 드레스를 밟았다.
✓③ 말을 탄 여자로부터 친절한 대답을 들었다.
④ 할머니에게 집에 데려다 달라고 부탁했다.
⑤ 할머니를 천사라고 생각했다.

Why? 왜 정답일까?

(C) 'The lady gave no reply, but stared coldly at her, leaving without saying a word.'에서 Amy는 말을 탄 여자에게 천사인지 물었지만 여자로부터 아무런 대답도 듣지 못했다고 하므로, 내용과 일치하지 않는 것은 ③ '말을 탄 여자로부터 친절한 대답을 들었다.'이다.

Why? 왜 오답일까?

① (A) '"Then, I am going to find one!" said Amy.'의 내용과 일치한다.
② (B) '~ Amy stepped on her dress by mistake.'의 내용과 일치한다.
④ (D) '"I am tired! Will you take me home, Grandma?" she asked.'의 내용과 일치한다.
⑤ (D) '"Well, Grandma, you are an angel to me because you always stay by my side," said Amy.'의 내용과 일치한다.

MEMO

MEMO